MANAGEMENT INFORMATION SYSTEMS

Girdhar Joshi

Principal Consultant & Director
BNG Infotech Mumbai

OXFORD

UNIVERSITY PRESS

OXFORD
UNIVERSITY PRESS

Oxford University Press is a department of the University of Oxford.
It furthers the University's objective of excellence in research, scholarship,
and education by publishing worldwide. Oxford is a registered trade mark of
Oxford University Press in the UK and in certain other countries.

Published in India by
Oxford University Press
22 Workspace, 2nd Floor, 1/22 Asaf Ali Road, New Delhi 110 002

First published in 2013
11th impression 2022

ISBN-13: 978-0-19-808099-2
ISBN-10: 0-19-808099-9

Typeset in Baskerville
by E-Edit Infotech Private Limited, Chennai
Printed in India by Rakmo Press, New Delhi 110 020

For product information and current price, please visit www.india.oup.com

To,
Parth

Preface

Information technology (IT) has taken a prime position in our professional and personal lives. It has had a significant impact on the quality of life and has touched all walks of life—offices, factories, communications, entertainment, education, health care, inventory, and transportation. Organizations have come to depend on information systems (IS) for the management of business operations. A management information system (MIS) is an organized approach to studying the information needs of an organization's management at every level of decision-making. With the backing of information technology, information systems help businesses gain competitive advantages and meet organizational objectives.

Educational institutes worldwide felt it necessary to introduce MIS as a discipline for students seeking higher education. MIS as a discipline gained acceptance in the US, UK, and Australian business schools as early as the 1960s. Departments were established in higher educational colleges to educate and inform students of the applications of computers in business and government functions. The discipline came into prominence in India in the 1990s with the emergence and awareness of the all-round applications of computers in business.

For students of business management, irrespective of whether they major in finance, marketing, operations, personnel, or information technology, the study of MIS would be invaluable to their career. Today, MIS is not only taught as a core subject, but also offered as a specialization. A subject that started with the study of critical information support to business managers has evolved into the study of more complex topics such as knowledge management, intelligent systems, artificial intelligence in business, web technology, and mobile computing.

Most books that students refer to for MIS have been written by western authors; most of the examples and cases have a western perspective too. Hence, a need was felt for a book that is written for students in the Indian subcontinent, which explains the conceptual topics through numerous business applications, using examples and case studies of Indian companies, so that students can easily relate to and understand the subject more comprehensively. The book also had to cover the latest developments in the IT arena and include emerging platforms and technologies—mobile computing and m-commerce—to name a few.

ABOUT THE BOOK

This book primarily caters to the requirement of postgraduate students pursuing business studies. Students will be able to appreciate the concept of information systems and the applications of computer technology in business. Business managers and systems managers may also find the book useful while planning the implementation of information systems. They can benefit from the real-life cases discussed and relate to them when using these systems to carry out day-to-day managerial tasks.

The book deals with the latest developments in the field of information technology, information systems, e-commerce, and mobile computing. Topics on the mission-critical applications of IT in various business and service sectors have been included, which will make the students aware of such applications in the representative sectors. As mobile technology is taking centre stage in information distribution and business applications, a separate chapter has been dedicated to the study of mobile computing.

PEDAGOGICAL FEATURES

The book has been written in a simple language with a problem-solving approach and has been presented in a user-friendly manner. Wherever possible, concepts have been explained with the help of real-life business examples, figures, illustrations, and tables. The business cases and scenarios, abundantly used in the book, refer to the latest applications in information systems, and have been adapted from interviews with chief information officers (CIOs), news items, and case studies from online and print media. It is replete with business cases from companies such as Bank of Baroda, Archies, Infosys, ONGC, IDBI Bank, Snapdeal.com, CEAT, Standard Chartered Bank, Wipro, Maruti Udyog, Titan Industries, TCI, and Videocon.

Each chapter contains the following pedagogical features :

Learning objectives   Learning objectives have been provided at the beginning of each chapter to enable students in understanding what they are going to learn in the chapter.

Chapter-opening case study   A chapter-opening case describing a real-world business scenario that establishes the theme and importance of the chapter.

Exhibits   Real-life business situations and scenarios have been used in abundance throughout the book, which will expose students to the uses of IT in enhancing business decision-making.

Figures   Wherever possible, concepts have been illustrated with the help of figures and drawings, which will leave an indelible impression on the students.

Tables   Tables have been provided at relevant places to give a bird's eye view of the various definitions and comparisons used in several topics.

Summary   Key points in the chapter have been revisited so that students can strengthen their understanding of the concepts.

Key terms   The key terms defined at the end of every chapter will help students recollect the important points at the time of revision.

Concept review questions   Self-assessment exercises in the form of concept review questions will help the students test their knowledge.

Critical thinking questions   Attempting the critical thinking questions found at the end of the chapter will help students think beyond what is covered in the text and further improve their analytical skills.

MIS development   At the end of each chapter, a practical business problem exercise is provided that will enable students to utilize the IS knowledge gained in the chapter. This will provide scope for interesting practical sessions for further classroom discussion.

Chapter-end case study   Each chapter ends with a real-life business case study in which students can apply the concepts learnt in the chapter. Discussion questions given at the end of the case study enhance the understanding of the points dealt with.

COVERAGE AND STRUCTURE

The book is divided into five parts. It covers topics of current interest to the student and prepares them to appreciate the field of management information systems. It attempts to simplify the subject as much as possible so that the student can grasp the complex field of computer technology. The chapters also strengthen the students' foundation in IT and IS, and prepares them for discussion on further technological concepts.

Part 1, *Concepts and structure of MIS*, includes three chapters.
   Chapter 1 introduces the subject to the students and defines information systems with respect to the diverse managerial functions. Students can understand the direct connection between information systems and management functions.
   Chapter 2 illustrates the role of MIS in an organization. Students would appreciate the importance of IS in effective and efficient management of businesses. The chapter discusses trends in MIS—the evolution from accounting systems to enterprise systems, knowledge management, and artificial intelligence.
   In *Chapter 3*, students will comprehend how IT can be used to play strategic roles in an organization. The chapter talks about how IS can be used for building pivotal advantages, bringing in organizational change, and reengineering business processes.

Part 2, *Information technology infrastructure*, includes four chapters.
   Chapters 4 and *5* discuss hardware and software infrastructure and the latest trends in this field. The numerous topics explained include a discussion on basic computer architecture and the various types of software, their system and applications, office productivity, and groupware.
   Chapter 6 gives an exhaustive explanation of database management concepts. The latest trends in data management—data mining, data warehousing, and online analytical processing—have been examined.
   Chapter 7 throws light on telecommunication and networking, which assume importance with the advent of the Internet and mobile technology.

Part 3, *Information system applications*, includes seven chapters.
   Chapter 8 encompasses the applications of e-business and elaborates on these applications for the many organizational functions.
   Chapter 9 comprises enterprise systems such as enterprise resource management (ERP), supply chain management (SCM), and customer relationship management (CRM) that support business

processes. The latest trends in business applications, for example, software-as-a-service (SaaS), e-procurement, etc., have been discussed in the chapter.

Chapter 10 is devoted to the study of mission-critical applications for the service sector. Some of the representative sectors (banking, insurance, transportation, hospitality, etc.) have been covered.

Chapter 11 gives a clear picture of how businesses use the Internet and the emerging business initiatives. Students gain insight into the upcoming technologies and e-commerce business initiatives.

Chapter 12 brings to the fore the usefulness of information systems in helping business managers take decisions. This chapter discusses the decision-making process, decision support trends, and business intelligence tools.

Chapter 13 simplifies the concept of knowledge management and intelligent systems, which are a part of decision support systems (DSS) and bring about clarity in the subject.

Chapter 14 defines mobile computing and its business applications in detail, as nowadays computers are making way for smartphones, as far as distribution of information is concerned. Students will become aware of the latest developments in the field of mobile computing and the ways of sharing information using mobile devices.

Part 4, *Development of MIS*, includes two chapters.

Chapters 15 and *16* are dedicated to the planning, development, and implementation of information systems. They illustrate how systems and business strategies are developed to meet organizational objectives. Students will gain an understanding of the various implementation methodologies and strategies and relate them in their professional lives. These chapters discuss the system development life cycle and implementation approaches.

Part 5, *Management and challenges of MIS*, includes four chapters.

Chapter 17 analyses systems security and the threats and challenges involved. It also discusses the various tools for security control and elaborates on a disaster management policy in business.

Chapter 18 lays emphasis on the ethical, legal, and privacy issues, and dwells on the liabilities and accountability of systems developers, users, and managers.

Chapter 19 aids in the understanding of the human aspect of information systems. It explains the evolution of IS functions in a business organization and discusses the role and responsibilities of a chief information officer (CIO).

Chapter 20 brings to light global challenges and opportunities and illustrates how information systems are designed to meet these global challenges.

ACKNOWLEDGEMENTS

I am grateful to a large number of friends from my profession, various universities, and business schools for inspiring me to write this book. I acknowledge the contribution and cooperation of my colleagues at BNG Infotech for allowing me to use their vast knowledge base.

I must thank the editorial team at Oxford University Press India for their untiring efforts in bringing out this book.

I pay my deepest gratitude to my parents who instilled values and confidence in me. I wish to thank my family, including my children, brothers, and sister for their love and well wishes.

I thank my learned readers and students and welcome suggestions for further improvement of the book.

Girdhar Joshi

Features of the Book

MOBILE COMPUTING

Mobile computing refers to the use of a variety of
tablets, etc.) that offer mobility to allow people to (
transmission to a
computing is a fo
on the move durin
wireless communi

M-COMMERCE

Mobile commerce (M-commerce) refers to conduc
network using mobile hand-held terminals such as m
to Laudon (2002), 'the use of wireless devices such as
appliances, to conduct e-commerce transactions ove
all e-commerce transactions are conducted over wir
transacted through mobile hand-held devices such
other digital devices. These devices can connect to th

NEW TECHNOLOGY

New emerging platforms and
technologies such as mobile
computing and m-commerce
that help widen the scope of
IT in business management
are discussed.

EXHIBITS

Numerous exhibits that
help illustrate the concepts
discussed are included.

EXHIBIT 3.1

Banks in India: Challenge to Establish Custom

The banking sector in India has experienced a rapid transformation. Just about a decade ago, this sector was limited
to nationalized and cooperative ba
by the entry of multinational banks

channels c
networking

EXHIBIT 14.1

Standard Chartered Bank Makes Mobi

When Standard Chartered, the London-headquartered
bank, took a conscious decision to move over to the iPhone
platform in May 2010, the device was nowhere close to

- ATM lo
- M-com
  - top

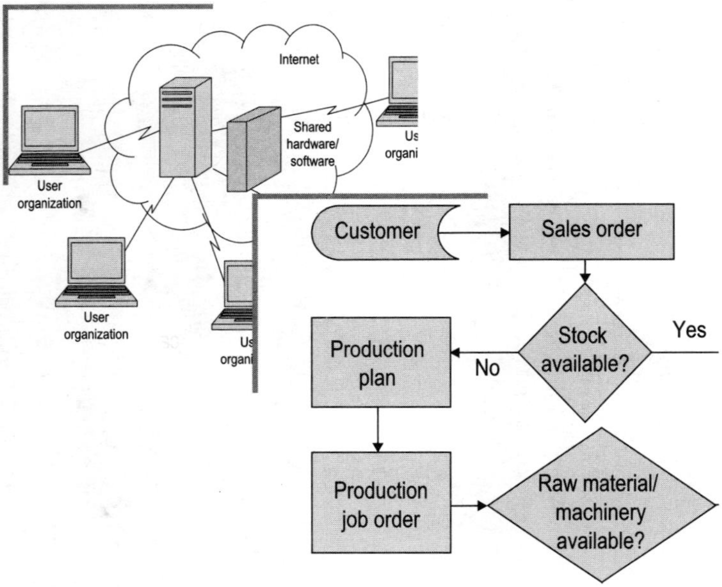

FIGURES AND FLOW CHARTS

A number of figures and
flow charts are provided
in the text to aid in clear
understanding of the
concepts discussed.

SUMMARY AND KEY TERMS

Summary and key terms are provided for quick revision of the important concepts and terms discussed in the chapter.

SUMMARY

The convergence of information and communication technolo- and Blu
gies (ICT) has brought about a major revolution in the working LAN. To
and lifestyle of people. The changin
cation industries, technologies, and
increase the decision alternatives
With the introduction of free marke

KEY TERMS

American National Standards Institute X12 (ANSI X12) A   **Circuit**
US standard for EDI communication.   com
Asynchronous transfer mode (ATM) A standard that   **Client–**
seamlessly and dynamically integrates voice, data, images,   a h
and video for transmission across the globe.   con
Broadband   A high speed telecommunication channel used   **Commu**

CONCEPT REVIEW QUESTIONS

1. What do you understand by strategic advantage? Explain with some examples.
2. What strategic role does informa in strategic planning?
3. What are the different types of various competitive forces and s

CRITICAL THINKING QUESTIONS

1. As a manager, you are being asked to develop e-business and e-commerce applications to gain competitive advantage in your company. How will you start and what reservation would you have about doing so?
2. Peter Keen, MIS author and consultant, said, 'We have learned that it is not technology that creates a competitive edge, but the management process that exploits technology.' What did he mean by this

END-CHAPTER QUESTIONS

Various concept review and critical thinking questions have been provided towards the end of each chapter that help in applying the concepts studied to real life situations.

PROJECTS

Numerous projects are provided under 'MIS Development' that enable better understanding of the use of IT tools in business decision making.

MIS DEVELOPMENT

eBay has been the standout leader in m-commerce with the iPhone applications they launched in 2008, and the Blackberry and Android applications launched in 2009 and 2010 respectively. In 2009, the company saw more than $600 million dollars in goods sold via mobile applications, which was a 200% increase from 2008. The launch of their app notified bidders with push alerts and SMS notifications when they had been outbid, and allowed them to cast another attempt

mobile app, with apparel, auto parts, cell
sories, sporting goods, and collectibles ra
five categories of purchased items.

Exercise

Dig the Internet further for m-commerc
What do you observe? What are the oth
that have not been discussed in this cha
trends in m-commerce applications an

CASE STUDIES

Various case studies and business problems that illustrate practical examples from the real business world are included from companies such as Archies, Infosys, Wipro, Amul, ONGC, Maruti Udyog, Videocon, Snapdeal.com, Titan Industries, etc.

CASE STUDY
Maruti Udyog—Developing an Automobile Finance System

In its constant endeavour to keep its financing system agile, the management of Maruti Suzuki India Limited (MSIL, formerly Maruti Udyog Limited), dentified the need to leverage the Internet-based enterprise e-commerce applications. An automobile financing system was developed to interact with the dealers as well as the alliance partners such as Citicorp Maruti, Maruti Countrywide, ICICI Bank, HDFC Bank, Kotak Mahindra, Sundaram Finance, Bank of Punjab, and IndusInd Bank.

About the organization
MSIL, a subsidiary of Suzuki Motor Corporation of Japan, is India's largest passenger car company, accounting for

150 variants ranging from people's ca
stylish hatchback, Ritz. MSIL is the ov
as Omni, Eeco, Alto, A-star, WagonF
Gypsy, Grand Vitara, SX4, and Swift
year 2009–10, MSIL became the or
to manufacture and sell one million
company has an employee strength
March 2012.
    Maruti Finance is one of the premi
by MSIL to tackle this challenge. It
financing deals to its customers with
dealer and alliance consortium.

Brief Contents

Detailed Contents

PART I: CONCEPTS AND STRUCTURE OF MIS

PART II: INFORMATION TECHNOLOGY INFRASTRUCTURE

PART III: INFORMATION SYSTEM APPLICATIONS

PART IV: DEVELOPMENT OF MIS

PART V: MANAGEMENT AND CHALLENGES OF MIS

List of Exhibits and Case Studies

Part I

Concepts and Structure of MIS

- Concepts of Information Systems

- MIS in Business

- Strategic Advantage of IT

1

Concepts of Information Systems

> *Business managers are moving from a tradition where they could avoid, delegate, or ignore decisions about IT to one where they cannot create a marketing, product, international, organization, or financial plan that does not involve such decisions.*
>
> **—PETER KEEN AND CRAIGG BALANCE**

LEARNING OBJECTIVES

After studying this chapter, you will be able to

- understand the concept of information systems
- define management information systems (MIS) and the three elements in MIS—management, information, and systems
- differentiate among various types of information systems
- understand the various components of information systems

EXHIBIT 1.1

Bank of Baroda: Powering Operations with a Technological Advantage

Bank of Baroda (BOB), India's fifth largest bank and prominent among the global top 200 banks, is backed by a century of financial experience. With assets in excess of ₹1,60,000 crore, the bank has a network of over 2800 branches and offices, and about 700 ATMs. BOB offers a wide range of banking products and financial services to 29 million global corporate and retail customers. It carries out the operations with the help of various delivery channels, specialized subsidiaries, and affiliates in the areas of investment banking, credit cards, and asset management. Today, BOB has an international presence across five continents with a network of 71 offices in 25 countries.

BOB began its transformational journey by migrating to Finacle core banking and e-banking solutions and replaced eight other disparate legacy systems across its branches in 18 countries. The bank's 'one solution, one strategy' stance was a strategic move to deter vendor-dependence that hampered its business users when they designed new products and updated business rules. With the advent of Finacle's centralized solution on the BOB scenario, the entire solution framework drew support from the bank's centralized data centre at Mumbai. This eliminated the need for 60 IT supervisors posted at 25 locations and the locally recruited support teams they led. This move had a direct impact on the bank's bottom line.

In its quest for a viable enterprise resource management (ERM) strategy, BOB is all geared up to leverage the IT environment provided by Finacle and is prepared to take the first self-assured steps in that direction. This was a move typical of a bank that aimed at aggressively minimizing costs and risks to gain a winning edge.

Manual MIS reporting and the ensuing delays at BOB's branches were increasingly being viewed as a deterrent to agile senior management responses. The bank leveraged Finacle's common application network to ensure branch-to-head office MIS reporting in real time. Consequently, an activity that spanned several weeks was completed within minutes. The reporting infrastructure also ensures that uniformity and consistency in reporting logic is maintained across the bank's branches. It also covers other applications such as enterprise-wide general ledger, risk management, anti-money laundering, cheque truncation, credit cards, mutual funds, online trading, data warehousing, customer relationship management, Society for Worldwide Interbank Financial Telecommunication (SWIFT) facility, real-time gross settlement (RTGS), national electronic funds transfer (NEFT), Internet payment gateway, global treasury, human resources management system, employee payroll, cash management, mobile banking, SMS delivery, retail depository, phone banking, and knowledge management, which are well integrated and provide a seamless experience to customers of all segments and lines of business. These applications also provide critical MIS through a data warehouse for making timely business decisions.

The bank's technology initiatives are clearly focused on the customer. The business transformation programme encompasses technology and is implemented by the bank with a view to provide convenience banking to its customers on a 24 × 7 basis in India and abroad. This is also enabled by means of deployment of a single core banking solution platform across the globe with integrated delivery channels such as ATM, Internet, phone, mobile, kiosk, and call centre.

Sources:
www.infosys.com/finacle/casestudies/casestudies.asp, last accessed on 31 August 2012.
http://www.bankofbaroda.com, last accessed on 31 August 2012.

BOB's initiative to implement Finacle is seen as a strategy towards leveraging IT tools for minimizing costs and risks, and to gain a winning edge in the now very competitive financial space. As illustrated in Exhibit 1.1, the bank's technological initiatives are clearly focused on the customer.

As students of business management, we are interested in studying about successful businesses, that is, those that are profitable and sustainable in the long run. Information systems (IS) and technologies are vital tools for successful businesses. Thus, the study of IS becomes imperative for a student of business management. In this book, we will understand the concept of IS and examine how it enables business processes and helps managers take effective decisions. This chapter will explain the concept of an IS, the various types of IS with respect to modern business management, and the components of an IS.

CONCEPT OF MANAGEMENT INFORMATION SYSTEMS

Whenever we come across the term 'information systems', it invariably brings to mind images of computers. Due to the advent and advancement of information technology (IT), computer-based information systems (CBIS) are playing an important role in business decision-making. Therefore, our course of study will revolve round CBIS. Information systems, aided by IT, play a strategic role in organizations. IT and IS are being used not only for automating existing processes and documentation, but also for reengineering obsolete processes and bringing in organizational changes.

It was only with the popularity of computers that IS departments were formalized and came to be known as electronic data processing (EDP) departments. They were also called management information system (MIS) departments, and were centrally coordinated, manned by computer and management expertise. Just as computer systems became hi-tech with the integration of the Internet, telecommunication, and multimedia technologies, EDP evolved into IT systems, and the IS department came to be known as the IT department. Today, IT systems are the backbone of most businesses. Large businesses have powerful IT departments that are headed by vice-presidents and directors.

The concept of MIS is a recent development, though businesses have been using information for several decades. With the advent of computers and communication technologies, it has been possible to generate and transmit large volumes of information across the globe on a real-time basis. MIS is made up of three components—management, information, and systems. In order to understand MIS, we will first discuss the three components individually.

Management

The managers of a company use information systems for performing various managerial tasks. These include organizing, planning, coordinating, and controlling resources. According to Koontz (1972), 'Management is the art of getting things done through and with people in formally organized groups'. Managers perceive business challenges in the environment and formulate strategies for responding to these challenges.

What are the challenges? Businesses are run under several constraints, laws, and government regulations. There are demand and supply equations, and resource constraints such as men, material, money, markets, and time. The manager has to deliver under tight work and time schedules. He/She plans his/her duties and allocates resources—human or financial—to coordinate work and achieve goals. The ultimate goal of an organization is to make profit and survive amidst tough competition.

Managerial responsibilities and duties vary at different levels of the organization. There are no concrete lines of demarcation; however, based on the types of jobs they perform or the nature of the decisions they take within the organization, managers are categorized into three types—senior level, middle level, and operational level. Anthony (1965) divides the managerial activities into the following three levels:

- Operational control (operating management)
- Management control (middle-level management)
- Strategic planning (top management)

Figure 1.1 depicts the levels in a management hierarchy and the managerial control they exercise.

Top executives and senior managers make long-term plans and strategies. Strategies are tactical manoeuvrings of situations that can be moulded according to the organization's preferences. Extending business to a new product line, setting up a plant to produce a sub-product, etc., are examples of long-term plans. The middle management carries out the plans and visions of the top managers. Their duties help them implement long-term plans and strategic plans. On the other hand, operational managers are responsible for monitoring the day-to-day activities. These involve carrying out transactions (e.g., sales, purchases), managing inventory, marketing, recruiting, retrenching people, collecting outstanding money from customers, and making payments to suppliers.

Kanter (1996) precisely establishes the interaction among the three levels of management. At the strategic planning level, the senior management formulates the policies, plans, and objectives of the company. These factors are passed down to the middle management where they are translated to specific revenue, cost, and profit goals. These tasks are then reviewed, analysed, and modified to meet the organizational objectives. Following this, the middle-level managers issue plans and schedule them to the operating management for carrying out the tasks.

The relationship among management, data, information, and information system is explained in Exhibit 1.2.

Information

Information is the next important element in MIS and is considered a valuable resource for the successful running of a business. Information has become so important in modern-day business management that some management scientists have even added it to the list of important resources of a business—money, men, materials, and machines. Information is data that is processed and

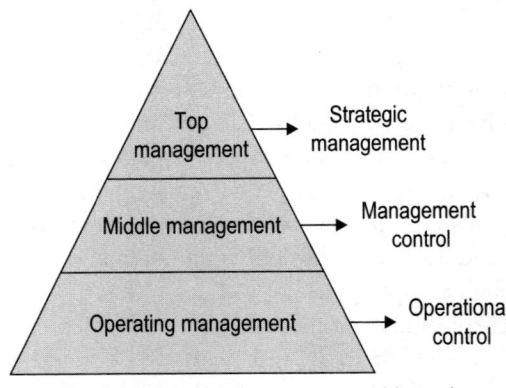

Fig. 1.1 Levels of management hierarchy

EXHIBIT 1.2

Information Systems at Girish & Co.

Girish Chandra runs a trading and distribution business. His firm, Girish & Co., has taken distributorship of major brands of gift items, perfumes, and music for the Delhi region, which includes the entire national capital region (NCR). The firm receives orders from retailers and consumers every day. The material is packed as per order and the pick-list is sent to the billing department for raising bills. Girish Chandra (management) wants to analyse sales data every month and asks his managers to compile a sales statement. He reviews the sales every month and quarter. Based on the sales trends, he discusses the plans and strategies with his managers. For the quarter ending June 2011, his manager has prepared a report (output) for the following sales data.

Girish & Co.
Statement of sales
Quarter ending June 2011

	April (₹)	May (₹)	June (₹)
Gifts	80,355	72,746	90,736
Perfumes	44,500	43,400	64,200
Music CDs	1,39,787	1,35,898	1,70,400

By studying this chart of information, we can deduce the following:

The billing clerk (people) scans (input method) each product during creation of a bill in the invoicing software (system) on a computer (technology) system. His system calculates (processing) the monthly sales of each type of product (data). The manager presents this report to his director. From this report, Chandra deduces that the sales of music CDs are better than the other products he deals with (information). It is evident from the chart that the sales in the month of June are higher than that of the previous month for all products (MIS). This chart helps him decide to keep more inventory of music CDs in June for the following year (decision support system).

(Hypothetical example based on author's personal experience.)

presented in different formats to assist decision-makers. Data, in contrast, are streams of raw facts representing events occurring in organizations or the physical environment, before they are organized and arranged in a form that people can understand and use (Laudon 2010).

System

The third element in the MIS is the system. A system is a set of elements that are combined together to achieve a common objective. These elements are input, process, and output; they are interdependent and interrelated. The input(s) are processed and converted into output(s). According to O'Brien (2006), a system is a group of interrelated components with a clearly defined boundary, working together towards a common goal by accepting inputs and producing outputs in an organized transformation process. The capturing of raw data from the environment that enters the system for processing is called input. The scanning of items at the billing counter by Girish & Co., in Exhibit 1.2 is a data input system. The conversion, manipulation, and analysis of raw inputs into processed data is called processing. In this example, each bill's sales value may not have mattered much to the manager. However, computing the total sales for the month becomes meaningful. The distribution of processed information in the form of a report is called output. The processed information provides some value to the manager. This output has helped him/her make a decision to buy more products for sale during the same month in the next year.

WHAT IS MANAGEMENT INFORMATION SYSTEM?

Having discussed the three components, we will define management information systems. MIS can be understood as a system that enables people to gather, consolidate, and compute data, and present the information in a meaningful and sensible format, either with the help of computers or manually. Laudon (2010) defines information system as a set of interrelated components that collect (retrieve), process, store, and distribute information to support decision-making, coordination, and control in an organization. It also helps managers analyse problems, visualize complex subjects, and find solutions.

There are three activities in information systems that produce the relevant information for managers. These activities are input, processing, and output. For example, as illustrated in Exhibit 1.2, Girish & Co., inputs data either by scanning each item at billing or by entering the item code in the system. This data is stored and then processed by a computer and organized

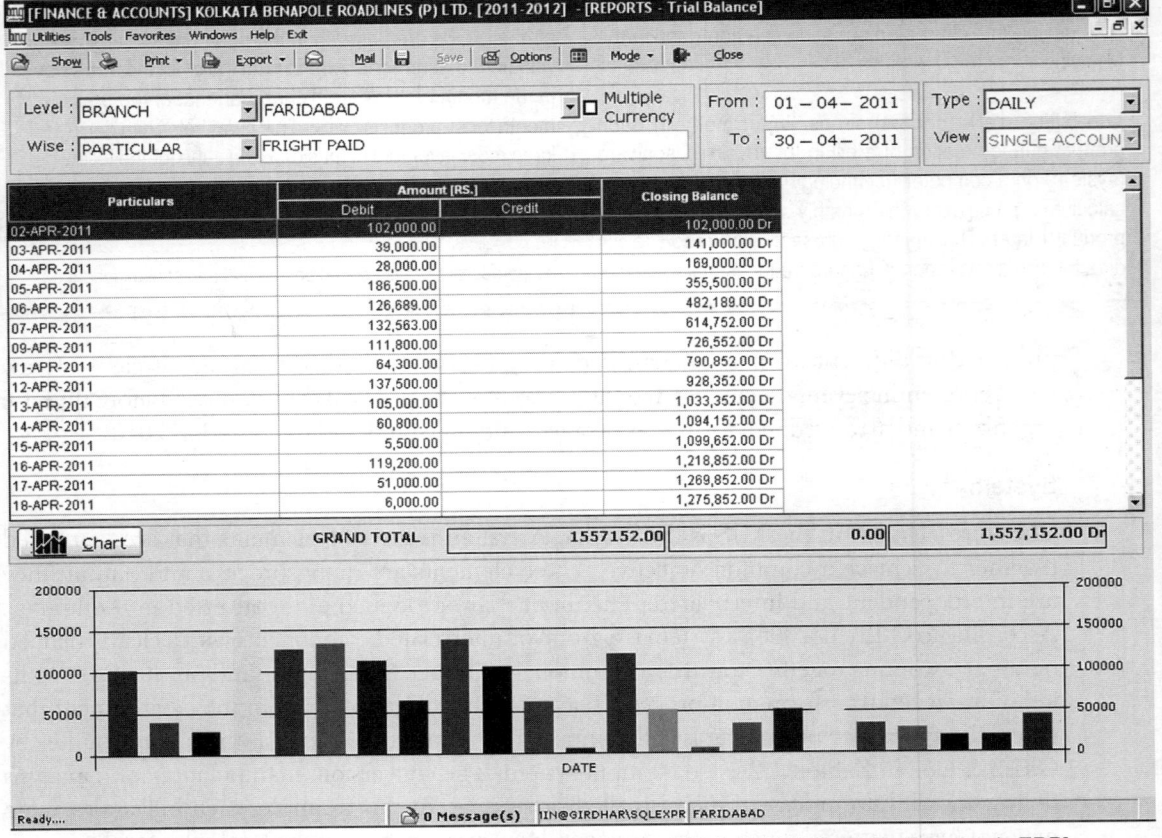

Fig. 1.2   Information presented in a variety of ways by an MIS tool [BNG Infotech, TransLogic ERP]

into an information format such as monthly sales figures and trends in sales. The management of the company then takes decisions to manage its business. The entire process of collection, processing, storage, and display of information for managerial decision-making forms a part of the MIS at Girish & Co.

Figure 1.2 illustrates how information is presented by information systems.

TYPES OF INFORMATION SYSTEMS

Information systems support the business processes of an organization. As there are several business processes, specialities, and levels in an organization, there can be several types of information systems. However, in the modern business context, applications can be broadly classified into six types of MIS. These six information systems are regrouped either as operational- or management-level information systems. Thus, we can call them either operations support systems or management support systems.

An information systems support is required at different levels of operations and management in the organization. As managers at different levels in organizations have different roles, responsibilities, and functions, based on management activity, we can categorize information systems in the following ways:

- Transaction processing systems (TPS)
- Office automation systems (OAS)
- Knowledge management systems (KMS)
- Management information system (MIS)
- Decision support system (DSS)
- Executive information system (EIS)

Figure 1.3 illustrates the classification of various information systems.

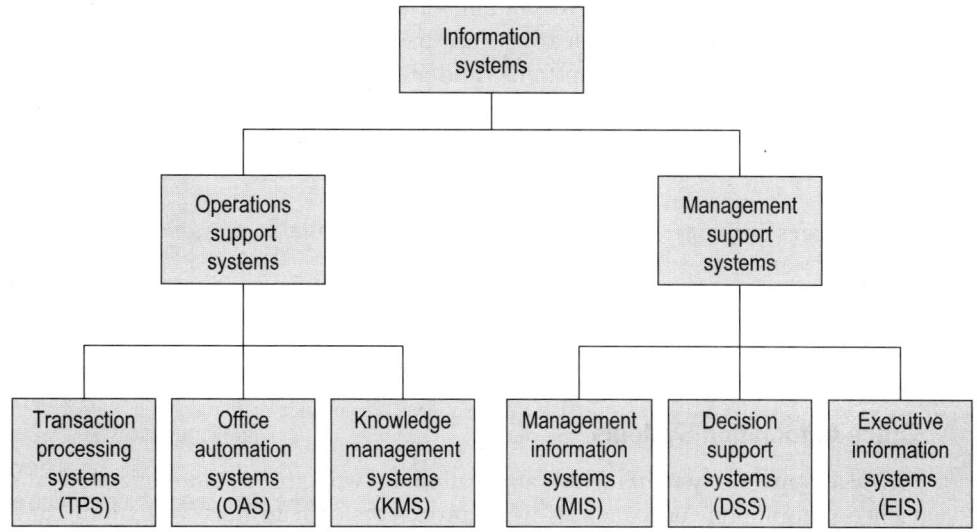

Fig. 1.3   Operations and management classifications of information systems

OPERATIONS SUPPORT SYSTEMS

Operations support systems cover those systems in which the basic data is generated and is later used for various internal and external purposes. For example, a bill generated by a sales system and a cheque payment voucher generated by a finance system are examples of operations support systems. Operations support systems cover the following:

- Transaction processing systems
- Office automation systems
- Knowledge management systems

Transaction Processing Systems

The everyday operations in an organization are managed by the operations personnel. They create basic documents such as bill, purchase order, material receipt note, and cheque. While creating these documents, certain predefined procedures are followed, data is gathered, and the transaction is completed. The personnel work on a predefined pattern. For example, every business organization has a system of billing that involves a number of predetermined steps, and the format of a bill is the same at a given period of time. These systems are called transaction processing systems (TPS).

TPS is the basic business system that works at the operational level of an organization. In the modern business environment, a TPS is a computerized system that performs and records the everyday routine transactions necessary to run the business. Examples of transaction processing include sales order processing system in a trading organization, hotel reservation system in a hotel business, out-patient registration system in a hospital, and payroll and financial transaction systems in all organizations. At the operational level, tasks are highly structured and well defined for functions such as sales, marketing, manufacturing, accounting, and purchases. The system conforms to these rules and generates primary data, which is further analysed at various levels of the management.

For example, Finacle's implementation at Bank of Baroda supports transaction processing of saving bank deposits, cheque clearing, cash payment, loan disbursement, etc., and thus ensures generation of basic data of a customer and his/her transactions.

Each of these TPS have dozens of subsystems. Figure 1.4 illustrates the various TPS and their subsystems. We will discuss these in greater detail in Chapter 2.

TPS have the following basic characteristics:

- Generates primary data that is further made available to other information systems for analysis
- Works on highly structured and predefined procedures
- Is routine and repetitive in nature
- Works at the operation level of the organization

Office Automation Systems

Office automation systems include applications for workgroup communications and productivity. Office automation tools such as word processors, spreadsheets, e-mailing, and storage and retrieval of electronic files come under this category. These applications not only cater to the communications requirements of office workers, but also help in the communication with external

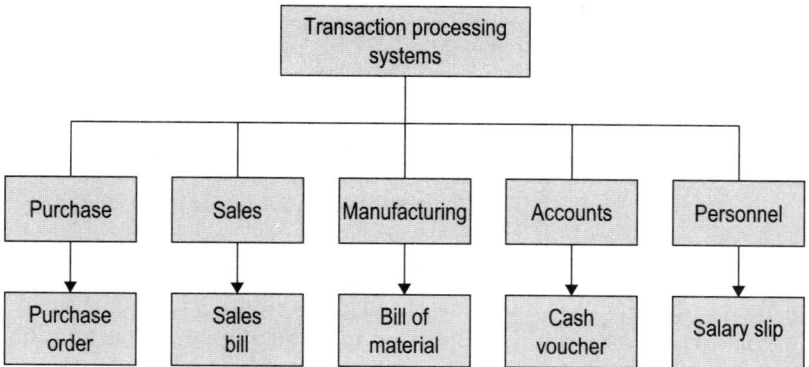

Fig. 1.4 Transaction processing system and its subsystems

stakeholders such as vendors, investors, and customers. Organizations also deploy enterprise collaboration for sharing and managing such files through local/wide area networks (LAN/ WAN) in the organization. For example, multiple users share a file over the Internet or LAN and update their tasks. Nowadays, a lot of communication is done through office automation systems such as e-mail, computer-enabled fax, and videoconferencing. The data generated by workers through these office automation tools further support MIS. An MS Excel worksheet in Fig. 1.5 illustrates a budget sheet of a firm.

Type	Customer	Orders Opening	Orders Current	Bills Pending	Bills Billing	Opening Balance		Receipt Against Bill	Receipt Advance	Outstanding Realised	Outstanding UnRealised	Outstanding Total
CUSTOMER												
	ASHOKA T	22472	0	0	22472	0	C	22472	0	0	0	0
	AVG	13484	0	13484	0	0	C	0	0	0	13484	13484
	CENTURY LTD	0	99903.72	0	99904	0	C	43652	0	56252	0	56252
	CENTURY MAN	0	105000	105000	0	136770	D	0	47250	136770	57750	194520
	DESHBANDHU ENGINEERING	233690	56180	289870	0	78652	D	67416	0	11236	289870	301106
	DEVI GEARS	420000	0	420000	0	120000	C	0	0	0	300000	300000
	FINE FILTERS	348600	0	348600	0	216125	C	0	0	0	132475	132475
	MACKSONS	77700	0	77700	0	25000	C	0	25000	0	27700	27700
	PUNEETA INTERNATIONAL	0	0	0	0	14607	D	14606.8	0	0.2	0	0.2
	RETILI FAB	189138	0	0	189395	90232	C	44203	0	145192	-90232	54960
	SPARCON	0	393750	393750	0	0	C	0	0	0	393750	393750
	LIVALIA	0	0	0	0	618	D	0	0	618	0	618
	MAHALAXMI	499999	0	499999	0	112854	C	0	0	0	387145	387145
	MEGA	0	0	0	0	25200	C	0	0	25200	0	25200
	MUMBAI	0	0	0	0	21000	D	0	0	21000	0	21000
	NEC HUBLI	0	0	0	0	10000	C	0	0	0	-10000	-10000
	NEETA JAMU	380000	0	380000	0	140000	C	0	0	0	240000	240000
	NORTHERN EAST	2134840	0	2134840	0	49440	D	0	0	49440	2134840	2184280
	OKARA	216000	0	216000	0	90000	C	0	0	0	126000	126000
	OKAY TEAM	0	0	0	0	15218	D	0	0	15218	0	15218
	RAJDOOT	105000	0	105000	0	55000	C	0	0	0	50000	50000
	REGAL	929250	0	929250	0	354000	C	0	0	0	575250	575250
	ROAD VIEWER	52500	0	52500	0	42000	C	0	0	0	10500	10500
	SADANA CARS	0	0	0	0	4500	D	0	0	4500	0	4500
	BLUE CLOTHS	0	0	0	0	3382	D	0	0	3382	0	3382
	CARE BIZ	50561.8	0	50561.8	0	0	C	0	0	0	50561.8	50561.8
	SHRIRAM	0	2809	0	2809	0	C	2809	0	0	0	0
	FOOTDESIGN	0	40449.6	0	40450	0	C	0	0	40450	0	40450
	GREENLAND	0	3370.8	0	3371	0	C	3371	0	0	0	0
	SRISHTI	0	24738.8	24738.8	0	0	C	0	0	0	24738.8	24738.8

Fig. 1.5 Use of spreadsheets for operations support

The following are the characteristics of office automation systems:

- They are productivity tools used by office staff.
- They enhance internal and external communication.

Knowledge Management Systems

Individuals build their expertise on a subject by understanding it through learning processes. The learning processes can be through study, interaction with groups, and also by coming across various situations in day-to-day work. Thus, knowledge refers to an individual's accumulation of information and expertise. Individuals having expertise and knowledge help organizations achieve their goals. However, what happens if an individual leaves an organization? The organization loses the knowledge along with the employee. In this fast-changing business environment with cut-throat competition, organizations cannot afford to lose important knowledge. Therefore, with highly efficient computer systems, organizations tend to build knowledge portals with the collective efforts of employees, research and development, and expertise.

Transaction processing systems do not cover the processes of knowledge discovery, storage, management, and dissemination. Knowledge base creation is the collaborative effort of experts and other employees. The collaborative activities are knowledge works and the system that promotes, preserves, distributes, and manages the knowledge works is known as a knowledge management system. For example, Siemens created a ShareNet portal for its employees to enter, store, update, and share knowledge, expertise, and inputs from the environment. The knowledge management website combines a data repository, a chat room, and a search engine. The employee can contribute to the effort of knowledge creation and search for knowledge sharing on various topics. This knowledge repository helped Siemens innovate and create an agile organization.

Let us summarize the characteristics of knowledge management:

- Knowledge is vested in individuals; hence, the risk of losing critical knowledge is always present.
- Knowledge base is an outcome of research and development, and employees' participation in knowledge base building.
- Knowledge management systems cannot be treated at par with MIS.
- Knowledge is very critical for organizations; they must promote and accumulate knowledge in a shared repository.
- Organizations need to invest in research and development.

MANAGEMENT SUPPORT SYSTEMS

Information systems that focus on providing information and support for effective and quick decision-making by managers are called management support systems. These systems work on the data generated by operations systems, which is further processed and converted into useful information. They comprise the following systems:

- Management information systems
- Decision support systems
- Executive information systems

Management Information Systems

Management information systems process data and convert it into information. They work on the primary data generated by the transaction processing systems. The system provides managers with reports and online access to the organization's current performance and historical records. MIS offer routine, periodical, and exception reports. Examples of exception reports include missing bills, goods sent to a branch but not received by them, difference in goods received from supplier and accepted by the company's inventory system, etc. These reports are simple and are not analytical in nature. Their orientation is internal, that is, they use the information generated by the transaction processing systems and knowledge work systems, as shown in Fig. 1.6. They do not look towards external environment or events. MIS have been in existence for the last four decades and are still appreciated as the most effective and efficient systems for business managers to carry out their management functions. Information systems have been developed for managers in charge of functional areas such as marketing, sales, purchase, production, material, accounts, and personnel.

The information systems covering these functional areas may be classified as follows:

- Hierarchical
- Horizontal
- Cross-functional

In hierarchical integration, the operational management-level systems feed data to middle-level management systems, and they in turn supply data to the strategic level. Horizontal integration

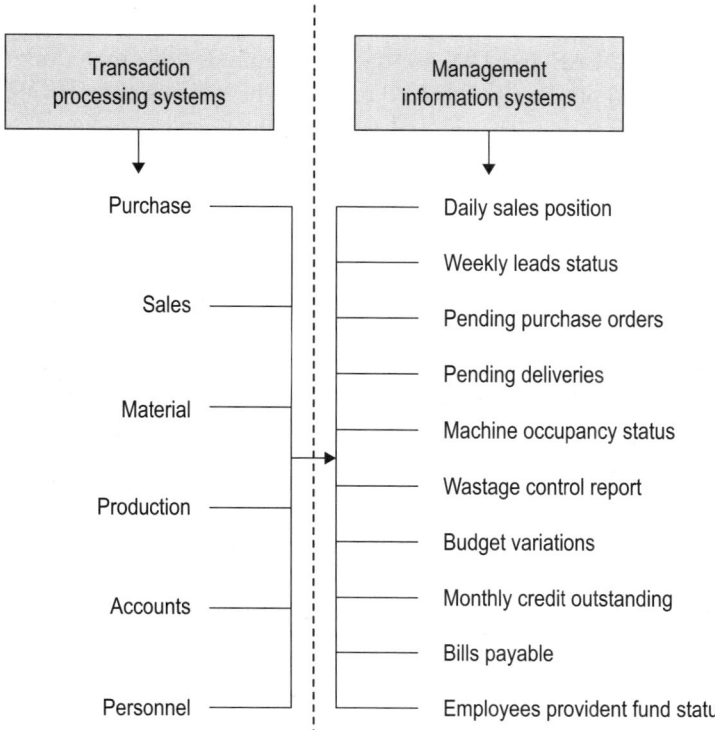

Fig. 1.6   MIS work on the data generated by TPS

refers to systems at the same level supporting other processes within the same functional area. Cross-functional integration refers to the use of data generated in one functional area for control and monitoring of the other. For example, if a financial system generates information of a particular customer having crossed his/her credit limit, the system at sales order processing may stop or send an alarm to the user.

We can summarize the characteristics of an MIS as follows:

- MIS do not generate any data. They work on data offered by TPS.
- MIS primarily serve the purpose of planning, controlling, and decision-making at the management level.
- This system provides managers with routine periodical reports and summaries.
- They work on internal data and do not consider external data.
- They provide fixed reports and, hence, are not much flexible in nature.
- Office automation systems such as word processors and spreadsheets support MIS.

Decision Support Systems

Data generated at the transaction processing level is processed to generate reports and graphs, and for further analysis by managers for making decisions. The information presented to the management is highly analytical. Decision support systems combine data and sophisticated analytical models or data analysis tools to support non-routine decision-making. They have more analytical power than other systems. By using tools such as online analytical processing (OLAP) and data warehousing (DW), users can derive reports by changing parameters, assumptions, and questions. OLAP and DW are database analysis tools that work on the huge data in the organization and produce the desired reports. The systems also provide sensitivity analysis, that is, 'what-if' analysis. In a what-if analysis, the manager can pose hypothetical questions regarding the future course of business, profitability, and product–market situations, and get analytical reports through these tools (see Exhibit 1.3).

EXHIBIT 1.3

How Krishna Engineering Corporation Uses Decision Support Systems

Krishna Engineering Corporation (KEC), headquartered at Patna, manufactures industrial blades and knives. The company has a large manufacturing unit. There are many cutting, hardening, and heat-treatment machines involved in the manufacture of blades. The firm bought a lathe machine 10 years ago at ₹2,00,000. This machine has recently started giving problems and needs to be maintained, at ₹1,00,000 every year. The new machine's current cost is ₹10,00,000. Obviously, on the new investment, the company calculates an investment cost in the form of 18% annual interest.

Krishna Kumar, the company's CEO, is interested in cost saving and profit maximization. The CEO wanted to have a system that can answer questions such as, 'What happens if we sell the printing machine and buy a new one at the new price?' 'Do we save money or end up spending more money?' Luckily, KEC had implemented an enterprise solution that offered analytical tools to answer his queries. The system offered DSS.

Additionally, this tool came handy to the marketing manager for his 'what-if analysis'. KEC has been advertising its products and manufacturing capabilities in newspapers, television channels, and had resorted to mass mailing for publicity of their products. Of late, they have also started web-marketing and search engine optimization, which bore the desired results. The m arketing manager of KEC uses the system to conduct what-if analysis to determine the media to be used to spend the advertising budget.

(Hypothetical example based on author's personal experience.)

Generally, a DSS serves at the senior management level. Systems at this level are designed to address non-routine decision-making by providing advanced graphics and presentations.

The characteristics of DSS can be summarized as follows:

- DSS are meant for managers taking non-routine decisions.
- DSS use internal TPS data, MIS reports, and other financial and revenue data for decision-making.
- They help the top management with an abstract and summary of the data in the graphical form.
- They use tools such as OLAP, DW, modelling, and sensitivity analysis for advanced decision-making.

Executive Information Systems

Executive information systems (EIS) provide critical information from a variety of internal and external sources to the top management for taking strategic decisions. Decisions concerned with strategy and long-term planning are made by the senior and top executive-level management. Strategic decisions are unique, non-repetitive, unplanned, and have a deep impact on the organization. The following are some examples of strategic decisions taken by the top management: relocating a production unit, venturing out to a new line of business, tie-ups and amalgamation, break-ups, and liquidation. EIS serve the top management with decisions that are unique, rapidly changing in nature, and not easily specified in advance.

EIS are supported by both TPS and DSS. By and large, executive information is presented in the form of graphs and abstract data by processing the internal and external data.

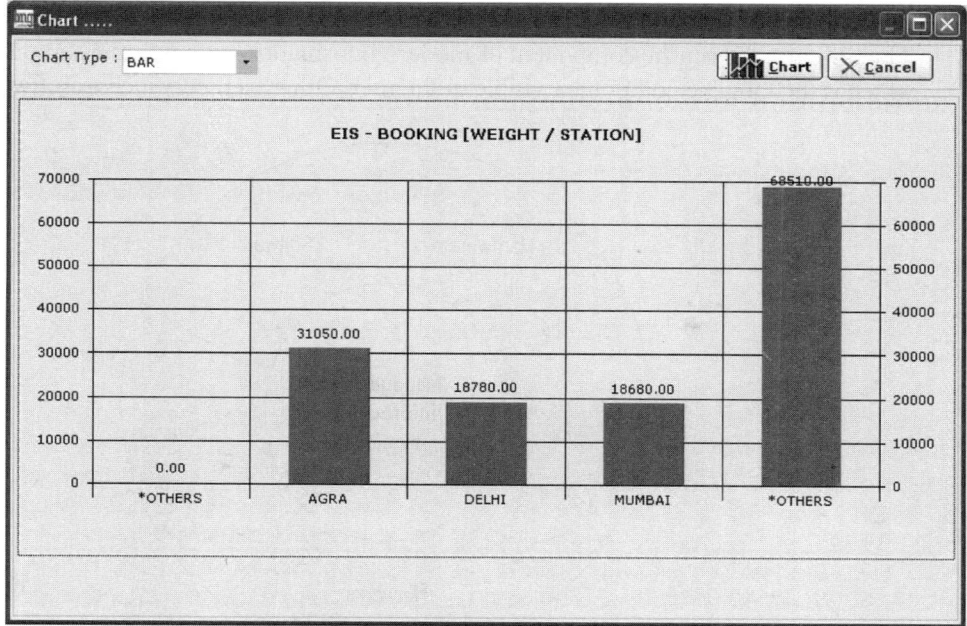

Fig. 1.7   Presentation of information by an EIS in a graphical form

Figure 1.7 illustrates an EIS report showing how much weight is moved by the logistics company per station in a given period of time. The information is presented in a graphical form and is summarized for the top management.

The characteristics of EIS can be summarized as follows:

- EIS are meant for the top management of the organization.
- EIS use internal financial and revenue data, and external data from government agencies and trade results.
- They help the management with an abstract and summary of the data, usually in a graphical form.
- They also use tools such as OLAP, DW, and sensitivity analysis.

COMPONENTS OF MANAGEMENT INFORMATION SYSTEMS

Having defined management information systems and understood the challenges of managing them, we must now know what constitutes an MIS. As discussed, the system concept applies to information management as well. The information system conforms to the input–process–output concept. It accepts input resources and processes them into information/output with the help of resources such as computers, applications, and people who manage the systems and convert the input into output. Business organizations have relied on information systems to communicate with human resources (people) using a variety of physical devices (hardware), information processing instructions (software), communication channels (networks), and stored data (data resources). There are five information technology components that are essential to build an information system, as illustrated in Fig. 1.8.

Hardware

The primary and central component of modern information systems is the computer hardware, which is the tangible component visible to the user. Other elements such as software, data, and

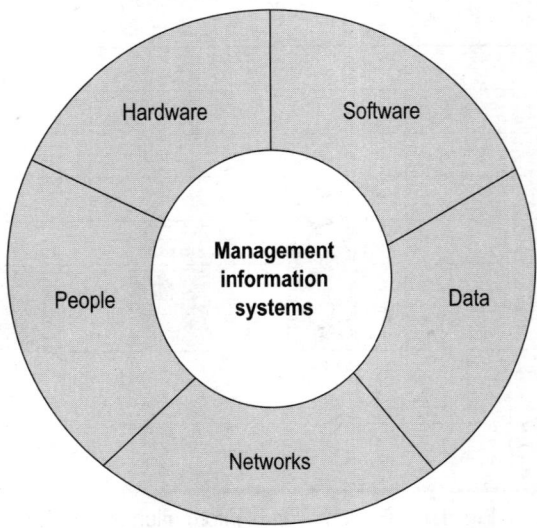

Fig. 1.8   Components of information systems

information are intangible assets. Computer hardware includes all the physical devices and equipment used in the processing of information.

In addition to resources such as desktops, laptops, and servers, hardware resources include peripherals such as printers and storage devices. We will discuss the various hardware systems used in modern information processing in Chapter 4.

Software

Software is a set of instructions given to the computer hardware to perform a specific task. These sets of instructions are called programs or applications. These applications are used for processing data and presenting it in a meaningful form to aid managerial decision-making. Software systems not only include applications but also system software, utilities, programming languages, procedures, and operating systems. We will discuss the concept of computer software in Chapter 5 and applications in Chapters 8–14.

Software can be broadly categorized into system software and application software.

System software The software that manages the resources of a computer system and provides utilities to manage creation, deletion, and storage of files, along with the software that controls various input and output devices, communication links, etc., is called system software. Various operating systems such as DOS, Windows, Linux, and Unix are examples of such software. In addition, various utilities such as Internet browsers and compress–decompress programs are a part of system software.

Application software Application software are programs that are directed towards the processing of information and produce a particular output. Software that is created to cater to business requirements and transaction processing is called application software. Word processors, spreadsheets, enterprise resource planning (ERP) systems, production planning systems, database management software, accounting software, and web-based ticket reservation software are examples of application software.

Data Resources

Data is the most indispensable component of an information system and a valuable resource for an organization. We have already defined data as streams of raw facts representing events occurring in the organization and environment before they have been organized and arranged into a meaningful form. However, data resources are more than just raw material for information systems. Data can be independent of applications and can be created, stored, and retrieved with the help of modern, sophisticated database management tools.

In any business transaction system, data is collected during the recording of transactions and processed and analysed later for management decision-making. The previously captured data is stored, processed, and analysed by using sophisticated applications, which may reveal complex relationships among sales, customers, costs, and profits. Data may be stored in many forms. Besides the traditional alphanumeric data that is composed of words and figures, the modern-day all-powerful database management systems can store, process, and analyse data in multimedia formats, that is, text, images, video, and audio data. Text data can be stored in text form, comprising words, sentences, and phrases; images data in the form of pictures and shapes; video data in the form of moving images; and audio data in the form of sounds and voice.

The data resides in a database. A database is a collection of related data that is stored in an organized and processed form so that it is available to many users for different purposes. We will discuss the various attributes of a database system, database administration, types of database, and some of the latest trends in database analysis such as OLAP, DW, and data mining (DM) in Chapter 6.

Networks

Networks and communication resources are fundamental components of computer-based MIS. We can hardly think of a modern successful business that does not rely on telecommunication technologies such as the Internet, intranet, and extranet. They provide a communication channel between two computers or a cluster of computers. Telecommunication networks consist of computers, communication processors, and other devices used to control the communication.

Computer networking is the science and technique of connecting two or more computers together to share files and documents and send messages. Local area network (LAN), wide area network (WAN), virtual private network (VPN), Internet, intranet, etc., are the various network systems that we will discuss in detail in Chapter 7. LAN technology is used to connect computers within an office to share applications, databases, and information. Organizations use multiple applications through LAN. WAN is used to connect offices across the city, country, or globe using several telecommunication channels. Computers can be connected through a wired medium or a wireless medium of telecommunication. Wireless fidelity (Wi-Fi), Radio frequency (RF), etc., are wireless systems of connecting networks. RF connectivity is gaining popularity because of the ease in erection and maintenance of the network. Using the Internet backbone, networks at the different offices of an organization are connected to one another. This is the technique behind the intranet. VPNs are established over leased telecommunication lines or an Internet backbone with high bandwidth. Bandwidth refers to the capacity of a telecommunication line to transmit a particular volume of data per unit of time.

People

Human resources are a very critical component of any MIS as they are instrumental in using and managing the systems. On the one hand, there are users such as accountants, salespeople, engineers, or managers who use information. These people spend their time creating, sharing, and disseminating the information within and outside the organization.

On the other hand, there are IT specialists who develop and manage information systems. These people include system analysts, software developers, database administrators, network managers, and system managers. System analysts understand business requirements and design systems accordingly. Software developers or programmers translate the business requirement document into an actual system by writing programs in modern-day programming languages.

INFORMATION SYSTEM ACTIVITIES

Information system activities refer to all the activities that occur during data processing. These activities are input, processing, output, data storage, and control. All information support systems

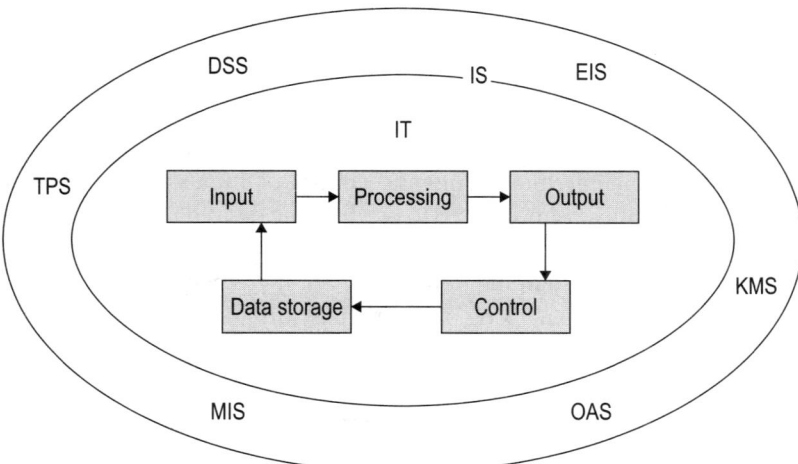

Fig. 1.9   Information system activities and information support systems

rest around these activities. Figure 1.9 illustrates them. The activities of an information system involve the following:

Input   Input refers to data entry activities. Before processing, data is collected and entered in the form of bills, product lists, material receipts, etc. The user collects or captures raw data from the environment and/or within the organization. The input process may be manual or automated. Data entry through barcode, radio frequency identification (RFID), and optical scanning are automated methods of data input. For example, physically entering the product code, name, quantity sold, and price in a bill processing system is a manual process. If the product details are entered by scanning a barcode or RFID tag on the product, it is an automated input process.

Processing   The conversion of raw input into information, and the subsequent manipulation and analysis is called processing. Processing activities may include calculating, comparing, sorting, classifying, and summarizing. To maintain accuracy and correctness of data in the information system, the data is periodically edited and manipulated. The data thus processed is converted into information for the consumption of end-users. For example, data related to each sales bill is computed for the entire month, and the sales summary and sales trends information are generated.

Output   The presentation of processed data, in the form of information to the users for consumption, is called output. The processed information is of some value to the user of an information system. The output in the required format helps in making the right decision. Common information formats include messages, reports, forms, and graphic images, which may be available in paper reports or electronic forms such as video, audio, or multimedia.

Data storage   Data refers to streams of raw facts representing events occurring in an organization or environment before they have been organized and arranged into a meaningful form. Information is the processed data on which future decisions and actions are based. Storage is the basic activity of any information system that retains data and information for future consumption by the managers. All forms of data, either in database files or electronic document files, are stored and retrieved whenever required.

Control Management of information systems calls for control of system performance. The system activities include monitoring and control of inputs, processing, output, and storage of data. The system must be monitored to produce the desired result. This is done through feedback generated at each activity. For example, if the number of outstanding purchase orders does not tally with the actual outstanding purchase order, there may be some mistake in data entry while receiving materials and knocking off a purchase order. This needs to be checked and corrected by the control system.

SUMMARY

An information system is the organized collection, processing, transmission, and dissemination of information in accordance with defined procedures, automated or manual. Management has been categorized into three levels—top management, middle management, and operating management—based on the types of tasks they perform and the decisions they take. The top management takes strategic decisions, the middle management exercises managerial control, and the operating management is interested in day-to-day transactions in the organization.

Broadly, there are six types of information systems that are regrouped as operations support systems and management support systems. The systems that support operations, namely transaction processing systems (TPS), office automation systems (OAS), and knowledge management systems (KMS), are categorized under operations support systems. Management information systems (MIS), decision support systems (DSS), and executive information systems (EIS) are part of management support systems. Transaction processing systems work at the operation level of the organization and MIS are used by middle-level managers who take day-to-day decisions. MIS work on the internal data collected by the TPS. Knowledge management systems are used by specialists and knowledge workers in the organization. DSS serve the top-level managers in making strategic decisions. EIS are also for the top management; they work on internal and external data and present reports in abstract and graphical forms.

Information systems have five components—hardware, software, data, networks, and people. These components are an integral part of any information system.

Information system activities include all the activities that occur during data processing. These activities are input, processing, output, data storage, and control. Information support systems rest around all these activities.

KEY TERMS

Application software Software that caters to the business requirements of data processing.

Competitive advantage Developing products, services, and capabilities that give the company an advantage over its competitors.

Cross-functional information system Information systems that draw information from multiple business functions in the organization.

Database Collection of records pertaining to the same set or object.

Decision support system An information system that supports decision-making with ad hoc, interactive modelling.

Electronic data processing Processing of data by electronic systems like computers to generate information for management decision-making.

Enterprise software Integrated suite of software to manage entire business operations.

Functional management Systems to manage various organizational functions such as sales and purchase.

Hierarchical integration A system in which the lower level of the system feeds data to the higher level.

Information system A system that produces information from a collection of data.

Knowledge management A system that promotes, preserves, distributes, and manages the knowledge works in an organization.

Operating system   A system that manages a computer's hard disk, memory, and file systems.

Operational control   Management control exercised by the operation-level managers.

Strategic control   Management control exercised by the top management for strategic issues.

Strategic decision   A unique, non-repetitive, unplanned decision that has a deep impact on the organization.

System   A set of elements that are grouped together to achieve a common objective.

System software   Software that manages the resources of a computer system and provides utilities to manage files creation, deletion, storage, etc.

CONCEPT REVIEW QUESTIONS

1. What do you understand by the term MIS? How does it assist managers in their everyday functioning?
2. How does data differ from information? Write brief notes with examples.
3. What do you mean by 'system'? What are the various elements of a system?
4. What is a system approach? Explain MIS as a system.
5. Describe the various levels of management with respect to the managerial tasks they perform.
6. What are the different types of management information systems from a management activity point of view?
7. What do you understand by transaction processing systems? Explain with examples.
8. Explain the term 'knowledge workers' with suitable examples.
9. What are the various components of MIS with respect to computer-based MIS.
10. Write short notes on the following:
    (a) OAS
    (b) TPS
    (c) KMS
    (d) DSS
    (e) EIS

CRITICAL THINKING QUESTIONS

1. Modern-day businesses cannot be managed without an efficient MIS in place. Critically examine this statement.
2. MIS is much beyond the computerization of business processes. Substantiate this statement with examples.
3. There are many types of information systems at Bank of Baroda (Exhibit 1.1). Identify them and explain the reasons for your choices.

MIS DEVELOPMENT

SM Perfume Corporation, a perfume manufacturing company, is owned by Sunil Mohanty. The company has its head office in New Delhi and two manufacturing units, one each in Aligarh, Uttar Pradesh and Haridwar, Uttarakhand. The company has one regional sales and distribution office in each of the four metropolitan cities. Each sales office is manned by a regional sales manager who collects orders from the distributors appointed in each state of the region. The logistics requirement is fulfilled by the regional distribution centre, which receives orders from distributors, routed through the sales managers incharge. The top management of the company requires day-to-day transaction data at the head office. The head office has received several complaints from distributors about delayed shipment of goods. On enquiry, the regional distribution hubs maintained that they dispatch the goods the same day they receive the sales orders from the regional sales managers. On further investigation, the regional sales managers figured out that the orders were manually dispatched from the distributors to the regional office. Following this, the regional office sends the orders to the head office for approval or authorization from the national sales head, who in turn routes the orders to the regional office for further processing. Moreover, the regional sales managers are unaware of the stock positions at each distribution centre.

Exercise

Design management information systems for SM Perfume Corporation, keeping in mind the data processing needs of each office, information requirements of each sales manager, and the requirements of the top management. How can the delay in order processing be reduced and how can sales managers get the stock position at the end of the day? What types of information would be required by the regional sales manager, national sales head, and managing director of the company? Design reports using spreadsheets for MIS, DSS, and EIS.

REFERENCES

Anthony, Robert, *Planning and Control Systems: A Framework for Analysis, Division of Research,* Graduate School of Business Administration, Harvard University, Cambridge, 1965.

Alter, Steven, *Information Systems—The Foundation of E-business,* Pearson Education, Singapore, 2004.

Davis, Gorden and Margethe Olson, *Management Information Systems,* McGraw-Hill, Singapore, 1996.

Goyal, D.P., *Management Information Systems—Managerial Perspectives,* Macmillan India Ltd, Delhi, 2006.

Jaiswal, Mahadeo and Monika Mittal, *Management Information Systems,* Oxford University Press, New Delhi, 2004.

Jawadekar, Waman S., *Management Information Systems: Text and Cases,* Tata McGraw-Hill, New Delhi, 2008.

Jerome Kanter, *Managing with Information,* Prentice-Hall, New Delhi, 1996.

Keen, Peter and Craigg Balance, *Online Profits: A Manager's Guide to Electronic Commerce,* Harvard Business School Press, Boston, 1997.

Koontz, Harold and Cyril O'Donnell, *Management,* McGraw-Hill International, New York, 1972.

Laudon, Kenneth and Jane Laudon, *Management Information Systems,* Pearson Education, Singapore, 2010.

Manzoni, Jean-Francois and Albert A. Angehr, *Understanding Organizational Dynamics of IT-Enabled Change, Research Paper,* http://www.calt.insead.edu/eis/documents, last accessed on 12 August 2011.

O'Brien, James, George Marakas, and Ramesh Behl, *Management Information Systems,* Tata McGraw-Hill, New Delhi, 2006.

CASE STUDY

Archies: Business Enablement with Information Systems

Archies Limited (Archies) was started by the Moolchandani brothers in 1979. It was launched as a greeting cards and gifts company with a very modest share capital and infrastructure. With the basic background in printing greeting cards and calendars of film personalities, the company evolved into the 'Hallmark' of India. By 2002, the company had strengthened its stable of products by adding multiple products such as gifts, perfumes, music cassettes, and photo albums. With a modest turnover of ₹40 crore in 1995, it has achieved a turnover of ₹157 crore in 2009–10. This achievement is despite the fact that the paper greeting cards industry has been facing intense competition from SMSes and e-greetings. Today, Archies can boast of the following:

- Archies is the largest retail chain in India in the greeting and gift segment with 168 stores in 48 cities and more than 300 franchisee stores.
- It has been a superbrand since the inception of the concept in India in 2003–04.
- It is Asia's largest greeting cards company and exports cards to Russia and Europe.
- Archies possesses exclusive licensing and marketing agreements with world-class brands such as American Greetings, Carte Blanche, and Fizzy Moon.
- Since 1988, it has influenced the way of expressing love on days such as Mother's Day, Father's Day, and Valentine's Day.
- The brand also created the concept of Friendship Day in August 1995.
- Greeting cards, as a segment, is growing annually in terms of value.

In the beginning of 2002, Archies had nine divisions, 11 distribution offices, 40 company-owned stores, and around 500 franchisee stores in the country. The company was vertically divided into nine major divisions as follows:

- Help-age division
- CRY division
- Gift division
- Perfume division
- Photo album division
- Paper flower division
- Office stationery division

- Printing division
- egreeting.com (an e-greetings division)

All nine divisions run as separate revenue centres. The 11 distribution offices across the country cater to the logistics requirement of 500-odd retail shops. Keeping pace with the retail boom, the company increased its number of stores from 40 in 2002 to 100 in 2009.

Archies faced several challenges and cut-throat competition from new emerging technologies such as e-greetings and SMSes. The new generation has an inherent liking for mobiles and electronic greetings. As a result, they switched over to new media, which is more efficient, prompt, and cost effective as well. The management of the company sensed this threat and recognized the importance of the Internet. The company mulled over the idea of restructuring the business. In order to keep pace with technology, archiesonline.com, the e-commerce division of Archies was created.

The functional departments encompassing the divisions at Archies include purchase, production, repacking, distribution, warehousing, accounting, information systems, human resource, taxation, machinery maintenance, and public relations. Archies' distributors visit the company's warehouses annually, before the beginning of the festival season. They browse through the new designs, select items they like, and confirm the order for the entire season.

Problem

The operations of the company were scattered over many functional divisions and geographical areas. Managing a big show without an efficient management information system (MIS) is a herculean task. Keeping a record of more than 1,00,000 inventory items at each warehouse and retail outlet was always an issue. Archies' management was always tech-savvy. This is evident from the fact that as early as 1990, they had registered their inventory on computers. The distribution billing was computerized using legacy software that was developed in-house. However, by the time the company became a 100-plus-stores organization, it could not just rely on its FoxPro-based legacy application, which was not efficient enough to handle the large number of records in its day-to-day operations. At the stores level, they needed proper electronic point-of-sales systems with user-friendly software packages. The problem was not just billing and stock keeping at the store front; it included gathering and analysis of data, valuation of stock, and preparation of statutory reports for investors and governments. Keeping a tab on stock movement,

analysing sales graphs of each store, and so on were crucial activities that Archies' management could not do without. In order to streamline these activities, Archies felt that they needed a proper MIS that could combine their retail and distribution operations.

Solution

The search began for the best, localized, comprehensive, but cost-effective software package that could cater to the entire needs of the management. A host of packages were evaluated keeping in mind these requirements. Delivery and implementation time were also important factors. The management zeroed in on BrainSoft, a local solution provider. The software vendor had a good presence in the segment and a localized product suitable for most retail and warehousing operations. After looking at the product features during a series of demonstrations, the senior managers of Archies were convinced about the product quality and felt that it suited their purpose. As the price was also attractive, the risks were minimum.

Archies commissioned IBM XEON servers E5506 quad core with dual processors and RAID5 systems that had around 500 GB hard disk and 8 GB RAM. Some 250 systems across nine divisions were connected at the corporate office. In some offices, cabled network was not available. Therefore, the IT department opted for wireless technology. As a result, WAN was established using a radio frequency (RF) transmission system.

Implementation

The decision taken by the management at Archies' was effective. The small vendor-consultant, who hardly had any big names on the customer list, had strong technical know-how and a stronger commitment to deliver, and thus, made it possible to implement the core modules within a mind-boggling time span of four months. This included system analysis, customization (mostly hardcore, which involved modification of the source code), data-porting, and training to the staff. There were around 75 major modifications and customizations in the software to accommodate the company's business functions. Around 100 new reports were drawn. Even the basic structure of product coding was changed. However, the strong will of the EDP team to implement a solution and the continuous support of the vendor organization were key factors behind the success of the project.

BrainSoft customized their distribution enterprise solution named 'Revive' to suit Archies' information system requirements. In the first phase, four information systems were implemented for the main functional areas—purchase, distribution, inventory, and accounts. The purchase system took care of purchase order generation and vendor evaluation systems. For order processing, handheld data capture units were used. The buyer visited Archies' warehouse and scanned an item of their choice. Later, this data was downloaded onto the computer. Goods were dispatched to them on the basis of the records in this computer. Inventory was streamlined by converting the opening stock data from legacy systems. The product code was 20 digits long, which represented the country code, company code, product code, and batch number. Similarly, finance and accounts were brought into the same system, as the company had been using the Tally software for accounts earlier.

As the implementation of an effective MIS involves change management in the organization, the constant support of the senior management was a key driver. A system task force (STF) was created, headed by Sanjay Harisinghani, General Manager, IT, and involved senior EDP and accounts managers of Archies and functional and technical heads of BrainSoft, who closely monitored the progress in MIS implementation.

Benefits

With the implementation of the MIS, all departments and functional areas were brought under one integrated solution. Duplicity in entering the same data into two different systems was eliminated. Similarly, systems executives who were earlier working on just sending and receiving data from Tally to their old system were allocated better jobs. By automating all divisions and departments, the huge investments on RF and optical fibre connections for intranet were utilized. The MIS system generated analytical reports on sales and stock of every store. Matrix reports on divisions–products and divisions–segments were available to the top management. Being in a business that is hugely impacted by new trends in the market, the top management was always interested in sales trends for different product lines. The following is the quantitative analysis of the changes:

- Increase in sales by 127% from 1996 to 2010.
- Investment blocked on inventories decreased by ₹61.5 million in 2010.
- Managing 168 stores in February 2010 as compared to 38 stores in 2002.
- Employee strength increased to 810, an increase of merely 15%, in spite of a sales growth of 127%.
- Increase in profits by 64% from 2002 to 2010.

Discussion Questions

1. What were the information issues before implementation of the integrated MIS at Archies?
2. From the perspective of the MIS, analyse the present division structure. Suggest a better structure that would benefit the management.
3. Classify the various systems at Archies into TPS, MIS, KMS, and DSS.
4. Identify the hardware, software, data, network, and people resources in these information systems.
5. Keeping in mind the competition from electronic media such as e-mail and SMS greetings, as a manager, what would you suggest to meet the challenges?

Sources:
'Archies powers retail outlets with new solution', http://www.cxotoday.com, last accessed on 26 October 2004.
'Archies to deploy connectivity solutions', http://www.cxotoday.com, last accessed on 12 September 2005.
Company's promotional material, interactions with management, and personal observations during consulting.
www.archiesonline.com, last accessed on 12 September 2005.

Note:
The cases used in this book are not intended to comment on the functioning or management style of the companies. They have been provided only for the purpose of learning.

2

MIS in Business

Technology is no longer an afterthought in forming business strategy, but the actual cause and driver.

—RAVI KALAKOTA AND MARCIA ROBINSON

LEARNING OBJECTIVES

After studying this chapter, you will be able to

- understand the role of management information systems (MIS) in an organization
- get acquainted with the trends in MIS
- understand various business processes
- define the scope of information systems from a functional perspective
- comprehend the challenges of managing information technology

EXHIBIT 2.1

Max Healthcare: Building Customer-centric IT Systems

Anyone who walks into a hospital for treatment of a problem, big or small, would want efficient and effective care, and transparent dealings. These are two parameters that are being increasingly considered by hospitals to measure themselves. The deployment of a state-of-the-art electronic health records (EHR) system at Max Healthcare Ltd, a well-known hospital chain in the national capital region (NCR), underscores this point.

'The EHR project was conceived with two major objectives', said chief information officer (CIO) Neena Pahuja, in an interview with CTO Forum. 'The first is quality of care and the second is continuity of care. These are probably the reasons that most hospitals worldwide go for EHR', she said. Besides achieving the twin objectives, this also helps the third-party administrator (TPA) in insurance claim assessment.

Dr Pervez Ahmed, chief executive officer (CEO) and managing director of Max Healthcare, said, 'Max Healthcare is striving to revolutionize healthcare delivery in India. In this effort, we were searching for a technology partner with a wide healthcare experience, who could assume the responsibilities for our IT solutions and implement an EHR that would comply with evidence-based medicine and clinical best practice standards, ensuring quality of patient care. Under a 10-year agreement, Perot Systems would be implementing and maintaining EHR.'

How EHR Helps Customers

Electronic health records begin when a patient seeks an appointment. The person may then get appropriate treatment either as an outpatient or an inpatient in the hospital. The EHR captures every step of the journey till the patient is cured/discharged. The information that is captured is exhaustive, and includes previous treatments, medications, allergies, and medicines that the patient should not be consuming, etc.

Patient-centred care is the core of all the activities. Widely acknowledged nationally and internationally for its quality patient care, Max has successfully implemented the medical excellence model through its clinical team of expert physicians and nurses who work together in an integrated manner, assessing patient needs, ordering tests, planning treatments, scheduling surgeries, monitoring progress, and planning for early discharge as well.

'We have a comprehensive performance measurement system for key processes—medical and services. Several process indicators are tracked uniformly across all hospitals and are regularly reviewed against preset targets to identify opportunities for improvement. Apart from this, a medical quality dashboard is placed for monitoring adverse events and clinical outcomes. We have recently developed an innovative, first of its kind scorecard for key clinical departments that track business, service, and clinical outcomes on an integrated platform,' said Dr Ahmed.

Right Medication, Right Patient, Right Time

Let us take an example to describe EHR's efficiency. From the patient's perspective, the EHR captures information on allergies. From the hospital's point of view, the EHR is used to store all available information on generics, dosage, any known allergies that have been reported in connection with those generics, and so on. The system then points out any instances of likely allergies or wrong dosage using the base data that has been fed into it.

All this helps ensure 'the right medication for the right patient at the right time,' said Pahuja. Keeping track of these data helps in easily monitoring which medication was given to which patient at what time. Every patient in the hospital will have a unique ID and the barcodes of the medication given to that patient will get associated with that ID. When a doctor prescribes a particular medicine to be administered at a particular time, after scanning the bar codes of the patient's unique ID and the medicine, the nurse will get an alert if the time at which the medicine was actually given does not fall within one hour of the time at which the medicine was meant to be given.

Customer-centric Approach

The EHR enables single window access to information of any given patient's care at any point in time, and helps analyse how a patient is responding to the prescribed treatment. This is the basic system that some of the progressive hospitals across the globe are trying to implement, because it brings in transparency. It also makes the doctors and nurses more accountable. They sign off every document, and look for every reaction before they sign off.

(Contd)

Exhibit 2.1 (Contd)

For patients, this would bring in many benefits. For instance, it significantly reduces the waiting period for the completion of the discharge processes. In some cases, the streamlined quality and continuity of care might even cut down the number of days the patient needs to stay in the hospital, thus improving the hospital's 'average days of stay' record.

Benefits

The EHR went live in August 2011, and so far, four hospitals have become a part of it, including three new hospitals that the chain started since then. While the main objectives of quality and continuity of care are being met, Pahuja expects some quantifiable financial benefits due to measures like moving towards a paperless office.

Pahuja's team has spent approximately 300 sessions on training the doctors and other personnel in using the EHR. While the flagship hospital at Saket in New Delhi needed change management handling, the new hospitals started implementing the EHR from the beginning. 'The doctors all like it', she said. The EHR was implemented by Dell Inc.'s IT services team, and Max Healthcare used an open-source product—WorldVistA, which was customized for Max Healthcare's specifications.

Analytics—The Road Ahead

In the near future, the hospital will continue to add more systems to the EHR. Radiology information system is one such project that will be integrated soon. It will use a speech-to-text software program and will also make specialist observations and dictated reports available within a matter of minutes. The integration with the EHR will also make the text version available very quickly to any other specialist that a patient needs to consult.

Later, the system may also allow Max to start looking at trends in instances of various diseases, their causes, the predisposition of various categories of people in terms of age, gender, diets, and perhaps, even socio-economic factors, and so on. This will be done to the level where doctors will identify which medicine is better for a person based on whether he is a wheat eater or a rice eater. These changes can be made possible with analytics.

Sources:

Arakali, Harichandan, 'Quality health care, the electronic way', http://www.thectoforum.com/content/quality-health-care-electronic-way, last accessed on 29 November 2011.

Sharma, Ankush, 'Perot Systems to enhance Max Healthcare service delivery', http://biztech2.in.com/news/healthcare/perot-systems-to-enhance-max-healthcare-service-delivery/65822/0, last accessed on 24 March 2012.

http://www.maxhealthcare.in/aboutus/totalpcare.html, last accessed on 24 March 2012.

http://www.maxhealthcare.in/pdf/applications_of_information_technology_in_hospital_healthcare.pdf, last accessed on 24 March 2012.

Max Healthcare implemented the EHR systems to achieve the objective of quality customer care (Exhibit 2.1). The case shows that organizations rely on information systems to run their businesses and drive innovation, growth, and customer satisfaction. They are built not only for managerial support, but also for customer fulfilment. The role of MIS has metamorphosed from a mere support system for the management into a customer-centric system.

In this chapter, we will discuss how information systems are used by organizations and the role they play in creating an efficient, innovative, and customer-centric business. We will also briefly discuss the trends in MIS.

ROLE OF MIS IN ORGANIZATIONS

Management information systems play a very important role at three stages in an organization. They ensure that the correct data is entered, processed, and further disseminated to the required places. They ensure accurate information at the right time to the management for taking the right decision. Management information systems help the management personnel by providing data for taking strategic decisions and enhancing the competitive advantage of the organization.

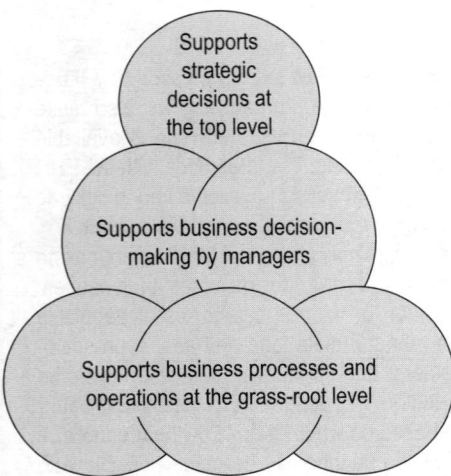

Fig. 2.1   Three vital roles of MIS in an organization

Thus, information systems play a very important role at the following three levels of management in an organization:

- At the grassroots level, they support its business processes and operations.
- They support decision-making by its managers.
- They provide support for strategic decisions taken by the top management.

This is shown in Fig. 2.1. A good MIS positively impacts an organization's functions, performance, and productivity. Today, the key to effective management of organizations is access to appropriate information and knowledge management. With the support of MIS, the management of all functions becomes efficient. Managers are alerted about exceptions and informed about probable trends in the various aspects of business. The efficiency of the business operations increases, as implementation of MIS throughout the organization brings in homogeneity and standardization. This helps people in understanding the terminology and inferring the same meaning, irrespective of the location. A well-designed and pervasively-implemented system motivates managers to use a variety of tools for better management of the organization. Computer-based MIS provides a relief from the monotonous work of recording, searching, processing, and computing data. It creates information-based work culture, leaves human resources with more quality time, and also improves their satisfaction levels. Though there have been instances in the past when employees felt insecure because of computers taking up most of the work that was repetitive and laborious in nature, it is possible to handle this kind of negative impact with proper training and counselling.

As described in Exhibit 2.2, the automation of point-of-sale (POS) billing at Study Apparels supports business process and operations, and creates a database. The periodical MIS reports to the middle managers help them in business decision-making. The top management of the firm

---

EXHIBIT 2.2

Study Apparels: Role of MIS in Retail Stores Management

Study Apparels is a multi-location retail store chain, exclusively targeted towards men's formal wear. Headquartered in New Delhi, the firm owns around 15 stores, primarily in major cities across the country. The management implemented MIS in all its stores and in back-office operations, warehouses, and accounts. MIS played vital roles in the following three ways:

Support business processes   The POS billing counter was automated. This facilitated unhindered billing, checkout, cash collection, and customer information collection. Post

POS automation, the employees were happy as they did not have to manually compile daily sales statements, inventory position, and stock replenishment statements.

Support decision-making   The store manager could analyse what was moving fast and which products were the slow-moving ones. Based on a computerized sales analysis statement, they could decide to demand the high-selling products from the central warehouse of the firm. The stock replenishment decision was also taken based on the reorder statement provided by the new MIS.

(Contd)

Exhibit 2.2 (Contd)

As the MIS helped capture customer information and maintained sales history for the customer, the manager could identify loyal customers and provide them extra benefits of discounts and freebies.

Support strategic decisions   The director of the firm started getting consolidated and comparative sales statements of all the stores on a regular basis. The director could easily make out that some products were selling better in one store, whereas, they were performing badly in another. He decided to discontinue shipping the poor-selling product to such stores. This also helped in taking a strategic decision of locating and relocating such stores. Fast and hassle-free checkout provided a satisfying shopping experience to the customers, who flocked in more numbers. Definitely, the implementation of MIS clearly provided a competitive advantage to Study Apparels.

(Hypothetical example based on author's personal experience.)

benefits by getting a complete view of the stores and customers across the country. The case gives examples of how MIS plays these roles in an organization.

TRENDS IN MIS

Historically, MIS was a management tool to help the management make informed decisions for business, based on the information gathered from all business departments. With the advent of computer-based information systems, technology has greatly improved the effectiveness of MIS. Applications of information systems have expanded greatly over the years, and the gambit of MIS now includes enterprise solutions, decision support systems (DSS), expert systems, knowledge management (KM), and so on.

Table 2.1 summarizes the trends in MIS, particularly with respect to the scenario in India. Until 1970, very few Indian businesses were using computers for data processing and information generation. The manual systems of transaction processing, record keeping, and accounting were used to generate information that the management needed for decision-making to run businesses. The accounts function was powerful to support the management with financial data and other data as well. With the introduction of computer-based data processing in the 1970s, the function was known as electronic data processing (EDP). The concept of MIS was conceived when businesses developed applications, keeping in view the predefined management reports that would give managers the information that they needed for decision-making.

Table 2.1   The expanding role of computer-based information systems

Year	Headed by	MIS activities
1950–1970	Data processing, accounting personnel	Manual systems of transaction processing, record-keeping, and accounting
1970–1980	EDP department	Data processing using computers, provided basic information about business
1980–1990	MIS department	Management information built for managerial decision-making
1990–2000	Systems department, system managers, vice-president (VP)	Executive information systems, decision support systems, expert systems, etc.
2000 onwards	CIO/CTO	Web-enabled enterprise and e-business systems

The concept of DSS was introduced to support managers with ad hoc reports, as MIS was not able to provide the same. This new form of MIS provided managers with interactive and summary reports for their decision-making processes. However, according to O'Brien (2007), it became evident that most of the top corporate executives did not directly use either the reports of MIS or the analytical modelling capabilities of DSS, and hence, the concepts of executive information systems (EIS) and expert systems were developed. These information systems were created to give top executives an easy way to get the required critical information, in a preferred format.

Finally, the growth of the Internet, intranet, and telecommunications at the beginning of this century, changed the capabilities of computing, and hence, information systems. Organizations started to use enterprise systems and web-enabled applications to run their businesses. These systems encompassed all features of MIS, DSS, EIS, etc.

BUSINESS PROCESSES

Business processes refer to the way the work in an organization is planned, distributed, and coordinated to produce a product or service. Business processes are a sequence of structured activities to perform a certain task. They consist of a concrete workflow of material, information, and knowledge, as a set of activities to, perform the job. For example, sales is a business function that covers processes such as identifying customers, accepting orders from them, and dispatching goods or performing services to them.

Every business consists of several processes. The related business processes are grouped under major functions such as sales, purchases, inventory management, warehousing, manufacturing, and personnel. Similarly, service delivery has a set of processes. For example, as illustrated in Exhibit 2.1, the hospital patient care processes include patient registration, doctor consultation, tests, diagnosis, and prescription. Table 2.2 describes some typical business processes for each of the functional areas of a business.

Some of the business processes are cross-functional, and require the contribution of more than one functional department of the business. For example, the purchase ordering system may require approval from the finance department for the budgetary outlay. Similarly, the sales orders processing may require approval from the finance department for the credit period or credit limit

Table 2.2 Examples of functional business processes

Functional area	Business process	Functional area	Business process
Purchase	Vendor identification	Manufacturing	Bill of materials and material requirements
	Quotations		Production scheduling
	Rate contract		Shop-floor control
	Purchase ordering		Quality control
Sales and marketing	Customer identification	Finance and accounting	Invoicing
	Price quotations		Paying suppliers
	Order acceptance		Receiving dues from customers
	Order processing		Recording business expenses
	Dispatch of goods		Making financial statements

validation of the customer, and approval from the production planning department to verify if the company has the spare production capacity to fulfil the order on time.

These processes are same for similar businesses across the world. However, the performance and efficiency of the business depends on how these processes are designed and coordinated by the employees. According to Laudon (2010), a company's business processes can be a source of competitive strength if they enable the company to innovate or execute better than its rivals. However, they can also become liabilities if they are based on outdated ways of working that impede organizational responsiveness and efficiency.

Business processes are managed with the help of IT so that they bring in efficiency and innovation. The concept of business process management is a holistic approach that is focused on aligning all aspects of an organization to fulfil the customer's needs. MIS supports business process management.

INFORMATION SYSTEMS FROM FUNCTIONAL PERSPECTIVE

We have discussed information systems from the point of view of managerial roles and responsibilities in Chapter 1. Now, we will discuss how MIS is used by organizations to manage business functions such as sales, purchase, material, finance, manufacturing, and personnel. Together, all these functions facilitate the process of buying, processing, and selling goods, as shown in Fig. 2.2.

The work distribution is based on these functions (also known as departments). All MIS are designed to support these functional systems. For each functional area, there are information system applications for transaction processing, operational control, and strategic planning. However, these business systems and sub-systems are not stand-alone or distinct processes. They are all part of the organizational system and are fully interdependent. Figure 2.3 depicts the interdependency of various systems through a flow chart.

We will discuss information systems for the following organizational functions:

- Purchase and vendor management systems
- Sales and marketing systems
- Material management systems
- Finance and accounting systems
- Manufacturing—production planning and control systems
- Human resource management systems

Purchase and Vendor Management Systems

Efficient purchasing and vendor management mean cost control and profit maximization. Business processes in the purchase department cover activities such as vendor identification, evaluation, request for quotation, rate contract, price finalization, and issuing purchase orders as illustrated

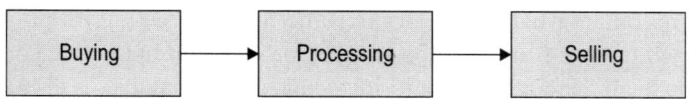

Fig. 2.2 Business as a system across all functions

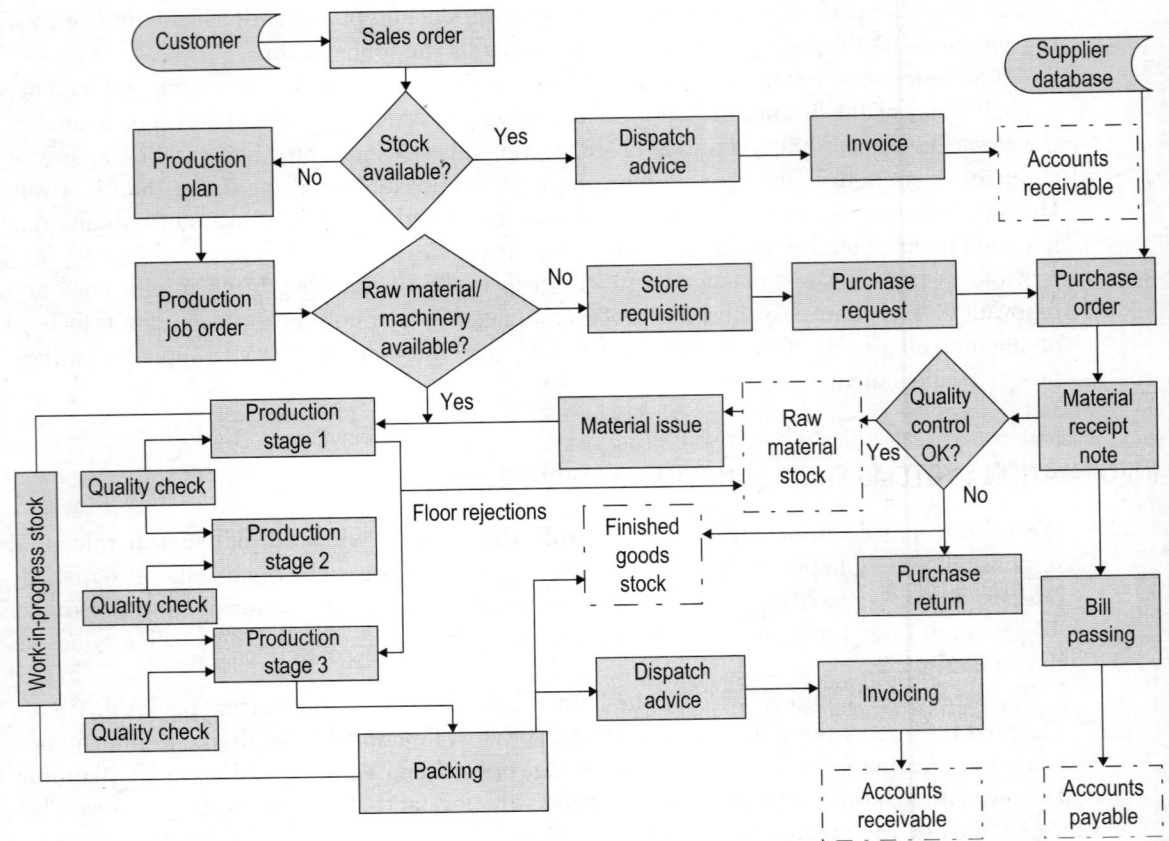

Fig. 2.3   Flow chart showing interdependency of various organizational systems [Joshi (2008)]

in Fig. 2.4. Internally, the purchase department plans purchases to be made during a particular time period. Purchase planning is based on a variety of factors such as sales data of the same period during the previous year or month, present demand, seasonal factors, and organizational planning. The purchase and vendor information systems generate periodical reports on pending supplies, short supplies, vendor performance analysis, purchase value estimation, purchase costing, purchase planning based on reorder, previous period requirements, open-to-buy (OTB), etc. These information systems bring efficiency in purchase functions and avoid chances of overstocking.

Sales and Marketing Systems

A major chunk of an organization's resources is spent on marketing of goods and services. According to Philip Kotler (1986), marketing is a social and managerial process by which individuals and groups obtain what they need and want through creating, offering, and exchanging products of value with others. Information systems for sales and marketing consist of functions related to marketing lead generation, orders, invoicing, and dispatches as illustrated in Fig. 2.5.

Sales and marketing cover activities related to product, price, promotion, and place. The choice of a product is based on the analysis of what sells most at a given point of time and place. Price

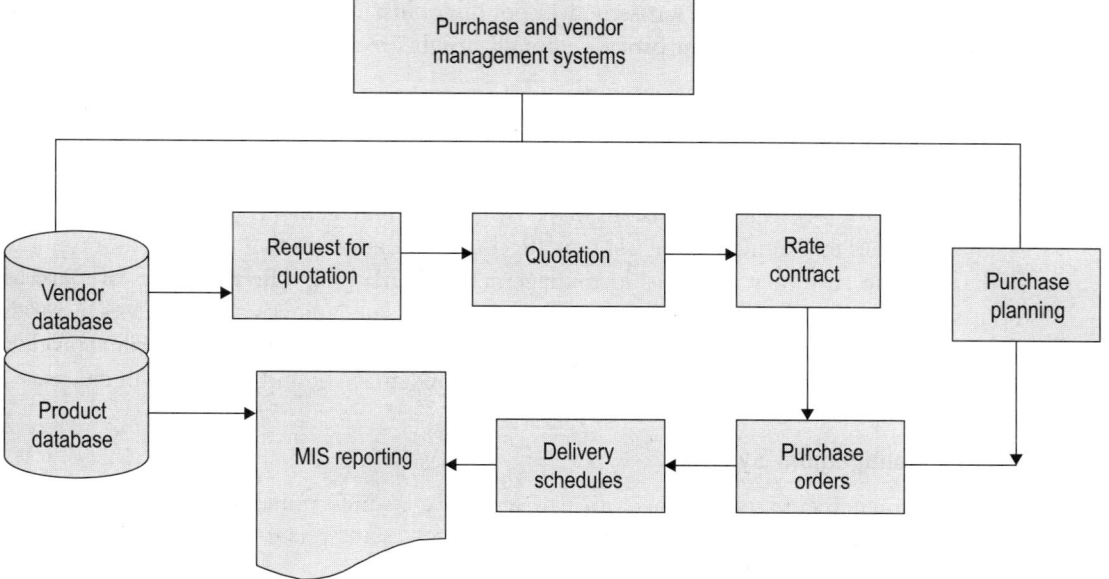

Fig. 2.4   Purchase systems and subsystems

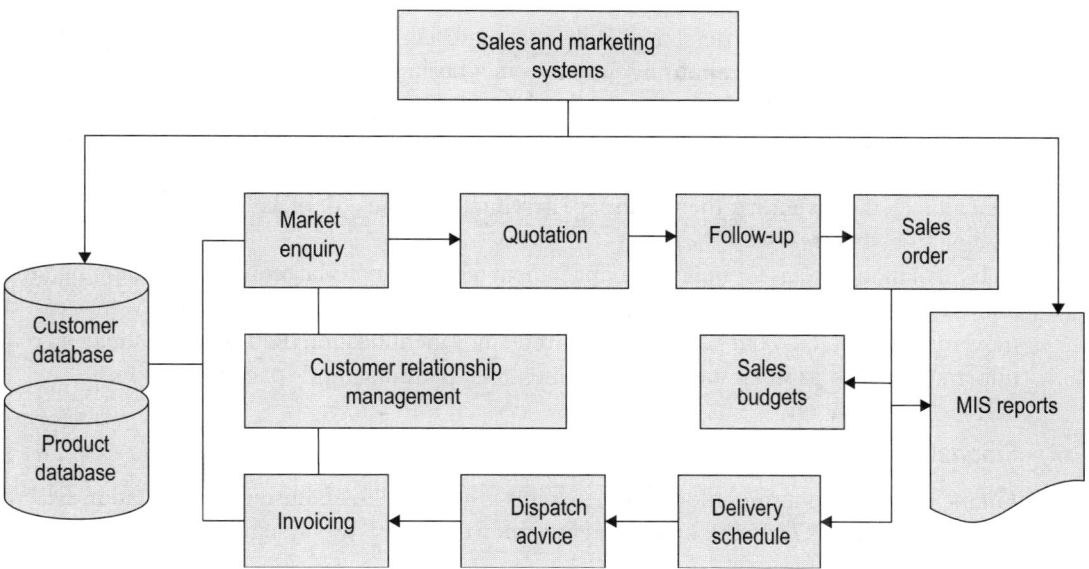

Fig. 2.5   Sales and marketing systems and subsystems

determination is a complex choice and is based on several factors. It is not based on just demand and supply. The system does an analysis of internal factors such as costs, margins, and quality of the product. External factors, such as competitors' price for a similar product, place, and time considerations of what a customer can pay, are also important factors for determination of prices. Similarly, the promotion mix is also decided on a number of factors. Advertising budgets, radio promotions, television advertisements, spot discounts, and promotional schemes are some of the areas where systems can provide enough insights to help the management choose the right promotion mix.

Modern marketing concepts emphasize on satisfying customers' needs and desires. The whole marketing process is now customer-centric, and is a deviation from the profit-centric approach of the older times. Therefore, analysis of internal and external data for a perfect marketing mix is very important for strategic decisions taken by the top management.

The sales and marketing transactions create customer databases that function as a repository of data for the customer relationship management (CRM) tool. The managers prepare MIS reports such as sales budgeting; daily, weekly, and monthly sales analysis; sales analysis by product categories, by customer types, by zone, and by salesperson; product grading (top n selling products), customer grading (top n customers); year-to-date (YtoD) analysis; and sales growth charts.

Material Management Systems

Material management is one of the critical systems of a business unit, and is more important for a manufacturing company. Material management involves answers to questions such as

- what to buy,
- when to buy, and
- how much to buy.

The material management systems provide analysis on the requirements of material based on the current customers' orders, availability of material in the warehouse, and capacity of the plant and warehouse. Warehousing functions in a business concern involve receipt, storage, and dispatch of goods. Though modern business management techniques talk about 'zero' or 'just-in-time' inventory, the storage function however, cannot be done away with. Inventories can be reduced but cannot be completely removed from the warehouse. Systems help in ascertaining the value of the inventory, the inventory carrying costs, the cost of last moment procurement in case of stock failure, etc.

Information systems for material management facilitate material requirement planning, storage, and control of inventory as illustrated in Fig. 2.6. Warehousing requires systems that can track movement of goods by bar codes or radio-frequency identification (RFID) tags. Managers require information such as stock status, stock value, stock planning, and space utilization.

Finance and Accounting Systems

Financial and accounting information systems are central to all business information systems as illustrated in Fig. 2.7. As the name suggests, they consist of two systems—financial systems and accounting systems.

Financial Information Systems

The financial system involves management, control, and monitoring of the financial health of the organization. It concentrates on budgetary controls, investments, and stakeholders' benefits. The basic function of a financial system is to see if the business is getting the right return on investment. The financial system answers questions such as 'Is the business profitable?', 'Is the business viable in the longer run?', 'Where to invest funds and how much?', and 'How can we

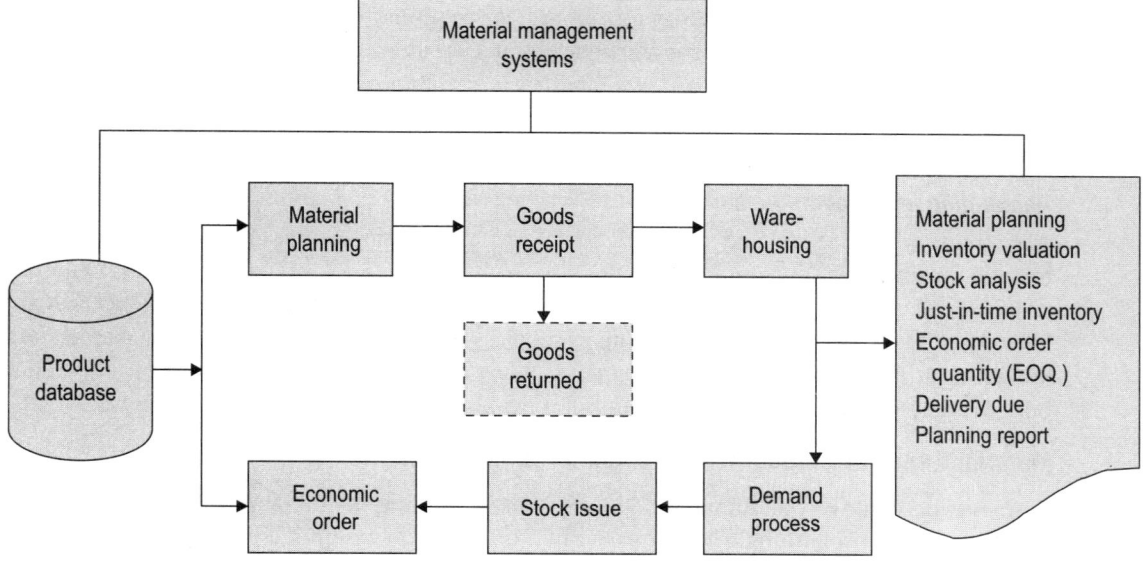

Fig. 2.6   Warehouse and inventory systems and subsystems

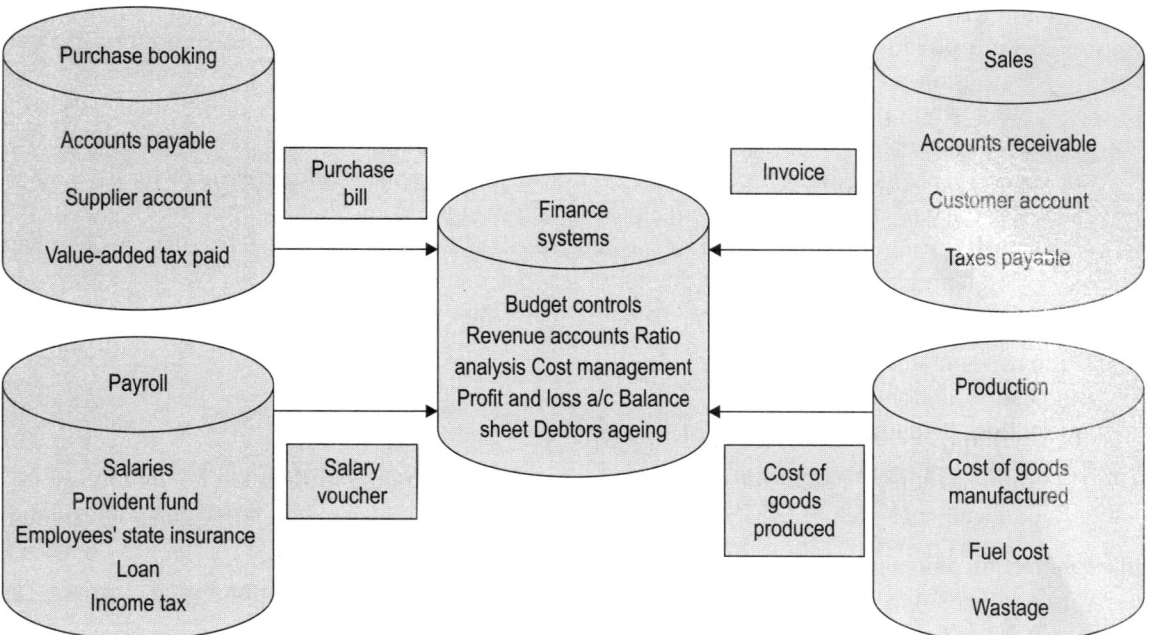

Fig. 2.7   Finance information system's interface with other systems

raise funds and what is the amount?' Jaiswal (2004) identifies the following key factors where financial information systems help in the integration of the process, technology, and information:

- Drive enterprise-wide profit improvement and shareholder value.

- Create a 'finance-on-demand' organization that is responsive, variable, focused, and resilient.
- Reduce the cost of finance through efficient transaction processing.
- Provide decision-makers at all levels with the right information, when and where they need it.
- Effectively manage risk and opportunity.

Accounting Information Systems

Accounting systems are related to the function of recording business transactions. Such transactions include receipt, payments, purchase, sales, etc. Accounting systems receive data from all other systems such as sales, purchases, and payroll. These are basic systems where data is generated and later processed to create financial statements such as balance-sheet, profit and loss accounts, ratio analysis, and funds and cash flow statements. They also produce reports such as trial balance, budget analysis, bills receivable analysis, bills payable analysis, and cost centre analysis.

Manufacturing—Production Planning and Control Systems

Systems that deal with planning, scheduling, and controlling of the manufacturing process are called production planning and control (PPC) information systems. Planning and scheduling refer to the system of deriving the right amount of goods to be produced within the constraints of manufacturing capacities and material resources. Controlling is the process of monitoring production so that it is as per the production planning and scheduling requirements. PPC systems provide information on operations and activities of an organization and thus facilitate the decision-making process of production managers.

Production planning systems help managers in production scheduling and planning, material planning, capacity planning, shop-floor planning, wastage control, manpower planning, etc. The systems in planning and scheduling advise the best plan of action for efficient manufacturing of goods.

Production information systems include all activities from the conception of a product to manufacturing and quality control as illustrated in Fig. 2.8. Such systems also involve plant location and layout decisions at the senior level of management.

Production information systems can be extended to service companies that produce and deliver services such as automobile repair workshops, hospitals, hospitality businesses, and software development and implementation services.

Human Resource Management Systems

Human resource systems deal with the human factor in an organization. The human resource management system (HRMS) is also known as personnel management or personnel information system. The HR functions involve the following:

- Manpower planning
- Staffing
- Training and development
- Performance appraisal
- Retirement
- Payroll

The information systems for HRMS deal with manpower recruitment, retention, and compensation. The systems include recruitment, posting, appraisals, promotions, transfers, payroll, etc. The subsystems of payroll are salary computation, tax computation, provident fund, employees' state insurance, loan, leave, attendance, perks and allowances, etc. They produce reports and maintain

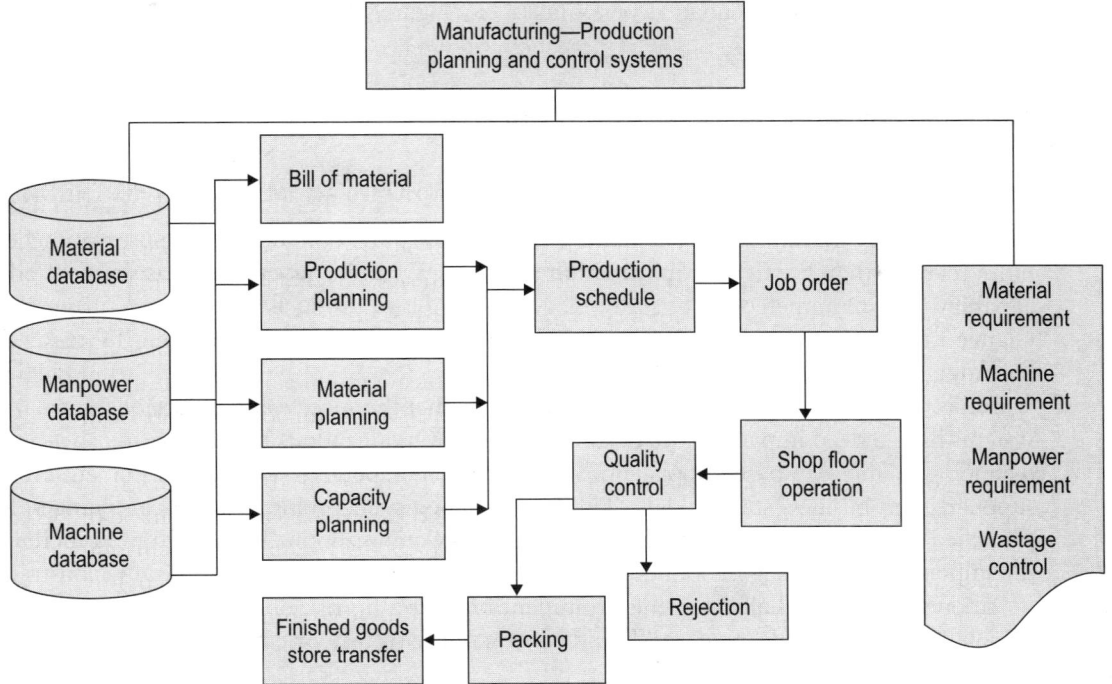

Fig. 2.8   Manufacturing and production systems and subsystems

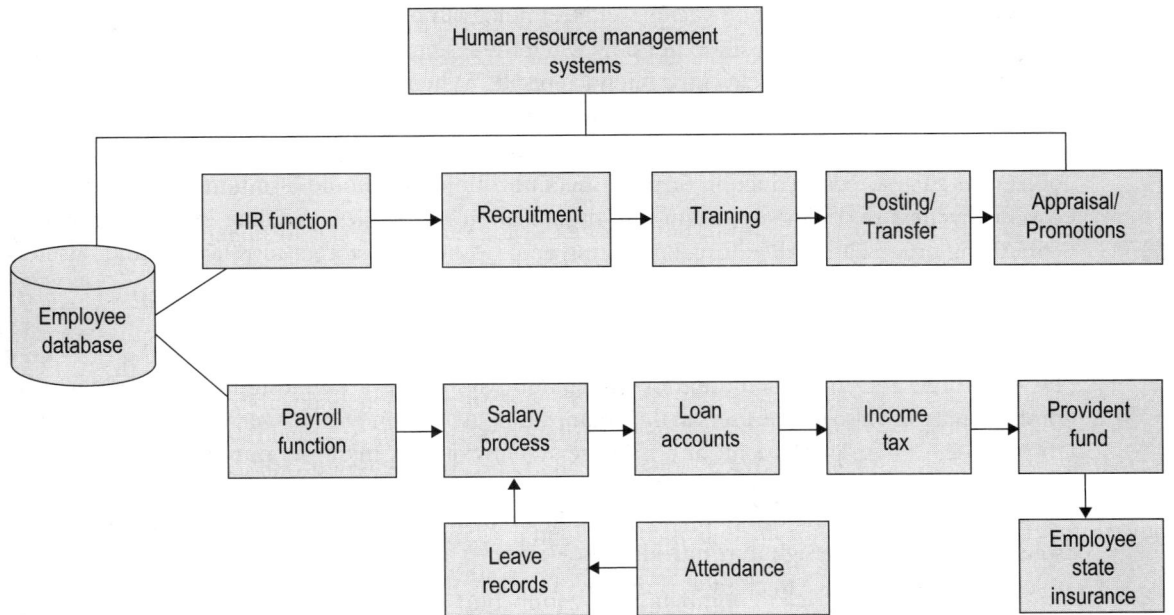

Fig. 2.9   Human resource management systems and subsystems

records of salary, leave, attendance, perks, taxes, etc. Figure 2.9 illustrates the various systems of the HRMS.

CHALLENGES OF MANAGING INFORMATION TECHNOLOGY

Manzoni (1998) maintains that 'over the last decade, the world has been changing so rapidly that one can no longer imagine managing in a steady state. The need to adapt and change continuously has become a given in managerial life. In no other domain has this observation been more relevant than the field of information technology.' In recent years, IT has skyrocketed in capability and plummeted in costs as well. New technology products emerge and current ones change rapidly. As a result of these rapid changes, the challenges of managing IT today are becoming increasingly complex.

Today, businesses are so heavily dependent on IT that the success and failure of information systems have a deep impact on the business's success. Organizations heavily use Internet-based technologies and web-based applications to meet the competitive requirements of customers, suppliers, and business stakeholders. The high acceptance, combined with rapid changes, has propelled IT into an increasingly strategic role in many organizations. This has further increased the importance of managing IT in organizations.

Among the many challenges, the prominent ones are the risk of failure of IT, developing IT solutions, IT security, ethics in IT, and careers in IT. We will briefly discuss these challenges involved in managing IT.

Risk of Failure

More often, we see information systems and technology implementation failures in organizations. Technology failures are measured not only when the systems implementation fail, but also when information systems fail to deliver the intended results. When information systems are not properly managed, they create both technological and business failures.

Therefore, the success of information systems should not only be measured in terms of intended objectives such as cost reduction or profit maximization, but should also be measured in terms of effectiveness of IT in supporting the organization's strategies, enabling business processes, enhancing organizational culture, enhancing employee and customer satisfaction, and business value.

Developing Solutions

Development and implementation of information systems is a daunting task not only for the professionals, but also for the users in the organization. As a business manager, you may be expected to propose, design, implement, and manage systems development in your career. Most of the time, managers face the dilemma of either developing a solution engaging professionals in-house or implementing a state-of-the-art IT solution available in the market. While implementing a solution, the system design may introduce new systems and discard old processes. This may lead to employees' resistance to change. Similarly, it is difficult to carry out a change to accommodate a function or business process once the system is developed and implemented.

Systems development and implementation in the modern era involves some methodical processes usually referred to as the systems development life cycle (SLDC). Figure 2.10 shows the

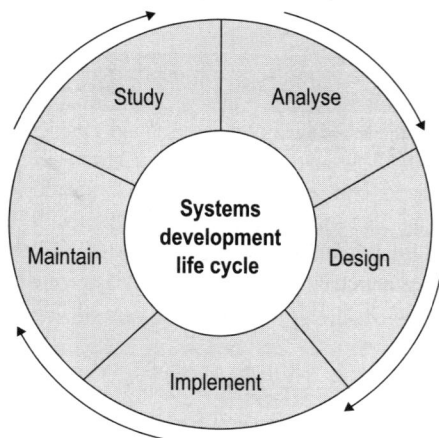

Fig. 2.10   Systems development life cycle as a multi-step process

important activities that are also called phases in the SDLC. These activities are study, analysis, design, implementation, and maintenance.

Security

The immense benefits provided by IT are drained out, if the security of the system is not managed properly. Today, organizations, small or large, are becoming dependent on information systems and IT so much that sometimes the very survival of an organization is affected by the information systems. These systems are vulnerable to a large number of potential threats due to networked computing, Internet access, telecommunications, and advanced software. It has now become easier for hackers to penetrate into the systems and steal valuable information. Data loss due to virus attack or hardware failure may adversely affect an organization.

The astronomical benefits of IT can only be reaped if the security challenges are dealt with by the organization in a strategic manner. Organizations must have appropriate defense strategies and exercise controls that are intended to prevent intentional and accidental hazards, improve incident recovery, and mitigate vulnerabilities. For example, Exhibit 2.3 illustrates how mobile and net banking have made banking susceptible to IT security threats.

EXHIBIT 2.3

E-commerce Transactions: Major Security Risks for Indian Banks

Rising e-commerce and mobile transactions have emerged as one of the major security threats for Indian banks. 'The risk of exposing confidential information is increasing as customers explore new channels for financial transactions through e-commerce and mobile banking. Smartphones are susceptible to hacking,' says a Symantec study.

The survey was commissioned by Symantec to understand security drivers, challenges, and adoption in Indian banking and financial services and insurance enterprises. It covered a sample of 100 respondents from banks, insurance enterprises, and broker houses, and was conducted during the period February–March 2011. The survey revealed that Indian financial service enterprises registered losses worth ₹6.9 crore on an average, due to security breaches every year. As part of the overall financial services segment, Indian banks saw their losses nearly double to ₹12.6 crore. Since November 2010, all phishing attacks have targeted the Indian banking sector. Phishing attacks on IDBI bank, ICICI bank, and others were reported in 2011.

'Indian customers are security conscious, but at times, they show negligence when it comes to online transactions. Banks need to implement robust security standards to prevent any form of attacks, internal or external,' says Muralidharan. R, chief operating officer, Dhanlaxmi Bank.

A customer of a leading bank told CXO that he lost ₹80,000 after he registered his credit card on a PayPal account. The bank registered a complaint by him, but did not give an assurance about paying the money back. PayPal returned the money though, after some time.

67% of the respondents who experienced a data breach lost man-hours, and 61% stated that they had lost customers subsequently. The survey also revealed that more than 80% of the respondents have faced downtime due to online attacks, and took an average of four hours to resume normal operations.

According to the Internet and Mobile Association of India (IAMAI), the Indian e-commerce market is growing at a rate of 47% and will touch ₹46,000 crore by December

(Contd)

Exhibit 2.3 (Contd)

2011. In May 2011, there were 1.1 crore mobile payment users in India, according to the Boston Consulting Group.

Rise in internal threats was another significant factor in security adoption as experienced by 15% of the respondents. The survey revealed that eight out of ten employees within an organization use endpoints, and that, currently 81% of smartphone users in these organizations access corporate information, and 57% use instant messaging. The survey reveals that a high percentage of corporate data is available to people through various devices. Hence, enterprises need to realign their IT risk framework.

Sources:
http://www.cxotoday.com/story/mobility-poses-security-risks-for-indian-banks/, last accessed on 23 August 2011.
www.aimai.in, last accessed on 23 August 2011.

Ethics

Information technology has become all pervasive and affects every walk of life. However, it has also created a risk of its unethical use. Ethics is about right and moral human behaviour. What is considered as proper, responsible, and harmless behaviour in the use and application of IT is guided by ethics.

The ethical use of IT relates to issues associated with individual privacy, work safety, intellectual property rights, fair treatment without any discrimination, etc. As such, human behaviour is best regulated and controlled by various legal provisions. Globally, various governments have enacted anti-spam acts to deter unsolicited emails, copyright acts to protect intellectual property rights, and information technology acts to address various concerns related to the IT field.

Careers

In the initial period of introduction of computers and IT in India, the general view of the people was that computerization brought job cuts and unemployment. However, with greater acceptance of IT by organizations, this is no longer the majority viewpoint. Rather, both service providers and service users in the IT sector have created interesting, challenging, and lucrative career opportunities for millions of people in the country. There are millions of jobs in IT such as product manufacturing, software development, system support and management, data management, network services, and Internet service providers. The job scope in the user market is also increasing as organizations are expanding their use of IT. For example, the requirement for programmers in new technologies increases as newer programming languages are introduced. The requirement for qualified IT professionals comes from millions of business organizations, government agencies, social organizations, etc. India's domestic IT market is growing at a rate of 15–17%, creating more jobs. According to N.R. Narayana Murthy, founder of Infosys, India needs 1.1 million IT professionals to cater to this requirement. There is a shortage of around 2,00,000 professionals in the IT sector. Moreover, computerization creates jobs for the technically qualified and trained manpower in other industries as well. Organizations give preference to people with computer knowledge.

SUMMARY

Information systems play key roles at three levels of management in an organization—they support business processes at the grass-root level, facilitate decision-making by middle management, and enable top management to take strategic decisions.

From a mere data processing function to expert systems, applications of information systems have expanded greatly over the years as they now cover enterprise solutions, decision support systems, expert systems, knowledge management, and so on. Business processes refer to the way the work in an organization is organized, distributed, and coordinated to produce a product or service.

Management information systems (MIS) are used by organizations to manage business functions such as sales, purchase, material, finance, manufacturing, and personnel. IS based on various organizational functions are part of

MIS. These functions are broadly classified into purchase and supply (P&S), sales and distribution (S&D), warehouse management system (WMS), finance and control (FICO), production planning and control (PPC), and human resource management systems (HRMS). These systems help managers create basic data that is cohesively linked with other systems.

As a result of rapid changes and high level acceptance of IS across the organization, the challenges of managing IT are becoming increasingly complex. These challenges include risk of failure of IT, development of IT, security threats, ethical concerns, and human resource-related concerns.

KEY TERMS

Business processes   Sequence of structured activities to perform a certain task.

Competitive advantage   Developing products, services, and capabilities that give the company an advantage over its competitors.

Cost centre analysis   Reports giving expenses and income of a particular centre such as a project or function.

Cross-functional   Business process that spreads to more than one business function.

Data warehousing   An integrated collection of data extracted from operational, historical, and other databases for processing and analysis to provide business intelligence.

Decision support systems (DSS)   An information system that supports decision-making with ad hoc, interactive modelling processes to reach a decision.

Enterprise solutions   Integrated cross-functional software to cover the entire business processes of a company.

Executive information systems (EIS)   A system that provides strategic information tailored to the needs of the executives and senior managers.

Expert system   A computer-based system that uses its knowledge about a specific complex application area and acts as an expert.

Financial statements   Reports presenting financial data of a company.

Just-in-time inventory   A modern concept of business management where minimum stock is stored at the production site.

Knowledge management (KM)   Organizing and sharing business information created within an organization.

Management challenges of IT   Challenges of managing IT in business as a result of rapid changes and other issues.

Manpower planning   Production systems that calculate how much human asset is required for the current batch of production.

Material requirement planning   System that calculates how much to buy to meet the raw material requirement of a particular order or batch of production.

Open-to-buy (OTB)   A system that calculates how much to buy based on certain sale criteria.

Performance appraisal   Concept of evaluating performance of an employee.

Ratio analysis   Financial reports presenting trends of income, expenses, profits, stocks, etc.

CONCEPT REVIEW QUESTIONS

1. Define the role of MIS and examine its impact on modern day businesses.
2. What trends do you notice in the evolution of MIS? Do the latest e-business applications fulfil the information requirements of managers?
3. What do you understand by business processes? Why it is necessary to understand business processes in order to understand MIS?
4. What are various organizational functions? Briefly explain any four business functions and point out the MIS needs of the same.
5. What are the various managerial challenges of information technology? Explain with suitable examples.

CRITICAL THINKING QUESTIONS

1. 'Technology is no longer an afterthought in forming a business strategy, but the actual cause and driver.' Explain this statement.
2. How have information systems in Indian businesses evolved since independence? What major change you visualize in the next 10 years?
3. Why do many companies still fail in using information systems in their entirety? How can they improve?

MIS DEVELOPMENT

Associated Plasmatron Pvt. Ltd is a Mumbai-based company, specializing in chemical coating products. The company has two manufacturing units that are always busy and engaged to their full capacity utilization. The company has implemented integrated software solutions to take care of the business processes of purchase order processing, sales order processing, inventory management, production planning, manufacturing processes, material management, and financial accounting. The company has an e-commerce portal, which is capable of receiving orders online. The orders are processed instantly and a confirmation is generated and sent to the customer. The system sends intimations to the logistics, manufacturing planning, and purchase departments for receipt of the said order. The production planning department then schedules the order for production and sends the material requirement plan to the purchase department and warehouse. The production manager can check the availability of raw material on his computer system and request the manager to replenish stock shortages. The job is put for actual production as per the schedule and the online e-commerce site is updated with real time data. The customer can see the status of his order by simply logging onto the site. As the product is ready, the intimation is sent automatically to the logistics manager and the sales head. The sales manager then makes a dispatch advice, which is sent through the integrated application suite to the warehouse and the finance department. The finance manager generates the invoice and the details are sent to dispatch for actual shipment of the goods. As the shipment begins, the customer receives an electronic mail to the effect and collects his goods from the transporters delivery office.

Amit Kudva, the CEO of the company, is able to access summary reports that present a graphical display of data representing the business operations of the company. The managers of the company access reports on a periodical, exceptional, or on demand basis. The customers and suppliers are able to access their data over the extranet that Plasmatron has established.

Exercise

1. Identify the various types of information systems being used by Associated Plasmatron.
2. How do information systems support (a) business operations, (b) business decision-making, (c) strategic advantage, (d) e-business initiative, and (e) e-commerce at Associated Plasmatron?

REFERENCES

Anthony, Robert, *Planning and Control Systems: A Framework for Analysis*, Division of Research, Graduate School of Business Administration, Harvard University, Cambridge, 1965.

Davis, Gorden and Margethe Olson, *Management Information Systems*, McGraw-Hill, Singapore, 1996.

Jaiswal, Mahadeo and Monika Mittal, *Management Information Systems*, Oxford University Press, New Delhi, 2004.

Joshi, Girdhar, *Information Technology for Retail*, Oxford University Press, New Delhi, 2008.

Kanter, Jerome, *Managing with Information*, Prentice-Hall, New Delhi, 1996.

Koontz, Harold and Cyril O'Donnel, *Management*, McGraw-Hill International, New York, 1972.

Laudon, Kenneth and Jane, Laudon, *Management Information Systems*, Pearson Education, Singapore, 2010.

Manzoni, Jean-Francois, and Albert A. Angehr, *Understanding Organizational Dynamics of IT-enabled Change*, accessed at http://www.calt.insead.edu/eis/documents, last accessed on 12 August 2011.

O'Brien, James, George Marakas, and Ramesh Behl, *Management Information Systems*, Tata McGraw-Hill, New Delhi, 2007.

Steven, Alter, *Information Systems—The Foundation of E-business*, Pearson Education, Singapore, 2004.

CASE STUDY

Bajaj Electricals Lights the Lamp of Organizational Agility

Mumbai-based Bajaj Electricals is a part of the reputed Bajaj Group. The consumer electrical products manufacturing company has 70 years of experience in the electrical market. With 30 branches, 600 distributors, and 3000 authorized dealers, Bajaj Electricals mainly operates through its strategic business units namely appliances, fans, lighting, luminaries, engineering and projects, and Morphy Richards.

Bajaj Electricals has experienced rapid growth recently, which brought home the realization that the 12-year old in-house legacy software may not be able to support the fast cumulative growth. Hence, the company implemented information systems that spanned the entire organization, its associates, customers, and suppliers. Before implementation of this project, inefficient procedures resulted in revenue losses as there was no forecasting or planning tool available. To eliminate these inefficiencies, the company deployed several business applications from Oracle. These included Oracle EBS ERP, DeMantra Demand Management, and Advanced Supply Chain Planning (ASCP) solution. Additionally, they deployed Oracle's i-Supplier to connect suppliers, Siebel CRM, and Oracle BI.

Objective

The main objective of the company for the implementation was to change the mindset of employees to adopt new processes. The company also realized that some of its business processes were outdated and inefficient as they were designed around 12 years ago. Pratap Gharge, CIO and VP of Bajaj Electricals, says, 'We did not want to merely replace software; our goal was to initiate actual business process improvements'.

Inefficient Business Processes Call for Revamp

The ERP suite automated most of the company's core business processes, including purchasing, inventory, sales order management, accounts payable, general ledger, fixed assets, and cash management modules. The Siebel CRM took care of opportunities, quotes, trade promotions, pricing, and sales order processing. The business intelligence (BI) tool had two parts, a daily BI tool for financial and procurement analysis, and an enterprise edition for sales analytics, dashboards, and reporting. The benefits observed within one year of implementation were reduction in the leakage of discounts delivery by 0.5% of turnover and reduction in the physical versus paper stock variance by 2%. The percentages may look low, but the total saving they contributed to was sufficient to cover the entire investment that was made.

Change Process

The company engaged PricewaterhouseCoopers (PwC) to conduct a study of all business processes, recommend improvements, and also to suggest an IT solution architecture to support future growth requirements.

PwC identified various areas for process improvements such as sales force effectiveness, streamlining pricing and discounting, logistics, warehousing and inventory handling, back office services, and product costing and sourcing. PwC also came up with a functional architecture supported by state-of-the-art application infrastructure.

The IT solution architecture recommended by PwC favoured various state-of-the-art applications from Oracle for different functional areas. These included Oracle ERP, Siebel CRM, Dementra for demand management, ASCP for supply chain management, Agile PLM, and Oracle BI.

However, Bajaj Electricals did not accept PwC's recommendation immediately. 'Internally, there was a feeling that we should also look at SAP as an alternative as some of our group companies were already using SAP,' says Gharge. To resolve this conflict, the company decided to form a cross-functional team, which evaluated both vendors over a course of six months.

The conclusion drawn was that Oracle had certain best-of-breed solutions, which met their requirements precisely. Choosing Oracle would also help the company protect its previous investment in JD Edwards.

Project Smile to Bring Enterprise-wide Transformation

The company decided to go ahead with the Oracle suite and the initiative was named 'Project Smile'. R. Ramakrishnan, executive director, Bajaj Electricals, says, 'Typically ERP projects are fraught with a lot of pain. We called it Project Smile as we wanted a transformed organization with smiling employees.'

Project Smile embodies simplification of processes, migration to new technologies, enterprise-wide integration, creation of a learning organization, and an effective work environment.

Implementation

In the first phase, the company decided to implement Oracle ERP (eBiz suite), some components of Siebel CRM,

Dementra for demand management, the ASCP solution, and BI components.

The Oracle e-Biz suite includes typical transaction processing areas such as financials, sales and distribution, purchasing, and inventory. Siebel CRM components are mainly targeted at improving sales force effectiveness. The sales opportunity management functionality of Siebel CRM will help various strategic business units (SBUs) of the company to track sales opportunities. This will also enhance lead management by allowing the sales leads generated to be deposited within a central repository and avoiding their loss even in cases where sales representatives quit the company. Siebel also has a trade promotion module, which helps to monitor the funds being used for various promotions. Its dynamic pricing feature is helping Bajaj Electricals overcome billing errors.

While Dementra and ASCP are helping the company to balance supply and forecast demand, the BI tools are deployed to filter intelligence for the top management.

Coupled with investment in Oracle Suite, the company has invested on Niagara-based servers from Sun Microsystems and is also using a cluster solution for automatic failover.

Software Integration—A Major Challenge

To ensure the success of Project Smile, Bajaj Electricals chose Oracle Consultancy as the implementation partner and Deloitte as the change management partner. 'The task of implementing three applications of such large scale simultaneously is obviously a daunting one. The process involves integration of different software, which turned out to be the key challenge. We had to make sure that all the software was communicating with each other seamlessly', says Gharge.

Sujit Sahu manager–direct sales, Oracle, says that some applications have in-built integration; for example, Dementra is already integrated with ASCP, while others have to be actively integrated. 'We are currently taking inputs from customers and plan to provide a process integration pack, which will offer out-of-the-box integration in case of certain critical applications like Siebel CRM,' he says. Deloitte's role will become important during the stage of user acceptance where it will have to conduct extensive training sessions for employees.

Lean and Efficient Organization

Project Smile was envisioned to bring about enterprise-wide efficiency and agility. All the three solutions implemented in the first phase are expected to leave the sales force with more time for the core sales promotion function, to strengthen the supply chain, and to improve overall visibility for top management. Ramakrishnan concludes, 'On the whole, we will create an organization which is quick, lean, and efficient.'

The business required improvement in back office operations along with timely and accurate MIS generation to be more responsive to market conditions. Streamlining pricing and discount schemes were deemed necessary for establishing a good customer relationship and to ensure proper control over price delivery. 'To rationalize cost and build operational efficiency, it was necessary to optimize inventory, improve warehouse management and logistics,' says Gharge.

It was conceived with the objective of simplifying business processes, migrating to new technology, innovating and integrating, learning orientation, and making the organization effective and efficient. The company is also planning to implement Oracle HRMS and Oracle Agile in the coming months. Bajaj Electricals bagged the CSI 2010 IT Excellence Award for its ERP implementation programme by Computer Society of India.

Discussion Questions

1. What types of MIS were implemented by Bajaj Electricals?
2. What roles do MIS play in Bajaj Electricals?
3. What was the major objective of implementing robust and expensive solutions from Oracle?
4. 'Project Smile was envisioned to bring about enterprise-wide efficiency and agility'. Was Bajaj Electricals successful in its objective? Elucidate.

Sources:
'Bajaj Electricals: Project smile', http://pcquest.ciol.com/content/implementation2010/2010/110060130.asp, last accessed on 27 February 2012.
'Bajaj Electricals bagged the CSI 2010 IT excellence award', http://www.dnserp.com/bajaj.htm, last accessed on 24 March 2012.
Pandya, Dhawani, 'Oracle Solutions lend agility to Bajaj Electricals', http://www.biztech2.in.com/casestudies/erp/oracle-solutions/bajaj-electricals/, last accessed on 23 January 2009.
'Project 'smile' brings end to end connectivity across Bajaj Electricals', http://www.cio.in/case-study/project-smile-brings-end-end-connectivity-across-bajaj-electricals, last accessed on 24 March 2012.

3

Strategic Advantage of IT

We are changing from a competitive environment in which mass-market products and services were standardized, long-lived, information-poor, and exchanged in one-time transactions, to an environment in which companies compete globally with niche market products and services that are individualized, short-lived, information-rich, and exchanged on an on-going basis with customers.

–Steven Goldman, Roger Nagel, and Kenneth Preis

LEARNING OBJECTIVES

After studying this chapter, you will be able to

- understand the fundamentals of strategic advantage
- appreciate the strategic role of information technology (IT)
- differentiate various types of strategies, competitive forces, and competitive strategies
- highlight the strategic usage of IT
- relate business value chain and strategic information systems
- understand the role of management information systems (MIS) in strategic business planning
- appreciate MIS as a tool for organizational change
- understand the concept of business process reengineering and differentiate it from process improvement
- appreciate the role of IT in business process reengineering

EXHIBIT 3.1

Banks in India: Challenge to Establish Customer Intimacy through IT

The banking sector in India has experienced a rapid transformation. Just about a decade ago, this sector was limited to nationalized and cooperative banks. This was followed by the entry of multinational banks; however, these were confined to serving only the elite few. One could regard the past as the 'medieval ages' of the banking industry, wherein every branch of the same bank acted as an independent information silo, and multichannel banking (automated teller machines, net banking, telebanking, etc.) was almost non-existent.

The opening up of the Indian banking sector to private players acted as 'the tipping point' for this transformation. The deregulatory efforts prompted many financial institutions (such as HDFC and ICICI) and non-financial institutions to enter the banking arena.

With the entry of private players into retail banking and with multinationals focusing on the individual consumer in a big way, the banking system underwent a phenomenal change. Multichannel banking gained prominence. For the first time, consumers had the choice of conducting transactions either the traditional way (through the bank branch), through automated teller machines (ATMs), telephones, or the Internet. Technology played a key role in providing this multi-service platform.

The entry of private players combined with the new Reserve Bank of India (RBI) guidelines forced nationalized banks to redefine their core banking strategy. Technology was central to this change and makes it easier for any company with the right channel infrastructure and money reserves to get into banking. This has been one of the major reasons behind this kind of competition from players who do not have a banking background.

Considering the fact that a significant number of Indian banks have settled with their core banking system (CBS), it is time for the Indian banking sector to use this as a launching pad to roll-out other IT initiatives mapped against their business priorities. Adequate liquidity, operational excellence, compliance adherence, and transformation in payment systems are identified as the top priority areas that Indian banks should adopt to continue to grow and keep competitors at bay. Consequently, IT will be a key enabler in putting these priorities in place.

N. Chandrasekaran, chief executive officer (CEO), Tata Consultancy Services, suggests leveraging upcoming channels of delivery, such as mobile banking, social networking, and also tapping the potential of advanced technologies like predictive analytics. Predictive analytics is a business intelligence technique that produces scores of a customer and is used for determining his/her behaviour and other business decision-making.

Investment in IT will supposedly drive and sustain the competitiveness of banking institutions in the future, and will transform payment systems. Among the major technology investment areas would be those that drive financial inclusion and help target the customer better in terms of service delivery and satisfaction. A combination of multiple technologies and platforms, such as mobile, applications, analytics, and cloud will be leveraged to further the much pursued financial inclusion drive of the banks. On the other hand, more investments will also go into initiatives targeted to 'understand the customer better'. 'We will also see areas like payments and compliance getting a pie of IT investments by banks', says Chandrasekaran.

Indian banks have realized that it no longer pays to have a 'transaction-based' operating model. This has led to the development of a relationship-oriented model of operations that focuses on customer-centric services. While banks have to ensure product superiority and operational excellence, the biggest challenge is to establish customer intimacy, without which the other two are meaningless.

'In the financial world, product superiority does not last long as it is relatively easy to copy products. So, the real strength comes from operational excellence and understanding the customer and developing rapport with him', says Gunit Chadha, managing director (MD) and CEO, IDBI Bank.

In this context, it is very important that banks identify and understand customer's needs. This will help banks in tailoring their products according to the customer's needs. Customer relationships have to be managed in the best possible manner as it will ensure that the customer comes back to the bank. In addition to good customer retention rates, it will also provide better income generation capability. This is because a major chunk of income of most banks comes from existing customers, rather than from new customers.

Banks are looking at newer ways to make a customer's banking experience more convenient, efficient, and effective.

(Contd)

Exhibit 3.1 (Contd)

They are using new technological tools and techniques to identify the customer's needs and are offering tailor-made products to match them.

Customer relationship management (CRM) solutions, if implemented and integrated correctly, can help in significantly improving customer satisfaction levels. Data warehousing can help in providing better transaction experiences for customers over different transaction channels. This is made possible because data warehousing helps bring all the transactions coming from different channels under a common roof. Data mining is the process of extracting information from a heap of diverse data. It helps banks analyse and measure customer transaction patterns and behaviour. This can help a lot in improving service levels and finding new business opportunities.

Risk assessment is another area where technology can play a major role. 'Using technology, banks are able to better assess risks like interest risks, liquidity risks, FOREX risks, etc. The other driver for using IT is that banks can reduce costs and reduce the time to market', says Rangesh Nair, country manager, financial services sector, IBM.

Sources:
Patrick, R. Anil, 'The new face of banking', http://www.network magazineindia.com/200305/tech1.shtml, last accessed on 19 November 2011.
'The biggest challenge is to establish customer intimacy', Interview of Gunit Chadha, MD, IDBI Bank, Network Magazine India, http://www.networkmagazineindia.com/200305/tech1. shtml, last accessed on 19 November 2011.
Raval, Abhishek, 'Business priorities that will drive upcoming banking tech initiatives', http://biztech3.in.com/nw/77B51/s/ 115002/12_Aug_2011/?utm_source= biztech2_12082011& utm_medium=newsletter, 12 August 2011, last accessed on 19 November 2011.

Why have new-age banks, such as HDFC, ICICI, and IDBI, invested a lot on information systems (IS) and technologies? Banks are looking at newer ways to make a customer's banking experience more convenient, efficient, and effective. They are using new technology, tools, and techniques to identify the customer's needs and are offering tailor-made products to match them. By doing so, these banks achieve operational excellence with quicker product and service development, launch better and new business models, ensure more customer satisfaction and intimacy, and improve their decision-making. Exhibit 3.1 illustrates that competitive advantage through customer intimacy is the key to the success of modern businesses.

In this chapter, our discussion will go beyond the use of IS for internal processes of the organization. We will learn to appreciate that IS are more than a set of computer technologies that help managers make and justify their decisions. We will understand the role of IS in the overall competitive advantage in the organization. This includes a study of how IT can change the way businesses compete and outperform their competitors.

FUNDAMENTALS OF STRATEGIC ADVANTAGE

Strategic advantage is defined as the competitive advantage that one business entity has over its rival entities within its competitive industry. According to Laudon (2010), doing things better than your competitors, charging less for superior products, and responding to customers and suppliers in real time, add up to higher sales and higher profits that your competitors cannot match. Achieving competitive advantage strengthens and positions a business better within the business environment. The competitive advantage theory suggests that states and businesses should pursue policies that create high-quality goods to sell at high prices in the market. Michael Porter (1985) emphasizes productivity growth as the focus of organizational strategies.

Competitive advantage occurs when an organization acquires or develops an attribute or combination of attributes that allows it to outperform its competitors. These attributes can include access to natural resources, such as high grade ores or inexpensive power; highly trained and skilled personnel human resources; or new technologies such as robotics and IT; and so on.

For example, HDFC Bank outperformed all nationalized banks by deploying state-of-the-art IT, for which the bank received the 6th IBA Banking Technology Award in 2011. Customer service was enhanced by providing IT-enabled services such as computerized statements, net banking, and ATMs. The bank attracted numerous customers and a majority of them are still loyal to it.

Therefore, competitive advantage is the ability to stay ahead of present or potential competition. Consequently, superior performance reached through competitive advantage will ensure market leadership. Additionally, it provides the understanding that resources held by a firm and the business strategy adopted by it will have a profound impact on generating competitive advantage. Powell (2005) views business strategy as the tool that manipulates the resources and creates competitive advantage. Hence, viable business strategy may not be adequate unless it possesses control over unique resources that have the ability to create such a unique advantage. Summarizing the view points, competitive advantage is a key determinant of superior performance and it will ensure survival and prominent placing in the market. Superior performance being the ultimate desired goal of a firm, competitive advantage becomes the foundation for achieving the same.

STRATEGIC ROLE OF INFORMATION TECHNOLOGY

The strategic role of IS involves using IT to develop and distribute products, services, and capabilities that give an organization a major advantage over its competition. IT has become such a prominent part of the modern business world that it can also contribute to competitive advantage by outperforming competitors. This can be achieved by adopting strategies and practices that enable reengineering business processes to bring in quality and efficiency. Implementation of enterprise applications weed out unwanted processes and introduce standard and time-tested processes adopted by successful organizations worldwide. The term 'competitive advantage' is the ability gained through attributes and resources to perform at a higher level than others in the same industry or market.

Since the beginning of organized businesses, the central problem was information transmission. This led to the rise of middlemen in the marketplace, which in turn, has been a significant impediment in gaining competitive advantage. By using the Internet as the medium of sales and purchase, and also the mode of information communication to the final consumer, businesses can gain competitive advantage through the creation of an effective online sales portal. In the past, this required extensive effort with regard to finding the right middleman and cultivating the relationship.

For example, MakeMyTrip launched an effective online travel portal and is one of the most successful businesses. Earlier, air and rail ticket booking was done either through middlemen or directly from the airline's/railway booking counter's ticket window, which was a very tedious and time-consuming process.

PORTER'S MODEL OF COMPETITIVE STRATEGIES

The IS that support and shape the competitive position of a business enterprise are called strategic information systems. The IS discussed earlier such as transaction processing systems, management information system, decision support system, and executive information system use IT to help an organization gain competitive edge. Michael Porter's (1985) classic model of competitive strategy defines how any business that wants to survive must develop and implement strategies to effectively counter the rivalry of competitors within its industry, the threat of new entrants into an industry and its markets, the threat posed by substitutes which may capture market share, the bargaining power of customers, and the bargaining power of suppliers.

We will briefly discuss these forces and strategies and see how IS can help develop these strategies and gain competitive advantage.

Competitive Forces

Michael Porter suggested five competitive forces in his famous model of competitive strategy. These forces are explained as follows:

Rivalry of competitors   Competitors are natural rivals. This rivalry often encourages proactive action and reaction from a competitor. Hence, firms require significant resources to meet the challenges posed by the competitors. For example, Godrej introduced a PUF-based refrigerator in the 1980s to meet the challenges posed by other manufacturers.

Threat of new entrants   New companies are launched with a sharp focus on the target segment of the existing firms. The old firm does not only have to compete with the existing competitors in the market but pose enough barriers to the new entrants in the market. This competitive force is very difficult to manage because a new firm may be launched unexpectedly and capture significant market share by the time the old firm gets ready for counter-attack. Further, new format businesses like the proliferation of the Internet has offered many ways for a new entrant to enter the market overnight, with significantly low costs.

Threat of substitutes   There are substitutes available for almost all the products. Rail journey is a substitute for air travel, Rasna and Roohafza are substitutes for Coke and Pepsi, and kulfi is a substitute for ice cream, to name a few. There are only a few products (salt, sugar, etc.) that have no direct substitutes. The substitutes sell more during periods of scarcity and inflation. This threat is difficult to manage as the choice of purchase rests in the hands of the customer.

Bargaining power of customers   Bargaining power of customers is another strong competitive force that a firm has to deal with. The customer has more bargaining power if a rival company's product is available at a better price or better quality. If the customer has a strong bargaining power, he/she can drive the prices of the product to a very low level or may even refuse to buy the same. For example, globally, airfares dropped sharply as a result of cut-throat competition. In India, many airlines are operating under losses, but are still providing low rates under strategic compulsions.

Bargaining power of suppliers   Suppliers' bargaining power is strong in times of scarcity of goods, or if the product has usage in emergency situations. The supplier with a strong bargaining power may push the price of goods and services to astronomical levels, or may sometimes refuse to supply the same. For example, oil prices increase during the time of war, as most of the oil resources are associated with the Gulf countries.

TYPES OF STRATEGIES

Figure 3.1 illustrates a conceptual framework on Porter's model to describe various strategies to confront competitive forces. Business firms can counter these competitive forces and threats with five basic competitive strategies. These strategies are as follows:

- Cost leadership strategy
- Differentiation strategy
- Innovation strategy
- Growth strategy
- Alliance strategy

Cost leadership strategy   Cost leadership refers to offering low-price products for the same quality and category as offered by the competitors. Companies adhering to cost leadership become low-cost producers and help suppliers or customers reduce their costs. For example, Tally Solutions offers Tally accounting software at such a low price that competitors either have to follow suit or exit from the packaged accounting software category.

Differentiation strategy   This refers to creating brand loyalty by developing new and unique products and services that are not easily duplicated by competitors. It entails finding a niche segment for products and services. A firm differentiates its products or works for reducing the differentiation advantage of competitors' products. For example, Dove soap is a premium-priced product and is targeted at a high-end market. This is differentiated as a soft soap for the soft skin of women.

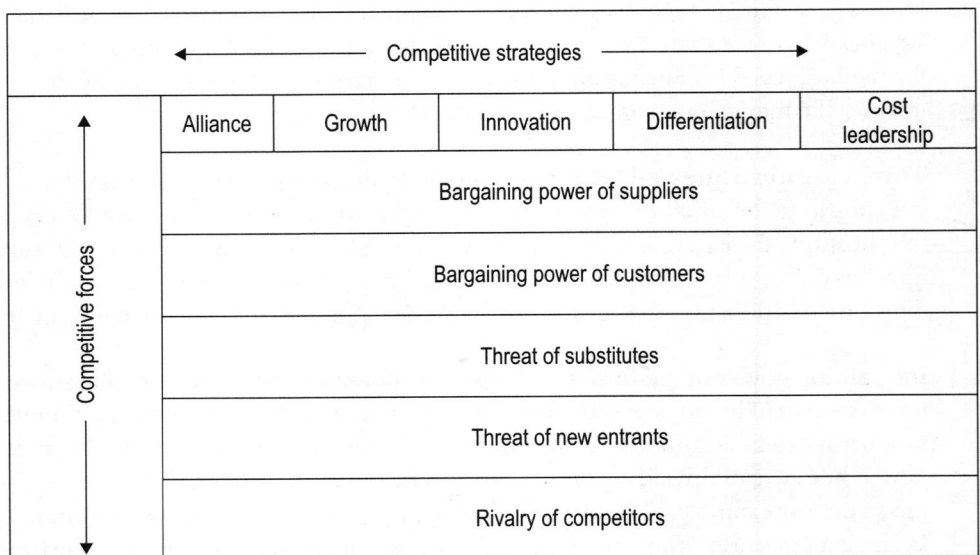

Fig. 3.1   Competitive strategies to counter competitive forces

Innovation strategy   In innovation strategy, the firm finds new ways of doing business that had not been done earlier in the industry. This may involve the development of unique products and services, or entry into unique markets or niche segments. Innovation may go beyond products and also cover introduction of radical changes into the production and distribution processes. For example, retail giants such as Shoppers Stop and Future Group launched innovative e-commerce portals for online retail sales.

Growth strategy   Growth strategies focus on enhancing production capacity, expanding into newer or global markets, diversifying into new products and services, etc. Pan-country or global presence will define competitive advantage for the firm as it signifies stability and confidence among customers. For example, Snapdeal.com started from one city and expanded to make an all-India presence within a very short period of 15 months.

Alliance strategy   Alliances are linkages and partnerships established with distributors, customers, suppliers, etc, for marketing and distribution of goods and services. At a higher level, it also includes mergers, acquisitions, joint ventures, etc. This boosts a company's image and hence helps in gaining competitive advantage over rivals in the industry. For example, many manufacturers in India are finding new online channels such as TradeIndia.com and IndiaMart.com, to promote and distribute their products. They are forming new alliances with other partners. For example, Dell Computers sell their products internationally through online channels.

STRATEGIC USAGE OF IT

Exhibit 3.2 illustrates the view point of international giants such as Dell and Cisco regarding the strategic usage of IT. As a student of MIS, you will appreciate how investment in information technology by Dell and Cisco directly supports their competitive strategies. We will discuss various strategies with examples of IT benefits.

EXHIBIT 3.2

Dell and Cisco: The Giants Reap the Benefits of the Competitive Advantage of IT

When Dell Corporations' CEO, Michael Dell, was asked, 'How important is information technology to Dell, and whether technology gives corporate buyers a competitive edge anymore?', he said, 'Just about anything in business can be either a sinkhole or a competitive advantage if you do it really, really bad or you do it really, really well. And information technology is an often misunderstood field. You have got a lot of people who don't know what they are doing and don't do it very well. For us, IT is a huge advantage. For Wal-Mart, GE, and many other companies, technology is a huge advantage and will continue to be so. Does that mean that you just pour money in and gold comes out? No, you can screw it up really bad.'

The argument that the computer is the primary mode for 'computing' will continue to become less relevant as computing becomes more ubiquitously embedded in different devices such as smartphones and notebooks. With the shift of computing devices towards smaller and embedded devices, the sales growth of computers has stagnated and will continue to drop. The next step for any computer reseller is to sell these smaller devices where the margins are small. Further, these products are also being sold by telecommunication companies (telcos) who have an advantage of giving the products for free for an extended communication service agreement. Here, telcos have the advantage of using these handheld devices as

(Contd)

Exhibit 3.2 (Contd)

loss leaders and making profits in service. Companies in emerging countries that have lower overhead costs can undercut Dell as a low-cost computer provider.

Dell's days of following a cost leadership strategy are over. Hence, Dell is planning on branching out to other products and services. Will it be successful? It depends on how Dell is planning on making these strategic moves—if Dell seriously intends to change top down (i.e., the entire organizational structure has to change), then there is a high possibility of its success. The company has to go through the painful change management process to successfully reinvent itself. IBM did the same in the 90s. Presently, Sony is going through that phase. Additionally, Dell is entering a crowded field where it does not have a first mover's advantage. It also lacks expertise in cloud computing. Odds are stacked against it and it will be worthwhile to watch how it manages to be successful in the next decade.

The IT department's role is to leverage the virtualized architecture and collaboration technology to quickly support each acquired company's business processes. For many years, Cisco has grown through acquisitions. Since 1993, the company has assimilated more than 130 smaller firms, including five in 2008 and three in 2009. The IT department's role is to leverage the virtualized architecture and collaboration technology to quickly support each acquired company's business processes. Thus, the IT department of Cisco, under the leadership of Rebecca Jacoby, the chief information officer, intends to lower the acquired company's costs, while enabling it to add value to Cisco.

According to an article titled 'Cisco: Collaboration Is Key to Business', the ultimate goal of Cisco's IT organization is to enable business growth and capabilities. IT plays a vital role within the organization, even as the company moves to an unusual committee-based management structure. IT is represented on all 60 committees on the new organization chart, which should help tie the department's top two initiatives—virtualization and collaboration—to the company's strategic business goals of asserting leadership across an ever-growing roster of businesses.

Virtualization Cisco's approach to virtualization encompasses both data centres and applications. By virtualizing servers in its data centres, Cisco is getting the same number of servers to do the work of more servers. At the application level, a service-oriented architecture enables Cisco to deploy many applications across a common infrastructure by means of web services.

Collaboration Collaboration technology will be critical to successfully execute Cisco's new organizational structure, which bulldozes operational silos, replacing them with a matrix of committees, councils, and boards. Cisco is taking a broad approach to collaboration—one that runs the gamut from social networking to video.

According to the article, Cisco's IT organization is enabling the company's push into the consumer products market. Manufacturing, distribution, and retailing of consumer products is essentially an exercise in supporting a global supply chain and a global distribution channel. Thus, with the focus on reducing both the acquisition cost and time to market cost, IT department seems to be adding 'strategic' value at Cisco.

Sources:
'Dell expands cloud computing and service strategy', *Dell's Cloud Strategy*, April 2010.
Sheelvant, Raj, 'Cisco's IT alignment with business', ServerWatch, October 2009, http://itstrategyblog.com/it-strategy/, last accessed on 19 August 2011.

Laudon (2002) describes that strategic IS change the goals, operations, products, services, or environmental relationship of organizations to help them gain an edge over competitors. They may even transform the business of organizations. The strategic usage of IT enables businesses to accommodate the impact of Internet-age firms and new information flows across the enterprise. Today, the emphasis is on exploring, identifying, and occupying new market niches before competitors can act.

The usage of and dependency on the Internet is so vast in present day businesses that more or less, every strategic move is highly impacted by the digital superhighway. Internet technologies have impacted industry structures so much that it is easier for competitors to compete on the basis of prices or enable new entrants to enter into the business.

For instance, startups such as Tehelka.com in India and WikiLeaks.org in the US started their business operations by pursuing online reporting as a strategic move. Some newspapers are more popular in the online version than in their print versions. Moreover, the coffee-table dictionary is losing its impact and the e-dictionary is gaining momentum.

Table 3.1 illustrates the various competitive strategies involving IT to counter competitive forces.

Companies create IS-based products and services to maintain product differentiation and innovation at a lower price. IT-supported product differentiation can prevent the competition from counter-attacks and the firms no longer have to just compete on the basis of costs. Similarly, with IT services, it is easier to create new market niches and expand the business in untapped areas. An information system can give companies a competitive advantage in sales and marketing by offering huge database of prospects which the company can mine to increase market penetration. By analysing the sales data, the IS give the business manager an insight into customers' tastes and preferences.

Deployment of enterprise-wide applications brings in efficiency in the organization. Efficient organizations are more sustainable and profitable than others. This can be a deterrent to new entrants in the industry as the nascent organization may not be in a position to deploy enterprise solutions owing to cost and investment factors. Therefore, implementation of enterprise solutions can be a move towards strategic advantage, thus outperforming competition.

For example, as seen in Exhibit 3.1, today, no bank can survive without the deployment of IT infrastructure. Banks having more sophisticated systems and greater customer intimacy are the only competitors to the former.

However, every strategic move by an organization does not have a long-lasting effect. This is because, as the organization starts gaining the advantage, the competitors comprehend its strategy. They may counter the move by a similar strategy or a superior one. This entails a constant struggle to achieve competitive advantage, which requires huge investment in terms of time and money of the organization.

Table 3.1   Competitive strategies to counter competitive forces

Basic strategies	Use of IT with examples
Cost leadership	• Use information technologies to reduce cost of business processes by automating process and bringing in efficiency. • Use IT to reduce the costs incurred by customers and suppliers by providing information through the Internet and direct access to firms' data.
Differentiation	• Develop IT portals for purchase of products and making online payments by credit cards. • Use IT for creating a niche market, for example, Indiatimes.com selling products at low price.
Innovation	• Cut unwanted processes by introducing IT applications, for example, firms allowing their suppliers to directly enter the invoice on their e-business portal and process payments. • Use IT to conquer new market segments, for example, retailers developing a virtual store along with a brick–mortar store.
Growth	• User enterprise online applications to manage business across the globe, for example, firms using ERP systems and controlling business. • Diversify and expand to other areas and product lines and manage it through IT.
Alliances	• Develop partnerships with companies in virgin geographies through your web portal and give access to product and services. • Create virtual organizations and sell and service through them.

Table 3.2   Usage of competitive strategies to gain business leadership

Strategy	Company	Strategic use of IT	Business benefits
Cost leadership	Tally Solutions	Web-based licensing and support	Market leader in packaged software
	Dell Computers	Online, customized orders	Low cost producer
	eBay.com	Online auctions	Prices set by purchaser
Differentiation	Tata Steel	Online e-biz portal access to business associates	Increase in market share
	DHL/DTDC	Customers online shipment tracking	Increase in market share
	Standard Chartered	Providing E-commerce solutions	Increase in market share
	Citibank	Developed ATM and Bank Debit Cards	Became largest bank in the US
Innovation	Philips India	SaaS implementation	Gives innovative edge in cost reduction
	Amazon.com	Online book store	Market leadership
Growth	HDFC Bank/ICICI Bank	Enterprise applications and Net banking services	Remarkable growth in business
	Wal-Mart	Network linking with stores and suppliers	Just-in-time inventory
	Citicorp	Intranet	Increase in global share
Alliance	Maruti Udyog	Centralized application for all workshops across the country	Centralized monitoring and control
	Red Hat	Participative development	Leader in open-source technology
	Procter & Gamble	Application linkage with suppliers	Reduced inventory costs
	Cisco Systems	Manufacturing alliances with associates	Market leadership

Table 3.2 depicts examples of global and Indian businesses using IT for gaining competitive advantage and therefore benefiting in their business.

SHORT-RANGE PLANNING

Most of the strategic planning is long-range planning, and might span over the lifetime of a product or a service in most cases. However, organizations need to monitor performance on a yearly basis. Thus, the long-term objectives are broken into short-term targets and planning is done according to the available budgets, capacities, and potentials. Short-range planning refers to the annual targets and objectives of an organization. These targets are set and achieved within the budgetary constraints.

Information systems, though tools for long-term strategic planning and control, also help in achieving short-range targets. They compare the actual expenditure with the budgeted expenditure and help the management with variance reports on which managers can take remedial actions. Similarly, the strategic information system built to outsmart competition can help in day-to-day monitoring and control. For example, an enterprise system that helps in achieving cost leadership by producing products at a lower cost by increasing efficiency, is also used as a short-term monitoring tool for achieving production targets.

VALUE CHAIN AND STRATEGIC INFORMATION SYSTEMS

Strategic IS can be deployed throughout the business value chain. A business value chain refers to all activities involved in a product's or service's purchase, manufacturing, storage, and sales including the support activities. Value chain analysis is the most common tool at the business level.

Value Chain Model

The value chain model was developed by Michael Porter (1985). It highlights the primary or support activities that add a margin of value to the company's products and services where IS can best be applied to achieve competitive advantage, and where IS are more likely to have a strategic impact. In other words, this model views a firm as a chain or a series of activities that adds value to its product or services at every step, and thus adds margin to the firm and its customers. In the value chain framework, some activities are primary activities and others are support processes. This framework can highlight where competitive strategies can best be applied with the help of IT.

The primary activities are directly related to the production and distribution of the firms' products and services. These include inbound logistics, operations, outbound logistics, marketing and sales, and customer service. Inbound logistics include receiving, storing, and issuing of materials to the manufacturing department. Operations involve manufacturing processes that transform raw material into finished goods. Outbound logistics include storing and distributing finished products. Marketing and sales involve promoting and selling the products. Customer service involves after sales service, maintenance, and other services provided to the customer.

Support activities make the delivery and production of the goods and services through primary activities possible and make use of the organization's infrastructure. These activities include administrative and financial management, human resource, technology development, and procurement of resources.

Organizations are said to have competitive advantage when they offer more value to their customers than the competitors. An IS could have a strategic impact when the deployment of the IS makes it possible to deliver the goods at a price lower than that of the competition, or at the same price, but with a higher value.

The availability of the Internet has made it possible to include an organizations' customers and suppliers into the value chain. The inclusion of customers and suppliers in the business value chain can be called the 'extended value chain'.

Value Chain and Information Systems Deployment

Figure 3.2 provides the value chain framework in a business organization and examples of where and how IS can be applied by a firm for attaining competitive advantage. This is one area where IS and IT have been instrumental in bringing in radical changes for process improvement and intra-disciplinary communication. For example, in administration and finance, companies can deploy systems for workflow intranet, messaging, financial controls, and budgeting systems. These systems improve intra-office communications, control of financial systems, and provide financial budgeting. Human resource management system and personnel intranet improve the employee–company relationship as they provide a self-service portal for intimation of leave, employee grievance redress platforms, etc. E-commerce and extranet portals provide access to customers and suppliers, which improves relations and makes the procurement system transparent.

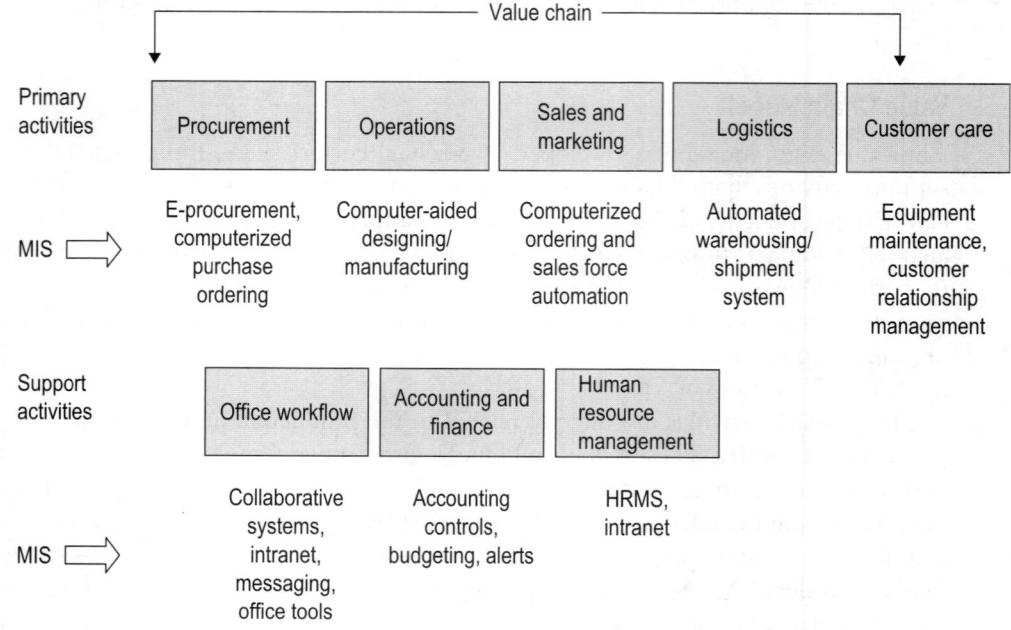

Fig. 3.2   Value chain and examples of strategic IS

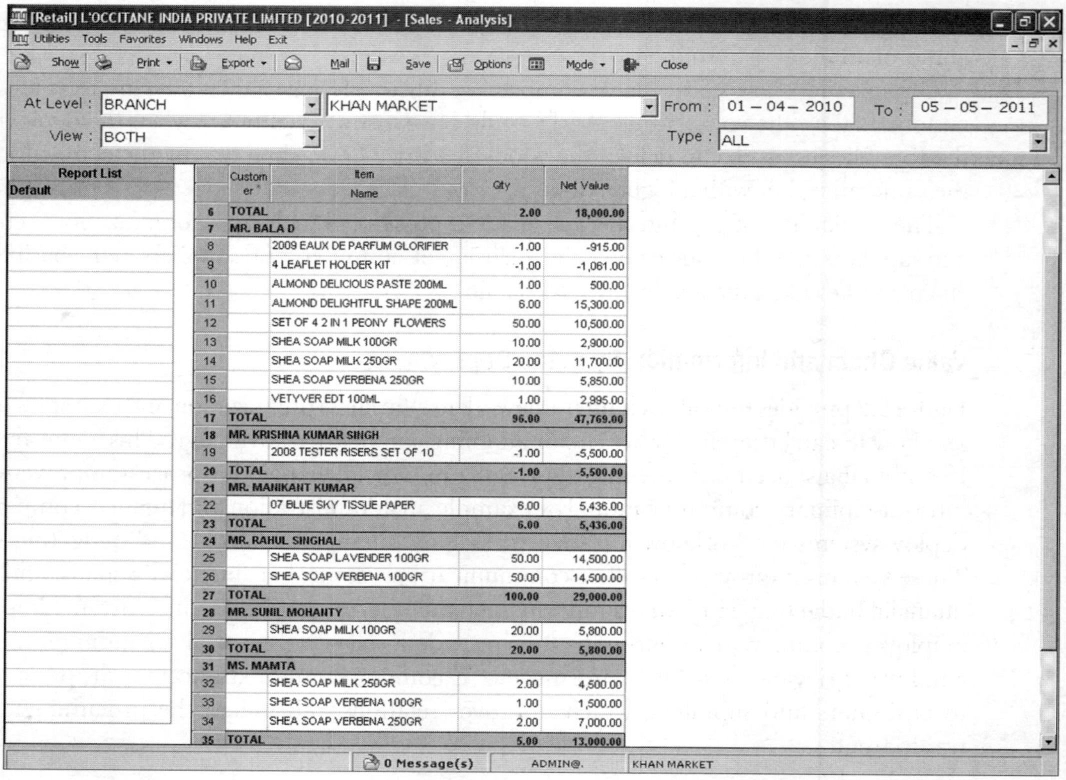

Fig. 3.3   CRM systems analyse customers' data to have customer insights

For primary activities, there are scores of IS that can be implemented for gaining strategic advantage. In case of inbound logistics, there can be automated warehousing systems. In large warehouses, the movement and storage of products can be tracked through radio frequency identification (RFID) systems. The manufacturing processes are controlled and managed by computer-aided manufacturing (CAM) and computer-aided design (CAD). Enterprise solutions for production planning and scheduling are common examples of IS deployment for competitive advantage. For the sales and marketing arena, there can be a variety of IS for internal and external value chains. Sales force automation provides for a strategic IS for the internal value chain. Better and efficient management of the sales force calls for a strong information and control system for the sales opportunity management. Customer order management system is another application that is used for improving links with the customer and thus gain strategic advantage. Customer relationship management is widely used to improve customer relations and understand the customer needs by having insights into a customer database, as illustrated in Fig. 3.3. CRM systems can provide analytical data on customers' tastes, preferences, and buying patterns and can be used to individually address a customer. Usually customers use the company's website to query about their orders, lodge complaints, evaluate products, and know about new products and services. Therefore, the intranet and web interface can effectively satisfy the customer and provide competitive advantage. Exhibit 3.3 provides an example of a company that gained competitive advantage by investing in IT.

EXHIBIT 3.3

Wal-Mart Gains Competitive Advantage by Investing in IT

Wal-Mart realized the benefits of IT as early as 1983, when it invested in a satellite network linking all its point-of-sales (POS) terminals in its retail stores. The POS terminals were equipped with indigenously developed software, as Wal-Mart opted for a very centralized development approach. The in-house development supported the ERP solutions running across the organization. In a short period of time, this system grew into a huge network, connecting all its retail stores, head office, warehouses, and even suppliers. The most innovative achievement was the introduction of just-in-time inventory control, which is otherwise unheard of in a retail scenario. When an item is sold by the store, a message is sent to the supplier of that item. This alerts the supplier and prompts him to include that item in the next shipment. This connectivity allowed Wal-Mart to reduce investment on excess inventory and handled the customer's requirement in an efficient way. Wal-Mart achieved operational efficiency and used it to offer lower costs and better quality products and services. These steps differentiated Wal-Mart from its competitors.

On the application part, instead of buying smaller systems, it preferred to build its own, and the company had the monetary power to develop ahead of the rest of its competition. Wal-Mart's main USP for in-house development was that the company competes on business process expertise. The retail giant considers its IT people, first as merchants, and later, as technologists. The IT persons are supposed to be experts in business processes of retail, merchandizing, and supply chain. This prevents the application of technology for technology's sake. Wal-Mart, while automating processes, eliminated lethargic processes. In other words, the retail giant does not automate bad processes. The philosophy is to weed out bad processes and see automation as a reengineering and change management tool.

Wal-Mart was not satisfied with its legendary supply-chain prowess. The company and its key suppliers began testing an online private trading hub that builds on the superbly efficient and sophisticated supply-chain technology that helped it become the world's largest retailer. The retail giant estimated its start-up costs between $13 million and $23 million for a supplier that ships 50 million tagged containers per year. Costs include RFID tags, readers, system integration, and changes to supply chain applications. The source said that cost-sharing discussions between Wal-Mart and its suppliers will be needed. The

(Contd)

Exhibit 3.3 (Contd)

tags, one of the key potential discussion points, currently range from 20 cents to 50 cents, according to analysts and consultants. Implementation of intranet and extranet to link its business with suppliers and customers pushed Wal-Mart way ahead of its competitors and enabled it to gain strategic advantage.

Sources:
'Retail's super supply chains,' 16 October 2000, http://www. informationweek.com/808/walmart.htm, last accessed on 19 November 2011.
Sliwa, Carol, 'Wal-Mart suppliers shoulder burden of daunting RFID effort', 10 November 2003, http://www.computerworld. com/s/article/86978/, last accessed on 19 November 2011.

MIS—STRATEGIC BUSINESS PLANNING

Companies, such as Wal-Mart (Exhibit 3.3), Cisco, Intel, IBM, and HP, made IT a part of their long-term strategic planning and made huge investments in it. Strategic business planning is a long-term planning process that is adopted by business houses in order to make the business sustainable and surge ahead of competition. Conditions such as market forces, technological changes, diversity of business, competition, and environmental threats, challenges, and opportunities force businesses to resort to long-term strategic plans.

Market forces   Market forces refer to changes in demand and supply, change in direction and growth of market, consumer behaviour, and emergence of new markets and substitutes.

Technological changes   Globally, technological breakthroughs have threatened existing businesses and created opportunities for new businesses.

Diversity of business   The scope and reach of business is ever-changing in the era of globalization. The variety of products, different market segments, various methods of manufacturing, multiple locations, various regulations of the states and the Centre, etc., add to the complexity of managing businesses.

Competition   Competition is the strongest factor affecting strategic planning and every business is affected by it. Competition is a natural phenomenon in business, and every business has to tackle it in a planned and proper way.

Environmental factors   Finally, environmental factors could be social, business, economic, industrial, government, regulatory, and technological factors that may present both threats and opportunities. These factors have a deep bearing on the fortunes of the businesses.

A business environment changes constantly. This factor makes strategic planning very complex. All the environmental factors mentioned earlier have a profound impact on businesses. MIS are designed to monitor and control these factors. MIS is designed to provide some insight into these factors so that the management can deal with them. Strategy formulation is the responsibility of the senior management. The senior management relies on MIS for information so that they can formulate long-term strategies to cope with the environmental challenges.

The business strategies may target products, market, finance, or overall growth in terms of sales and market capture. The organization may formulate and implement one strategy at a time. The task of MIS is to provide relevant information that would help the management in deciding the type of strategies the business needs at that point of time. The strategy is related to the current

Table 3.3 Usage of competitive strategies to gain business sustenance

Business conditions	Questions that a business manager must answer
Market forces	• How does demand for a product vary over a period of time?
	• Was my company able to meet those demands?
	• Are we geared up for a sudden surge of demand?
Technological changes	• What is the market share of the substitute product?
	• How equipped are we to adopt the new business format?
	• Can we switch over to the e-commerce model of business?
Diversity of business	• Are our systems capable of handling multiple company operations?
	• Can we expand and enhance our product reach to meet this new challenge?
Competition	• What is our market share vis-à-vis the competitor?
	• Is the low price policy suitable for current business?
	• Should we pitch our product to a different market niche?
Environmental factors	• Are we meeting the regulatory standards in our production processes?
	• Are we meeting the environmental factors?
	• Is the current product regulated and what is its life?

business scenario and the respective goals. MIS is supposed to provide current information about the status of business and that of the goals. It provides information on whether the business is on a growth path, stagnant, or is declining. MIS provides continuous assessment of business progress in terms of markets, sales, profits, and direction of business. Thus, MIS helps the top management in strategy formulation at each stage of the business. There can be several strategies for different areas of business. The business may require a mix of various strategies at different levels of management. For example, if the business is on a growth path, it would require a mix of good price, products, and new market strategies. If a business is showing a negative or a downward trend, it would need a mix of price discounts, sales promotions, and advertising strategies.

Table 3.3 displays various environmental forces and how they should be supported with the help of relevant answers by a suitable MIS. Based on these answers, the top management formulates a long-term strategy to sustain and grow in business.

Jawadekar (2006) has summarized the role of MIS in the top management strategy formulation, as follows. MIS supports by providing information to

- decide the goals and objectives,
- determine the correct status of future business and projects,
- provide the correct focus for the attention and action of the management,
- evolve, decide, and determine the mix of the strategies,
- evaluate the performance and give a critical feedback on the strategic failures,
- provide cost-benefit evaluation to decide on the choice of resources, the mobilization of resources, and the mix of resources, and
- generate the standards, norms, ratios, and yardsticks for measurement and control.

MIS—TOOL FOR ORGANIZATIONAL CHANGE

It is difficult to bring in sudden changes in the functioning and business processes of a live organization. The management may convert the event of IS implementation into an opportunity to bring in metamorphic changes in the organization. The implementation of the new IS can be a powerful instrument for organizational change, enabling organizations to redesign their structure, scope, authority centres, workflows, products, and services.

Table 3.4 describes some of the ways in which IT can be used to transform organizations and its business processes.

IT can bring in various degrees of organizational change, depending on how the management views and plans it. It can range from simply automating the processes, rationalizing the processes, reengineering, or a major paradigm shift. Organizational change carries both risks and rewards. The higher the risk, the bigger the reward. The most common forms of organizational changes while implementing IS are automation and rationalization. These changes are modest in nature and carry few risks and rewards. The organization simply automates the existing processes with

Table 3.4   Examples of organizational transformation through the use of information technology

IT-induced organizational change	Examples
The role of IT in a manufacturing enterprise has evolved from a support tool to a catalyst for change and the creator of new business paradigms, which gives rise to innovation. This has led to individualized mass-production.	Levi Strauss (US) manufactures customized jeans for its customers. Ashok Leyland transformed its manufacturing with the help of IT by bringing in innovation and agility.
IT has had a dramatic impact on our economy and has spurred innovation in many industries. Advancements in IT have influenced business processes in the telecommunication industry.	Airtel, Vodafone, and Idea Cellular are some new IT-based business models in mobile telecommunications.
Collaborative tools and workgroup applications have created virtual organizations; work is no longer tied to physical location and these tools facilitate anywhere, anytime access to knowledge and information.	NIIT pioneered the idea. Companies such as Infosys and Yahoo! India allow their employees to work from home.
The Internet has given rise to new business models, alternative marketing, order collection, and procurement channels for businesses.	'Rishte-hi-Rishte' marriage bureau transformed into matrimonial sites such as shaadi.com and Jeevansathi.com. Online shopping malls such as FlipKart and Jabong prospered.
Enterprise applications such as ERP, CRM, and SCM help reduce operational costs as workflows move from paper to digital media. They help organizations reduce costs, increase efficiency, and enhance profitability.	Behemoths such as ONGC, BHEL, and Indian Oil streamlined their operations and brought in efficiency through the use of ERP systems.
Global networks, intranets, and extranets have made real-time access to information a success. Globally networked organizations could bring in coherence in diverse business processes.	British Telecom India established global networks that are flexible; the company can expand these networks in accordance with the business needs.
Cloud computing propounds concepts of shared resources and makes the technology accessible to everyone while reducing the deployment cost drastically.	Maruti Suzuki India implemented cloud computing for its large network of dealers and service providers and hence managed to lower costs, increase management efficacy, and become more agile during peak loads.
IT has had a visible and widespread impact on process transformation in important industries such as transportation (airlines, railways), finance (online trading), banking (online banking), and medicine.	Companies such as Air India, Jet Airways, and Indian Railways offer online ticketing, which has simplified and improved the efficiency of the reservation process. Online stock trading in the Bombay Stock Exchange has transformed the way shares are traded.

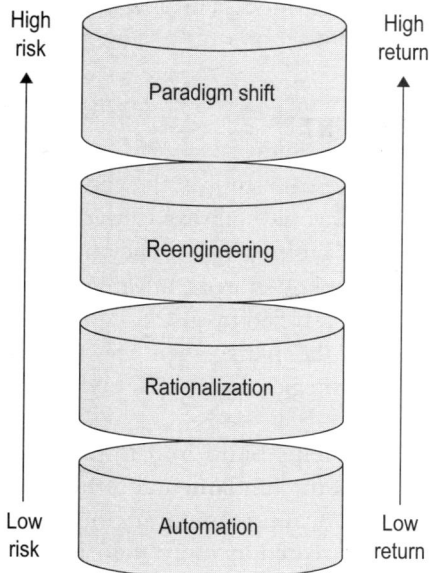

High
risk

High
return

Paradigm shift

Reengineering

Rationalization

Low
risk

Low
return

Automation

Fig. 3.4 Different types of changes and their risks and rewards

minor improvements. More comprehensive changes include reengineering and paradigm shifts. These changes carry high rewards but involve very high risk.

For example, with the new IS and applications in place, Indian banks simply did not automate the processes; rather, process reengineering had to be done. After computerization, the customer does not queue up at three different counters for cash withdrawal; rather, one teller performs all the three tasks of demand entry, signature verifications, and cash payments. The paradigm shift was visible with the introduction of ATM and net banking facilities.

Figure 3.4 illustrates the relationship between risk and returns with respect to the four types of changes that IT implementation can bring in an organization.

Automation is the basic form of change caused by computerization of the existing processes to speed up the tasks. This involves assisting employees in performing their tasks efficiently. Accounting, bookkeeping, preparing salary sheets, payslips, computerized passbooks by banks, and hotel and airline reservation systems are examples of automation of basic business processes.

The next stage of automation is rationalization, in which the organization streamlines standard operating procedures (SOP), eliminates visible bottlenecks, and sheds obsolete processes. The bottlenecks and obsolete procedures highlighted by automation are taken care of by rationalization. In rationalization of procedures, the automation makes the system more efficient and effective. For example, automation of banks brought in changes that eliminated the processes of queuing at multiple teller windows and simplified the processes of cash withdrawal and deposits. A web-based passenger reservation system by airlines is an example of rationalization.

A more radical organizational change is business process reengineering (BPR), in which business processes are analysed, simplified, and redesigned. It is a radical redesign of business processes, combining steps to cut waste and eliminate repetitive, paper-intensive tasks in order to improve costs, quality, and service. It maximizes the benefits of IT implementation. Reengineering is much more ambitious than rationalization of procedures, requiring new vision and rethinking. Net banking is an example of reengineering, wherein customers can carry out transactions such as funds transfers and bill payments from the comfort of their home or office. Similarly, web-based reservation systems by airlines is a rationalization of procedures; however, introduction of remote boarding passes is an example of process reengineering.

Paradigm shift is a more radical form of business change than reengineering. It involves rethinking the nature of the business and the nature of the whole organization. While rationalization and reengineering are limited to specific parts of business, paradigm shift can ultimately affect the nature of the entire business. For example, Apollo Hospitals are into the health care business. While processing the health insurance claims of their patients, they found it natural to have a separate wing for doing the same. Consequently, they ventured into health insurance with Munich Insurance as their international business partners. This is a paradigm shift as well as an expansion in their business.

BUSINESS PROCESS REENGINEERING AND PROCESS IMPROVEMENT

Globally, companies such as Oil and Natural Gas Corporation (see case study at the end of the chapter), Wal-Mart, Pepsico, Coke, ITC, McDonald's, and Subway have always viewed IT as a competitive differentiator and made it part of their long-term business plan. They used IT for BPR and process improvement. Businesses may use IT as a tool of strategic advantage and this is helpful in formulating strategic policies. They may also be satisfied by just using IT as a support system for the day-to-day operations of their business. If the management views IT as a major competitive differentiator, it would formulate business strategies that use IT to develop capabilities to gain competitive advantage.

One of the major strategic uses of IT is in BPR. BPR helps build and implement competitive strategies. Michael Hammer (1990) defines BPR as the fundamental rethinking and radical redesign, to achieve dramatic improvements in the critical contemporary measures of performance such as cost, quality, service, and speed. It is treated as more than just an improvement in business processes. It is an approach for redesigning the way work is done to better support the organization's mission and reduce costs. Reengineering starts with a high-level assessment of the organization's mission, strategic goals, and customer needs. Basic questions are asked, such as, 'Does our mission need to be redefined?', 'Are our strategic goals aligned with our mission?', 'Who are our customers?' An organization may find that it is operating on questionable assumptions, particularly, in terms of the wants and needs of its customers. Only after the organization rethinks what it should be doing, does it decide how best to do it.

There is a high degree of risk involved in making radical changes to an organization's business processes to dramatically improve efficiency and effectiveness. Just like the potential gains of successful reengineering are very high, so are its risks in case of failure. Reengineering differs from process improvement, as the latter is a slow and a low-key affair in the organization. Table 3.5 differentiates between process improvement and process reengineering.

Table 3.5   Difference between business process improvement and business process reengineering

Business process improvement	Business process reengineering
Changes are continuous and incremental	Changes are one time but radical in nature
Automates and reduces existing processes	Recreates brand new processes
Low cost, hence low risk	High cost, hence high risks
Implementation time is less	Implementation time is more
Involves technology to improve processes	Involves workflow change
Scope is narrow and within functions	Scope is broad and cross-functional
Management involves the past and present	Reengineering is done for the future
Does have some impact on the culture of the organization	Involves cultural and structural changes
Changes are advised by the lower management	Changes are initiated from the top management
Multiple processes are improved or managed simultaneously	One process is worked upon and completed at a time
IT collaborates to improve processes	IT is optional to effect change

For effective reengineering of business processes, the senior management needs to develop a broad strategic vision that calls for redesigned business processes.

ROLE OF INFORMATION TECHNOLOGY IN BPR

IT plays a significant role in reengineering most business processes. The speed, processing capabilities, connectivity of computers across the organization, and the Internet can substantially increase the efficiency of business processes. For example, many companies worldwide have used ERP to reengineer, automate, and integrate their business processes such as manufacturing, distribution, finance, and human resources. They have reaped impressive gains and benefits in business. Michael Hammer (1990) maintains that while implementing computer-based IS, the major challenge for managers is to obliterate non value-adding work, rather than using technology for automating these processes. The computerization process should render these non value-adding processes as obsolete.

Any exercise to design and build an IS is preceded by the exercise of BPR. As the implementation of MIS may have an impact on organizational goals and mission, a rethinking is required on the management's part. The business itself may undergo a qualitative change in terms of focus, work culture, and value system. MIS takes care of performance parameters such as data capture, processing, analysis, and reporting, which are set as per new missions and goals. The decision support systems are integrated in the business process and are made available to users at the click of a button.

IT has historically played an important role in the reengineering concept. It is considered by some as a major enabler for new forms of working and collaborating within an organization and across organizational borders.

The following attributes of IT contribute to the BPR effort in an organization:

- Shared databases, making information available at many places
- Expert systems, allowing generalists to perform specialist tasks
- Telecommunication networks, allowing organizations to be centralized and decentralized at the same time
- Decision support tools, allowing decision-making to be a part of everybody's job
- Wireless data communication and portable computers, allowing field personnel to work independently
- Interactive e-commerce portals, facilitating immediate contact with potential buyers
- Automatic identification and tracking, allowing objects to tell where they are, instead of requiring to be found
- High performance computing, allowing rethinking and revisioning organizational objectives
- Advent of mobile computing and m-commerce, making organizations more agile and gaining acceptance in the corporate world

Earlier, workflow management systems were considered as a significant contributor to improved process efficiency. Workflow management is the process of streamlining business procedures so that documents can be moved easily and efficiently from one location to another. ERP vendors, such as SAP, JD Edwards, Oracle, and PeopleSoft, are positioning their solutions as vehicles for business process redesign and improvement.

BPR is not always about finding a newfangled way of doing business, but at times just sifting through what has really worked over the years. That is what shipping-to-telecom major Essar

Limited realized a few years ago. Its projects division had almost a dozen orders to execute with a purchase budget of $3.5 billion and that is when it decided to go back to something that had worked for it in the past—a central purchase team. V. N. Paradkar, CEO, Global Supplies of Essar, says that in the mid-1990s, there was a similar team in place that handled procurement for all group projects. Once those projects were completed, the team was disbanded and split among the individual locations. When things slumped about a decade later, the group decided to reassemble this team. As the volumes are significantly larger, this enables the team to get special deals with suppliers (*Economic Times*, 10 April 2009).

SUMMARY

Strategic advantage is defined as the competitive advantage that one business entity has over its rivals within an industry. Competitive advantage occurs when an organization acquires or develops an attribute or combination of attributes that allows it to outperform its competitors. Competitive advantage is a key determinant of superior performance and ensures survival and prominent placing in the market. Superior performance being the ultimate desired goal of a firm, competitive advantage becomes the foundation for highlighting the significant importance to develop the same. The strategic role of information systems (IS) involves using information technology (IT) to develop and distribute products, services, and capabilities that give an organization major advantage over its competition.

Porter's (1985) classic model of competitive strategy defines five types of strategies to counter five types of competitive forces. These include (a) the rivalry of competitors within its industry, (b) the threat of new entrants into an industry and its markets, (c) the threat posed by substitutes who may capture market share, (d) the bargaining power of customers, and (e) the bargaining power of suppliers. Business firms can counter these competitive forces and threats with five basic competitive strategies. These strategies are (a) cost leadership strategy, (b) differentiation strategy, (c) innovation strategy, (d) growth strategy, and (e) alliance strategy.

Strategic usage of IT enables businesses to accommodate the impact of Internet-age firms and new information flows across the enterprise. Today, the emphasis is on exploring, identifying, and occupying new market niches before competitors act. Companies create IS-based products and services to sustain at a lower price, and carry out product differentiation and innovation. IT-supported product differentiation can prevent the competition from counter-attacks and the firms no longer have to compete merely on the basis of costs.

The value chain model highlights the primary or support activities that add a margin of value to a company's products and services where IS can best be applied to achieve a competitive advantage, and where IS are more likely to have a strategic impact. In the value chain framework, some activities are primary activities and others are support processes. Primary activities include inbound logistics, operations, outbound logistics, marketing and sales, and customer service. Support activities include administrative and financial management, human resource, technology development, and procurement of resources.

Strategic business planning is a long-term planning process that has been adopted by business houses to make the business sustainable and surge ahead of competition. MIS is designed to provide some insight into environmental factors so that the management can deal with them. Strategy formulation is the responsibility of the senior management. The senior management relies on MIS for information so that they can formulate long-term strategies to cope with environmental challenges better.

The management may convert the event of IS implementation into an opportunity to bring in metamorphic changes in the organization. Implementation of new IS can be a powerful instrument for organizational change, enabling organizations to redesign their structure, scope, authority centres, workflows, products, and services. IT can bring in various degrees of organizational change depending on how the management views it and plans it. It can be simply automating the processes, rationalization of processes, reengineering, or a major paradigm shift.

Business process reengineering (BPR) is defined as the fundamental rethinking and radical redesign to achieve dramatic improvements in the critical contemporary measures of performance such as cost, quality, service, and speed. Making radical changes in the business processes to dramatically improve efficiency and effectiveness involves a high degree of risk. Just as the potential gains of successful reengineering are very high, so are its risks in case of failure. IT plays a significant role in reengineering most business processes. The speed, processing capabilities, connectivity of computers across the organization, and the Internet technology can substantially increase the efficiency of business processes.

KEY TERMS

Cloud computing   A method of computing in which the hardware or software resources are shared over the network.

Distributed computing   A form of decentralized processing made possible by a network of computers.

Mobile computing   A form of computing that connects a mobile device such as laptop, palmtop, and iPhone with the central server and permits processing.

Strategic advantage   Developing products, services, and capabilities that give the company an advantage over its competitors.

Strategic IS   Information systems that provide a firm with competitive products and services that give it a strategic advantage.

Value chain model   Primary or support activities that add a margin of value to the company's products and services where information systems can best be applied to achieve competitive advantage.

Workflow   The way work is performed, usually defined by an information system.

CONCEPT REVIEW QUESTIONS

1. What do you understand by strategic advantage? Explain with some examples.
2. What strategic role does information technology play in strategic planning?
3. What are the different types of strategies? Explain various competitive forces and strategies.
4. How can IT be strategically used for attaining competitive advantage?
5. What do you understand by business value chain? How can a strategic IS take care of the value chain?
6. Why could a business use IT to increase switching costs and increase loyalty among customers and suppliers?
7. 'MIS offers much more than simple automation of business processes.' Explain this statement in the light of the role of MIS in strategic business planning.
8. How can MIS be used to make changes in the business structure of a company?
9. What is business process reengineering? What strategic role can IS play in BPR?

CRITICAL THINKING QUESTIONS

1. As a manager, you are being asked to develop e-business and e-commerce applications to gain competitive advantage in your company. How will you start and what reservation would you have about doing so?
2. Peter Keen, MIS author and consultant, said, 'We have learned that it is not technology that creates a competitive edge, but the management process that exploits technology.' What did he mean by this statement? Do you agree? If not, why?
3. 'Information technology cannot help an organization gain any strategic advantage, because most competitive advantages do not last more than a few years and soon become a strategic necessity that raises the stakes of the game.' Critically examine this statement.

MIS DEVELOPMENT

Business process reengineering is not an easy task. For reengineering of business processes effectively, the senior management needs to develop a broad strategic vision that calls for redesigned business processes. As you already know, it involves high risks of failure, but also offers great rewards. Many business processes, especially in the firms and public utility departments handled by the government, are still very complex and involve many slow and lousy procedures. For example, the driving license issuing process of the transport departments of various states in India is a long and lethargic one. Before obtaining a driving licence, the candidate visits at least 15 counters. The flow chart in Fig. 3.5 shows the process of obtaining a driving licence from the regional transport authority of any state.

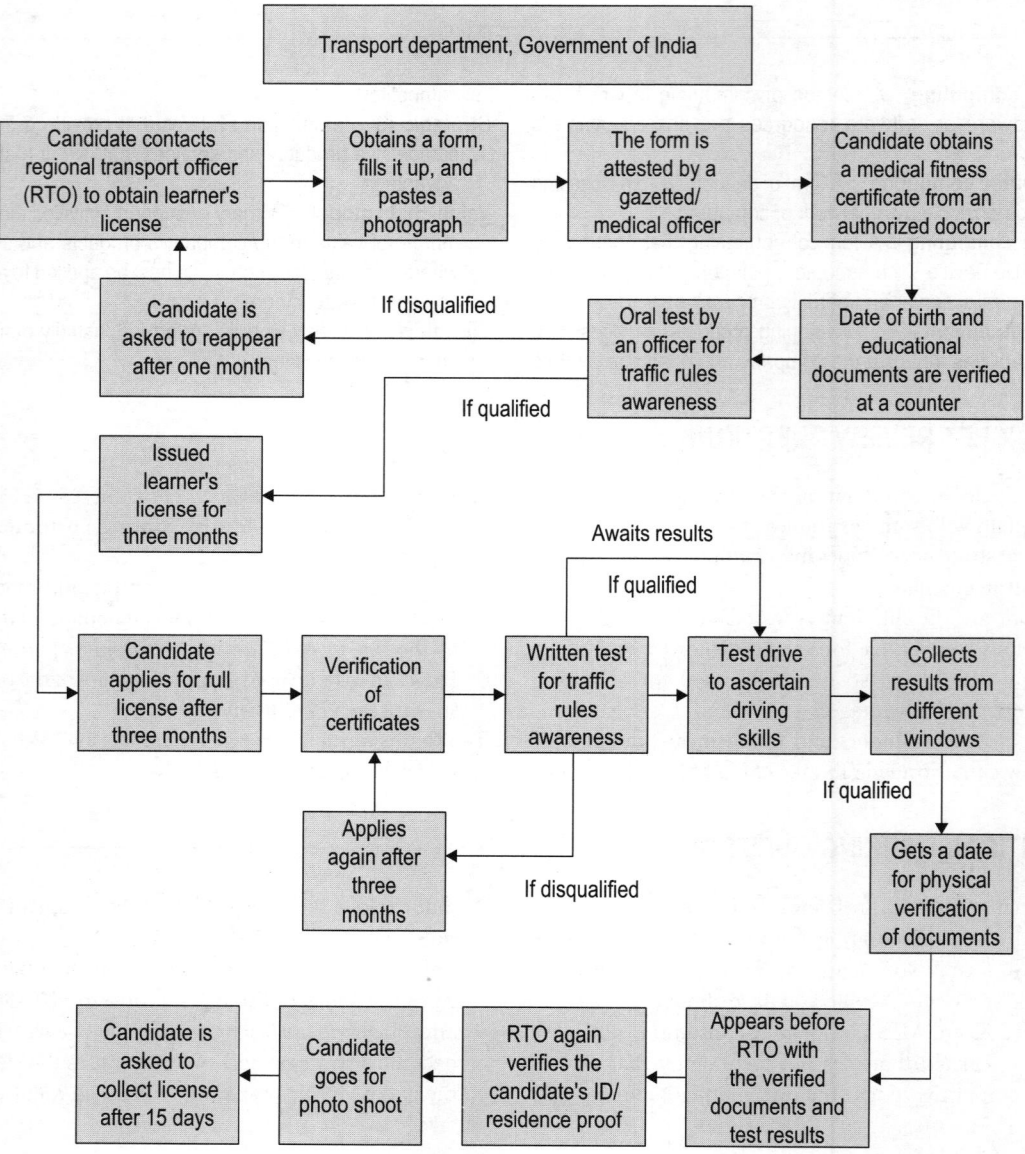

Fig. 3.5   Driving license issuing process

Exercise

Assume that the transport department of your State approaches you for reengineering the driving licence issue process. Discuss among your peer groups and rethink over this issue. Draw a new flow chart reengineering the complete process. Reduce the steps in acquiring driving licenses. Redraw the processes and plan so that licence seekers have to just visit three to four windows to get their licences.

REFERENCES

Alter, Steven, *Information Systems—The Foundation of E-business*, Pearson Education, Singapore, 2004.

Goldman, Steven, Roger Nagel, and Kenneth Preis, *Agile Competitors and Virtual Organizations: Strategies for Enriching the Customer*, Van Nostrand Reinhold, New York, 1995.

Gorden, Davis and Margethe Olson, *Management Information Systems*, The McGraw-Hill Book Company, Singapore, 1996.

Hamm, Steve and Marcia Stepneck, *From Reengineering to E-engineering*, Business Week, March 1999.

Hammer, Michael, 'Reengineering the Corporation', *Harvard Business Review*, 1990.

Jawadekar, Waman S., *Management Information Systems: Text and Cases*, Tata McGraw-Hill, New Delhi, 2008.

Laudon, Ken and Jane Laudon, *Management Information Systems*, Pearson Education, Singapore, 2002.

Laudon, Ken, Jane Laudon, and Rajanish Dass, *Management Information Systems*, Pearson Education, Singapore, 2010.

O'Brien, James A., George M. Marakas, and Ramesh Behl, *Management Information Systems*, Tata McGraw-Hill, New Delhi, 2006.

Porter, Michael, *Competitive Advantage*, Free Press, New York, 1985.

Powell, Thomas C., 'Organizational Alignment as Competitive Advantage', *Strategic Management Journal*, www.thomaspowell.co.uk/article_pdfs, last accessed on 10 May 2011.

Sangani, Priyanka, 'Indian Companies go for Business Process Reengineering', Economic Times, http://articles.economictimes.indiatimes.com/2009-04-10/news/27641202_1_bpr-business-process-reengineering-raw-materials, last accessed on 10 April 2009.

Smith, Howard and Peter Fingar, *Business Process Management: The Third Wave*, Meghan-Kiffer Press, Tampa, 2003.

http://www.managementsciences.co.za/downloads/, last accessed on 26 March 2011.

CASE STUDY

ONGC: A Case of Business Process Reengineering with IT

When ONGC Limited, India's largest oil exploration and production company, set out to completely transform its business, it turned to IT enterprise solutions. As a result, the company was able to overcome the challenge of standardizing business processes across its 500-plus locations.

ONGC, a Fortune 500 company, is one of the *Navratna* companies of India (*Navratna* was the title given originally to nine public sector enterprises [PSEs] identified by the Government of India in 1997 as 'public sector companies that have comparative advantages', giving them greater autonomy to compete in the global market so as to 'support [them] in their drive to become global giants'); and its dedicated team of nearly 33,000 professionals are responsible for this. With market capitalization of over ₹1,00,000 crore, ONGC contributes more than 80% of India's oil and gas production. The company has adopted progressive policies in scientific planning, acquisition, utilization, training, and motivation of the team. It has a unique distinction of being a company with in-house service capabilities in all activity areas of exploration and production of oil and gas and related services. ONGC spans across 10 countries outside India, from Russia to Venezuela.

Issue

Deriving business benefits from IT is not new to ONGC. As early as 1996, the company undertook Project *Kuber*, wherein it implemented SAP R/3 ERP system for its finance function. Thereafter, in December 1999, ONGC started another project, Project *Shramik*, where it deployed SAP for automation of all HR modules, including payroll and administration. The implementation started in mid-2000 and it was expected to go live by mid-2004. ONGC used a PC-based legacy system for material management, project monitoring, and maintenance planning. Information is as valuable as oil for any organization and sometimes, harder to locate. ONGC felt the need for a solution using IT to streamline the business process, and integrate all the information along the business process of enterprise core business.

However, such piecemeal implementations were never going to be enough. Subir Raha, chairman and managing director (CMD) of ONGC in 2001, was intent on integrating all the functions of the company under one umbrella. His motto was 'one data, one system'. Raha had his reasons. Despite the earlier implementation, the company suffered from lack of availability of real-time information. Monthly reports generated were not enough to take forward-looking managerial decisions.

Project

Subsequently, Project ICE (information for consolidation and efficiency) was born. A six-month study, undertaken by software major SAP, recommended that all operations and offshore business operations of ONGC had to be integrated into a single ERP system. Besides core activities like drilling, this also sought to include associated activities such as mudding and cementing, which most global energy companies tend to outsource.

The move towards an ERP package was to enable the availability of information on a real-time basis and eliminate duplicate activities across the organization. Keeping this as an imperative, ONGC aims to take maximum advantage of the state-of-the art technology for leveraging productivity and thereby, profits. Overall, ONGC has kept aside ₹1000 crore to invest in IT. In addition to ₹95 crore invested in SAP implementation, ONGC is also looking to invest ₹45 crore every year towards software implementation. Another ₹600 crore was earmarked for the establishment of a communication and control network. The rest of the amount will be spent on EPNet, its exploration and production network, being implemented in two phases by Schlumberger. 'The project is all about data capture as part of all transactions. If there is an invoice drawn up somewhere, it is automatically fed into the system as data, so is a payslip or the day's measurement of oil from a well ... and the beauty is that it would all be available on tap', said Raha. This will, in turn, facilitate decision support, better operation control, and efficient cost management.

Project Objectives

Optimization and standardization of the business process was the primary objective. Post implementation, it was expected to have more efficient operations to improve productivity. Integration of all systems was necessary to provide the data validation to ensure that the correct numbers are sent to the integrated systems. The oil giant wanted integration and extension of the value chain of the business.

Solution

mySAP.com™ e-business solutions was proposed to be implemented over the next 30 months across five regions of ONGC for over 8500 users. It includes solutions covering financials, corporate financial management, business intelligence, supplier relationship management, enterprise portals (for workplace), upstream oil and gas requirements, strategic enterprise management, and product lifecycle management. ONGC was using a human resource package (*Shramik*) and a financial package (*Kuber*) from SAP earlier. The reasons why SAP was chosen was that it has experience with global oil and gas production companies. SAP India signed its largest ever deal in ONGC for implementation of the ICE project. The deal worth ₹950 crore would provide a comprehensive

IT-enabled system for the oil and gas PSU—right from its wellheads all the way to its boardrooms. It was also the largest consulting deal for SAP Asia Pacific. In terms of sheer size (with 8500 licensed users across ONGC), it would be Asia's largest ERP project.

The mySAP business suite and the SAP for oil and gas solution portfolio, including the SAP® strategic enterprise management (SAP SEM®) application, SAP business information warehouse component (part of the SAP NetWeaver® business intelligence component), and SAP portal were implemented. The enterprise-wide project was designed to integrate with existing SAP financials and human resource solutions used in more than 500 ONGC locations. SAP solutions support ONGC's exploration, production, maintenance, procurement, finance, payroll, sales, offshore logistics, joint ventures, treasury, and quality management. The implementation also includes other SAP solutions, such as the collaboration projects suite, supplier relationship management, and upstream oil and gas exploration and production solutions.

Roll-out

Project team consultants from SAP played a critical role in the roll-out and education of users. It was excellent knowledge transfer process from SAP consultants. SAP Consulting blended expertise with ability to improvize as complexities of project required them to do so. By the time the project was completed in May 2005, the team had added other geographical locations and functions to the implementation, making new solutions available to a total of 13,000 users—65% more than the user base originally planned. The idea was to attract the hard target at first and make it successful so that all the others would fall in line. The first day of a quarter was a go-live date set for the production and drilling facility of ONGC. The project was spread across India and in the Arabian Sea with a cost of approximately $100 million. Finally, the system was implemented in the corporate centre in New Delhi with a backup centre in Mumbai.

Business Process Reengineering

More than 200 end-to-end processes were replaced with redesigned and pragmatic processes. The new processes yielded unparalleled insights into operations, real-time reporting on oil exploration and production, inventory, financial analysis, and accurate and efficiently delivered data. The business process solutions met stringent regulatory controls, considering ONGC's state ownership, yet remained adaptable enough for users throughout the value chain. For example, in the area of procurement, the team built in validations to ensure that users could place a purchase order only with an approved requisition and available budget.

To make sure the change management happened without any problem, the new solution meant that paper-based contracts and vendor payments were complemented by electronic transactions and workers had to begin using the new system. Moreover, to ensure compliance and data integrity, the project team implemented built-in checks to make sure users followed the correct procedures when entering data and identifying themselves. The daily and weekly reports replaced quarterly data and facilitated real-time reconciliation. Process-oriented redefinition of work roles and duties were assigned and this resulted in greater transparency and accountability. In addition, the company now sends out payments for purchased products only after invoice verification. Likewise, payments for services are made only after service entries have been completed and the project's progress has been updated.

Benefits

A key benefit of the new solution is that it creates high visibility for critical data. The new solution ensures that critical operational data is available online for all levels of management. One of the benefits of using SAP was the launch of reverse auction process, the first PSU to do so. Termed as 'live action cockpit' (LAC), the system will enable ONGC to collect and compare price and bid information of various suppliers in a real-time, open bidding environment. The reverse auction will ensure transparency in the tendering process and thereby, generate confidence amongst the bidders. It will also add speed to the process of procurement that will allow ONGC to source the best-in-class technology. On the basis of the pilot project, it is estimated that reverse auction will be able to accrue a cost saving of nearly 10%. The reverse auction process enables supplier selection process by facilitating vendors worldwide to participate in the bidding process seamlessly.

The potent combination of a new business culture supported by a new IT tool and the flexibility to adopt new business innovations, along with an in-house leadership capability, prepares ONGC to explore new frontiers, including joint ventures overseas. ONGC has also implemented the employee self-service (ESS) functionality of the mySAP ERP solution, thereby, expanding its reach to cover 36,000 users, making it one of the largest ESS implementations in India. ESS—christened *Samparc*, meaning connect—facilitates

employees to apply for leave, submit their claims, and view their payment details online. For ONGC, SAP solutions have equipped the world's second-largest oil exploration and production company with reliable and available data that it needs to manage the magnitude of the challenges in the 21st century.

The following were the achievements in a nutshell:

- Improved visibility across the enterprise, spanning the globe
- Improved ability to compete through the strategic use of new IT platform
- Rapid acceptance and improved performance by workers
- Improved and disciplined approach to accounting, procurement, and financial systems
- Reengineering business processes across different business functions from exploration to production to sales and offshore joint ventures
- Disaster recovery solution for the corporate data centre
- Integration of real-time and history data of SAP, EPINet, and VRC

Discussion Questions

1. Do you agree with the arguments made in this case in support of the business process reengineering provided by IT in business? Why or why not?
2. How has SAP implementation helped ONGC achieve business process reengineering?
3. What strategic advantages has ONGC been able to gain by relying on IT and IS?
4. Find out some other Indian companies that have used IT strategically and gained competitive advantage. Illustrate how they went about it.

Sources:

http://infotech.indiatimes.com/articleshow/943355.cms, last accessed on 20 November 2011.

http://www.brplindia.in/news_erp_sap.htm, last accessed on 20 November 2011.

http://www.ongc.net/archives1.asp?fold=archives%5CMarch04&file1=feature_article&file2=feature_article3.txt, last accessed on 20 November 2011.

www.ongcindia.com, last accessed on 20 November 2011.

http://www.ongc.net/press_release1_new.asp?fold=press, last accessed on 20 November 2011.

http://www.sapendusers.com/oilIndia.php, last accessed on 20 November 2011.

http://www.slideshare.net/swapnilsaurav/business-process-reengineering-ongc, last accessed on 20 November 2011.

Part II

Information Technology Infrastructure

- Hardware Resources

- Software Resources

- Data Resources

- Networks and Telecommunications

CHAPTER

4

Hardware Resources

Computer technology is becoming so powerful and integrated into daily experiences that it can appear almost invisible to the user. Social interfaces are being developed to model the interaction between people and computers using familiar human behaviour. People increasingly will interact with the computer in more intuitive and effortless ways—through writing, speech, touch, eye movements, and other gestures.

—Ted Selker

LEARNING OBJECTIVES

After studying this chapter, you will be able to

- define information technology (IT) infrastructure and understand its components
- recapitulate the history of the evolution of computers
- differentiate among the computers of different generations
- appreciate the revolution in digital computing with the invention of the microcomputer
- classify computers in the present-day context
- define a basic computer hardware architecture
- understand the trends in the hardware platform
- comprehend the concepts of grid, cloud, and mobile computing

EXHIBIT 4.1

Cloud Computing Fuels Hardware Spending

Gartner's latest figures (as of 2011) put the number of installed personal computers (PC) worldwide as just having surpassed 150 crore units and at a growth rate of just under 12% annually. It is expected to surpass 200 crore units by early 2014.

The world's installed base of PCs remains heavily concentrated in mature markets. However, emerging markets will claim an increasingly larger share of the world's installed base going forward as the rapidly rising PC penetration in emerging markets continues to drive a strong double-digit PC growth.

'Mature markets such as the United States, Western Europe, and Japan currently account for 58% of the world's installed PCs, but these markets only account for 15% of the world's population,' said George Shiffler, research director at Gartner. 'There is a startling difference in the per capita PC penetration between mature and emerging markets. Of course, much of this difference reflects the disparity in average living standards between mature and emerging markets. However, rapid economic development across emerging markets is not only narrowing the disparity in average living standards, but also closing the difference in per capita PC penetration between mature and emerging markets.'

'Emerging market governments are also increasingly committed to reducing the digital divide by promoting PC use among their citizens through a variety of means, including providing PCs directly to the less affluent', said Luis Anavitarte, research vice-president at Gartner. 'While mature markets accounted for just under 60% of the first billion installed PCs, we expect emerging markets to account for approximately 70% of the next billion

installed PCs.'

According to the International Data Corporation (IDC), the move to cloud computing is driving significant spending on data centre hardware to support private cloud initiatives of businesses. In fact, IDC also predicts that private cloud hardware spending will draw public cloud hardware spending and that server hardware revenue for public cloud computing will grow from ₹58.2 crore in 2009 to ₹71.8 crore in 2014, and server hardware revenue for the larger private cloud market will grow from ₹260 crore to ₹570 crore in the same period.

The irony of this phenomenon is that cloud computing may drive up the number of servers in the data centre, even though many organizations are looking to cloud computing to reduce the hardware footprint in the same area. However, building all those new cloud services, both public and private, also requires building the platforms to run them. Ultimately, the adoption of cloud computing could diminish the number of servers deployed in proportion to the number of users served, but that might not happen until the late 2010s or even early 2020s.

Sources:
Linthicum, David, 'Why cloud adoption is driving hardware growth, not slowing it', http://www.infoworld.com/d/cloud-computing/why-cloud-adoption-driving-hardware-growth-not-slowing-it-616, last accessed on 26 August 2011.
http://www.gartner.com/6447088, last accessed on 10 March 2011.
http://www.gizmag.com/global-pc-installed-base-passes-1-billion/9569/, last accessed on 26 August 2011.
www.ciol.com/technology/storage/News-reports, last accessed on 26 August 2011.

Gartner, the renowned international research firm, estimated an installation base of 200 crore PCs worldwide and ever increasing server hardware revenue as indicators of strong information technology (IT) hardware infrastructure (Exhibit 4.1). Corporations are still spending huge money on IT and telecommunication equipment, which are enabling information systems and providing a platform for IT applications. Rapid hardware and software developments accelerate the emergence of new system models that reduce the physical size of the systems, but entrust massive computing power into them. Today, computer hardware comes in a variety of processing capabilities, storage capacities, and computing powers.

Computer-based information systems (CBIS) are developed for and revolve around computer technology. In this chapter, we will briefly touch upon the invention and evolution of computers and understand their basic architecture. Further, we will discuss the latest trends in computer technology, high-end servers, and the concept of cloud computing.

INFORMATION TECHNOLOGY INFRASTRUCTURE

Information technology infrastructure refers to the technological resources that provide a platform for the organization's information system applications. IT infrastructure resources include computer hardware, software, data, and telecommunication and network equipment.

According to Laudon (2010), IT infrastructure consists of a set of physical devices and software applications that are required to operate the entire enterprise. However, IT infrastructure is also a set of firm-wide services budgeted by management, comprising both human and technical capabilities.

The infrastructure equipment and services include the following:

- Computer hardware is a platform used to provide computing services. It includes PCs, large mainframes, laptop computers, personal digital assistants (PDAs), and smartphones.
- System and application software services provide system capabilities such as operating systems, software development tools, system management utilities, and collaboration tools. They also provide enterprise-wide capabilities such as enterprise resource planning (ERP), supply chain management, customer relationship management, and knowledge management.
- Data management tools, applications, and services that store, manage, and analyse organizational data.
- Telecommunications and network equipment and services that provide data, voice, and video connectivity, including Internet equipment and services.

In this chapter, we will discuss the various computer hardware platforms.

EVOLUTION OF COMPUTERS—A BRIEF HISTORY

Charles Babbage, a French mathematician, is known as the father of computers. He designed his mechanical device in 1835, which he called the 'analytical engine'. Babbage drew inspiration from the centuries' old abacus, which was used for counting numbers. Babbage's machine could only perform very simple arithmetic calculations. He replaced the abacus beads with mechanical gears, which were similar to the arithmetic logic unit of modern computers. However, there are scores of known and unknown contributors who later improved upon this machine and invented digital systems. For instance, as a military necessity, during World War II, there were many developments in the digital arena. Electronic circuits, relays, capacitors, and vacuum tubes replaced mechanical parts. There were many developments and improvements on Babbage's machine. The most noticeable improvement over Babbage's machine was the invention of the electronic numerical integrator and computer (ENIAC) in 1945 by John Mauchly and J. Presper at the University of Pennsylvania. ENIAC was the first electronic general purpose machine and was 1000 times faster than other contemporary computers.

The electronic discrete variable automatic computer (EDVAC), designed by John von Neumann, a Hungarian–American mathematician, was the basis of the modern computer. Most mainframes and minicomputers were developed around this architecture, which was the most suitable for digital computing. Even today, most contemporary computers use this architecture. We can call this the first generation of computers.

Based on the period of their inventions and the technology used, computers are known to belong to different generations. The first generation of computers, called mainframes, came out in 1952. The first computer for commercial use was launched by IBM, which was called IBM701 Mainframe. These machines were huge, weighed around 30 tonnes, had 18,000 vacuum tubes to operate them, and occupied more space than what could be accommodated in a 400-square feet room. These computers only understood zeros and ones as the programming language. A programming language is an instruction code to the computer that gets translated into the binary numbers—0 and 1. These computers used a machine-level language, which later came to be known as the first generation computer language (as the instructions were given to the computer in 0s and 1s). However, programming and operating these computers was a strenuous job. It took hundreds and thousands of man-days to write even a small program for simple calculations.

The period from 1960 to 1970 was the period of the second generation of computers or minicomputers. In 1960, Digital Equipment Corporation developed a computer with a keyboard and a monitor that was commercially available. These were called minicomputers because of their smaller size when compared to the mainframe. In 1969, Data General launched 'Nova', which was the first 16-bit minicomputer. These computers offered relatively more features, and were easy to program, use, and maintain. The programming language also matured from the first-generation machine language to the second generation, called the assembly language. Assembly language was more programmer-friendly. It was converted into machine language (to be understood by the computer) by a converter program in the computer. We will discuss these languages in detail later in this book.

With the invention of the microprocessor by Ted Hoff and F. Foggin at Intel Corporation in the early 1970s, computer technology underwent a sea change. The third generation of computers that came into the picture were called microcomputers because they used microprocessors. These computers were extremely small in size, had much more processing speed, and could store information in magnetic disks. Thus, these computers were called personal computers or PCs, as any person could buy and use them. In 1971, Intel Corporation released the first microprocessor, Intel 4004, which was made for a Japanese calculator company. Later, in 1975, Intel 8080 was used to build MITS Altair, the personal computer. This was the first time that Paul Allen and his friend Bill Gates developed a BASIC interpreter for Altair and later, both friends formed Microsoft. It was only in August 1981 that IBM released its first PC and used an Intel 8088 microprocessor, which had a speed of 4.77 MHz. This computer was developed on a memory chip that could store 1024 bits of data, which is equal to 1 kilobyte. Almost at the same time, floppy disks were introduced. These were the first generation floppy diskettes that were 8 inches in size. IBM (then known as International Business Machines) standardized the configuration of the PC.

The journey of PCs started with Intel Corporation introducing the tiny microprocessor or integrated chip (IC) by the code name, 8088. The technology was improved continuously. The size became smaller while the speed and efficiency doubled and quadrupled with every new release. It is said that if the automobile industry had made progress like that of computers, we would have a car the size of a match box with the speed of a jet, within 40 years.

The fast evolution of microcomputers was due to the invention of the microchip known as an integrated circuit (IC). In this technology, the computer logic is 'burnt into' the layers of the microprocessor. A chip, the size of your thumb nail, is enough to hold enough logic to run the computer programs we have in our computer. The pace of evolution of computers was always followed by development in the field of peripheral devices. Peripheral devices include input, output, and storage equipment such as mouse, monitor, printer, and hard disk. Monitors evolved from monochromes and high-resolution colour to liquid crystal displays (LCDs) and thin-film transistors (TFTs). Similarly, the graphic user interface (GUI)-based operating system software came along with a mouse. The headache of memorizing DOS commands had gone. Printers evolved from the ubiquitous dot matrix to inkjet and laser jet printers. Similarly, the largest hard disks available in 1988 had a 10 megabyte (MB) capacity. Today, a PC is available with a 1 terabyte (TB) or 1000 gigabyte (GB), that is, 10,00,000 MB space. This development has been phenomenal.

Computing power, which has been doubling every 18 months, has improved the performance of microprocessors over 25,000 times since their invention 30 years ago. Computing power refers to how fast a computer can perform a task. With easy-to-use software, a computer can crunch numbers, analyse vast pools of data, or simulate complex physical and logical processes with animated drawings, sound, and even tactile feedback.

CATEGORIES OF COMPUTERS

The categorization of computers as mainframe, mini, and micro does not represent today's computer systems that are based on the microprocessor technology. Therefore, a more appropriate classification will be to categorize them as microcomputers, network servers, and supercomputers.

Microcomputers

Microcomputers are pervasively used systems that cater to our personal needs as well as in the corporate sector. Though, they are also called personal computers, their usage is widespread in modern businesses. Their computing power has surpassed the power of the first generation minis and mainframes. Microcomputers come in many forms such as laptops, notebooks, desktops, and even palmtops. They are used as powerful workstations and run applications such as computer-aided design (CAD) and computer-aided manufacturing (CAM).

Network servers

Modern global businesses require high-end computers for their data processing needs. Eventually, they rely on high-end computers, commonly known as 'servers', which serve clients with data and applications in a client–server environment. These machines are comparatively less costly, and easy to maintain and operate. They are used to host large websites, business applications requiring high computing power, and corporate intranets and extranets. Nowadays, we usually hear about servers with multiple processors and hot swappable multiple hard disks, and redundant array of independent disks (RAID)-compliant systems. For example, XEON and Blade are high-end servers that use Intel XEON processors, multi-processors (up to four processors), and hot swappable hard disks (RAID-compliant).

According to Simpson (1997), 'burgeoning data warehouses and related applications such as data mining and online analytical processing are forcing IT shops into higher and higher levels of server configurations. Similarly, Internet-based applications, such as web servers and electronic commerce, are forcing IT managers to push the envelope of processing, speed, storage capacity, and other applications, fuelling the growth of high-end servers.'

Supercomputers

Supercomputers are highly sophisticated and powerful systems that are used for tasks requiring complex calculations and very high speed. Though supercomputers are said to be of massive computing power and used for government agencies for applications such as weather forecasting, military defence systems, and astronomy, they are now being used by global businesses as well for data warehousing and data mining. Supercomputers use parallel processing architectures in which interconnected multiple processors work in tandem. Supercomputers can perform millions and trillions of instructions or operations per second. There are supercomputers that can calculate in trillions of floating-point operations per second (teraflops), which use thousands of microprocessors in parallel processing designs.

According to O'Brien (2006), 'the use of symmetric multiprocessing (SMP) and distributed shared memory (DSM) designs of smaller numbers of interconnected microprocessors has spawned a breed of mini-supercomputers with prices that start in hundreds of thousands of dollars'. This has made supercomputers affordable for businesses worldwide. For example, IBM RS/6000 SP with multiple processors is a supercomputer used by Charles Schwab & Co., in the US. The US-based Oak Ridge national laboratory uses Cray XT5-HE supercomputer. The Blue Gene/P supercomputer at Argonne national lab runs over 2,50,000 processors.

Based on the price affordability of supercomputers, Ken (1997) maintains that supercomputers have now become 'scalable servers' at the top end of the product lines that start with desktop workstations. Market-driven companies like IBM have a much broader focus than just building the world's fastest computer, and the software of the desktop computer has a much greater overlap with that of the supercomputer than it used to, because both are built from the same cache-based microprocessors.

India joined the league of supercomputers with a supercomputer named 'Param', invented by the Centre for Development of Advanced Computing (C-DAC). Besides this, Eka is a supercomputer built in India and used by Computational Research Laboratories in Pune and is owned by Tata Sons. More on this is given in Exhibit 4.2.

EXHIBIT 4.2

Indian Supercomputers Enter Global Top 500

With India leaving a mark in every sector of the technology field, the country has shown its importance in the super-computing race too. Eight of the top 500 supercomputers are from India with Tata Group's Eka, a Hewlett Packard (HP)-based system leading the race with the 13th rank.

Following Eka is C-DAC's Param supercomputer at the 68th rank and the IBM-based eServer Blue Gene solution of the Indian Institute of Science at the 213th rank. As Faisal Paul, country manager, HPC and OS/L, said, 'Though the company is yet to make a mark in terms

(Contd)

Exhibit 4.2 (Contd)

of capacity of a supercomputer globally, wherein tags such as Blue Jeans and Cray dominate, in the rest which consist of 94% of high performance computing (HPC), we have a significant position.'

Earlier the fastest super computer of India was the 2007-built Eka at the Tata-owned computational research laboratories in Pune. Eka uses HP's supercomputing technology. In January 2011, the Indian IT major, Wipro technologies, developed India's fastest super computer, SAGA 220, for the Indian Space Research Organization (ISRO). The super computer was built at the Vikram Sarabhai Space Centre (VSSC) in Thiruvananthapuram. SAGA-220 (Supercomputer for Aerospace with GPU Architecture 220 teraflops) used by space scientists for solving complex aerospace problems, is to be India's fastest supercomputer in terms of theoretical peak performance of 220 teraflops (trillion floating point operations per second).

SAGA-220 is fully designed and built by VSSC using commercially available hardware, open-source software components, and in-house developments. The system uses 400 NVIDIA Tesla 2070 GPUs and 400 Intel Quad Core Xeon CPUs supplied by Wipro with a high speed interconnect, costing ₹14 crore to build. With each GPU and CPU providing a performance of 500 gigaflops and 50 gigaflops respectively, the theoretical peak performance of the system amounts to 220 teraflops.

Sources:
Silicon India, 'ISRO builds supercomputer', http://www.silicon india.com/shownews/ISRO_builds_Indias_fastest_super computer-nid-83003-cid-30.html, last accessed on 9 September 2011.
'Wipro builds fastest supercomputer', http://www.socioparivar. wordpresss.com/2011, last accessed on 9 September 2011.
http://www.ciol.com/News-Reports/, last accessed on 9 September 2011.

Table 4.1   Evolution of computers and the computing era

Computing technology	Year of introduction	Technology
General-purpose mainframe computers	1959	IBM 1401, 7090
Minicomputers	1965	DEC PDP-11, VAX
Personal computers	1981	IBM PC on Intel 8088
Network computing	1991	Introduction of network software such as Novel LAN and Windows NT
Enterprise computing	1995	Use of transmission control protocol/Internet protocol (TCP/IP), enterprise resource planning (ERP), enterprise risk management (ERM)
Cloud computing	2000	Sharing of hardware, software, and other resources

Table 4.1 illustrates the periodic evolution of computer technologies.

COMPUTER SYSTEM ARCHITECTURE

As students of business management, we need to understand only the basic concepts of computer systems, which will help us in being more effective users. The basic computer system is a set of interrelated elements that perform the basic system functions of input, processing, output, storage, and control. Figure 4.1 illustrates the basic computer architecture, which conforms to the input–process–output system concept of computers and explains the basic input, output, and storage devices.

Having understood the computer architecture, we will briefly explain the important elements in a computer system.

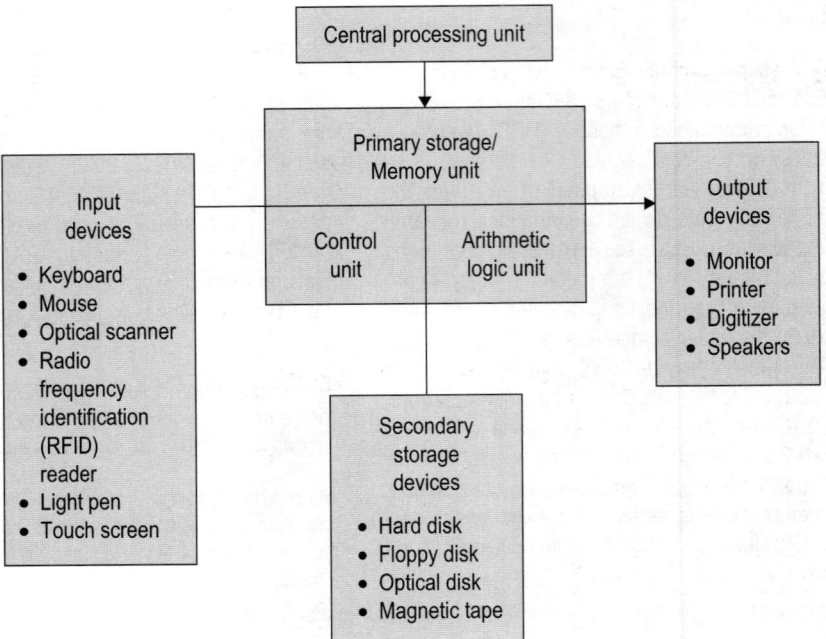

Fig. 4.1   Basic computer architecture and peripheral devices

Central Processing Unit

The central processing unit (CPU) is the main processing component of a computer system. The CPU consists of three main units—an arithmetic logic unit (ALU), a control unit, and a primary storage unit. The ALU performs all the arithmetic and logical calculations in the computer; it can add, subtract, multiply, and divide numbers. It can also understand logical calculations and negative numbers. The control unit controls and coordinates the various parts and components of a computer (the input and output devices, storage units, and other internal units).

Primary Storage

This unit of a computer performs the function of storage. The storage of the operating system, the program at work during an operation, and the data related to that operation occurs in the primary storage area. This is also known as the memory of a computer system. The primary storage is supported by secondary storage devices such as hard disks and optical disks. The functions of a memory unit are to

- store all the data to be processed;
- store data and results during the intermediate stages of processing;
- hold the data after processing until it is transferred to an output device or saved permanently in the hard disk; and
- hold instructions from a program for on-going processing.

There are two types of memory systems in the computer—read only memory (ROM) and random access memory (RAM).

Read only memory   This is permanent memory and the retrieval is sequential in nature; the system can access the second block of memory data only after reading the first block. The data or information in this memory is fused in the chip and information about the computer is stored in a program called BIOS (basic input/output system). You must have noticed some information getting displayed on the screen of your computer when it starts. This information comes from the ROM part of the memory.

Random access memory   This is temporary memory. It is called random because it can be accessed and retrieved randomly from any location in the memory area. This memory is used to store data or applications when the system is working. For example, after starting the computer, it retrieves the operating system files from the hard disk, brings it in the RAM area, and executes the commands. In the same way, if you are working on a spreadsheet like Excel, your Excel application, which was stored and remained dormant in the hard disk, comes to the RAM, and you can start working on it. The data that you enter in the Excel worksheet remains in this volatile memory until you press the save button and permanently write it on the disk. If you have not saved your work and the computer is accidentally switched off, the work done will be lost.

The unit of measurement of memory is byte. Information in the form of a word, symbol, image, or character is stored and processed in the form of binary digits. A binary digit is called a bit and is represented by either 0 or 1. All characters and symbols are in the form of zeros and ones. The computer system has been designed using only two electrical signals—the presence (1) and the absence (0) of an electrical pulse, which is either an 'on' or 'off' state of the electrical signal. For storing each character, a unique representation in the form of 0 and 1 is used. With two bits, four (2^2) different symbols—00, 01, 10, and 11 can be represented. With 3 bits, eight (2^3) representations are used in the form of 000, 010, 011, 001,100, 101, 110, and 111. Thus, the computer internally stores information in 8 bits, up to 256 (2^8) representations.

Broadly, there are two 8-bit coding schemes. These are extended binary coded decimal interchange code or EBCDIC (pronounced 'eb-sa-dic') and American standard code for information interchange or ASCII (pronounced 'as-kee'). Both the systems use various combinations of bits to form bytes that represent characters of the alphabet, symbols, and images. These coding standards are given in Table 4.2.

To represent numbers internally, most computers use two bytes, four bytes, or eight bytes. Hence, the 16-bit, 32-bit, or 64-bit systems concept originated. Eight bits form one byte or character. Consider the following conversion table:

8 bits	= 1 byte	1024 megabytes	= 1 gigabyte (GB)
1024 bytes	= 1 kilobyte (kB)	1024 gigabytes	= 1 terabyte (TB)
1024 kilobytes	= 1 megabyte (MB)		

Computer processing speed   As memory is measured in bits and bytes, computer speed is measured in word-length. Word-length is the number of bits a computer processes at a time. If a computer has a word-length of 16 bits, it can process 16 bits or two bytes at a time. As we have seen in the Intel-chip table, a Pentium computer has a 32-bit word-length, and this means that it can process up to four bytes at a time. The chip speed is guided and affected by the clock speed of the computer. This is the internal speed and is measured in megahertz (MHz), which refers

Table 4.2 Coding standards in EBCDIC and ASCII

Character	EBCDIC	ASCII	Character	EBCDIC	ASCII
A	11000001	10100001	S	11100010	10110011
B	11000010	10100010	T	11100011	10110100
C	11000011	10100011	U	11100100	10110101
D	11000100	10100100	V	11100101	10110110
E	11000101	10100101	W	11100110	10110111
F	11000110	10100110	X	11100111	10111000
G	11000111	10100111	Y	11101000	10111001
H	11001000	10101000	Z	11101001	10111010
I	11001001	10101001	0	11110000	01010000
J	11010001	10101010	1	11110001	01010001
K	11010010	10101011	2	11110010	01010010
L	11010011	10101100	3	11110011	01010011
M	11010100	10101101	4	11110100	01010100
N	11010101	10101110	5	11110101	01010101
O	11010110	10101111	6	11110110	01010110
P	11010111	10110000	7	11110111	01010111
Q	11011000	10110001	8	11111000	01011000
R	11011001	10110010	9	11111001	01011001

to millions of cycles per second. If a computer has a clock speed of 2600 MHz, it means it can perform 2600 million cycles per second. Cycles refers to the frequency at which the CPU is running.

Secondary Storage

The secondary storage devices such as hard disk, floppy disk, magnetic disk, magnetic tape, optical disk, and pen drive support the computer data storage function. These devices store data and software applications needed for processing. Secondary storage devices such as magnetic disks and magnetic tapes come with a large capacity to store data.

RAID Technology

This concept was first defined by Patterson, Gibson, and Katz at the University of California, Berkeley in 1987. RAID, an acronym for redundant array of independent disks, is a technology that provides increased storage reliability through redundancy, and combines multiple disk drive components into a logical unit where all the drives in the array are interdependent. They combine scores of small hard disk drives and their control microprocessor into a single unit. Nowadays, servers have multiple data storage devices that are programmed to work simultaneously. This is called RAID storage. RAID units provide large capacities with high access speeds as the data is accessed in parallel over multiple paths from many disks.

RAID technology divides and replicates data among multiple hard disk drives. The different schemes or architectures are called RAID, followed by a number (e.g., RAID 0, RAID 1, ..., RAID 5). When multiple physical disks are set up to use RAID technology, they are said to be in a RAID array. This array distributes data across multiple disks, but the array is seen by the computer user and operating system as one single disk (Fig. 4.2).

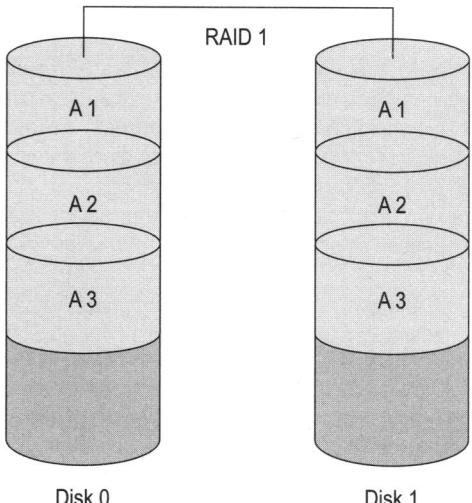

Disk 0   Disk 1

Fig. 4.2   RAID 1—mirroring of hard disks
in RAID technology

RAID 0 provides improved performance and additional storage, but there is no redundancy or fault tolerance. So, as per the RAID definition, it is not a true RAID. However, because of the similarities to RAID, the data is written to multiple disks. RAID 0 does not implement error checking, so any error is left uncorrected. More disks in the array means higher bandwidth but also greater risk of data loss.

In RAID 1, data is written identically to multiple disks (a 'mirrored set'). Although many implementations create sets of two disks, some sets may contain three or more disks. An array provides fault tolerance from disk errors or failures and continues to operate as long as at least one drive in the mirrored set is functioning. Using RAID 1 with a separate controller for each disk is also called duplexing. Distributed parity is used in RAID as a way to increase fault tolerance. It requires all drives but one to be present to operate; drive failure requires replacement, but the array is not destroyed by a single drive failure. Upon drive failure, any subsequent reads can be calculated from the distributed parity such that the drive failure is masked from the end user. The array will have data loss in the event of a second drive failure and is vulnerable until the data that was on the failed drive is rebuilt onto a replacement drive. A single drive failure in the set will result in reduced performance of the entire set until the failed drive has been replaced and rebuilt.

Exhibit 4.3 discusses cloud computing and migration of media to the cloud.

EXHIBIT 4.3

TV is Moving to the Clouds in the United States, Clouds Trudging Uphill in India

Television (TV) is moving to the cloud. It is inevitable, just as other kinds of media from books to music are increasingly delivered over the Internet. Netflix, Hulu, and even Apple TV are making inroads when it comes to distributing

(Contd)

Exhibit 4.3 (Contd)

traditional TV shows and movies to Internet-connected screens. YouTube is increasingly grabbing our attention, accounting for 7% of the total time spent on the Internet in the US.

Nevertheless, the TV (and movie) industry is proving to be more resistant to change than any other form of media. Change will come, but it will not happen as quickly as it is with music, news, or books.

The TV industry is digging in. Starz is walking away from its content deal with Netflix. Hulu seems to be treading water while it tries to sell itself. Even Apple is having a hard time changing the model. It recently stepped back from its attempts to offer TV show rentals (a move we saw coming a month ago) because the TV networks only participated half-heartedly.

However, does anyone really doubt that eventually the Internet will triumph here to smash the rigid program guide that cable and satellite companies shove down our throats? Most of us only watch a few dozen channels regularly, yet we pay for 500. If we could subscribe on a per channel or per show basis, many of us would do so. It's just so obvious that the better experience starts with letting people watch what they want, when they want, on whatever device they want—whether that's their TV, laptop, iPad, or mobile phone. However, that is not enough. TV in the cloud is not just about shifting distribution. It is about making it easier to find and share new shows, and change the way we view them. It is about making TV smarter (who said it's an idiot box?). Unlike the Smartphone, which could only have emerged to leverage the Internet, TV has no 'smart content' to leverage. The 'smartness' has to be not in the box but in the programming.

The cloud computing scenario in India is not as rosy as in the US. Small and medium businesses (SMBs) in India are planning to spend more than $2 million on information and communication technology (ICT) in 2011 and there is an anticipated growth of nearly five times this spending by 2014, according to a research by New York-based Access Markets International (AMI) Partners. Still, cloud-based solution is trudging behind in the SMB segment.

Only 8% of medium businesses currently use cloud-based ERP solutions, whereas the use of this type of application by small businesses (SBs—companies with 99 employees or less) is nearly non-existent. There are several reasons for this relatively sluggish adoption. 'Indian SMBs are uncomfortable with data being housed on servers of remote third-party locations', says Ashima Sharma, research associate, AMI Bangalore. 'Additional concerns are platform lock-in, worries about reliability and performance, data governance, integration, and management.' Due to these concerns, widespread desire to implement these types of technology is lacking.

Of the few SMBs using an ERP solution, manufacturing SMBs are the forerunners. Cloud vendors need to have an aggressive sales strategy to convince these SMBs to adopt these solutions. Additionally, even though vendors are pushing the on-demand option, it has been noted that India channel partners seem traditionally less receptive to change, and are therefore sluggish in promoting the cloud option. If ERP solutions are to gain a strong foothold, Indian SMBs must not only be willing to embrace the technology, but also channel partners.

There is reason to believe that this change in attitude is forthcoming. According to a recent AMI survey, there is considerable anticipated growth in spending on ICT. 'With credit tightening and revenues falling, Indian SMBs are looking to reduce their infrastructure costs, while investing in areas that directly impact revenue, efficiency, and productivity', says Sharma. 'A cloud ERP solution is attractive to these SMBs because it is easier to implement, deploy and maintain, reducing time and cost expenditures.' In the next 12 months, 13% of the Indian SMBs stated that they plan to adopt some type of on-demand ERP solution.

Cloud computing has taken ERP solutions to a new level and has the potential to change the way Indian SMBs operate. As IT infrastructure among most Indian SMBs is minimal, they are prime candidates to move this entire phase of their business to a cloud solution. Widespread acceptance of an ERP cloud solution will happen in stages for Indian SMBs after the resolution of the issues associated with the deployment. The new innovating trends in cloud ERP will ensure maturity and dependability in the technology. This will bring better governance, reliability, seamless functionality, and security.

Sources:

'ERP cloud solutions are facing an uphill battle with India SMBs: AMI', http://www.cxotoday.com/story/erp-cloud-solutions-are-facing-an-uphill-battle-with-india-smbs-ami/, last accessed on 19 September 2011.

Schonfeld, Erik, 'TV in the cloud', http://techcrunch.com/2011/09/04/tv-cloud/, last accessed on 19 September 2011.

TRENDS IN HARDWARE PLATFORM

Exhibit 4.3 explains how media and entertainment, for example, television programmes, will be available on the Internet. It is a step ahead of computer resources such as hardware, applications, data, and services being offered as shared resources via the Internet. The concept of grid and cloud computing emerged with the view to share these expensive resources and includes paying for the usage as per individual requirements. Though the cost of computer hardware has reduced over time, the cost of computing services such as consulting, system integration, and software are very high. The multi-channel delivery of data and information has increased the overall expenditure of an organization. For example, employees now use sophisticated applications on a variety of hardware in laptops, desktops, hand-held mobile terminals, and smartphones.

As organizations had to integrate the data and information available on separate platforms such as mobiles, computers, intranet, Internet, enterprise applications, and legacy systems, organizations worked towards building a more resilient infrastructure that could withstand the enormous data load, as well as lower the impact of increasing costs. To meet these challenges, concepts such as grid computing, cloud computing, and digital mobile computing emerged as the new trends in hardware platform.

Grid Computing

Grid computing is a form of distributed computing whereby a 'virtual supercomputer' is composed of many networked but loosely coupled computers acting together to perform very large tasks. Grid computing uses a cluster of computers. Cluster computing also uses a set of loosely connected computers that work together like one computer to perform a large task. What distinguishes grid computing from conventional high-performance computing systems like cluster computing is that grids tend to be more loosely coupled, heterogeneous, and geographically dispersed. According to Laudon (2010), grid computing involves connecting geographically remote computers into a single network to create a virtual supercomputer by combining the computational power of all the computers on the grid. Figure 4.3 shows such a system.

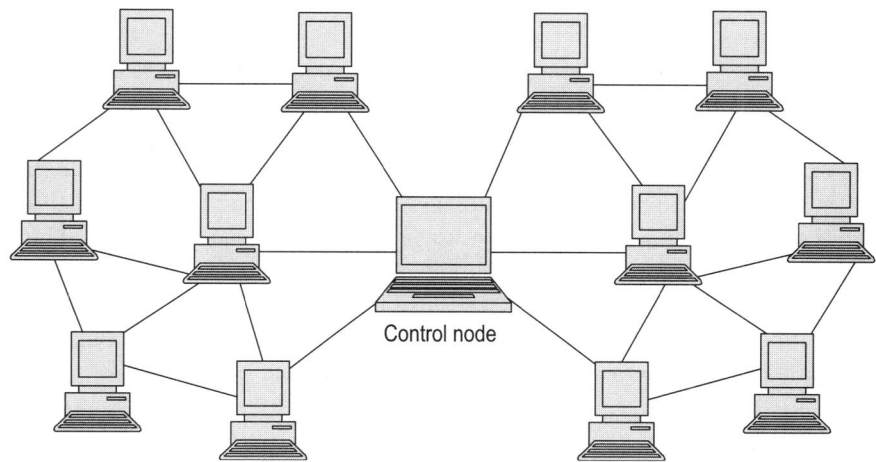

Control node

Fig. 4.3   Grid computing system

Grid computing was possible only with the availability of high-speed broadband Internet, which facilitated connecting various computers economically. This is possible with the help of a software program that controls and allocates resources on the grid. The software helps communication between clients and servers. The server software breaks the data and information into smaller packets and then parcels them to the grid. The client computer performs their normal tasks while running the grid applications in the background.

The primary advantage of grid computing is that each node is a normal desktop hardware, which, when combined in a grid, can produce a computing resource similar to a multiprocessor supercomputer, but at a much lower cost.

Cloud Computing

The latest phenomenon in the IT workspace is the concept of sharing resources to cut costs and leverage high yields by using a superior technology, which would otherwise have been difficult to afford. This concept is of relatively recent origin and managers can benefit by introducing cloud technology in the organizations they serve. Cloud computing describes a new supplement, consumption, and delivery model for IT services based on the Internet. It typically involves over-the-Internet provision of dynamically scalable and often virtualized resources. These resources are virtual and scalable in the sense that they can upgrade or degrade themselves depending on the user's requirement. For example, if an application or user requires more memory, the system supplies the same from the unutilized memory in the shared pool.

Cloud computing is an Internet-based computing, whereby shared resources, hardware, software, and information are provided to users on demand.

Cloud computing is a great leap forward following the shift from mainframe to client–server in the early 1980s. Today, high-speed broadband connection has arrived at every corporate house's doorstep. More computing powers at minimum costs can be leveraged through cloud computing.

The term 'cloud' is used as a metaphor for the Internet, based on the cloud drawing that is used to represent the Internet/web network, as illustrated in Fig. 4.4. Typically, cloud computing providers deliver common hardware infrastructure, business applications, security firewalls, etc., that are accessed from another web service or software like a web browser, while the software and data are stored on servers.

Most types of cloud computing infrastructure consist of services delivered through common centres and built on servers. Clouds often appear as single points of access for consumers' computing needs. Commercial offerings are generally expected to meet the service quality requirements of customers, and typically include service level agreements with the vendor.

In general, cloud computing customers do not own the physical infrastructure; instead, they avoid capital expenditure by renting usage from a third-party provider. The users do not have expertise in and control over the technology infrastructure. They consume resources as a service and pay only for the resources that they use. Many cloud computing offerings employ the utility computing model, which is analogous to how traditional utility services (e.g., electricity) are consumed, while others bill on a subscription basis.

Advantages

The flexibility of cloud computing helps users to rapidly and inexpensively upgrade or degrade technological infrastructure resources, depending on organizational requirements. It provides

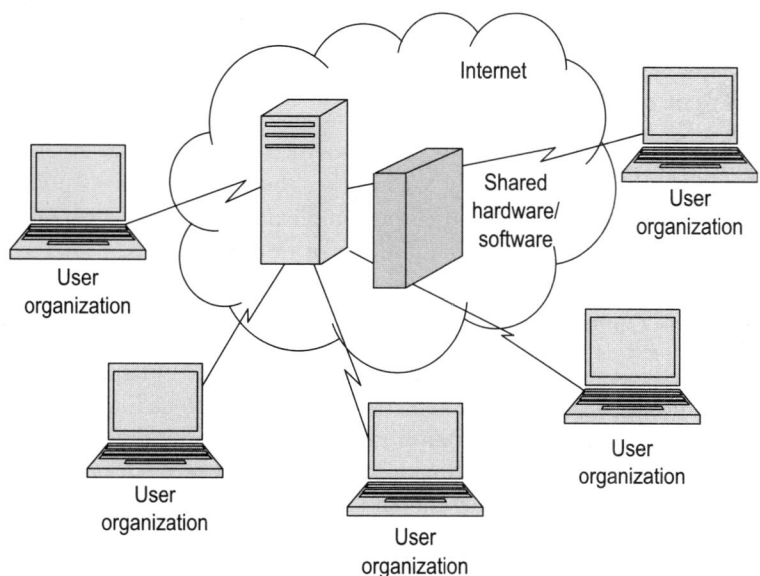

Fig. 4.4   Cloud computing

utilization and efficiency improvements for systems that are often underutilized in the organization. The following are some advantages:

- Cost is claimed to be greatly reduced and capital expenditure is converted to operational expenditure. This ostensibly lowers barriers to entry, as infrastructure is typically provided by a third party and does not need to be purchased for one-time or infrequent intensive computing tasks. Pricing is purely usage-based and fewer IT skills are required for implementation. Multitenancy enables sharing of resources and costs across a large pool of users.
- As infrastructure is off-site (typically provided by a third-party) and accessed via the Internet, users can connect from anywhere. Device and location independence enable users to access systems using a web browser, regardless of their location or what device they are using (e.g., PC, mobile).
- As the computer resources are centralized, users can benefit from the economy of scale. For instance, shared and economical server farms, electricity, high Internet bandwidth, security, etc., are available to users.
- Reliability is improved if multiple redundant sites are used, which makes well-designed cloud computing suitable for business continuity and disaster recovery. Scalability is achieved through dynamic (on-demand) provisioning of resources. Performance is constantly monitored, and loosely-coupled architectures are constructed using web services as the system interface. One of the most important new methods for overcoming performance bottlenecks for a large class of applications is data parallel programming on a distributed data grid.
- Security is often as good as or better than the traditional systems, partly because providers are able to devote resources to solving security issues that many customers cannot afford. Security is also improved due to centralization of data. Cloud computing applications are easier to

maintain, since they don't have to be installed on each user's computer. They are easier to support and improve since the changes reach the clients instantly.

- The usage of cloud computing resources is measurable and is metered per client and application on a daily, weekly, monthly, and annual basis. This enables clients to choose a cloud vendor on the basis of cost and reliability.

However, there can be concerns about loss of control over and the lack of security for certain sensitive data. Providers typically log accesses, but accessing the audit logs themselves can be difficult or impossible. Furthermore, the complexity of security is greatly increased when data is distributed over a wider area and a number of devices.

Digital Mobile Computing

The most recent development in the networked workplace is digital mobile computing. The latest communication devices, for instance, mobile phones such as BlackBerry and iPhone come with many functions of a hand-held computer. Besides oral communication, these devices are capable of transmission of data, net surfing, e-mail, exchange of data, etc. They can be configured to connect to corporate servers and send and receive data. While on the move, high-flying executives can process information and take decisions. There are increasing instances of business computing moving from PCs to these mobile devices, thus enabling managers to monitor and coordinate their tasks. We will discuss mobile computing in detail in Chapter 14.

SUMMARY

IT infrastructure refers to the technological resources that provide a platform for the organization's IS applications. IT infrastructure resources include computer hardware, software, data, and telecommunication and network equipment. The journey of computers started in 1835 with Charles Babbage's mechanical device called analytical engine. The first generation of computers, called mainframes, came out in 1952. IBM launched its first mainframe, IBM701. The period between 1960 and 1970 was the era of minicomputers. In 1969, Data General launched Nova, which was the first 16-bit minicomputer. In the 1970s, the third generation of computers came into the picture, and were called microcomputers because they used microprocessors. The rapid evolution of microcomputers can be attributed to the invention of the microchip, called integrated circuits (ICs).

An appropriate classification of computers in the modern context would be microcomputers, network servers, and supercomputers. Microcomputers come in various forms such as laptops, notebooks, desktops, and even palmtops. Modern global businesses require high-end computers for their data processing needs and rely on high-end computers, commonly known as 'servers' that serve clients with data and applications in a client–server environment. Supercomputers

are highly sophisticated and powerful systems that are used for tasks requiring complex calculations and very high speed. They are now being used by global businesses for data warehousing and data mining. Supercomputers use a parallel processing architecture in which interconnected multiple processors work in tandem. They can perform millions and trillions of instructions or operations per second.

The basic computer system is a set of interrelated elements that perform the fundamental system functions of input, processing, output, storage, and control. The central processing unit (CPU) is the main processing component of a computer system. The CPU consists of three main units—arithmetic logic unit (ALU), a control unit, and a primary storage unit. The primary storage unit of a computer performs the function of storage or memory. There are two types of memory systems in the computer—ROM and RAM. The unit of measurement of memory is byte. Any information is stored and processed in the form of binary digits. A binary digit is called a 'bit' and is represented by either 0 or 1.

The secondary storage devices include hard disks, floppy disks, magnetic tapes, pen drives, etc. RAID, an acronym for redundant array of independent disks, is a technology that provides increased storage reliability through redundancy, combining multiple disk drives components into a logical unit where all drives in the array are interdependent.

To meet costs, enormous data loads, and network challenges, concepts such as grid computing, cloud computing, and mobile computing emerged as the new trends in the hardware platform. Grid computing is a form of distributed computing whereby a 'virtual supercomputer' is composed of many networked, but loosely coupled computers acting together to perform very large tasks.

Cloud computing is a form of Internet-based computing, whereby shared resources, hardware, software, and information are provided to users on demand. Typical cloud computing providers deliver common hardware infrastructure, business applications, security firewalls, etc., that are accessed from another web service or software like a web browser, while the software and data are stored on servers.

The most recent development in the networked workplace is digital mobile computing. The latest communication devices such as BlackBerry and iPhone offer the same functionality as that of a hand-held computer.

KEY TERMS

Analytical engine   Name given to the first computer by Charles Babbage.

Assembly language   The second generation language used for minicomputers.

BASIC interpreter   A software program that could work as a disk operating system.

Cloud computing   An Internet-based computing, whereby shared resources, hardware, software, and information are provided to users on demand.

Floating point operations   Capacity to perform instructions or operations per second.

Grid computing   A form of distributed computing whereby a 'virtual supercomputer' is composed of many networked, but loosely coupled computers acting together to perform very large tasks.

Integrated circuits   Microchips having the capability to write programs on the chip.

Machine-level language   The first generation language used for mainframe computers where instructions were given using binary digits 0 and 1.

Mainframe   The first generation of computers, which used machine-level language for programming.

Microcomputer   The third generation computers, which use modern programming languages and are user-friendly.

Minicomputer   The second generation of computers that used assembly-level language and were comparatively smaller that mainframes.

Mobile computing   Use of digital communication devices such as BlackBerry and iPhone for connecting with the corporate network.

Network servers   High-end computers with multiple processors and hard disks, which act as servers for other computers with resources, files, and applications.

Parallel processing   A processing architecture in which interconnected multiple processors work in tandem.

RAID technology   Redundant access array, a technology that provides increased storage reliability through redundancy, combining multiple disk drives components into a logical unit where all drives in the array are interdependent.

Shared resources   The concept of sharing computer resources such as memory, storage, and applications.

Supercomputers   Highly sophisticated and powerful systems that are used for tasks requiring complex calculations and very high speed.

Symmetric multiprocessing   Interconnected multiple processors working in tandem, with the technology used by supercomputers.

CONCEPT REVIEW QUESTIONS

1. Write a brief note on the evolution of computers.
2. What are the current trends in the development and use of the major types of computers?
3. Define the basic computer system architecture and explain the input and output devices with examples.
4. What do you understand by cloud computing? Explain with examples.
5. What is grid computing? How is it different from cloud computing?
6. Write short notes on the following:
   (a) Random access memory (RAM)
   (b) Read only memory (ROM)
   (c) Arithmetic logic unit (ALU)
   (d) Parallel processing
   (e) Redundant arrays of inexpensive disks (RAID)

CRITICAL THINKING QUESTIONS

1. Will the convergence of personal digital assistants (PDAs), notebook PCs, and mobile phones produce an information appliance that will make all of those categories obsolete? Why or why not?
2. Do you agree that supercomputers have replaced mainframes?
3. What processor, memory, magnetic disk storage, and video display capabilities would you require for a computer that you will use in your new business?
4. Conduct some research over the Internet and find out companies that still use mainframe computers for their vast computational needs.

MIS DEVELOPMENT

In the campus interview this year, you have been selected as Manager–Systems by an upcoming company, which is a startup, but belongs to a well-known business group of the country. The company has sufficient budget for capital expenditure and the promoters are willing to spend on the right technology assets and excellent human resources. The business operations of the company are yet to commence and all the machinery and information technology assets are yet to be procured. You have been given the responsibility of setting up the IT department. The chief executive officer (CEO) of the company explains the following business model to you.

The company is into manufacturing of men's wear. The products will compete with major brands in the country. The company has set up a business objective to be among the top three brands in this category, in the country within the next three years. For achieving this, the company plans to heavily advertise and promote themselves in both the print and electronic media. To meet the demands thus generated, the company is setting up two manufacturing units, one each in Rudrapur in Uttarakhand and Karur in Tamil Nadu. The manufacturing units will distribute the goods to 20 distribution hubs, located in all the major cities and state capitals. These distribution hubs will serve as replenishment centres for all garment retailers in their regions. From day one, the operations of the company will be computerized. The company plans to install computers at each manufacturing unit, all distribution hubs, and the corporate office in Mumbai that takes care of procurement, accounting, and human resource functions. Besides the CEO, there will be seven directors who will like to see everything online on their systems.

Exercise

Identify the entire hardware requirements for the company, including the directors and the CEO. Prepare a comparative list of best brands, with the best prices, value-added services, after-sales support, and maintenance costs. Which brands would you like to go for? Figure out the computer specifications with speed, memory, storage, network servers, Internet bandwidth, and backup devices requirements for the entire company. Present this requirement specification sheet to your CEO for his/her approval and sanctioning of budget for your department.

BIBLIOGRAPHY AND WEB RESOURCES

Joshi, Girdhar, *Information Technology for Retail*, Oxford University Press, New Delhi, 2009.

Kennedy, Ken, 'A nationwide parallel computing environment' *Communications of the ACM*, ACM, New York, November, 1997.

Laudon, Ken, Jane Laudon, and Rajnish Dass, *Management Information Systems*, Pearson Education, Singapore, 2010.

O'Brien, James A., George M. Marakas, and Ramesh Behl, *Management Information Systems*, Tata McGraw-Hill, New Delhi, 2006.

Patterson, David A., Garth Gibson, and Randy H. Katz, *A Case for Redundant Arrays of Inexpensive Disks (RAID)*, University of California, Berkley, 1988.

Selker, Ted, 'New paradigms for using computers', *Communications of the ACM*, ACM, New York, August 1996.

www.ibm.com, last accessed on 26 August 2011.

CASE STUDY

Great Eastern: How Software Induced Hardware Acquisitions

Great Eastern Impex Pvt. Ltd (GEIPL) was promoted by P.C. Jain, chairman of the company, way back in 1983 as a company providing retail support with its product marking, labelling, and barcoding items. GEIPL is the first company in India to introduce product identification through barcodes. The company is a leading systems integrator and solution provider of Auto-ID technologies (Barcode, RFID, EAS, and labelling solutions) to help organizations efficiently move goods and information across the supply chain and improve business productivity and profits. As of today, the company boasts of expertise of over 25 years in delivering value and innovation to multitude of customers in manufacturing, distribution, and retail businesses.

Some of the brands that the company is dealing with include Toshiba TEC, Japan; Unitech Electronics, Taiwan; PDC Inc., USA; Motorola Solutions Inc., USA; Avery Dennison Inc., USA; UPM Raflatac Inc., Finland, Alien Technologies Inc., USA, etc. These brands are some of the best in the world and offer time-tested solutions.

The Auto-ID technology was well appreciated and accepted in India. With the increase in demand, GEIPL expanded its operations in the country by creating regional offices. The company has nationwide service support capability with strategically located regional offices in the national capital region (NCR), Mumbai, Pune, Bangalore, Chennai, Hyderabad, Kolkata, and Ludhiana. These offices made their own sales and also catered to the large dealer-network. GEIPL manufactures gun labels and barcode labels on its own at a state-of-the-art manufacturing plant setup at Udyog Vihar in Gurgaon, adjacent to New Delhi. The plant is an ISO 9001:2008 certified facility. The company is one of the largest RFID, barcode labels, tickets, tags and printing ribbon manufacturer (converter).

Industry
MIS support through Auto-ID technology

Solution Area
Enterprise software application for manufacturing, procurement, order processing, and finance management

Problem
Managing countrywide operations and sales network without proper management information systems in place was found to be very difficult. However, Jain, though belonging to an older generation, was modern in his outlook and approach towards technology. In 1990, he got the MIS software created with the help of an in-house team of programmers on a DOS platform with FoxPro. This program mainly catered to sales billing and debtors' management, and could well suffice the needs of the company for a couple of years.

However, at the turn of the century, when the retail boom started taking place, the requirement increased heavily. The need for an integrated system was felt, which could provide proper management of sales accounting, order processing, debtors, creditors, inventory, servicing of equipment, production planning and control, wastage control, distribution management, etc. The emphasis was on order processing and recovery of accounts receivables. Timely recovery of dues was necessary to strengthen the revenue and funds flow of the company. Moreover, the system did not have any query builder, which could work on user definable parameters.

Solution Implementation
GEIPL started looking for an integrated enterprise application that could serve all its functions and cater to the needs of the next decade. A host of application packages from various vendors were evaluated. The international ERP packages were very costly to implement and required a lot of time and effort. Finally, the management of GEIPL shortlisted a New Delhi-based solution provider. The order was given to BrainSoft Solutions Pvt. Ltd for a custom-made ERP to suit GEIPL requirements.

It was a custom-built development and carried the full software development life cycle approach. The system study took three months and the review and approval of the same took more time. An ERP implementation task force that had five members from GEIPL was created. Jain, Rajiv Bawa, finance manager, Subir Kochhar, general manager, Bua Singh, sales manager, and Naveen Sharma, IT manager from GEIPL and technical head, and Deepak Negi, system analyst from BrainSoft were members of the task force. The BrainSoft team developed application packages using Visual Basic Version 6 with an Oracle 8i relational database management system (RDBMS).

Solutions were developed for eight key areas clubbed under eight major modules of ERP, namely, purchase and supply, sales and distribution, warehouse and inventory, finance and accounts, HR and payroll, production planning and control, service management, and fixed assets management. The core modules of purchase, sales, inventory and finance were implemented first and went live in one year. Three months' data was repunched in the new system to check the accuracy and robustness of the system. Later, production planning, service management, and human resource applications were implemented. Rest of the branch implementation was taken up only in the third year of implementation.

Benefits

By implementing ERP, GEIPL achieved major benefits in two difficult areas. The first was order processing. Now, customer orders could be easily tracked and scheduled for production or dispatch. The query generator provides a list of pending orders based on multiple parameters, which was earlier difficult to do. The second area was collection of outstanding dues from debtors. Now, the ERP provided periodic report on outstanding and ageing of bills. Moreover, checks have been put on the creation of invoices if the total outstanding dues are more than the permitted credit limits to dealers and customers.

Issue

Before the implementation of ERP, the company had around 10 PCs, out of which one was being used for the current billing application, another for account software, and the rest were being used for word processing and spreadsheet activities. Based on the requirement calculated by the IT manager along with the system analyst, the company procured one IBM XEON server, and upgraded the present systems with high memory and storage capacity. Within a period of 24 months, that is, at the end of completion of implementation, the company had around 55 PCs. When branch implementation was completed in the following year, they procured another 20 personal computers.

Discussion Questions

1. Put yourself in the shoes of the IT manager and estimate the entire requirement of hardware, operating systems, networking devices, peripherals, etc., for GEIPL.
2. How can ERP implementation increase the purchase of sophisticated hardware?
3. Do you think the company's decision to build their own customized application was right? Why or why not?
4. 'Software requirements always push hardware development and inventions.' Do you agree? Support your answer with examples.

Source:

www.geipl.com, last accessed on 17 February 2013. Interactions with the management and staff of GEIPL, and personal observations during software implementation. The contribution of Shakti Jain, managing director, is highly appreciated.

5

Software Resources

A radical shift is occurring in corporate computing – think of it as the recentralization of management. It's a step back towards the 1970s, when a data-processing manager could sit at the console and track all the technology assets of the corporation. Then came the 1980s and early 1990s. Departments got their own PCs and software; client/server networks sprang up all across companies. ...Three things have happened in the past few years: the Internet boom inspired businesses to connect all those networks; companies put on their intranets essential applications without which their businesses could not function; and it become apparent that maintaining PCs on a network is very, very expensive. Such changes create an urgent need for centralization.

—**David Kirkpatrick**

LEARNING OBJECTIVES

After studying this chapter, you will be able to

- define and understand the various trends in software
- classify the different types of software and appreciate their capabilities
- identify various application and system software
- differentiate among programming languages and appreciate the various programming tools
- describe common business applications and office productivity software
- define groupware and understand its emergence as a collaborative tool

EXHIBIT 5.1

Linux: Open-source Operating System Makes Inroads Globally

Believe it or not, the gigantic, ever-growing cluster of servers that power Google's search and other applications, runs Linux. Of course, in typical fashion, Google was not content to simply run an out-of-the-box version on its own hardware. Instead, the search giant had its engineers devise a customized version of Ubuntu, referred to within the company as 'Goobuntu'. Cisco Systems, the computer networking and routing giant, switched to Linux after vowing to use Microsoft's Active Directory solution for its servers.

Electronics giant, Panasonic, is another household name that uses Linux in powering some of its operations. Panasonic used Linux only after Windows NT proved inadequate for what the company needed—voicemail systems, in this case. In addition to performing development work on Linux itself, IBM is known to use it internally on desktops and servers. IBM also ran a TV advertising campaign in 2006 called 'IBM supports Linux 100 per cent'. Online book and electronics retail behemoth, Amazon.com, is said to 'use Linux in nearly every corner of its business', according to ZD Net. After Amazon 'began to use Linux in 2000 for basic tasks', Linux began spreading through the company, notably the company's database system.

In 2007, European car maker, Peugeot, announced that it was set to deploy upto 20,000 copies of Novell Desktop Linux and 2500 copies of SuSe Linux Enterprise Server. LinuxJournal.com wrote that Tommy Hilfiger Corporation chose eOneGroup and Linux for its new e-business infrastructure way back in 2001. Company representatives were quoted as saying that 'we saved significantly on the time and expense of deploying this total infrastructure', as opposed to if another operating system provider had been chosen. Travelocity is yet another Internet business powered by Linux servers. According to Network World,

Travelocity management cited their desire 'to improve our flexibility and really decrease our time to market' as the chief reasons for choosing Linux over other alternatives.

When Mumbai-based Unit Trust of India (UTI) wanted to set up a call centre, the bank settled on Linux for its servers, even as it continues to use Windows on its personal computers (PCs). 'The openness of the system appealed to us,' says UTI President V.K. Ramani. The shift in government's policy in favour of open-source software has spurred more businesses to use Linux. One convert is state-owned Life Insurance Corporation (LIC) of India, which switched its servers to Linux in 2005. With the $2 million in savings from using the free software, LIC began adding more computers. It had 70,000 PCs, all running Linux, and by 2006, it was expected to have more than 1,00,000 PCs. Others are taking a more measured approach. The Cotton Hill Girls High School in Thiruvananthapuram did not appear to be at the vanguard of anything related to information technology. Yet, the 71-year-old school embraced Linux. The school is one of the 2600 schools in Kerala that are making the shift. Over the next two years, computer science based on Linux software will be made mandatory in all of the state's high schools.

Sources:

Bort, Julie, 'Travelocity's flight to open system', 10 November 2003, http://www.networkworld.com/ee2/2003/1110qa.html, last accessed on 11 September 2011.

'Linux spreads its wings in India', http://www.businessweek.com/stories/2006-10-01/linux-spreads-its-wings-in-india, last accessed on 11 September 2011.

'50 places Linux running you might not expect', http://www.focus.com/fyi/50-paces-linux-running-you-might-not-expect, last accessed on 11 September 2011

The Unit Trust of India, Life Insurance Corporation of India, Tommy Hilfiger Corporation, and others choose to run their systems on Linux (Exhibit 5.1). Among thousand others, Linux is a piece of software that makes a computer work as it is desired to work. In this chapter, we will discuss software resources, which are the second components of information technology infrastructure discussed in Chapter 4.

The visible and tangible part of a computer system is the hardware, and the intangible part that works silently in the form of instructions to perform a certain task or control a certain part of the hardware is known as software. Software is an important part of any computer system. We can compare software with the blood and life of a person.

SOFTWARE

Software is a general term used for various programs used to perform a given task or operate, control, and manage computers and related devices. In other words, software is a set of instructions to the computer to perform a certain task; it resides in the computer in the coded form as binary digits of 0 and 1. Windows, Word, Excel, SAP, Tally, QuickBooks, Unix, Linux, Visual Basic, .NET, Oracle database, Forms, etc., are all examples of software. Software can also be defined as a set of instructions given to a computer, in the form of functions, to receive inputs and manipulate them to produce the desired output. Help files, user manuals, etc., meant for users to understand the software system, are a part of the software.

TYPES OF SOFTWARE

Software programs perform two types of functions in a computer system: one, managing the computer's hardware and filing system, and controlling the attached peripheral devices; and the other, performing business application functions, which users use to do their day-to-day work. On the basis of the functions provided by the software, it can be broadly classified into two categories:

- System software
- Application software

According to Goyal (2006), 'System software consists of sets of programs to support the efficient use of hardware resources that include primary and secondary memory, display devices, printers, communication links, and other peripherals. It also interprets and executes application software.' Operating systems and utility programs are examples of system software.

Application software refers to programs that actually process data to generate information. All business applications such as accounting and inventory management programs come under this category.

Systems software and application software are interrelated and interact closely with each other. As depicted in Fig. 5.1, systems software (e.g., operating system) serves as an intermediary between hardware and application software.

Figure 5.2 gives a comprehensive overview of the major categories of software systems. Suitable examples have been given for each type of software.

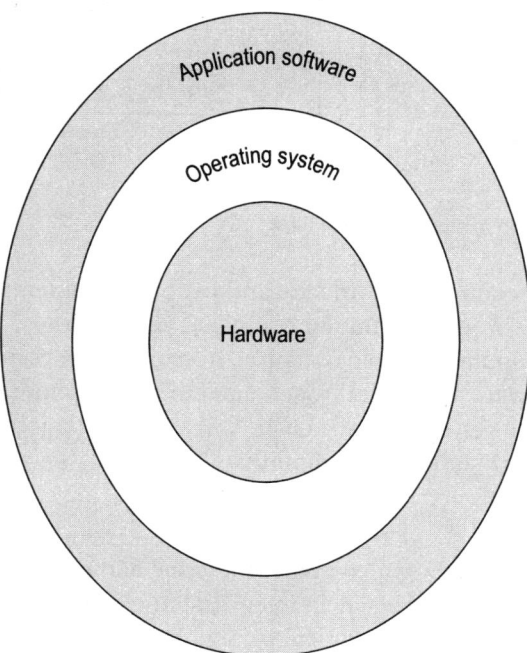

Fig. 5.1   Hardware and various software layers in a computer system

System Software

System software manages computer resources, file systems, other hardware peripherals, and communication

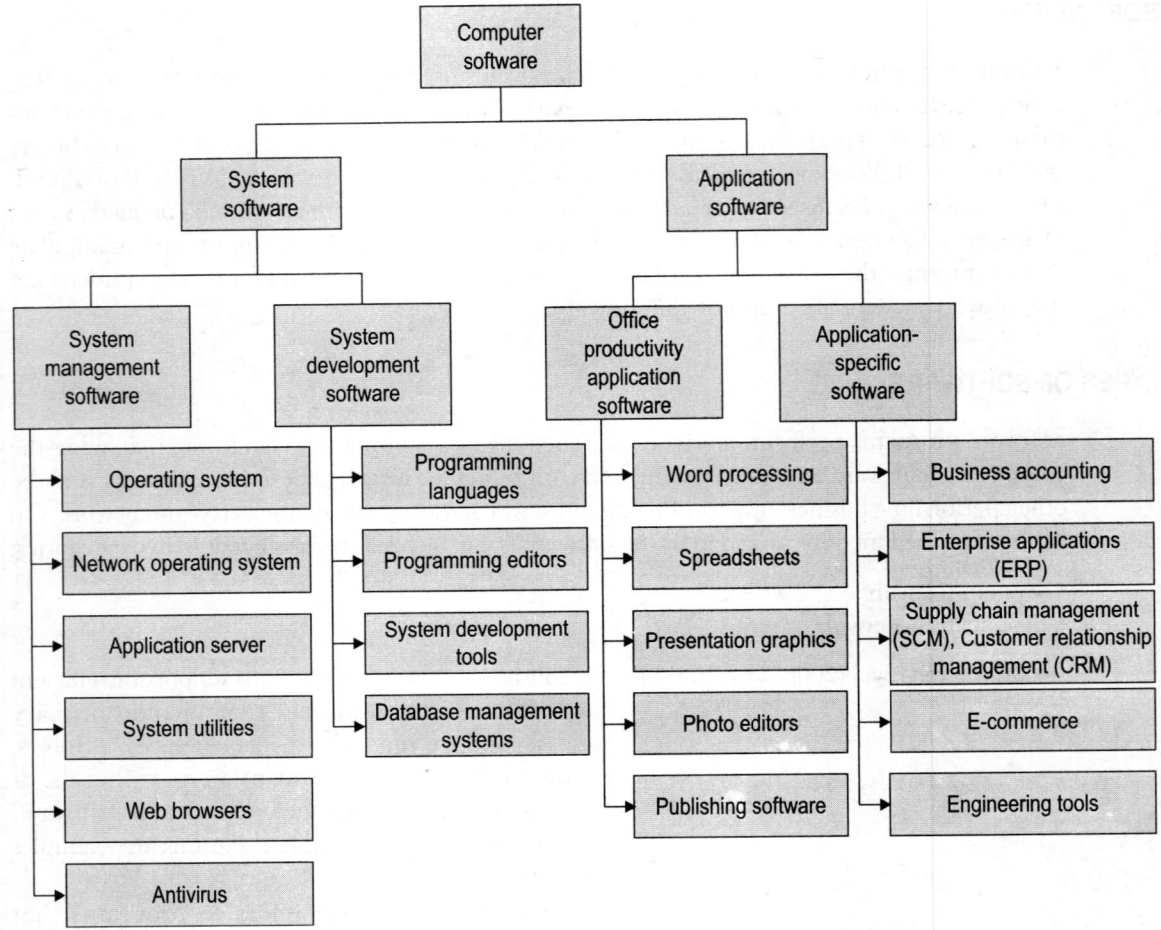

Fig. 5.2   Classification of software with examples of each type

links. The software programs that manage and control the hardware and various file systems are called system software. Operating systems, browsers, utilities, compilers, device drivers, etc., are examples of system software. As the computer technology evolved from mainframes to mini, and mini to microcomputers, systems software also went through major metamorphosis. Initially, the mainframe did not have an operating system at all. Later, Unix was introduced and become a very popular operating system for mainframes and minis.

Operating Systems

The basic function of operating systems (OS) is to manage a computer's internal and external resources such as memory, files, and peripheral devices. They help in creating directories and folders, and copying, deleting, and moving files from one physical storage unit to another. Operating systems offer various utilities to configure the computer according to environmental settings such as date formats, numbering system, and memory management. They also help in adding new programs to and removing unwanted programs from a computer. The various devices attached with a computer are linked through drivers in association with the computer's operating system. DOS, Windows, Linux, Unix, Novell, and Mac are the most popular operating systems in the world.

MS-DOS With the invention of microcomputers, the disk operating system (DOS) was introduced. IBM developed the first DOS for its PCs. It was known as PC DOS (IBM outsourced the development of PC DOS to Bill Gates and his friend, Paul Allen). Later, Microsoft launched MS-DOS for microcomputers. MS-DOS was a 16-bit operating system (i.e., it could address data in chunks of 16 bits at a time) and supported IBM PC standards. It could handle a maximum application size of 640 kB in its memory and could run only one program at a time (as opposed to multitasking in Windows).

MS-Windows Windows is an operating system that overcomes the constraints of DOS. Microsoft launched its second generation of Windows OS in 1995 as Windows 95, which was completely based on a graphic user interface (GUI), with true multitasking, networking, multimedia, and many other capabilities. Multitasking refers to the ability to perform multiple tasks simultaneously. MS-Windows is a 32-bit operating system with more capabilities such as fax, email, scheduling, and Internet browsing. Windows can run programs written for DOS as well as those that utilize more than 640 kB of memory through its extended memory management concept. The Windows family of operating systems became popular for modern PCs.

Later, microsoft launched Windows 98, Windows 2000, Windows ME (Millennium Edition), Windows XP (eXPerience), Windows Vista, and Windows 7 (launched in 2009). Each of the subsequent versions of Windows had some modifications, improvements, and enhancements from the earlier versions. For instance, Windows 7 combines the ease of XP and security of Vista.

Mac OS X Apple Macintosh, which was launched in 1976, had a GUI-based operating system. Mac OS can only run on Mac machines and is immensely popular with the Mac users. Mac OS X is the latest operating system from Apple for iMac. Macintosh systems are mainly used for publishing work.

Linux Microsoft had monopoly over the PC operating systems market, until Linux was launched at the turn of the century. The Linux kernel was developed by Linus Torvalds in 1991. The kernel is the core of the software, around which developers can build tools and utilities. Linux supports open-source technology and is a freeware. This means that nobody owns rights over it legally. The open-source concept propagates non-proprietary rights on the product and allows developments, additions, and improvements in the software by any user, mentor, or developer of the system. It can be redistributed along with the improved source code. The source code of Linux is available and one can create additional tools around the Linux OS. Linux can run on major processors developed by corporations such as Intel, Motorola, SPARK, and Alpha. Linux being a freeware, any development can be around its basic kernel and the developer cannot charge for the kernel, though they may sell the upgraded function they have developed around the kernel.

The use and development of Linux is supported by Sun Microsystems and IBM, in particular, and Oracle, HP, and others in general. It aimed to champion the cause of open-source technology and counter the monopoly of Microsoft's Windows in the market. Initially, it faced some hitches;

however, now, Linux is gaining acceptance and is quite popular for web-based applications. It is a popular operating system for web servers.

Network Operating Systems

Network operating systems (NOS) are operating systems that manage communication between two or more computers in a network. Along with Windows 95, Microsoft introduced Windows-NT as the operating system for the networks. Windows NT gave the flexibility and ease of a GUI (mouse compatibility) and secured local networks. In the subsequent versions, the network capabilities were merged with Windows 2000, Windows 2003, and Windows 2008 operating systems. For instance, Windows 2000 integrated the capability of Windows NT for secured networking. It can work on PCs, laptops, and servers.

Novell   Just as Microsoft had monopoly over DOS for PCs, Novell Corp had monopoly over NOS. Novell Netware is a very popular, strong, sturdy, and secure NOS. Novell Netware offers the capability to network diskless nodes with dedicated Novell servers.

UNIX   UNIX and XENIX are operating systems that support single machines and multiple servers under networks. Primarily, they are suitable for mainframes and minicomputers. UNIX was developed by Bell Laboratories in 1969, primarily to make it run over networks and offers functionalities such as multitasking, and interactive and multi-user options. UNIX is still regarded as a very secure and robust operating system that runs on large networks and high-end servers. UNIX is being offered as Solaris by Sun Microsystems and AIX by IBM.

Web Browsers

Any word wide web page opens only on a web browser. Thus, web browsers work as an operating system for web pages. Today, web browsers are the most important tools for users visiting a website. Microsoft Internet Explorer, Mozilla Firefox, and Google Chrome are the most powerful and feature-rich browsers.

Other System Management Software

There are many programs that are used to manage, control, and analyse a computer system. These are either available as a distinct software or are included as a part of operating systems. These programs are called utilities. While application software help manage business processes, write text or letters, listen to music, etc., the utilities focus more on the computer infrastructure. Some examples of computer software utilities are file compression software (WinZip or WinRAR), disk compression and fragmentation utilities, windows registry cleaners (CC Cleaner), backup utilities, disk restore utilities, cryptographic utilities to encrypt and decrypt data, etc. Antivirus vaccines or virus cleaners (Norton, AVG, etc.) are the most popular utilities used to clean systems from viruses.

Another set of system software is 'middleware', which provides an interface between an operating system and the application programs. According to O'Brien (2006), 'Middleware is software that helps diverse software applications and networked computer systems exchange data and work together more efficiently. For example, application servers such as BEA's WebLogic and IBM's WebSphere help web based e-business and e-commerce applications run much faster and more efficiently on computers using Windows, Unix, and other operating systems.'

Table 5.1 Comparison of system software offered by various companies

Software category	What it does	Offered by	Product name
Operating system	Manages PC, networks	Microsoft	Windows
		Red Hat and others	Linux
Network management	Network operating system	Sun Microsystems	Solaris
		IBM	AIX
RDBMS	Manages data and data warehouses	IBM	DB2
		Oracle Corp	Oracle 9i
		Microsoft	SQL Server
Application server	Manages data between business applications and the web	IBM	WebSphere
		BEA	WebLogic
Network management	Monitors networks to keep them up and running	HP	OpenView
		IBM	Tivoli
Groupware	Manages everything from email to e-calendars	IBM	Lotus Notes
		Microsoft	Microsoft Exchange
Development tools	Develops software for business and web	IBM	Java
		Microsoft	VB.Net
Antivirus	Protects systems from virus attacks	Symantec	Norton
	Scans for and gives notifications about viruses in the system	Quick Heal Tech	Quick Heal

Table 5.1 compares several types of system software offered by various companies and the tasks they are used for.

Programming Languages and Tools

Computer software is written using programming languages and tools. These programming languages have some methodology that is followed by programmers when they write the code. For example, programming in machine language, which uses binary codes of 0 and 1, follows a method specific to that programming language. All operating systems and utilities are written using a programming language. Some texts may classify programming languages under application software. However, as we appreciate that these are tools for system development and management, we will categorize and discuss them under the 'system software' section.

For mainframes and minicomputers, which are first and second generation computers respectively, programming was done either using machine language or assembly language. These languages were used by scientists and engineers for developing scientific applications. They were both the creators and users of the programs at the same time. The programs were mainly meant for numerical calculations using scientific formulae, arithmetical rules, and logic. It was a very time-consuming and cumbersome job to write programs using these low-level languages. Eventually, the languages evolved to high-level languages, popularly known as third generation (3GL) and fourth generation languages (4GL). Table 5.2 gives examples of these languages.

Machine language Machine language is the first generation computer programming language, which was used in the early stages of computer evolution. It was machine-specific and machine-dependent. In this language, the programming was done using binary digits, 0 and 1, in various combinations. This is the lowest level of any programming language. The programming used to address the location code of data, instructions, and every switch and indicator used by the program. This made programming very tedious and error-prone.

Table 5.2   Four generations of programming languages with examples

Programming language	What it uses	Example
Machine language	Binary coded instructions	1010 11001 1011 11010 1100 11011
Assembly language	Symbolic coded instructions	LOD B ADD C STR A
High-level languages	Brief statements or commands such as INPUT, GET, and PRINT	A = B + C 10 INPUT B, 20 INPUT C, 30 PRINT A
Fourth generation languages	Natural and non-procedural statements	SUM NUMBERS (B, C)

Assembly language   Assembly or assembler languages are the second generation languages used for computer programming. These languages were developed to reduce the difficulties in the machine language. Instead of directly using binary digits, abbreviated forms of instructions were used. In assembly language, an assembler or a language translator was used, which converted the instructions into machine language. For example ADD (for addition) and SUB (for subtraction) were used as program instructions, which were translated by the assembler into 0s and 1s. The assembler was written in machine language and translated the assembly instructions into machine-readable coded instructions.

Assembly languages were also machine-oriented and machine-dependent. Therefore, a program written for one machine was not reusable for another machine. Some programming is still done in assembly language, especially for system programming, where the instructions are required to be machine-specific. Assembly codes are also faster and more efficient in execution.

High-level languages   At the later stages of development of computer systems, the focus shifted from machine-specific to user-oriented languages. More simplified languages called high-level languages, evolved. The high-level languages are also called third generation languages. In these languages, one can write software for both micro and mainframe computers. C, Common business oriented language (COBOL), Formula Translation (Fortran), Beginner's all-purpose symbolic instruction code (BASIC), and Pascal are the main third generation languages that became popular in system programming, database development, and application programming. System programming is the development of tools, compilers, utilities, and operating systems. Database programming is the development of database management systems such as dBase, FoxPro, Access, and Oracle. Application programming is the development of systems to perform a certain task and capture, manipulate, and retrieve data from databases.

High-level languages use 'statements' or 'commands', which are microinstructions and are translated into machine language by high-level translator programs called compilers or interpreters. These programming languages are much easier than assembly languages. Compilers convert the normal English-like phrases into binary language that the machines understand. Various software packages, such as word processors, spreadsheets, and other business applications, are developed using these languages. High-level languages are not machine-dependent, that is, a program is not rewritten to be installed on a new computer system. Though a high-level language requires more computer time to translate the instructions into machine language, the advantages outweigh this single disadvantage. The following are some of the most popular high-level languages:

C   It is a structured language, which was developed as part of the Unix operating system. C combines some features of assembly language with machine portability. An advanced form of C, called C++, is more popular as a programming language for object-oriented software development.

COBOL   It is an English-like language developed for business data processing.

Fortran   It was developed for solving mathematical and scientific problems.

BASIC   It is a very simple language that was developed and widely used for interactive programming for PCs.

Pascal   Named after Blaise Pascal, this structured language was used for both scientific and business applications.

LISP   Acronym for 'list processor', LISP is a language especially popular for artificial intelligence applications. LISP was developed in the early 1960s by John McCarthy at Massachusetts Institute of Technology (MIT).

Ada   Developed in the late 1970s and early 1980s for the US defence department, Ada was designed to be a general-purpose language for everything from business applications to rocket guidance systems.

Prolog   Short for 'programming logic', Prolog is a language based on formal logic. Unlike traditional programming languages that are based on performing sequences of commands, Prolog is based on defining and then solving logical formulae.

Fourth generation languages   The third generation languages needed deep procedural details and step-by-step instructions to carry out a task. The job of the programmer was not only to tell the computer what to do, but also to instruct it on how to do the same. Besides, these languages were not capable of handling GUI and multimedia convergence. Therefore, computer technologists worldwide developed more languages to overcome these drawbacks. These languages were called fourth generation languages (4GLs). Visual C++, Visual Basic, Oracle Developer Tools, SQL, PowerBuilder, FrontPage, Java, J2EE, CGI-Perl, PHP, .NET, etc., are some examples of 4GLs.

The 4GLs are non-procedural and more like natural English. These languages require the programmer or user to specify the result they want, and the computer determines the sequence of instructions needed. Natural language refers to a language that we speak. In the command line, the programmer tells the computer what to do. The 'how to do it' part is taken care of by the machine when the programming codes are compiled and assembled by the specialized tools provided in the language kit.

Figures 5.3 and 5.4 illustrate the simplicity with which programs are written in 4GLs and object-oriented programming (OOP) languages.

The 4GLs became popular due to their ease in writing programs. The lines of codes (LoC) that are needed to be written to create a function in different languages reduced sharply as the languages evolved. Table 5.3 shows an example of how the LoC drops sharply per function-point. Function-point is a measure of the complexity of the software.

```
'-------------------------------------------------------------
' Procedure : LastDay
' DateTime  : 19-Oct-2006
' Developer : Sunil Mohanty
' Purpose   : Return Last Date of Month and Year
' Modify History :
' Date        Dr/Cr        Developer  Details
'-------------------------------------------------------------

Public Function fniLastDay(p_intMonth As Integer, p_intYear As Integer) As Integer
On Error GoTo ErrorHandler

    Select Case p_intMonth
       Case 1, 3, 5, 7, 8, 10, 12
          LastDay = 31
       Case 2
          If p_intYear Mod 4 = 0 Then
             LastDay = 29
          Else
             LastDay = 28
          End If
       Case 4, 6, 9, 11
          LastDay = 30
End Select
Exit Function
ErrorHandler:
   Err.Raise Err.Number, Err.Source, Err.Description
End Function
```

Fig. 5.3 Sample of Visual Basic program for printing the last day, month, and year of any English calendar

```
SELECT item_name FROM itemtable WHERE item_name LIKE 'shirt%';

SELECT customer_name FROM transactiontable WHERE amount = 10000
AND vatamount=500;
```

Fig. 5.4 Simple query written in an SQL to locate an item from a database

Object-oriented Programming Languages

Some 4GLs such as Visual Basic, VC++, and Java offer software development in a highly advanced form of programming called object-oriented programming. In this programming method, the data and procedures are tied together into objects. Thus, an object consists of a data element and an action that works on that data. For example, an object-oriented program to calculate the interest on an outstanding debt of a firm will tie together the data (outstanding debt) and the operation (calculate interest) in the program itself. Object-oriented programming languages are different from other languages as they combine data and procedures into objects, whereas the other programming languages separate data from the procedures.

Table 5.3   Programming languages complexity table

Programming languages in descending order of complexities			
Language	**Intended use**	**Complexity**	**Function-points**
Assembly	General	Highly specific, related to the target processor	320
C	System	Procedural	128
Fortran	Application	Generic, imperative, object-oriented	105
C++	Application, system	Generic, imperative, object-oriented	56
Java	Application, web	Generic, imperative, object-oriented, concurrent	55
Visual Basic	Application	Component-oriented, event-driven	35
Other 4GLs—Perl, Smaltalk, and Python	Application, web, scripting	Functional, generic, object-oriented, reflective	20

Object-oriented languages are easier to use and very efficient in GUI programming. Another benefit is the reusability of objects. Hence, they are the most widely-used programming languages today.

Web Development Languages and Services

Hypertext mark-up language (HTML) and extensible mark-up language (XML) are programming systems used for development of websites requiring multimedia pages. HTML inserts control codes within a document at specific points that create links (hyperlinks) to other parts of that document or any other document on the web.

Many modern software systems such as word processors, spreadsheets, and, databases facilitate automatic conversion of documents into HTML format. Specialized tools such as Microsoft FrontPage and Lotus FastSite offer designing of web pages in HTML without formally using HTML language (see Fig. 5.5).

Extensible mark-up language (XML) is not a web designing language as such, but it is a set of rules for encoding a document in machine readable form. XML describes the contents of web pages by applying 'tags' to data. Thus, XML is a service that makes website information more searchable, sortable, and easier to analyse. For example, if the website of your college has XML tags hidden with words such as 'college', 'MBA', 'education', it will make the search faster.

Java, .NET, PHP, etc., are various programming languages that are used for websites, Internet, and intranet development. Java, an object-oriented programming language created by Sun Microsystems, is revolutionizing the development of e-commerce applications. Java applications consist of small application programs called applets. Applications developed in Java can be executed by any hardware, operating systems, and network in the world. This kind of flexibility and mobility, coupled with secure and robust applications makes Java very popular. The latest version of Java is called J2EE (Java2 Enterprise Edition).

ASP.NET or Active Server Pages is a web development tool used for creating large e-commerce sites, corporate intranets, and browser-based business applications from the Microsoft stable. .NET offers a strong framework for building rich GUI and is easy to use for programmers. ASP was built for web applications. ASP.NET and J2EE are seen at par when it comes to program development.

Hypertext preprocessor (PHP) is a general-purpose, server-side scripting language, originally designed for web development to produce dynamic web pages. PHP code is embedded into the HTML source document and interpreted by a web server with a PHP processor module,

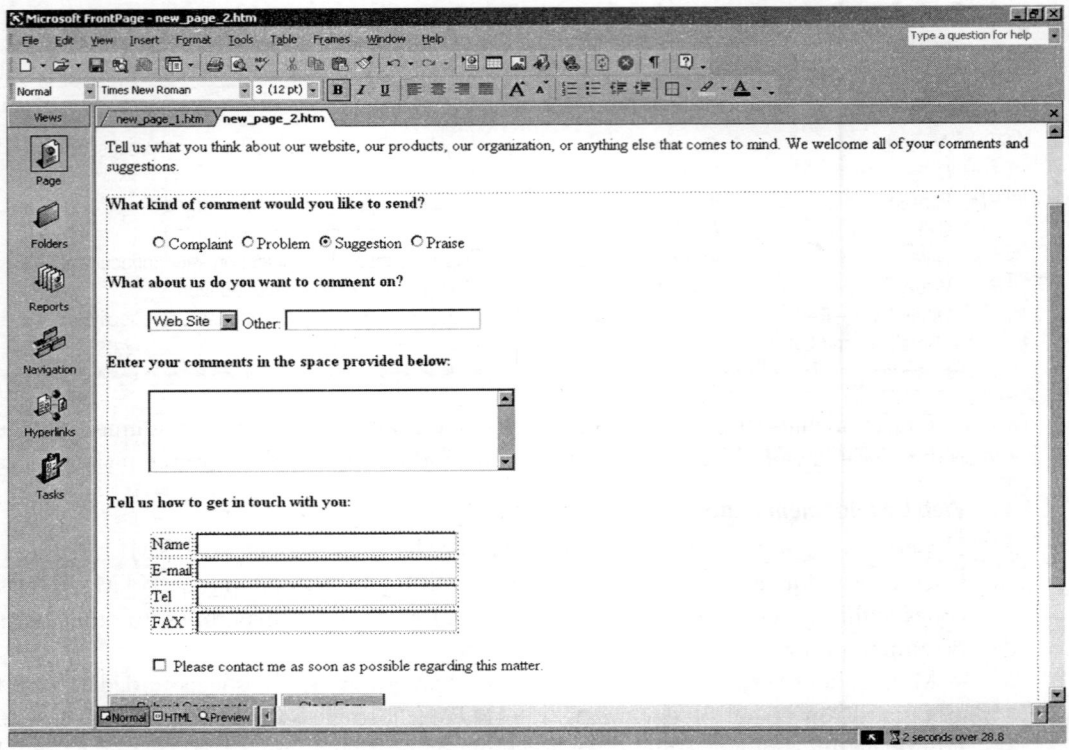

Fig. 5.5 Microsoft FrontPage tool available with Microsoft Office provides a step-by-step approach to web page designing

which generates the web page document. It is especially suited to server-side web development where PHP is an open-source product and generally runs on a web server. See Table 5.4 for a comparative study of these three languages

Application Software

Application software is a program created to perform certain tasks for the end-users. These tasks can be, for example, maintaining a fee register in a school, keeping transaction records of an account holder in a bank, creating bills at the point-of-sale location, managing inventory at the warehouse, playing music or a movie file, a database system allowing users to construct a database structure, etc.

Various software packages such as Tally, RetailPRO, SAP, Oracle Applications, MS-Office, OpenOffice, LotusNotes, QuickBooks, Microsoft Outlook, and Finacle are examples of application software. All these applications are off-the-shelf (OTS) software. These software applications are developed by a programmer for the purpose of mass-selling them as a generic product to some end-users. This is in contrast with the concept of developing tailor-made or customized software as per the specifications of some user organization. Usually, the customized software is owned by the organization that gets it developed. On the other hand, the OTS software are sold, leased, or licensed to the end-user, but the intellectual property rights (IPR) of the product remain with the vendor who develops the product.

Table 5.4 Comparison of J2EE, ASP.NET, and PHP programming tools

J2EE features	ASP.NET features	PHP features
• A standard that is built by Sun Microsystems and others • An evolution of Java application development technology • Has a complex application development environment • Runs on any operating system and application server with minor adjustments • Handles complex, high-volume, high-transaction applications • Tools can be difficult to use • Favoured by large international vendors • May cost more to build, deploy, and manage applications • Can be integrated with a range of tools and application servers • Being complex, it is difficult to develop GUI quickly • Appreciated as a robust and fail-safe application development tool • Lacks built-in support for web services and standards • Has a proven track record • Difficult to use for quick-turnaround, low-cost, and mass-market projects	• A product suite developed by Microsoft Corporation • An evolution of Windows DNA–Active server pages development technology • Easy-to-use tools for programmers • Framework needs more adjustment for running on browsers other than Explorer • Has a strong framework for building rich GUI • Major deviation from earlier Microsoft tools, so steep learning process • Flexibility of development in many international languages • New runtime infrastructure lacks maturity • Provides flexibility and offers templates for quick development • Tightly integrated with Microsoft OS and enterprise software • May not be as robust in scalability and transaction processing capability • May cost less, unified management, less expensive tools • Choice of integrated development environment limited • Has built-in support for web service standards	• PHP (Hypertext Preprocessor, originally Personal Home Page) is an open source web scripting language • Extremely easy-to-use tools for web development • Better suited for web pages development • Easy to learn and recommended for beginners in programming • Offers advanced features for professional programmers • Applications run on many web browsers and support many web servers • Not so robust in scalability and transaction processing capability • Application development may cost less, as PHP programmers are easily available • Not suitable for writing large client–server applications • Influenced by Pearl, C, and Java • Most used server site programming script

Business Application Software

There are hundreds of business application software available for various businesses. The business application software support transaction processing, reengineering, and automation of critical processes and provide data for management decision support. Besides enterprise solutions such as customer relationship management (CRM), supply chain management (SCM), and enterprise resource planning (ERP), there are various e-business application packages for business functions such as accounting, human resource, procurement, sales order processing, and manufacturing. Other packages are available for decision support functions, online analytical processing (OLAP), data mining, or knowledge management systems. Figure 5.6 depicts a dashboard application.

Business applications will be discussed in detail in Chapters 8, 9, and 10. Table 5.5 compares several types of application software offered by various companies and the tasks they are used for.

Office Productivity Software

Office productivity software are general-purpose applications that are used in offices for writing documents, letters, emails, tabulation work, designing presentations, scheduling meetings, etc.

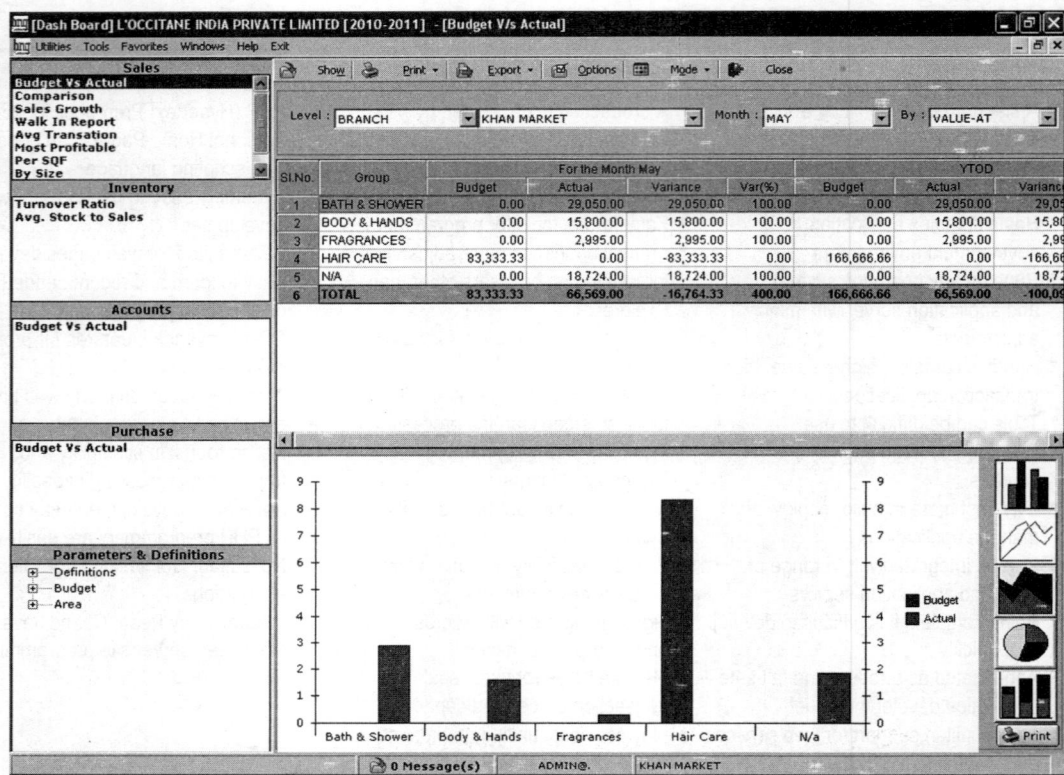

Fig. 5.6   Business application software showing data with graphical presentation [Loccitane India and BNG Infotech, BNG Business Suite, www.bng.co.in]

Table 5.5   Comparison of business application software offered by various companies

Software category	Offered by	Product name	What it does
Accounting	Tally Solutions	Tally ERP 9	Manages financial accounting, inventory, and sales reporting
	Busy Solutions	Busy	Manages financial accounting, inventory, and sales reporting
	R.K. Softwares	Miracle	Manages financial accounting and inventory
	Sapphire Systems	Infor FMS	Manages financial accounting, inventory, and sales reporting
Manufacturing	SAP India	SAP B-One	Production planning, scheduling, shop floor
	Mawai Infotech	Mawai TERM 8.1	Manufacturing systems
	Netsoft	Impact	Manufacturing and trading accounting systems
	BNG Infotech	Business Suite	Order processing, purchase, sales, production planning and scheduling, shop-floor
Retail	Ginny Systems	Ginsys	Point-of-sales (POS) management for multi-format retail
	BNG Infotech	BNGpro	POS management, specializes in garments
	Polaris	Retail Excel	Retail management, POS solutions for super stores
	Shawman software	ShawMan	Specializes in hospitality retail segment
Human resource	HRMantra Software	HRMantra	Provides mobile-based payroll accounting systems
	Adrenalin eSystems	Adrenalin	Human resource management system (HRMS) and payroll accounting

Table 5.6 Components of four major program suites available globally

Software category	Microsoft Office	Lotus SmartSuite	Corel WordPerfect	OpenOffice	Softek (India)
Word processor	Word	WordPro	WordPerfect	StarWriter	AKSHAR (Hindi), SoftWORD
Spreadsheet	Excel	1–2–3	Quattro Pro	StarCalc	SoftCalc
Presentation graphics	PowerPoint	Freelance	Presentations	StarImpress	–
Database manager	Access	Approach	Paradox	StarBase	DevBase, SoftBase
Personal scheduler	Outlook	Organizer	Corel Central	StarSchedule	–

Most general-purpose office productivity suites of software come bundled from various vendors. Microsoft Office, Lotus SmartSuite, Corel WordPerfect Office, and Sun OpenOffice are examples of such bundled suites. Table 5.6 illustrates software suites from major international vendors.

The introduction of PCs in the mid-1980s replaced the ubiquitous typewriter in offices. Even today, most PCs are being used for document writing, editing, and storage. Word processing software changed the face of letters. Most word processing packages possess desktop publishing capabilities. They offer functionalities such as spelling check, autocorrection, dictionaries, thesaurus, translation, and mail merge.

Electronic spreadsheet software such as MS Excel, Lotus 1-2-3, and Quattro Pro offer very strong functionalities in tabulation, calculation, analysis, and modelling. Developing a worksheet involves designing its format by entering data in cells, that is, cross junction of rows and columns and defining relationships of various cells. The relationship is defined by entering formulae. Electronic spreadsheets prove to be excellent MIS tools if you use macros in the worksheet. You can use spreadsheets for advance analysis such as what-if analysis, break-even analysis, scenario analysis, and loan modelling. Electronic spreadsheet is known to be the most widely used MIS tool in the world. Most packages offer graphical display of data as seen in Fig. 5.7.

PowerPoint is the most widely used graphic presentation software available in MS-Office. Presentation software help convert numeric data into graphics display such as line graphs, bar graphs, and pie charts. Most of these packages facilitate multimedia presentations of graphics, photo, animation, audio, and video clubbed into the presentation, and thus, enrich the total experience of presenting your viewpoint. They offer easy-to-use capabilities and templates for slide shows, which are mostly used for corporate presentations and training. Figure 5.8 illustrates how presentation can give a 3D view of the data.

Along with word processor, email management software is a must-have for individuals as well as organizations. Millions of people now depend on email software to communicate with each other by sending and receiving email messages with all types of attachments through the Internet. Email providers such as Hotmail, Yahoo!, Gmail, WebMail, and Rediffmail not only provide free email services, but also offer inbuilt email managers. Besides offering mail management functions, desktop email software also provide personal organizers and schedulers. Personal information managers such as Lotus Organizer and Microsoft Outlook help users store, organize, and retrieve information about customers, prospects, and peer groups. They also facilitate scheduling and managing appointments, meetings, and tasks. Microsoft Outlook is the most commonly used email manager and task scheduler (see Fig. 5.9).

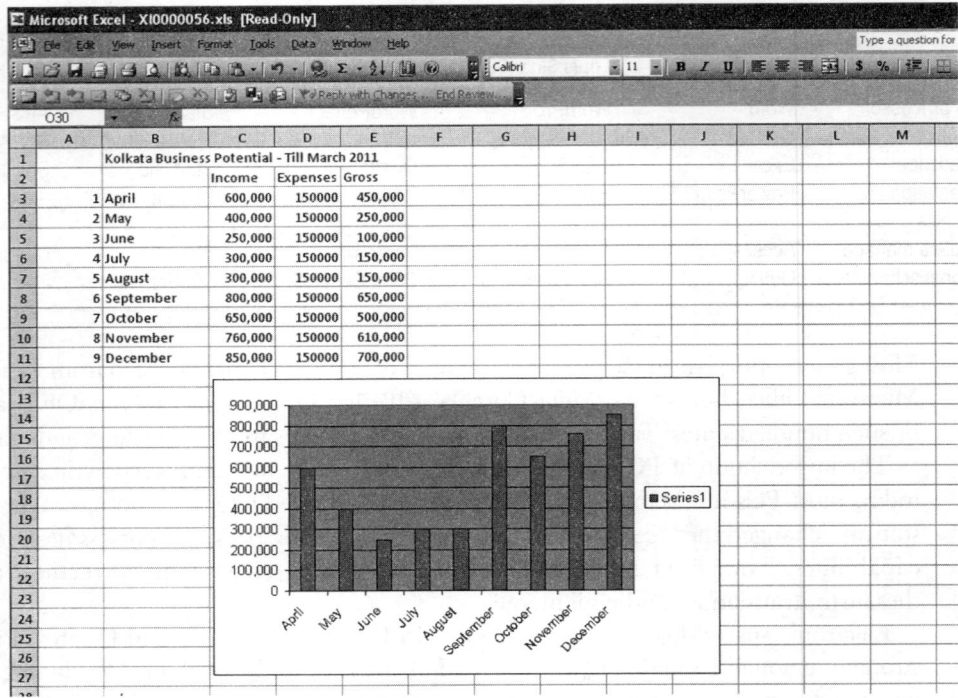

Fig. 5.7   Electronic spreadsheet

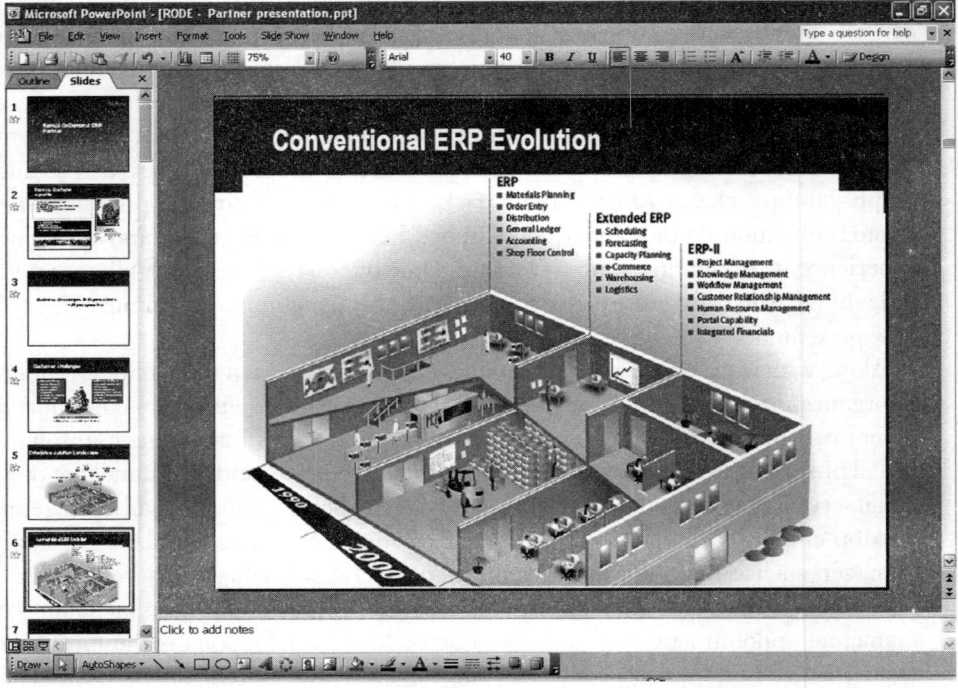

Fig. 5.8   Microsoft PowerPoint [Ramco presentation (2010)]

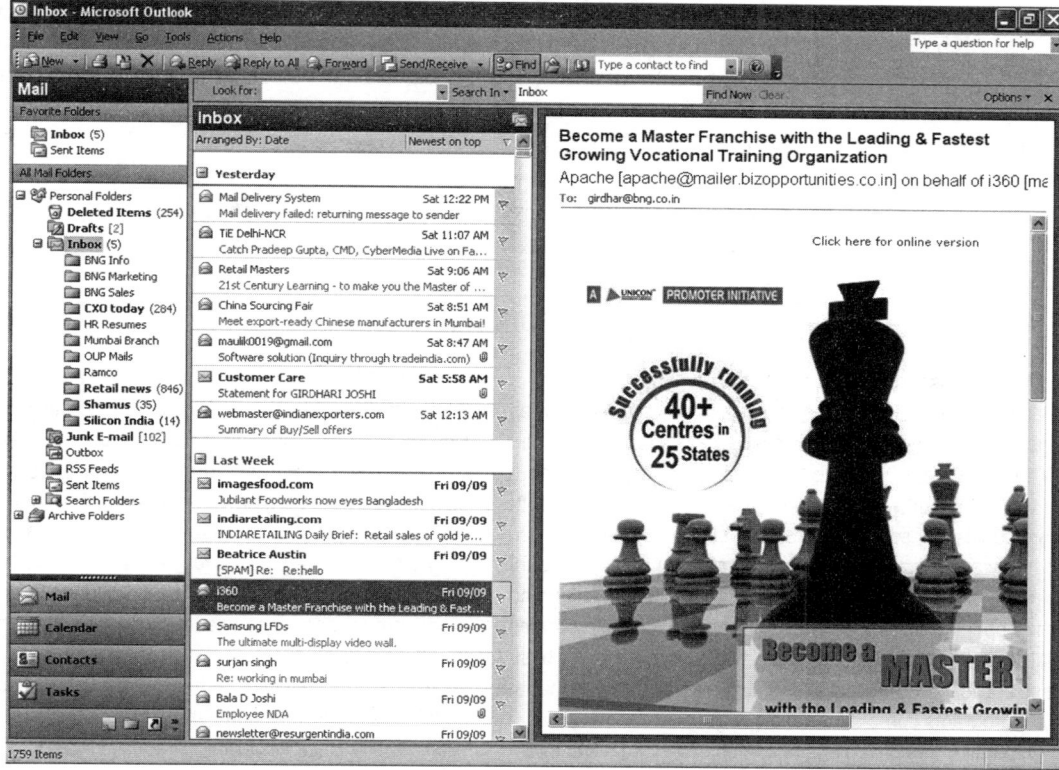

Fig. 5.9   Microsoft Outlook

Groupware

Groupware is a specialized software suite for office collaboration. Collaboration software helps workgroups and teams work together to accomplish group assignments. According to O'Brien (2006), 'Groupware is a category of general-purpose application software that combines a variety of software features and functions to facilitate collaboration'. For example, Microsoft Exchange, Lotus Notes, Novell GroupWise, etc., support collaboration through electronic mail, discussion forums, databases, scheduling, task management, audio, and videoconferencing.

Groupware (also referred to as collaborative software) is computer software designed to help people involved in a common task to achieve the set goals. The design intent of collaborative software is to transform the way documents and rich media are shared to enable more effective team collaboration. While groupware or collaborative software pertains to the technological elements of computer supported cooperative work, collaborative work systems become a useful analytical tool to understand the behavioural and organizational variables (Wilson 1991). Groupware products use the Internet and corporate intranets to make collaboration possible on a global scale by teams located anywhere in the world. For example, team members may use the Internet for email, to work on a joint project, or participate in a discussion forum.

In the early 1990s, the first groupware commercial products began delivering on their promises, and big companies such as Boeing and IBM started using electronic meeting systems to leverage key internal projects. Lotus Notes appeared as a major example of that product category, allowing remote group collaboration when the Internet was still in its infancy. Kirkpatrick (1992), then wrote, 'If groupware really makes a difference in productivity long term, the very definition of an office may change. You will be able to work efficiently as a member of a group wherever you have your computer. As computers become smaller and more powerful, that will mean anywhere.'

Microsoft Windows SharePoint™ Services and IBM's WebSphere are two recent additions to collaborative software systems. Both these products allow teams to quickly create sophisticated websites for information sharing and document collaboration.

SUMMARY

Software is a set of instructions to the computer to perform a certain task; it resides in the computer in the coded form as binary digits of 0 and 1. On the basis of the functions provided by the software, it can be broadly classified into two categories—system software and application software. System software consists of sets of programs to support the efficient use of hardware resources that include primary and secondary memory, display devices, printers, communication links, and other peripherals. Application software refers to programs that actually process data to generate information. All business applications such as accounting and inventory management programs come under this category.

Operating systems manage computers' internal and external resources such as memory, files, and peripherals devices. DOS, Windows, Linux, UNIX, Novell, and Mac are the most popular operating systems in the world. There are many programs that are used to manage, control, and analyse a computer system. These are either available as a distinct software or are included as a part of operating systems. These programs are called utilities. Another set of system software is 'middleware', which provides an interface between an operating system and various application programs.

Computer software is written using some programming language and tools. These programming languages have some method that is followed by programmers when they write the code. For the mainframes and minicomputers, which are first and second generation computers respectively, programming was done either using machine language or assembly language. High-level languages are popularly known as third generation (3GL) and fourth generation languages

(4GL). C, COBOL, Fortran, BASIC, and Pascal are the main third generation languages. Visual C++, Visual Basic, Oracle Developer Tools, SQL, PowerBuilder, FrontPage, Java, J2EE, CGI-Perl, PHP, .NET, etc., are some examples of 4GLs. In object-oriented programming language, the data and procedures are tied together into objects. HTML and XML are programming systems used for websites development requiring multimedia pages. Java, .NET, PHP, etc., are various programming languages used for websites, the Internet, and Intranet development.

Application software is a program created to perform certain tasks for the end-users. Various software packages such as Tally, RetailPRO, SAP, Oracle Applications, MS-Office, OpenOffice, LotusNotes, QuickBooks, Microsoft Outlook, and Finacle are examples of application software. Besides enterprise solutions such as customer relationship management (CRM), supply chain management (SCM), and enterprise resource planning (ERP), there are various e-business applications packages for business functions such as accounting, human resource, procurement, sales order processing, and manufacturing. Office productivity software is a general-purpose application used in offices for writing documents, letters, emails, tabulation work, designing presentations, scheduling meetings, etc. Groupware is a specialized software suite for office collaboration. Collaboration software helps workgroups and teams to accomplish group assignments. Microsoft Exchange, Lotus Notes, Novell GroupWise, Microsoft Windows SharePoint™ Services, IBM's WebSphere, etc., support collaboration through email, discussion forums, databases, scheduling, task management, audio and videoconferencing, etc.

KEY TERMS

Application software Programs that process data to generate information.

Assembly language A second generation programming language that utilizes symbols to represent operation codes and storage locations.

Binary codes   Programming codes written as 0 and 1, which are binary digits.

Collaborative software   A software designed to help people involved in a common task to achieve goals.

Compilers   Programs that translate a high-level programming language into a machine language program.

Device drivers   Software programs that control the functioning of a device attached with a computer.

Extensible mark-up language (XML)   A set of rules for encoding a document in machine-readable form.

Fourth generation languages (4GLs)   Programming languages that are easier to use, also known as non-procedural or natural languages.

Freeware   Software available for free that supports the open-source concept.

Graphic user interface (GUI)   A software interface that relies on icons, bars, buttons, boxes, and other images to start a computer task for the user.

High-level language   A programming language that utilizes macro instructions and statements that closely resemble natural English.

Hypertext mark-up language (HTML)   A popular language for creating hypertext and hypermedia documents for the web.

Machine language   A programming language where instructions are expressed in machine language consisting of 0s and 1s.

Middleware   A software that provides an interface between an operating system and the application programs.

Multimedia   Graphics, photo, animation, audio, and video clubbed into one.

Multitasking   Ability to perform multiple tasks simultaneously.

Network operating systems (NOS)   Operating systems for networks (LAN) that manage communication between two or more computers in a network.

Object-oriented programming (OOP)   A language used to develop programs that create and use objects to perform information processing tasks.

Off-the-shelf (OTS) software   Software applications developed by a programmer for the purpose of mass-selling them as a generic product to some end-users.

Open-source technology   A technology propagating non-proprietary rights on the product that allows developments, additions, and improvements in the software by any other user.

Spreadsheet macros   A series of commands and functions that are stored in the spreadsheet program and can be run whenever required to perform a task.

System programming   The development of tools, compilers, utilities, and operating systems, etc.

System software   A set of programs to support the efficient use of hardware resources.

Utility software   Programs that are used to manage, control, and use computer file systems such as file backup and compression.

Web browsers   Applications for surfing through the Internet, with utilities for emailing, downloading files, chat, etc.

CONCEPT REVIEW QUESTIONS

1. Define software and differentiate the various software systems.
2. What do you understand by system software? Explain any three system software.
3. What are the primary functions offered by operating systems? How do they differ from utility software?
4. Explain application software with examples.
5. What is a business application software? How do they help managers in decision-making?
6. Which are the office productivity software applications and how do they help increase productivity of a user?
7. What do you understand by collaboration software?

CRITICAL THINKING QUESTIONS

1. What are the major trends in software development? What capabilities do you expect to see in future software packages?
2. Should a web browser be integrated into an operating system? Justify your answer.
3. Do you think Linux will replace Windows in the future? What do you think about Linux as an operating system for networks?
4. Though open-source operating system and Open-Office are freeware, why have they not gained acceptance in a big way?

MIS DEVELOPMENT

Brainsoft Solutions Pvt. Ltd is a software development firm. The firm has developed proprietary software products for various business segments such as manufacturing, retail, and transportation. The promotion mix of the company's marketing policy consists of telecalling by in-house staff, online promotion, and search engine optimization on Google and Yahoo!, advertisements in print media such as trade magazines, and sending monthly journals of trade associations to their members. Besides this, the company also participates in trade shows and exhibitions, which help generate business. As such, the company generates many leads and receives inquiries. Out of those leads, only a few materialize. Table 5.7 lists the promotional elements along with the number of instances, calls generated, expenses per instance, and calls converted into leads per month.

Table 5.7   Promotion mix

Promotion head	No. of instances	Calls generated	Expenses per instance	Calls converted
Telecallers	2	120	16,500	3
Google promotion	1	3	10,000	1
Yahoo! promotion	2	3	9500	1
Visual advertisements	15	10	3000	2
Trade India online	12	12	1000	6
Sulekha online	12	9	1000	3
Direct sales	3	15	22,000	3
Dealers	3	6	17,700	2
Trade shows	1	50	1,50,000	4
Trade association magazine	2	4	10,000	1
Images retail	1	3	10,000	0.5
SME magazine	1	3	9500	0.5
Retailer magazine	1	2	10,000	0.25

The following data is also relevant:

- Besides the direct marketing expenses, the company also incurs direct operational costs in installation and implementation of the software packages.
- The average sales revenue per deal is ₹1,75,000. The direct operational costs per deal is ₹90,000.
- The company incurs administrative costs that are 50% of the total sales plus operational costs.

Exercise

Spreadsheets are capable of performing many analyses like 'what-if'. In a what-if analysis, you can see the resultant change, if the value of a factor is changed. You can change various values in formulae and achieve the goal.

Create a spreadsheet in Excel and apply what-if analysis on this data. Determine which mode of promotion is most profitable for the company.

1. How much gross profit does the company make from spending on each promotional head?
2. If the overall budget for promotion is increased by threefold, what will be the sales revenue and profit earned by the company?
3. Figure out if the company's profit and loss statement is in profit at the aforementioned revenue and expenditure.
4. How can the company increase its profit?

REFERENCES

Davis, Gorden and Margethe Olson, *Management Information Systems*, McGraw-Hill, Singapore, 1996.

Goyal, D.P., *Management Information Systems—Managerial Perspectives*, Macmillan India, Delhi, 2006.

Jawadekar, Waman S., *Management Information Systems: Text and Cases*, Tata McGraw-Hill, New Delhi, 2008.

Jawadekar, Waman S., *Software Engineering*, Tata McGraw-Hill, New Delhi, 2004.

Joshi, Girdhar, *Information Technology for Retail*, Oxford University Press, New Delhi, 2008.

Kirkpatrick, David, 'Back to the future with centralized computing', *Fortune*, November 1997.

Laudon, Ken and Jane Laudon, *Management Information Systems*, Pearson Education, Singapore, 2002.

Laudon, Ken, Jane Laudon, and Rajanish Dass, *Management Information Systems*, Pearson Education, Singapore, 2010.

O'Brien, James A., George M. Marakas, and Ramesh Behl, *Management Information Systems*, Tata McGraw-Hill, New Delhi, 2007.

O'Brien, *Management Information Systems*, McGraw-Hill/Irwin, New York, 2006.

Selker, Ted, 'New paradigms for using computers', *Communications of the ACM*, August 1996.

Sliwa, Carol, '.Net vs Java', *Computerworld*, May 2002.

Wilson, P., *Computer Supported Cooperative Work: An Introduction*, Kluwer Academic Publication, 1991.

Kirkpatrick, David and Losee, S., 'Here comes the payoff', 1992, http://money.cnn.com/magazines/fortune/fortune_archive/1992/03/23/76204/index.htm, last accessed on 17 May 2011.

CASE STUDY

Infosys: Improving Project Delivery with Enterprise Collaboration Suite

Infosys Technologies, a global IT firm, needed to make it easier for its geographically dispersed team members to share information. The company chose Microsoft Share-Point Server 2010 as the foundation for its enterprise-wide collaboration platform. With it, Infosys expects to improve productivity and customer service, simplify IT management, and reduce costs.

Company

Infosys Limited (NASDAQ:INFY) was started in 1981 by seven people with a seed capital of just $250 in Bangalore, India. Today, the company is a global leader in the 'next generation' of IT and consulting with revenues of $6.35 billion. Infosys defines, designs, and delivers technology-enabled business solutions for Global 2000 companies. Infosys also provides a complete range of services by leveraging its domain, business expertise, and strategic alliances with leading technology providers.

Infosys is a global leader in IT consulting. With nearly 1,15,000 employees, it operates from more than 50 offices and development centres around the world.

The company's offerings span business and technology consulting, application services, systems integration, product engineering, custom software development, maintenance, reengineering, independent testing and validation services, IT infrastructure services, and business process outsourcing. 'Finacle' is the one of the best known products from Infosys' stable.

Business Needs

Infosys software engineering project teams involve people from multiple offices, who relied on file-share based methods for storing and sharing information, including requests for proposals (RFP), budgetary worksheets, and source code. Information existed in silos—on local and network file shares, storage appliances, and in Microsoft Office SharePoint Server 2007-based portal sites. With customers located in different time zones, it was challenging for teams to access project information on-demand, to respond to customers' needs. Due to security concerns, employees were not allowed to expose data on file servers over the Internet, making it impossible for those working from customer sites to access documents.

'Our SharePoint sites were the only easy and protected way to share confidential information,' explained a practice manager at Infosys. However, Infosys had not implemented centralized provisioning or management of its SharePoint sites, nor were these sites exposed on the company's extranet. Infosys operated 1200 servers, each server farm had its own administrator, and management costs were high. 'Departments asked for more storage, better backup, better virus protection, and access to the SharePoint sites over the extranet. We also risked losing data as individual administrators followed their own backup regimens. We couldn't sustain this environment and provide capabilities users needed without a centralized farm and simpler administration', said a practice manager. Sites also contained many custom-built applications that weren't aligned to the IT departments' standard guidelines.

Solution

In 2009, Infosys began to implement a collaboration platform, called Infosys collaboration platform (ICP), based on MS SharePoint Server 2010. Infosys went for SharePoint without any custom coding. For instance, using the new version's co-authoring features, a dispersed team member can simultaneously work on RFPs and budgets.

Microsoft Office Web Apps, the online lightweight version of the MS Office 2010 program, can be used by employees to edit and share documents stored in Share-Point Server 2010, and employees can render MS Visio diagrams within a web browser.

Infosys also plans to take advantage of the managed metadata capabilities of SharePoint Server 2010 to apply tags to documents. This makes it easier for employees to find information. Finally, Infosys is consolidating manage-ment of its SharePoint Server environment with its central IT department. The newer version of the product provides the company with enhanced capabilities of monitoring server performance and usage, including a unified logging database. The SharePoint health analyser enables adminis-trators to schedule automatic checks for potential configura-tion, performance, and usage problems in the server farm, and the sandboxed solutions feature of SharePoint server helps the IT department protect the integrity of the server farm and give site collection administrators the authority to manage the applications in their site collection. The company plans to deploy ICP for its employees by 2010.

Benefits

The SharePoint server-based ICP environment will make it easier for Infosys employees to share information and respond to customers. Sites will be centrally managed, and administration will be easier and cheaper.

More effective collaboration   Infosys will use ICP as the central location for employees to store and share project-related information. Using Office Web Apps and Visio Services in the SharePoint server, employees will have continual access to information. With this, collaboration will happen more easily among Infosys development centres and customer time zones. With nearly 1,00,000 MS Office users, many using different versions of the software, Office Web Apps will help the company overcome document version compatibility challenge.

Higher productivity   Easier access to information will help boost employees productivity and overall responsiveness

to customers. They will be able to improve productivity because teams will have easy access to accurate data, that they can deliver to the customer.

'Infosys is going to use Office Web Apps extensively and we expect it to drastically reduce the time it takes to complete RFPs and budgets.', said a project leader.

Streamlined IT management   With the SharePoint server deployment, Infosys will transfer management of all the company SharePoint sites to the central IT department. 'If a department wants to increase its storage space, it will be easy. Backups and virus protection will be performed according to the company standards,' said a project leader. 'With the SharePoint server, our insight into the performance of the system is much easier. This is critical to ensuring server health. The SharePoint health analyser helps us fix configuration and performance issues with out-of-the-box tools. Infosys also expects to cut costs through centralized management. 'With SharePoint Server 2010 and ICP, we will reduce our overall time spent on administration by 30–40%', opined the project leader.

Discussion Questions

1. 'Collaboration software help workgroups and teams work together to accomplish group assignments.' Comment on this in the light of the Infosys case study.
2. How did Infosys benefit by implementing SharePoint Server, the collaboration software suite from Microsoft?
3. What were the problems faced and anticipated by Infosys before deciding on a collaboration software implementation?
4. Do you think groupware such as 'SharePoint' and 'WebSphere' are only for giants like Infosys? Can small and medium enterprises (SMEs) implement and benefit from such collaboration software?

Sources:

http://visio.microsoft.com/en-us/Customer_Evidence/Customer_ Case_Studies/Pages/default.aspx, last accessed on 10 October 2011.

http://www.slideshare.net/msitpro/infosys-final, last accessed on 10 October 2011.

http://www.infosys.com/aboutus, last accessed on 10 October 2011.

Many organizations have amassed vast amounts of data that employees use to unlock valuable secrets to enable the organization to compete successfully. Some organizations do this extremely well, but others are quite ineffective. To use analytic tools to improve organizational decision-making, a foundational data architecture and enterprise architecture must be in place...

—**Efraim Turban**

LEARNING OBJECTIVES

After studying this chapter, you will be able to

- understand the concept of database
- realize the disadvantages of traditional file processing systems
- explain the database management approach
- define various database management systems (DBMS)
- understand the functions of DBMS
- differentiate between the various types of database systems
- get acquainted with a step-by-step approach to designing a database
- describe client–server and distributed databases
- learn how to manage databases
- understand the latest trends in using databases such as data warehousing, data mining, web mining, and online analytical processing

EXHIBIT 6.1

Asian Paints: Informatica PowerCenter Manages Data Resources

Asian Paints is India's largest and Asia's third largest paint company, with a turnover of ₹77.06 billion. The group has a reputation in the corporate world for professionalism and fast-track growth. The Mumbai-headquartered company operates in 17 countries and has 23 paint manufacturing facilities in the world, servicing consumers in over 65 countries. Besides Asian Paints, the group operates around the world through its subsidiaries such as Berger International, Apco Coatings, SCIB Paints, and Taubmans. Forbes ranked Asian Paints among the 'Best under a Billion' companies in Asia in 2005, 2006, and 2007. Asian Paints is the only paint company in the world to receive this recognition.

In July 2010, Asian Paints implemented PowerCenter, the data management tool for cost calculations. The company saw it as the ideal solution to empower users with real-time actionable business insight to help improve costing and hence, pricing. PowerCenter delivers a view of costing data across multiple disparate systems to power critical pricing and marketing decisions, cost-saving measures, inventory valuations, demand forecasts, and income projections. The new product costing system is the latest part of a larger deployment of the Informatica platform at Asian Paints, which has standardized Informatica for data integration enterprise-wide.

'The new product costing system has transformed our operational efficiency,' said Maulik Desai, senior manager (system development) of Asian Paints. 'With the Informatica platform, Asian Paints has been able to achieve a degree of flexibility we used to dream of, greatly increasing our pricing accuracy. For example, if there is a change in the price of one of the raw materials, we can immediately see its impact on the selling price of the paint. We can play around with an infinite number of 'what if?' scenarios.'

Asian Paints has sourced its data management software from Informatica Corporation, one of the providers of data integration software. PowerCenter and the integral component of the Informatica Platform have helped Asian Paints create a highly unified product costing system. The Informatica solution is vital to the company's market responsiveness and continued success.

The use of the data management tool has enabled Asian Paints to slash the time required to run its sophisticated costing model from 24 hours to just 20 minutes, nearly a 99% reduction in time. At Asian Paints, the data management solution delivers a consistent, trusted view of costing data.

It increases productivity and opportunities for analytical insight, with product costs now calculated concurrently, rather than sequentially, across all Asian Paints business units and five paint manufacturing plants in India. The tool lowers operating costs since critical data is now integrated and delivered in the right format at the right time. The solution simplifies decision-making around ingredients and formulae by enabling the setting of varied alternatives across products and production facilities.

Informatica PowerCenter has replaced the legacy standalone pricing system at Asian Paints that was prone to extensive and costly manual intervention and opportunities for errors.

Sources:
http://www.cxotoday.com/story/asian-paints-implements-informatica-powercenter/, last accessed on 30 August 2010.
www.asianpaints.com, last accessed on 24 August 2010.
www.indiainfoline.com/Asian-Paints-implements/4914270746, last accessed on 24 August 2010.

Asian Paints' initiative to implement a data management tool illustrates the importance of data management in a business (Exhibit 6.1). The company was unable to bring in operational efficiency through prompt costing because of scattered data and inflexibility of the existing costing systems. The data was fragmented across scores of units and was inconsistent and redundant. The way organizations store, organize, and manage their data has tremendous impact on the competitive advantage they have.

This case suggests that the management of the company was able to determine that efficiency was reduced because it could not obtain consistent and quick information for product costing, which was one of the critical factors in their business. The company had invested on one of the best data management tools from Informatica for storing, organizing, and analysing costing data and making it available to users across the organization.

Data is a vital organizational resource that needs to be managed like other business assets. Therefore, in this chapter, we will discuss how data is created, captured, stored, and managed with the help of software known as database management systems (DBMS).

DATABASE

Before we discuss DBMS, let us understand the concept of data and how it is organized in a database for use in an information system. Data refers to raw strings of facts which, if organized, can be converted into information. Data is also defined as a representation of facts or concepts that are processed and converted into information. Data is logically organized into characters, fields, records, files, and databases, as illustrated in Fig. 6.1.

The computer system organizes data in a hypothetical hierarchy starting with characters and growing into fields, records, tables, and databases. The basic logical data element is the character, which consists of a single letter of the alphabet (A–Z), a numeral, (0–9), or a symbol. The data *field* is the name of a column that represents the data in that column. It is also known as a data item. For example, in Fig. 6.1, name, month, basic, etc., are fields. The data under a data field represents similar facts.

A *record* is a collection of related data. A single row in a database table is known as a record. A row contains different elements of data. As in the aforementioned example, all the data in the first row belongs to B. Murthy. All related records are stored in a *data file* or *table*. Thus, a payroll file contains data related to the salary records of the employees. These files or tables are frequently used by applications for the storage, retrieval, and processing of information. Storage of data, in

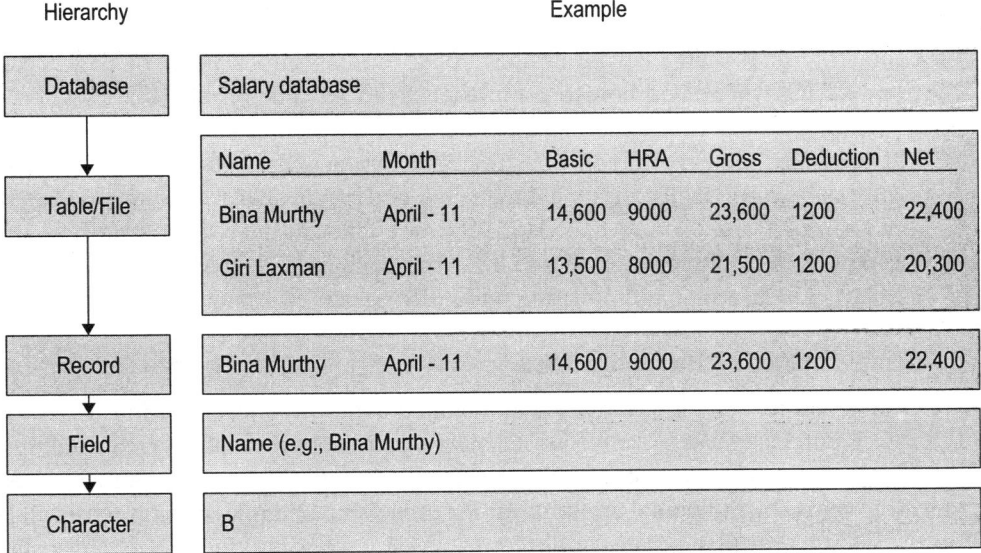

Fig. 6.1   Examples of logical data elements in a database

paper or electronic files, for future use, analysis, and retrieval is called *database*. It is a collection of 'related' information, stored so that it is available to many users for different purposes.

A database is where data resides. A computer database gives us a form of electronic filing system, which has many ways of cross referencing. Electronic filing can be of different types such as storing in spreadsheets, text formats, application-specific files, or an independent database system. Cross referencing allows users to refer and retrieve data in multiple ways. A database has the following implicit properties:

- Data is about places, objects, or things. It consists of facts and figures. A database represents some aspect of the real world. A change in the real world reflects in the dataset.
- A database is a logically coherent collection of data. The facts represent some meaning. Unrelated and random collection of facts cannot be called a database. For example, a data file containing population details of a city will only have data related to the population of that city. It cannot contain data about the eruption of a volcano in Japan. These are random and unrelated facts.
- A database has a specific purpose. Data is always collected with an objective in mind. A database is designed, built, and managed by a group of users through applications that users are interested in.

TRADITIONAL FILE PROCESSING SYSTEMS

The following are the systems of data storage and management: paper-based, text, electronic files (e.g., spreadsheets), and specialized database files (used for specific applications). For example, a database can be maintained in an Excel worksheet as illustrated in Fig. 6.2. Similarly, COBOL programming uses specialized data files that can only be used by the specific programs. The storage and management of data in such files is called file processing system. If an organization maintains a large amount of data in the form of text, electronic spreadsheets, or specialized database files, there will be an enormous number of files, within a very short period of time, containing data. Large corporates have data running into millions of pages. Nobody knows what is lying where, and how to get it when required. The problem arises when this data has to be managed, retrieved, and analysed.

Data stored in such traditional file processing systems cannot be properly managed, is difficult to process, involves high costs for maintenance, and is inflexible. Every organization that performs any form of transaction creates data. However, efficient analysis of data becomes impossible because of poor file management. Thus, the concept of a DBMS, which stores the data in a well-structured format and processes and retrieves data in an efficient manner, was introduced.

Disadvantages of Traditional Files

Organizations—small or large—accumulate data at every level. Various transaction systems, such as purchases, sales, manufacturing, payroll, and stock movement, create multiple documents and hence, multiple types of data. This data is used by the respective groups of users; related files are required by individual applications for processing and information retrieval. For example, the sales department creates hundreds of files related to products, prices, discounts, schemes, customer, taxes, sales persons, enquiries, quotations, customer orders, order terms and conditions, order confirmations, delivery schedules, dispatch advices, invoices, etc. Similarly, the purchase

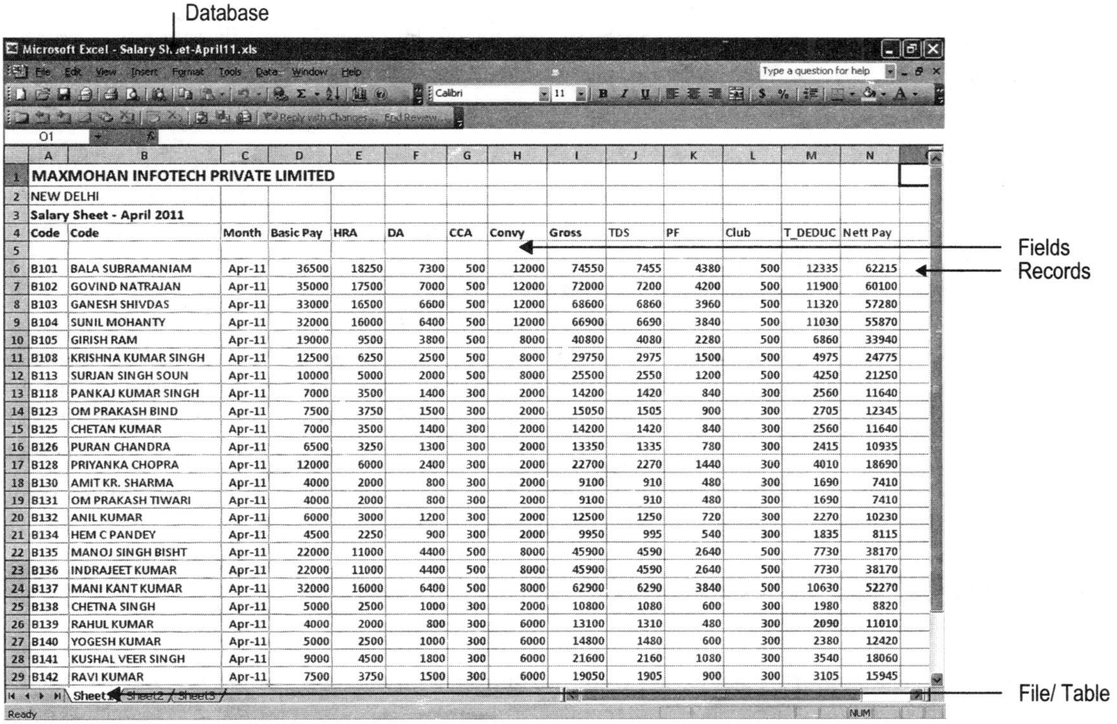

Database

Fig. 6.2   Data maintained in an MS Excel worksheet file

department also creates files related to products, prices, vendors, purchase orders, etc. Some of these files are created multiple times. In addition, the product and tax rates files can be created by both the sales and purchase departments. This leads to duplicity and redundancy of files. Laudon (2010) summarized the major problems in keeping data in traditional file environments—data redundancy and inconsistency, program–data dependence, lack of flexibility, poor security, and lack of data sharing and availability.

Data redundancy   Redundancy or duplicity of data refers to maintenance of duplicate data files and records by various departments or sections across the organization. This leads to inefficiency as well as storage-related problems. Within the same file, there could be instances of duplicate data records. The presence of such duplicate records is known as data redundancy. For example, if customer names and addresses are stored in different database files, it may result in problems of updating the records at various places. If all the files are not updated at the same time, the result of data retrieval may show inconsistent records.

Lack of flexibility   Traditional file storage methods are not flexible and the data structure format may also differ from one file to another. Independent electronic file systems such as spreadsheets and text files give only limited flexibility in the process of retrieving data. Having data in independent files makes it difficult to provide end-users with information for ad hoc requests that require accessing the data stored in several different files. This is, most of the time, a very costly and ineffective process. This is because the program thus created only caters to that particular data file.

Poor security   Traditional file system methods are not completely secure. Paper files can easily get lost and electronic text or spreadsheets can be modified or deleted despite being protected by passwords. Moreover, in traditional systems, the management does not exercise control over data. Electronic files can be modified without leaving a trace of the changes made.

Lack of data sharing   Lack of easy sharing of data forces departments to create and maintain their own sets of data, which in turn, leads to duplicity and redundancy. As pieces of information are available at different places and in different files, it is impossible to share or make the data available to others on a real-time basis.

Program–data dependence   The data stored in electronic files can be modified, processed, and retrieved only by programs specifically written for them. Data cannot exist independently; for example, the data existing in an Excel sheet can only be used and retrieved by an Excel application. Similarly, many third generation languages that are used for programming (e.g., BASIC) store data only in files that are read and modified by the same program. It thus makes the data and the program cohesively interdependent. We cannot use a third application to manipulate the data. Such manipulation and programming is very costly and time-consuming.

APPROACH TO DATABASE MANAGEMENT

The various disadvantages of traditional file systems paved the way for the creation of database systems that are more flexible, secure, and independent in their functioning. The database management approach consolidates records previously stored in separate files, into a common pool of data elements that provide data for many applications. Such carefully arranged files make it easy to obtain data from the data repository. Even a non-programmer can use a data repository and retrieve data by using certain inbuilt tools in the repository. The system that gives tools to create, store, process, modify, update, and retrieve data from the repository is called a database management system. Such a system stores data within it and helps in the management of data through updating, retrieval, deletion, etc., by providing special tools to do so. It stores data in one location or file instead of multiple files and locations. Data within a single location serves multiple applications, users, and systems within the organization.

For example, Asian Paints' data management initiative consolidates and processes data from various units and business functions and calculates a product's price on a real-time basis. An example of a database management approach is given in Fig. 6.3.

Advantages of Database Approach

In a traditional file system where the data is stored in text format, it is not possible to easily index the records and retrieve relevant information quickly. Moreover, the same data may be scattered across multiple files. The disadvantages of traditional file processing systems are taken care of in the database approach. The database approach helps in the following ways:

- It eliminates redundancy and duplicity. (Redundancy is the multiple presence of the same record in the database.)

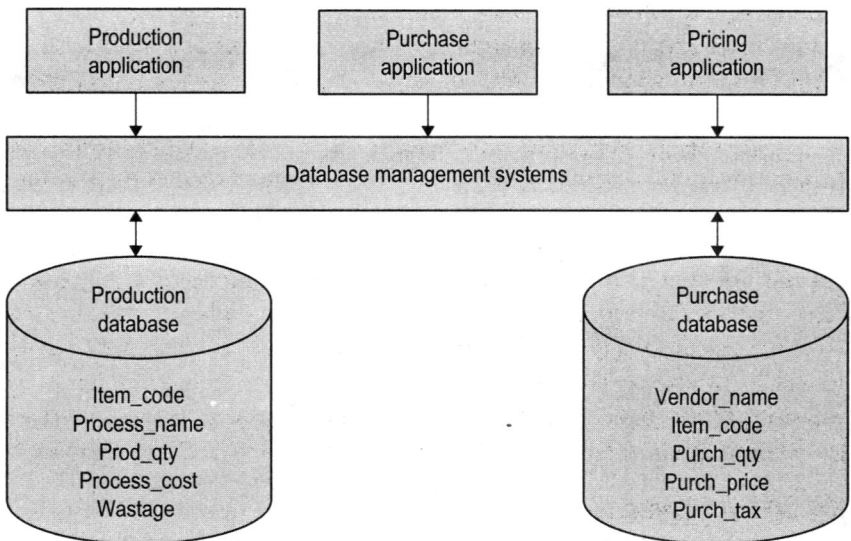

Fig. 6.3 Database management approach in product price calculation

- It controls data inconsistency.
- It facilitates sharing of data by many people across the organization or geographical area.
- It enforces standards. Information is stored and retrieved in standard formats.
- It maintains integrity, that is, two tables containing similar information will not have contradictory records.
- Security restrictions can be applied on a database. Unwanted users cannot perform any action on the database.

DATABASE MANAGEMENT SYSTEMS

The Census Commission of India manages its huge database with DevInfo, a database management and presentation tool, as illustrated in Exhibit 6.2. DBMS is the main software tool of the database approach as it controls the creation, maintenance, storage, and usage of data within an organization, as well as its end-users. The management of data in a database is carried out by general purpose software packages such as dBase, FoxPro, MS Access, Ingress, Sybase, MSDE, SQL Anywhere, FireBird, Lotus Approach, and Corel Paradox. There are some high-end DBMS that are used for mainframes and servers such as Oracle 10g, IBM DB2, MS SQL Server, and MySQL (a popular open-source DBMS).

Laudon (2010) stated that DBMS relieves the programmer and end-user from the task of understanding where and how the data is actually stored by separating the logical and physical views of the data. The logical view presents data as they would be perceived by end-users or business specialists, while the physical view shows how data is actually organized and structured on physical storage media.

EXHIBIT 6.2

India Census 2011: It is all about Database Management

The government of India takes up the gigantic task of population enumeration every 10 years. Indian Census 2011 is the 15th in an unbroken series since 1872 and the seventh after independence. It was carried out from 9–28 February 2011. One of the essential features of a population enumeration is that each person is enumerated and his/ her individual particulars are collected in a form having 29 field categories. The reference date for Census of India 2011 is 00:00 hours of 1 March 2011.

Census 2011 covered 35 states/union territories, 640 districts, 5924 sub-districts, 7935 towns, and 6,40,867 villages. In Census 2001, the corresponding figures were 593 districts, 5463 sub-districts, 5161 towns and 6,38,588 villages. In 1901, India's population was about 238.4 million; this increased by more than four times in 110 years to touch 1210 million in 2011. Once the huge data was entered in the database, the census commissioner of India (CCI) presented an animated dashboard giving a single view consolidated report on the census results. This has been developed

using DevInfo database technology. CensusInfo is a major adaptation of DevInfo. DevInfo technology was adopted for the 2001 census and used to present and display the provisional results in 2002. UNICEF is supporting the data dissemination of Census of India 2011 results, which includes development of a dissemination strategy and software support for dissemination of census data in a user-friendly manner to enable quicker and easy dissemination of the census data to users. DevInfo was selected among other data display software, in part, because it was free and endorsed by the UN. Building on the experience of India and other countries, the United Nations Statistics Division, in partnership with UNICEF and UNFPA, commissioned the development of an enhanced version of CensusInfo to help countries disseminate census data on CD and on the web.

Sources:
http://censusindia.gov.in/, http://www.censusindia.net, http://www.census2011.co.in, last accessed on 30 September 2011.

Functions

The following are the three major functions of a DBMS:

- Creation of new databases and database applications
- Maintenance of the quality of data
- Usage of the database to provide end-users with the information they need.

These functions are carried out through inbuilt tools, such as tables, forms, queries, and reports, that are available in any DBMS. Database management systems not only help in the management of stored data, but also in the storage of queries (to manipulate and retrieve data), forms (for data entry or retrieval), and report files (the format in which the data is placed and presented).

Components

A DBMS consists of the following major components through which the aforementioned functions are performed:

Data table   Database development involves defining and organizing the contents, relationships, and structure of the data table. A data table functions as a repository of data in the database. The DBMS have a data definition capability to specify the structure of the contents of the database. It is used to create database tables and to define the characteristics of the fields in each table. The information about data field is stored in the data dictionary provided by the DBMS. As records

Table 6.1   Database table showing product prices as viewed by an end-user

P_code	Product_name	Group	Cost_price	Trnf_price	Deal_price	Sale_price	MRP
S0001	Shirt cotton F/S	Gar	900.0	1990.00	1490.00	2290.00	2990.00
S0111	Luxor pen	Sta	22.00	34.00	44.00	55.00	55.00
P0112	Natraj pencil	Sta	11.50	12.50	14.00	15.00	16.00
P0113	F/Pen waterman	Sta	125.00	143.00	184.00	190.00	210.00
T0294	Trousers grey 32	Gar	1248.00	1998.00	1780.00	1500.00	2150.00

of the same subject are placed in one data table, multiple tables are placed under one database. Table 6.1 displays a product price table.

Forms   Database application development involves using DBMS to develop prototypes of queries, forms, and reports. The database maintenance function is performed using forms, which serve as an interface between the users and the database. They are bridges that connect the user (involved in data entry or viewing of reports) and the invisible databases at the back end. We create forms to easily enter, view, or modify data. They can fetch data from one or more tables and display it on the computer screen in a format specified by the user. They provide captions, space, and dialogues for data entry or retrieval.

Queries   DBMS offer database interrogation capabilities. The interrogation is done through queries to find and retrieve data that meet the conditions specified by the user. Queries can also fetch records from multiple tables, update or delete multiple records at the same time, and perform predefined tasks or customized calculations on the data. In other words, queries maintain program instructions to retrieve data in the desired quantity and quality. The query language feature allows us to easily obtain immediate responses to ad hoc data requests.

Most DBMS offer a structured query language (SQL) feature, which makes the retrieval of data very simple. The basic form of an SQL query is as follows—SELECT...FROM... WHERE...

SELECT... (list the data field you want to retrieve) FROM... (list the files or tables from which the data is to be retrieved) WHERE... (specify conditions that limit the search to those data records that satisfy the condition).

Most DBMS provide a graphical user interface (GUI) point-and-click method for query generation, which are translated by the DBMS into SQL commands. Figure 6.4 displays a query generator in Microsoft Access.

Reports   Reports are created to retrieve the desired data from data tables using queries for specific needs. The data is consolidated either on screen or in print format. Thus, a report is an effective way of presenting data in a printed format. It is a formal, presentable, usually printed document that lists the data in a formatted manner.

Microsoft Access and other DBMS include capabilities for report generation so that the queried data can be displayed in a more structured and formatted way. Access also has the capacity of developing desktop applications, which include tools for creating data entry screens, reports, and writing the back-end logic for transaction processing.

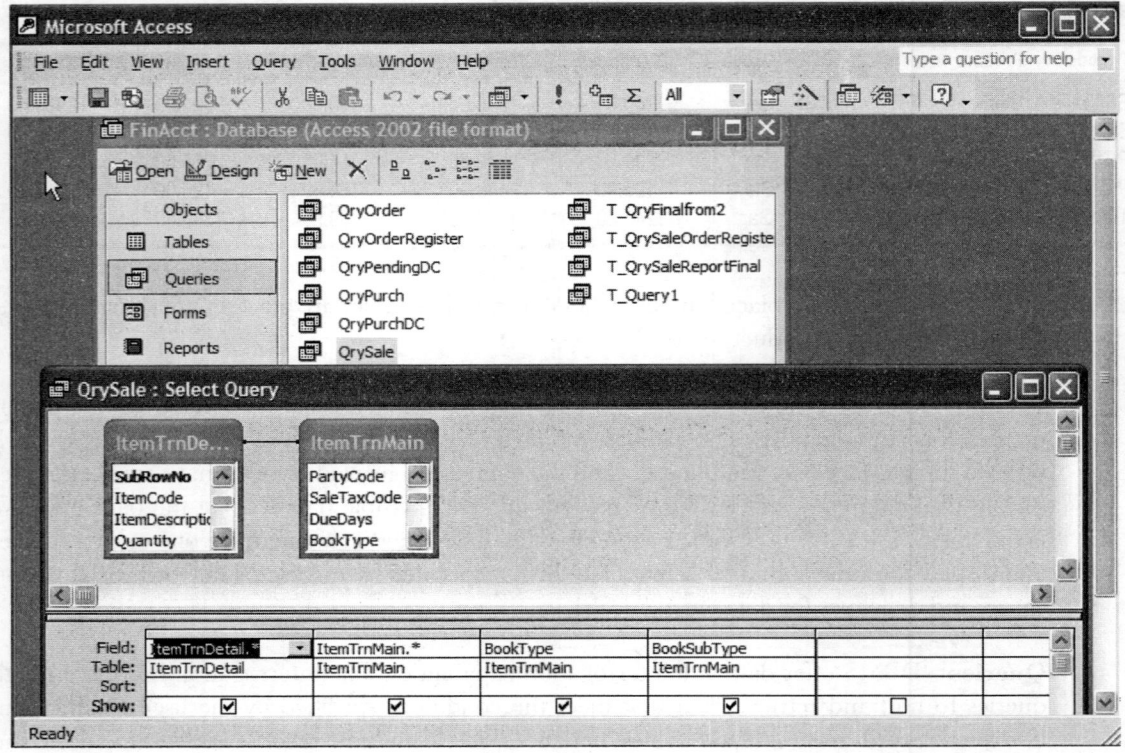

Fig. 6.4   GUI-based query generator in MS Access

Types

The census commission of India 2011 covered 35 states/union territories, 640 districts, 5924 sub-districts, 7935 towns, and 6,40,867 villages, and collected data for and reached out to 1210 million people (see Exhibit 6.2). Imagine how difficult it would be to get any information from such massive data if the data was not stored in an organized, structured, and logical manner. Based on the complexity of the database, various data structures and access methods have been devised to efficiently organize and retrieve data using information systems.

According to O'Brien (2007), the relationship among the many individual data elements stored in databases are based on one of several data structures or models. DBMS packages are designed to use a specific data structure to provide end-users with quick, easy access to information stored in databases. The following are the five fundamental database structures: hierarchical, network, relational, object-oriented, and multidimensional. We will not discuss the first two as they were only in use for mainframes in the early stage of DBMS evolution. These types of databases are now considered outdated and no longer used for building database-driven applications. They are less flexible compared to modern-day relational DBMS. Their major drawback was the difficulty in establishing a relationship between two database files containing related records.

However, some of the older system-run applications were built around these databases. The Y2K syndrome caused many companies to shed these applications and port their data into new databases.

RELATIONAL DATABASE MANAGEMENT SYSTEMS

The relational model is the most widely used DBMS. Relational database management systems (RDBMS) are so called because one table in a database has a relationship with another table. This data model is based on relational calculus. The relational model allows data to be represented in a simple table (row–column format). A table is referred to as a relation. In a relational database, data is arranged in files called database tables. A table is composed of a number of rows and columns. A row is called a record and a column is called a field. Thus, the data of one table can be related to the data in another table, if both the tables share a common data element. Simply said, in an RDBMS, each data table has a relationship with other tables.

Relational database management systems have much more flexibility in processing data for queries, combining information from different sources. RDBMS allow the addition and editing of data without disturbing the old data or bringing about any change in the programmed application. Microsoft Access, MS SQL Server, Oracle, DB2, etc., are some of the widely used RDBMS. MySQL is a popular open-source RDBMS.

To understand the relationship concept clearly, let us understand the following terms: entity, attributes, values, and primary key. We can explain this relationship with the help of an example. The database table, Table 6.1 can be explained in RDBMS terms. To understand the concept, this table is divided into two tables, as shown in Fig. 6.5.

This database has separate tables for the entities 'product' and 'price'. An entity refers to a person, place, thing, event, or concept, about which information is recorded. In Table 6.5, product and price are the two entities. The attributes describe the entities meaningfully. For 'product', the code, name, and group are attributes that describe the entities. Though seemingly independent, these tables have a relationship between them (refer to Fig. 6.6). The diagram that describes the relationship among the entities is called an entity–relationship diagram or E–R diagram. There is a common element—P_code—in both the tables, which relates to one (or more) record(s) of one table with one (or more) record(s) of the other table. The field for P_code in the 'Product' table uniquely identifies each record and is called the key field. Each table in a relational database has one field that is designated as its primary key. This key field is the unique identifier for the information in any row of the table and cannot be duplicated.

In the tables, the RDBMS can retrieve and display a product name from the 'Product' table and sales price from the 'Price' table by using the common P_code number field to join the two tables, as shown in Fig. 6.6.

Advantages

The relational database model is very popular because it offers significant advantages over other database systems. Some of the advantages are as follows:

Structural independence   Structural independence means that the changes in the database structure do not hamper the data accessing process. Any change in the structure of the database does not affect the database's data access mechanism in any way. The application programs, therefore, do not need any modification even if the structure is modified. As there is no need for navigational arrangement for data access, this database offers complete structural independence.

P_code	Product_name	Group
S0001	Shirt cotton F/S	Garmt
S0011	Luxor pen	Staty
P0001	Natraj pencil HB	Staty
P0012	Fountain pen Waterman	Staty
T0003	Trouser 34/BL	Garmt

Table: Product

Key field
(Primary key)

Columns
(Attributes/Fields)

Table: Price

P_code	Cost_price	Tranf_price	Dealer_price	Sales_price	MRP
S0001	900.00	1240.00	1600.00	1900.00	1999.00
S0011	90.00	111.00	125.00	133.00	140.00
P0001	1.25	136.00	1.50	2.00	2.00
P0012	122.00	145.00	170.00	180.00	190.00
T0003	1890.00	2210.00	2300.00	2500.00	2590.00

Fig. 6.5 Joining the product and price tables in a relational database

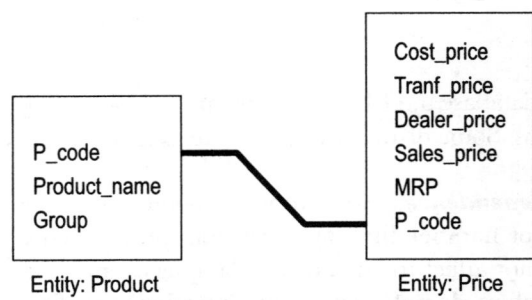

Entity: Product

Entity: Price

Fig. 6.6 Relationship between two different tables

Simplicity of design and use   Relational databases run independent of application, data, and structure. They are said to possess data independence and structural independence. Therefore, design and implementation is easier.

Advanced query capabilities   Querying a relational database is very simple, highly efficient, and very powerful. It supports SQL because both, SQL and RDBMS, have strong foundations in relational algebra and relational calculus.

OBJECT-ORIENTED DATABASE MANAGEMENT SYSTEMS

Traditional DBMS and RDBMS can only store and process fully structured data in the form of text and numbers. They are not capable of storing and manipulating multimedia files such as HTML text, images, graphics, voice, video, and movies. Now, data is also stored and available in various multimedia forms, thanks to the Internet. Besides the traditional structured data, data comes in the form of HTML text, images, graphics, voice, etc., which may need to be stored and retrieved for various applications. These unstructured databases are being handled using the latest breakthrough in database technology—object-oriented DBMS (OODBMS). Multimedia web pages having data, text, images, sound, etc., are examples of OODBMS.

OODBMS are able to store data as objects that can be retrieved and shared. They store the data and the procedures that act on that data as objects that can be automatically retrieved and shared. They are becoming popular because they can be used to manage various multimedia components and Java applets that are used in web applications.

Though OODBMS can handle large chunks of a variety of data, they are not as efficient as RDBMS. This is the reason why RDBMS are still preferred by technologists for storage, processing, and retrieval of large amounts of data containing numbers and characters.

MULTIDIMENSIONAL DATABASE MANAGEMENT SYSTEMS

Multidimensional database structures are data cubes that display information having more than one dimension. According to O'Brien (2007), the multidimensional database structure is a variation of the relational model that uses multidimensional structures to organize data and express the relationship between data. Each cell within a multidimensional structure contains aggregated data related to elements along each of its dimensions. These databases present data elements in compact and easy ways that have many interrelationships.

DATABASE DESIGNING

Database designing is a very structured but complex process. When designing a database, one has to keep in mind the purpose of the database, determine the scope and structure of the tables, identify unique keys, and determine the relationship between various tables. Large organizations entrust the task of database development to a database administrator (DBA). The database developers use the data definition language (DDL) in DBMS (e.g., Oracle 9i or DB2) to develop and specify the data contents, relationships, and structure of each database.

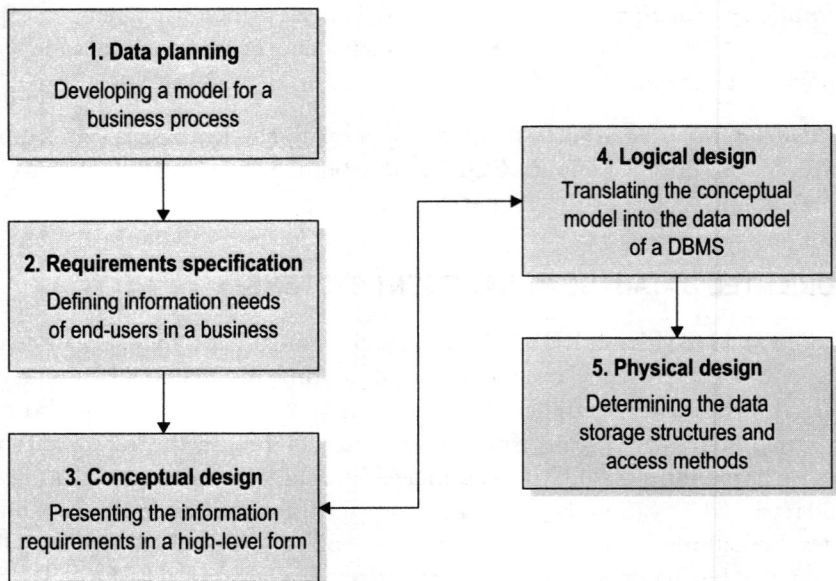

Fig. 6.7   Process and steps involved

Database development involves data planning and database design activities. Data models that support business processes are used to develop databases that meet the information needs of the end-users in an organization. Figure 6.7 illustrates the complete database development process.

The database designer first develops a conceptual model. The conceptual model is independent of user applications, hardware, and DBMS. Users, managers, and database designers view data from their own perspectives. Based on these views, we understand them as conceptual, logical, and physical data models. Conceptual views indicate the relationship between entities as needed to support the basic business process. These data models then serve as logical frameworks called schemas and subschemas, on which the physical design of a database rests. The schema is an overall logical view of the relationship among data elements. The logical views present the data that is seen by the user. The physical model is a framework of how the data is stored in the database on a physical device. Figure 6.8 illustrates all the three models of a database. Let us assume that the organization wants to build a database for invoices. With this example, we will explain the entire process of database design. The designer defines entities such as customer, item, invoice, and tax rate.

Data Planning

The database designer must have a clear understanding of the purpose for which the database is being created, the relationship among the data, the type of data, and how the data will be used. The DBA should initiate a plan to collect the data needs of each person in the organization. It is necessary to further investigate how the data is processed and used by people in performing their tasks. This kind of meaningful assembly of entities with their attributes is called data dictionary. This exercise is carried out for each functional department in the organization.

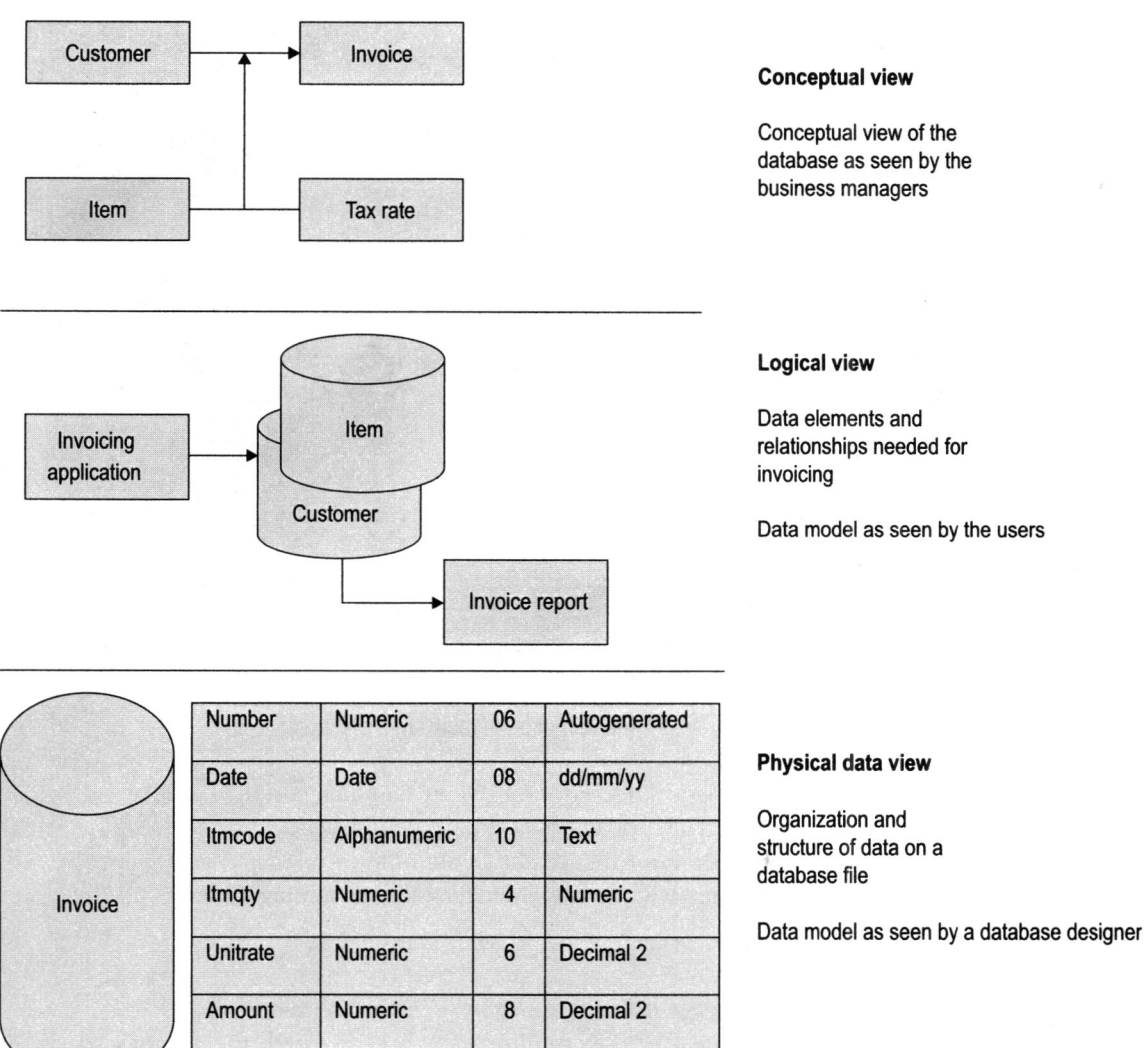

Conceptual view

Conceptual view of the database as seen by the business managers

Logical view

Data elements and relationships needed for invoicing

Data model as seen by the users

Physical data view

Organization and structure of data on a database file

Data model as seen by a database designer

Fig. 6.8   Examples of conceptual, logical, and physical database views

Let us go back to the example of invoice database creation. The database manager's task is to collect all the types of data entities and determine their description and spell out their uses in the operation. The entities—customer, item, invoice—should be described by their attributes details, as shown here:

Entity   : Invoice
Attribute's name   : Invoice_number
Primary key   : Yes, number
Source   : Self-generating sequence number
Characteristics   : Numeric, maximum 6 characters

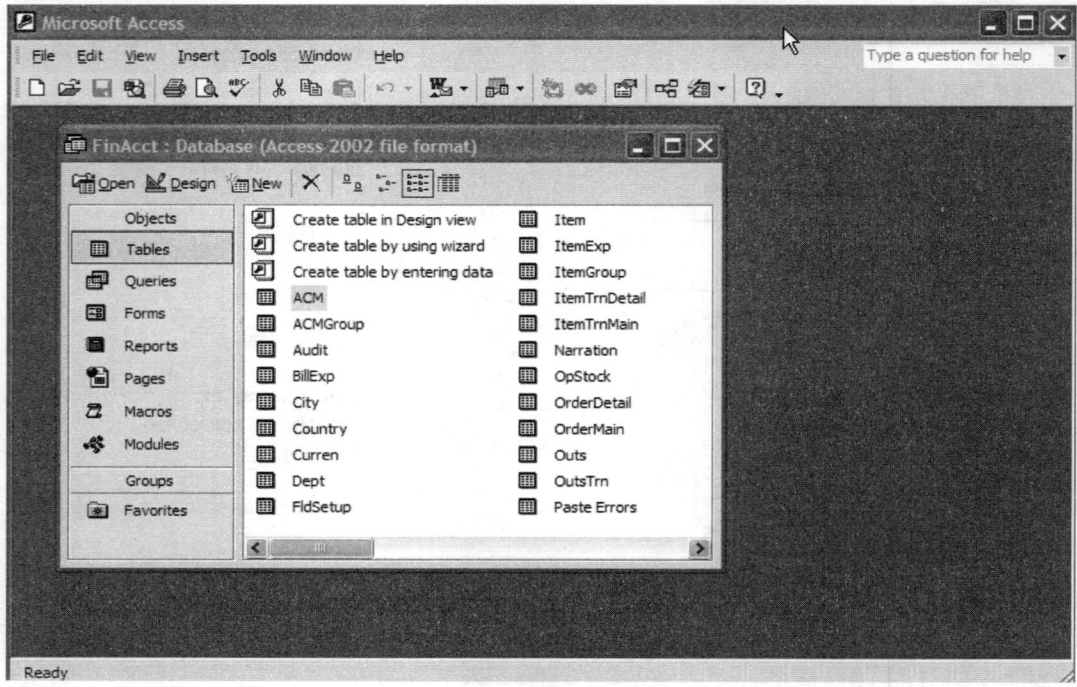

Fig. 6.9   MS Access allows creation of tables in a database

Use   : Bill sequence, reference for bill outstanding, customer ledger
Security   : Access to all, updates by accounts department
Important   : Reference value, hence not changeable
Attribute relationship: Associated with customer ledger, bill outstanding table

Figure 6.9 shows a group of entities created in MS Access.

Relational Identity

Once the data analysis is done and user requirements are specified, the database designer determines how the data elements in the database are to be grouped. The design process identifies a relationship among data elements and the most efficient way of grouping data elements together to meet the information systems' requirements. In this process, the grouped data are organized, refined, and streamlined to weed out redundant data elements and unwanted many-to-many entity relationships.

Considering the aforementioned example, the 'invoice' database may have many tables. The database designer may design just one 'invoice' table as seen in Table 6.2. However, this table has many anomalies. There should not be any duplicate or redundant records and fields containing similar data. The database designer splits this table and goes through a process called normalization.

Normalization

It is the process of simplifying the data structure by replacing it with smaller and multiple data structures. This is done for the sake of reducing complexities and making the database

Table 6.2   Data table for invoice database created by the database designer

Invoice no.	Invoice date	Cust_code	Cust_name	Cust_address	Item code	Item name	Quantity	Unit rate	Amount	Tax	Net amount
10001	30/9/1	C0022	SIMPO	114, Sa.	T0101	Mobile	02	2450	4900	490	5390
10001	30/9/1	C0022	SIMPO	114, Sa.	T0112	Battery	02	0500	1000	100	1100

tables free from duplicate records and fields containing similar data. The process of creating small, stable yet flexible, and adaptive data structures from a complex group of data is called normalization. A relation is established among various tables by using a common element in the data tables.

The process of normalization takes place in three steps known as the first normal form (1NF), second normal form (2NF), and third normal form (3NF). A table is in 1NF if there are no duplicated rows and each cell is single-valued. In this table, each attribute consists of a single fact about an entity.

A table is in 2NF if it is in 1NF and all non-key attributes are dependent on all the keys. All columns should depend on the primary key only. This means that all the data items in a table are uniquely associated with a specific data item. Similarly, a table is in 3NF if it qualifies for 2NF and each column in that table is dependent on the entire primary key.

In the invoice database example, the database designer splits the table further to achieve normalization. If multiple items are sold to the same customer, the customer code, name, and address is repeated in the table. This table of data is not normalized as there is repetition of data values for the same invoice. The relationship contains repeating data groups because there can be many items on a single invoice. The first step towards normalization is to break down the invoice into smaller relations, each of which describes a single entity (as seen Table 6.3). The 'customer' table contains basic details about the customer; the 'item' table holds product details. The sales data can spread across a number of tables. The bill number, date, and customer code can be elements in the main sales table, whereas, the item break-ups with quantity, price, taxes, and discounts can be stored in another table.

We can understand the normalization process with the example of the invoice database. Before normalization, this database will look like the one shown in Table 6.3.

The database designer applies rules of normalization to Table 6.3 and in a step by step approach, the table is split into the following four tables, as shown in Tables 6.4–6.7.

By splitting the data into four tables, we have eliminated the update anomaly, and by introducing a primary key, the insertion anomaly has been eliminated. According to Laudon (2010), relational database systems try to enforce referential integrity rules to ensure that the relationships between coupled tables remain consistent. Referential integrity is a property of data, which when satisfied,

Table 6.3   Un-normalized data table for the invoice database

Invoice no.	Invoice date	Cust_code	Cust_name	Cust_address	Item code	Item name	Quantity	Unit rate	Amount	Tax	Net amount
10001	30/9/1	C0022	SIMPO	114, Sa.	T0101	Mobile	02	2450	4900	490	5390
10001	30/9/1	C0022	SIMPO	114, Sa.	T0112	Battery	02	0500	1000	100	1100

Table 6.4   Customer table

Cust_code	Cust_name	Cust_address
C0022	Simposium Trades	114, Savitri Nagar
C0023	Dynamic Enterprises	65, Krishna Nagar

Primary key

Table 6.5   Item table

Item code	Item name	UOM
T0101	Mobile	Each
T0112	Battery	Each
T0113	Headset	Each

Primary key

Table 6.6   Invoice header table

Invoice no.	Invoice date
10001	30/9/11
10002	01/10/11

Primary key

Table 6.7   Data table for invoice broken down into four smaller relations after normalization

Invoice no.	Cust_code	Item code	Quantity	Unit rate	Amount	Tax	Net amount
10001	C0022	T0101	02	2450	4900	490	5390
10001	C0022	T0112	02	0500	1000	100	1100

Primary key   Foreign keys

requires every value of one attribute (column) of a relation (table) to exist as a value of another attribute in a different or same attribute or table. When one table has a foreign key that points to another table, you may not add a record to the table with the foreign key unless there is a corresponding record in the linked table.

Entity–Relationship Diagram

The main attribute of RDBMS is their ability to establish a relationship with various tables. Where data is required from more than one table at a time, the system processes and picks data from all sources (tables). The link is pre-established in the database and is done on the basis of the common fields in the tables. If two tables requiring a relationship do not have a common field, it is said to be a bad structure. Therefore, to establish a relationship, the designer inserts a common field in both the tables. Figure 6.10 shows a simple entity–relationship diagram for the database model shown in Table 6.3.

Physical Database Model

As the number of tables has been determined, the next step is to decide the structure of the database table. Each table indicates information about the subject and each field in a table contains its individual attributes. Database architecture affects the speed of storing and recovering records, the speed of processing data, and the complexities in updating and modifying data. While creating

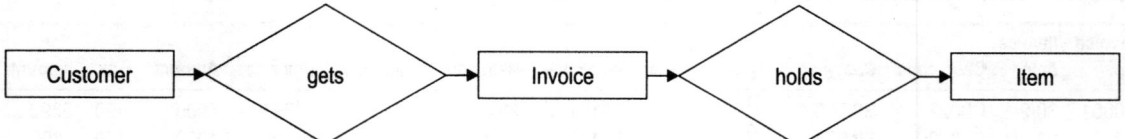

Fig. 6.10   Entity–relationship diagram among entities item, invoice, and customer

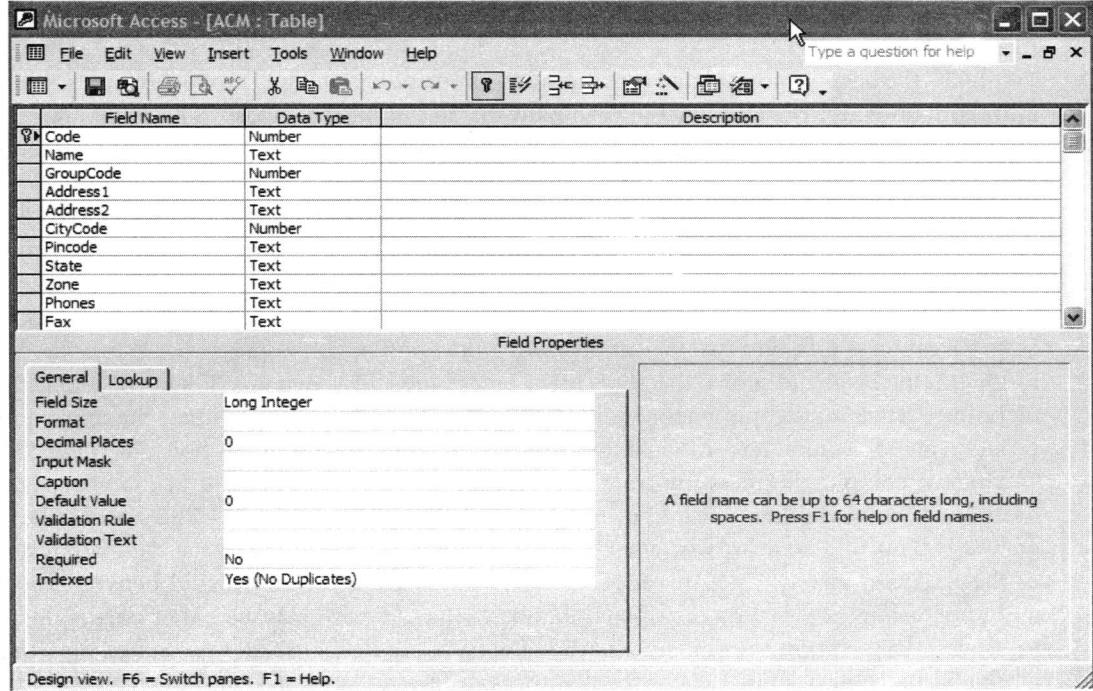

Fig. 6.11   Table design format in MS Access

a database structure, the designer decides on the name of the data fields, data types, such as text, memo, number, date, time, currency, auto-number, logical (yes/no), and hyperlinks, and defines field properties. Figure 6.11 shows the creation of a table in MS Access, where the table created (ACM), has a number of attributes. While structuring a database table, one has to

- relate each field directly to the subject of the table;
- include all the information required of the subject;
- ensure that the fields for information are broken into the smallest logical parts, for example, customer name can be stored in three parts—name, middle name, and surname; and
- ascertain that good structures do not store calculated data in a field within the same table.

CLIENT–SERVER AND DISTRIBUTED DATABASE

Database designing takes care of how data is distributed in a decentralized processing environment. The MIS may have a decentralized database with multiple processors in a client–server network. According to Jawadekar (2005), the system architecture from the 1960s to the 1980s was grossly inadequate, inefficient, and incapable of handling the latest business requirements. The technologies involved in computing, storing, programming, processing, communicating, and presenting the processed results were so advanced that one could build a new architecture called client–server. A client–server architecture is a distributed, cooperative, processing environment where the entire task of processing is divided in a manner such that there is a demand on the system through a client and there is a server in the system to serve the demand.

VLCC, the beauty and personal care products company, has multiple production units, salons, and distribution centres. How does the company manage its huge database? The company works on a client–server architecture and a distributed database concept. A database that is stored in more than one physical location is called a distributed database.

The client–server architecture has two components—client and server—in which the client makes a request to the server and the server then processes the request and serves the client by offering the result. The clients and servers are connected to each other through a network component, which handles communications between the two. In the client–server architecture, the application is split into two logical divisions—data and its processing logic. While the data resides on the back-end server, the application processing logic, such as validations, application of business rules, and computation, is placed in the client device. Sometimes, the application is put on an application server to gain more efficiency and throughput, as shown in Fig. 6.12.

Modern complex business information systems may have data present at more than one location. A database that is stored in more than one physical location is called a distributed database. This is in contrast with the client–server architecture, in which the database resides in the database server, while the application and processing are distributed between clients and application servers. In a distributed database, the database may be either partitioned or replicated. In the partition strategy, a part of the database is stored and maintained physically at different locations, so that each remote processor has the necessary data to serve its clients. Another strategy is to replicate (i.e., duplicate in its entirety) the central database at all remote locations. This is shown in Fig. 6.13.

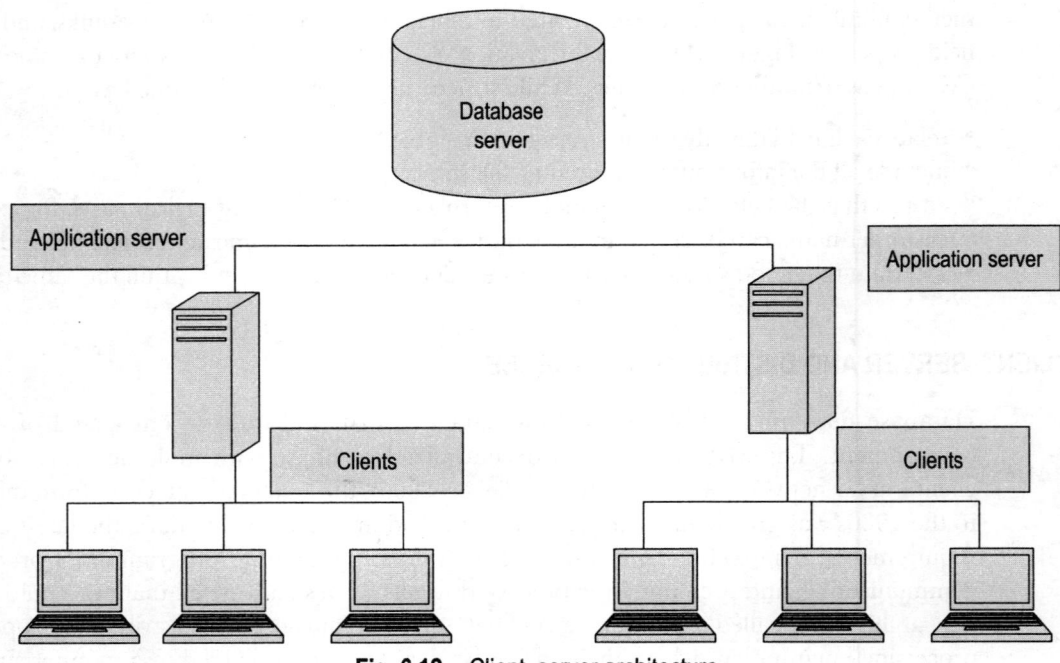

Fig. 6.12   Client–server architecture

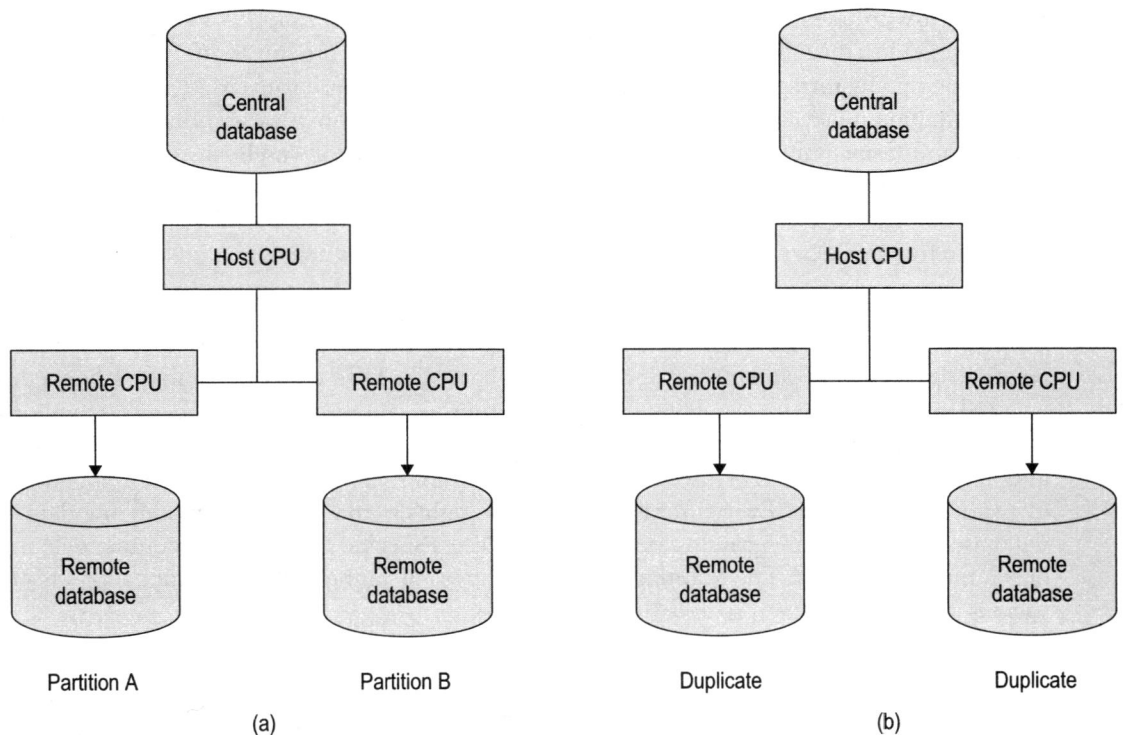

Fig. 6.13   Distributed databases (a) Central database partitioned (b) Central database replicated

Saurashtra Roadways (Bangalore) uses the partition strategy of distributed database systems. The transport company has around 60 booking and delivery offices, uses different databases in their regional and delivery branches, so that each branch can work independently. At the end of the day, the branch data is appended to the central database at their head office in Mumbai. This strategy has reduced the vulnerability of a single massive database at the central site and has reduced the usage of Internet broadband to a great extent. The broadband is used only when data is updated to the central server at the end of the day. The users also get faster database access.

According to Jaiswal and Mittal (2004), distributed databases are becoming an attractive alternative in today's computing environment. This is because the distributed nature of many businesses relies on information for its operation and thus, distributed databases are considered a valuable asset to their company. The parallel nature of distributed systems not only reduces processing costs, but also in some cases, may actually boost performance.

MANAGING DATABASES

Globally, data resourcing has become one of the most sought after assets for companies. Companies want to ensure that their data remains accurate, reliable, and readily available to users when needed. This requires special policies and procedures for data management. There are various safeguards that the management may take. These safeguards include proper information policies, database administration, data governance, data quality assurance, and database tuning.

Information policies   Information policies specify how an organization views its data resources. According to Laudon (2010), an information policy specifies the organization's rules for sharing, disseminating, acquiring, standardizing, classifying, and making an inventory of information. An information policy lays out specific procedures and accountabilities, identifying which users and organizational units can share information, where information can be distributed, and who is responsible for updating and maintaining the information. For example, organizations do not want employees to see sensitive data about other employees' salary or financial profit–loss figures. They can frame policies to restrict information-sharing on these issues.

Database administration   In large organizations, the person who implements an organization's information policies is called the database administrator. The DBA is responsible for the design, creation, maintenance, and monitoring of the database. The DBA creates a database schema that is stored in the data dictionary. They create an appropriate storage structure and access methods, that is, queries written to access data from the database. A corporate database is handled, used, and accessed by hundreds of users across the organization. The security of such a database is of prime consideration. Every user is not given the rights to manipulate or modify the data. A database is protected by granting permission to access specific tasks such as editing, deleting, or adding new records. The granting of different types of authorization for data access to the various users of the system is done by the DBA.

Data governance   IBM coined the phrase 'data governance'; it deals with the policies and processes for managing the availability, usability, integrity, and security of the data accumulated in an enterprise. Data governance lays special emphasis on promoting privacy, security, data quality, and compliance with government regulations.

Data quality assurance   An organization takes steps to ensure that the data is accurate and remains reliable. One of the tasks to ensure maintenance of data quality is to specify the integrity constraints. A database manager specifies integrity constraints in the database. Constraints are inbuilt checks in a database that prevent wrong data from being entered or modified in the database. If the database is properly designed and proper data standards are established, duplication or inconsistent data elements would be minimal. With proper integrity constraints in place, input errors are removed at the input stage.

For example, if a particular constraint is applied on the 'item name' data field that specifies 'not null', it will not accept any blank entry into the database. In other words, a record having no item name, cannot be entered by the user. Constraints are an integral part of RDBMS. As per the Gartner 2007 report, more than 25% of the critical data in large Fortune 1000 companies' databases are inaccurate or incomplete, including bad product codes, product names, faulty inventory descriptions, erroneous financial data, incorrect supplier information, or incorrect supplier data.

Database tuning   A database needs control and periodic maintenance. Periodical data tuning is a database maintenance process to re-index data and weed out unwanted or redundant data, to index files for fast access, etc. All these efforts improve data quality. Data quality audit may precede data tuning. This audit is a structured survey of the accuracy and level of completeness of the data. Data cleansing is carried out to detect and correct data that is incorrect, incomplete, improperly formatted, or redundant in a database. This process not only corrects errors but also enforces consistency among different sets of data.

LATEST TRENDS IN DATABASE MANAGEMENT

In Exhibit 6.3, we can see how databases and business decisions are cohesively related. Over a period of time, organizations accumulate large volumes and variety of data. As organizations grow from single-unit, single-location business firms to multi-unit, multi-product, multi-location, and transglobal behemoths, they create and consume large volumes of data. For their complex information needs, they not only process internal data, but also consider external data for decision support and strategic decision-making. The complex and competitive nature of present-day organizations has forced them to go beyond simple data analysis of such transactional data. Large organizations worldwide have graduated from simple transaction processing systems to special capability tools such as online transaction processing (OLTP), OLAP, data warehousing (DW), and data mining (DM), to name a few.

EXHIBIT 6.3

Using Databases to Improve Business Decision-making

The MIS is supported by databases in its endeavour to support the management in decision-making. All database models play the same role in the MIS; however, with the latest computer hardware and software capabilities, RDBMS have become popular. The concept of end-user computing is easily implemented with the database approach to an information system. Business decisions, information processes, and databases are cohesively interrelated. Some examples are given in the following table:

Business decisions	Information processes	Databases
What should be bought?	Sales transaction data analysis to find customers' tastes and preferences	Sales data with product and customer databases
How should it be bought?	Data collection on products, prices, and vendors; creation of quotations and contract signup	Supplier and quotation databases
How much should be bought?	Purchase forecasting, planning, and auto-purchase ordering systems	Sales and production databases, open-to-buy analysis
When should it be bought?	Purchase order generation based on requirement planning and replenishment	Purchase and stock databases
How many orders are pending?	Sales order processing, dispatch advice, invoicing	Customer orders and sales databases
Which salesmen should be awarded?	Lead generation and order closer systems	Lead, salesman, and order confirmation databases
What sales promotion activity should be decided?	Recording of leads and orders for various promotional activities	Lead and order confirmation databases
Which geographical area or customer is more profitable?	Sales processes, ordering systems, and logistic systems	Sales, customer, and logistic expenses databases

(Contd)

Exhibit 6.3 (Contd)

How much debt is outstanding?	Accounts receivable processes	Sales and receipts databases
How much profits have been made?	General ledger transaction processing	Sales, purchases, expenses, assets, and taxation databases
Are we over investing on inventory?	Inventory information processing	Inventory database
Are our employees satisfied? What is the employee attrition rate?	Human resource management system	Human resource database
How much do we spend on employee welfare?	Human resource information systems	Payroll and accounting database
What is the worth of assets owned by the organization?	Assets processing application	Assets database

Data Warehousing

Large organizations are plagued with the problem of ever increasing amounts of data that is indispensable. Data warehousing (DW) refers to a single, centralized, and unified repository of data that works across the enterprise. Such data is collected throughout the life of the organization, and is scattered and stored in large but incompatible data repositories.

According to Laudon (2010), a data warehouse is a database that stores current and historical data that is of potential interest to decision-makers throughout the company. The data originates in core operational transaction systems, such as sales, accounts, manufacturing, and payroll, and may include data from web transactions. As such, the data warehouse consolidates and standardizes information from different operational databases so that the information can be used across the enterprise for decision-making (as shown in Fig. 6.14).

For example, DCM Shriram Consolidated Ltd (DSCL, the erstwhile Delhi Cloth Mills) was earlier using legacy systems running on COBOL, FoxPro, or C applications for transaction processing systems. There was huge data available in spreadsheets such as Lotus 1-2-3, QuatroPro, and MS Excel. Later, DSCL implemented SAP R/3 across all its divisions. Besides the latest core transaction data in complex RDBMS, they own data in HTML websites and XML graphics databases. DSCL wants to retain that data and undertake its analysis for looking at their profitability trends, product life cycle, and other general trends in complex business environments. The solution for DSCL lies in data warehousing.

Data from diverse documents and sources is clubbed into one database. Later, it is standardized and normalized into one data model. Standardization involves complying with a single system of keeping data. For example, the date in old databases may be written as 'yy/mm/dd', 'mm/dd/yyyy', or 'ddmmyyyy'. Therefore, the task involved in standardization is the application of a single date type to all the data in the data warehouse. Normalization refers to the removal of all duplicate data, which has crept in because of a variety of data sources. The duplicate, redundant, and unwanted data is removed.

Finally, the data is consolidated and stored in a data warehouse and made available to different users across the organization. The subject-based or summarized data can also be moved into data

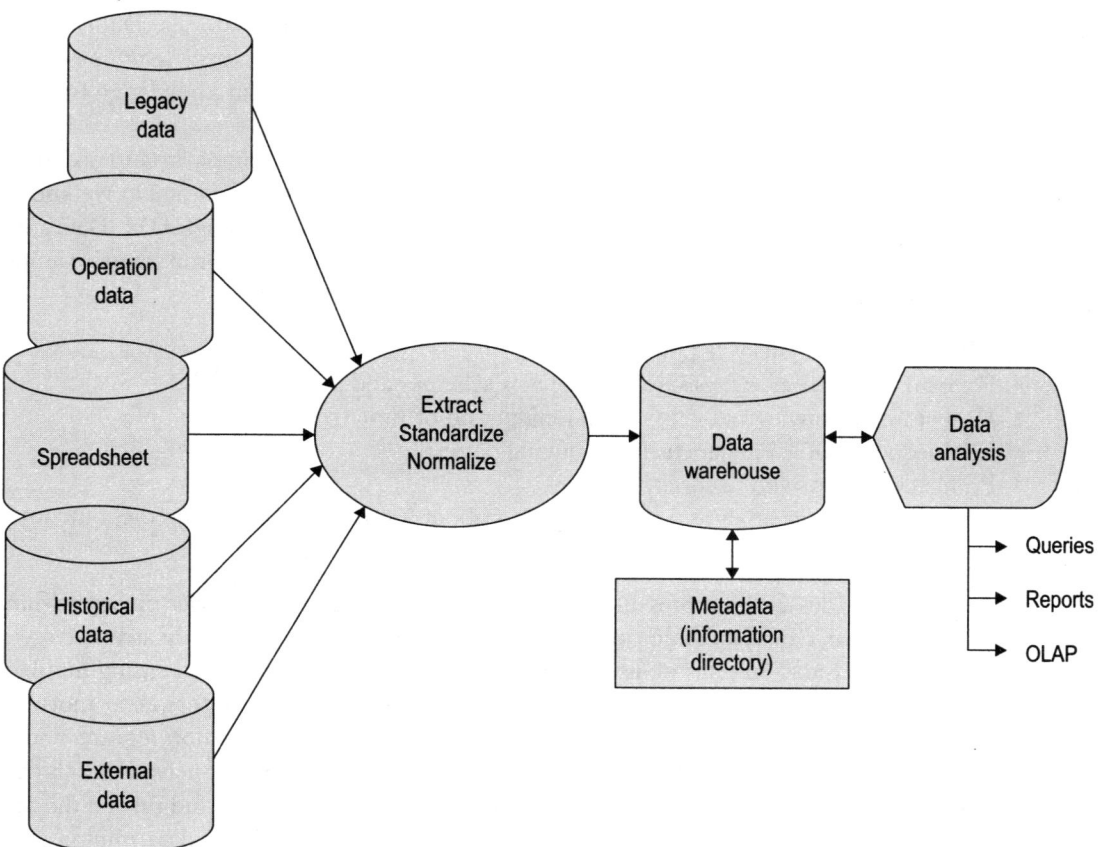

Fig. 6.14   Functioning of a data warehouse

marts. Data marts are subsets of a data warehouse, in which organizations move selective data for a particular user group. There can be different data marts for different types of data such as finance, marketing, sales, and accounting. For a data warehouse, metadata is maintained. Metadata refers to description about the data. It provides information about a certain item's content. For example, an image may include metadata that describes how large the picture is, its colour schemes, the image resolution, the date and time of creation of the image, etc. Similarly, a text document's metadata may contain information about its length, author, date of creation, and a short summary of the document.

Finally, data analysis tools, for example, data mining, web mining, OLAP, OLTP, etc., are provided for analytical reporting.

Data Mining

Data mining (DM) is the process of extracting data from data warehouses. Due to the very complex data structures in a data warehouse, there cannot be a single application or tool to extract the required data. DM involves a variety of data extraction processes. Most of the time, data extraction is performed by running ad hoc queries. According to Turban (2006), data mining is a term used to describe knowledge discovery in databases. Data mining is a process that uses statistical, mathematical, artificial intelligence, and machine-learning techniques to extract and identify useful information and subsequent knowledge from large databases'.

Answers to complex questions (e.g., how has product 101 fared in comparison to product 102 in the last four years and in particular in the northern and southern zones? Do we know the product's life cycle path during the last ten years?) are possible only through DM. Data mining processes help in the discovery of new knowledge, patterns, and strategies from massive amounts of data. Companies use data mining tools for the following processes:

- Discover product life cycle patterns
- Perform 'promotion-analysis' to identify new schemes and product bundling
- Find customer buying patterns over a long period of time
- Find sequence of events in customer buying patterns
- Profile customers with accuracy
- Conduct predictive analysis (i.e., assumptions about future conditions to predict outcomes of events)

For example, Idea Cellular presented an interesting story at a mobile service providers summit at Kuala Lumpur, Malaysia, The company was trying to understand why the average revenue per user (ARPU) and minutes of use (MOU) were declining despite an increasing number of subscribers. The company opined that a key predictive variable for a person to move away from the network was their time on the VLR (VLR stands for visitor location register, and time on VLR means how often the user has his SIM card connected to the GSM network). In layman's terms, it indicates how often a user has plugged his SIM into the phone and turned the phone on. This type of insight would not have been possible without rigorous data mining at Idea Cellular.

Web Mining

The web is a gigantic source of data, especially external data that businesses need for strategic planning and decision-making. We are aware of how frequently we go to search engines to search for information, be it business or educational. The collection and analysis of useful patterns and information from the world wide web (WWW) is called web mining. Web mining is the application of data mining techniques to discover patterns from the web. Modern businesses turn to web mining to understand customer behaviour, evaluate the effectiveness of their website, or quantify the success of a marketing campaign. A lot of research is being carried out using Google Trends and Google Insights to meet business and educational needs.

Web mining establishes patterns in data through exploration of contents, structure, and usages (as shown in Fig. 6.15). It is the process of extracting knowledge from the contents present on web pages, which may include text, images, audio, and video data.

This technology has many advantages, making it attractive to corporations, including government agencies. The process has enabled e-commerce, to carry out personalized marketing,

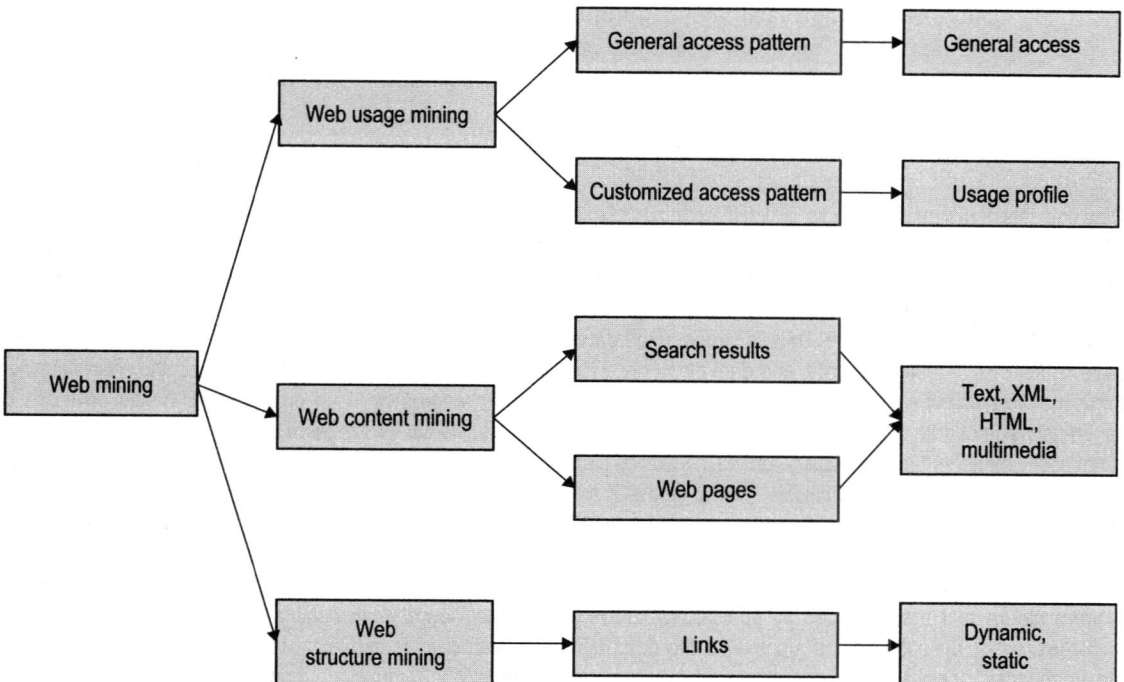

Fig. 6.15   Web mining exploration of usage, content, and structure

which eventually results in higher trade volumes. Government agencies are using this technology to classify threats and fight terrorism. Companies can establish better customer relationship by giving them exactly what they need. They can understand the needs of the customer better and can thus react to customer needs faster.

Online Analytical Processing

Online analytical processing (OLAP) is a multidimensional data analysis tool to process and filter out data from multiple databases. Multidimensional data analysis refers to viewing the same data in multiple ways. Most of the latest enterprise applications (e.g., ERP, SCM, and CRM) come with such analytical tools, which can act on the enterprise database and derive complex reports. These applications provide additional analysis (beyond the normal day-to-day descriptions) and present summarized reports for a business organization. OLAP enables users to obtain online answers to ad hoc queries in a fairly rapid amount of time, even when data is being updated in a large database.

OLAP tools are provided with the ability to present multidimensional reports. Each aspect of information such as product, model, brand, pricing, cost, region, and period, represents a different dimension.

For example, you may want a matrix report showing sales of product per retail store on one axis and sales figures for each brand on the other axis. This multidimensional report will be possible with the OLAP tool.

Thus, OLAP tools facilitate creation of data cubes that present a multidimensional view of data. The OLAP tools work on various advanced analytical models such as quantitative analysis, sensitivity analysis, what-if analysis, transport model analysis, and linear programming tools.

SUMMARY

Data consists of raw strings of facts, which if organized, make information. Data involves facts and figures about some object or event. Storage of the data in a structured manner so that it can be retrieved, processed, and presented to those who require it is called database. Data is stored in the database in the form of tables, records, and data elements. This forms the hierarchy of a data system in the database.

The storage of data in physical form, text, or spreadsheet is not easily manageable, is difficult to process, involves high costs of maintenance, and is inflexible. The database management approach consolidates records previously stored in separate files into a common pool of data elements that provide data for many applications. Large databases of a modern nature that are managed by specialized software packages, which consolidate and manipulate the data, and are independent of any application, are called database management systems (DBMS). DBMS provide us with tools to add, modify, delete, and retrieve data in the database.

The following are the three major functions of a DBMS:

- Creation of new databases and database applications
- Maintenance of the quality of the data
- Provide end-users with the information they need

These functions are carried out through inbuilt tools, such as tables, forms, queries, and reports, that are available in any DBMS.

DBMS can be grouped into three types. The most used and admired are relational database management systems (RDBMS). RDBMS provide a tool to establish the relationship between two or more data tables within the database. This DBMS is the most secured, and one can apply constraints and authorizations to prevent duplication of records and unauthorized entry into the database. Microsoft Access, MS SQL Server, Oracle, DB2, etc., are some of the widely used RDBMS. MySQL is a popular open-source relational DBMS. Besides the traditional structured data, the data is also present as HTML text, images, graphics, voice, etc., which may need storage and retrieval for various applications. These unstructured databases are handled using the latest breakthrough in database technology—object-oriented

DBMS (OODBMS). The third and the latest type of DBMS are multidimensional database structures, which are data cubes displaying information having more than one dimension.

Database designing involves data planning and database design activities. Data models that support business processes are used to develop databases that meet the information needs of the end-users in an organization. Based on these data views, we categorize them as conceptual, logical, and physical data models. The conceptual view indicates a relation between entities that is needed to support the basic business process. These data models then serve as logical frameworks called schemas and subschemas, on which the physical design of a database rests. The schema is an overall logical view of relationship among data elements. The logical views present the data that is seen by the user. The physical model is a framework of how the data is stored on a physical device in the database. The design process identifies relationship among data elements and the most efficient way of grouping data elements together to meet information systems requirements. The process of creating small, stable yet flexible, and adaptive data structures from complex groups of data is called normalization. The main attribute of RDBMS is their capability to establish a relationship with various tables and is known as an entity–relationship diagram.

An MIS may have a decentralized database with multiple processors in a client–server network. In client–server architecture, the data resides on back-end servers; the application processing logic, such as validations, application of business rules, and computation, is placed in the client device. A database that is stored in more than one physical location is called a distributed database. Managing data resources warrants proper information policy and procedures. These safeguards are proper information policies, database administration, data governance, data quality assurance, and database tuning.

The need to integrate and process large chunks of data gave birth to the concept of online analytical processing (OLAP), data warehousing (DW), and data mining (DM). The latest trend in database management is the consolidation of various internal and external data into one large repository. Creating of DW involves extracting data from various databases and diverse documents, standardizing the data by applying common rules, and normalizing data by removing duplicate records and tables. The consolidated data is then processed and reports generated using tools such as OLAP, query generators, and data mining. The collection and analysis of useful patterns and information from the world wide web is called web mining.

KEY TERMS

Data dictionary   A database that contains descriptions concerning the structure, data elements, interrelationships, and other characteristics of a database.

Data elements   A string of data under a data attribute/field.

Data mining   The practices of extracting and analysing data from a data warehouse to find hidden patterns and trends.

Data modelling   A process where the relationships between data elements are identified and defined to develop data models.

Data resource management   An activity that applies IT and management tools to manage an organization's data resources.

Data structures   The method of organizing records in a database.

Data warehouse   An integrated collection of data extracted from operational, historical, or external databases that are cleaned, transformed, and documented for retrieval and analysis.

Database administration   An IT function that includes responsibility for developing and maintaining the organization's database and data dictionary.

Database maintenance   The activity of addition, modification, and upkeep of records in a database.

Database management approach   A way of storing and processing data in which independent files are consolidated into a common database of records available to various users.

Distributed database   A database that is stored in more than one physical location.

Entity–relationship (E–R) diagrams   Diagrams that describe the relationship between the entities in a database.

File processing systems   These organize data into specialized files of data records that are designed for processing by only specific application programs, in contrast to DBMS.

Hypermedia database   A database that can contain multiple forms of media, including text, graphics, video, and sound.

Metadata   Description about some data, document, or object by providing additions information about a certain item's content.

Online analytical processing   Capability of an MIS that allows interactive examination and manipulation of large amount of data.

Online transaction processing   A transaction processing system that allows real-time processing of data.

Primary key   A key field that is a unique identifier for all the information in any row of the table and cannot be duplicated.

Query language   Program instructions to retrieve data in the desired quantity and quality.

Relational database management systems   A relationship calculus that establishes the relationship between one table in a database and the other tables.

Web mining   Collection and analysis of useful patterns and information from the world wide web.

CONCEPT REVIEW QUESTIONS

1. Define the concept of a database and explain the basic characteristics of a database with examples.
2. What are the disadvantages of a file processing system? What is the alternative to the file approach?
3. What is the database approach? Enumerate its advantages.
4. What do you understand by database management systems? How do DBMS work in a business organization?
5. What are the different types of databases? Explain object-oriented databases.
6. Differentiate between DBMS and RDBMS. Why has RDBMS gained popularity with database managers?
7. What are the steps involved in designing a database? Explain relation identity and normalization with examples.
8. Are databases in a client–server architecture and distributed databases one and the same? If not, what is the basic difference?
9. Management of databases is much more than what a DBA does. Explain.
10. What do you understand by OLAP?
11. Explain data warehousing and differentiate between data warehousing and data mining.

CRITICAL THINKING QUESTIONS

1. Why is the object-oriented database model gaining acceptance for developing applications and managing hypermedia databases on business websites?
2. 'Data resources are as important as any other business asset.' Critically examine this statement and give examples to substantiate your point of view.
3. How have the Internet, intranet, and extranets affected the types and uses of data resources available to business managers? What are the other trends affecting data resource management?

MIS DEVELOPMENT

Well Protecto Security Inc., is a Mumbai-based firm that is into manpower consultancy and security systems. The company has a personnel base of 300 security guards who are deployed for VIP security on a regular basis and for seminars, exhibitions, and film shootings on a daily basis. The company generates revenue by deployment of security guards on a man-month and man-day basis. Besides this, the firm sells security equipment such as metal detectors and CCTVs. The security guards are on the company's permanent payroll, and are given salary and allowances as per company rules. The firm manages its payroll on a spreadsheet. Due to the presence of a large workforce and compliance to regulatory requirements of provident fund, employee state insurance, etc., the firm wants a proper database management for this purpose. The company approaches you to design a database for this purpose. The following information was given to you as the project specifications and usage requirements:

- The employee information sheet has name, father's name, date of birth, date of joining, sex, permanent address, local address, experience in terms of the number of completed years as on joining date, marital status, spouse's name, number of dependent members in the family, bank account number, bank name, provident fund account number, ESI number, introducer's/guarantor's name, guarantor's address, employee e-mail ID, job status, and grade.
- The components of the payroll include allowances and deductions. Besides basic pay, it has house rent allowance, dearness allowance, city allowance, conveyance allowance, medical allowance, and dress allowance. The deduction heads are provident fund, ESI, income tax, and welfare fund.
- There are three job states—temporary, permanent, and retired. The four grades for the security guards are probationer, executive, supervisor, and managerial.
- The business process rules have been defined in Table 6.8.
- The medical and dress allowances are respectively fixed as ₹1200 and ₹500 per month, for all categories of employees.

Table 6.8   Business process rules for salary calculation

Emp. grade	Basic	HRA	DA	City	Conveyance
Probationer	3000	40% of Basic	20% of Basic	10% of Basic	22% of Basic
Executive	5000	40% of Basic	20% of Basic	20% of Basic	22% of Basic
Supervisor	7000	50% of Basic	20% of Basic	25% of Basic	25% of Basic
Manager	9000	50% of Basic	25% of Basic	25% of Basic	30% of Basic

- The provident fund is deducted as 12% of basic, ESI is deducted as 2% of basic, and welfare fund contribution is ₹100 per month.
- Income tax is deducted as per income tax rules. Presently, at the given salary, only managers qualify for deductions. Hence, the management wants to deduct only ₹1500 per month on an ad hoc basis.

Exercise

1. Use Microsoft Access to design database tables for the aforementioned payroll database.
2. Use employee code, category number, and grade

number as unique keys for database tables.

3. Carry out normalization up to the third normal form for tables so that no table has any anomaly.

4. Enter some imaginary data in the database and create two reports: (a) Salary sheet for January (b) Salary slip for Glad Stone

REFERENCES

Gartner Inc., *Dirty Data is a Business Problem, Not an IT problem*, Sydney, 2007.

Gorden, Davis and Margethe Olson, *Management Information Systems*, The McGraw-Hill Book Company, Singapore, 1996.

Goyal, D. P., *Management Information Systems—Managerial Perspectives*, Macmillan India Ltd, Delhi, 2006.

Hay, David C., *Requirement Analysis: From Business View to Analysis*, Prentice Hall, New York, 2003.

Jaiswal, Mahadeo and Monika Mittal, *Management Information Systems*, Oxford University Press, New Delhi, 2004.

Jawadekar, Waman S., *Management Information Systems*, Tata McGraw-Hill, New Delhi, 2008.

Laudon, Ken, Jane Laudon, and Rajanish Dass, *Management Information System*, Pearson, Singapore, 2010.

O'Brien, James A., George M. Marakas, and Ramesh Behl, *Management Information Systems*, Tata McGraw-Hill, New Delhi, 2007.

Turban, Efraim, Jay Aronson, and Ting-Peng Liang, *Decision Support Systems and Intelligent Systems*, Pearson, Singapore, 2005.

http://www.sonamine.com/home/index.php?option=com_wordpress&p=315&Itemid=70, *Social Network Model Versus Data Mining Model*, last accessed on 2 October 2011.

CASE STUDY

Pantaloon: Fortifying Databases with SAP ERP

More than eight years after it forayed into the retail business, Pantaloon Retail decided to implement SAP to keep itself competitive in the rapidly growing Indian retail market.

Company

Pantaloon Retail India Limited (PRIL) is the flagship enterprise of the Future Group, with a presence across multiple lines of business. The company owns and manages multiple retail formats that cater to a wide cross-section of Indian society. Headquartered in Mumbai, the company operates through 16 million square feet of retail space, has over 1000 stores across 73 cities in India, and employs over 30,000 people. The company registered a turnover of ₹4097 crore for the financial year ending June 2011.

Pantaloon Retail forayed into retail in 1997 with the launching of its fashion retail chain, Pantaloons in Kolkata. In 2001, it launched Big Bazaar, a hypermarket chain. This was followed by Food Bazaar, a food and grocery chain. Next up was Central, a first of its kind located in the heart of major Indian cities. Some of its other businesses include Collection-i (home improvement products), E-Zone (consumer electronics), Depot (books, music, gifts and stationary), aLL (a little larger, fashion apparel for plus-sized individuals), Shoe Factory (footwear), and Blue Sky (fashion accessories). The group's subsidiary companies include Home Solutions Retail India Ltd, Pantaloon Industries Ltd, Galaxy Entertainment, and Indus League Clothing. The group also has joint ventures with a number of partners including French retailer Etam group, Lee Cooper, Manipal Healthcare, Talwalkar's, Gini & Jony, and Liberty Shoes. Planet Retail, a group company, owns the franchisee of international brands such as Marks & Spencer, Debenhams, Next, and Guess in India. As on March 2011, the company was operating 148 Big Bazaar stores, 169 Food Bazaar stores, among other formats, in over 70 cities across the country. As a focussed entity driving the growth of the group's value retail business, Pantaloon Retail aims to continue delivering more value to its customers, supply partners, stakeholders, and communities across the country and shape the growth of modern retail in India.

The group's speciality retail formats include supermarket chain—Food Bazaar, sportswear retailer—Planet Sports, electronics retailer—eZone, home improvement chain—Home Town, and rural retail chain—Aadhaar, among others. It also operates the popular shopping portal, www.futurebazaar.com.

Problems

Store operations have never been as important to retailers as they are now. Customer data acquisition and insight into customer databases are what retail businesses are all about. Successful retailers are those who know that the battle for customers is only won at the frontline, which, in the case of a retail chain, is at its stores. Pantaloon was regularly opening stores in the metros and there was an urgent need for a reliable enterprise-wide application to help run its businesses effectively. The basic need was to have a robust transaction management system and an enterprise-wide platform to run the operations. As it owned a plethora of retail divisions, brands, and outlets, data management was really an issue. The company was looking for a solution that would bring all of its businesses and processes together on a unified database management. After a comprehensive evaluation of different options and software companies, the management at Pantaloon decided to go in for SAP.

Solution

Pantaloon banked on some qualities of SAP retail solutions that supports product development, which includes ideation, trend analysis, and collaboration with partners in the supply chain; sourcing and procurement, which involves working with manufacturers to fulfil orders according to strategic merchandising plans and optimize cost, quality, and speed variables that must be weighted differently as business needs, buying plans, and market demand patterns change; managing the supply chain, which involves handling the logistics of moving finished goods from the source to stores and overseeing global trade and procurement requirements; selling goods across a variety of channels to customers, which requires marketing and brand management; managing mark-downs and capturing customer reactions, analysing data, and using it to optimize the next phase of the design process.

The SAP solutions and services implemented included SAP® General Ledger application and SAP General Ledger Migration service for subsequent implementation of document splitting tools. The implementation was outsourced to a third party. It was done by the SAP Consulting team with help from Novasoft, which is based out of Singapore. Pantaloon also provided some assistance to the project. About 24 qualified people worked on the SAP implementation. This project was headed by Pantaloon's chief information technology officer. SAP was chosen as the outsourcing party on a turnkey basis.

Three Phases

The SAP implementation was not a single-phase process. The project was divided into three phases.

The first phase involved blueprinting existing processes and mapping them to the desired state. In this phase, the entire project team worked on the current processes within the structure of the organization, and analysed and drafted them. This blueprint was later used in the formation of new states of the solution. As SAP would combine all the processes, every one of these had to be evaluated.

In the second phase, the SAP platform was developed with the help of Novasoft's template, which was predefined by SAP after evaluation of Pantaloon's needs and expertise in retail solutions. The last phase of this project was for stores to switch over to the new system and for current data to be ported. Before the SAP implementation, all the data was unorganized. This data had to be migrated to the new SAP application.

Key Challenges

The key challenges in this project were not in the implementation. Rather, difficulties were faced during data migration and in managing the interim period when the project was underway for about six months. Migrating unorganized data to an organized format is a challenging task. The key challenges were to

- improve financial tracking and reporting for all retail locations and business levels;
- enhance decision-making by providing more granular, real-time information;
- support financial accounting needs of a rapidly expanding retail business; and
- expedite the reconciliation and closing processes.

Benefits

Pantaloon has not been able to see the immediate benefits of this implementation. This application certainly has long-term benefits, which will be seen when the performance of various aspects is analysed. It was too early to calculate the return on investment. They have already started working on merchandise assortment planning, auto-replenishment, and purchase orders. The following key benefits were achieved:

- Total cost of ownership significantly reduced infrastructure and processing costs
- Reduced database growth by around 500 GB per year via document summarization at profit-centre level
- Completed project on time, in just six months
- Financial and strategic benefits—greater business insights through more accurate and timely financial information
- Lower costs via convergence of financial accounting and controlling
- Enhanced data quality
- Easier compliance with regulatory requirements via the SAP parallel accounting feature
- Operational benefits—greater visibility of AR and AP throughout profit centres

- Increased business transparency via drilldown reporting capabilities
- Real-time, continuous reconciliation of cost elements and expense accounts, freeing up personnel for more value-added activities
- Ability to close books 15% to 20% faster and 5% to 10% reduction in accounts receivables

Maintenance and Hardware

This application is currently being used by around 1200 employees across the organization. For maintaining this implementation and its related applications, Pantaloon has an in-house team and has outsourced ABAP resources. They are also in the process of setting up a SAP Competency Centre. The system runs on a HP Superdome server on HP UNIX 11i and the database is Oracle. The cost of this project was about $10 million.

Discussion Questions

1. What were the basic problems faced by Pantaloon? Analyse and state if these problems were because of database issues.
2. What kind of database and database servers does Pantaloon use?
3. Why is database technology so important for a business like Pantaloon Retail?
4. How does Pantaloon currently benefit from the SAP implementation in terms of data warehousing?

Sources:
'SAP business transformation study', www.sap.com/india/solutions, last accessed on 9 October, 2011.
Shah, Kushal, 'Pantaloons fortifies its armour with SAP', *Network Magazine*, March 2007.
http://www.pantaloonretail.in, last accessed on 11 October 2011.

Networks and Telecommunications

As the possibilities in such low-cost technology began to explode, firms across retail, banking and communications found that information technology (IT) could well be their missing link in connecting with people who were often illiterate and located in distant villages, dirt-road miles away from the nearest market. And reform-minded bureaucrats found that such technology, untouched as it was by the legacies of the sarkar raj, could be a powerful leverage for better public service. IT could play a bigger and more powerful role in the economy than anyone had guessed or attempted before. At the same time networks transmitting this information have become intricately intertwined and ubiquitous, especially with the rise of fibre optic and broadband technology. Communication is becoming wireless, lighter than air, with cellular telephony and an alphabet soup of technologies such as Wi-Fi and WiMax.

—Nandan Nilekani

LEARNING OBJECTIVES

After studying this chapter, you will be able to

- understand the trends in telecommunication and networking technologies
- define computer networks
- differentiate various types of networks
- understand network and communication protocols
- know about the various communication media
- understand wireless technology used to connect networks
- gather knowledge about basic networking devices
- appreciate the Internet revolution, its architecture, and services
- learn about radio frequency identification (RFID) technology and its functions
- understand the business applications of RFID

EXHIBIT 7.1

Indian Railways: Connecting with Passengers in a Wireless Way

Indian Railways, in its pursuit to serve its clients better, has realized the importance of connecting with them. The profit-making government enterprise is facing tough competition from air travel in the premium category of first and second classes air-conditioned traveller segment.

Rail travellers can now get e-tickets on their cell phones and would not have to carry printouts of tickets. Called m-ticket, it can be booked by passengers having Internet facility by downloading the mobile ticketing application on their cell phones from the Railways' new web portal. A passenger can book train tickets through a mobile phone and carry the display ticket sent to their cell phone through a short message service (SMS). Indian Railways' web portal, www.indianrailways.gov.in, provides a plethora of services to its clients. The new facility is part of those services. The m-ticket service was launched in July 2011, by Mamta Banerjee, former Union Railway Minister and the Chief Minister of West Bengal.

The portal aims at consolidating all the services and information into a single window web-interface for the public. On completion of booking and payment formalities, an SMS containing the ticket details will be sent to the user, which is referred to as mobile reservation message (MRM). The cost of the MRM will be borne by the Indian Railways. The facility of booking e-tickets through the web portal will be available from 12.30 a.m. to 11.30 p.m. on all days. In addition to the facility of e-ticketing provided by the new portal, no travel agents have been allowed so that passengers can have ease of booking during peak hours, that is, morning 8.00 a.m. to 10.00 a.m.

Sources:
'Now get railway e-ticket on your cell phone', *The Times of India*, 9 July 2011.
www.indianrail.gov.in, last accessed on 15 October 2011.

Exhibit 7.1 on Indian Railways' initiatives to connect with their customers provides an insight into how businesses, in order to create long-term sustainability and strategic advantage, need to adopt the latest technologies. With the introduction of computerized reservation systems in the late 1980s, the web-based online reservation, train enquiry, and e-tickets on mobile phones, the Indian Railways has understood the need for customer service through IT and unified communication technology. Using information and communication technology (ICT) for public benefit has definitely boosted the image of the government behemoth, which is considered to be the biggest employment generator in the country.

Thus, the study of information systems is incomplete without understanding networks supported by telecommunications, as virtually, every computer is a part of a network and each network is a part of other greater networks. As future business managers, we need to understand networks and communication technology to help us make the right decisions.

TRENDS IN TELECOMMUNICATION TECHNOLOGIES

Computers were invented to help scientists and mathematicians perform complex and time-consuming calculations. They were not originally meant for what they perform today. They were designed for carrying out large and complex calculations, but today their role transcends computation. They have evolved from mere computing devices to playing a key technological role in telecommunication services. The coming together of computing and communication technologies is called convergence of ICT. The integration of these two industries brought about a major revolution in our lifestyles. For instance, communication with the help of computers has brought about a major change in mobile communication. Further, the use of computers in the field of satellite image processing, travel and aviation, healthcare, etc., has transformed the life of the common man.

As Messerschmitt (1999) rightly summarizes, 'when computers are networked, two industries—computing and communication—converge, and the result is vastly more than the sum of the parts. Suddenly, computing applications became available to business-to-business coordination and commerce, for small and large organizations. The Internet creates a public place without geographic boundaries, cyberspace, where ordinary citizens can interact, publish their ideas, and engage in the purchase of goods and services. In short, the impact of both computing and communication on our society and organizational structures is greatly magnified.'

The changing trends in telecommunication industries, technologies, and applications significantly increase the decision alternatives for business managers.

Industry Trends

Globally, the telecommunication industry has changed from being government-regulated monopolies to a free market with increasingly competitive suppliers of services. Until recently, the telecom sector in India was owned and regulated by the government. With the introduction of the free market economy in 1990s, the industry saw the birth of new telecom giants. These companies provided not only telephone services, but also cellular phone service, cable TV, mobile radio, and Internet access.

As a result of innovations in IT and unrestricted connectivity through the Internet, telephone and computer networks have converged into a single digital network. Telecom providers such as Airtel, Tata, and Reliance offer data transmission, Internet access, wireless telephone services, dish television, as well as voice services. Table 7.1 illustrates telecom companies who provided multiple services in the post-liberalization era.

Technology Trends

Technology is changing at a fast pace. According to Laudon (2010), both voice and data communication networks have become more powerful (faster), more portable (smaller and mobile), and less expensive. The normal Internet speed offered has increased from 28 kbps to 3.1 Mbps for personal users. Various technological breakthroughs have pushed organizations towards building client–server networks based on open system architecture. The open systems use common standards for hardware, software, applications, and networking so that products and services from

Table 7.1   Examples of Indian telecom companies providing a spectrum of services

Company	Landline telephone	Internet services	Cable TV	Radio
Bharti Airtel	Airtel fixed line	Airtel broadband	Airtel digital TV	–
Tata Teleservices	Tata Walky	Tata photon/broadband	Tata Sky	–
Idea Cellular (part of Aditya Birla Group)	–	Idea netsetter	–	–
Sistema Shyam Telecom	–	MBlaze broadband	MTS TV (mobile)	–
Reliance Communications	Reliance WLL	Reliance broadnet/ netconnect	Reliance digital TV	92.7 FM
Vodafone Essar	–	Vodafone broadband	–	–

various vendors are compatible. These systems provide greater connectivity and interoperability, which means easy to communicate and share information even in the diverse nature of computer hardware, software, and databases. The telecommunication system is changing from wire-based to wireless technology. Satellite transmission facilitates smooth and unhindered transmission of huge quantity of data, audio, and video over global networks.

Hence, the telecommunication networks are rapidly converting to digital transmission which facilitates higher transmission speeds, larger information throughput, much lower error rates, and greater economy in the form of cheaper services globally.

Business Application Trends

The advancements and trends in telecommunications technology are changing the way telecom is being used in businesses. According to O'Brien (2007), the trend towards introducing more vendors, services, Internet technologies, and open systems, and the rapid growth of the Internet, the world wide web, and corporate intranets and extranets dramatically increase the number of feasible telecommunications applications.

BUSINESS VALUE OF TELECOMMUNICATION NETWORKS

What are the benefits that a business can achieve by investing in telecommunication networks? Business houses can gain several benefits by using the Internet, intranet, and other forms of telecommunications as networks can help reduce costs, shorten communication time, facilitate sharing of documents, encourage collaboration among employees and offices, and help develop new business formats including new products and services.

Telecommunications and networks are vital to the majority of businesses today, as they serve as the foundation for electronic commerce and the digital economy. Organizations can connect to their suppliers and customers, which reduces lead time and increases partners' satisfaction. For example, Walmart is networked with its suppliers. As an item is sold at the retail outlets, a message is automatically sent to the supplier of the item. It prompts the supplier to despatch the product to the retail giant. Therefore, the retailer saves time on sending purchase orders and minimizes the risk of delayed supplies.

Networks facilitate employees' workgroups tasks and collaboration. The same file or system can be shared by many employees working at multiple locations. For example, Pidilite Industries has connected its sales force by the Internet and extranet. The sales order is created by a sales executive and viewed and authorized by the sales manager working at a different location. Thus, they are able to transmit the sales orders to the warehouse for despatch of goods.

Inter-office communication has been greatly supported by telecommunications. Concepts such as teleconferencing, web meetings, webinars (like seminars) induce reductions in travelling costs, as they allow customers, suppliers, and employees to participate in meetings and collaborate on joint projects.

COMPUTER NETWORKS

Computers are interconnected to share resources such as data, files, information, and equipment (printers and scanners). They can be connected through cables and other wireless communication media for transmission of data, graphics, images, etc. Fundamentally, a network of computers consists of the following components:

- One or more host or server computers which store and process information, and provide network resources such as network operating system (NOS) and other communication software.
- The client computers, which are connected to the server or host computer. They use network resources but do not provide them (network resources).
- Communication lines through which data and voice are transmitted between the connected computers. These lines can be telephone lines, twisted pair, coaxial cables, wireless radio signals, or wireless local area networks.
- Peripheral equipment to facilitate communication, devices such as modems, switches, multiplexers, and controllers.
- Communication software and NOS, which control the various input-output processes such as Windows Server, Linux, and Novel Netware.

Figure 7.1 further illustrates computer network systems using these components.

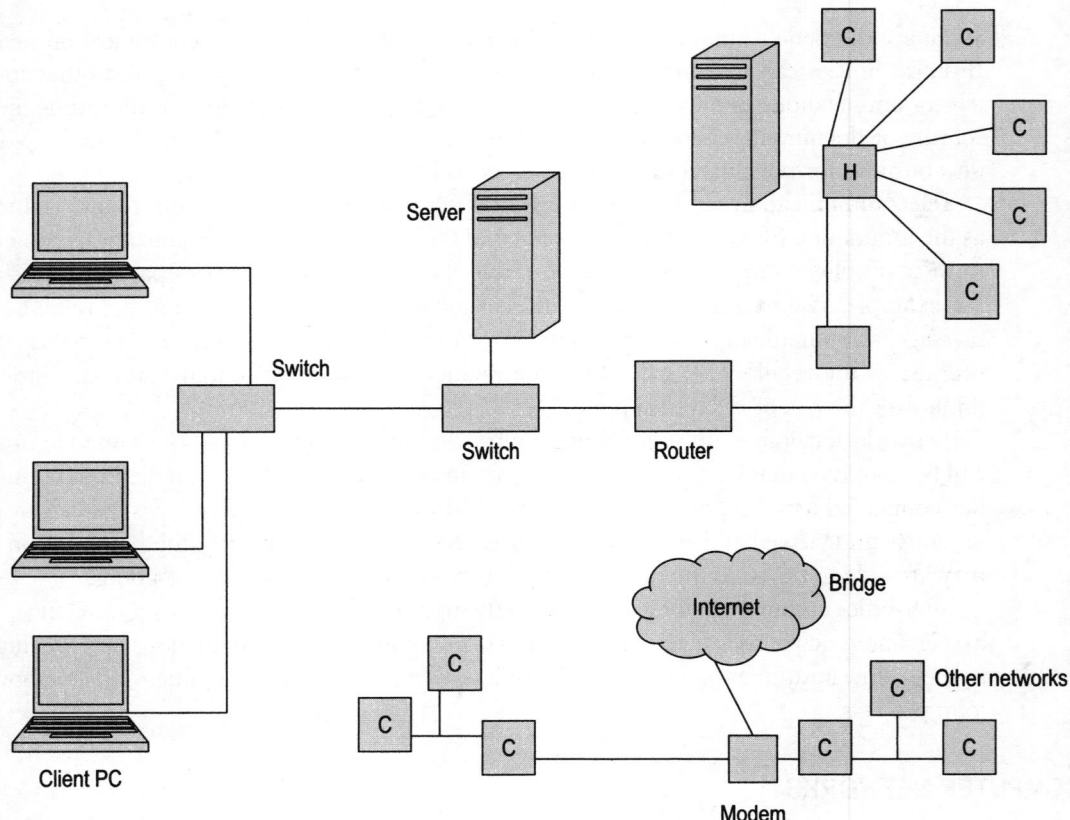

Fig. 7.1　Components of a basic computer network

Types of Networks

Networks can be best classified on the basis of their geographical reach. The geographical reach refers to the distance between various computer resources, connectivity, and the medium of communication they use.

Local Area Networks

Local area network (LAN) refers to networking among computers located within a limited distance, usually one floor or nearby floors in the same building. LAN connects PCs to share printers, data, and applications on a high bandwidth line. LAN capabilities are defined and managed by NOS, which route and manage the communications on the network. Windows NT, Windows 2003 Server, Windows XP, Novell Netware, Linux, and OS2 Warp Servers are examples of NOS. LANs are distinguished from other networks based on their size and their transmission technology. They usually consist of systems that occupy one room, building, or two adjacent buildings within a campus. They run on twisted pair or coaxial cables, operating at 10 to 100 Mbps speed.

Wide Area Networks

Wide area networks (WANs) are spread over broad geographical areas, that is, city, country, or continental level. They help in long-distance transmission of data, voice, image, and video. While LANs use their own resources, WANs connect many LANs and use private and public resources. The major distinction of WANs is that they work over multiple communication channels such as switched and dedicated lines, and microwave and satellite communications. Switched lines are telephone lines that a person can access from his/her PC to transmit data to another PC. Dedicated lines, also called leased lines, are continuously available for transmission. Figure 7.2 illustrates how a WAN connects different LANs.

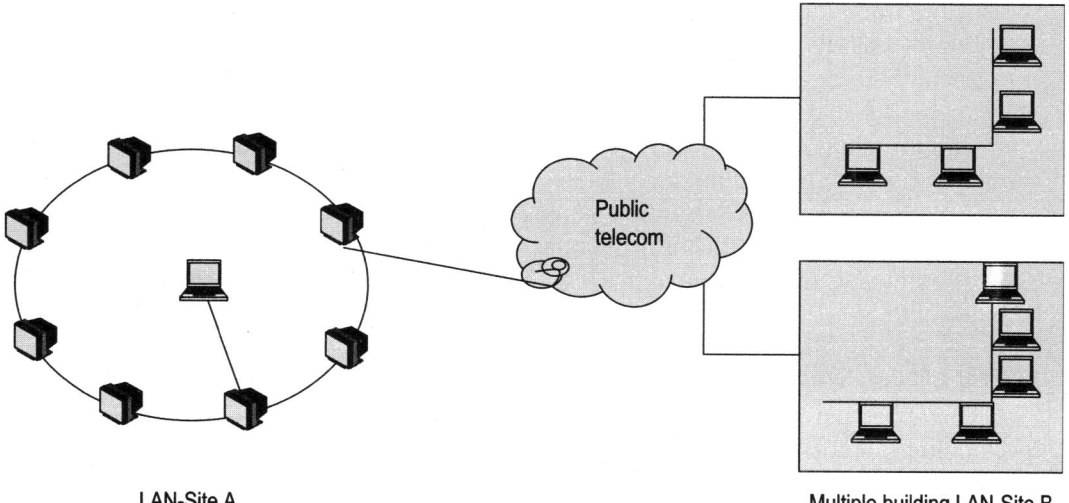

LAN-Site A   Multiple building LAN-Site B

Fig. 7.2   A typical WAN connecting various LANs

The latest revolution in telecommunication transcends all hindrances and provides a service called asynchronous transfer mode (ATM) which seamlessly and dynamically integrates voice, data, images, and video for transmission across the globe. ATM can transmit up to 2.5 GB of data per second. The latest development on high capacity service is the digital subscriber line (DSL), which operates over existing copper telephone lines to carry voice, data, and video. These high-speed transmission technologies are called broadband.

Most companies having operations in multiple cities and countries possess their own WAN. Companies such as Jindal Steels and Hero Group have connected their offices in all the metros through WAN using almost all the communication channels such as fibre optic and radio frequency for the last mile operation. The 'last mile' or 'last kilometre' is the final leg of delivering connectivity from a telecommunications provider to a customer. This phrase is therefore often used by the telecommunications industries. Last mile in telecommunication refers to connecting the customer's office with the telecom provider's infrastructure, which is usually not connected with cables.

Client–Server Networks

We discussed client–server computing in Chapter 6 from the point of view of database management. Client–server computing is a distributed computing architecture where some of the processing power is vested with the client computer. Client–server networks involve a server (usually a high-end computer) and clients (other computers connected with the server). Clients are also called workstations or nodes. The server is the centralized machine which stores and shares the network resources with the clients. Servers run on various NOS such as Unix, Linux, Windows 2000, Windows-XP, and Novell Netware.

Processing based on client–server architecture is called distributed processing. Distributed processing is the use of multiple computers linked by communications networks. This is in contrast with centralized processing in which processing is done by one large central computer, usually a mini or a mainframe. Client–server computing splits the workload between the client and the server. Both are located on the networks and the tasks that are best suited are assigned to them. Servers are usually dedicated server computers that store and process data and also perform back-end functions not visible to users, such as managing network and sharing resources. Clients are normal desktops and laptops and normally process the client portion, that is, the user interface of the applications.

According to Jaiswal (2004), the advantages of client–server networks are: centralized security for network resources, scalability (i.e., the network can be expanded more easily), centralized network management, resource sharing, user management, and more efficient use of network bandwidth.

Peer-to-peer Networks

Peer-to-peer networks involve two or more computers that are connected through some communication channel. In this type of network, each computer is a host as well as a client. These types of networks are established for simple files and printer sharing and usually in a small network set-up. It supports less than 10 computers. The main advantage of such networks is that they are easy to set up and are cost effective, as no additional resources such as hardware or software are required. However, the biggest disadvantage is that networks based on peer-to-peer architecture are not secured.

Virtual Private Networks

Virtual private networks (VPNs) are close private networks owned and managed by a single organization that uses public Internet backbone as the communication infrastructure. They are secured by network firewalls, encryption, and other security features.

In order to understand VPNs, let us first understand private networks and hybrid networks. Private networks connect two sites on a LAN cable or, if the sites are at a distance, on WAN connectivity, using dedicated lease telecom lines. These types of networks are highly secured, but expensive. Hybrid networks use private Internet as well as public Internet for connecting their sites. The internal communication happens through the leased lines, but all external communications are conducted through the Internet. In other words, the sites which are not of critical nature are connected using the public Internet backbone. These networks, when established over high-speed dedicated/leased lines, are known as 'intranet'.

Exhibit 7.2 discusses how Filatex benefited by using VPN over public Internet, secured by a firewall. They could run their enterprise applications on these networks while sharing data and information, with a very high speed through a secured network using high bandwidth communication lines. Figure 7.3 shows a VPN.

Intranets and Extranets

Intranets are private or internal networks owned by organizations that provide access to data and facilitate information sharing across their various offices. Intranets are created using the Internet as a backbone or over other private and public communication channels. These networks are

---

EXHIBIT 7.2

Filatex India: Leveraging Benefits with VPN

New Delhi-based Filatex India Ltd (FIL), a company involved in manufacturing various types of man-made synthetic fibres, learnt the benefits and incorporated VPN quite early. The company was incorporated in 1990. It is considered to be a pioneer in the manufacture of mono filament yarn and special polyester filament yarns like micro denier polyester filament yarn in the Indian market.

The company has two manufacturing units, one each in Noida and Silvassa. Besides its head office in New Delhi, the company has marketing offices in Mumbai and Surat.

In 2006, the company switched over to Ramco Marshall, an enterprise solution, from a legacy system which was in place for decades. The company planned to run the application in all manufacturing units, sales offices, and the corporate office and leverage the full potential of an ERP. Achieving this goal required a major reorganization and standardization of business practices and a new network infrastructure.

This new infrastructure had two critical requirements—high bandwidth and the ability to deliver applications over that bandwidth. As a normal Internet-shared broadband was ruled out due to security and efficiency reasons, setting-up of VPNs was agreed upon by the management and the experts. Filatex used Internet links that provided flexible many-to-many connections on a 64 kbps line. The network was secured by firewalls at the desired point of connection with the Internet. Establishing the VPN not only enabled Filatex to use the enterprise application in all its branches, units, and divisions, but also reduced communication costs across the enterprise. Thus, VPN provides secured private network of computers across the offices of Filatex India Ltd.

(Based on author's interactions.)

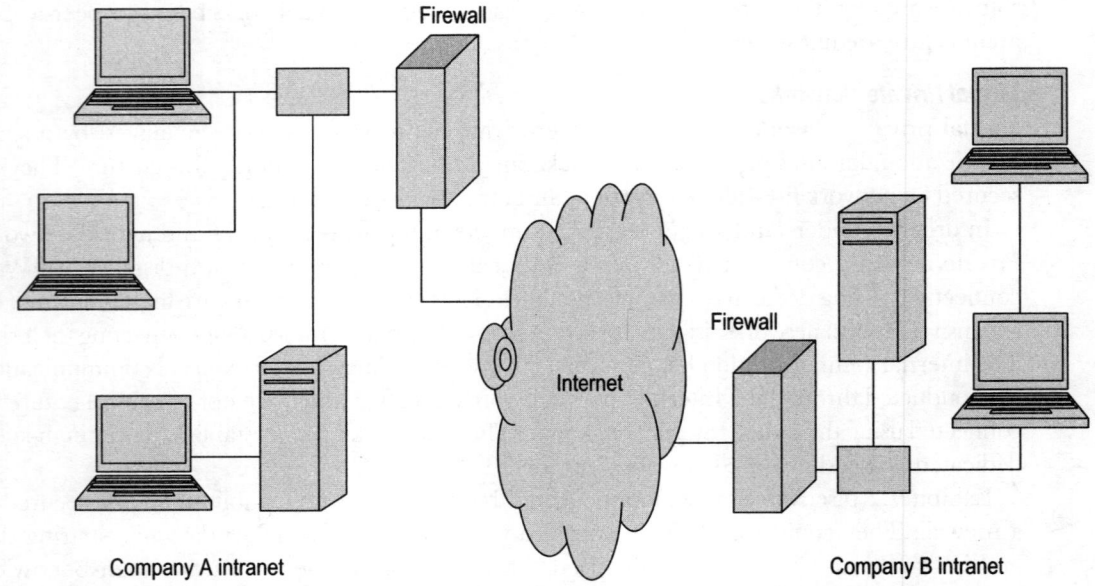

Fig. 7.3　Network diagram showing VPNs protected by firewalls

secured with firewalls to prevent unwanted elements from gaining unauthorized access to an organization's private networks. The firewall consists of specialized hardware and software placed between the organization's network and the external network. The hardware firewall is a device with RAM, processor, and ethernet ports and is placed between the organization's server and external network connected through the Internet. The software is installed in the user's computer to prevent access to unwanted programs such as Trojans and spam mails. The software can also be configured to prohibit users from accessing certain websites.

A firm creates an extranet to allow authorized vendors and customers to have limited access to its internal network, that is, the intranet. Both intranets and extranets reduce costs and bring in efficiency by allowing business associates to participate in business process and be proactive in decision-making. For example, Wal-Mart has linked its extranet to suppliers, who get an alert the moment a piece of their product is sold in the store. They take steps to replenish the product in the next lot of supplies made to Wal-Mart.

NETWORK AND COMMUNICATION PROTOCOLS

Protocols are rules and laws governing communications between two networking devices and systems. Behrouz (2002) simplifies protocols 'as a set of rules that govern data communication. It represents an agreement between the communicating devices. Without a protocol, two devices may be connected but not communicating'.

In telecommunication networks, hardware and software from different manufacturers need to work together to transmit information. The communication will be complete only when different systems adhere to a common set of rules called protocols. We will briefly discuss open systems interconnection (OSI) protocols governing networking, and transmission control protocol/Internet protocol (TCP/IP) governing Internet, packet-switching technology for data transmission, and electronic data interchange (EDI) to exchange information electronically.

Open Systems Interconnection

Open systems interconnection (OSI) is an international standard organization (ISO) standard that covers the complete network communication aspect. An open system is a model that allows any two different systems to communicate, regardless of their architecture. Products from different vendors work on different standards. The OSI model opens communication among different systems without requiring changes in the logic of their hardware and software. According to Behrouz (2002), 'the OSI model is not a protocol; it is a model for understanding and designing a network architecture that is flexible, robust, and interoperable'.

Transmission Control Protocol/Internet Protocol

Transmission control protocol/Internet protocol (TCP/IP) is a networking standard by which computers on the Internet connect with each other. It is the most widely used and accepted protocol by corporate networks worldwide. It uses a suite of protocols in which the main are TCP and IP. TCP handles the movement of data between computers. As such, TCP establishes a connection between the computers, sequences the transfer of packets, and acknowledges the packets sent. On the other hand, IP performs the delivery of packets and takes the responsibility of disassembling and reassembling of packets during transmission.

The TCP/IP protocol suite is made of five layers—physical, data link, network, transport, and application. An upper-level protocol is supported by a lower-level protocol. The first layer is 'application' that provides end-user functionality by translating the messages into user software for displaying on the screen. Hyptertext transfer protocol (HTTP) is an example of one such protocol. The second layer is 'transport' that provides reliable end-to-end message delivery function. At this layer, TCP/IP breaks down application data into TCP packets. The third layer, 'Internet protocol' (IP) receives data from TCP layer and breaks the packets down further. It contains the header with address information. The fourth layer is network interface that handles addressing issues. The last interface is physical layer that defines basic electrical transmission characteristics for sending the actual signals. Figure 7.4 illustrates how the five layers of TCP/IP reference model for communication work between two computers.

Packet Switching

Packet switching is a method of breaking digital communication messages into fixed-or variable-length parcels called packets. These packets are sent to the destination along different available communication paths and reassembled. Prior to the development of the packet-switching technology, computer networks used dedicated telephone circuits to communicate with a remote computer, similar to regular telephone communication. This was called circuit-switch technique and a complete point-to-point circuit was assembled before the communication could proceed. The circuit-switch technology was expensive as it wasted the communication channel by not utilizing or underutilizing the circuit. In this case, the circuit was always maintained, regardless of whether data was sent or not.

In packet switching, the packets include information for directing the packet to the right destination and for checking transmission errors along with the data. The packets are transmitted

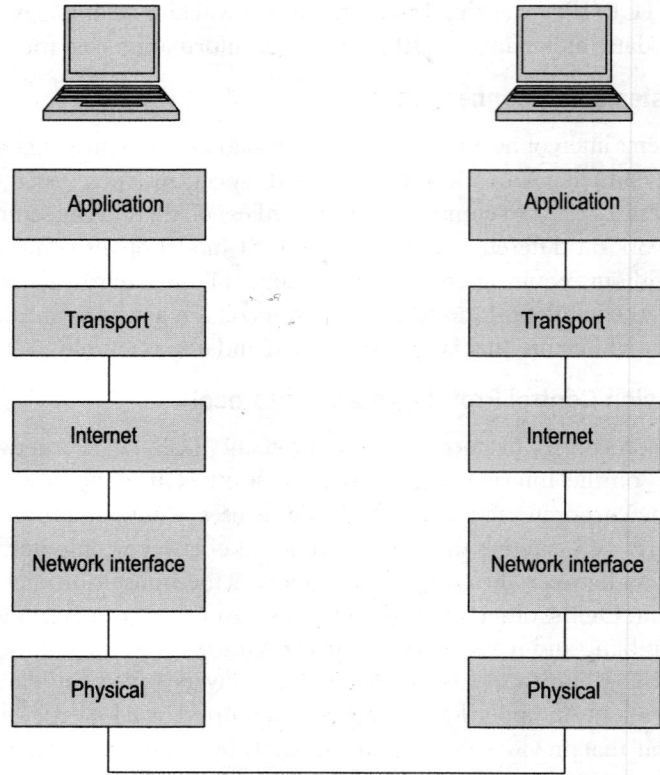

Fig. 7.4   Working of the five layers of TCP/IP model

over various channels using routers and each packet travels independently. While the X.25 protocol breaks the message into 128 character long packets, the packets are of variable lengths in case of the frame relay technology.

Electronic Data Interchange

The process of transmitting data between two computers is known as electronic data interchange (EDI). Using EDI, trading partners establish computer-to-computer links that enable them to exchange information electronically. EDI is the electronic transfer of processable data from one computer to another using an agreed standard to structure the data.

EDI can be conducted between computers of the same organization (as in case of data transfer from the retail point-of-sale (POS) to the head office servers) or between computers of two different organizations such as vendors and customers. In this case, standard transaction documents such as invoices and purchase orders are transmitted through a telecommunication network and accepted electronically at the other end (Joshi 2009). This eliminates the need for printing and paperwork. In doing so, computers at both ends conform to certain standard formats of data. Presently, there are two most widely used standards:

• Electronic data interchange for administration, commerce, and transport (EDIFACT)—international standard for EDI communications

- American national standards institute X12 (ANSI X12)—US standards for EDI communication

There should not be any confusion regarding EDI and email. In EDI, the data is transmitted in the actual structured format (with distinct homogenous fields) and is received in the same format in the database at the receiving end; while email sends data in an unstructured text format like letters.

TELECOMMUNICATION MEDIA

Computers and other telecommunication devices use electrical signals to represent data. These signals can be transmitted from one device to another in the form of electromagnetic force. These electromagnetic signals need some media through which they can travel. This media can be vacuum, air, or metal. For our study, we divide the media into physical and wireless media. Physical media includes various types of cabled media such as twisted pairs, coaxial cables, and optical fibre. Wireless media covers wireless technologies such as microwaves, satellite, cellular, Wi-Fi, and bluetooth.

Wired media, also known as guided media, is the physical conduit between two or more devices. Twisted pair and coaxial cables use copper wire as a conductor for electromagnetic signals in the form of electric current. Optical fibre is made of glass or plastic cables that transport signals in the form of light.

Twisted pair   Twisted pair cables are a set of two or more insulated copper cables. The name of these cables is 'twisted' because the pair of cables is twisted with each other. The normal LAN cable comes in a pair of five twisted pairs and is called Cat-5 UTP (unshielded twisted pair) cable. Cat-5 refers to category five and is used to transmit data up to 100 Mbps. These cables are connected through a connecter called UTP connecter. Twisted pairs are more popular in LANs.

Coaxial cable   Coaxial cable is made of two cables; one is the central solid wire, usually made of copper and is covered by the other cable made up of a mesh or a metal foil. Television cables are the best examples of coaxial cables. These cables are connected with bayonet network connector (BNC). In this category of connectors, T-connectors are used to branch off a cable for connection with a computer device. The terminators—the connectors that terminate the network—are used at the last end of the cable. Though coaxial cables can carry signals of higher frequency, they are used less because of the changing network topologies. A topology defines the layout of computers in a network. These layouts are in the form of ring, star, etc. The topologies are referred to by the same name.

Fibre optics   While twisted pair and coaxial cables carry signals in the form of electric current, optic cables carry signals in the form of light. The fibre optics use cables consisting of one or more hair-thin filaments of glass fibre, wrapped in a protective jacket. They can conduct pulses of visible light elements called photons, generated by lasers. One end of the cable is connected to a device emitting light and the other end is fitted to a photosensitive device for receiving and translating light into electromagnetic current to make it usable for computers.

As they are lighter in weight, fibre optic cables are a hundred times more efficient than twisted pair or coaxial cables in conducting transmission. Their data error is also very less compared to others in this category.

WIRELESS COMPUTER NETWORKS

Wireless transmission is based on radio signals of various frequencies. Wireless media is also known as unguided media as the electromagnetic waves are broadcast through air or water. Any device which has a receiving capability can receive and translate the waves into some sort of data. Wireless transmission that sends signals through air, water, or space without any physical cable has become an increasingly popular alternative to cabled transmission channels because of their reach and cost-efficiency. Today, common technologies for wireless data transmission include microwave transmission, communication satellites, paging, cellular telephones, and mobile data networks. Radio frequencies (RF) are radio waves carrying data. They can travel long distances through any media and do not require line-of-sight connectivity. Radio waves travel from a very small frequency of 3 kHz to 30 GHz. We will briefly discuss radio frequency, microwave, satellites, wireless local area network, Bluetooth, worldwide interoperability for microwave access (WiMAX), and radio frequency.

Microwave

Microwave systems transmit high-frequency radio signals through the atmosphere and are widely used for high-volume, long-distance, and point-to-point communication. Microwave communication channels require line-of-sight transmission and reception equipment. The towers containing antenna are placed at high places such as hill tops or tall buildings so that the signals can cover a large area. Microwaves move in one direction at a time, so two transmitters and receivers are placed to receive and send signals simultaneously. To increase the distance covered by microwaves, repeaters are installed on each antenna.

Satellite Communication

Satellite communication works like microwave. They are typically used for transmission of large, geographically-dispersed organizations that would be difficult to network using cabling media or terrestrial microwave. The satellites are placed in stationary orbits, approximately 22,000 miles above the equator. They are powered by solar panels and can transmit microwave signals at a rate of several hundred megabytes per second (mbps). The satellite orbiting the earth functions as a very large antenna/receiver. Figure 7.5 illustrates how a communication satellite works.

As in terrestrial microwave, in satellite transmission, the signals travel straight in line-of-sight; however, because of the satellite, the reach is increased dramatically. These types of microwave can cover any corner of the earth and the leasing time or frequencies on the satellite provide a cost-effective way of communication.

There are many other satellite technologies which are being implemented by corporates to improve business communication. For example, many companies are using VSAT (very small aperture terminal) to connect their offices via satellite links. Some of the satellite networks use many low-earth orbit satellites that orbit at an altitude of just 500 miles above the earth.

In 2010, the Indian premier league (IPL) used Internet and VSAT communication to display matches online in theatres with the help of UFO Moviez, a specialist of satellite-based digital delivery of movies. They used VSAT services of Hughes Communications across the country (*Source*: Financial Express).

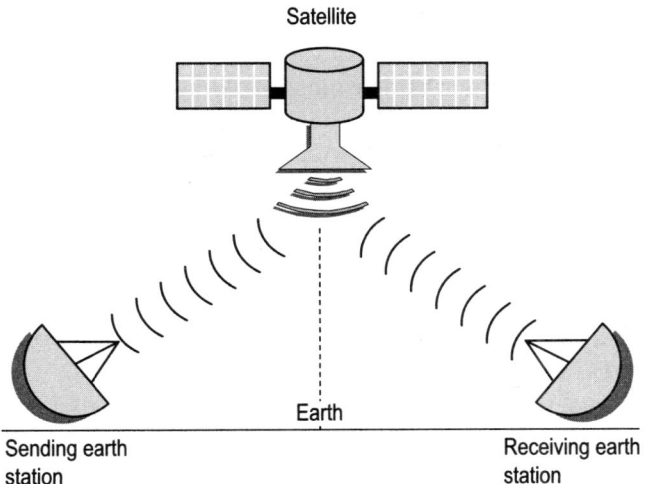

Fig. 7.5   Example of a satellite communication system

Wireless Local Area Network

Wireless local area networks (WLANs) are becoming popular as they save the hassles of wiring and laying conduits for twisted pair and coaxial cables. Repairing faults and damages to wiring is often difficult and costly. Many times, office work arrangement requires relocation of workstations, which may require relaying of cables for LAN. The solution for such problems lies in wireless LAN, using wireless technologies such as Wi-Fi and Bluetooth.

Wi-Fi is an open-standard wireless radio-wave technology, technically known as IEEE 802.11b. Wi-Fi is faster and cheaper than the standard ethernet-based LANs. Wi-Fi supports speeds of 54–100 Mbps and spans across a range of 30–50 metres. However, the range can be increased by using tower-mounted antennae. Wi-Fi WLAN enable laptops, PCs, PDAs, and other devices equipped with Wi-Fi modems to easily connect to the LAN and the Internet. In Wi-Fi-enabled LANs, the wireless devices connect with the wired LAN using a Wi-Fi modem called access point. The access point consists of a radio receiver/transmitter and an antenna that acts as a link to the wired network. Presently, most of the laptops come with an inbuilt Wi-fi card.

For example, at Great Eastern Impex, the systems in the warehouse are connected using Wi-Fi LAN technology. The portable data terminals, used for scanning of goods, send the data to the system via Bluetooth technology.

Bluetooth

Bluetooth is yet another short-range wireless technology used for local area networking. It links up to eight devices within a 10 metre area using low-power, radio-based communication and can transmit up to 722 kbps. Electronic devices such as cell phones, pagers, computers, and printers are equipped with Bluetooth technology. For example, you can give a print command to a printer from a laptop connected with Bluetooth. There are Bluetooth-enabled keyboards, mouse, USB drives, etc., available in the market.

WiMAX

At many places in the country (even advanced country like the US), there is no fixed broadband connectivity for Internet access. The range of Wi-Fi is very limited. To solve this problem, IEEE developed new standards of wireless networks transmission called the worldwide interoperability for microwave access (WiMAX). WiMAX has a wireless access range of up to 31 miles, compared to 300 feet for Wi-fi.

The bandwidth and range of WiMAX make it suitable for the following potential applications:

- Providing portable mobile broadband connectivity across cities and countries through a variety of devices
- Providing a wireless alternative to cable and digital subscriber line (DSL) for 'last mile' broadband access
- Providing data, telecommunications (voice over Internet protocol, VoIP), and Internet protocol television (IPTV) services
- Providing Internet connectivity as part of a business infrastructure plan

WiMAX can provide at-home or mobile Internet access across cities or countries. In many cases, this has resulted in competition in markets which typically only had access through an existing incumbent DSL (or similar) operator. Additionally, given the relatively low costs associated with the deployment of a WiMAX network (in comparison with 3G); it is now economically viable to provide last-mile broadband Internet access in remote locations.

NETWORKING DEVICES

Connecting many computers over a network is done through hubs and switches. Devices such as repeaters and bridges are used to enhance the signals and connect such networks. They work as bridges between various computers. Similarly, connecting two networks is called internetworking, and the devices needed to connect them are routers and gateways. We will briefly cover the essential equipment used in networking.

Hubs and switches   Hubs are the oldest devices used to connect computers on a network. With advancement in technology, switches have replaced hubs. Their main aim is to provide a junction for data transmission from one direction to another.

Repeaters   Repeaters regenerate a weakening signal on the network path. Signals on a network can travel a fixed distance and slow down. A repeater is installed at the designated link which receives the signal before it becomes too weak or corrupts. The repeater regenerates the original bit pattern and puts the strengthened signal back on the track.

Bridges   Bridges are used to connect two networks using the same protocol. They can divide a large network into smaller manageable segments. Bridges can also keep traffic of each LAN separate. Thus, they play a role in filtering the traffic and managing congestion on the network.

Routers   Routers are hardware devices or software that act like a station on the network. They are intelligent devices than repeaters and bridges. The software in them determines several paths between the addresses and the best path of current data transmission.

Gateways   Gateways are the entrance points for another network in a network path. In the Internet, the gateway node works as a link between networks using different protocols. Gateways can accept a packet formatted for one protocol and convert it into a packet formatted for another protocol.

INTERNET REVOLUTION

The explosive growth of the Internet in a short period of time has impacted computing and telecommunication in a big way. The Internet has touched every aspect of life that it has become indispensable for individuals as well as businesses. It has evolved into a global information superhighway. It will not be an exaggeration to divide the time period as before Internet (BI) and after Internet (AI).

The Internet is constantly expanding, as more and more businesses and other organizations and their users, computers, and networks join its global web. Thousands of businesses, educational, and research networks now connect millions of computer systems and users in more than 200 countries to each other. For example, as per one estimate by Internet World Stats, the worldwide population of Internet users was estimated at around 2095 million in March 2011, which is around 32% of the world population. In India, the number of users is estimated at 100 million, which is roughly 8% of the total population of the country.

Definition

The Internet is known as the network of the networks. It is a self-regulatory, self-managed large network of thousands of smaller networks, in which each computer is a node as well as a server. Internet works on the telecommunication backbone and has global reach. To connect to the Internet, one has to connect to the local Internet service provider (ISP) through telephone lines connected through the modem in the computer. The telecommunication lines can be a digital subscriber line (DSL) which operates over the existing telephone lines to carry voice, data, and video at a high transmission rate. Alternatively, there are cable Internet connections, which use coaxial cables like a cable TV, and provide higher bandwidth. The computer and communication devices should agree to TCP/IP.

The Internet is based on client–server architecture. The rules and language of connection are written in the browser we use. The browser helps connect your client computer with the web server at a distant location. Internet is another form of client–server computing, in which, client processing and storage capability are very minimal. Most of storage and processing happens at the server end. The client downloads the interface forms, application, and data from the server over the network and completes his/her task. In the client–server architecture, the web servers store and retrieve information, and manage data, applications, and security. The client is the interface between the user and the web server and it displays the information through a core browser or application. Take the example of a web-based e-mail like yahoo mail. The web server hosts complete data, runs Yahoo email management application, and provides security to your email data. The computer terminal on which you work runs Windows Internet Explorer (as browser), is a client of the web server, which functions as an interface between the user and the web server.

No one owns the Internet. However, international Internet policies are established by a number of professional organizations and government bodies. The Internet architecture board (IAB) helps define the overall structure of the Internet; the Internet corporation for assigned names and numbers (ICANN) assigns IP addresses; and the WWW consortium (W3C) sets hypertext mark-up language (HTML) and other programming standards for the web.

Applications and Tools

The Internet offers a variety of applications and tools. The most popular applications are e-mail, instant messaging, participating in newsgroups and social networking sites, file transfers, and browsing sites on the world wide web. The phenomenon of Internet-based services cannot be understood without understanding the WWW. We will discuss the WWW in Chapter 11on e-commerce. Each of these services is managed by one or more software programs. For example, there is email management software such as MS-Outlook and Google Chrome for browsing, which we have already discussed in Chapter 5.

For businesses, the Internet has evolved from just an electronic information exchange to a broad platform for strategic business applications. The Internet has become a major tool for business collaboration among business associates, customer support, electronic commerce, and application support. Organizations are using the Internet for marketing, sales, and customer relationship management (CRM). Enterprise applications such as manufacturing, human resource, and accounting are implemented on corporate networks over the Internet. Besides support function for existing businesses, the Internet provides a platform for new business models.

The Internet is being widely used for long-distance telephony for the advantage of cost saving. It is done by using VoIP, which delivers voice data in the digital form using packet switching. The calls are made to travel over corporate networks based on the Internet protocol or the public Internet. For example Skype, Google, etc., provide free VoIP. Table 7.2 summarizes the major applications of the Internet.

Table 7.2   Examples of most popular applications of the Internet

Application	Purpose
Browsing	Surfing through thousands of websites for information, research, and entertainment
E-mail	The most common activity on the Internet. Exchange email messages with colleagues, friends, family, etc.
Networking	Participate in discussion groups, newsgroups, and network socially with common interest groups
Publish	Post your profile, creative work, credentials, or pictures on the web for others to read and view
Shopping	Buy and sell anything through various e-commerce sites, auction sites, and service providers
Download	Download pictures, movies, music, freeware, tools, and transfer data files
Videoconferencing and VoIP	Conduct videoconferencing, make long-distance calls—using voice over IP technology of the Internet
Run business application	Use the Internet to run business applications for multi-office multi-city operations
Launch new business	Start a new business or service over the Internet backbone

Future of Internet—Internet Protocol Version 6 and Internet2

The massive growth and expansion of the Internet has forced computer scientists and technocrats to think about newer protocols, addressing systems, and a high bandwidth version of the Internet. The present IP addresses, which use a 32-bit address system, can support only 2^{32} addresses, and are going to be exhausted soon. To meet this challenge, Internet protocol version 6 (IPv6) has been developed by the Internet engineering task force (IETF). The IPv6 uses 128-bit addresses, so that the new address space supports 2^{128} addresses. This expansion allows for many more devices and users on the Internet as well as extra flexibility in allocating addresses and efficiency for routing traffic.

Similarly, Internet2 is a futuristic road map that can be followed when the next stage of innovation in the current Internet takes place. This is a US-based initiative by a consortium led by universities working in partnership with the industry and government to develop and deploy advanced network applications and technologies. The consortium representing 200 universities, private businesses, and government agencies in the USA, is working on a new version of the Internet. It would be a high-performance network that uses an entirely different infrastructure than the public Internet of the day. The research group is working on a high performance backbone network with bandwidth ranging from 2.5 gigabytes per second (Gbps) to 9.6 Gbps. The target is to develop new technology for the more effective routing system, high levels of services, advanced application for distributed computing, virtual laboratories, digital libraries, etc.

RADIO FREQUENCY IDENTIFICATION TECHNOLOGY

Radio frequency identification (RFID) can be part of any information system that requires data capturing and transmission over a wireless media. It would be extremely beneficial for students of management to know the latest technology and understand the benefits so that they can implement automatic data capture system for various business uses such as inventory management, supply chain management, and assets tracking.

RFID is a new generation technology for data capture and communication, which is being used effectively in modern businesses. This technology uses radio communication to uniquely identify and transmit data relating to an item, object, or an individual. Radio communication works on radio waves or frequencies emitted by one part (tag) of the device and accepted and read by the other part (reader). The radio frequencies are unique in nature; hence, the data transmitted is clearly identifiable. Radio frequency tags can be put on a product or implanted on any living animal.

Invented in 1948, it was first used during the Second World War by the US Army for identification of friend or foe (IFF) aircrafts. This technology gained commercial acceptance during the 1980s and the 1990s. In an RFID system, the data is carried in suitable transponders, commonly known as RF tags, and is retrieved at the appropriate time and place by means of an antenna and a transceiver/reader, in order to satisfy a particular application need. RFID systems allow for non-contact reading or writing of data and are highly effective in manufacturing and other hostile environments where other technologies cannot survive.

Hardware Components

The RFID hardware has the following two components:

- Tag: Programmed to carry unique data
- Reader: For communicating with the tag

Tag   The RFID tag is a microchip transponder, that is, it acts as a transmitter and a responder. It can transmit the data when powered by an electrical source and respond to a call by the reader. Tag contains the following four components:

- A processor for executing instructions
- Memory for storing data
- Source of electricity to charge the circuits
- A transmitter for data communication

RFID tags are either active or passive. Active RFID tags are self-powered. They are powered by an internal battery and the tag data can be rewritten or modified. These tags can be read from a larger communication distance and they have a larger memory size. These types of tags are used in applications that require faster data access from a relatively long distance. Highway toll applications are one area where these tags are useful. However, these tags are very expensive at present.

Passive RFID tags do not have their own internal power source; hence, they require external power. They operate without a separate external power source and obtain operating power generated from the reader. The transponder is powered by an electromagnetic signal transmitted by the reader. The signal charges an internal capacitor on the tag. This supplies power to communicate with the reader. The low-frequency passive tags operate at a frequency of 125–134 khz. The distance they cover ranges from a few centimetres to a few metres. The high-frequency tags run at a frequency of 13.5 MHz and cover a relatively higher distance. Passive tags are consequently much lighter than active tags, less expensive, and offer a virtually unlimited operational lifetime.

As a result, passive RFID tags have shorter read ranges than active tags and require a higher-powered reader. Read-only tags are passive and are programmed with a unique set of data and cannot be modified. The higher performance of high-frequency RFID systems incurs higher system costs.

Reader   As the name suggests, it is an electronic device that reads or communicates with the tag. It consists of the following:

- Antenna: It produces radio waves for communication with the tag. The shape and number depends on the read range and permissible strength of the signal. In case of handheld readers, antennas are integrated with the reader.
- Signal processors: They enable understanding and communicating the reads
- Embedded software: It processes the reads from the tags and communicates with the middleware

The antenna emits radio signals to read and write data to the RF tag. Antennae are the conduits between the tag and the transceiver. They can be built into a door frame to receive tag data from persons or things passing through the door. The electromagnetic field produced by an antenna can be constantly present when multiple tags are expected continually. If constant interrogation is not required, the field can be activated by a sensor device.

The antenna, when packaged with the transceiver and decoder, becomes a reader (interrogator), which can be configured either as a handheld or a fixed-mount device. The reader emits radio waves, depending upon its power output and the radio frequency used. When an RFID tag passes through this radio frequency zone, it detects the reader, which decodes the data encoded in the tag's circuit and the data is passed to the host computer for processing.

Functioning

The RFID tag is put on an object that needs identification. An RFID reader communicates with the tag using radio waves. The identification code on the tag is read and communicated to the back-end system for making useful business decisions (see Fig. 7.6).

According to Rangarajan (2005), an RFID hardware interacts with an IT infrastructure through a middleware comprising hardware, application, and the interface. The RFID hardware generates event data. This refers to the number to identify the object being read. Further, this data is sourced from the hardware, filtered, adopted, and logged. Then, the data becomes usable for processing in the existing enterprise systems. For example, time and location details associated are added to this data. The existing enterprise system like ERP is one component of an IT infrastructure. Business process analytics is the layer where this data is utilized to meet the objective for which the RFID system has been deployed. An enterprise would like the RFID network to connect to enterprise systems such as ERP, supply chain management (SCM), CRM, or WMS (warehouse management systems) or any other third party applications. It provides libraries of adapters and application programming interface for other technologies.

RFID generates a data stream to bridge the gap between the physical flow of goods and the information flow in the IT systems. This data is made available in existing ERP or some other applications—enterprise software. It presents crucial strategic opportunities that enhance the performance of the business. This opportunity has to be exploited by a business analytics application. The application provides an interface to the business user to derive the benefit out of the investments for employing RFID technology in the enterprise (Joshi, 2009).

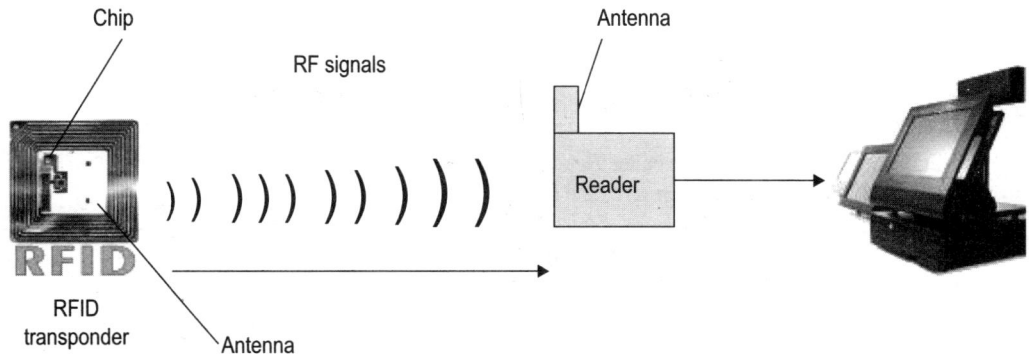

Fig. 7.6 Functioning of an RFID system

Benefits

There are enormous benefits that can be derived out of RFID systems in modern business management. There are innumerable uses of RFID in all walks of life and applications as varied as access and security control, livestock identification, inventory control, children's identification at amusement parks, wildlife animal identification, airline baggage tracking, automated vehicle identification, toll collection, etc. They are providing significant improvements in productivity, efficiency, and convenience to organizations and consumers across the globe. RFID is extensively being used in retail for electronic article surveillance as an anti-theft measure. Big Bazaar, as illustrated in Exhibit 7.3, illustrates how the retail giant gained from implementing RFID-based security check system.

Today, RFID has become indispensable for a wide range of automated data collection and identification applications. It is difficult to imagine work without RFID in certain situations. RFID systems play significant role in warehouse management. The transaction processing system in a warehouse can be automated with the help of RFID technology. We can implement the system in tracking fast moving consumer goods in the supply chain management. It is now widely used across a multitude of industry sectors, and inventory tracking is a major application of RFID

EXHIBIT 7.3

Big Bazaar: Security Check Prohibits Shoplifting

Big Bazaar is a well-known chain of hypermarkets in India, which caters to every family's needs. This retail chain is a subsidiary belong to the Future Group and is touted to be an answer to the United States' Wal-Mart. Big Bazaar owns more than 100 stores all over the country with an amalgamation of Indian *bazaars'* feel and touch, with a convenience and choice of the modern retail facilities.

Industry experts opine that organized retail crimes such as shoplifting, theft by internal employees, credit card fraud, gift card fraud, and price tag switching cost the US about $30 billion a year. According to the 21st annual retail theft survey conducted by Jack L. Hayes International, a loss-prevention consulting firm, 22 major retailers lost more than $6 billion to shoplifters and dishonest employees in 2008. On the upside, a record 9,04,226 thieves were apprehended, up 7.26% from 2007. Of them, 8,32,106 were shoplifters and 72,120 were dishonest employees.

The retail crime scene in India is no better. Retail security companies such as Adtech, Sensormatic, and Checkpoint are offering comprehensive solutions. Sensormatic EAS using the patented Acousto-magnetic technology is designed to help retailers prevent shrinkage and shoplifting using advanced digital technology. It helps them to increase sales by open merchandising opportunities while reducing shoplifting and internal theft. Most of India's retail chains rely on Sensormatic. The RFID-powered security check at each exit of Big Bazaar uses electronic article surveillance (EAS) system, which detects the products that has attached tags.

When implementing EAS, every expensive product is fitted with an RFID tag. The tag is deactivated or removed when it is billed at the checkout counter. However, if any unauthorized person takes the product out without billing it, the sensors fitted at the exit raise an alarm. The shoplifter can be apprehended with the product. By implementing the EAS, Big Bazaar drastically reduced shoplifting and thus increased profitability.

Sources:

'Big Bazaar', http://ekikrat.in/Big-Bazaar, last accessed on 8 April 2012.

jparker, 'Annual retail theft', http://retailnotes.wordpress.com/2009/09/02/annual-retail-theft-survey/, last accessed on 8 April 2012.

'Tyco Retail Solutions protects 40 billion items', http://www.sensormatic.com/WhoWeAre/prDetail.aspx?id=303, last accessed on 8 April 2012.

http://adtechindia.com/products/eas-solutions.html, last accessed on 8 April 2012.

http://www.fbi.gov/news/stories/2011/january/retail_010311, last accessed on 8 April 2012.

technology. The visibility provided by this technology allows an accurate knowledge on the inventory level by eliminating the discrepancy between inventory record and physical inventory. Each product is fitted with an RFID tag, which transmits a signal and is captured by the reader. The signal linked with the item code traces the location of the product. If the product is moved from its location, the reader detects the movement and updates the computer database accordingly.

RFID system offers a lot of advantages over manual system and other form of product identification and data capture. The following are some advantages:

- The RFID systems use the no-contact, non-line-of-sight technology. The data can be read from a distance. Non-line-of-sight means the tag and reader communication will still be established, even if they are not facing each other.
- The tags have a read-write capability; hence, data can be upgraded continuously.
- RFID tags can be read through a variety of substances such as paint, crusted grime, snow, fog, ice, and other visually and environmentally challenging conditions. At such locations, barcodes or other optically read technologies would be useless.
- RFID tags can also be read in difficult circumstances and at remarkable speed. The response is typically less than 100 milliseconds.
- Multiple tags can be read at once and in bulk, thus, making mass reading possible. Therefore, any speeding source tag cannot skip the reader.
- It can be embedded into any non-metallic surface.

Although RFID is a costlier technology, it provides considerable benefits. There has been a lot of technological advancements in this field, but the process of evolution for commercially-viable solutions is still on. There are regular revisions in the standards for tags, reader, air interface, and data handling. This phenomenon, coupled with the lack of relevant RFID expertise in industry, poses a risk to all those organizations seeking to garner benefits offered by technology.

SUMMARY

The convergence of information and communication technologies (ICT) has brought about a major revolution in the working and lifestyle of people. The changing trends in telecommunication industries, technologies, and applications significantly increase the decision alternatives for business managers. With the introduction of free market economy in India in the 1990s, the industry saw the birth of new telecom giants and new technologies. Telecommunications system is changing from wire-based to wireless technology. The great changes in industry and technology trends in telecommunications are changing the way telecom is being used in businesses.

Networks are interconnected computers used to share data, files, information, and equipment such as printer and scanner, which are connected through cables and other communication media for transmission of data, graphics, images, etc. Networks are differentiated on the basis of their reach and size. Different types of networks include local area network (LAN), wide area network (WAN), client–server, intranet, extranet, and virtual private networks (VPN). Data communication between computers and networks is done through creation of VPNs, which are most secured and private networks using public telecom backbone.

Protocols are rules and laws governing connectivity issues and help connect two devices and systems from different manufacturers. The commonly used networking protocols are OSI and TCP/IP. OSI protocols are used for networking and TCP/IP are used for the Internet. Packet switching is a method of breaking digital communication messages into fixed or variable-length parcels called packets. Electronic data interchange (EDI) is a structured transmission of data from one system to another.

The media used to connect various computer and networks are of two types. One is guided through various types of cables and wires. The other is called wireless. In wireless radio frequency, microwave and satellite are used. Wi-Fi and Bluetooth are wireless technologies used to connect LAN. To connect various computers and networks, networking devices such as repeaters, bridges, hubs, switches, and routers are used.

The explosive growth of the Internet in a short period of time has impacted computing and telecommunication in a big way. Internet is known as the network of the networks. It offers a variety of applications and tools. The most popular applications are e-mail, instant messaging, participating in newsgroups, and social networking sites, file transfers, and browsing sites on the world wide web. The Internet is being widely used for long-distance telephony for cost saving by using VoIP technology. The massive growth and expansion of the Internet has forced computer scientists and technocrats to think about newer protocols, addressing systems, and high bandwidth version of the Internet. IPv6 and Internet2 are the steps in this direction.

Radio frequency identification (RFID) is a new generation technology for data capture and communication, which is being used effectively in modern businesses. This technology uses radio communication to uniquely identify and transmit data relating to an item, object, or an individual. The RFID hardware has just two components. Tag is programmed to carry unique data. An RFID tag is a microchip transponder. RFID tags are either active or passive. Readers are used for communicating with the tag. This is an electronic device that reads signals and communicates with the tag. An RFID tag is put on an object that needs identification. An RFID reader communicates with the tag using radio waves. The identification code on the tag is read and communicated to the back-end system for making useful business decisions. There are innumerable uses of RFID in all walks of life, and applications as varied as access and security control, livestock identification, inventory control, kids identifications at amusement parks, wildlife animal identification, airline baggage tracking, automated vehicle identification, and toll collection.

KEY TERMS

American National Standards Institute X12 (ANSI X12) A US standard for EDI communication.

Asynchronous transfer mode (ATM) A standard that seamlessly and dynamically integrates voice, data, images, and video for transmission across the globe.

Broadband A high speed telecommunication channel used for the Internet.

Circuit-switch technique Dedicated telephone circuits to communicate with the remote computer.

Client–Server network Networks using a server (usually a high-end computer) and clients (other computers connected with the server).

Communication protocol A set of rules that govern data communication.

Cyberspace A public virtual place provided by the Internet without geographic boundaries where ordinary citizens can interact, publish their ideas, and engage in business.

Digital subscribers line (DSL) A type of telecommunication line.

Electronic data interchange (EDI) The electronic transfer of data from one computer to another using an agreed standard, to structure the data.

Electronic data interchange for administration, commerce, and transport (EDIFACT) International standard for EDI communications.

Extranet Private networks extended over other networks of suppliers and customers.

Hypertext transmission protocol (HTTP) A protocol that provides end-user functionality by translating the messages into user software for displaying on his/her screen.

Information superhighway The concept of an advanced high-speed Internet-like network that connects individuals, houses, businesses, etc., with interactive voice, video, data, and multimedia communication.

Internet2 A futuristic road map that can be followed when the next stage of innovation in the current Internet takes place.

Interoperability Easy to communicate and share information even among diverse computer hardware, software, and databases.

Intranet Private networks over public Internet backbone.

IPv6 (Internet protocol version 6) An Internet protocol that uses 128-bit addresses, so the new address space supports many computers on the network.

Local area network (LAN) A network that connects computers at small locations.

Microwaves High-frequency radio signals through the atmosphere used for high-volume, long-distance, point-to-point communication.

Network firewalls A security mechanism consisting of hardware and software to protect a network of computers.

Networks An interconnected system of computers, terminals, and communication channels and devices.

Open systems interconnection (OSI) An open-systems

model that allows any two different systems to communicate regardless of their architecture.

Packet switching   A method of breaking digital communication messages into fixed or variable-length parcels called packets.

Radio frequency identification (RFID)   An automatic data capture device that works on radio waves.

Social networking   A form of networking by people over the Internet that is also used by companies for marketing and finding their target segment.

Transmission control protocol/Internet protocol (TCP/IP)   A suite of telecommunication network standards used by the Internet.

Voice over Internet protocol (VoIP)   A protocol that delivers voice data in digital form using packet switching.

Virtual private network (VPN)   A private network using public Internet.

Wide area network (WAN)   A network that connects computers in a larger space like multiple cities.

Wi-Fi   An open-standard wireless radio wave technology.

CONCEPT REVIEW QUESTIONS

1. How is the telecommunication technology progressing? What are the various trends in this industry?
2. Explain local area network (LAN) and wide area network (WAN) with suitable examples.
3. Explain intranet, extranet, and virtual private network (VPN) with suitable examples.
4. What is electronic data interchange (EDI)? How does it function?
5. What are the widely-used standards for connecting networks through Internet?
6. Which are the wireless technologies of connecting LANs?
7. What is the 'last mile' concept in networks?
8. Explain client–server networking in layman's terms.
9. What are the various services and tools provided by the Internet for modern businesses?
10. What is radio frequency identification (RFID)? Explain their functioning.
11. How can RFID technologies help in transactions processing at a warehouse?

CRITICAL THINKING QUESTIONS

1. 'Computers would have been just calculators if telecommunications had not collaborated with them to create telecommunication revolution.' Critically examine this statement and explain with suitable examples.
2. Which are the different fields where computers and communication technologies converge to make an impact on the society as well as businesses?
3. 'Internet has brought in revolution in personal, social, and professional life of a person.' Examine this statement and give suitable examples.

MIS DEVELOPMENT

Shah Enterprises Ltd is a multi-unit and multi-product company that is into manufacture, distribution, and retail of men's garments. The operations of the company are scattered over the country. The company has its head office in Mumbai, and four manufacturing units, one each in Karur in Tamil Nadu, Gandhidham in Gujarat, Pant nagar in Uttrakhand, and Singur in Kolkata. The company has 200 hundred retail outlets, exclusively selling its own brands. Some sixteen distribution warehouses support these retail outlets in terms of replenishment of inventory. These distribution centres are located strategically in major state capitals and are supported by the company's four manufacturing units. The retail outlets are located in tier-two and tier-three cities in India.

The company plans to establish a high-speed network covering all units, warehouses, and retail outlets to run its newly-procured enterprise application, point of sales software, and corporate intranet. Some of the cities are not connected with broadband telecommunication cables. At least half a dozen warehouses are functioning from very old buildings where laying of physical cables is not possible. In his ambitious plan, the managing director of the company wants to connect some suppliers with the company's network, so that they are aware of the raw material's inventory position on an everyday basis. The

ERP vendor has reported two Mbps as the minimum requirement for running the software, while the point of sale (POS) can run over 512 kbps broadband lines. The managing director of the company is particularly concerned about the security of the networks and wants a completely secured intranet.

Exercise

Create a network blueprint for the company. Indicate which technology would be used to connect the local offices, inter-cities, and inter-state units. What will be the most economical solution to provide optimum speed and uptime?

REFERENCES

Forouzan, Behrouz A., *Data Communications and Networking*, Tata McGraw-Hill, New Delhi, 2003.

'IPL shows in theatres under lens', *Financial Express*, New Delhi, 14 April 2010, last accessed on 10 October 2011.

Jaiswal, Mahadeo and Monika Mittal, *Management Information Systems*, Oxford University Press, New Delhi, 2004.

Joshi, Girdhar, *Information Technology for Retail*, Oxford University Press, New Delhi, 2009.

Laudon Ken, Jane Laudon, and Rajanish Dass, *Management Information System*, Pearson Education, Singapore 2010.

Messerschmitt, David, *Network Applications: A Guide to the New Computing Infrastructure*, Morgan Kaufmann, San Francisco, 1999.

Nilekani, Nandan, *Imagining India—Ideas for the New Century*, Penguin, New Delhi, 2008.

O'Brien, James A., George M. Marakas, and Ramesh Behl, *Management Information Systems*, Tata McGraw-Hill, New Delhi, 2007.

Rangarajan, T.S., Pradeep Misra, and Sumit Talwar, 'The success tag', *Retail Biz*, November, 2005.

The EDI Handbook: Trading in the 1990s, International Data Exchange Association, http://www.gslis.utexas.edu/~ssoy/pubs/l389c5a.htm, accessed on 16 October 2011

'Internet world stats, usage statistics', http://www.internet worldstats.com/stats.htm, last accessed on 10 October 2011.

http://en.wikipedia.org/wiki/WiMAX, last accessed on 10 October 2011.

http://www.internet2.edu/, last accessed on 10 October 2011.

CASE STUDY

Application of Information and Communication Technologies at Amul: Bridging the Digital Divide

The term 'digital divide' has always fascinated the Indian IT Industry. Both the government and the social organizations from the private sector have launched various schemes to take 'IT to the masses'. Amul has been one of the first organizations to use IT-enabled transactions for masses.

The use of information and communication technologies (ICT) in the rural areas of Gujarat by Gujarat Cooperative Milk Marketing Federation Ltd (GCMMFL), popularly known as Amul, has made the operation of the dairy industry different. While it has always been argued that investments related to ICT made in rural India are not effective, the case of Amul proves that 'where there is a will, there is a way'. Amul has become rural India's flag bearer in the IT revolution. This system makes it easy for the farmers to get the cash payment as soon as the milk is delivered. The Amul experience indicates that, if properly designed and implemented, the rural poor can benefit from ICT platforms. Customization of IT platforms for use in rural communities is emerging as a major opportunity for change.

Organization

Amul Dairy was formed in 1946. It was initially named Kaira District Co-operative Milk Producers Union Ltd. It was located in Anand, a small town in Gujarat and began with just two village dairy cooperative societies and 247 litres of milk. Amul grew in strength due to the inspired leadership of Tribhuvandas Patel, its founder chairman, and the committed professionalism of Dr Verghese Kurien, who was entrusted with the task of running the dairy from 1950.

As Amul was a successful cooperative movement, it was decided that the same approach should become the basis of a national dairy development policy. The success of Amul could be attributed to four important factors—a) the farmers owned the dairy, b) their elected representatives managed the village societies and the district union, c) they employed professionals to operate the dairy and manage its business, and d) the cooperatives were sensitive to the needs of farmers and responsive to their demands.

In 1965, the National Dairy Development Board was set up with the basic objective of replicating the Amul model. Dr Kurien, who was later regarded as father of the 'white revolution', was chosen to head the institution as its chairman and was asked to replicate this model throughout the country.

Amul Model

The Amul model of dairy development is a three-tiered structure with the dairy cooperative societies at the village level, federated under a milk union at the district level and a federation of member unions at the state level. GCMMF, which was formed in 1973, is the sole marketer for the entire range of Amul products. GCMMF consists of 12 affiliated member dairies, district milk unions, and has its own manufacturing unit called Mother Dairy at Gandhinagar with the largest network in food industry. It is supported by marketing and distribution of liquid milk and a variety of products under the brand, Amul.

The movement, which started at Amul Dairy in Gujarat, is now replicated in 70,000 villages in about 200 districts of India. The National Diary Development Board (NDDB) has drawn up a programme to double milk collection in the next six years. This sharp increase requires an extensive educational programme that should reach millions of farmers and dairy workers. This case shows how the education can be delivered through rural Internet kiosks, created for the dairy sector. GCMMF, being a pioneer in the dairy industry, became the industry standard.

Operations

The village milk cooperative is a society of primary producers. A milk producer becomes a member by buying a share from the cooperative after agreeing to sell milk only to it. Each society has a milk collection centre. There are one million farmers organized into village milk producer's cooperative societies and the procurement of milk is 13 million litres per day. The GCMMF—Amul has taken the initiative of installing the AMCUS or the automatic milk collection unit systems at village societies to enhance the transparency of transactions between the farmer and the cooperative society. These systems not only ensured the transparency but also gave cooperative societies a unique advantage by reducing the processing time to 10% of what it used to be earlier. GCMMF got the entire supplier information through systems integration. The information related to members, fat content, volume of the milk procured, and the amount payable to the member are accessible to the cooperative society in the form of a database. There are 10,755 village cooperatives in Gujarat that are now able to collect 6.1 million litres of milk from 2 million members. Thanks to the use of IT, both transparency and trust have been enhanced.

Use of Information Technology

'Information technology is our thrust area from our inception, because we are marketing perishable goods. There is every chance that we may collapse in between if we don't understand the market realities and the village farmers. There should be a 24 x 7 information flow in between us and the remaining nodes of our supply chain,' says Rathod, divisional manager, Amul.

The IT-related initiatives that GCMMF undertook include an ERP initiative to integrate the market-related activities. Web initiatives made the consumer aware of Amul. 'Online stores and portal activities such as sending emails, and greetings gave the consumer a better picture of Amul. AMCUS empowers farmers by employing IT at village cooperative societies. IT increases the transparency levels in the system and builds the trust among the farmers. Making the system automatic could remove the intermediaries. The use of IT platforms reduces the potential for discretionary decisions.

The success of AMCUS prompted the GCMMF to aggressively employ IT to capture the end-to-end data. GCMMF planned to cover all aspects of the value chain. These plans supported integration of the value chain activities destined towards 'better management practices'. These efforts of GCMMF triggered the changes in the villages; farmers kept themselves open for the changes.

The dairy information and services kiosk (DISK) is another initiative that was started by GCMMFL with the help of the Indian Institute of Management, Ahmedabad (IIM-A). There are many more in the pipeline of GCMMFL's IT initiatives. Various initiatives such as enterprise-wide integrated application systems (EIAS) to integrate the distribution side of the supply chain, and DISK—to upgrade the application at the milk collection centres and to connect them to the Internet to access a specialized dairy portal with content delivered in the local language have already started giving the fruits to the rural poor. These attempts have persuaded the rural folks to actively participate in the IT revolution of the dairy industry.

GCMMF has embarked on IT as a thrust area for gaining a competitive edge in its global business operations. With a view of handling the rapid growth and data volumes that needed to be effectively managed, GCMMF developed the information systems plan. This plan was a step-by-step planning document that envisaged information strategy as an integral part of the business strategy through end-to-end total quality management.

Accordingly, a system for improving the milk procurement system was conceived. All the current systems were redesigned and reorganized as per the need and all activities were focused towards capturing the important data that is vital for decision-making. From the beginning, the implementation of the plan went in a big way. The implementation of AMCUS gave GCMMF adequate experience for the deeper exploitation of IT. 'Amul is not a food company, it is an IT company in the food business,' is a saying at GCMMF.

Experience and Initiatives

The initial success of GCMMF gave confidence to experiment with newer initiatives. Various activities like total quality management (TQM) do have their role of getting IT to the rural front. The TQM drive in GCMMF triggered a lot of innovative plans to improve the entitlements of various stakeholders. At the grass-roots level, it is essential to ensure that the implementation is flawless. GCMMF employed the same approach that was used to make the distribution chain effective. This approach helped in developing the required internal competencies to transform the village society into a technology user community. The DISK model has built upon the existing application by expanding the database of the milk societies to include a complete history of milk cattle owned by the member farmers. The details such as the breed and a history of diseases, inoculation, and artificial insemination are maintained in the system. The data history on milk production by individual farmers is also available in the database at the collection centres. This model has been designed by IIM-A. 'The test of an organization is not its genius but its capacity to make common people achieve uncommon performances,' said Chaudhary of GCMMF. This is the idea behind the AMCUS, DISK, as well as the other programmes were being initiated by GCMMF successfully and they made the maximum of what they are intended to be.

Working and Challenges

The GCMMF business involves daily collection of milk at 25 supply centres in Gujarat; the production of butter, cheese, ice cream, baby food, and milk powder; the marketing of these products through 50 sales offices throughout India; and distribution through a network of 4000 stockists who, in turn, supply to 5,00,000 retail outlets. Notwithstanding the traditional nature of its business, the management decided to adopt 'IT integration' as a strategic thrust in 1995. GCMMF, being an apex organization with 12 unions with their own manufacturing units, consists of 2.1 million milk producing members who supply milk twice a day to the respective cooperative societies in the village. The manual process of collecting the milk was practised at AMCUS.

GCMMF identified the complexity of the operations of the societies. The farmers were vexed up with the traditional set-up because of human mistakes in calculations and started doubting the system itself. This led GCMMF to look into the problem seriously. To get the best deal to the cooperatives, they employed some software companies to automate the whole process. However, these initiatives were not without challenges. For instance, GCMMF had to give the systems at free of cost for AMCUS to some cooperative villages to convince the cynical farmers about the benefits of IT. These efforts of GCMMF paid off and the villagers recognized the importance of AMCUS. This helped the diffusion of IT into the rural communities.

Advantages

The time taken to collect the milk in a society ranges from five to six hours, averaging about five minutes per member after installing AMCUS. There is a comparative reduction of more than 75% of time spent on each deal. Each farmer is getting paid for the milk deposited in society's counter immediately on a real-time basis. Villagers were able to send their e-mails from AMCUS to anywhere in the world and DISK was expected to arrive at the village cooperatives in the year 2003, enabling the villagers to learn from the Internet and connect with enterprise systems of GCMMF. The DISK project, conceptualized by IIM-A, will have interconnectivity to a dairy portal at the district level, and serve the information to village cooperative society members. The application software provides cooperatives with the following:

- Data analysis and decision support to help rural milk collection society in improving its performance
- Data analysis to improve the productivity yield from the cattle
- Facilities for farmers to place orders for goods and services offered by different agencies in the dairying sector and collaboration on subjects of interest

The basic requirements of DISK are already met by the village cooperatives. There might be an upgrade required for the software and hardware in place, and an Internet connection would be required. For the portal at the unions, a small server and a leased line would be needed. The union portal can be implemented at a central location at one of the NDDB servers. Projects such as decision support systems and data mining packages are in pipeline of GCMMF action plan.

Economic Benefits

At GCMMF, there is average milk collection of ₹452.80 million litres from 2.2 million farmers. The AMCUS benefits the farmer community by saving ₹1159.4 million per year. The economic benefits do not include the knowledge and skill development, quality improvement, and the remaining subjective parameters. The AMCUS, when implemented in 2500 villages, might benefit the farmers when the DISK becomes operational, because of providing the farmers with the right and required education. The successful utilization of IT to bridge the digital divide has aptly been described by Dr M. V. Kurien as, 'Computers were not created for poverty reduction; hence, it is futile to except that the world will be a better place if we all had access to computers and the Internet but information is power and it stands to reason that if this power is shared equitably all will benefit'. Amul makes about 10 million payments every day, amounting to transactions worth ₹170 million in cash. More than 500 trucks move the milk from villages to 200 dairy processing plants, twice a day. The IT initiatives of Amul started in 1994 and IT became the major thrust area of GCMMF as it facilitates improvement in operational efficiency. Since then, GCMMF is marching ahead in a big way, starting from AMCUS to today's DISK.

Critical Success Factors

One of the critical factors that contributed to the success of the project has been the participation of the beneficiaries and the systematic communication. The village farmers assembling at a pre-specified location in the village discuss with the secretaries of the cooperative societies and tell them about the problem areas. The secretary of the society will ensure that action will be taken. Moreover, the village members elect the village cooperative boards. It is purely

a democratic set-up, which empowers the people.

All the external assessment proved that the AMCUS systems were effective. The model is getting replicated in other states. As the user feedback has been positive, GCMMF and village cooperatives are replicating this in other locations. The feedback system is giving them the right inputs for the improvement of the cooperative societies. The TQM measures of kaizen and quality circles are enabling the villagers to push forward their ideas to the higher officials, and they in turn are trying to resolve the issues when they come up. The ISO certifications are continuing at the district unions of GCMMF and are now moving to villages. The TQM initiative that is passed to the village cooperatives by GCMMF transformed them in a major way.

Discussion Questions

1. How do you think that Amul's deployment of ICT in supply chain management helped bridge the digital divide and benefited the rural poor?
2. What were the IT-related initiatives that Amul undertook in the cooperative's business management?
3. 'Amul's ICT initiatives not only helped its supply resources but immensely helped the cooperative to gain strategic advantage.' What do you think about this statement? Substantiate your answer with examples.
4. Make out a case for any other business organization, particularly a cooperative, which can replicate the success of Amul.
5. 'Amul is not a food company; it is an IT company in the food business'. Do you agree with this statement? Why or why not?

Sources:
'Amul story', http://www.planningcommission.nic.in/reports/sereport/ser/stdy_ict/2_intro.pdf; http://www.authorstream.com/anjusha786-138867-amul-entertainment; last accessed on 12 October 2011.
'ICT application in a dairy industry: The e-experience of Amul,' http://www.citeseerx.ist.psu.edu/viewdoc/download?doi, last accessed on 11 October 2011.
http://www.amul.com/m/bridge-the-digital-divide-innovation-at-the-grass-roots, last accessed on 15 October 2011.
http://www.nisearch.com/search/pdf/amul; http://www.amul.com/m/about-us, last accessed on 12 October 2011.

Part III

Information System Applications

- E-business Applications

- Enterprise Systems

- Applications for Service Sector

- E-commerce

- Decision Support Systems

- Knowledge Management and Intelligent Systems

- Mobile Computing and M-commerce

8

E-business Applications

> *Really difficult business problems always have many aspects. Often a major decision depends on an impromptu search for one or two key pieces of auxiliary information and a quick ad hoc analysis of several possible scenarios. You need software tools that easily combine and recombine data from many sources. You need Internet access for all kinds of research. Widely scattered people need to be able to collaborate and work the data in different ways.*
>
> **—BILL GATES**

LEARNING OBJECTIVES

After studying this chapter, you will be able to

- appreciate the meaning and scope of e-business enterprise
- distinguish various e-business applications
- define transaction processing systems (TPS) applications, e-communication, and e-collaboration
- appreciate cross-functional systems
- define the scope of marketing applications, and sales and distribution systems
- understand material management applications, finance, financial control applications, production planning, and control applications
- appreciate human resource management systems

EXHIBIT 8.1

Tata Refractories: Synergy between Technology and Business Processes

Tata Refractories Ltd (TRL) is India's leading refractories producer. It was established in 1958 and is located at Belpahar in the district of Jharsuguda in Odisha. TRL has been successfully meeting the needs of customers in steel, cement, glass, copper, zinc, aluminium, and petrochem industries for over five decades. Well known for their quality as well as customer satisfaction and performance, TRL products have found ready acceptance in USA, Chile, Zambia, Zimbabwe, South Africa, Middle East, and the Gulf countries.

TRL turned to information technology (IT) to push itself ahead in the competition. Today, the entire business process of the company is designed and driven by technology. TRL implemented Baan IV C4 enterprise resource planning (ERP) to gain real-time access to important data and to streamline business operations. A perfect synergy between IT systems and business processes is considered the ideal technology investment. Any investment in technology can only be justified if the user company experiences significant benefits to its overall business. After all, what would be the purpose of IT in a business if it fails to become a business facilitator?

TRL started its IT initiatives with a definite purpose. Right from the beginning, the management of the company knew that there was a need for an integrated system covering all the processes in the organization to achieve its objectives. After evaluating several packages, the company decided to implement Baan IV C4. 'We were looking for a solution having a module that could be localized to Indian taxation and duty structure norms. Baan's solution met most of our requirements', said C.D. Kamath, managing director of TRL.

The big task ahead was to reach a sophisticated level of technology with very little experience. Apart from selecting key users, the ERP implementation process was considered an opportunity to reengineer business processes. 'We were keen on a solution that did not need too much customization', explained Kamath. The pre-implementation process also involved creating awareness and allocating budgets.

Change Management
The first step towards implementation was to familiarize employees with the changes that were likely to take place post-implementation. In order to create a wave of change within the organization, TRL called the initiative, *Parivartan*

(meaning change). The implementation also involved coordinating with all concerned user departments to iron out any gaps in the implementation.

Baan typically follows a two-tier approach to any big-bang implementation. The first is the 'as is' approach, which studies existing processes in the organization and suggests various changes that would speeden them up. The second is the 'to be' approach that outlines details of the changes that are likely to occur in the workflow process. 'Both our approaches are basically meant to suggest the best alternative based on reference models picked up from all over the world. The system provides a bird's eye view of the workflow existing within the organization', said Ravi Kathuria, Baan's marketing director.

With Baan being the implementation partner, TRL focused on business issues rather than technical issues. 'There was a clear synergy between what we wanted to achieve in terms of processes and the use of the right technology to achieve the same', says Kamath. The implementation took place in a span of seven months with intensive knowledge transfer from the technology consultant to users, together with post-implementation handholding and stabilisation.

TRL also integrated its Baan ERP with a BlackBerry application for SMS alerts. The objective of the SMS solution was to send alert messaging from the field sales force about account receivables from debtors to be updated in the Baan ERP financial application at the very moment a cheque or bank draft was collected by the sales executive.

Benefits
Apart from achieving a complete turnaround in internal processes, TRL benefitted in other ways from its ERP implementation. From an organization where the use of computers was confined to a few key people, TRL emerged as an organization where the entire business was driven by the use of IT. Easing the whole process was some excellent training, change management initiatives, and the advantage of not having to deal with legacy systems.

By going in for a big-bang implementation, TR adopted the best business practices followed the world over to cut costs, streamline core activities, and gain a significant competitive advantage. 'An integrated ERP solution

(Contd)

Exhibit 8.1 (Contd)

automates the entire business process and helps decision-makers get a holistic view of the organization. The implementation of Baan's system increased the responsiveness of the company to changing business environments, thereby resulting in greater customer satisfaction', concludes Kamath.

There have been several noticeable benefits for TRL: finalization of monthly accounts by the second day of the following month; transparency of inventory, enabling faster turnover; and reduction in communication costs. TR's change from a supplier of refractory products to a complete service provider was thus successfully mapped and delivered through the Baan ERP system.

Sources:
Padmanabhan, Chitra, 'Tata Refractories: Another ERP success story', www.expresscomputeronline.com/20040517/ebusiness 01.shtml, last accessed on 17 May 2004.
'Tatas strike while the Iron is hot', *Economic Times*, http://www. articles.economictimes.indiatimes.com›Collections, last accessed on 10 December 2011.
www.avontechnologies.com/.../Case%20Study%20-%20 TRL_SMS.pdf, last accessed on 17 May 2004.

By implementing ERP, TRL not only achieved a complete turnaround in the internal processes, but also emerged as an organization where the entire business was driven by the use of IT. As it grew in size, TRL began to use various e-business applications and adopt Baan ERP, CRM, and BlackBerry applications to optimize their performance and profits. As students of business management, you must be aware of the various applications of ERP, which you will use during the course of your career. In Chapter 2, we briefly discussed management information systems (MIS) for various functional areas of management. This chapter will introduce you to business applications that support essential processes in the functional areas of business.

E-BUSINESS ENTERPRISE

With the emergence of computer technologies and the Internet, business organizations have undergone sea changes in their culture and structures. The new organization, known as e-business enterprise, enables employees, business partners, professionals, and other groups to perform business operations electronically, anytime and anywhere. The Internet has given e-businesses cutting-edge abilities to increase business value. It has opened new channels for businesses, shifting the focus from brick and mortar to virtual organizations. It has not only empowered customers and suppliers, but has also reduced the cost of business operations by eliminating paper-driven processes, and bringing about faster communication and effective collaborative working.

E-business enterprises are more process-driven, technology-enabled, and use information and knowledge to gain competitive advantages. According to Jawadekar (2007), the e-business enterprise is lean in number, flat in structure, broad in scope, and a learning organization. Most of the features in these enterprises are electronic; they use digital technologies and work on databases, knowledge bases, directories, and document repositories.

E-business has given birth to a new model of business and has brought about transformation in the existing enterprise. These transformations are mentioned here:

- Domestic business to global business
- Industrial economy to service economy
- Paper document-driven processes to paperless electronic transactions processes

E-BUSINESS APPLICATIONS

E-business applications refer to the use of the Internet and information technologies to support electronic commerce, communication within an enterprise, and collaborations. Sawhney and Zabin (2001) opine, 'contrary to popular opinion, e-business is not synonymous with e-commerce. E-business is much broader in scope, going beyond transactions to signify use of the Net, in combination with other technologies and forms of electronic communication, to enable any type of business activity'.

The scope of e-business is limited to executing the core business processes of the organization. These processes would have external interfaces such as suppliers, customers, business partners, and professionals. The core business processes are sales, procurement, material management, manufacturing, distribution, accounting, etc. Thus, e-business applications would cover the following: transaction processing systems (TPS), e-communications, and e-collaborations.

Transaction Processing Systems

The MIS model for e-business applications considers transaction processing as the basis for building an MIS. These applications work on a database model, that is, the application development is done over a database. The applications are meant for basic transaction processing. Business documents are generated using these applications, which also build a database of transaction records. These transactions include events that occur as part of carrying out businesses: sales, purchase, payment, receipts, etc.

The application has a query system, which processes and retrieves data in the desired format and style. The system generates the status of various business elements such as stock status, payment status, order, and so on. The system also generates real-time documents, for example, invoices, purchase orders, sales orders, dispatch advices, delivery notes, payment vouchers, etc. These applications also provide analytical information on various transactions. The analyses can be used to determine various trends and results such as sales trends, expenses trends, and inventory trends over a period of time.

An organization's internal and statutory requirements determine the types of reports generated from the system. The corporate management is interested in efficiency, profitability, and endurance of the organization. While ensuring organizational stability and growth, they have to comply with the statutory requirements. Therefore, statutory reports are generated for submission of information and taxes to the government.

Figure 8.1 illustrates the various business applications that serve the needs of the functional areas of a business (i.e., marketing, sales, material, production planning, finance, human resource, etc.).

E-communication

In an e-business enterprise, electronic communication is the backbone of all processes. Today, the most widely-used messaging systems are e-mail and voicemail. For real-time communication for multiple team members, video conferencing, voice conferencing, and electronic meeting systems are more popular.

Offline communication tools include web publishing, bulletin board systems, and paging systems. Web publishing uses websites and portals for publishing documents, catalogues, drawings,

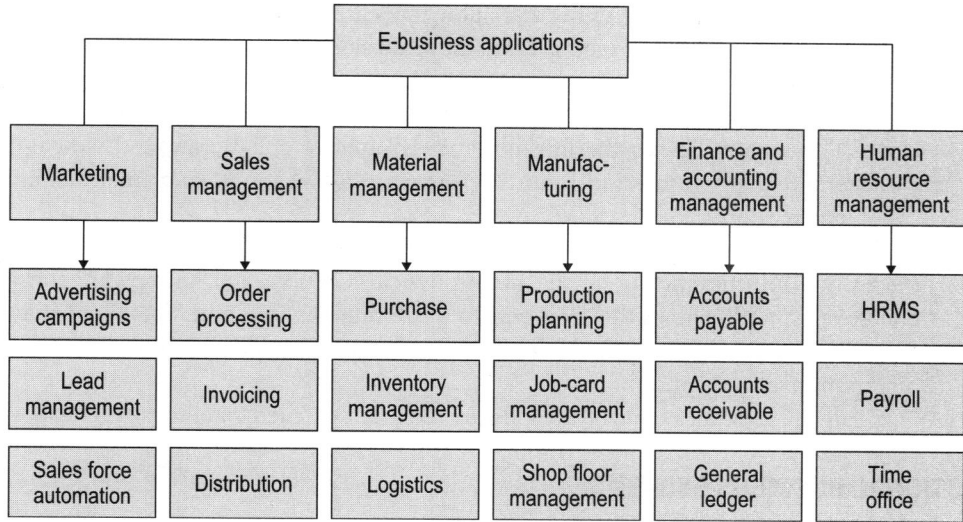

Fig. 8.1   E-business applications systems and their subsystems

pictures, and other information. E-communication channels are capable of sending messages, documents, and files in any format over the Internet.

E-collaboration

E-collaboration systems are cross-functional information systems that enhance communication, coordination, and collaboration among the various teams and workgroups in the organization. Information technologies, especially the Internet, provide tools to collaborate with various resources and workgroups. In an organization, collaboration refers to communication of ideas, sharing of resources, and coordination of work among workgroups. These capabilities help to

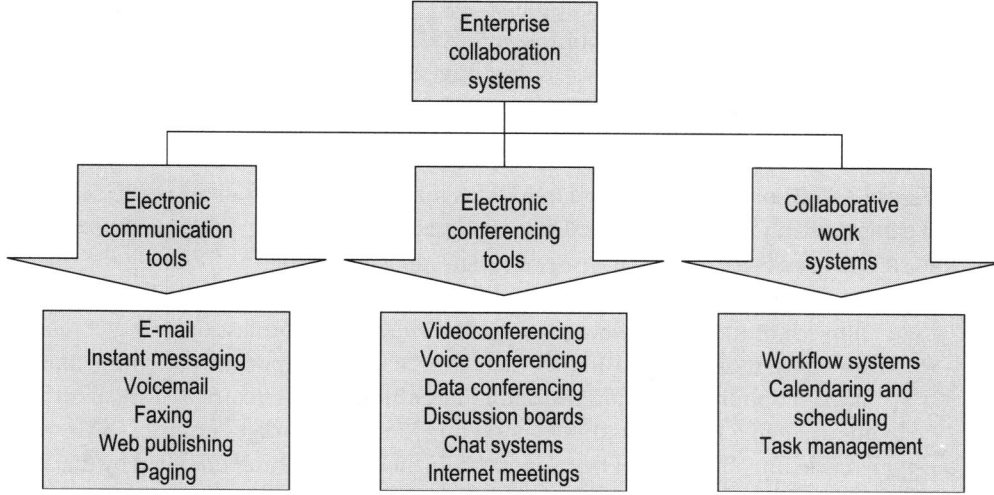

Fig. 8.2   Software tools for enterprise collaboration systems

create collaborative work systems that allow the team members to work together and cooperate with one another on their projects. Thus, they can share their wisdom, knowledge, and experience among the group members.

For example, employees, consultants, and professionals working on a project form a virtual team. The team relies on the intranet and extranet to collaborate and view e-mails, and for videoconferencing, discussion forums, groupware applications, and multimedia databases, to share information.

E-collaboration works on an Internet platform and uses web technologies; the members of the workgroup may not be at the same physical location. The groupware software increases effectiveness and enables the members to share information, and create and share documents. Lotus Notes, Novell GroupWare, Microsoft Exchange, Netscape Communicator, etc., are examples of groupware applications.

Figure 8.2 illustrates some of the software tools that are used for enterprise collaboration systems.

FUNCTIONAL BUSINESS SYSTEMS

Businesses have many functions to perform in order to buy, store, manufacture, and sell products or services. Now, our aim is to understand how information systems support these business functions and help them achieve success. As a student of business management, you must understand how information systems are used in a particular industry and how they support those functions.

Marketing Applications

Marketing is a pre-sales business activity. It involves identifying the target segment before starting sales initiatives. Marketing application tools help marketing staff identify, execute, and replicate effective marketing initiatives across sales channels. They can assign, schedule, and track marketing campaign activities and measure campaign performances. With marketing applications in place, the manager can integrate their pre-sales, marketing, and service processes more effectively and present an image of professionalism to the customers.

We will discuss IT tools and applications that support lead generation tools such as e-mail marketing and search engine optimization (SEO); and lead management tools like sales force automation (SFA) systems that use computing and Internet technologies to automate marketing activities for management support.

Prospecting, Leads, and Opportunity Management

Figure 8.3 illustrates how a typical marketing application covers all the processes from prospecting (i.e., identifying target customers) to negotiating and ordering. The marketing application uses basic data that is created during prospecting. Applications such as SFA help the sales staff manage more leads and also close more deals. This provides access to a complete view of a customer's data online or offline. SFA leverages tools that enable sales professionals to get real-time access to leads and close more deals faster. The staff can capture important sales information to uncover new business opportunities and use lead analysis reports to create precise sales forecasts.

Leads are generated through telemarketing, tenders, market enquiries, SMS marketing, bulk e-mail marketing, SEO, etc. These leads are further scanned and qualified by the authorized staff. Leads are also generated by the sales staff in the form of enquiries, which are recorded in the

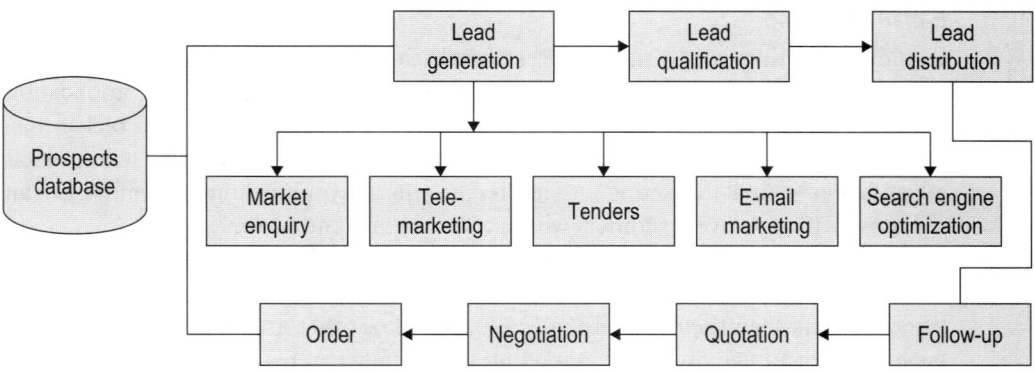

Fig. 8.3   TPS for marketing functions

computer for carrying out further action on them. Applications provide the functionality to track prospective customers and then convert them into qualified leads. The leads, once qualified, are then routed to the relevant salesperson or team for follow-up, as shown in Fig. 8.4. The system manages the sales opportunity funnel. The sales opportunity funnel determines sales leads in the pipeline that can be finalized by a certain date.

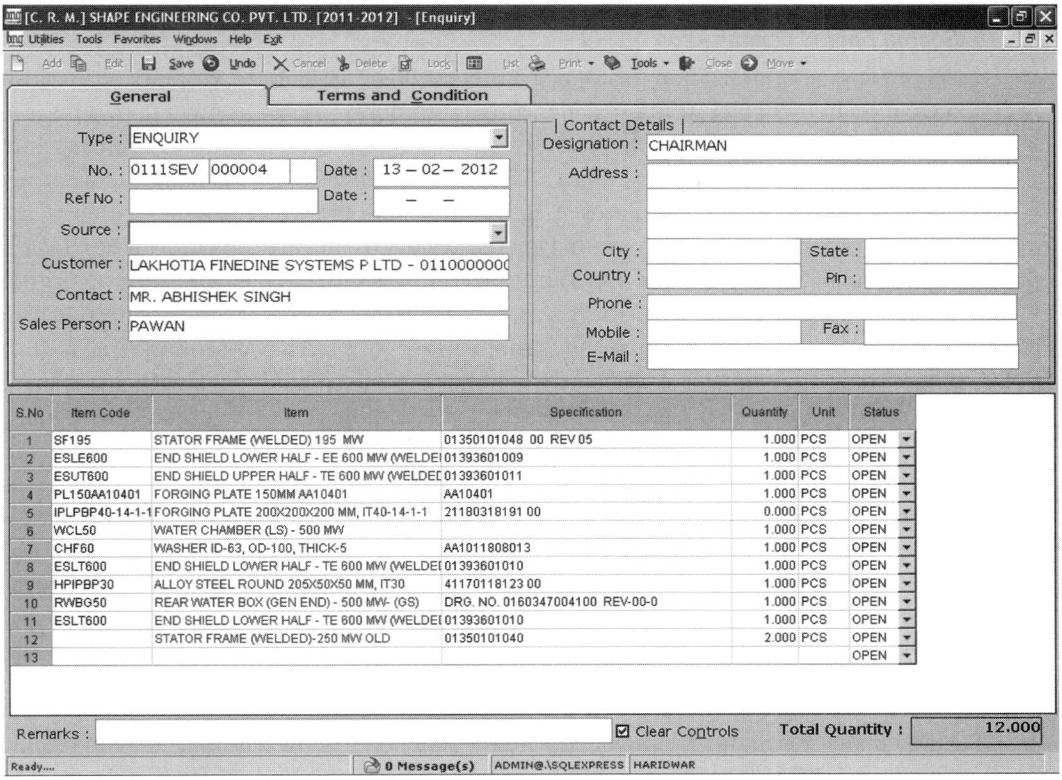

Fig. 8.4   Use of marketing applications to manage leads and opportunities

E-mail Marketing

E-mail marketing is a form of direct marketing that uses electronic mail as a means of communicating commercial messages to an audience. E-mail marketing applications facilitate sending bulk e-mails to a number of prospects at a time. The applications pick e-mail addresses from an existing database, which is usually provided by the companies selling databases. The advantage of e-mail marketing is that it is cost-effective and the intended message can be sent to millions of prospective customers within a very short span of time.

The advantage of e-mail marketing is that the return on investment can be tracked and is believed to be high, when done properly. However, this is treated as second best to search marketing. Internet users scan their e-mails and only read those that are of interest to them. Hence, the biggest disadvantage of e-mail marketing is that they can be rejected or not delivered because of their spam nature. Various legislatures, especially in the US, have passed anti-spam laws that prohibit unsolicited e-mails.

An alternative to e-mail marketing is opt-in or permission marketing, wherein the advertiser sends e-mails to only customers who have consented to receive the communiqué. A common example of permission marketing is a newsletter sent to an advertising firm's customers. Such newsletters inform customers of upcoming events, promotions, or new products. In this type of advertising, a company that wants to send a newsletter to their customers may ask them at the time of purchase, if they would like to receive the newsletter.

Search Engine Optimization

Search engine optimization (SEO) is the process of improving the visibility of a website or web page in search engines, using specific words, commonly known as meta tags. This is an unpaid form of Internet marketing. When an Internet user keys specific words in popular search engines (e.g., Google, Yahoo!, AltaVista, Bing, Ask, etc.), the crawlers track servers and web pages having that key word, and populates those page addresses on the search engines' results. Crawlers are software programs that find pages having the key words that are used in searches. Leading search engines such as Google, Bing, and Yahoo!, use crawlers to find pages for their algorithmic search results. Pages that are linked from other search engine-indexed pages do not need to be submitted because they are found automatically. Another form of search engine marketing is the paid form where web pages appear in lists only when they have been paid for. This includes the key words (names of websites) in a search engine's database and thus ensures guaranteed appearance. The more frequently a site appears on the top of a listing, the more customers or visitors it will get.

Optimizing a website may involve submission of meta words continuously to various search engines, domains, and public networking sites. This also involves editing the site's content, HTML, and the associated coding to increase its relevance to specific keywords and for removing barriers to the indexing activities of search engines. To get effective results, the SEO promotion should register the activity regularly, as every competitor endeavours to get their site on top of the listing and in the process, a company may be relegated down in the results.

Account Management

Marketing applications are provided with the function to view past and current account activity, including contact information, communications, price quotes, and negotiation details. The account information is updated at every stage of interaction with the customer during a sales cycle. All

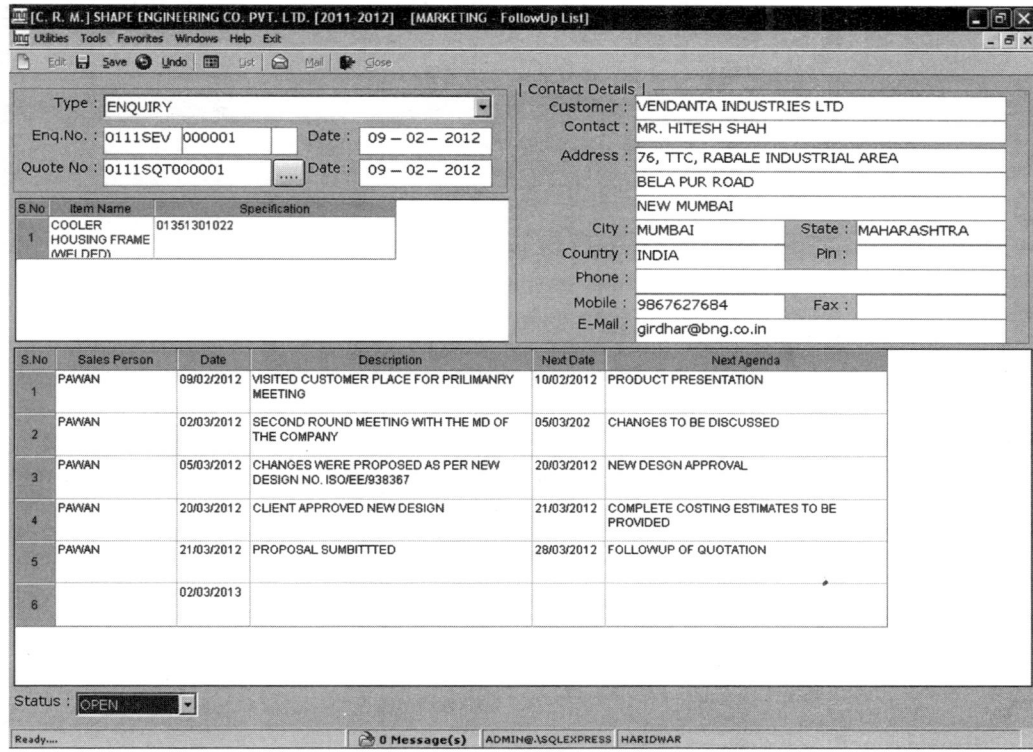

Fig. 8.5   Recording and viewing of customer communications

communications with the prospective customer are maintained in the system at all stages of lead follow-up, as depicted in Fig. 8.5.

Worldwide, companies are taking the help of SFA, the sales contact management software that connects salespeople to marketing websites on the Internet and intranet. This not only increases the personal productivity and efficiency of salespeople, but also speeds up the database building process, which is available for analysis of the marketing heads. Sales managers benefit from improved delivery and quality of information, and the support and guidance they provide to their subordinates.

Figure 8.6 shows Zoho CRM, one of the scores of applications available for SFA.

Sales and Distribution Applications

Sales involve order processing, invoicing, and outbound logistics that result in the transfer of title of ownership of goods and services to the customer. The various sales and distribution TPS include order confirmation, delivery scheduler, dispatch advice, invoicing, and sales budgeting. Sales analysis provides the information for a decision support system (DSS) to a manager. Figure 8.7 illustrates various sales information systems.

Sales applications help in decision analysis. Day-to-day decisions are taken on pricing, order acceptance, stock allocation to order, discounts, commissions, payment terms, etc. These decisions

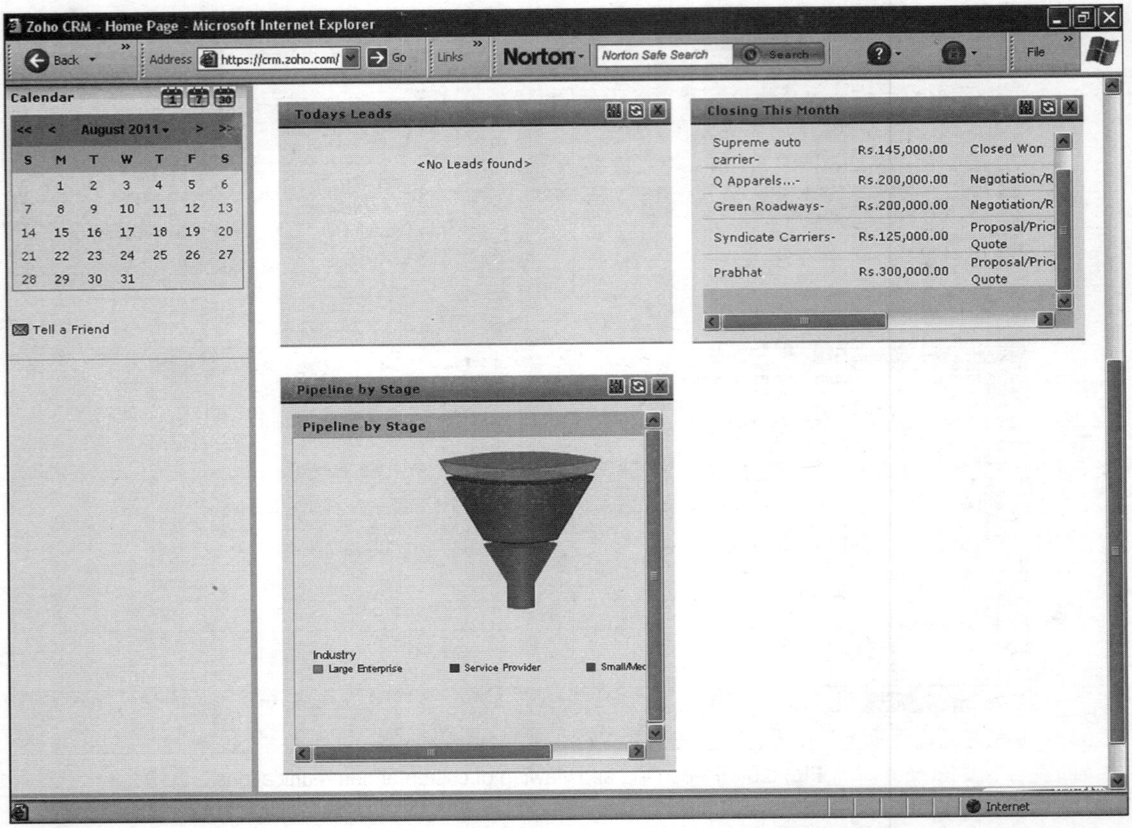

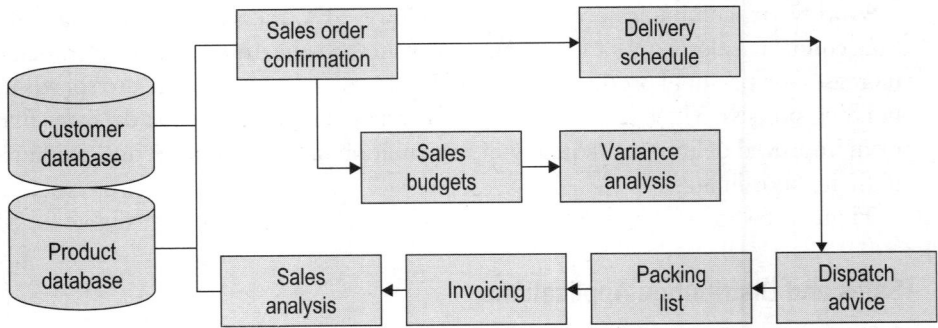

Fig. 8.6   Recording and viewing of complete customer communications [Zoho CRM, www.crm.zoho.com]

Fig. 8.7   TPS for sales and distribution

are of routine nature and are based on predefined rules; therefore, they are made with the help of DSS offered by the application. Strategic or tactical decisions are related to price increase or decrease, launching of new products, packaging, distribution channels, product positioning, segmentation, etc. Besides analysis for the management, as shown in Fig. 8.8, applications also help create statutory reports and returns related to taxation and excise duty, which are submitted to various government agencies.

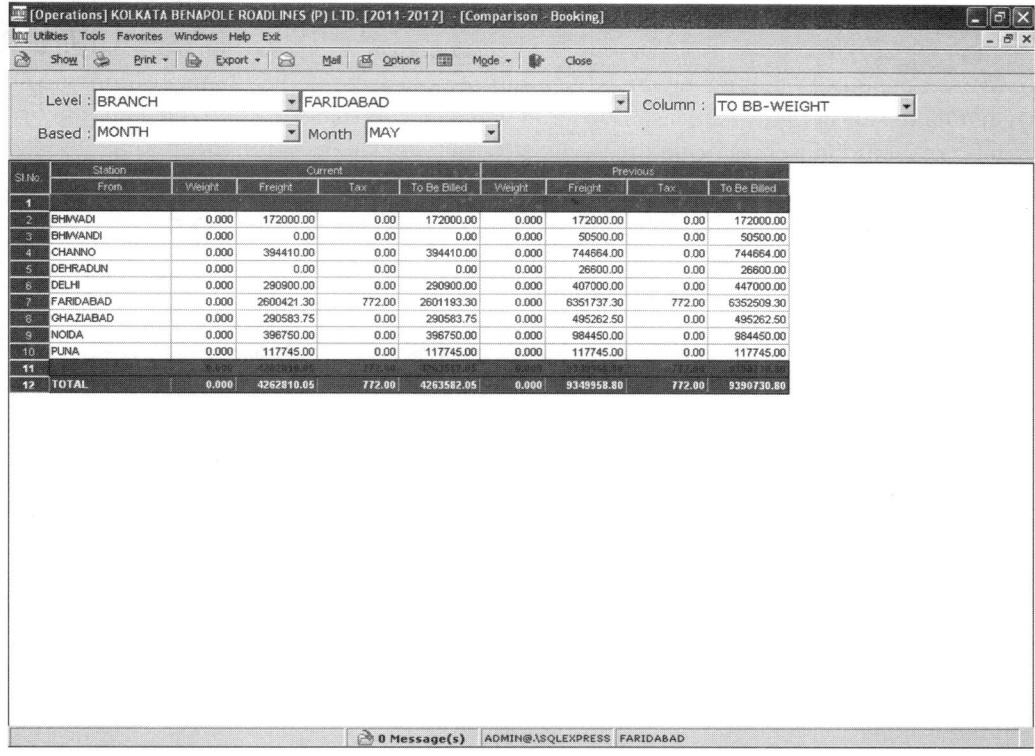

Fig. 8.8   Application displaying branch-wise booking comparison of a transport company

The e-business applications not only streamline and support business processes, but also help cut costs and achieve profitability.

For example, TRL, as illustrated in Exhibit 8.1, achieved a reduction in communication costs (by ₹20 lakh per annum) since the output data relating to customers and suppliers is hosted on the Internet.

Material Management Applications

The scope of the material management system includes the complete process of material procurement, storage, and control of inventory. It covers material requirement planning, vendor management, and warehousing functions, as shown in Fig. 8.9. Material management systems ensure availability of material to the production department at the right time and in the right quantity. It provides analysis on requirement of materials based on the number of customer orders in hand, availability of material in the warehouse, and the capacity of the plant and warehouse. The warehousing functions in a business concern involve receipt, storage, and dispatch of goods. Effective material management systems ensure the least investment in inventories and minimum inventory carrying costs. Modern business management techniques talk about 'zero' or JIT inventory; however, the storage function cannot be done away with. Inventories can be reduced but not completely removed from the warehouse. Such systems help in managing JIT inventories as well, besides helping in ascertaining the inventory value,

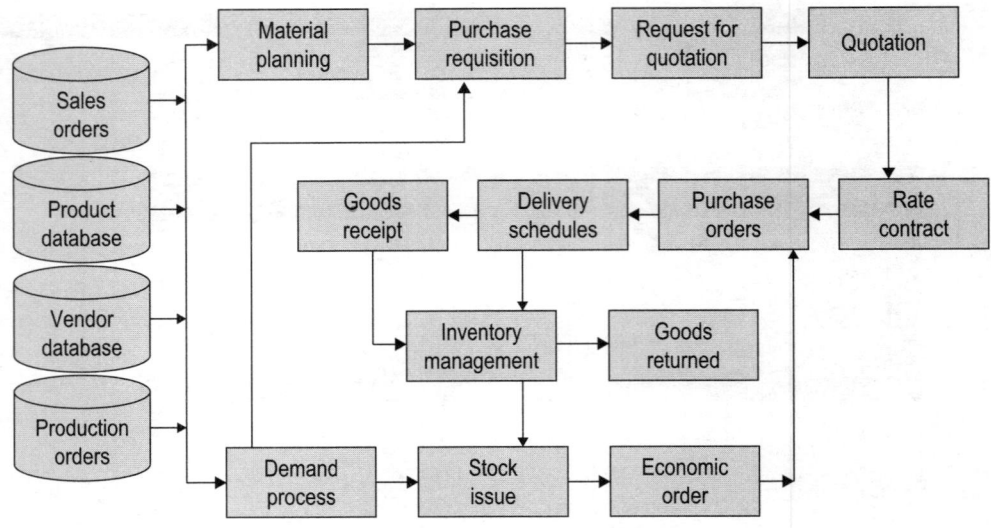

Fig. 8.9   Material management TPS

the inventory carrying costs, cost of last-moment procurement in case of stock failure, etc. As an example, Exhibit 8.2 illustrates how HP ships computers to customers quickly and keeps inventory costs low.

EXHIBIT 8.2

ERP Keeps Inventory Updated at HP

According to Jean-Luc Meyer of Hewlett-Packard (HP), the PC business is like the fruit business. As every following day, fresh fruits become less valuable, the ever-decreasing PC prices make the business as much challenging. Computer technologies develop so quickly that computers in the shelf become technically outdated quickly. To help the company sell its computers at full price, HP created a sophisticated supply chain management system that produces PCs as per order and the company ships them to customers within 48 hours.

The new ERP system automates the process. Orders are placed through the systems, which in turn forward the data to HP's production and delivery application. The supply chain management system is also linked to some of HP's suppliers. For example, a contract manufacturer in California receives the orders from HP. Their system checks the credit outstanding to the customer and then validates the order. Once everything is fine, the authorized order is sent to the production control module. This system prints a job-order for the assembly technicians and a store requisition note to the warehouse of the contract manufacturer. The spare parts are thus shipped to the assembly floor, along with the job order. The assembly technicians then assemble the computer and send it to the testing workstation. The job order also has a checklist for add-ons and is inspected accordingly. The new computer system is packed, boxed, tagged, bar coded, and then shipped. The activities are monitored over the Internet using an enterprise software.

The ERP system at HP enables customers to receive their computers quickly while HP minimizes production costs and faults. The system helps in reduction of over stocking of parts and finished products. The order processing system is so efficient that HP has been able to reduce the waiting time for new orders. Suppliers can also monitor the stock of their products through an interface available to them. The contract manufacturers do not have to keep huge inventories and have thus helped in the implementation of the just-in-time (JIT) inventory concept.

Sources:
O'Connor, Roy J., 'Keeping inventory fresh', *Upside*, June 2000.
Wailgum, Thomas, *The CIO Magazine*, www.cio.com, April 2008.

There are many processes involved in complete material management. Some of the applications described here are based on these processes.

Forecasting and Planning

When to buy? How much to buy? The answers to these questions lie in purchase forecasting and planning. Purchase planning is a meticulous task based on careful analysis of material requirements to fulfil the orders in hand, materials required at the production floor, and materials available at the warehouse. An efficient material management application takes into account factors such as minimum order quantity (MOQ), economic order quantity (EOQ), reorder level (ROL), quantity on hold (QOH), stock allocation, and goods in transit. In a manufacturing set-up, material planning is also determined by the production capacity of the plant. In a trading organization, 'how much to buy' is answered by taking into account the previous period's sales with seasonal variations, projected sales, and organizational goals in terms of sales turnover. Purchase planning is based on demand forecasting, reordering level of products, and sales estimations (as part of procurement management).

Figure 8.10 provides a snapshot of material requirement generated by a material-planning application.

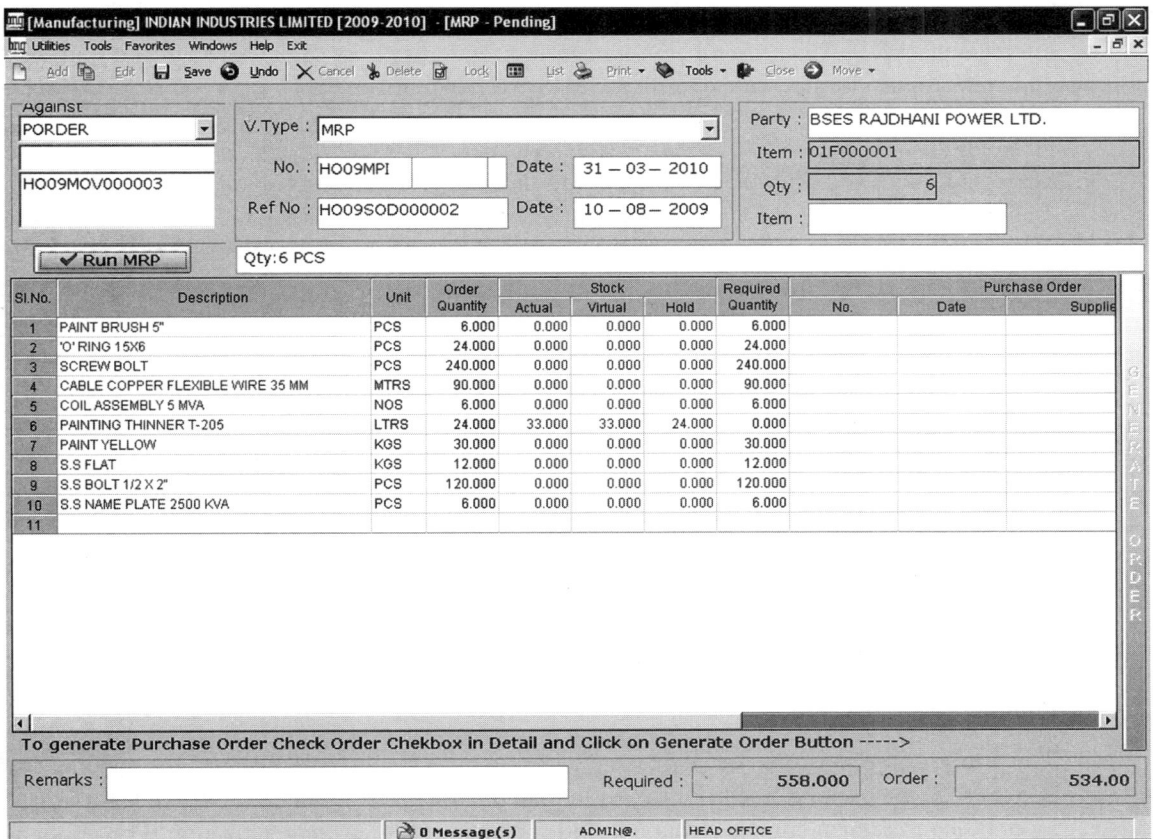

Fig. 8.10   Material requirement generated by the application

Material Procurement

Procurement involves the complete process of ordering to receive material. It includes evaluating and selecting the vendor, floating enquiries, generating comparative charts for comparing prices and terms of various suppliers, and generating purchase orders (POs). The system maps items with procurement terms and constraints (e.g., lead time, lot size, etc). The individual suppliers' purchase order terms and conditions are defined. The systems facilitate floating of enquiries known as request for quotation (RFQ). The auto mailing feature enables sending of automatic mails to pre-configured addresses in the supplier database.

Quotations received from various vendors are tabulated to create a comparative chart. The system calculates the least price (L1) based on quantifiable attributes of the quotation. Non-quantifiable attributes such as 'good quality' and 'nearest location' are not considered by the system for calculating the least price. The purchase department consolidates or splits the purchase requests received from the warehouse. This request is known by names such as indent, requisition, purchase request, or demand note.

Purchase order   These are raised by the supplier for supply of material, as seen in Fig. 8.11. POs are based on purchase requests, which in turn, are results of material planning. Efficient purchase ordering applications allow e-mail or electronic transmission of purchase orders to suppliers. Enterprise applications facilitate transmission of PO data through electronic data interchange (EDI), which uses a standard format understood by applications at the suppliers' end. The applications provide a purchase MIS (as shown in Fig. 8.12).

Inventory Control

Storage of goods and control of inventory is the next important function in material management. The major functions of inventory control involve receiving of goods from vendors, carrying out inspections, issuing goods for sales or production, and returning defective items or excess material to the vendor.

Stock movements in a warehouse happen through inward and outward processes. On receipt of goods from vendors, a document called material receipt note (MRN) is created. Inventory is reduced due to stock-out functions like goods issue notes (GIN). This function facilitates issue of goods to selected departments. Thus, proper control and management of inventory is the central objective of material management.

Applications providing analytical reports on inventory control function as a DSS for the management. The system helps in planning, decision-making, and improving business efficiency. Some of the important MIS/DSS are provided on the basis of stock variance reports, price variance reports, supplier performances, pending purchase orders, purchase trends, stock statements, inventory valuations, stock movements, and minimum, maximum, and reorder levels of inventory. These analyses are generated through a query builder, as shown in Fig. 8.13.

Finance and Accounts

The primary objective of financial management is to meet the financial needs of the organization and manage the working capital for the business to be sustainable in the long term. It takes care of money (finances), men (human resources), and machines (assets) in an organization. This helps the management not only in decision-making (based on analysis of internal transactional data), but also

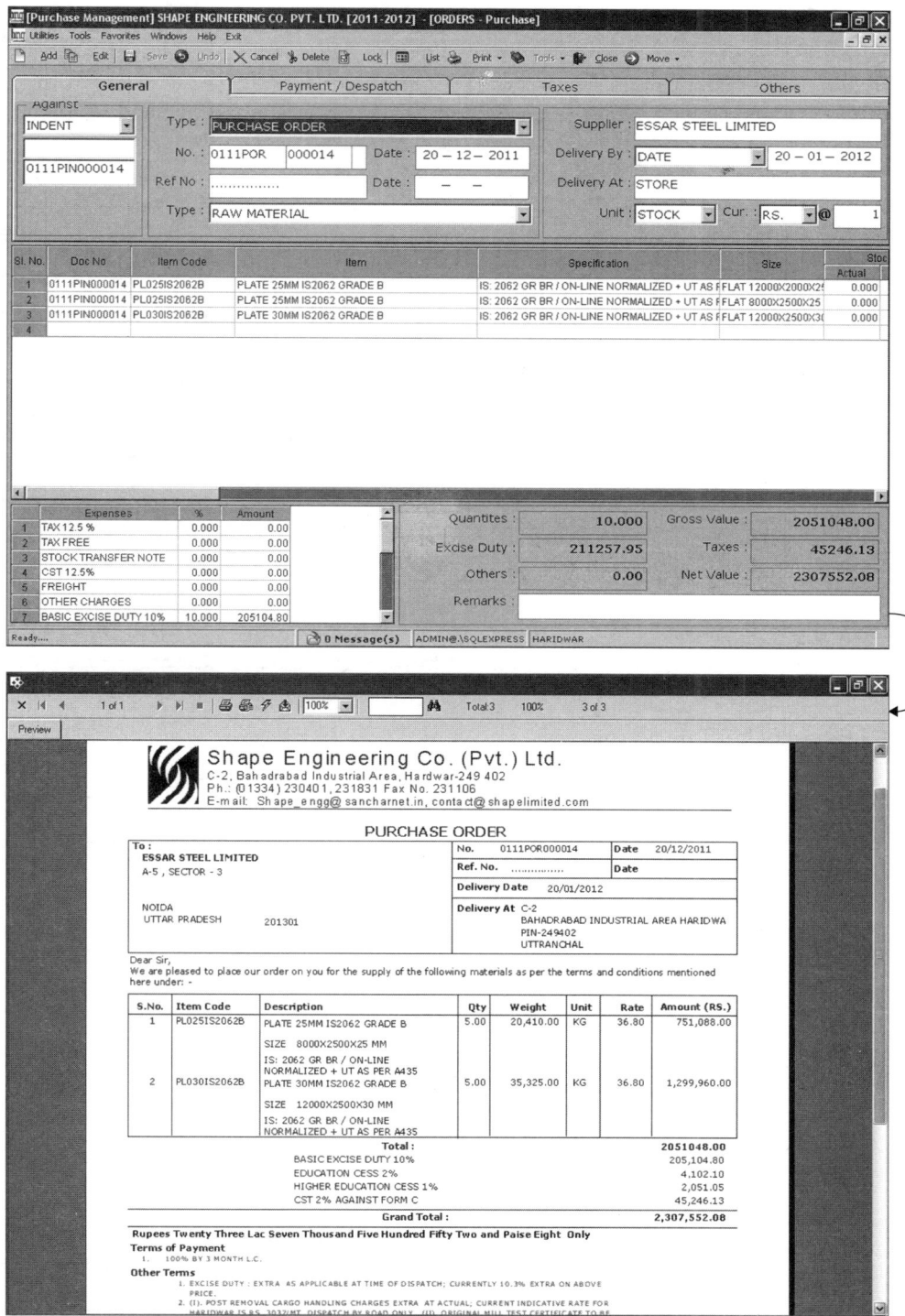

Fig. 8.11   Purchase ordering systems provide electronic as well as paper-based POs

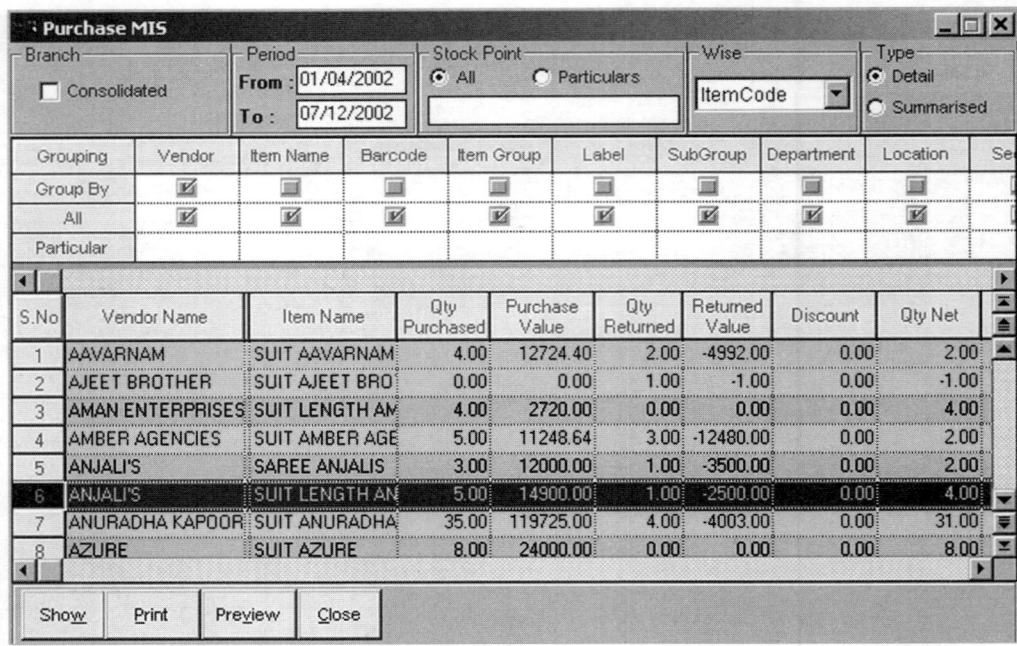

Fig. 8.12   Purchase MIS generated by the system

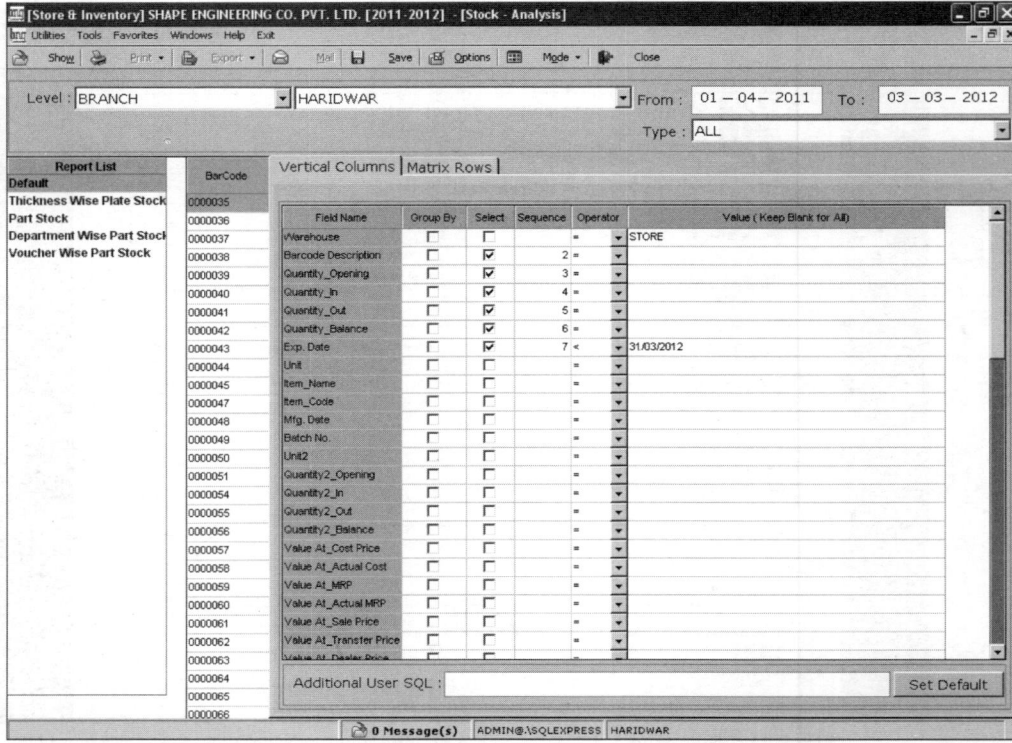

Fig. 8.13   Application tools and query builders for inventory analysis

in strategic decision-making, which is the result of external and internal data analysis. Information systems for finance offer measurable benefits in terms of cost reductions, profit maximization, and revenue realization. The information provided through financial functions helps the management have better control over its affairs, offers better competitive advantages, and long-term business sustenance. The finance department is expected to be more responsive than others when it comes to budgeting and forecasting; they thus manage risks to mitigate their effects. This department also works effectively by supporting the value chain. With organizations metamorphosing from single location, single-unit businesses to huge global giants, keeping track of human resources and managing assets have become a critical aspect of finance information systems.

Financial applications cover various TPS and generate reports for MIS and DSS (as shown in Fig. 8.14).

Transaction Processing Systems for General Ledger

A general ledger (GL) is central to the accounting system. It provides a platform for transaction entry, processing, and consolidation of data pulled up from other systems such as sales and purchases. Transactions related to receipts and payments are facilitated through transaction vouchers (as shown in Fig. 8.15).

The GL receives data from the *accounts receivable* and *accounts payable* systems. Accounts receivable systems involve complete processing of customers bills, generation of recovery plans, pending payments from individual customers, and ageing of debts up to the latest details. This helps in the cash flow management of the organization, which is crucial for efficiency, effectiveness, and long-term sustenance of the organization. A financially sound organization can have a competitive

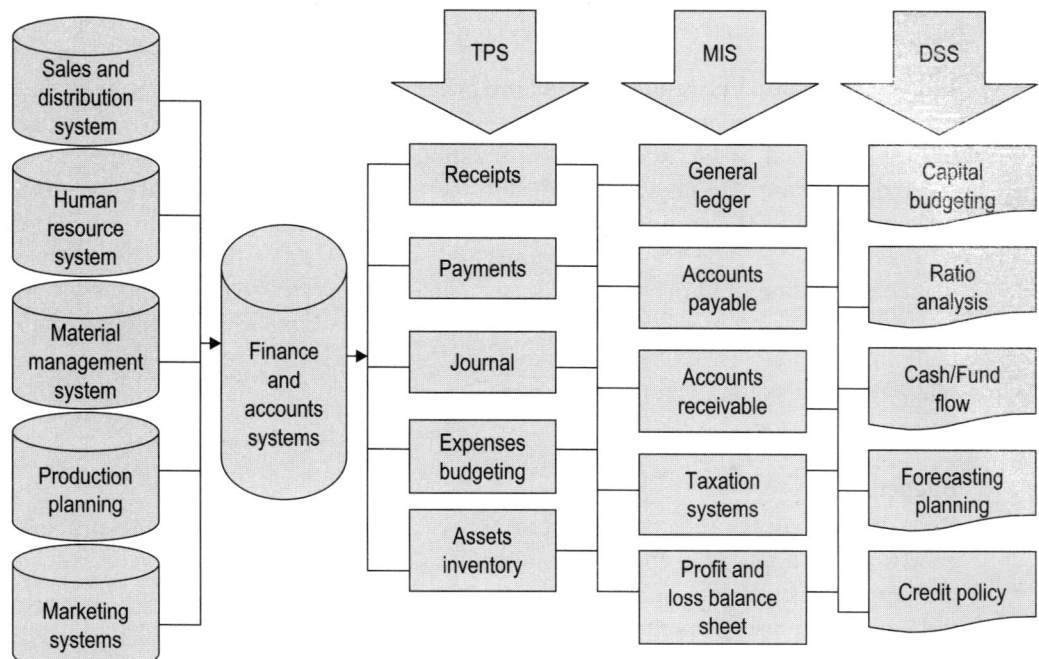

Fig. 8.14 Finance applications showing their relationship with TPS, MIS, and DSS

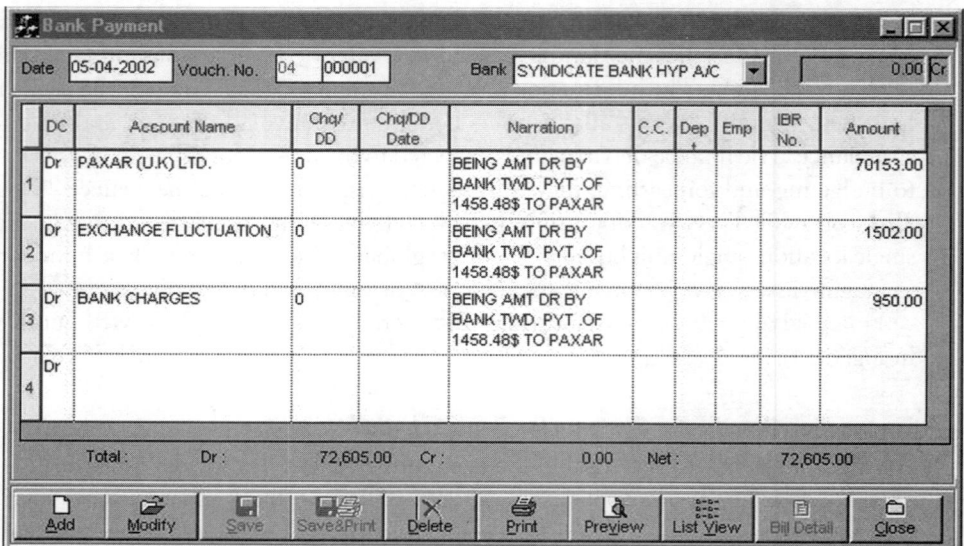

Fig. 8.15   Transaction system for bank payment voucher [Brainsoft India Inc.]

edge and work towards satisfying its customers and employees. Outstanding bills are assets of the organization in the hands of their customers. Accounts receivable systems help finance managers plan the recovery of these assets and also maintain cash flows. Ageing and recovery plan reports generated by the system help managers plan expenditures in advance, as illustrated in Fig. 8.16. Accounts payable systems involve complete processing of suppliers bills, generation of payment schedules, pending payments to vendors, and ageing of their bills.

Interrelationship between financial and other systems   Finance applications are dependent on other applications such as sales, purchases, and human resources. Data is automatically entered into the financial system at the time of creation of a transaction. For example, when a bill is created, it updates the sales database, customer database, and other heads like taxes, etc. The activity itself pushes data into bills receivables. The data is now available in the 'bills receivables' module for further processing, monitoring, and control. Most of the time, the finance personnel in an organization want to scrutinize the data before it is posted to the financial systems. For such systems, the application may provide 'data pull' procedures. Similarly, in a purchase transaction, the material receipt note (MRN) is authorized and the data is transferred to financial accounting (i.e., bills payables account). Figure 8.17 shows the interrelationship among the important accounting information systems.

Budgeting

Budgets and cost controls are an important part of higher levels of financial management. A good financial application comprehensively offers budgeting and analysis on cost centres. Budgets are permitted outlays on individual heads of expenditures. Organizations plan in advance as to how much must be spent on what. The budgets are set on the basis of past experience and future probable, planned, and unplanned expenditures. Budgeting systems help organizations to set budgets and compare actual expenditures periodically. Variance analysis over budgeted

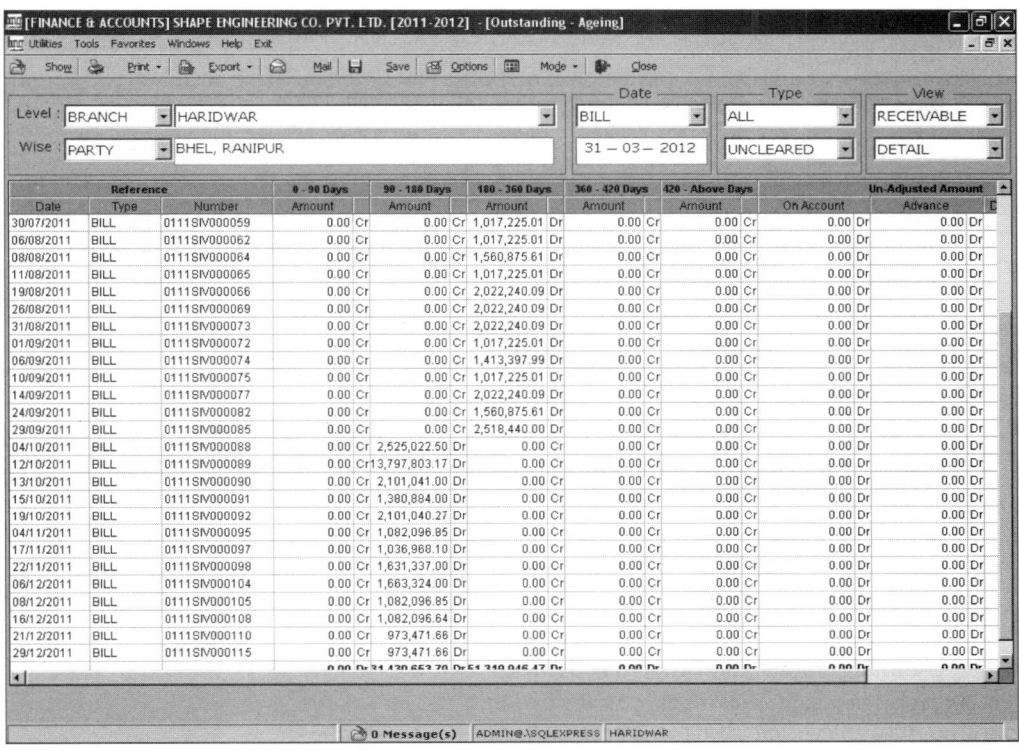

Fig. 8.16   Ageing of debt receivables

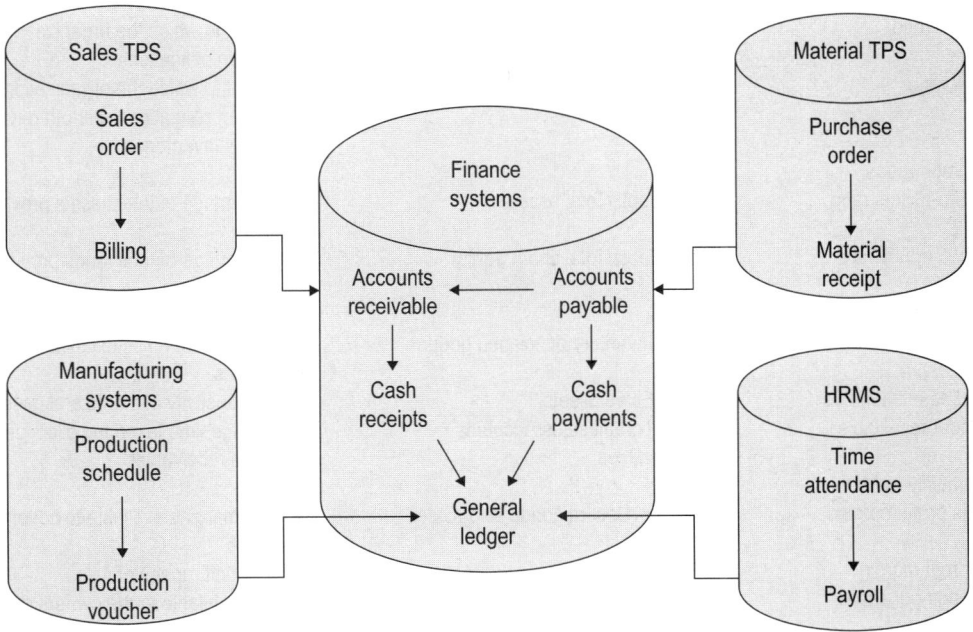

Fig. 8.17   Financial systems' interrelationship with other TPS

expenditures helps maintain them within permitted levels so that remedial action can be taken if the budgets overshoot.

Taxation and Statutory Reporting

A major portion of any financial application is devoted to taxation and tax reporting. Taxation is an indispensable part of accounting systems. The tax systems are very complex and tend to change frequently, at least once in a year. There are local, state, and central taxes. Proper accounting of all these taxes is carried out and periodical information in the form of 'returns' is sent to the government. These taxes include excise duty (ED) on manufactured goods, sales tax, value added tax (VAT) on traded goods, service tax on services rendered to the customer, and tax deducted at source (TDS) on payments made to service providers and suppliers of services.

Ratio Analysis

Ratio analyses reflect the financial position of a company. Most strategic decisions related to an organization are based on and influenced by the financial position of the company. The financial health of the company is presented by analytical reporting in the form of financial funds flows and ratio analysis. Financial ratio analysis is the most widely used method for determining an organization's strengths and weaknesses. These are dependent on the investment, financing, and dividend areas. As the functional areas of business are interrelated, financial ratios can signal strengths or weaknesses in management, production, research and development, marketing, or computer information system activities.

Table 8.1   Ratio analysis provided by financial applications

Ratio	Method of calculation	Significance
Liquidity ratios		
Current ratio	Current assets/Current liabilities	The extent to which the organization can meet its short-term obligations
Quick ratio	(Current assets – Inventory)/ Current liabilities	The extent to which the organization can meet its short-term obligations, without relying upon the sale of its inventories
Leverage ratios		
Debt-to-assets ratio	Total debts/Total assets	The percentage of total assets provided by creditors
Debt-to-equity ratio	Total debts/Total share equity	The percentage of total funds provided by creditors versus owners
Activity ratios		
Inventory turnover ratio	Sales/Inventory of finished goods	Whether the firm holds excessive stocks of inventories
Fixed assets turnover	Sales/Fixed assets	Sales productivity of plants and assets
Account receivable turnover	Annual credit sales/Accounts receivables	The average time taken to collect debts or accounts receivables
Profitability ratios		
Gross profit margins	(Sales – Cost of goods sold)/Sales	The total margins available to cover operating expenses
Net profit margin	Net income/Sales	Profit per unit rupees of sales
Earnings per share	Net income/Number of shares in equity shares	Earnings available to the owners of equity stocks

An organization's income statement and balance sheet are used to compute the financial ratios. Financial ratios reflect the position of a business at a particular point of time. The two key financial ratios that indicate whether a firm's financing decisions have been effective or not are the debt-to-equity ratio and the debt-to-total assets ratio. Ratios are grouped under common ratios, liquidity ratios, leverage ratios, activity ratios, and profitability ratios. Some of the most commonly used analyses on flows and ratios are given in Table 8.1.

Fixed Assets Management

Organizations need fixed assets such as machinery, land, buildings, and vehicles, among others, to run their business operations. Hence, they accumulate a large number of assets during their lifetime. Assets are used, depreciated, and transferred from one location to another. Keeping track of the assets becomes a nightmare, especially if the organization is large, multi-locational, and has several units. Assets management systems take care of such complexities. This module maintains a history of the asset since its purchase. It links all the expenses incurred on repairs and maintenance of the assets. Annual depreciation is calculated as per the laws and rules. These systems also provide advanced analytical reports on replacement costs and realization values of assets.

Assets value and depreciation charts are part of balance sheets and submitted to the government as a statutory report. Financial applications are expected to deliver these functionalities.

HUMAN RESOURCE MANAGEMENT

Human resource management systems (HRMS) or personnel management systems (PMS) deal with the human aspect of the organization. The primary objective of the human resource management (HRM) function is to provide the required human resources with relevant experience and expertise to all the functional departments. HRM works towards employee recruitment, training, motivation, retention, and development. A satisfied employee is going to serve the customer better. This modern concept of human management, coupled with information technology as a tool and enabler of systems, has brought HRM to the fore of the organization. IT is playing a key role in people management and HR departments are discarding costly, time-consuming manual processes, and adapting IT-enabled HRMS.

The deployment of HRMS over a corporate intranet allows employees to receive and send valuable information to their respective departments. They can apply online for leave, enter tour programmes, obtain travel information, view the status of their applications, scrutinize salary slips, and other relevant files. HR departments can train their employees by providing online content and videos, and instruct employees on various occasions.

The HR activities in an organization can be divided into two—HR functions and payroll functions. HR functions cover non-financial activities related to employee recruitment, training, placement, transfers, appraisals, promotions, and retirement. Payroll activities relate to financial aspects such as remuneration, leave, loan, perks, provident fund (PF), employee state insurance (ESI), and income tax computation and deductions. Figure 8.18 illustrates both the functions of HRMS.

Human Resource Functions

Human resource management applications take care of workforce development in the organization. It enables managers to better understand what exactly is required from the workforce. The tool

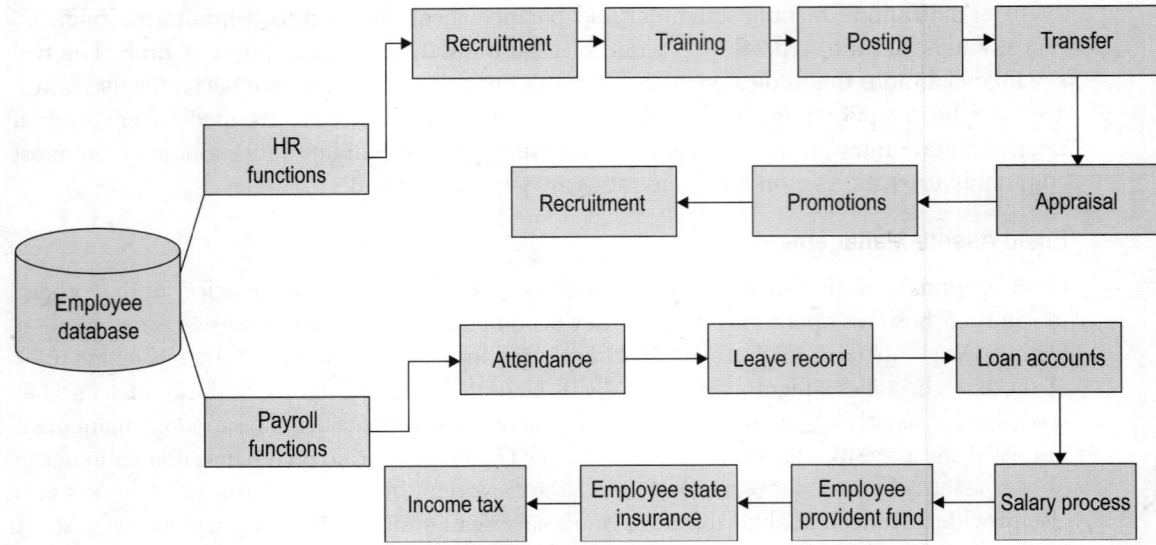

Fig. 8.18   Human resource management systems

reduces costs, improves recruitment of skilled staff, streamlines union grievances, improves workforce morale, and reduces time spent on generating statutory information to the government.

The recruitment process involves handling requisitions from departments, advertising vacancies, and matching candidate profiles against requirements. It also includes interview and selection of candidates. Training is provided to the selected candidates. The HR module facilitates creation of training schedules, assignment of employees to the schedule, assignment of departments to the schedule, and collection of feedback regarding the training, training history, and instructor details. Employee postings, transfers, promotions and maintenance of leave records are handled by the systems. Appraisal of employees is an important part of any human resource system. Appraisal consists of questions related to an employee's job and work environment, their personal goals and achievements in the workplace, which are answered by the employees themselves, and graded by their seniors. Retirement, gratuity, and related issues are also handled efficiently with a proper HRM application in place.

Internet-based online systems involve online solicitation of applications, interviews, and recruitment. Figure 8.19 displays the kind of employee information that is entered in the HRMS application.

Payroll Functions

Payroll is a subsystem of HRMS. It takes care of salary, attendance, leave, bonus, overtime, advances, and income tax computation functions. Employee provident funds (EPF) and ESI are the two welfare measures for employees; every HRM system provides procedures for these. For PF and ESI, periodical reports and documents are submitted to the respective regulatory bodies.

HRMS applications interface with attendance marking systems, commonly known as time access machines, for automated attendance marking. Income tax planning, deductions, and e-returns are an important part of any payroll system, as shown in Fig. 8.20 and Exhibit 8.3.

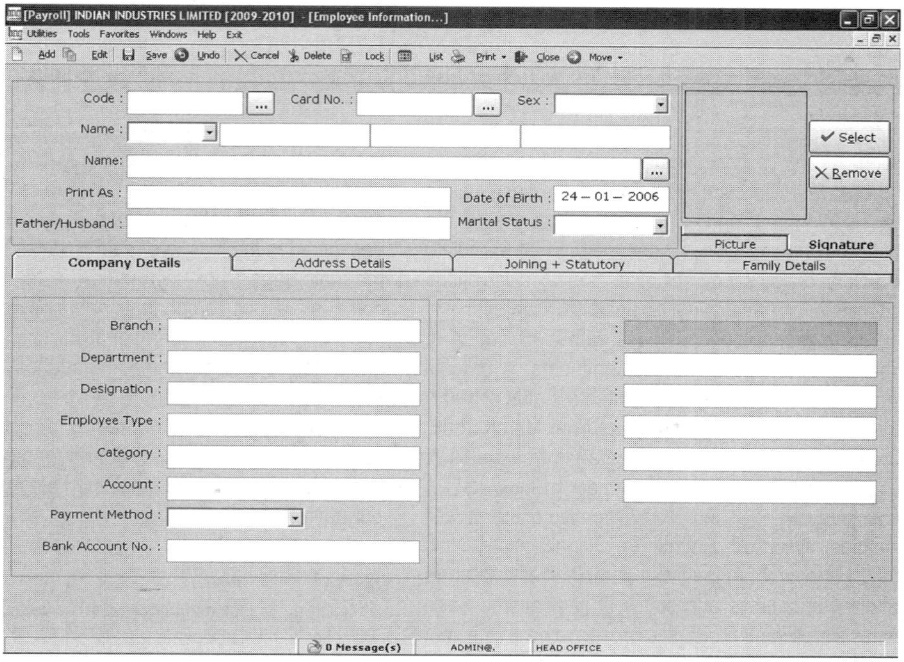

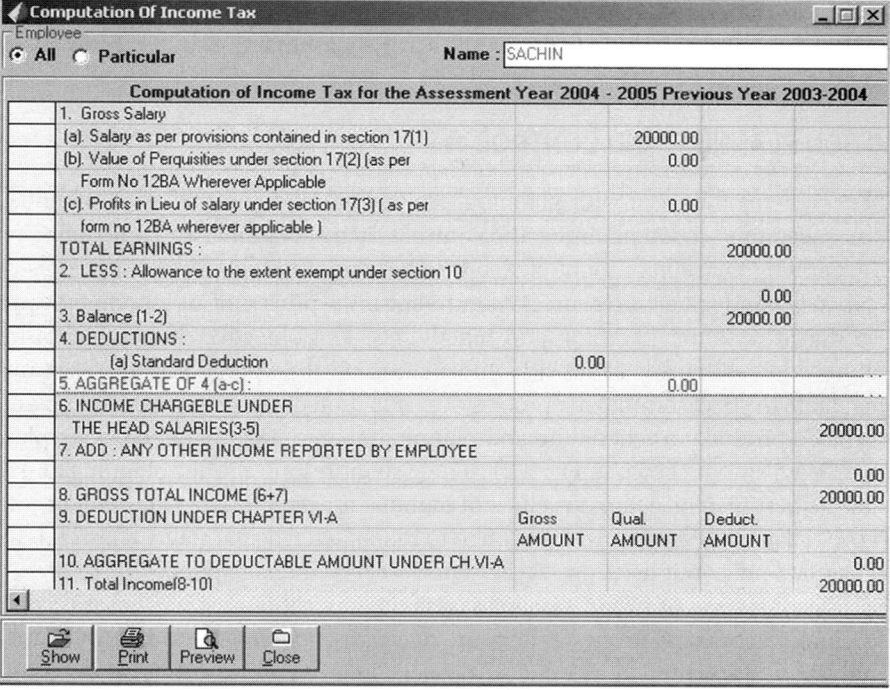

Fig. 8.19   Employee profile building in an HRM application

Fig. 8.20   Tax planning and computation in HRMS applications

EXHIBIT 8.3

Sage Helps Winjit Tech Improve Payroll Processing

Sage India has successfully deployed Sage Pocket, a payroll application, at Winjit Technologies to automate the company's payroll processes. With over 70 employees, the Nasik-based software development and consulting company uses the application to compute salaries, generate payslips, calculate PF and ESI, and also keep track of income tax calculations and deductions, and maintain a record of investments.

Winjit is a technology business with a presence in more than 30 countries across all continents. With local offices around the globe, Winjit attainted a status of 100% export oriented unit (EOU) with effect from March 2006, which has helped the company enjoy a tax-free status. It is now called a software technology park of India (STPI) unit. K. Ashwin, founder and chief executive officer, Winjit Technologies, remarked, 'Payroll is a crucial activity which is repeated every month involving complexities related to calculations, deductions and statutory regulations. Sage Pocket has simplified the task and proven to be an efficient and effective way of payroll in our organization.'

Payroll processing being an error prone activity, the HR team at Winjit faced typical challenges in the computation of salaries including variable pay. Errors were common in the full and final settlement and increased when employees joined in the middle of a term as the processes were manual. Sage Pocket enabled the team to accurately compute various components of the payroll function, thus improving the overall operational efficiency. Winjit has also integrated its biometric time and attendance records with the Sage Pocket payroll.

Thomas Abraham, managing director, Sage India stated, 'Sage Pocket is positioned for small and medium businesses in India and small markets like Nasik's adopt our payroll solution'.

Sources:
CXO Today Magazine, March 2010, www.cxotoday.com, last accessed on 10 December 2011.
www.winjit.com, last accessed on 10 December 2011.

Statutory reports and income tax certificates are also provided by the system. HRMS provide MIS reports on salary, arrears, bonus, leave encashment, gratuity, and pension, and statutory reports on PF, ESI, income tax, etc.

PRODUCTION PLANNING AND CONTROL

The systems that deal with planning, scheduling, and controlling of manufacturing processes are called production planning and control systems. Planning and scheduling refer to the system of deriving the right amount of goods to be produced within the constraints of manufacturing capacities and material resources. Controlling is the process of monitoring the production process, so that it is as per planning and scheduling. The objective of manufacturing or production application systems is to provide information on the operations of an organization, and thus facilitate the decision-making process of production managers. Production planning applications provide production scheduling and planning, material planning, capacity planning, shop floor planning, etc., as shown in Fig. 8.21. The systems responsible for planning and scheduling advise on the best plan of action for efficient manufacturing of goods. Production control applications cover all activities from product design to manufacturing to quality control. It also involves plant location and layout decisions at the senior level of management.

The objectives of production management applications include ensuring optimum utilization of manufacturing capacity, minimum rejections, maximum uptime of plant and machinery, minimum wastage, and meeting of delivery time. Manufacturing information systems provide exception reports, based on which the management can take control and remedial actions.

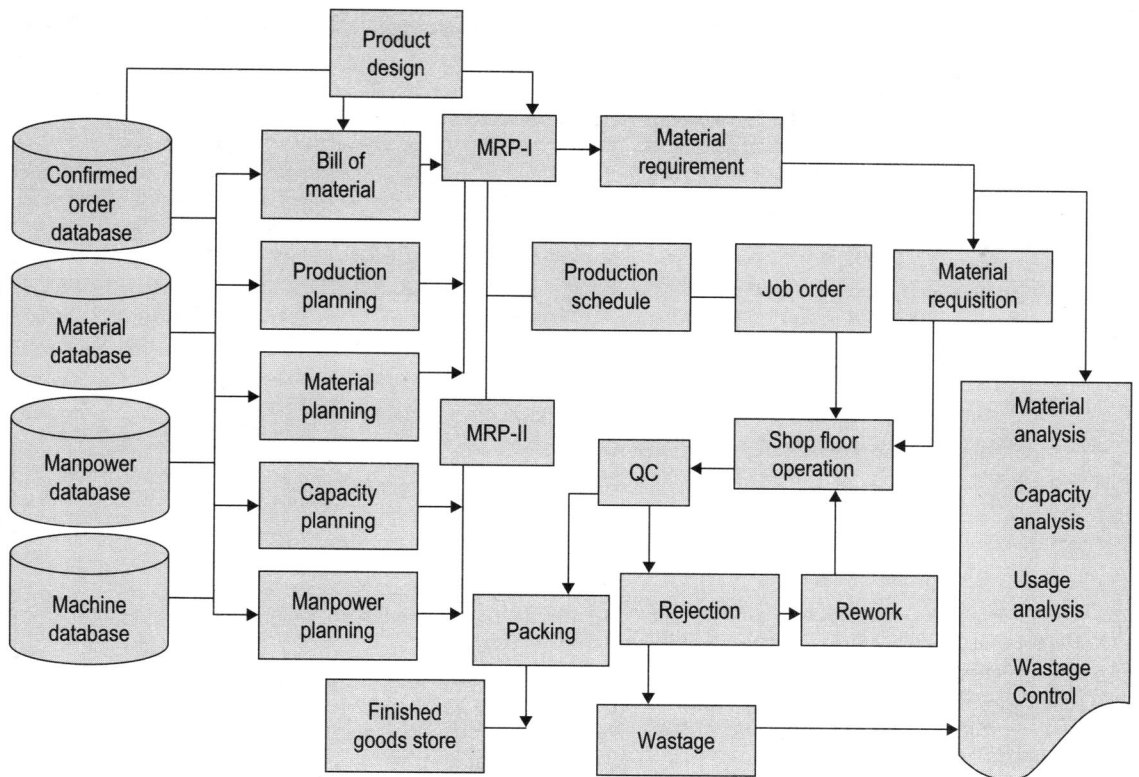

Fig. 8.21   Production planning and control applications and TPS

The tasks involved in production processes begin with production planning and material requirement planning, which is based on confirmed orders received from the sales department. The material requirement planning (MRP) system considers a confirmed order quantity and bill of the material for calculation of the material requirement. Most enterprise applications know this by MRP-I (i.e., the first phase of material requirement planning). The second part is machine capacity planning and manpower planning, which is covered under MRP-II. A job card is generated for daily production or a batch of production in a discreet manufacturing process. Discreet manufacturing refers to the process where each sub-assembly or component is manufactured separately and then assembled to make the main product. Contrast this with a flow manufacturing process, wherein the complete product is manufactured in one instance. For example, manufacturing of soap is a flow-manufacturing process, whereas manufacturing of air conditioners is a discreet manufacturing process. Figure 8.22 displays a job card layout screen. The shop floor management allows users to record the quantity of goods manufactured at each production stage.

Production planning and control applications keep account of what is produced in a unit of time (one day or each hour of a day). They help in the generation of material requirements and usages at the shop floor. In addition, they take care of rejections during production processes and wastages during conversion processes, when semi-finished goods are moved from one process

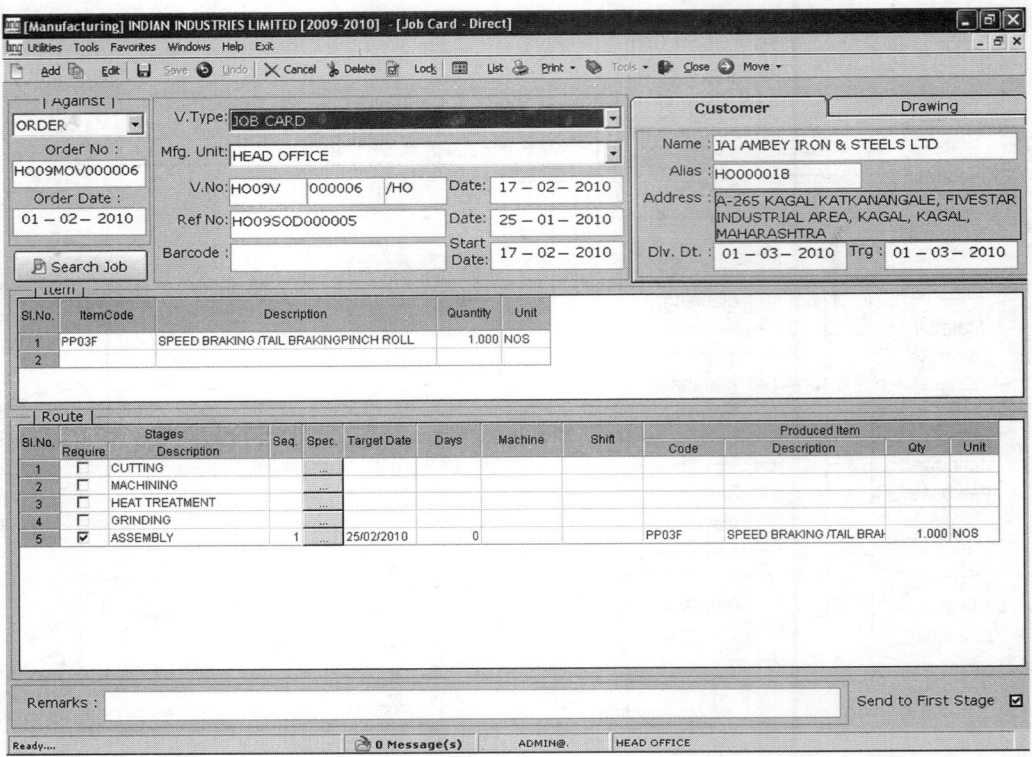

Fig. 8.22   Job card in production planning and control applications [BNG Infotech]

to another. The TPS allows the recording machinery to breakdown incidences, usage of power, fuel, and other consumables during a production process. Based on analysis of such data, the management is able to take remedial actions and control measures to bring in efficiency in the production function. For example, TRL, as illustrated in Exhibit 8.1, achieved efficiency in work in progress (WIP), inventory management, and wastage control by using an e-business application for production.

One of the most important types of information provided by the manufacturing application is the tracking of job information on a particular machine, workstation, time, or process. The management seeks crucial information from the system related to the status of a job or customer order in terms of production stage, job schedules, load status on a machine or assembly line, material availability for a batch of production, work in progress, and quantum of wastages during production process.

Computer-aided manufacturing (CAM) is another concept that integrates manufacturing and computers with the objective of simplifying production processes, product design, and factory activities. It automates production processes and integrates them with business functions using computers and other information technology products.

According to O'Brien (2007), 'The overall goal of computer-integrated manufacturing and such manufacturing information system is to create flexible, agile manufacturing processes that efficiently produce products of the highest quality. Implementing such manufacturing concepts

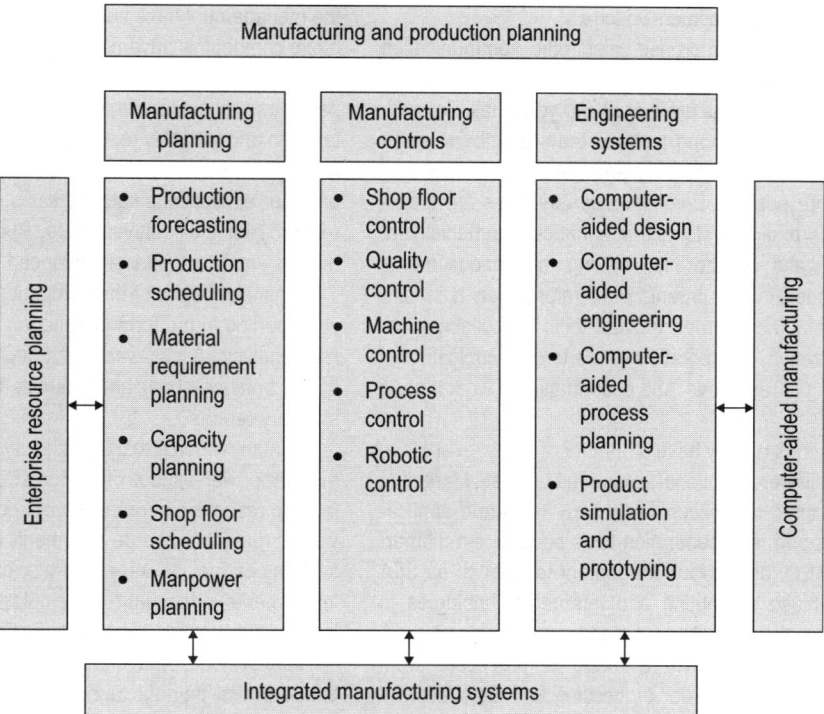

Fig. 8.23 Managing manufacturing and planning processes using enterprise systems

enables a company to quickly respond to and fulfil customer requirements with high-quality products and services.'

The complete planning and manufacturing processes involved can be managed and controlled with the help of enterprise resource planning applications and computer-aided engineering as depicted in Fig. 8.23.

Therefore, all manufacturing and production planning applications help managers in material, human resource, and machines planning, and efficiently execute jobs in a timely manner. The applications provide recording of all events in the production processes, which in turn, build the database. Based on analysis of such data, the management is able to take remedial actions and control measures to bring in efficiency in the production function.

SUMMARY

The new category of organizations, known as e-business enterprises, enable employees, business partners, professionals, and groups to perform business operations electronically, anytime and anywhere. E-business enterprises are more process-driven, technology-enabled, and use information and knowledge to gain competitive advantages. Their applications include the use of the Internet and information technologies to support electronic commerce, enterprise communications, and collaborations.

Thus, e-business applications cover TPS, e-communications, and e-collaborations. The MIS model of the e-business application considers transaction processing as the basis of building such a system. The TPS also generates real-time documents such as invoices, purchase orders, sales orders, dispatch advice, delivery notes, payment vouchers.

In an e-business enterprise, electronic communication is the backbone of all processes. Today, the most widely used messaging systems are e-mail and voicemail. For real-time communication among multiple team members, video conferencing, voice conferencing, and electronic meeting systems are more popular. E-collaboration systems are cross-functional information systems that enhance communication, coordination, and collaboration among the various teams and workgroups in the organization. Information technologies, especially the Internet, provide tools for collaboration. In an organization, collaboration refers to communication of ideas, sharing of resources, and coordination of work among workgroups.

Organizations usually have a number of software applications for the different functional areas of a business. Marketing applications offer information technology tools and applications that support lead generation tools such as e-mail marketing and SEO, and lead management tools such as SFA systems that use computing and Internet technologies to automate marketing activities for management support.

Sales applications cover a range of processes from customer acquisition to order processing and distribution of goods. The sales applications allow transaction processing functions such as sales order confirmation, dispatch advice, and billing. MIS and DSS offer tools for sales budgeting, quota management, sales forecasting, and sales analysis. These applications work as decision support tools.

The material management system takes care of the processes involved in material procurement, storage, and control of inventory. It covers material requirement planning, vendor management, and inventory control functions. Material management applications answer questions such as when to buy and how much to buy. Procurement involves evaluating and selecting vendors, floating enquiries, comparing prices, and generating purchase orders. Storage of goods and control of inventory is another function of material management.

The information provided through financial functions helps the management have better control over its affairs, and thus offers competitive advantages and long-term business sustenance. Financial applications cover general ledger, accounts payables, accounts receivables, budgeting and allocations, taxation and statutory reporting, ratio and funds analysis, and fixed assets management. A finance application is dependent on other applications such as sales, purchases, and human resource for their relevant data. Budgets and cost controls are an important part of advanced financial management. The financial health of the company is presented by analytical reporting in the form of various financial funds flows and ratio analysis. Assets value and depreciation charts are part of the balance sheet and submitted to the government as statutory reports.

Human resource management systems (HRMS) deal with the manpower aspect of the organization. The HR department is responsible for employee recruitment, training, motivation, retention, and development. Payroll activities related to finances include keeping track of remuneration, leaves, loans, perks, provident fund, employee state insurance, and income tax computation and deductions.

The systems that deal with planning, scheduling, and controlling of manufacturing process are called production planning and control systems. Planning and scheduling refer to the system of deriving the right amount of goods to be produced within the constraints of manufacturing capacities and material resources. Production planning and control applications provide the following facilities—production scheduling and planning, material planning, capacity planning, and shop floor planning. The systems involved in planning and scheduling offer the best plan of action for efficient manufacturing of goods. Production planning and control (PPC) applications keep an account of what is produced in a particular unit of time. The application allows the recording machinery to breakdown incidences, use of power, fuel, and other consumables during a production process. Based on analysis of such data, the management is able to take remedial actions and control measures to bring in efficiency in the production function.

KEY TERMS

Anti-spam laws　Laws that govern and regulate unsolicited e-mails.

Capacity planning　A feature of e-business applications that allows planning of materials and other resources in the automation of the manufacturing process.

Collaborative work systems　Systems that allow group work and thus facilitate knowledge-creation and sharing.

E-business enterprise　An IT and Internet-enabled organization that supports employees, business partners, professionals, and other groups in performing business operations electronically, anytime and anywhere.

E-collaboration Cross-functional information systems that enhance communication, coordination, and collaboration among the various teams and work groups in the organization.

E-communication Electronic messaging systems including e-mail, voicemail, video conferencing, voice conferencing, and electronic meeting systems.

Economic order quantity (EOQ) The stock to be ordered that incurs the least cost for procurement and storage.

E-mail marketing A form of direct marketing, which uses electronic mail as a means of communicating commercial messages to an audience.

Groupware application An Internet-based application that allows users to use, share, and collaborate from any location.

Meta tags Specific words that are used to improve the visibility of a website in the process of search engine optimization.

Multimedia database A database containing text, images, sound, video, etc.

Quantity on hold (QOH) An inventory of quantity that is reserved for any other order or process.

Search engine optimization (SEO) Process of improving visibility of a website by promoting it on various search engines.

CONCEPT REVIEW QUESTIONS

1. What is an e-business enterprise?
2. What do you understand by e-collaboration? What are the various collaboration tools used in businesses?
3. What are the several e-business applications that you may recommend to a mid-size business to help it survive and succeed in a competitive environment?
4. Explain the various features commonly available in a marketing application.
5. What would you like to have in a sales force automation application?
6. What functionalities are provided in an application for distribution management?
7. What features would you look into when purchasing an application to manage raw materials for your company?
8. Explain the salient features of a finance application.
9. What are the salient features of a HRM application?
10. How can an organization achieve efficiency in wastage control by using a production planning and control application?

CRITICAL THINKING QUESTIONS

1. 'Manufacturing is a complex activity in business. Optimum utilization of men, machines, and material is possible only with a comprehensive production planning and control application.' Critically examine this statement with relevant examples.
2. Construct a database of employees' salary sheets for a month using MS Excel.
3. What types of MIS reports can better explain the efficiency of operations and financial health of an organization?
4. For each business function, draw an MIS report that the departmental head would be interested in viewing on a day-to-day basis.

MIS DEVELOPMENT

Ratio analyses reflect the financial health of a company. Most strategic decisions related to an organization are based on and influenced by the financial position of the company. As a student of business management, you must understand that mere profit-making is not enough for the long-term sustenance of an organization. It is mandatory for all public limited companies to publish their financial results. You may find them in newspapers and in the websites of these companies.

Exercise

Collect information about three companies (at least), preferably competitors, operating in the same field. Examine their financial results, including net sales, gross profit, income before tax and depreciation, and net profit. Analyse the financial strengths and weaknesses of the companies based on these results. Do the following ratio analysis and compare the results of one company with another.

- Current ratio
- Debt-to-assets ratio
- Debt-to-equity ratio
- Inventory turnover ratio
- Accounts receivable turnover
- Net profit ratio
- Equity earning ratio (Earnings per share)

Indicate what these ratio analyses signify with respect to each company. You may use an MS Excel worksheet.

REFERENCES

Alter, Steven, *Information Systems—The Foundation of E-business*, Pearson Education, Singapore, 2004.

Gates, Bill, *Business @ the Speed of Thought*, Warner Books, New York, 1999.

Gordon, Davis and Margethe Olson, *Management Information Systems*, The McGraw-Hill Book Company, Singapore, 1996.

Goyal, D.P., *Management Information Systems—Managerial Perspectives*, Macmillan India Ltd, New Delhi, 2006.

Jaiswal, Mahadeo and Monika Mital, *Management Information Systems*, Oxford University Press, New Delhi, 2004.

Jawadekar, Waman S., *Management Information Systems, Text and Cases*, Tata McGraw-Hill, New Delhi, 2007.

Joshi, Girdhar, *Information Technology for Retail*, Oxford University Press, New Delhi, 2009.

O'Brien, James, George Marakas, and Ramesh Behl, *Management Information Systems*, Tata McGraw-Hill, New Delhi, 2007.

Sawhney, Mohanbir and Jeff Zabin, *The Seven Steps to Nirvana: Strategic Insights into e-Business Transformation*, McGraw-Hill, New York, 2001.

http://www.brainpulse.com/search_engine_promotion_india/search_engine_promotion_india.php, last accessed on 5 March 2011.

http://www.crm.zoho.com, last accessed on 26 February 2013.

CASE STUDY

Madura Garments: The Perfect Software for Business Processes

Madura Garments is the proud owner of premium brands such as Louis Philippe, Van Heusen, and Allen Solly. The group consists of eight factories, a warehouse, over 120 exclusive franchisee showrooms, 15 agents, 22 distributors, and 3,500 retail outlets spread across the country. The Bengaluru-based Madura Garments, which is part of Indian Rayon, wanted to resort to complete business process automation and transform it into an e-business. They also added other applications to reduce lead times and have better response mechanisms. Madura Garments implemented SAP to manage their e-business processes and supply chain, and to control inventories and returns in a highly competitive branded garments market.

The daunting task in front of N.P. Singh, vice-president, information technology, was that hundreds of stock-keeping units (SKUs) had to be sold within four to six weeks. Otherwise, whatever was left had to be cleared at a discount of up to 50%. As this was a business where the planning-to-sales cycles could be as long as six to nine months, the challenge was to keep the level of unsold stocks (returns) between 5 and 10%, which was a condition that every garment-maker

had to deal with. Returns up to this level were acceptable as it was impossible to get the forecasts completely right; but anything higher began to hurt.

The returns in Madura's case were as high as 30%, and this was high enough to hurt the bottom line. The problem was apparent. 'Users across functions identified operational problems and the absence of timely MIS as two major issues', says Singh. The drawbacks of the legacy system included lack of updated information due to non-integrated systems, difficulty in modifying current systems for new information requirements related to product development and impending technology obsolescence (INGRES, COBOL, and FOXPRO were the platforms). The legacy systems were mainly developed for stock management, general ledger maintenance, and employee records, and were using platforms such as COBOL and FoxPro, which have become obsolete now. The latest ERP platform provided flexibility to upgrade the system to meet the latest management and user requirements.

In 2005, Madura Garments planned three IT initiatives. The first one was the development of an enterprise portal, which made knowledge management easier and self-service among employees possible. The second was the implementation of radio frequency identification (RFID) in retail and warehouses for inventory management, and the third was the implementation of a comprehensive CRM solution. However, the presence of a multiple legacy system was making integration and modification complex and cumbersome. Moreover, the company was incurring high costs in maintaining the IT infrastructure. As a matter of fact, there were times when the warehousing system would show one figure that would be totally different from the consolidated figure at the corporate level.

In November 2008, Madura Garments decided to implement Oracle's Retek for its retail business. Retek rolled out in 40 Allen Solly stores, and in all Louis Philippe and Van Heusen stores by March 2009. The Retek solution assists in retail merchandise management, allocation of stock to store, setting up of promotions, merchandise, items, and demand planning. What is important is that Retek has been interfaced with SAP for financial transactions.

It was critical that Madura Garments had complete visibility of the supply chain. It also needed more accurate forecasting, better matching of demand and production, and smoother interfaces with distributors and retailers. It needed to wire up everything—production, forecasting, and distribution, smartly.

Having analysed the various implementation needs at the organization, Singh knew that SAP, which already had over 200 installations of SAP R/3 in India alone, was the right partner for triggering e-business initiatives at Madura Garments. Hence, the company started with ERP from SAP. It decided to go in for an industry and inventory-specific solution called apparel and footwear solution (AFS) comprising SAP R/3 and AF3.

Now, a traditional ERP attempts to integrate all functions on to a single platform to serve the specific needs of all the departments. Consequently, it takes care of the 'enterprise' part (in its acronym) reasonably well. The trouble is with the 'planning' part. There, it does not quite live up to its promise.

SAP had two great aces up its sleeves—advance planning and optimization module or APO (a forecasting application) and business intelligence and warehousing module or BIW (a data warehousing and decision support application)—that took care of planning and top management decision-making concerns.

As both the applications were from SAP, it meant that integration was going to be easier. It also added a web-based customer interface on top of the ERP system.

This would make sure that it captured data from external sources (distributors, retailers, suppliers) in addition to what ERP gathered from within the organization.

Method of Implementation

Madura Garments formed a project team comprising a consultant from PwC (which is now IBM business consulting services.) Besides, a joint team was formed with SAP India as well. 'It is because of the industry expertise [that] SAP had', says Singh. A 30-member core team comprising 15 consultants and an equal number of specialists from the company was formed to oversee the operations. Madura also hired four to five programmers and trained them in advanced business application programming (ABAP—the SAP language). They had to perform the customization during implementation.

In a Nutshell

Company Madura Garments, one of the fastest growing branded apparel companies with a turnover of ₹395 crore, increasing by over 30% per annum

Industry Garment and textiles

SAP solution SAP R/3 plus AFS ERP, SAP APO, and SAP BIW

Number of outlets and stores covered 120 franchisee showrooms and 3,500 retail outlets

Implementation partners Consultants from SAP and PwC

Number of end-users Around 200

Objectives of the implementation Bridging the information gap to bring about efficient data flow and increase order fulfilment rate

Server 3 Sun Fire V880R, 2 IBM RS6000 Dual CPU

Operating systems Sun Fire runs on Solaris 8 and IBM RS6000 runs AIX 5.1

Cost of implementation ₹9 crore, inclusive of hardware, software, and training

Key areas of benefits	Pre-ERP	Post-ERP
Order fulfilment	70%	90%
Order release-dispatch	22 days	18 days
Inventory (% of sales)	13%	11.7%
Receivables	55 days	40–45 days
Unsold stock	Around 30%	10%

As Madura Garments wanted all the processes to be automated, the customization team came in handy. For example, the entry of SKUs into the ERP system is manual. 'However, that would have been very cumbersome', says Singh. Hence, the team developed a barcode scanning module. It was essentially a software that would collect and load data automatically into the ERP system from a barcode scanner.

The team then integrated its existing web-based ordering process with the ERP system. Today, Madura Garments does not entertain any orders offline. Distributors and agents can place orders, check the status of their orders, and even check the accounts with the company, by simply logging in. With this, the team had integrated a large chunk of the supply chain with ERP at its core.

Simultaneously, it went about integrating the top management's MIS requirements so that it could cull out data from the back end and present it to the bosses faster and more accurately than ever before. This included information such as profitability across brands and channels, sales off takes (sales turnover), and working capital status.

While implementing the solution, Madura set certain milestones. When the materials management module was implemented, it insisted that SAP AG fly an expert from its headquarters in Germany for auditing that milestone. Only after the audit, did they move to the next stage. As a result, the company was able to stabilize the system within 12 months.

'SAP implementation has changed the way we conduct our business by bringing in transparency and doing away with islands with tenuous connections to each other', says Singh. In the process, Madura Garments has also reduced its response time to internal and external customers. 'We are now able to sense, act, and respond efficiently to ever-changing markets.'

Presently, senior executives can monitor variations between annual budget plan and monthly plans, which ensure coordinated monitoring of top line and bottom line growth, thus resulting in improved profitability. The implementation has also brought an integrated order management, revenue recognition, and account receivables functionality, and at the same time, it has eliminated non-value adding functions such as reconciliation and consolidation.

'Profitability assessment for each showroom, brand, and customer can be done in the system', says Singh. The new system can also suggest replenishment based on these parameters and also generate weekly control reports on sales and inventory for each showroom. Moreover, sales returns can be linked to original sales orders.

The numbers at Madura tell the entire story. Order fulfilment rose up from 70 to 90%, order release-to-dispatch time was down from 22 to 18 days, inventory was down from 13% of sales to 11.7%, and showroom receivables reduced from 55 to 45 days.

Discussion Questions

1. Identify the processes that Madura Garments automated in order to achieve e-business status.
2. What were the problem areas that the management could foresee before implementing the applications?
3. Madura Garments used a number of applications for order processing, distribution, retail, inventory control, etc., as evident from the case. Identify the types of information required by the top management of the company that could be used for taking strategic decisions.
4. Do you think Madura is an e-business enterprise? Fortify your answers with examples from the case study.
5. What benefits has the company achieved post-implementation of this e-business initiative?

Sources:

Das, Stuti, 'Madura Garments: Tech in time, saves…', http://dqindia.ciol.com/content/casestudy/2009/109022104.asp, last accessed on 21 February 2009.

Kumar, Sunil, 'Madura Garments charts IT roadmap', http://www.cxotoday.com/story/madura-garments-charts-it-roadmap/, last accessed on 18 February 2013.

Press report at http://www.adityabirla.com/media/press_reports/20050304_madura_garments.htm, last accessed on 4 March 2012.

Singh, Abhinav, 'Madura Garments changes the way it works', http://www.expresscomputeronline.com/20050221/management01.shtml, last accessed on 21 February 2009.

9

Enterprise Systems

> People don't like to change, and ERP asks them to change how they do their jobs. That is why the value of ERP is so hard to pin down. The software is less important than the changes companies make in the ways they do business. If you use ERP to improve the ways your people take orders and manufacture, ship and bill for goods, you will see value from the software. If you simply install the software without trying to improve the ways people do their jobs, you may not see any value at all—indeed, the new software could slow you down by simply replacing the old software that everyone knew with new software that no one does
>
> —CHRISTOPHER KOCH

LEARNING OBJECTIVES

After studying this chapter, you will be able to

- define enterprise systems
- understand enterprise resource planning (ERP) systems
- appreciate the advantages, challenges, and trends in ERP systems
- get acquainted with the concept of software as a service (SaaS)
- define supply chain management
- describe the IT tools for a supply chain
- comprehend the role of supply chain management (SCM) applications and trends in SCM
- get a clear picture of e-procurement
- define and appreciate customer relationship management (CRM)
- explain the concept of customer relations
- define CRM applications such as sales, marketing, support, and loyalty
- understand the advantages of using CRM applications and the latest trends in CRM

EXHIBIT 9.1

Tata Power: The Power of ERP Behind Success

Tata Power (the erstwhile Tata Electric), established in 1910, pioneered the generation of electricity in India. The company has been associated with the growing legacy of Mumbai as a business city for almost a century now. Mumbai's growth has been literally powered by Tata Power's reliable power supply. It was mainly a 'Mumbai-centric bulk supplier' before privatization; post-privatization, it grabbed on to the big opportunity.

Today, Tata Power is India's largest integrated private power company with consolidated revenues of ₹19,450.76 crore for the fiscal year ended 31 March 2011. It has an installed power generation capacity of over 3120 MW and a presence across the entire value chain (thermal, hydro, solar, and wind) in generation, transmission, distribution, and trading. Apart from Mumbai and New Delhi, the company has emerged as a pioneer in the Indian power sector, with an impressive track record. It has also been a frontrunner in introducing state-of-the-art power technologies. Among its achievements, the company has to its credit the installation of India's first 500 MW unit at Trombay, the first 150 MW pumped storage unit at Bhira, a flue gas desulphurization plant for pollution control at Trombay, and is now bringing up the first 800 MW super-critical unit at Mundra, Gujarat. The company has a customer base of 22,000 in Mumbai and has acquired 6,00,000 consumers, post-privatization in New Delhi, by distributing through subsidiary companies.

With privatization in the power sector, the company could foresee several untapped opportunities. With the new roadmap in place, they brought in several changes across the company and ERP implementation was one of them. Before implementing ERP, Tata Power had various legacy systems in operation; however, to keep pace with their growth plans, they felt that an ERP solution was essential.

When Tata Power decided to implement ERP in 2001–02, SAP was the only company with an ERP solution for the power sector, and hence, became an obvious choice. SAP was being considered across all companies of the Tata Group and hence, the comfort factor was obvious. In addition, they could negotiate a good price, thus making it an ideal choice. Tata Power became the first utility company in India to implement an industry-specific ERP solution. They had to gear up their systems to cater to their vastly increased customer base, integrate the complete business process chain, and improve efficiencies in operations and maintenance.

The SAP implementation partners were none other than Tata Technologies. The SAP R/3 implementation covered all power generation processes and distribution across all locations, nearly 28 in number; the complete supply chain; centralized procurement; vendor management; complete cash cycle; centralized accounting; project management, budgeting, and monitoring; plant defect notification and work order management; HR organizational and personnel administration, and customer management and bill-processing. At Tata Power, SAP R/3 became the first utility implementation in India.

The company benefitted in four major areas—cycle time reduction, inventory reduction, manpower reduction (thereby making people available for redeployment), and most importantly, in providing better quality information. Implementing SAP R/3 reduced the procurement cycle time—41 days to 17 days (material procurement), 90 days to 14 days (capital procurement), and 38 days to 8 days (accounts closing cycle time, which is annual, in SAP). It caused stock reduction by ₹28 crore at major stocking locations and human resource savings due to centralization and automation of processes. The billing integrity index improved from 3% to 1.83% and the billing complaints response index improved from 90% to 99%.

Sources:

Lal, Aparna, 'ERP propels Tata Power', http://www.ciol.com/ciol/news/25647/erp-propels-tata-power, last accessed on 5 January 2013.

http://www.indiainfoline.com/Markets/Company/Fundamentals/Directors-Report/Tata-Chemicals-Ltd/500770, last accessed on 16 October 2011.

http://www.sapag.co.in, last accessed on 16 October 2011.

http://www.tatapower.com/aboutus, last accessed on 16 October 2011.

Tata Power's initiative (Exhibit 9.1) to implement ERP as a measure to meet requirements in the post-liberalization era and to bring in efficiency and control over business transactions highlights the importance of enterprise applications in modern businesses. The company achieved efficiencies in the form of cycle time reduction, inventory reduction, better manpower or human resource utilization, and better quality information, post ERP implementation.

We can observe from the case that Tata Power not only brought in efficiency in operations, but also benefitted economically.

ENTERPRISE SYSTEMS

When organizations are small, they use general-purpose office productivity applications for keeping records and maintaining documents in word processors, spreadsheets, etc. As the needs grow, they build mission-critical applications for individual processes or departments such as billing, inventory management, purchase functions, or accounting. As all these applications are developed over a period of time and in a piecemeal manner, they seldom 'talk' to each other. This leads to duplicity of data and sometimes, inconsistency in reports. When organizations grow in size and become complex in nature, these standalone legacy applications do not serve their entire needs; therefore, larger and integrated systems are built to cover the entire organizational requirements.

To solve this problem, organizations build enterprise systems to provide company-wide integration. Integrated solutions that are used across diverse functional areas and geographical expanses in large organizations are known as enterprise systems. Such systems are based on a single platform, compatible databases, and computer systems. Enterprise resource planning (ERP), supply chain management (SCM), and customer relationship management (CRM) are some examples of enterprise systems. Figure 9.1 illustrates enterprise systems and their sub-systems.

Enterprise Resource Planning

Enterprise resource planning (ERP) systems are integrated software suites built on a common platform and unified database covering the entire organizational information requirements. They serve as a cross-functional enterprise backbone that integrates and automates many internal business processes and information systems within the manufacturing, logistics, distribution, accounting, and human resource aspects of the organization. Cross-functional business processes are organizational functions that are scattered over more than one business process. According to De Gues (1988), ERP is the technological backbone of e-business, an enterprise-wide transaction framework with links into sales order processing, inventory management and control, production and distribution planning, and finance.

ERP systems give an integrated real-time view of an organization's core business processes, such as order processing, inventory control, and production, which are tied together by the ERP application software and a common database maintained by the database management system. The ERP application software consists of integrated modules for production planning and control, sales and distribution, finance and accounting, and human resource management. Each module is supported by a number of sub-modules created for each business process, such as production planning, shop floor management, order processing, sales budgeting, logistics, accounts receivables, accounts payables, and payroll. Figure 9.2 illustrates the various modules of an ERP system.

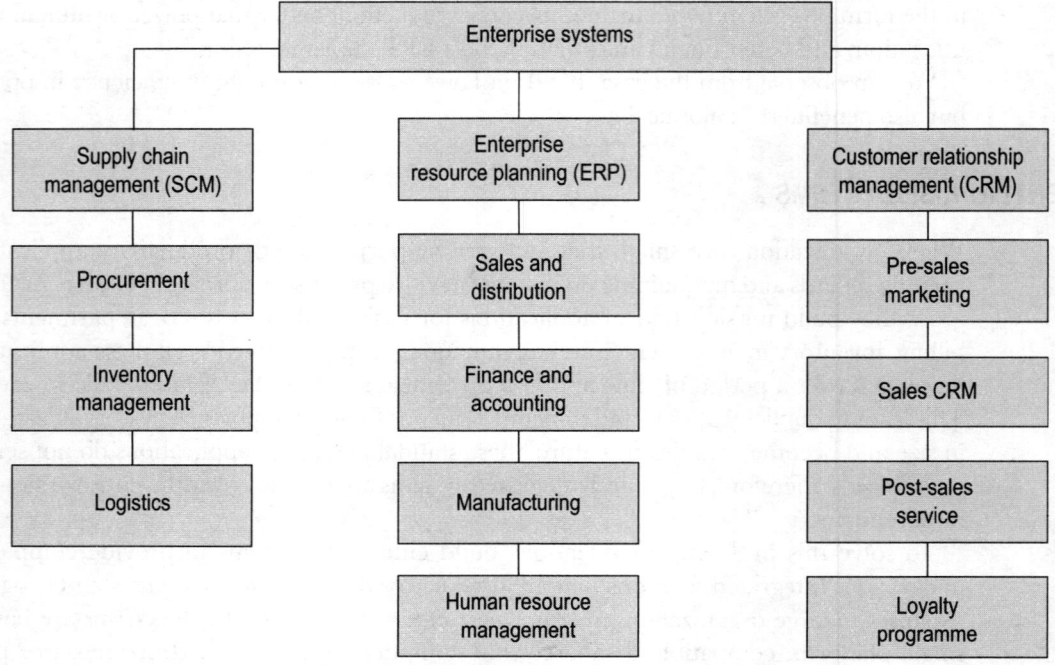

Fig. 9.1   Enterprise systems and their sub-systems

Thus, ERP systems perform the following functions:

- Integrate various processes in the organization and provide consistency across the value chain.
- Provide an opportunity to implement processes that are the best practices in the industry.
- Work on a consistent and unified data model for the entire enterprise. A unified data model is a single database or set of databases that communicate with each other in terms of data exchange.
- Integrate key business processes into a single application software. For example, the distribution module takes care of customer order processing, dispatches, billing, and delivery management, which are critical business processes.

For example, Tata Power's SAP R/3 provided the best practices that could be adopted by any electricity production and distribution company. The ERP integrated business processes include power generation, distribution, procurement, vendor management, billing, cash receipts and disbursement, budgeting and monitoring, and finance.

Major international ERP products include SAP R/3, SAP-B1, SAP Business ByDesign, Oracle Manufacturing, Oracle Financial, Oracle E-Business Suite, PeopleSoft (now acquired by Oracle), SSA Global, JDA, JD Edwards, Microsoft Dynamics, Xapta, Sage Accpac, MFG/PRO, NetSuite, Plex, Deacom, Epicor, Syspro, IFS, etc. There are hundreds of Indian ERP products; however, the most well known are Ramco Marshall, Ramco OnDemand, ESS eBizframe, ICICI Orion, Infosys Finacle, TCS Banc, and Polaris RetailExcel.

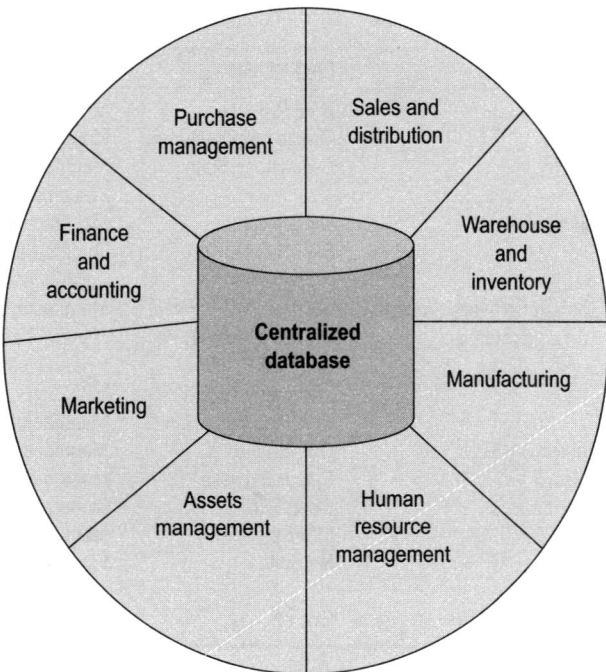

Fig. 9.2   Application modules with a centralized
database in an ERP system

Table 9.1 compares the different types of ERP software offered by various companies and the niche segments they cater to.

ERP systems generate significant business benefits by integrating diverse business processes and provide consistent reporting; at the same time, they are difficult to implement and come at a high upfront price, thus posing many challenges.

Advantages

The advantages of ERP systems are numerous. ERP places the whole information system on a single compatible platform, which brings in efficiency and effectiveness in the management of the organization. Organizations find great business value in the use of ERP by changing and reengineering age-old systems.

Enterprise uniformity   ERP systems help in creating and maintaining uniform organization structures, systems, and procedures throughout the geographical area. A uniform organizational structure refers to the type of system in which everyone uses similar processes and informatics. Lack of standard and company-wide business processes may prevent companies from leveraging the benefits of ERP and responding quickly to market changes. For example, Samsung uses similar systems, procedures, and documents for purchases throughout the world. Similarly, Coca-Cola uses similar distribution processes throughout the globe.

Table 9.1   Comparison of ERP software offered by various companies

ERP category	Offered by	Product name	Niche segment
Client/server/ on-premise ERP	SAP AG	SAP R/3	Manufacturing, finance, and distribution
	Oracle	Oracle Manufacturing	Manufacturing and distribution
	Oracle	E-Business Suite	Manufacturing, finance, distribution, and e-commerce
	Microsoft	Dynamics	Manufacturing, finance, and distribution
	SAP AG	SAP B-One	Targeted at SME segment for finance, distribution, and light manufacturing
	Eastern Software Systems	eBizframe	Manufacturing systems
	Ramco Systems	Ramco Marshall	Manufacturing and trading accounting systems
	Sage	Sage ERP 300 (formerly AccPac)	Finance, sales, and production planning
Software as a service (SaaS)/on demand	SAP AG	Business ByDesign	Manufacturing, finance, and distribution
	Ramco Systems	OnDemand	Manufacturing, finance, and distribution
	Epicor	Epicor Express	Manufacturing, finance, and distribution
	OpenSource	OpenERP	Manufacturing and distribution
	Infor	InforSyteline	Manufacturing, finance, and distribution
	NetSuite	NetSuite	Finance and distribution, and light manufacturing
	Everest Software	Everest	For distribution available as SaaS

Unified information architecture   ERP systems work around a single unified architecture, which helps organizations in forming common and standardized definitions and formats that are accepted by the whole organization. They work on a single integrated repository or database for key business processes. For example, Marks & Spencer and Wills Lifestyle use the same application on the Windows platform in all their offices.

Change agent   At times, organizations want to get rid of the old, lethargic, and costly paper-friendly systems, and introduce new and more efficient systems that are in sync with the changing times. However, they find it very difficult to introduce such modern systems. Implementation of ERP systems works as a catalyst to reengineer work processes within the organization. They work as a change agent and bring in more efficient systems and operations. For example, introduction of the banking software in State Bank of India brought in e-statements and the old paper-based passbook systems could be easily discarded.

Improved decision support   ERP systems not only automate key transaction processes, but also improve management reporting and decision-making. Critical reports are structured around cross-functional business processes and provided to managers, thus enabling them to make timely and correct decisions. For example, deciding how much must be bought based on the previous month's sales figure may result in reporting from the entire supply chain, which involves purchase systems on one hand, and inventory and distribution on the other. Another example is that of Pantaloon Retail, which gained greater insight into its business and improved decision-making by implementing SAP a few years ago.

Efficient operations   ERP systems are built around the best business practices that induce customer-driven and vendor-oriented work culture. Today, organizations work on customers'

demands. By integrating discrete business processes, such as sales, finance, production, and logistics, the entire organization can efficiently respond to customer requests for maximizing production. Modern management concepts, such as zero inventory, just-in-time inventory, and zero budgeting, have been introduced to make the organization efficient. For instance, we have observed in our opening case about Tata Power how the company reduced cycle time and brought about efficiency in their operations.

Connecting with the outside world   ERP systems not only smoothen and streamline internal operations but also connect with the outside world that is, customers and vendors. Both these external bodies may have access to the relevant part of the system through a secured extranet. For example, Wal-Mart allows the system to create an automatic purchase order on a vendor. The vendor instantly receives orders as the stock goes below reorder level at the warehouse. Similarly, the organization knows in advance what needs to be delivered as the vendor proactively processes the order.

Challenges

Though ERP systems offer a lot of advantages, and improve organizational coordination, efficiency and decision-making, the costs and risks are also considerable. They not only require large investment on technologies, but also force fundamental changes in the business processes, and are difficult to implement.

Daunting implementation   Implementation is the toughest part of ERP systems. This not only requires changes in the current system, but also a deep understanding and analysis of the existing business processes of the company. Failure to understand a critical business process may lead to faulty implementation and hence, the organization may not be able to reap the fruits of its investments. According to Joshi (2009), a smaller organization can implement ERP systems in 12 to 18 months; however, it may take a large corporate firm about three to five years to implement ERP fully. If the company loses confidence and patience, it will not be able to achieve a higher level of functional and business process integration.

High upfront costs   ERP systems are very costly. There are large upfront costs that are highly visible. Upfront costs are direct costs such as hardware, software licences, and training and implementation costs. According to Omar (1997), hardware and software costs are a small part of total costs, and the costs of developing new business processes (reengineering) and preparing employees for the new system (training and change management) make up the bulk of implementing a new ERP system. Converting the data from previous legacy systems to the new cross-functional ERP system is another major category of ERP implementation costs. Sometimes, it is difficult to justify the investments as the benefits are not quantifiable in the beginning.

Belated ROI   As ERP systems take a long time for implementation, the benefits start showing only later, and the return on investment (ROI) takes a long time. Initially, due to process changes and introduction of new processes, the disadvantages are more prominent than the advantages. Once the system stabilizes and there is wide acceptance of the new processes and procedures, the qualitative or quantitative benefits start surfacing. The average ROI in Indian businesses is expected to be between five to ten years. For example, Godrej Industries Ltd, which implemented MFG/PRO, expected a ROI in five to seven years.

Resistance to change   Resistance to change is a rule rather than an exception. This is more so because of dramatic changes in the processes or introduction of new processes. This resistance comes not only from employees, but also from customers and suppliers as well. They may also have to go through additional processes or documentation. For instance, a customer may not like a mandatory process of 'order confirmation' from his vendor, which may involve review of sales order or changes in some terms. Similarly, employee resistance can be highlighted with several instances, for example, employees of many Indian banks resorting to strikes in the 1980s–90s against the introduction of computerization.

Inflexibility   ERP systems are complex because of the existence of thousands of business rules and logic that have been defined for hundreds of processes. If the software does not support a business process, it can be customized to suit the same. As various business rules and logic pertaining to different functional modules are intertwined, a change in one place will affect functioning at other places. As ERP systems are very complex, too much customization may degrade system performance and efficiency. The optimum benefits may be derived by implementing the standard processes offered by the system and modifying internal processes. For example, when Tata Refractories implemented Baan, they used Baan's approach of 'as is', in which they studied the existing processes and suggested changes to speeden them.

Trends

Led by the customer relationship management (CRM) and business intelligence requirements of an organization, ERP systems are still evolving and reaching new heights. According to De Gues (1988), 'Today, ERP is still evolving—adapting to development in technology and the demands of the market. Four important trends are shaping ERP's continuing evolution—improvements in integration and flexibility, extensions to e-business applications, a broader reach to new users, and the adoption of Internet technologies'. Today, ERP vendors are delivering more value by offering flexible, web-enabled systems capable of integration with other systems. Software as a service (SaaS) is a new phenomenon in the ERP space.

Flexible ERP   During the 1990s, the industry saw inflexible and segment-oriented ERP systems, which were built for the niche segment. However, during the beginning of this century, organizations demanded more flexible and standard applications that made the software easier to integrate with other applications. This was the era of the one-size-fits-all kind of ERP systems. The launch of SAP R/3 in 2002 by SAP AG signified the end of this era. Similarly, some companies, such as Oracle, PeopleSoft, and Microsoft, launched flexible and configurable ERP applications. Exhibit 9.2 illustrates how Pidilite gained from implementing SAP and Lotus Notes for its operations.

Web-enabled ERP   The next development in the ERP arena is web-enabling of ERP software. According to O'Brien (2007), the growth of the Internet and corporate intranets and extranets prompted software companies to use Internet technologies to build web interfaces and networking capabilities into ERP systems. The availability and pervasiveness of Internet technology pushed

EXHIBIT 9.2

Pidilite Industries: The Business Value of ERP

Since its inception in 1959, Pidilite has been a pioneer and market leader in adhesives and industrial speciality chemicals. With annual sales of about ₹2200 crore in 2009–10, and 2900 employees, the company is a market leader and its brands, Fevicol, Steelgrip, Acron, Dr Fixit, Fevitite, and M-seal, are household names in India. Pidilite invests a fairly large amount of its resources on the research and development of its products and processes. The quality of their products is assured and supported by a well-defined, structured, and focused quality assurance system that is continuously audited and upgraded in line with the organization's quality policy. In a recent *Economic Times* report, Pidilite ranked 131 among the top 500 companies in India.

The company has an extensive distribution network over 2000 distributors, servicing 4,00,000 dealers and retailers in all parts of the country. Given this extensive network, the company faces the big challenge of collecting feedback and information from the market.

Pidilite implemented SAP R/3 ERP in 2001 and IBM Lotus Notes later for streamlining its operations and getting better information flow. The company gained great business value by implementing both systems. Zoeb Adenwala, Chief of IT, said that ERP has improved customer service, reduced working capital, standardized processes, reduced inventory, and provided a centralized set-up from the previous distributed model. Pidilite has integrated various marketing and sales applications with the back-end ERP systems, thereby greatly reducing turnaround time. To quote an example, Pidilite developed a Lotus Domino-based application that enables employees to get approvals for customer orders quickly. For instance, when a customer order is booked, the same is recorded in the ERP back-end. If the credit limit for the order is exceeded, then a Lotus Notes application, linked to the ERP back-end, sends an e-mail to the concerned supervisor for approval. The supervisor sends an approval through the same Lotus

Notes application and when the order is confirmed, it is again recorded by the ERP system.

'Earlier it would take four to five days to complete the order approval cycle; now the same gets done in four to five hours. Notes Workflow replaces the paper approval process and managers have access to Notes application 24 × 7, even when out of office,' says Adenwala.

Pidilite used the ERP experience for gaining strategic advantages and dished out new products to meet competition. As the sales executives directly record market feedback into this system, it helps the company to come out with new and better products quickly. The marketing department picks up the feedback and passes it on to the R&D department, which then works out the feasibility of introducing a new product. In this manner, Pidilite is able to constantly innovate and has cut down the time taken to introduce new products into the market. For instance, the company launched a new product variant, the 5 mg Feviquick stick. This product is one of the fastest-selling products from the company, today. The company had a 20 gm pack that cost ₹25. However, the feedback that the company received was that this packaging size did not meet the needs of those customers who wanted to use the adhesive only once, as the rest of the quantity would then go waste. Hence, the company worked out a smaller packaging; a 5 mg tube served as a single-use product. 'The market response to this product has been tremendous, it is an instant hit,' says Adenwala.

Sources:
'Making paperwork less of a burden', http://www-07.ibm.com/in/casestudies-sw/case_pidilite.html, last accessed on 18 October 2011.
Pereira, Brian, 'Making ROI in ERP happen', *Network Magazine*, October 2003, www.networkmagazineindia.com/200310/coverstory02.shtml, last accessed on 18 October 2011.
http://www.pidilite.com, last accessed on 18 October 2011.

vendors to design links between key business systems of the organizations and their customers and suppliers. With the growing importance of CRM applications, internal ERP induced links with external, focused applications such as SCM and CRM.

Mobile-enabled ERP   The mobile device market is changing with mind-boggling advancements in a very short span of time. There are iPads, iPhones, smartphones, and many more business tools. Thus, ERP suites have to keep pace with the ever-growing mobile segment. ERP vendors may design interfaces with such mobile devices and deliver critical information and reports on smartphones. According to Drew Robb (2011), mobile applications will continue to proliferate, driving functionality out towards employees. Mobile and other self-service options lower costs and increase transaction quality while improving timeliness.

SOFTWARE AS A SERVICE

A major development in the ERP space is that ERP software is being offered as a service over the Internet using cloud computing technology. Given the complexities in implementation and maintenance of a large ERP, organizations have evaluated the option of a third party in creating, implementing, and maintaining enterprise solutions, which are web-based and available on rental basis. As the huge upfront costs are a deterrent to ERP deployment, the technology providers have addressed the cost issue with an innovative method of hosting. In fact, this hosting method has bypassed one of the intermediaries in ERP application deployment, which has helped in cutting costs.

Under a pay-as-you-go model, customers gain access to desired applications developed and managed by the application service provider (ASP) company. In addition to implementation and maintenance support, all necessary application and database management software as well as connectivity are provided by the service provider company. Under this method, the ERP applications are not deployed on-site of business firms. Instead, all the data related to processing and resource management are hosted on the data servers or data centres of the ERP software companies. This enables the business firms to access the ERP software round the clock as per their requirements, using Internet connectivity via a browser.

This new form of ERP application as a hosted service has given birth to the software as a service (SaaS) model. Presently, major ERP software companies are offering SaaS modules. For example, SAP has recently launched SAP By Design, Ramco OnDemand ERP, OpenSource ERP, SaaS.com, etc. These are some of the vendors providing ERP on SaaS platform.

Evolution

The disadvantages of legacy software developed in a piecemeal manner led to the invention of integrated, single-platform solutions called 'enterprise solutions'. Enterprise solutions were launched under the name of ERP and started coming into the market in the mid 1980s. They have been surviving and flourishing for several years now. Their longevity is testimony to the fact that ERP applications are far more efficient, versatile, and integrated. Prior to the ERP era, organizations built software by clubbing some business functions to plan and compute material requirements (Joshi 2009).

ERP applications can also handle multitasking in large-sized business enterprises. ERP applications are designed as per the businesses' requirement and their unique needs make the ERP a highly customizable and configurable program. However, these customized features have made it an expensive piece of software, keeping it out of reach of business enterprises and firms that are concerned about affordability. Thus, the ERP evolved into the SaaS model that was available in the market on a pay-per-use basis.

SaaS is a pure subscription model where the service company (vendor) provides the delivery platform, ongoing software updates, and the server infrastructure. This is in contrast to the traditional software license model, in which the user company buys licences of application software and database software, and sets up server and workstation infrastructure.

Advantages

SaaS is a relatively new model but is likely to emerge as a futuristic technology with the advancement in web technologies and Internet penetration. We enumerate certain advantages of using a SaaS model:

- SaaS user enterprises are free from setting up a large dedicated IT department and technical staff. It immensely cuts down the fixed costs in the deployment of ERP applications.
- Further, the SaaS provider companies extend their support in the field of data security and management, technical faults, and other technical services, thus helping the firms focus on their core business strengths.
- The initial set-up costs are low, as SaaS is used on a pay-per-use basis.
- Organizations can use SaaS as an upgrade on existing client–server applications.
- For companies having multiple locations and which are into businesses or services that would be delivered more effectively over the Internet, SaaS is a better model to work on.
- SaaS solutions offer mature and rich functionalities as they understand the complexities of delivering SaaS in a multi-customer environment.
- The user organization carries minimum risks due to two factors: one, the initial set-up costs are low in comparison with client–server ERP systems–two, if the user organization thinks that the solution does not fit its requirements, the services can be discontinued anytime.

Exhibit 9.3 illustrates how a Bengaluru auto component company benefitted from SaaS solutions from Ramco OnDemand ERP.

EXHIBIT 9.3

SaaS Implementation in a Bengaluru-based Auto Component Company

Ramco OnDemand ERP was successfully launched for a leading automobile component manufacturer having its headquarters in Bengaluru. The company aims to be a market leader in its operating regions including Eastern Europe and India. Ramco Systems aimed at deploying an ERP solution that could enable the auto component manufacturing company to standardize and streamline their business processes across the organization and ensure efficient management reporting. Ramco OnDemand ERP helps the manufacturer draw their disparate processes together, efficiently controlling their purchases, production schedules, inventories, finance, and MIS. The company's manufacturing processes are efficiently handled by the discrete production module, integrating the entire complex process plan, and managing high complexities in the bill of material (BOM) through product structure. End-to-end inventory lot and serial traceability was achieved by allocating unique numbers to each item. External and internal suppliers are differentiated by grouping supplier accounts and reports and these can be extracted accordingly.

Business Challenges
There were many business challenges such as handling complex and intricate manufacturing processes, tracking inventory on high priority, managing internal and external suppliers, and handling and tracking excise gate passes offered to suppliers.

Benefits
After implementation of SaaS ERP, the company reaped benefits in the form of streamlined business processes, improved response time and productivity, better organizational planning and control, reduced operating and inventory cost, and enhanced material tracking.

(Hypothetical example based on author's personal experience.)

SUPPLY CHAIN MANAGEMENT

The total supply chain functions of an organization involve movement of goods from the supplier to the end customer. This means managing suppliers on one hand and distribution channels on the other. The flow of goods from suppliers to the organizations and then further to the end consumer involves complete supply processes. Simply put, supply chain management (SCM) is the process of making the right goods available to the right people at the right time and right place at the right costs.

According to Laudon (2010), 'A firm's supply chain is a network of organizations and business processes for procuring raw materials, transforming these materials into intermediate and finished products, and distributing the finished products to customers. It links suppliers, manufacturers, distribution centres, retail outlets, and customers to supply goods and services from source through consumption'.

For example, ColorPlus, the manufacturer of premium quality men's garments has a manufacturing unit in Chennai. The fashion brand sells across the country through retailers and company-owned retail outlets. The company sources raw material, such as fabric, buttons, zippers, threads, packing bags, and packing boxes, from various suppliers. The suppliers of ColorPlus may have further suppliers. Similarly, the finished goods from ColorPlus reach the end consumers through intermediaries such as stockists, distributors, and retailers. This is a complete supply chain for ColorPlus garments. As seen in Fig. 9.3, the upstream (backward) supply chain consists of suppliers and their suppliers, while the downstream (forward) supply chain consists of stockists, distributors, retailers, and end consumers. Materials, information, and cash flow through the supply chain in both directions, as seen in Fig. 9.3.

The objective of supply chain management is to manage the flow of products through distribution centres and warehouses to ensure that the products are delivered to the right locations in the most efficient manner. Kalambi (1999) summarizes the objectives of a successful supply chain management as follows:

• Integrating information
• Analysing this information to trigger a corresponding product transition
• Creating a nimble and responsive planning and execution process
• Enabling global process visibility and coordination among supply chain partners
• Improving overall throughput and asset utilization
• Empowering people to identify and solve problems proactively

Information Technology Tools

SCM is a cross-functional enterprise system that uses information technology to link an organization's business processes and business partners such as suppliers, distributors, and customers. The goal of SCM is to bring in efficiency in procurement and to meet the demands

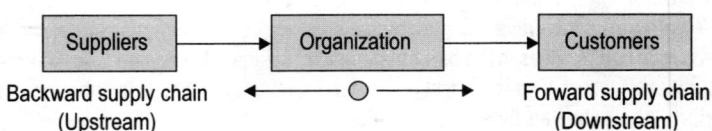

Fig. 9.3   Total supply chain system

of customers effectively. Hence, the need is to plan, manage, and optimize inventory and capacity in a company's operations and communicate the planning and inventory information among the various levels of suppliers and customers.

The IT functions in a value chain involve efficient inventory management through a systemic approach applied across the supply chain partners. It focuses on the need to look at value delivery to the customer. SCM tools cover the complete process of flow of goods from raw material (from the supplier) to finished product (from the manufacturer), warehouse, and end customers through the logistic processes (see Fig. 9.4). This complete supply chain life cycle can be identified as buy–make–move–store–sell. IT systems provide a set of integrated applications, tools, and capabilities that give strategic insight into current processes of an organization, and help remove bottlenecks and inefficiencies. The organization can respond faster to customers' demands and gain competitive advantages. Therefore, it helps keep profits high and reduces leakages by way of improvement in productivity.

SCM software and Internet technologies can help integrate and reengineer SCM processes that support the supply chain life cycle. Figure 9.4 illustrates the basic framework of SCM, which constitutes partners, processes, tools, and life cycle.

SCM tools provide people across the supply chain, visibility into customer demand and the delivery of goods, helping them make faster, better business decisions and take the best course of action when adjustments are necessary. With features such as automatic notification and alerts, they easily keep tabs on inventory, helping sustain optimal item levels, without holding up funds in

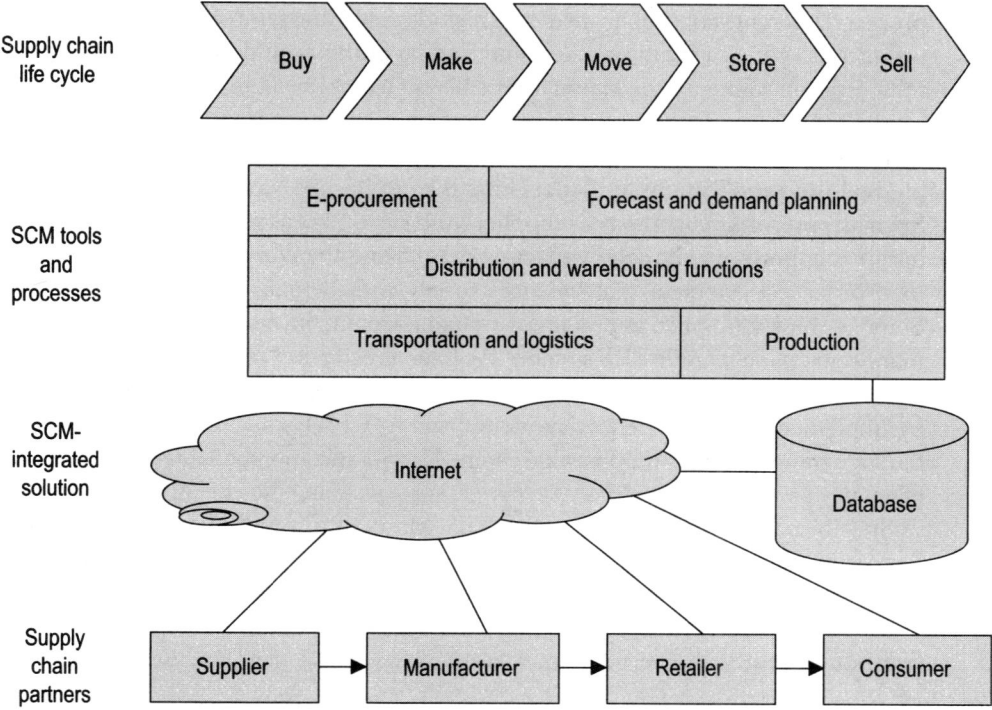

Fig. 9.4   Constitution of supply chain management

the warehouse. The procurement team can plan purchasing at favourable terms and in a timely manner, thus controlling costs and ensuring that the organization meets its customer commitments.

Role of SCM Applications

SCM software can help organizations in either planning supplies or executing supply chain activities. Different modelling and planning tools work in synchronization with each module of SCM. Various tools, such as advance planning and scheduling, offer the promise of extending the benefits of ERP systems beyond transaction data processing. These tools employ constraint-based technologies that enable them to examine the constraints that an organization faces, such as storage capacity, distribution points, and transportation modes. With this technology, companies and members of the supply chain can streamline delivery schedules together and react quickly to sudden changes in variables such as material supply, storage capacity, transportation resources, or customer changes.

For example, in Exhibit 9.3, if the Bengaluru-based auto component company receives an unexpectedly large order, it will have a widespread impact on the entire supply chain operations. They have to order additional raw material, which will involve more logistics and transportation, and would require more warehouse space. The manufacturing will also be affected as it will require more capacity in terms of machines, human resources, and energy. Thus, the entire process may need rescheduling. This critical task is demand planning in the SCM, which determines how much product a business needs to make to satisfy the customers' needs.

Supply chain execution systems manage the various activities involved in the supply chain process. Different supply chain activities include delivering sales or services to customers, shipping products, negotiating with suppliers and trading partners, and managing inventories. The SCM solutions help connect information from different teams managing these activities. In doing so, they can help empower people to perform with optimal productivity, maintain profitable relationships with vendors and business partners, and satisfy customers. The new enterprise solutions, which are real-time applications, are addressing the entire supply chain through extended enterprise. Such an enterprise encompasses suppliers and customers as well. These solutions are capable of optimizing both material and capacity, while taking the constraints into account. They involve total order management that balances supply with demand and supports virtual enterprises. Some of these tools, such as procurement management, inventory management, and distribution management, are part of ERP systems. We have already discussed these applications in Chapter 8 .

The story of ITC Wills Lifestyle, as illustrated in Exhibit 9.4 shows how the company benefitted by implementing radio frequency identification (RFID) and European article number (EAN) barcode standards in its supply value chain. The organization benefitted by increasing per person efficiency and improving customer service, supply chain efficiencies, and inventory velocity.

Specialized SCM software, such as i2, Manhattan, and Manugistic, offer planning and forecasting capabilities. The latest ERP packages, such as Oracle's E-Business Suite, SAP's mySAP, and JDA, include SCM modules.

E-procurement

E-procurement is one of the major enablers of SCM. B2B e-procurement technologies allow web-enabled procurement markets to automate communications and collaboration among

EXHIBIT 9.4

Wills Lifestyle: The Best Supply Chain Practices

ITC's Lifestyle Retailing Business Division (LRBD), a major Indian garment manufacturer, has established a nation-wide retailing presence through its Wills Lifestyle chain of exclusive specialty stores. Wills Lifestyle, the fashion destination, offers a tempting choice of Wills Classic work wear, Wills Sport relaxed wear, Wills Clublife evening wear, fashion accessories, Essenza Di Wills—an exclusive range of fine fragrances and bath and body care products, and Fiama Di Wills—a range of premium shampoos and shower gels. Wills Lifestyle has also introduced Wills Signature designer wear, designed by leading designers of the country.

ITC Lifestyle is adding technology to its mix of style and branding. The company has implemented RFID and EAN. Uniform Code Council (UCC) barcode standards are aimed at improving customer experience and increasing supply chain efficiency. This is a step towards implementing collaborative supply chain practices and global standards by adopting the universal EAN barcode and RFID. EAN and UCC standards enable common and unambiguous identification of garments and other general merchandise by retailers, manufacturers, and their distribution supply chain trading partners. The use of common barcodes on physical goods in conjunction with electronic information flow using global identification standards for ordering, invoicing, dispatching, etc., streamlines business processes and eliminates frequent manual errors, thus saving avoidable administrative costs.

Wills Lifestyle can establish collaborative supply chain processes that result in automated, vendor-managed replenishment cycles, real-time stocks and returnable management, inventory tracking, sales forecasting based on actual consumption, efficient product introductions, category management, etc. 'The adoption of EAN barcodes by all players in the industry is an essential step in streamlining business processes which eliminate costs besides facilitating compliance with international best practices,' says Ravi Mathur, chief executive officer, EAN India. However, RFID implementation does not necessarily mean departure from barcodes. Though ITC is aggressive on RFID, as of December 2007, it does not intend to do away with the barcodes completely. According to Bansal, although RFID is an enabling technology, it may not completely replace barcodes in the near future. However, its use is surely going to proliferate as the costs come down, and the number of successful implementations go up to augment the end-users' confidence. He further adds that RFID has the potential to enable a higher level of automation in the garments industry, thereby providing a tool for increased responsiveness required for a sustained competitive advantage.

The process started in April 2007 when the printing of tags and tagging of merchandise at manufacturing locations began. Subsequently, the two regional distribution centres (RDCs) began using RFID by June 2007. With the launch of the autumn–winter '07 collection, the Wills Lifestyle Store at the Metropolitan Mall in Gurgaon became the first store to be enabled for billing through RFID. The ambit of RFID implementation also included aligning and modifying existing systems to accommodate new technology.

By implementing RFID technology, Wills Lifestyle set out to increase efficiency per person as its main objective, and subsequently improve customer service, supply chain efficiencies, and inventory velocity, thus enabling lesser stock-out situations. The company has been able to handle the increased scale of operations, and witnessed increased warehouse efficiency, reduced physical handling of garments, elimination of manual scanning, and thus, ensured high accuracy.

Sources:
'ITC Wills Lifestyle: Increasing the style quotient', *Data Quest*, 15 December 2007.
'Garment majors go for collaborative supply chain', www.gs1india. org/news/Press%20Release%20-%20Garments.doc, last accessed on 29 April 2012.
http://www.itcportal.com/itc-business/fmcg/lifestyle-retailing.aspx, last accessed on 29 April 2012.

partners trading on the Internet. The Internet provides a platform for achieving organizational efficiency with optimum use of time, money, and labour. E-procurement refers to the processing of purchase order systems through the Internet. According to Jaiswal (2004), in the true sense, e-procurement is not just putting the purchasing decisions online, but also includes suppliers in the purchasing network, broadening the range of employees who can carry out transactions, and emphasizing effective supplier relationship. Thus, information technology has changed the supply chain management concept in a big way.

E-procurement has many advantages over the traditional procurement system. It reduces purchase ordering cost and order cycle time. There is no paper work; hence, the data is more accurate. Employees prefer to work on Internet-based applications than write purchase orders by hand. This increases their satisfaction. Organizations make more profits by saving on purchases than selling on high margins. The supplier relationship is improved by focusing on a limited number of suppliers and making more purchases from them.

Functioning of E-procurement Systems

E-procurement is accomplished through a B2B collaboration module. The buyer and supplier business applications may be independent, but the buyer's enterprise system or e-commerce site has a vendor registration. Alternatively, an Internet-based middleware is developed in the form of an e-portal, which works as a link between the customer and the supplier's database. Suppliers are registered at the e-procurement site and are given identities, rights, and privileges to access information.

The customer sends a request for quotation (RFQ) to the suppliers through the e-portal. This also works like a tendering process, wherein the requirements are displayed in the web portal as tender documents. The suppliers access the RFQ and respond with their quotation. The quotations are received only through the portal; however, organizations may also entertain quotations through mails and manual paper processes and enter them in the system. The purchaser then compares the quotations received and shortlists the suppliers based on their prices, terms, and quality of products.

Purchase orders (POs) are created using the e-procurement web application. The supplier accesses the PO on the site. Alternatively, the PO data may be directly sent to the supplier's database using electronic data interchange (EDI).

The supplier dispatches goods and creates a goods dispatch document through the e-commerce portal. The information is available to the customer on a real-time basis. The delivery information on the Internet is captured by the customer's database. The goods are received by the customer and an acknowledgement is sent to the supplier, which can be accessed by the supplier. In many cases, the suppliers have access to a customer's database through the extranet and can send an advice of dispatch.

Trends

SCM has evolved through many phases. During the 1960s, SCM referred to fragmented processes such as demand forecasting, purchasing, and requirement planning while the 1980s saw the inclusion of warehousing, distribution, and channel functions as its core processes. During the 1990s, transportation and logistics also became a part of SCM. In the new century, we see the integration of all the functions with IT as the enabler of the system (Chaturvedi 2004).

Prior to the Internet era, SCM information flow was restricted to internal supply chain systems for purchase, material management, manufacturing, and distribution. It was not possible to share information smoothly with external supply chain partners, such as suppliers, distributors, and logistic providers, as they used incompatible systems. Due to the advent of IT in general and the Internet technologies in particular, SCM has evolved from an internal process to an integrated external process. According to Laudon (2010), some supply chain integration is supplied inexpensively using Internet technology. Firms use intranets to improve coordination among their internal supply chain processes, and they use extranets to coordinate supply chain processes shared with their business partners.

The new trends in SCM are pushed by widespread applications of intranets and extranets. These advancements allow all members of the value chain to instantly communicate with each other and reschedule and readjust purchasing, logistics, manufacturing, and distribution. The partners in supply chain will be able to collaborate online through the web-based SCM tools. Koudsi (2000) forecasts, 'The supplier-facing applications arena will see the continual growth of public as well as private networks that transform linear and inflexible supply chain into nonlinear and dynamic fulfilment networks. Supplier-facing applications will also evolve along another dimension: from automation and integration of supply chain to collaborative sourcing, planning, and design across their supplier network'.

CUSTOMER RELATIONSHIP MANAGEMENT

Hotel Holiday Inn learnt that retaining customers through loyalty programmes and customer care would bring back the guests to their hotels (see Exhibit 9.5). The 'bucket theory of marketing' by

EXHIBIT 9.5

Holiday Inn: Plugging the Hole in the Bucket

With more than 4400 properties located in over 100 countries, Intercontinental Hotel Group (IHG) has some of the best-known hotel brands in the world. The group owns 4400 hotels and seven brands—Intercontinental, Crown Plaza, Hotel Indigo, Holiday Inn, Holiday Inn Express, StayBridge, and Candlewood. From an iconic family hotel—Holiday Inn to Crown Plaza, the place to meet for business—IHG brands are some of the most respected hotels in the industry. How did they earn that respect? 'By ensuring that everything about our hotels makes them the first choice for guests, from the softness of our pillows to our leading rewards programme,' says a senior executive at Holiday Inn.

The customer loyalty programme launched by the hotel chain rewarded its guests. Loyal guests were given preferential rooms and offered discounts on repeat visits. They were offered complimentary food vouchers and drinks in the fabulous bars of the hotel. Guests earning high points in the reward programme were allowed to bring additional companions. In this manner, the hotel chain was always able to maintain near full occupancy of its million-odd rooms across the globe.

In an interview, James L. Schorr, then executive vice-president of marketing at Holiday Inn, illustrates a point.

He stated that he was famous at Holiday Inns for what's called the 'bucket theory of marketing'. By this, he meant that marketing can be thought of as a big bucket. It is what the sales, advertising, and promotion programmes do that pours business into the top of the bucket. As long as these programmes are effective, the bucket stays full. However, 'There is only one problem,' he said, 'there is a hole in the bucket'. When the business is running well and the hotel is delivering on its promises, the hole is small and few customers are leaving. However, when the operation is weak and customers are not satisfied with what they get, people start falling out of the bucket through the holes faster than they can be poured in through the top.

Therefore, the right customer relationship strategy calls for plugging the hole in the bucket. Retain more customers than you can acquire.

Sources:
Zeithaml, Valarie A. and Mary Jo Bitner, *Services Marketing: Integrating Customer Focus across the Firm*, Tata McGraw-Hill, New Delhi, 2006.
http://www.holidayinn.com/hotels/us/en/global/support/about_ihg, last accessed on 29 April 2012.

the hotel's vice-president indicates that marketing programmes fail if customers exit due to bad customer relationship management (CRM).

Markets are fast transforming from being seller-driven to being buyer-driven. Modern enterprises adopt customer-focused business approaches in which the customer is treated like the proverbial 'king'. According to a research finding, creating a new customer is six times costlier than retaining an old one. According to Pareto's principle or the '80/20 rule', 20% of the existing customers give 80% of the business. Organizations pay more attention to maintaining relationships with existing customers than investing more in creating new customers. In a highly competitive market, customer loyalty plays an important role in business continuity, profitability, and competitive advantage.

Customer Relationship

Customer relationship refers to keeping in touch with the customer, providing personalized services, and thus, cultivating loyalty. According to Jawadekar (2007), with rapid globalization and product differentiation becoming less relevant and competitive, customer relationship is now the key enabler for moving the business ahead. Customer relationship has become a factor in gaining a competitive advantage. In an ever-changing world, organizations adopt customer-centric approaches of doing business.

Customer relationship is not an event, but a process of acquisition, enhancement, and retention of customers through the organizational life cycle. Figure 9.5 displays the three phases in customer relationship. A new customer is acquired by contact management, sales prospecting, selling, direct marketing, and order fulfilment. Customer value is enhanced by keeping the customer happy by providing superior services, cross-selling, and up-selling. The value is supposed to be enhanced if customers find it attractive to buy again. To retain a customer, organizations proactively identify and reward their most valuable and loyal customers. The business is expanded by targeted and relationship marketing programmes.

An organization gets to know its customer through various contact points or touch points, where both of them come across each other. These touch points include initial interactions while running promotional campaigns, selling of goods, and finally at service delivery in the customer value chain. Figure 9.6 displays the customer value chain showing touch points where the organization's employees come across the customer.

According to Norris (2000), 'Managing the full range of customer relationship involves two related objectives: one, to provide the organization and all of its customer-facing employees with

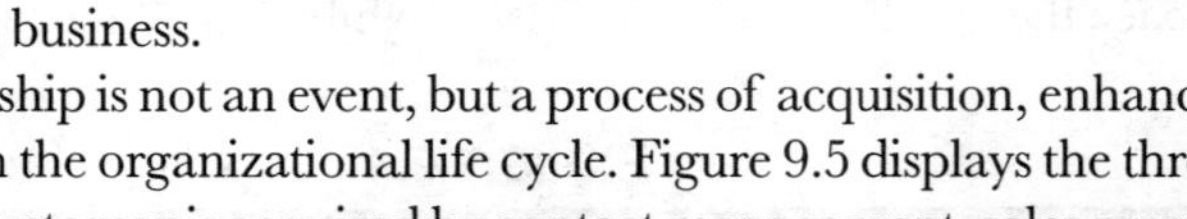

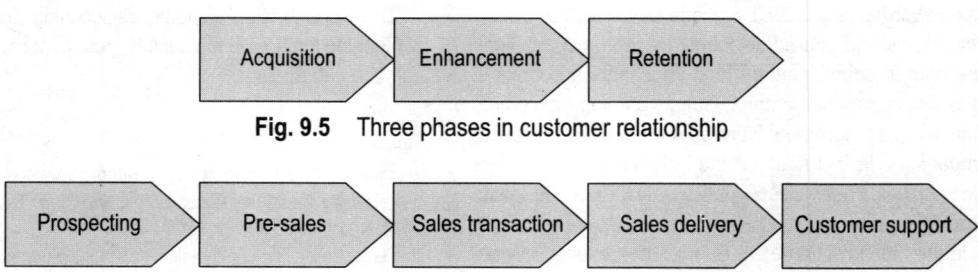

Fig. 9.5   Three phases in customer relationship

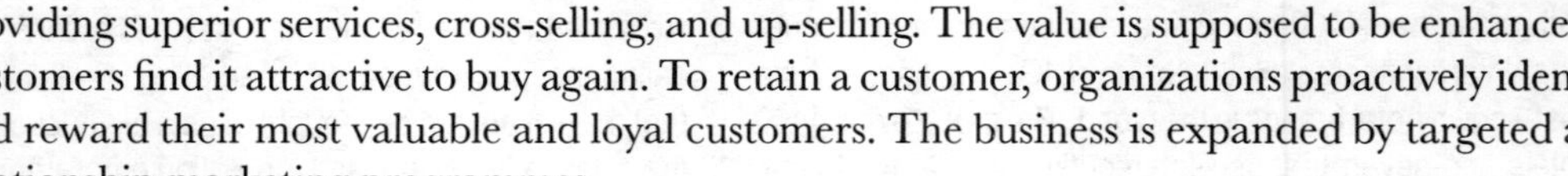

Fig. 9.6   Customer value chain providing touch points

a single, complete view of every customer at every touch point and across all channels; and two, to provide the customer with a single, complete view of the company and its extended channels'.

Thus, a customer relationship programme takes care of the customer throughout its value chain. This helps the organization retain the customer and increase business and profitability with the customer, which in turn, is the foundation for its success.

Customer Relationship Management Systems

CRM systems are processes and technologies that are used for managing relationships with customers across business functions. CRM systems help capture and integrate customer data from all over the organization, consolidate and analyse the data, and then disseminate the results to various systems and contact points in the customer value chain. According to Laudon (2010), 'Well-designed CRM systems provide a single enterprise view of customers that is useful for improving both sales and customer service. Such systems likewise provide customers with a single view of the company regardless of what touch point the customer uses'.

CRM systems involve the use of IT to create cross-functional enterprise systems to automate and integrate many customer-centric business processes such as contact and accounts management, sales force automation, marketing, customer loyalty programmes, and post-sales customer services. There are a number of CRM applications available in the market. Siebel Systems, Oracle, Microsoft, PeopleSoft, SAP AG, etc., are some of the international CRM software vendors. We will discuss CRM systems under four categories. Figure 9.7 provides a framework of CRM systems.

Sales Force Automation

Sales force automation (SFA) is the most widely used CRM application in the world. The SFA module of CRM systems helps sales staff manage more leads and increase productivity. The

Fig. 9.7 Various CRM application modules

module leverages tools that enable sales professionals to get real-time access to leads and close more deals, faster. Salespersons can capture important sales information to uncover new business opportunities and use pipeline analysis reports to create precise sales forecasts. The sales CRM gives them real-time access to a single common view of the customer, enabling them to manage customer account and schedule meetings.

A sales CRM application provides functionalities for account and contact management, lead and opportunity management, quotation generation, customer communication, defining sales targets, forecasting and sales analytics, and offline and mobile device access of sales data. There are scores of sales force automation packages available in the market. Salesforce.com, Open CRM, etc. are the most widely used web-based SFA software.

Figure 9.8 illustrates some communication with a customer and leads management function in the CRM software.

Marketing

The marketing module of CRM systems provides a clearer view of customers and more informed marketing investments. This module offers the option of creating segments of customers based on distinct benefit groups and then marketing to one or more of the identified segments using a workflow-driven model. The system provides tools to help marketing managers identify, execute, and replicate effective marketing initiatives across sales channels. As such, CRM applications support direct marketing campaigns by providing capabilities to segment a customer and execute a promotion plan like e-mailing.

The marketing modules of CRM cover the following:

- Customer segmentation
- Campaign planning and execution
- Data extraction and refinement

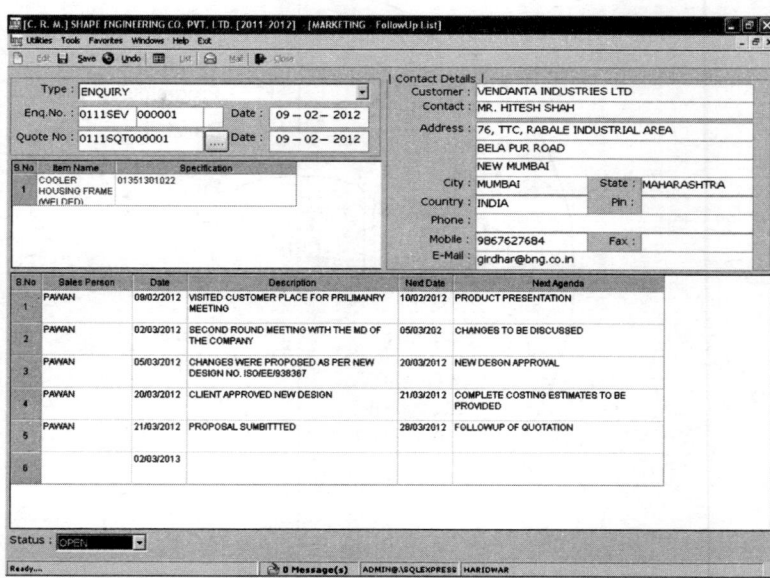

Fig. 9.8 Leads and opportunities management in a CRM application

- Analytics and reporting
- Marketing/Sales collaboration tools
- Information sharing portals

Loyalty Programmes

Loyalty programmes offer rewards and incentives to customers for their loyalty to the organization, which further help the organization retain their customers. Enhancing and optimizing customer retention is a major business strategy and the primary objective of any CRM system. Therefore, organizations worldwide, especially in hospitality, aviation, and retail businesses, invariably resort to customer loyalty programmes that offer rewards to loyal customers and help them retain the customer.

Loyalty programmes may have infinite permutations and combinations of discounts and rewards. For instance, offers such as buy two shirts and get one free, buy goods worth ₹5000 and get coupons worth ₹500 (which the customer can redeem on next purchases), buy goods worth a specific amount and get lifetime discounts on all purchases, etc., are examples in this regard. Shoppers Stop runs the 'First Citizen' club and rewards loyal customers and promotes repeat purchases. Westside, a retail chain of the Tata Group, has 'Club West' for its loyal customers. Similarly, Reliance Retail, D&A, and Study By Janak, formed a buyers' club and register their customers as members of the club. A customer holding a loyalty card of the club is offered special discounts on next purchases and gifts on their anniversaries. L'Occitane India, an international cosmetic brand chain in India has a fantastic loyalty programme that rewards customers on buying goods above a certain value. CRM captures interesting data about the customer to run a loyalty programme, as depicted in Fig. 9.9.

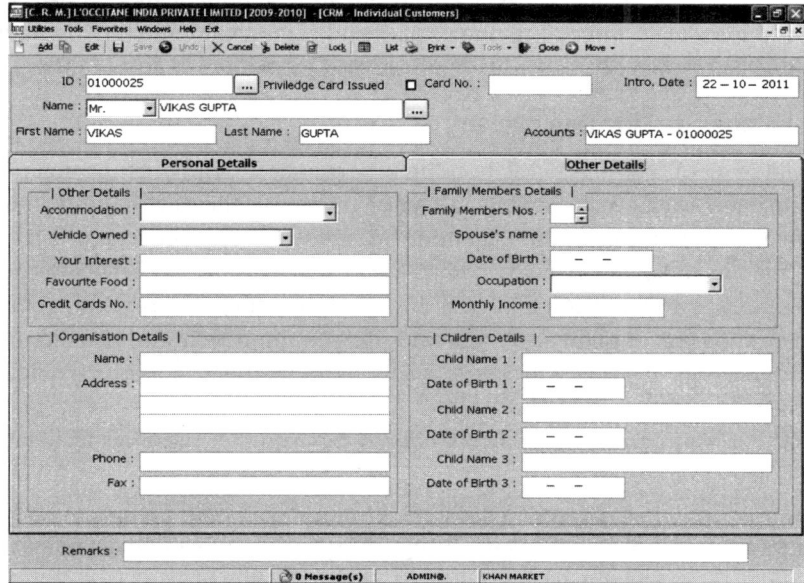

Fig. 9.9 Customer loyalty programme running on information
captured by the CRM system [www.bng.co.in]

Customer Service

After successful marketing and sales initiatives, the responsibility of the organization is to serve the customer better and handle service complaints. Through CRM applications, the organization can respond faster to customer service issues and empower service organizations to anticipate, address, and deliver consistent and efficient customer care that contributes to long-term business profitability. The customer service module of CRM systems provide information and tools to manage call centres, complaint handling, help desks, and customer support functions. These systems help customer service managers to create, assign, and manage service requests. As the CRM database gives a 360-degree view of the customer, the help desk can better support and satisfy a customer. The web-based self-service capabilities of CRM enables customers to easily access personalized support information.

For example, the Airtel website (www.airtel.in) is provided with self-service functions, wherein we can make payments, view previous bills, current unbilled amount, pending payments, and last payments made, and buy new connections, recharge, and lodge a complaint.

The customer service and support module of CRM covers account and contact management, customer service request, allocation of service request, performance of service and scheduling, and service reporting and analytics. The functions of a customer service CRM can be summarized as follows:

- Manage and track customer service requests from initial contact through resolution.
- Automatically link incoming enquiries to the appropriate customer service request file.
- Send requests to a queuing area where they can be accessed directly by teams and individuals.
- Automatically route service requests to the appropriate representative for action.
- Quickly search a knowledgebase that contains solutions to the most common service problems.
- Accurately bill for support incidents by creating and managing service contracts.
- Keep tabs on customer e-mail messages and generate automatic responses when appropriate.
- Generate reports that identify demonstrated service needs and evaluate service performance.

Advantages of CRM Deployment

Deployment of a customer relationship programme aids an organization in many ways. It helps organizations achieve customer satisfaction, empower their teams, and develop their businesses. It inculcates the culture of customer-oriented business processes. Availability of customer information and database helps in improving marketing and its effectiveness. Customer behaviour, tastes, and preferences are analysed through transactional data. With CRM applications tools, organizations can capitalize on customer insight, improve front-line efficiency and effectiveness, streamline critical business processes across customer touch points, and quickly adapt to changing business and customer needs.

We can summarize the benefits offered by customer relationship enabled by information technology as follows:

Improved access to customer information   Organizations view and update a wealth of customer data, which covers contact details, accounts, sales, personal information, complaint records, service records, and history of customer interaction. Organizations disseminate and share this information across teams and departments, which give a 360-degree view of the customer. With so much more information available at the click of a mouse to service workers and salespeople, it is possible to respond to a client's concerns quickly. This boosts customer satisfaction, breeds loyalty, and ultimately leads to more revenue and more profits for the organization.

More responsive customer service A happy customer breeds employee satisfaction and hence, enhances employee morale. An employee of the organization likes to serve a happy customer more than a dissatisfied customer. The response time is much less and service personnel find it motivating to serve the customer.

Streamlined business processes CRM applications not only centralize customer sales and service information, and provide analytical reports on customer data, but also provide well-structured and defined business processes to follow. For example, there are well-defined steps for complaint handling systems in a mobile service company. The employee simply follows those steps and completes the process of complaint recording, allocation, service delivery, and compliance system.

Enhanced forecasting capability Based on sales transactional data, customers' spending patterns, history of promotional effectiveness, etc., CRM applications provide important tools for sales forecasting. The user can analyse and forecast future opportunities in real time. For example, the user can analyse sales data of a particular month in the previous three years. The pattern of sales may certainly signify some trends. This gives the management the ability to spot trends as they develop, leading to more informed decision-making.

Connectivity anytime, anywhere E-CRM enables users to access customer data through the web. The sales team can create data while on transit and access data from the server connected through the Internet. Customers can have access to the CRM application through the Internet and browse through important pricing decisions, promotional offers, etc. Post-sales, customers can login to register complaints and give suggestions. This reduces direct customer interaction and dependency on employees. Similarly, solutions can be offered remotely using a variety of devices, including mobile-based terminals, mobiles, iPhones, and Smartphones.

Table 9.2 compares some CRM applications offered by different companies and the functionalities they offer.

Trends

Despite the availability of mature CRM solutions, it is not very widely used in Indian companies. Only companies in banking, financial services, and insurance (BFSI), telecom, and BPO businesses in India are using CRM extensively. Most companies that have implemented ERP systems are using CRM at the operational level. However, slowly, Indian companies are becoming more customer-centric. It is only now that the use of technology to automate customer processes such as sales, marketing, and after-sales services is getting due attention.

The infrastructure strategies survey conducted by Network Magazine and the Indian Market Research Bureau (IMRB) among Indian CIOs reveals that only 13% of the companies have CRM as an IT priority. Among companies that have already invested in enterprise applications

Table 9.2 Comparison of CRM software offered by various companies

Offered by	Product name	Website	Modules offered
Siebel System Software India	Siebel CRM	www.siebel.com/crm	• Sales force automation • Marketing automation • Call centre and service • Business analytics • Hosted CRM
Oracle India	Oracle CRM	www.crmondemand/oracle.com	• Sales CRM • Marketing CRM • Customer support CRM • On demand CRM
Adapt India	Adapt CRM	www.adapt-india.com	• Account/Customer database • Activity database • Sales opportunity/Pipeline management • Service ticket tracking • Marketing campaign
Microsoft India	Microsoft CRM	www.microsoft.com/	• Sales CRM • Marketing CRM • Customer support CRM
Talisma Corporation	Talisma CRM	www.talisma.com	• Sales CRM • Marketing CRM • Customer support CRM • Hosted CRM
Sales Force.com	Salesforce.com CRM	www.salesforce.com	• Sales force cloud • Marketing cloud • Help desk cloud • Customer service cloud
Ramco Systems	Ramco OnDemand CRM	www.ramcoondemand.com	• Sales CRM
Sage Software India	Sage CRM	www.sagesoftware.co.in	• Sales CRM • Marketing CRM • Customer support CRM • Mobile solutions • CRM cloud
CRM 24 × 7	CRM 24 × 7	www.crm24×7.com	• Sales force • Help desk • Customer service • Contact centre
Zoho	Zoho Online CRM	www.zoho.com	• Sales force CRM

or are planning to invest, only 23% have prioritized CRM. About 19% of the companies plan to dedicate a part of their planned investments to CRM (Gupta 2004).

The global trends in CRM can be attributed to four types of applications being used by organizations. Most companies start with operational CRM applications such as sales force automation and customer service centres. Organizations at the second stage implement analytical CRM using various analytical tools like data mining to extract customer data for targeted marketing campaigns. The next advancement in the CRM space is use of collaborative CRM in which business partners and customers collaborate with each other for self-service and feedback. This is also known by partner relationship management, which uses CRM tools for collaborative service among organizations and partners. Finally, web-based CRM portals are in use for giving customers access to information. The intranet and extranet-based CRM systems are helpful in operational, analytical, and collaborative applications.

Table 9.3 shows these four categories of CRM with their functionalities and the business value they provide.

Table 9.3   Trends in CRM implementation

Types of CRM	Functionalities	Business value
Operational CRM	Supports marketing, sales, and service functions, customer targeting, pricing, marketing campaign management, etc.	• Supports a variety of customer-oriented business processes and facilitates customer interaction with greater convenience through a variety of channels, including phone, fax, e-mail, chat, and mobile devices • Synchronizes customer interactions consistently across all channels
Analytical CRM	Provides customer value analysis, customer retention rate analysis, and sales forecasting	• Provides analytical insights into customer data and relies on in-depth customer history, customer intelligence, tastes, and preferences from the data warehouse • Analyses transaction patterns and predicts customer behaviour for better customer relationship • Facilitates customer interaction with relevant information and tailor-made offerings
Collaborative CRM	Provides a collaborative platform by integration with internal enterprise systems and databases, and with front-end web systems	• Allows the enterprise to response faster to customer needs • Provides a means to conduct interactive, collaborative, and personalized interactions and communications on an integrated platform • Improves efficiency and integration throughout the supply chain
Web-based CRM	Gives access to customers and employees through a web-based CRM portal	• Provides real-time assessment of customer interactions, analysis, and interpretations • Empowers all employees to respond swiftly to customer demands • Transforms the organization to become customer-focused

SUMMARY

The enterprise systems are based on single platform, compatible databases, and computer systems. Enterprise resource planning (ERP), supply chain management (SCM), and customer relationship management (CRM) are examples of enterprise systems. ERP systems are integrated software suites built on a common platform and a unified database covering the entire organizational information requirements.

ERP systems generate significant business benefits by integrating diverse business processes and provide consistent reporting; however, at the same time, they are difficult to implement and come at a high upfront price, thus posing many challenges. ERP systems help in creating and maintaining uniform organization structures, form common and standardized definitions and formats, work as catalysts to reengineer the work processes within the organization, and also improve management reporting and decision-making. ERP systems are built around the best business practices and induce customer-driven and vendor-oriented work culture; and also connect with customers and vendors.

ERP systems not only require large investments on technologies, but also force fundamental changes in the business processes, and are difficult to implement. The challenges include daunting implementation, high upfront costs, delayed returns on investment (ROI), resistance to change, and inflexibility.

Four important trends are shaping ERP's continuing

evolution—improvements in integration and flexibility, extensions to e-business applications, a broader reach to new users, and the adoption of Internet technologies. The new form of ERP applications as hosted services has given birth to software as a service (SaaS) model. Under a pay-as-you-go model, the customers gain access to desired applications developed and managed by the application service provider (ASP) company.

The total supply chain functions of an organization involve movement of goods from the supplier to the end customer. IT functions in a value chain involve efficient inventory management through a systemic approach applied across the supply chain partners. It focuses on the need to look at value delivery to the customer. Supply chain management (SCM) software can either help organizations in planning the supplies or executing the supply chain activities. Supply chain execution systems manage the various activities involved in the supply chain process. Delivering sales or services to customers, shipping products, negotiating with suppliers and trading partners, managing inventory, etc, are the different supply chain activities.

E-procurement is one of the major enablers of supply chain management. B2B e-procurement technologies allow web-enabled procurement markets to automate communications and collaborations among partners trading on the Internet. E-procurement is accomplished through a B2B business collaboration module.

The new trends in SCM are pushed by the widespread applications of intranets and extranets. These advancements allow all members of the value chain to instantly communicate with each other and reschedule and readjust purchasing, logistics, manufacturing, and distribution as per requirements.

Customer relationship refers to keeping in touch with the customer, providing personalized services, and thus, cultivating loyalty. Customer relationship is not an event, but a process of acquisition, enhancement, and retention of customer through the organization's life cycle. CRM systems help capture and integrate customer data from all over the organization, consolidate and analyse the data, and then disseminate the results to various systems and contact points in the customer value chain. Customer relationship management (CRM) systems involve that use of information technology to create cross-functional enterprise systems to automate and integrate many customer-centric business processes such as contact and accounts management, sales force automation, marketing, customer loyalty programmes, and post-sale customer services.

CRM systems facilitate organizations to delight their customers, empower their teams, and develop their businesses. It inculcates the culture of customer-oriented business processes. Some of the major advantages are improved access to customer information, more responsive services, streamlined business processes, enhanced forecasting capability, and connectivity—anywhere, anytime.

The worldwide trends in CRM can be attributed to four types of applications being used by organizations. These CRM applications are operational, analytical, collaborative, and web-based systems.

KEY TERMS

Analytical CRM   Use of analytical tools like data mining to extract customer data for targeted marketing campaigns.

Application service provider (ASP)   Applications developed and managed by vendors and available on clouds or rental model.

Change agent   An advantage of ERP systems as they act as catalysts to reengineer the work processes within the organization.

Collaborative CRM   A customer relationship management (CRM) system in which business partners and customers collaborate for self-service and feedback.

Customer loyalty programmes   A programme that offers rewards to loyal customers and helps organizations retain them.

Customer relationship management (CRM)   Systems that help capture and integrate customer data from all over the organization, consolidate and analyse the data, and then disseminate the results to various systems and contact points in the customer value chain.

Customer touch-points   Instances where a customer comes into contact with an organization.

Enterprise resource planning (ERP)   An integrated software suite built on a common platform and unified database covering the entire organizational information requirements.

Enterprise systems   Integrated solutions used across diverse functional areas and geographical expanses in large organizations.

Enterprise uniformity   Maintaining uniform organization structures, systems, and procedures throughout the geographical area.

e-Procurement   Technologies that allow web-enabled

procurement, automated communications, and collaboration among partners trading on the Internet.

Mobile-enabled ERP   Enterprise systems that can be interfaced with mobile smartphones to deliver information to the user.

Operational CRM   The beginning level of CRM where the organization uses an application like sales force automation.

Return on investment (ROI)   Benefits in terms of value from investments on enterprise systems.

Software as a service (SaaS)   A service offering software on clouds as a pay-as-you-use or rental model.

Supply chain execution systems   Systems that manage the various activities involved in the supply chain process.

Supply chain life cycle   A buy–make–move–store–sell cycle in a supply chain activity.

Supply chain management (SCM)   A cross-functional enterprise system that uses information technology to link organizations' business processes and business partners such as suppliers, distributors, and customers.

Web-enabled ERP   Use of Internet technologies to build web interfaces and networking capabilities into ERP systems.

CONCEPT REVIEW QUESTIONS

1. Explain the core role of enterprise systems, such as enterprise resource planning (ERP), supply chain management (SCM), and customer relationship management (CRM) solutions, in the management of business.
2. Explain ERP and the advantages of ERP solutions.
3. What are the various challenges of using ERP systems?
4. What are the latest trends in ERP systems? Explain the concept of SaaS.
5. What do you understand by supply chain management (SCM)?
6. What are the IT tools available for SCM? Explain their role in supply chain management.
7. What trends do you see in SCM in Indian companies?
8. Why has customer relationship management assumed high importance in modern enterprises?
9. Which are the various CRM management software modules available? Explain in detail.
10. What advantages do you see in deploying a CRM tool in your organization?
11. What trends to you foresee in CRM applications in India?

CRITICAL THINKING QUESTIONS

1. 'ERP systems are indispensable for modern businesses.' Do you agree with this statement? Why or why not? Justify your answer with suitable reasons, facts, and figures.
2. 'Information technology is the enabler of supply chain management systems.' Comment on this in the light of how SCM has been benefitted by IT tools.
3. 'In spite of the availability of mature CRM solutions, it is not very widely used in Indian companies.' Do you really think so? Why or why not?
4. For a business to survive, all modern businesses need to be customer-focused. Critically examine this statement.

MIS DEVELOPMENT

There are hundreds of ERP software available worldwide. Some of them have already been referred to in the chapter. These ERP solutions cater to various industry segments in terms of their applicability, affordability, complexity, and comprehensibility (coverage of business processes).

Exercise

Collect information about ERP packages through Internet search engines, print media, and company brochures. Categorize these packages into three—tier 1, tier 2, and tier 3. You can categorize the most complex, most comprehensive, or the most expensive as tier 1, and so on. From the vendors' websites, find out their customers. Tabulate the information in the format given in Table 9.4. Do you see a relationship between the category of the package and the business size of their customer?

Table 9.4 ERP packages and their customers

ERP category	ERP name	Web URL	Indian/ International	Customer's name
Tier 1	A			
	B			
	C			
	D			
Tier 2	T			
	X			
	Y			
	Z			
Tier 3	1			
	2			
	3			
	4			
	5			
	6			
	7			

REFERENCES

Caulfield, Brian, 'Toward a more perfect (and realistic) e-business', *Business 2.0*, January 2002.

Chaturvedi, B.M., *Supply Chain Management—An introduction*, ICFAI Books, New Delhi, 2004.

De Gues, Arie, 'Planning as learning', *Harvard Business Review*, March–April 1988.

Digby, James, '*50* facts about customer experience', http://returnonbehavior.com/2010/10/, last accessed on 23 March 2011.

El Sawy, Omar and Gene Bowles, 'Redesigning the customer support process for the electronic economy: Insights from storage dimensions', *MIS Quarterly*, December 1997.

Gupta, Soutiman Das, 'CRM—The Indian Experience', http://www.networkmagazineindia.com/200505/coverstory03.shtml, last accessed on 24 October 2011.

Jaiswal, Mahadeo and Monika Mittal, *Management Information Systems*, Oxford University Press, New Delhi, 2004.

Jawadekar, Waman S., *Management Information Systems: Text and Cases*, Tata McGraw-Hill, New Delhi, 2007.

Joshi, Girdhar, *Information Technology for Retail*, Oxford University Press, New Delhi, 2009.

Kalambi, N.M. and Sam Bansal, 'Why supply chain management', *Data Quest*, April 1999.

Koch, Christopher, 'ERP Basics', http://www.cio.com/research/erp/edit/erpbasic.html, last accessed on 17 January 2006.

Koudsi, Suzanne, 'Actually it's like brain surgery', *Fortune*, 20 March 2000.

Krigsman, Michael, '5 critical points for ERP success', www.zdnet.com/blog/ projectfailures, last accessed on 23 March 2011.

Laudon, Ken, Jane Laudon, and Rajneesh Dass, *Management Information System*, Pearson Education, Singapore, 2010.

O'Brien, James A., George M. Marakas and Ramesh Behl, *Management Information Systems*, Tata McGraw-Hill, New Delhi, 2007.

'Magic quadrant for midmarket and tier 2-oriented ERP for product-centric companies, Gartner Inc., 4 June 2009, http://www.gartner.com/id=1006412, last accessed on 29 April 2012.

'MySAP CRM', www.mysap.com, last accessed on 24 October 2011.

Norris, Grant, James Hurley, Kenneth Hartley, John Dunleavy, and John Balls, *E-Business and ERP: Transforming the Enterprise*, John Wiley & Sons, New York, 2000.

Robb, Drew, 'Top 10 trends in ERP', http://www.enterpriseappstoday.com/erp/the-top-10-trends-in-erp-1.html, last accessed on 18 October 2011.

BNG Infotech, www.bng.co.in, last accessed on 24 October 2011.

http://www.erp.asia/erp-failures.asp, last accessed on 23 March 2011.

CASE STUDY

Tata Chemicals: Innovative Way to Customer Relationship

Established in 1939, Tata Chemicals Limited (TCL) has manufacturing facilities in India, UK, Kenya, and USA. TCL started off with the creation of a plant in Mithapur, Gujarat, India that would raise a wealth of marine chemicals from the ocean. From these humble beginnings, it spread its operations across four continents and a market-leading international business was created. Today, TCL is a global company with interests in businesses that focus on LIFE—living, industry, and farm essentials. The story of the company is about harnessing the fruits of science for goals that go beyond business.

Through its living essentials portfolio, the company has had a positive impact on the lives of millions of Indians. TCL is the pioneer and market leader in India's branded iodised salt segment. With the introduction of an innovative, low-cost, nanotechnology-based water purifier, it is providing affordable, safe drinking water to the masses. TCL is the world's second largest producer of soda ash with manufacturing facilities in Asia, Europe, Africa, and North America. The company's industry essentials product range provides key ingredients to some of the world's largest manufacturers of glass, detergents, and other industrial products. With its farm essentials portfolio, the company has carved a niche in India as a crop nutrients provider. It is a leading manufacturer of urea and phosphatic fertilizers and, through its subsidiary, Rallis, has a strong position in the crop protection business.

The TCL innovation centre is home to world-class research and development capabilities in the emerging areas of nanotechnology and biotechnology. The company's centre for agri-solutions and technology provides advice on farming solutions and crop nutrition practices.

The company has also entered into a joint venture with Singapore's Temasek life sciences laboratory (Joil) to develop *jatropha* seedlings to enable capability of biofuels. In line with its mission, 'serving society through science', the company is applying its expertise in sciences, to develop high-tech and sustainable products.

TCL had already implemented SAP with modules such as sales and distribution, purchase, HR, and CRM. Online access to dealers and suppliers are already SAP-enabled. The company had already begun reaping the benefits.

Problem

TCL recently rolled out a small IT initiative, which it believes could have big implications in terms of servicing its customers in the days ahead. Earlier, TCL had to constantly interact with its sales force, distributors, and vendors for business purposes. TCL's distributors often depended on the salespeople or regional office representatives for basic information about dispatches and pending invoices. These salespeople or company employees acted as intermediaries, who would look into the system and extract the required information manually.

Beyond office hours, it would be really difficult for employees to get this information, and many a time, trucks would land up in storage warehouses late at night, which created hassles and delays due to lack of information. As the hazard kept growing, it became necessary to address it. Vikas Gadre, chief information officer, TCL, came up with a very innovative fix for this problem. He decided to connect the interactive voice response (IVR) to the company's SAP ERP, which gave them the perfect solution to cater to the needs of the employees, distributors, and customers.

Solution

TCL undertook the ambitious 'Project Manthan', which is a process that seeks improvement in all areas. The improving trend is on target in most areas and performance and capability improvement is seen as well. The process is on in waves; each wave stretches over two to three months and covers four to five units of the plant. The unit teams brainstorm, meet customers, suppliers, even competitors, and then crystallize their ideas on how to save costs and improve functioning. Ideas are then prioritized to act upon and bring results within a specified time frame. Several people are involved in this process as it builds capability among employees. Project Manthan has completed one full cycle and one full year.

Connected to the ERP through a middleware, the IVR system allows the users to dial its toll free number. Upon successful authorization, TCL customers can query the ERP system and get information varying from order and delivery status of their shipment, payment matters, and other transactional details.

As the new system eliminates the human element at their end, it brings in a greater degree of transparency to the entire process. Though a seemingly simple initiative, the new system is expected to have significant implications in terms of availability of information at TCL.

TCL uses a system developed by MobileOne, a company based in Hyderabad. The calling number '1800' is sourced from Tata Indicom and the IVR engine has been developed collaboratively by MobileOne's offices in India and Germany. This engine sits on top of middleware and then connects with the Tata Indicom number.

Challenges

The implementation, which was executed in phases, came with its own share of challenges. It took three months to connect the IVR solution to the ERP system. The roll-out got extended due to the training and handholding involved.

Due to financial constraints, TCL had to cut down on a lot of initial ideas during the implementation. Gadre says, 'One of the challenges is that people resist listening to a robotic voice to get information. In spite of the information being very relevant, the human touch is missing. The development of the IVR engine itself was a challenge. It required a lot of programming in SAP so that relevant information was extracted and made available. There were also challenges in terms of response time because if the IVR query queue is large, then it puts pressure on the production system, so we had to make a decision about this as to how to prioritize queries on a busy day or during peak hours'.

Benefits

IVR can be used very effectively for secondary phase data capture. The engine developed by TCL has a facility to call back the distributor as well. The engine is not merely equipped to receive calls; it can also call back the distributor and ask for information.

TCL is planning to extend the IVR implementation for employee self-service. 'One of the extensions that we are trying is to modularize the IVR engine and then Tata Indicom could offer it to other Tata Group companies on a SaaS model. The journey is still on in that direction,' says Gadre, mapping out the future plan.

At a time when most organizations are going in for cost consolidation and containment, IVR can be really useful. In companies that have many regional branches and wide-spread buyers, a lot of work can be completely eliminated with the use of IVR. On a concluding note, Gadre says, 'It is one more step towards cost containment for organizations as it eliminates unproductive use of man force'.

Discussion Questions

1. What factors were responsible for Tata Chemicals implementing interactive voice response systems?
2. Explain how SAP ERP must have had an impact on the functioning of Tata Chemicals?
3. What do you think is the supply chain of TCL? How would TCL have benefitted by implementing a SCM solution?
4. What were the challenges faced by TCL in implementing IVR?

Sources:

Choudhary, Rajendra, 'Tata Chemicals connects IVR system to its ERP', http://www.expresscomputeronline.com/20081117/expressintelligententerprise16.shtml, last accessed on 24 October 2011.

Desai, Jasmine, 'IVR to the rescue at Tata Chemicals', http://biztech2.in.com/casestudies/communication/ivr-to-the-rescue-at-tata-chemicals/53062/0, published on 29 April 2009, last accessed on 24 October 2011.

'The churning', http://www.tatachemicals.com/media/interviews/200301jan/200301_churning.htm, published on April 2003, last accessed on 23 October 2011.

http://www.tatachemicals.com/aboutus, last accessed on 24 October 2011.

10

Applications for Service Sector

‘
To have any kind of national-level working approach to technology, we must start with the government. But when it comes to computerization with the state, we cannot build new systems over a creaky base—we have to first reinvent our state processes to increase our efficiencies rather than merely computerizing what exists. We also need to ensure that people can actually access these systems effectively; else IT-enabled governance will be little more than a showcase project.
’

—NANDAN NILEKANI

LEARNING OBJECTIVES

After studying this chapter, you will be able to

- appreciate the concept of service and understand the differences between services and products
- understand service management systems and the service process cycle
- get an overview of MIS for major service sectors
- understand the applications in logistics and transportation
- comprehend the applications in hospitality and health care management
- learn about the applications in the aviation sector
- understand the applications in construction and real estate, banking, and insurance sectors

EXHIBIT 10.1

SL Raheja Hospital Mumbai: Managing Hospital Workflow with Soarian MedSuite

Health care information systems (HIS) have become necessary in hospitals. There are increasing technical enhancements in this solution to provide better clinical and administrative results. HIS, which is currently implemented in tertiary care hospitals, will soon find a place in primary and secondary care hospitals. In September 2010, Siemens Information Systems Ltd (SISL) announced the launch of its cutting-edge Soarian MedSuite HIS for the first time in India. The system has been successfully implemented at SL Raheja Hospital in Mumbai. Soarian MedSuite, an innovative and scalable HIS solution, helps hospitals to provide better patient care and drive clinical excellence by effectively integrating various processes.

Commenting on this pioneering technology, Dr Uma Nambiar, chief executive officer, SL Raheja Hospital said, 'Our goal is to provide seamless patient care through IT-enabled process optimization and leverage an advanced clinical informatics solution that can help us drive quality initiatives in the hospital and also measure and improve patient outcomes.' She also added, 'Siemens, the global technology leader had the perfect solution, which was tailor-made for our requirement and thus it was our chosen partner for this implementation.'

Siemens IT Solutions and Services is a leading international provider of IT solutions and services. Soarian MedSuite from SISL is an innovative and scalable HIS that helps hospitals worldwide increase efficiency by arming caregivers with integrated tools to manage administrative, clinical, and financial processes. The key differentiator for Soarian MedSuite from a business perspective is that the solution is based on hospital workflows and not on discrete modules. The workflow can be configured to reflect changes in business processes. Additionally, the solution has a clinical focus and was developed by a health care organization. In fact, the application is role-based and can be easily configured according to the various roles in a hospital. Further, the solution's implementation methodology is based on the global experience of Siemens in implementing similar health care solutions.

The HIS is a built-in workflow engine that provides flexibility for the system to address process improvements. It has a built-in interface engine, which facilitates interoperability with other third-party applications. It can be accessed from virtually anywhere and at any time, as physicians can easily connect to the system, from either inside or outside the hospital. Soarian MedSuite's key differentiator comes from its advanced technology platform that combines service-oriented architecture (SOA), rich Internet application (RIA), built-in interface engine, and health care process management (a business process management engine) integrated with the business logic of the application to deliver a deeper, richer, and unique 'role-based application' to health care institutions. Its adaptable, service-oriented architecture is based on a secure, open platform that is standards-based, easily integrated, and leverages widely-accepted technologies.

The HIS received the Best HIS Solution award at the health care IT Awards 2011 by NASSCOM, in collaboration with KPMG. The award recognized the impact of the solution for enhanced patient experience and faster delivery of medication at the hospital.

According to D. Ragavan—executive vice-president, Siemens Healthcare—in general, IT adoption in hospitals is at a nascent stage. Traditionally, HIS solutions have primarily focused on administrative and revenue cycle management. However, overall adoption of IT by physicians has been slow, and this is one of the major challenges. Additionally, the market is highly fragmented with multiple health care providers. This makes it difficult to deploy IT. Further, the public health care system is not adequately developed and investment in IT is generally not considered as a strategic requirement to drive businesses.

Benefits

How did SL Raheja Hospitals benefit from the HIS solution? They had a clinical focus. After its implementation, they have successfully demonstrated positive outcomes such as reduction in waiting time for discharge, increase in bed management efficiency, decrease in turnaround time of laboratory results, reduction in average length of stay, and reduction in unbilled charges for discharged patients.

Future of Hospital Management Systems

Ragavan opines that several government initiatives are likely to drive IT adoption in health care as various telemedicine projects have been launched in India. Further, the introduction of health smart card schemes will also drive information and communication technologies (ICT) investments. Some

(Contd)

Exhibit 10.1 (Contd)

states have initiated projects to digitize patient records in public hospitals and link them to a central database. In states such as Gujarat, Maharashtra, and Tamil Nadu, health care IT projects have been initiated in public hospitals.

Industry veterans anticipate that there will be tremendous changes in the Indian HIS market with increased spending in IT, primarily by private corporate hospitals, consolidation among HIS vendors including entry of global players, opportunities in cloud computing and software as a service (SaaS), and opportunities in telemedicine/telehealth.

Sources:
Interview of D Ragavan, executive vice-president, Siemens Healthcare *in Express Healthcare*, http://www.siemens.co.in/en/news_press/index/september16.htm, last accessed on 26 October 2011.
http://www.expresshealthcare.in/201108/market03.shtml, last accessed on 28 December 2012.
http://www.nasscom.in/best-healthcare-information-systems-his-solutions, last accessed on 26 October 2011.
www.siemens.com/it-solutions, last accessed on 26 October 2011.

SL Raheja Hospitals implemented the hospital management system (HMS) from Siemens and covered the hospital's entire workflow system (Exhibit 10.1). The objective of providing seamless patient care through IT-enabled process optimization and leveraging an advanced clinical informatics solution was fulfilled. You can see from the aforementioned case that IT initiatives helped in service delivery, drove quality initiatives, and also improved patient outcomes by reducing the waiting time for discharge, quickening laboratory results, and improving bed management at SL Raheja Hospitals.

The service sector in India accounts for more than half of India's GDP, as per 2010 figures. According to the national portal of the government of India (http://business.gov.in), in 2009–2010, the share of services in India's GDP was 55.2% (63.4% including the construction sector). The fact that the service sector accounts for more than half the GDP marks a watershed in the evolution of the Indian economy and takes it closer to the fundamentals of a developed economy. Services or the tertiary sector of the economy covers a gamut of activities such as telecom, banking and finance, insurance, media and entertainment, aviation and travel, health care, hospitality, real estate, transportation, security, management and technical consultancy among several others.

As the economy grows, employment and welfare take a paradigm shift towards the service sector. In the initial stages of economic evolution, the economy and the employment depended mainly on the agrarian sector. Consequently, people got engaged in the production and trading of agricultural produce. However, as the economy developed, the agrarian economy metamorphosed into a manufacturing economy. At very advanced stages of the economy, the manufacturing economy transforms into a service economy, and hence, becomes a major employment and revenue generator. Most of you are likely to be employed in service industries such as banking, insurance, aviation, hospitality, health care, logistics, transportation, finance, real estate, power, and public distribution. In this chapter, we will be discussing the applications in some of these sectors.

SERVICE VS PRODUCT

The management of service businesses calls for a distinctive service delivery to gain a competitive advantage. To understand the service delivery concept, it is necessary to understand the differences between a service and a product.

There is a basic difference between a product and a service delivery. A product is manufactured in the factory and then delivered to the customer. Thus, these are two distinct and separate activities. However, in case of services, the creation and delivery of services go hand-in-hand. Hence, MIS, which are normally found in manufacturing and trading organizations, are not suitable for the service sector. Today, enterprise solutions are implemented on the basis of maximum fitment and suitability for a particular industry segment. Though generic applications for accounting and human resources may be common for both the sectors, the mission-critical applications will always differ. According to Jawadekar (2008), most of the service industries have front-end facilities to serve the customer to meet their immediate needs and make them comfortable for their service demands. Any human interaction is knowledge-based and hence, information-dependent. All the systems that make human interactions effective and comfortable are mission-critical applications, and a service industry has to provide these to offer the most satisfying services. Mission-critical applications are built around the business strategy.

A product is tangible, while a service is intangible. A product has a unit of measurement such as per piece, kilogram, metre, or square decimetre; however, the service may be billed as per instance or per hour of service, like a doctor's or lawyer's fee. A product can be stored as an inventory item and sold at a later date. However, the service is rendered on demand and cannot be stored. The quality control of a product is possible on the parameters of predefined standards; however, the service quality is dependent on the quality of the human resource rendering the service. A product can be produced, sold, and consumed in stages, while a service has to be produced, sold, and consumed simultaneously.

Concept of Service

Service is defined by Kotler (1989) as 'an activity or a benefit that one part can offer to another which is essentially intangible and does not result in the ownership of anything. Its production may not be tied to a physical product'. A service has the following characteristics or attributes:

Intangibility   All services are fully intangible, that is, they do not have any physical existence. They can only be seen or observed when they are being performed by a service provider and received by a customer. For example, a body massage by a masseur at a spa can be seen as being delivered and received but cannot be displayed.

Inseparability   In case of a service delivery, both the provider and receiver must be present at the site of service. Zeithaml (2006) argues that the service process cannot be executed unless both are present at the site of a service experience. As the production and consumption of a service are simultaneous processes, the service provider and the receiver become inseparable. For example, when we take a flight service, the service provider's staff—pilot, stewardess, attendants, and the passengers—are present at the time of journey.

Storage   Being intangible, services cannot be stored like goods; the latter can be stored in a warehouse. For example, in a hospital, a doctor offers services on an hourly basis. A day's services cannot be stored and used the next day.

Inconsistency   Service performances are inconsistent. As the service process is intangible, it can vary from one service delivery to another. Thus, it becomes difficult to standardize the service delivery process. Every service experience is different because it is based on individual quality, expectations, and environment of the service delivery. However, this is not true for the services that are automated. These include a bank ATM, web-based rail reservations, and online check-in at airports.

Service Management Systems

All services are defined by a process that has various steps; each step adds value to the service. All the steps can be categorized into various stages, based on the role they play in the process. These stages together build a service process cycle.

The service process has five stages—initiation for service, transition to service, pre-service, service consumption, and post-service feedback. All the steps in a service delivery process are categorized under these five stages. Figure 10.1 displays this cycle and the service management stages.

Initiation of service   The objective of this stage is to convince the customer to avail the services. In this stage, the service provider answers queries, records query details, and lays down conditions to avail the queries. The system captures the data, ascertains the service requirement, creates a quotation for service offer, generates a service ticket, and puts the service in a queue. For example, in health care services, the patient seeks information on doctors, diagnostics, timings, and fees.

Transition to service   The objective is to establish technical and commercial feasibility, and obtain customer acceptance. The service provider system checks for availability of resources and validates the service requirements. The service requirements are matched with commercial and technical viability, and operational feasibility. It also checks for any mandatory documents or goods

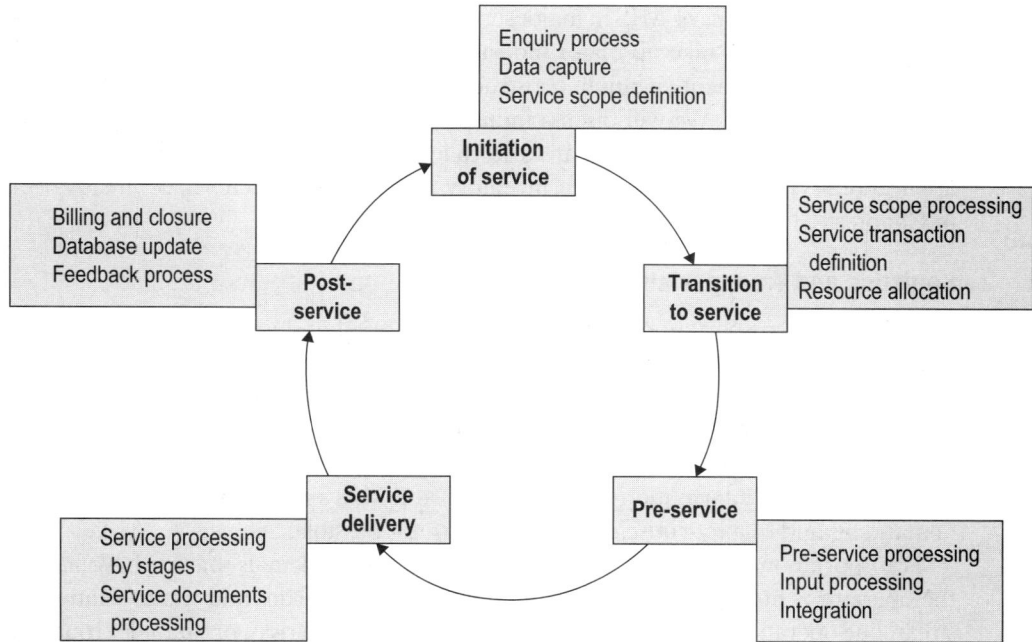

Fig. 10.1   Service process cycle and service management system

required for the service. Once everything is in place, the system obtains a formal acceptance. For example, a patient takes an appointment with a consultant doctor and ensures his/her availability on the desired day and time.

Pre-service   At this stage, the service offer is given an identity with the customer. All previous submissions are inspected and verified. A service or a job identity number is issued for the record. For example, a patient visits the hospital and registers at the outpatient department (or the relevant department) and gets a registration slip/card. In some cases, the patients get themselves admitted in the hospital.

Service delivery   This is the actual stage of delivery of service. The objective is to complete the service in an efficient and satisfying manner to the customer. This involves executing all the necessary transactions, collecting records, and updating the database for future reporting and analysis. For example, the doctor examines the patient and recommends further tests or investigation, or prescribes medicines, thus, fully satisfying the patient.

Post-service feedback   The objective of this stage is to collect data and information about a service for decision-making and improvement. The system collects feedback and suggestions, bills the customer for the services, processes payment, and updates all relevant records. For example, a patient who is discharged from the hospital after getting fully checked for his/her condition, may sometimes have to revisit the doctor for feedback.

MIS FOR SERVICE SECTORS

Having understood the concept of service and service management systems, we can now discuss the various applications of MIS in major service industries. Though there are numerous industries in this sector, we will take up major industries, such as logistics and transportation, hospitality, health care management, aviation, construction and real estate, banking services, and insurance sector, for discussion. We will discuss industry-specific applications that describe the workflow management. These applications are also called 'mission-critical' for the sector. The common applications systems (e.g., accounting, inventory, human resource, etc.) have already been discussed in Chapter 8.

Logistics and Transportation

Logistics and transportation is the service backbone of industries. The Indian transportation and logistics sector evolved from a totally disorganized sector, represented mostly by individual truck owners, to a healthy and organized logistics industry. With the entry of multinational manufacturing corporations and distributing companies, Indian transport and logistics operators are upgrading themselves to keep pace with their new customers' demands. Without the help of state-of-the-art information technology (IT) and MIS applications, providing services to such demanding and quality-conscious companies is not possible.

Transportation is a high-risk business and there are incidentals that are beyond the control of the operator. Thus, the objective of an application for logistics and transportation would be to streamline operations and provide mission-critical reports on risks, profitability, route analysis, cost of movements of goods, vehicle performance, etc. The workflow management of the transport and logistics industry managed by an enterprise system offers the following:

- Transport operations covering transportation workflow processes of consignment booking, dispatch, movement, and delivery
- Marketing and lead management for sales force
- Customer relationship management and post-delivery interaction with the customer
- Fleet management and truck maintenance
- Warehouse management with RFID technology
- Consignment tracking with web-based interfaces
- Vehicle tracking with GPS/GSM technology

Figure 10.2 illustrates the various modules in a logistics and transportation management application.

The IT applications in transportation and logistics can be used to create strategic advantages and help the organization work towards customer satisfaction and profit maximization, which are the perennial objectives of any business organization.

The operation module is used by operation workers who are responsible for basic transaction data creation and generation of documents that travel with the goods. The process flow of a transport business starts with receipt of goods for movement. The goods are booked for dispatch and a goods receipt or consignment note is generated. Goods booked at various places are collected to a central loading point and a manifest (a document that lists the consignments) is created for each destination. The transport company either uses its own fleet of lorries for transportation or hires a vehicle from the lorry owners. In the first instance, a trip sheet is created, while, a lorry-hire document is made for the hired vehicles. On arrival of the lorry at the destination, the system is made to record the same. Later, when goods are unloaded from the truck, an unloading chart is created. On delivery of goods to the consignee, a delivery note is made. All these documents complete the process flow and the transaction data is created. Figure 10.3 illustrates consignment note creation in a logistics application.

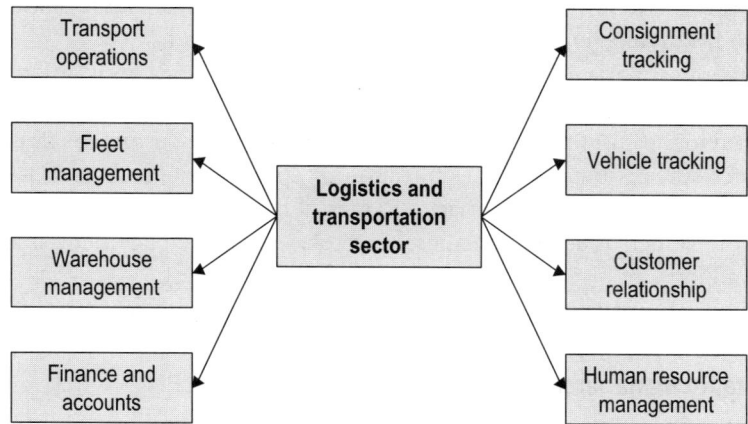

Fig. 10.2   Applications in the logistics and transportation sector

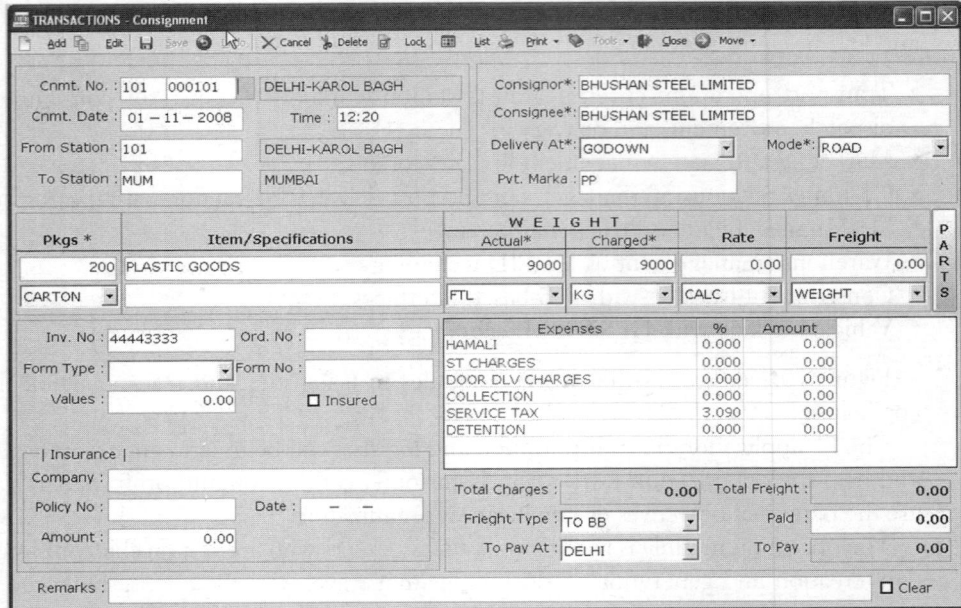

Fig. 10.3   Consignment booking—an applications in transportation business
[BNG Infotech, www.bng.co.in]

The trucks are the most critical assets of a transport company. The fleet management module of the application covers reminders and alerts for renewable documents such as permits, insurance, and road taxes. It takes care of preventive maintenance schedule of vehicles, vehicle purchase and depreciation history, breakdowns and accidents history, etc. The application takes care of vehicle tyres, which incur a major expenditure and are subject to pilferage and theft as well. The vehicles demand frequent servicing and repair. The application comprises a workshop management module, which covers repair, servicing, and maintenance of vehicles. The MIS would provide reports on preventive and periodical service status of each vehicle. Figure 10.4 shows a fleet management application for transport owners.

Warehouse management is an integral part of logistics applications. The logistics service provider renders space (as part of the service) in the warehouse to its customer. The goods are delivered to the customer or any other location as per the customer's directions. The application facilitates systems for optimum utilization of space, periodical stock statements for the client, calculation of rentals, and service charges. These functions are supported by other generic applications such as accounting, customer relationship management, marketing, and sales force applications.

Exhibit 10.2 explains how the problems faced by Okay Logistic Pvt. Ltd were smoothened out.

Hospitality Management

The hospitality industry encompasses hotels, motels, inns, resorts, lodges, hostels, guest houses, ranches, suites, service apartments, etc. A hotel is one place where the customer looks for distinctive services. This sector can create competitive advantages by offering better services at both back office

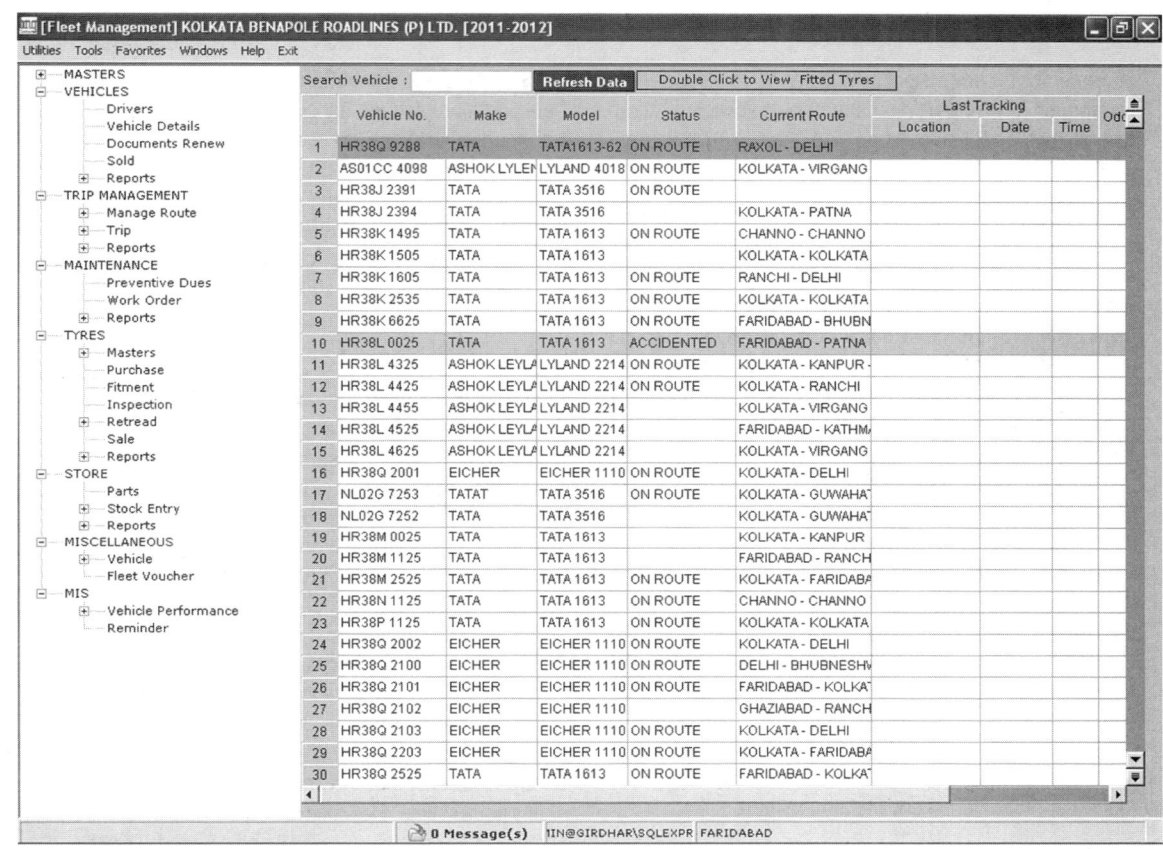

Fig. 10.4   Vehicle tracking module in fleet management application [BNG Infotech, www.bng.co.in]

OKAY Logistics: Okaying Business Process with Logistics Application
Industry: Logistics and Transportation

Organization

Incorporated in 1978 by two young enterprising brothers, (Late) O.K. Subramanian and O.K. Vasudevan, with a solitary office in Kochi, Okay Logistics Pvt. Ltd has grown into a premier transport organization with more than 31 branches located in important cities of India with strategic partners in other parts of the country. While the head office continues to be in Kochi, the regional offices in Chennai, Mumbai, Kolkata, and New Delhi provide the necessary administrative infrastructure for a country-wide efficient organization.

The company has a fleet of around 350 vehicles of different makes, sizes, and types, in addition to a large number of

vehicles hired on a contract basis. The fleet comprises light, medium, and multi-axle vehicles with both open high-sided deck and containerized bodies of sizes ranging 14–30 feet in length and 7–8 feet in width. These vehicles are ideal for shipment of part loads and unpacked or partially packed goods such as machinery and sensitive or valuable items. The company has adequate warehousing facilities at many of their branches and is therefore, in a position to provide storage facility for their customers' goods.

In an effort to move with the times and meet the growing demand of IT-enabled end-to-end solutions, the group has expanded services in the area of supply chain

(Contd)

Exhibit 10.2 (Contd)

management, comprising procurement, transportation, warehousing, inventory management, packaging, scrap and salvage disposal, and handling.

Issues

For several years, Okay Logistics has been maintaining all documents and reports on paper as none of the business processes were computerized. The business operations were controlled and managed from the Mumbai corporate office, although the head office at Kochi required all the financial data. The financial analysis and auditing functions were carried out at the head office. The company used to send financial data in the form of paper reports and documents for auditing. This process took many days and sometimes, weeks. The billing was centralized but the debt recovery was delegated to the concerned branches. At the branch level, however, there was no mechanism to find debt ageing and bills due for submission. In a transport business, the profit comes from and goes into vehicles. Proper maintenance of vehicles is necessary to sustain long-term profitability. Therefore, keeping track of each vehicle was of utmost importance. However, as the company owned a large fleet of trucks, it was difficult to keep track of renewable documents, preventive maintenance, wear and tear of tyres, and profitability of each truck. On any day in a month, more than 95% of the fleet was on the road.

Solution

Vineeth Vasudevan, managing director of the company and a young blood in the company's board, dreamt of a paperless office with seamless flow of information and data across the head office and branches. He looked for some industry-standard applications, which could meet the entire requirements of transport operations, consignment tracking for the customer, vehicle tracking for the fleet, fleet management, and accounting and consolidation of reports for auditing at the head office in Kochi.

Implementation

Okay Logistics evaluated a couple of industry-specific solutions. After a few rounds of presentations and negotiations, the management finally zeroed in on BNG Logics Suite, a standard software suite available for logistics and transportation companies in India. The management felt that the application could meet their complete requirements for transportation freight management, fleet management, and accounting. For vehicle tracking, the company implemented another GPS-based application, which could track the movements of a truck.

BNG Infotech implemented the online solution for transportation management. The modules covered were transport operations covering consignment creation, manifest, lorry hiring, unloading, delivery, and acknowledgement. The fleet management took care of the large fleet of vehicles and covered reminders for renewable documents, alternatives for preventive maintenance, workshop management, spare parts inventory management, tyre accounts, and truck profitability.

Benefits

After implementation of the application, Okay Logistics was able to receive and consolidate the complete data at the corporate office. The same data was replicated at the head office at Kochi for auditing. Bills were raised from Mumbai on behalf of all branches. Now, the branches were able to get the billing data and outstanding reminders on time for follow-up and debt recovery. With the automated system of billing, the company was able to submit bills to customers within a very short period. This process accelerated the debt collection and hence, strengthened cash flow.

Following the implementation, there was hardly any instance when a vehicle's insurance premium was not renewed before it expired. They could see that the trucks were giving better mileage and tyre pilferage had stopped. At any point of time, the traffic manager could enter the tyre number and see the total miles it had covered. They could change the tyre for better performance of the truck. The customers could track their consignment by just logging on to the company's website. All the trucks that were equipped with a GPS tracking system could be tracked along their route. This helped in better planning and management of the freight-loading process.

Discussion Questions

1. Why is transportation called a high-risk business? What IT measures do you suggest to mitigate the risks?
2. What are the various modules of a complete transportation and logistics information management system? Mention the functionalities offered by each of them.
3. What benefits did Okay Logistics get by implementing the application for its business processes?

Sources:

Personal observations of the author during consulting and implementation of solutions, contributions by Vineeth Vasudevan, Director.

www.okaytransport.com, last accessed on 5 November 2011.

and customer touch points by implementing IT tools and applications. There are comprehensive software suites consisting of integrated modules for various aspects of hotel management. The software is sometimes referred to as property management system in the hotel industry.

A hospitality management application covers the following business processes and functions:

- Hotel room reservation software
- Hotel lodging and billing application (front office)
- Call accounting module
- Point-of-sales (POS) for restaurant, bar, room service, housekeeping, etc.
- Other billing services such as conference, banquet, and car rentals
- Inventory management system
- Finance and accounting application
- Human resource management system

Figure 10.5 illustrates the different modules of a hospitality management application.

The room reservation systems are usually web-based, where the customer books the room on a self-service basis. Alternatively, there are desktop applications providing reservation facilities, which are operated by the front desk staff of the hotel. The web reservation system is integrated with the desktop application for reservation and lodging and the billing application. The reservation system provides information such as number of rooms available, expected arrivals, pickup reminder pop-ups, tentative booking, and room blocking system. These features are available in most of the hotel management applications.

The lodging applications cover functionalities such as reservation, check-in, shifting of rooms, check-out, and preparation of extra bills with split or complement options. For better service, the system provides a handy occupancy chart, as shown in Fig. 10.6.

The POS application provides services and billing at a restaurant of the hotel. The functionalities included are direct billing (in which the bills are created in one stroke), running order billing (in which a kitchen order ticket is first created and the bill is printed on finalization), and flexi-rate billing (in which there is no fixed rate for any item). For example, 'package food' billing is flexi billing, where the rates can differ from time to time.

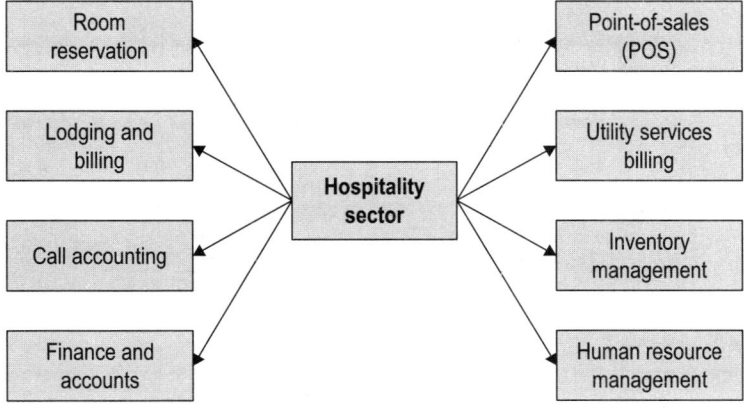

Fig. 10.5 Applications in hospitality sector

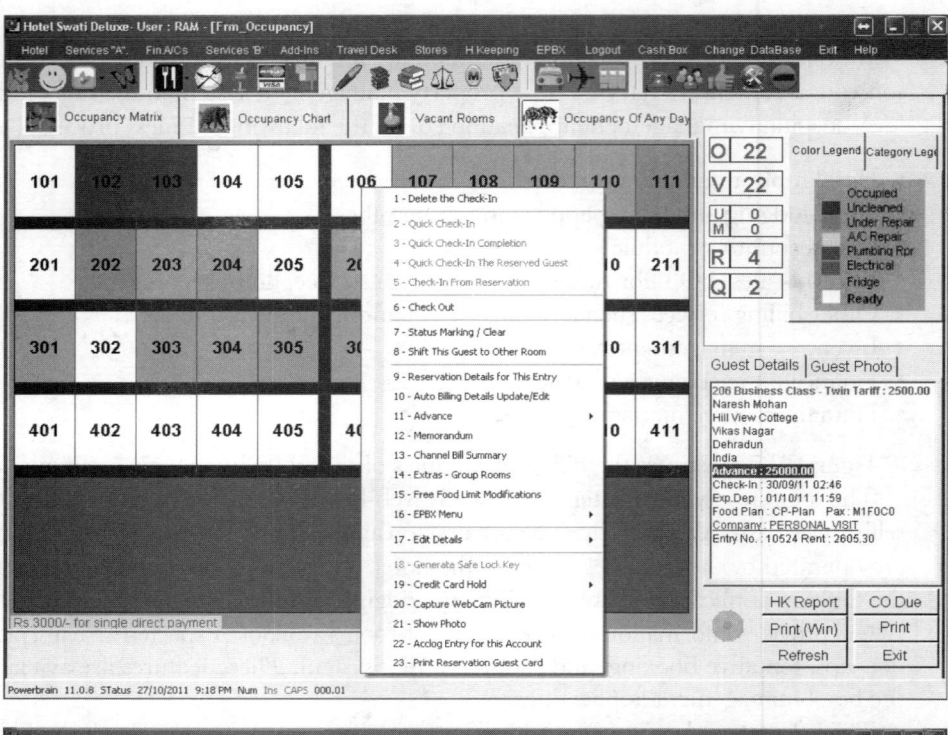

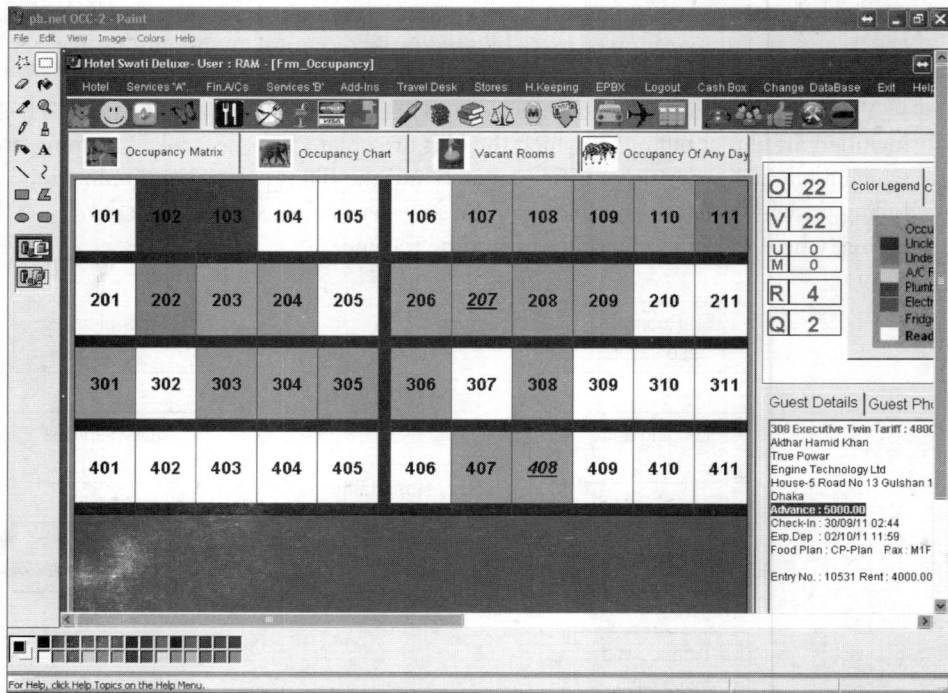

Fig. 10.6　MIS support by hotel management applications [PowerBrain Software,
www.powerbrainsoftware.com]

Hotels provide calling facilities from rooms. Such outstation calls are routed through their EPABX system and billed to the customer at checkout. A good hotel management application is integrated with the EPABX and provides telephone call billing. Similarly, hotels organize and support a lot of other services such as conferences, travels, and also rent out space for parties and banquets. An efficient hospitality application supports tracking of car rentals, ticket purchases, travel agent accounts, booking, and follow-up conferences. Hotel business process-specific applications are supported by generic modules such as purchase, inventory, human resource, and accounting.

Exhibit 10.3 explains how the management processes were streamlined at Swati Garden Hut Hotel.

EXHIBIT 10.3

Swati Garden Hut Hotel: Bringing Customer Satisfaction with IT

Swati Garden Hut Hotel, located in New Delhi, is a 75-room budget hotel in the heart of the city in one of the busiest commercial districts. The hotel used to arrange bookings for their customers manually. Most of the bookings were walk-in or through local agents. The hotel felt the need for proper coordination and management to handle the paper-dependent business processes.

Requirements

The hotel management thought of providing distinctive services for their loyal customers. Providing satisfactory services from reservation to lodging and checkout was thought to be a key task for the continuation of business. The lodging process was a complex job to handle and manage satisfactorily, as it was very difficult to communicate between entities. The hotel required an effective management system for booking and checking the availability of rooms. The management started evaluating hotel management applications that could provide facilities for the following:

- Reservation and cancellation of booking by the hotel staff
- Self-reservation by customers (login system for customers)
- Registration (check-in) for customers
- Searching and checking the availability of rooms for customers
- Generation of bills—manually or automatically
- Service—laundry/restaurant bill generation

Solution

The hotel management decided to implement a hotel application from PowerBrain Software to meet their requirements. The application was used to manage the daily transactions of a hotel, which included room billing, restaurant billing, reservations, enquiry, and a complete accounting module. The application also featured restaurant and room maintenance modules.

Benefits

With the web-based reservation system, Swati Garden Hotel became more transparent in its offerings. The hotel saw a sudden spurt in bookings and hence, a steep upward growth path in sales. The occupancy level of their hotel rose up to 90%. They could analyse from the new application that they got repeat business from the customers. As the POS activities at the annexed resto-bar were integrated with the application, the management could see consolidated cash flow into the business. The prudent hotel management saw increase in the number of customers and concentrated more on matching customer perception with expectations.

Discussion Questions

1. What makes you think that by implementing a hotel application, Swati Garden Hut's operations became transparent?
2. What are the various modules of a hospitality information management system? Mention the functionalities offered by each of them.
3. What benefits did Swati Garden Hut get by implementing the application for its business processes?

Source:
www.powerbrainsoftware.com, last accessed on 31 December 2012 (Contribution of Ramanathan is acknowledged).

Health Care Management

Hospitals are service organizations where the customer perceptions and expectations of service is of the highest degree. Hospitals are required to run as business institutions by following the mission of providing the best health care for people. The scope of services now includes consulting, health care guidance, preventive care, post clinical attention, and advice. The management of the hospitals strive to provide distinctive services to a wide range of customers whose service expectations and perceptions are varied. The customer can easily discriminate between the quality of care and quality of caring, being treated medically and being treated personally, and being served at the least cost and being served with efficiency and effectiveness.

Health care organizations own critical resources that include operation theatres, radiology laboratories, X-ray machines, sonography equipment, CT scan machines, hospital beds, etc. These resources have to be managed through meticulous planning and control by the management. There are critical manpower resources such as surgeons, physicians, anaesthetists, radiologists, and nursing staff. Hospitals strive to provide the highest degree of emergency services, which have an impact on the perception and expectation of the customer. Therefore, an effective resource planning is a must with highly advanced IT applications that are available for the health care sector.

A health care management application covers the following business processes and functions:

Front desk operations   Patients' primary record, out-patient department (OPD) appointments, in-patient department (IPD) admissions, ward allotments, resource availability views, doctor visit charges, IPD/OPD billing estimates, and medical claims

Hospital administration   Resources scheduling, security levels, and duty roster

Electronic medical record (EMR)   Patient history, online drug prescriptions, and patient education through images

Laboratory management   Sample collection, test, test–cost analysis, and radiology

Billing   Automated billing system, insurance claim settlements, and settlement of bills

Nursing and ward management   Nursing staff scheduling, ward/room/bed maintenance plan, patient movement, occupancy status, visitor details, ward management, discharge summary, and birth and death registration

Blood bank management   Donor registration, donors database, blood samples, blood inventory management, procedure, and transfer

Housekeeping module   Kitchen management, food distribution, commodity requirement, stock maintenance, and linen maintenance

Operation theatre   Operation gradation and scheduling, anaesthetist report, endoscopies, and OT material requirement

Psychiatry   Diagnosis, family history, patient follow-up, rating scale, subjective analysis, and treatment history

Pharmacy   Medicine database, purchase, sales, and inventory management

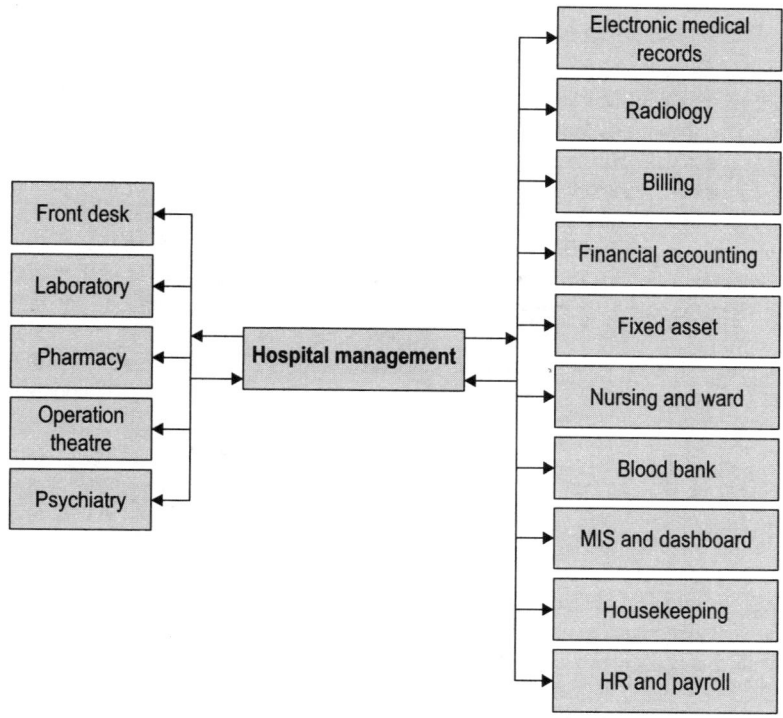

Fig. 10.7   Hospital management applications and their modules
[Axis Softech, www.axissoftech.com]

Figure 10.7 displays the various modules of a health care management application. Exhibit 10.4 describes how a web-based hospital information system was able to cater to the requirements at the Sikkim Manipal Hospital.

EXHIBIT 10.4

Sikkim Manipal Hospital: Curing with IT Application
Industry: Health Care Management

Central Referral Hospital

Sikkim Manipal Institute of Medical Sciences (SMIMS), located at Tadong, is a constituent college of the Sikkim Manipal University (SMU). SMIMS offers MBBS, undergraduate courses in nursing and physiotherapy, and postgraduate programmes in microbiology, biochemistry, physiology, and anatomy. The Central Referral Hospital (CRH) and Sir Tashi Namgyal Memorial (STNM) hospital, Gangtok offer clinical training opportunities to students. The Sikkim Manipal University of Health, Medical, and Technological Sciences was established in 1995. It is the

first government–private initiative in the region. SMU is recognized by the University Grants Commission and approved by the government of India. SMU offers quality education to students from north and north-eastern parts of India. Established with the aim of imparting exemplary educational opportunities and health care services in Sikkim, it is a first of its kind in the country with collaboration between the private and public sectors.

In 2005, the vice chancellor of SMU decided to automate the 500-plus bed CRH. The challenge was to adopt a package that was completely web-based with a centralized

(Contd)

Exhibit 10.4 (Contd)

database so that multiple locations could be managed with the same package. Another challenge was to make the project completely system-independent and location-free. The vice chancellor, being a technical czar, wanted the system to be robust and comprehensive enough to bring in efficiency in the processes and build a database for decision support. User management was given extra thrust for security and user log maintenance. After closely looking at the portfolios of various vendors, the hospital management zeroed in on Axis Softech, a New Delhi-based firm providing hospitality solutions. The firm was chosen for their expertise in the development of web-based applications.

Solution

Based on the hospital's business process flow and user requirements, Axis developed a web-based hospital information system to cater to the complete requirements of the organization. The hospital implemented modules such as front desk (OPD), EMR, laboratory, radiology, billing, nursing and ward management, operation theatre, housekeeping, blood bank, payroll, and accounting.

Automation of the help desk or OPD helped the front office in executing the hospital's functions and helped create a patient database. Computerization of EMRs helped in easy storage, retrieval, and printing of the records. The lab machines were directly integrated with the software to transfer the details and records to build the hospital MIS. Laboratory automation addressed the issue of transfer of test results to the doctors and the billing department. In the same way, radiology was integrated with the customers' database.

Billing is one of the most important modules of the entire HMS, which internally interacts with most of the cross-functional modules and fetches data to generate reports. The data related to any other services availed by the customer at different departments is automatically passed on to the billing department. This enhanced the efficiency and reduced the possibilities of errors in billing.

Once the patient is admitted for in-house treatment, the nursing and ward management has the most important role to play. SMIMS implemented this module,

which takes care of the entire in-house operations and database management. Information about availability of beds and stock of required blood groups are critical issues. After connecting the blood bank with the rest of the departments, the hospital was able to get timely information on blood requirements, donations, stock, etc. The housekeeping module controlled the entire gamut of housekeeping, which includes kitchen and other consumables. Scheduling of operations and requirement of equipment is another critical area for a hospital system. SMIMS linked its operation theatre with the rest of the enterprise resource planning (ERP) modules. This facilitated the planning and scheduling of patients' operations and resulted in reduced waiting time.

Besides the business process modules in SMIMS, the company implemented other supporting modules (e.g., accounts and finance, human resource, stores, etc.). In hospitals, human resources such as specialists, surgeons, and consultants are of critical nature, and need to be managed in a planned way.

The hospital developed an MIS dashboard to prepare graphical and summary reports for the senior management. This module facilitated a 360-degree view of all the activities of the hospital while providing graphical reports for the most critical operations. The module generates reports that are helpful in providing distinctive and responsive services to the customer.

Discussion Questions

1. Why are hospital information systems so critical as compared to other service industries?
2. What are the various modules of a complete hospital information management system? Mention the functionalities offered by each of them.
3. What are the benefits derived by the SMIMS management by implementing the application at the CRH?

Sources:
Contribution of Gyanesh Kumar, Axis Softech, acknowledged.
www.axissoftech.com, last accessed on 5 November 2011.
www.smims.smu.edu.in, last accessed on 5 November 2011.

Aviation Sector

The aviation sector consists of airline companies that are directed towards the movement of passengers and goods. The expectations and perceptions about the service of an airline are always high. A customer expects punctuality, on-schedule arrivals and departures, convenience, better and competitive prices, comfort, on-board food quality, amiable treatment by ground staff and crew members, etc. The service perception may also include assistance in travel planning, drop and pickup facility to the airport, etc.

In times of changing and competitive business conditions, 'fly profitably' is the motto for every airline. Profitability can be achieved by implementing information systems that provide robust financial tools that conform to the best practices of the industry and which have the ability to provide the right data output for decision-making.

The information system application for aviation sector would cover the following major modules:

- Passenger ticketing and reservation systems
- Passenger revenue accounting
- Aircraft maintenance
- Financial management
- Cargo solutions
- Miscellaneous billing solutions
- Human resource management

Figure 10.8 illustrates the various modules in an aviation management application.

Today, every airline offers online ticketing and reservation systems as a strategy to woo more customers. The web-based reservation systems offer flexible and intelligent fare options.

Passenger revenue accounting is an area that requires applications with rich functions that deliver real business values. The solutions address the business pains of stakeholders in finance through revenue accounting. A good application in airlines management offers a module-based and highly scalable system that leverages the best practices in the industry. They come up with powerful business intelligence capabilities and end-to-end functionalities to deliver real business value to the airline. They empower the airlines to transform the revenue accounting function from a transaction processing environment to a strategic tool, thus enabling them to devise competitive strategies to succeed in the marketplace.

The cargo solution suite covers the complete needs of the airline cargo business, right from allotment management, reservations, space control, operations, and tracking to revenue accounting, ground handling, and electronic data interchange (EDI) communications.

Besides customer ticketing and revenue collection, there are hundreds of other contractual obligations—agents' accounts, ground handling, engineering services, on-board food—that an airline has to manage. The miscellaneous billing solution module of an airline application provides

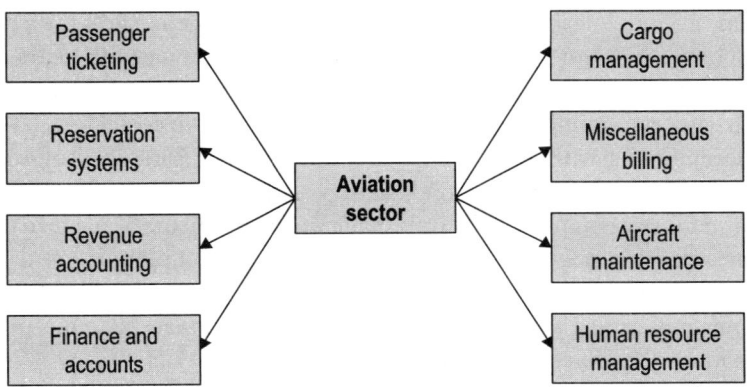

Fig. 10.8   Applications in aviation sector

settlement processes as per the International Air Transport Association's (IATA) guidelines. Simplified interline settlement (SIS) is a new guideline for miscellaneous billing settlements. As miscellaneous billing is one of the least automated areas for process optimizations, compliance for these standards is posing significant challenges for many airlines. While compliance needs to be addressed, standardization and centralization through SIS provides a unique opportunity to airlines and other service providers to reengineer their current billing processes, thereby, reducing billing costs and improving cash flows.

The miscellaneous billing solution module provides an opportunity to not only achieve SIS compliance without significantly changing internal IT systems, but also enables appropriate financial controls to restrict revenue and cost leakages. It ensures that miscellaneous revenues from contractual as well as ad hoc services (ground handling, engineering) can be defined and managed.

Passenger safety is associated with aircraft maintenance and upkeep. Any airlines information system would provide modules for aircraft maintenance. The safety aspect of the business calls for a dedicated MIS to provide decision support system for purchases, planned replacement, investment on maintenance, and management of critical spare parts for the planes. The module would provide periodical reports on preventive maintenance, maintenance schedule, etc.

Construction and Real Estate

Construction and real estate services are one of the largest and highly developing sectors in India. Real estate encompasses land and building, such as commercial and residential structures, roadways, and ports. Construction is the process of building new infrastructure on real estate. Given their close interlinks, these sectors are often treated as one. Far from being a single activity, large-scale real estate development is a feat of multitasking by a wide host of professionals, including financial analysts, legal experts, project managers, construction managers, design engineers, and project architects, amongst others.

The sector, as a whole, has been performing very well over the past decade, especially given the property prices rally experienced in most developed economies. India is currently the second fastest-growing economy in the world. The Indian construction industry has been playing a vital role in the overall economic development of the country, growing at over 20% compound annual growth rate (CAGR) over the past five years and contributing 8% to the gross domestic product (GDP). In 2005, the sector generated around 31 million jobs, of which only one million were generated by the organized sector. The industry has matured to a large sector, with great complexity and an increasing institutional ownership structure. The increased complexity of the industry and real estate principles and processes created a demand for systems to effectively manage the components of a construction project, including business development, estimation, cost control, project planning and scheduling, negotiation, and labour relations.

A mission-critical application for construction and real estate business processes would offer the following modules and features:

Land development   Covers land acquisition, development details, appointing agents, sanctions, etc.

Project management   Creation of project identity and configuring all the details with regards to the budget, payment schedules, accessories, etc., for the project

Project engineering   Central module that takes care of projects, sub-projects, contracts, and work orders

Documents management   Knowledge management module for an organization that stores, indexes, and retrieves documents

Finance   Covers the complete financial transactions and statutory reports, analysis on financial health of the organization

Purchase   Covers the purchase of construction material

Legal   Capture legal details related to the land bank created by the land development group as well as legal documentation for a project

Liaison   Updates details regarding clearance and sanction for properties, sub-properties, projects, and sub-projects

Human resource   Covers the human aspect of the organization

Call centre   Used by front desk/help desk for calls related to business leads and complaints regarding property and projects

Sales   Module for sales of land, building, projects, and units

Rentals   Covers all rental and leasing activities of the company including tenant database, renewals, etc.

Property management   Covers the post-construction activities and functionalities to raise payment requisitions, raise the billing to the end customer, and issue receipts for money collected for maintenance, etc.

Dashboards   MIS reports covering all aspects of construction and real estate, presenting 360-degree view of customers, projects, and property

Figure 10.9 illustrates the various modules in a construction and real estate management application.

The *property development module* is used by a select group of users who are responsible for the identification of land databases. The functionality in this module allows users to capture details of the land bank, log information regarding the various details of the land, (e.g., pricing negotiation details), analyse payments that have been made to parties for the land, etc. It maintains the land bank (the listing and status of land acquired, acquirable by the company) from which a property is developed into a project. It manages information on properties for acquisition, creates agents and manages the details of the agent profile, monitors business development payment approvals, searches for property details, status of various land sanctions, etc.

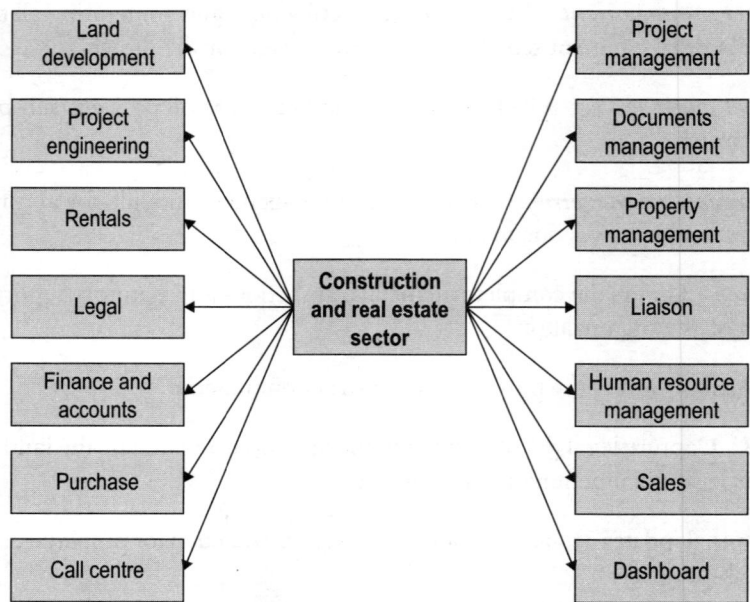

Fig. 10.9   Applications in construction and real estate sector

The *project management module* creates identities of all projects and subprojects. Once business development is initiated on a property and the legal or liaisoning department gives the clearance to start the project, the project module will configure all the necessary details with regard to the budget, payment schedules, accessories, etc., for the project. All the units that fall under this project/sub-project would inherit all these details.

The *project engineering module* is the core of the application. This module contains various sub-modules, which are used by project engineers, site engineers, and various other members of the project engineering group to update real-time and accurate information of ongoing projects, initiation of payments, etc. The module allows storing of details about projects and sub-projects, issue of work orders, creation of material demand note, receipt of material, and updating of inventory. This module facilitates payment requisitions to contractors, consultants, suppliers, miscellaneous expenses, and transporters.

The *documents management module* enables capture of enhanced knowledge and dissemination across the enterprise with advanced knowledge structuring, querying, and document management services. In this module, the complete information is maintained in a repository, which is indexed and can be searched. Information storage follows a workflow that allows a document to be reviewed and authorized before being published. The *legal module* is used by the legal department to capture the legal details related to the land bank created by the business development group as well as legal documentation for a project or sub-project that is to be initiated. Payment requisitions related to the legal expenses of the company with respect to property or a project are also initiated from this module. It permits complete property documentation and authorizes the payments to be made. It manages all legal documents relating to properties, projects, and sub-projects. The module provides functionality to approve payment requisitions raised by legal users.

The real estate business involves a lot of liaison work with government agencies. The liaison group will work on the sanction details with reference to a property, as created by the legal department. They will update the status of each sanction so that the management and legal departments are informed about where the approvals are updated in the process. It also updates the details of clearance and sanction for properties, sub-properties, projects, and sub-projects, raises payment requisitions with reference to the government NOCs, etc. The *call centre module* is typically used by the front desk/call centre. This module keeps a record of all lead-related or other calls received.

The *rental module* is used to manage all rental/leasing activity of the company. Term sheets, tenant data, rental agreements, stock of available units, etc., are all managed from this module. Receipts and payments related to leasing activities can be managed using this module. Various reports and search criteria enable the user to handle the day-to-day activities. It maintains rental stock details such as project, sub-project, unit, owner details, and accessories details. It generates rental bills based on selected conditions and issues receipts for deposit, rental, and lease. The application would be able to create rental statuses, rental arrears, renewal dues, enhancements dues, etc.

The *property management module* is used by the group that would be maintaining and managing the properties after the construction phase is over and all the units are handed over to the customers. This module contains all the necessary functionalities to raise payment requisitions, raise the billing to the end customer, and issue receipts for money collected for maintenance of the property. It manages contracts related to the property being managed.

The *dashboard module* provides a complete view of the business in just one click. The summarized and quick reports provide the basis for decision support.

Banking Services

Banking is a complete customer-oriented business that thrives on customer acquisition and retention. As such, banking solutions must satisfy the needs of multiple customer segments, geographies, and service levels, efficiently and effectively.

Banking services encompass a wide range of financial products based on the types of customers such as individuals, institutions, corporates, and investors. Based on the services and financial products offered by banks, their business activities are grouped as follows:

- Retail banking
- Consumer banking
- Wealth management
- Corporate banking
- Investment banking
- Trade finance
- Islamic banking
- Functional services
- Accounting backbone
- Infrastructure management

Globally, banks rely on technology to help them streamline business processes, meet increasing regulatory compliance demands, and improve cost efficiency, while providing greater value to customers. The core banking solutions offered by various vendors across the globe are sets of integrated solutions that automate all aspects of core banking operations across entities, languages, and currencies. The solution helps financial institutions quickly introduce new products and efficiently manage changes in existing products. The solutions support a variety of products, including savings accounts, checking accounts, overdraft accounts, term deposit accounts, and a variety of lending products, including personal loans, corporate loans, and mortgages, along with a full complement of transactional services incorporating remittances, foreign exchange, drafts, banker's cheques, cards, and trade finances. These capabilities are accessible through multiple channels, from branches to call centres to mobile banking and the web. The solution integrates front, middle, and back-office processes in real time, providing bankers throughout the organization with complete, timely, and actionable information about customer relationships and providing a single view of the bank to the customer.

The banking applications are offered in a variety of ways. Today, banking solutions encompass enterprise banking solutions, web-based online banking solutions, ATM services, credit cards services, and mobile banking solutions. These solutions are totally customer-centric. The customer expects the service to be delivered in a smooth, problem-free, efficient, and timely manner. The manager of the bank aims to fulfil the bank's business goals; therefore, the MIS designed would be expected to fulfil all these requirements.

Most of the core banking solutions from vendors are easy to integrate, scalable, enterprise-wide solutions that handle large transaction volumes on a round-the-clock basis. These solutions automate banking processes and provide customer service, thereby, maximizing operational efficiency and minimizing risks. Figure 10.10 illustrates the various modules offered by a core banking application. Exhibit 10.5 discusses the core banking solution used by **IDBI Bank**.

Insurance Sector

The insurance sector in India has gone through a sea change due to deregulation and liberalization of the financial market, providing business opportunities for multinational players. Apart from the challenges of deregulation, consolidation, and convergence of financial services worldwide, insurance of all kinds such as life, health, and property has established

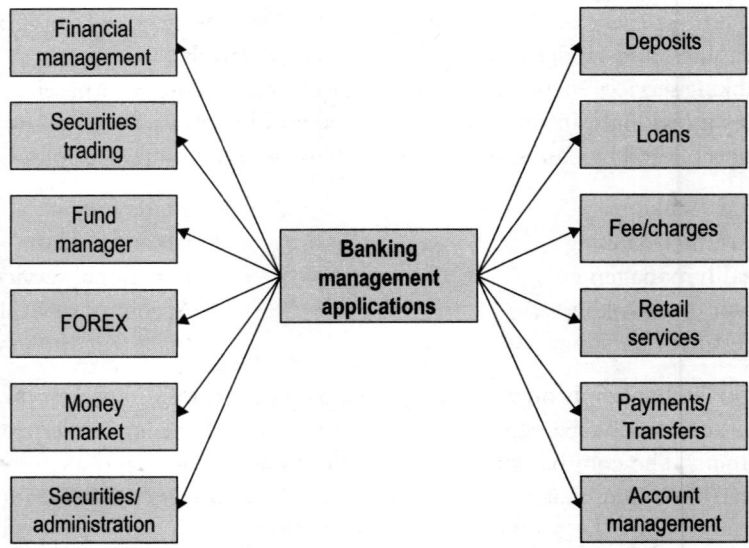

Fig. 10.10   Applications in core banking operations

EXHIBIT 10.5

IDBI Bank: Technology-enabled Agile Banking

Headquartered in Mumbai, IDBI Bank today rides on a robust business strategy, a highly competent and dedicated workforce, and a state-of-the-art IT platform to structure and deliver personalized and innovative banking services and customized financial solutions to its clients across various delivery channels. The bank promoted by industrial development bank of India began with an equity capital base of ₹1000 million in November 1995. Today, IDBI Bank Ltd is a universal bank with its operations driven by a cutting edge core banking IT platform. The bank offers personalized banking and financial solutions to its clients in the retail and corporate banking arena through its large network of branches and ATMs, spread across the length and breadth of India. The bank has also set up an overseas branch at Dubai and has plans to open representative offices in various other parts of the globe for cashing in on emerging global opportunities.

As on 31 March 2011, the bank had a network of 816 branches and 1372 ATMs. The bank's total business, during FY 2010–11, reached ₹3,37,584 crore, the balance sheet reached ₹2,53,377 crore, while it earned a net profit of ₹1650 crore.

Key Business Drivers

The vision of IDBI Bank is to set global standards of excellence and to build the most valued financial conglomerate. In January 2001, following a change in the top management of the bank, the bank redrew its strategy as it felt a strong need to upgrade the technology platform, which would enable it to transform itself to meet the challenges of the future.

Retail Banking Initiatives

IDBI Bank had started operations as a bank catering primarily to the corporate clientele. This strategy was redrawn in early 2001 to focus on the exciting arena of retail banking. At that time, the bank had only 53 branches and 79 ATMs nationwide. The need of the hour was to have a technology platform that would seamlessly scale up and at the same time enable the bank to reach out to its customers through multiple delivery channels. Scalability was important because of the expected explosion in transaction volumes, customer accounts, etc., that accompany consumer banking business. The seamless offering of delivery channels was important because customers need and demand not just access, but also a unified view of their interactions with the bank through multiple delivery channels. In short, the need was to have a completely integrated solution, which would cater to consumer banking requirements while providing comprehensive business banking functionalities to cater to the bank's corporate customers.

IDBI Bank was earlier using a centralized system from Kindle. However, to meet its new strategic initiatives and specific thrust on retail banking, this core banking system needed to be replaced.

Business Agility and Time-to-market

IDBI Bank wanted to have a solution that would not only be quick and easy to deploy but also provide the bank the flexibility to launch new products and services easily. Being fully aware that typical core banking implementations lasted 12–18 months, the bank was keen to choose a solution that gave it a time-to-market advantage. They needed to choose a technology partner who had a track record of deploying core banking solutions significantly faster. Furthermore, along with the speed of implementation, an extremely robust solution was required. Achieving technology-driven business agility was one of the key drivers for the bank.

Solution Overview

After a detailed and rigorous evaluation, Finacle from Infosys was deployed at IDBI Bank to power its retail and corporate banking, trade finance, as well as consumer and business e-banking operations. The core banking solution runs on high availability Unix-based servers from Sun Microsystems and interfaces seamlessly with the bank's other applications such as ATMs, telebanking solution, and Internet banking.

Infosys deployed Finacle core banking solution in a record time frame of five and half months across the entire bank. Going live with Finacle in record time has gained IDBI Bank critical time-to market advantage and the ability to roll out products much faster than ever before. For example, IDBI Bank introduced the concept of 'welcome kit' in the Indian banking industry, consisting of all the deliverables a customer expects on day one such as cheque book, Internet, and phone banking access details. This has

(Contd)

Exhibit 10.5 (Contd)

enabled IDBI Bank to open accounts on the fly unlike other banks where the customer needs to wait for a week or more to get these.

Discussion Questions
1. With features like net banking, the entire banking applications have become customer-centric. Critically examine this statement.
2. How do you think that IDBI became innovative in its approach after implementing the online IT application?

3. What are the benefits derived by the IDBI management by implementing the core banking application?

Sources:
'IDBI Bank reinvents itself', 11 October 2004, http://www.idbibank.com/aboutus.asp, last accessed on 5 November 2011.
http://www.infosys.com/finacle/solutions/Pages/corebanking.aspx, last accessed on 5 November 2011.
http://www.accessmylibrary.com/coms2/summary_0286-14546008_ITM, last accessed on 5 November 2011.

itself. The Indian insurance sector has witnessed significant growth; the number of life policies in force has increased nearly twelve-fold during the period 2000–2010, and health insurance policies nearly twenty five-fold. Factors such as better terms, availability of a wide variety of products, and government incentives have boosted the growth of the industry.

Data released by the Insurance Regulatory and Development Authority (IRDA) indicates that 23 life insurers registered ₹18,282.86 crore (US $4.1 billion) by writing new policies from April–June 2011. The state-owned Life Insurance Corporation (LIC) of India collected premiums worth about ₹13,341.97 crore (US $3 billion), while its private peers collected ₹4940.89 crore (US $1.1 billion) as new first-year premium during the period. Currently, in India, only two million people (0.2% of the total population of more than 1 billion) are covered under mediclaim; on the other hand, in developed nations like USA, about 75% of the total population is covered under an insurance scheme. This reflects that there is enormous scope for growth of the insurance sector in India. With the arrival of more and more private companies in the sector, the situation may change soon.

In the insurance sector, customer expectations revolve around the quality of the risk coverage and the process of claim settlement. The service perceptions differ and are based on the types of insurance cover the customer has opted for. The use of IT applications may help in expediting policy processing and claim settlements, thus enhancing customer satisfaction. Hence, the MIS in the insurance business revolves around the information needs during the launch of a new product, policy processing, risk coverage, and risk settlement.

A robust and comprehensive enterprise application for insurance management covers the following modules and business processes. Figure 10.11 illustrates the various modules in an insurance management application:

- Insurance policy management system
- Insurance agency management system
- Claims management system
- Content management system module
- Endorsements management system
- Insurance document management system
- Insurance accounting and auditing
- Business intelligence
- Policy registration and quotations engine
- Workflow solutions

Insurance policy management system   This module ensures policy registration and communication between the insurer and the insured. It is intended to be a vehicle for exploration

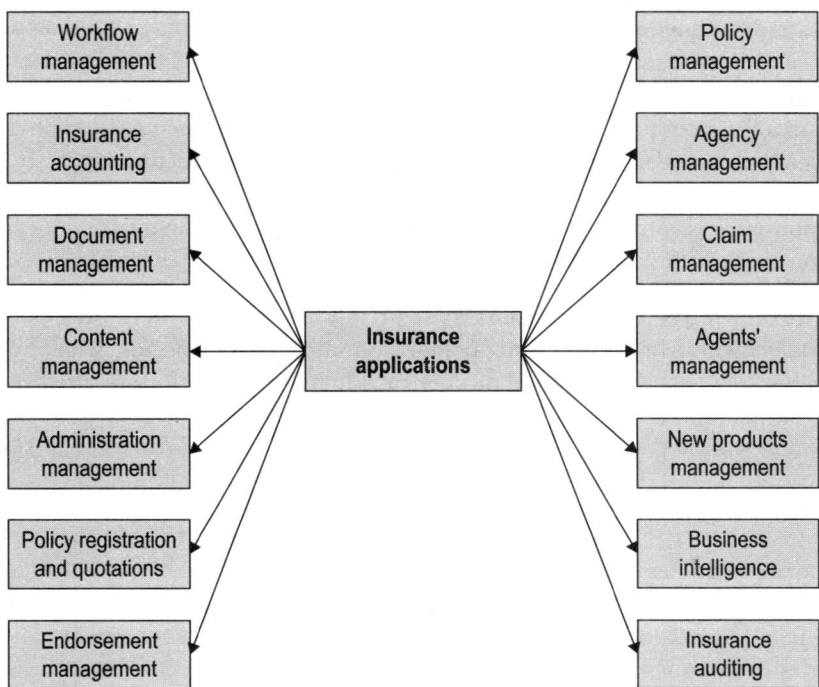

Fig. 10.11   Applications in insurance sector

and discussion of policy issues and is aimed, in particular, at enhancing communication among health policy researchers, legislators, decision-makers, and professionals concerned with developing, implementing, and analysing health policies. Policy quotations engine is an on-demand quotation management feature coupled with detailed profit optimization and approval management system. With the quotation engine, you can automate the sales and service processes that are currently being performed using a hybrid of spreadsheets, documents, and e-mails with little or no process control. Policy renewals and policy cancellation can be managed through the insurance policy management system.

Insurance agency management system   This module facilitates an insurance company to address relationships with its product distribution channels. Insurance businesses heavily depend on the agencies and agent system. The agency management system provides a solution to manage and help in the growth of an insurance agency, and to assist in the day-to-day management. The system keeps track of activities from policy registration to claim processing. The data of all the agents, their commissions, their policies status updates, etc., are taken care of by this module. The insurance agency system facilitates smooth workflow and makes the processes faster and efficient. The web-based interface provides an online working environment for agents.

Claims management system   This module ensures that claims are processed quickly and efficiently. It improves operator productivity by providing user flexibility while processing claims. The claim ageing tool shows the status of thousands of claims. The claims system uses an electronic filing system for primary and secondary payers and helps in quick resubmission for claim rejections.

Content management system   This module is used for managing the capture, storage, security, revision control, retrieval, distribution, preservation, and destruction of documents and content. It especially manages the content imported into or generated from within an organization in the course of its operation, and controls access to this content from outside. The content management system is designed to manage unstructured content or semi-structured data, so that the organization can more effectively meet business goals, serve its customers a competitive advantage, improve responsiveness, and protect itself against non-compliance, lawsuits, uncoordinated departments, or turnover within the organization.

Endorsements management system   This module facilitates policy endorsements. Endorsements to a title insurance policy are attachments to the policy that may correct or modify a previously issued title policy, or alter or modify the provisions of the exceptions, conditions, and stipulations so that the insured party receives greater coverage than would exist under the terms of the unendorsed title policy. Endorsements create a greater liability for the title insurance underwriter, and therefore, most endorsements require an additional charge to be collected in excess of the usual title insurance premium.

Insurance document management system   This is a secure file upload management system with an inbuilt audit tracking. The system has the capability for surveyors or hospital administration to upload mandatory, mission-critical documents. It is important to maintain documents so as to retrieve them quickly. The documents can be retrieved at any time and are indexed in a database for quick searches. This system is designed to create an audit trail of all document uploads, manage the process of document approval, and track viewer profile attributes.

Insurance accounting and auditing   This is quite a complicated task, given the fact that there are many issues with regulation, taxes, filing, commissions, brokers, underwriters, endorsements, etc. The applications are intended for insurance accounting systems and insurance billing systems that automate a part of this task and help build better and more flexible solutions. As insurance is a highly regulated industry, audit controls are very important. Thus, the application provides audit control solutions that will help track and control business issues within the organization.

Business intelligence   This module provides reporting and charting solutions to analyse and interpret complex insurance data. Individual customers' demographic details are very important for the insurer. Hence, this module analyses past data for better decision-making and helps make more informed decisions.

SUMMARY

Services or the tertiary sector of the economy covers a wide range of activities such as telecom, banking and finance, insurance, media and entertainment, aviation and travel, health care, hospitality, real estate, transportation, security, management and technical consultancy among several others. There is a basic difference between product and service delivery. A product is manufactured in the factory and then delivered to the customer. Thus, these are two distinct activities. However, in case of services, the creation and delivery of service go hand-in-hand. Hence, MIS normally used in manufacturing and trading organizations may not be suitable for the service sector.

The service process has five stages—initiation for service, transition to service, pre-service, service consumption, and post-service feedback. All the steps in a service delivery process are grouped into these five stages.

The objective of an application for logistics and transportation would be to streamline operations and provide mission-critical reports on risks, profitability, route analysis, cost of movements of goods, vehicle performance, etc. The workflow management of the transport and logistics industry managed by an enterprise system offers the following features: transport operations, marketing and lead generation, fleet management, customer care, warehouse management, consignment tracking, and vehicle tracking.

A hospitality management application covers the following business processes and functions—hotel room reservation software, hotel lodging and billing application (front office), call accounting module, point-of-sales (POS) for restaurant, bar, room service, house-keeping, etc., and other billing services such as conference, banquet, car rentals, inventory management system, finance and accounting application, and human resource management system.

Hospitals provide the highest degree of emergency services, which in turn have an impact on the perception and expectation of a customer. Therefore, an effective resource planning is a must with highly advanced IT applications available for the health care sector. The modules covered are front desk operations—patients' primary record, OPD/IPD appointments, laboratory management, billing, nursing and ward management, blood bank management, housekeeping module, operation theatre, psychiatry, pharmacy, etc.

The applications of the aviation sector information system cover major modules such as passenger ticketing and reservation systems, passenger revenue accounting, cargo solutions, miscellaneous billing solutions, aircraft maintenance,

financial management, and human resource management.

Construction and real estate services are one of the largest and highly developing sectors. A mission-critical application for construction and real estate business processes would offer modules and features such as land development, project management, project engineering, documents management, finance, purchase, sales, legal, liaison, human resource, call centre, rentals, and property management.

Banking is a complete customer-oriented business that thrives on customer acquisition and retention. As such, banking solutions must satisfy the needs of multiple customer segments, geographies, and service levels, efficiently and effectively. The solutions support a variety of products including savings accounts, checking accounts, overdraft accounts, term deposit accounts, and a variety of lending products including personal loans, corporate loans, and mortgages, along with a full complement of transactional services incorporating remittances, foreign exchange, drafts, banker's cheques, cards, and trade finances.

In the insurance sector, customer expectations revolve around the quality of risk coverage and the process of claim settlement. A robust and comprehensive enterprise application for insurance management covers these modules and business processes such as insurance policy management system, claims management systems, insurance agency management system, endorsements management system, policy registration and quotations engine, content management system module, insurance document management system, insurance accounting and auditing, workflow solutions, and business intelligence.

KEY TERMS

Customer touch points Instances in a service delivery where the customer comes in contact with the organization.

Distinctive service Making service better than the competitors, thus gaining a competitive advantage.

Mission-critical applications Applications that are designed

to perform a specific task and workflow in an industry.

Responsive service A service process that fulfils the customer's expectations and resolves queries.

Workflow management The sequential nature of processes in a business, usually supported by business applications.

CONCEPT REVIEW QUESTIONS

1. What makes the service sector different from the manufacturing sector?
2. What are the various service attributes that distinguish a service from a product?
3. Explain the various steps in a service management system.
4. Explain the various modules and features of IT applications in the logistics and transportation sector.
5. What are the modules and features of IT applications in the hospitality sector?
6. Explain how IS applications help in the workflow management of the health care sector.

7. What are the critical modules and functionalities provided by applications in the aviation sector?
8. Explain how IS applications help workflow management in the construction and real estate sector.

9. What are the mission-critical applications of information systems in the banking and finance sector?
10. Explain the various modules and features of IT applications in the insurance sector.

CRITICAL THINKING QUESTIONS

1. Identify the features that distinguish an application for the service industry from the manufacturing industry.
2. How would you control the quality of service through MIS support? Explain with examples any one service industry.

3. 'Most of the applications for the service industry come up with a built-in workflow engine that provides flexibility for the system to address process improvements.' Substantiate this statement with the help of examples.

MIS DEVELOPMENT

In this chapter, we discussed the workflow and information systems applications for some representative sectors in the service industry. There are many other such sectors in the service industry.

Exercise

Make a list of those which have not been discussed here.

Browse and identify available software applications for each of those industries. Define the workflow and applications for each sector and detail the functionalities provided by these software applications.

REFERENCES

Jawadekar W.S., *Management Information Systems*, Tata McGraw-Hill, New Delhi, 2007.

Kotler, Phillip, *Marketing Management*, Tata McGraw-Hill, New Delhi, 1989.

Nilekani, Nandan, *Imagining India—Ideas for the New Century*, Penguin, New Delhi, 2008.

O'Brien, James A., George M. Marakas, and Ramesh Behl, *Management Information Systems*, Tata McGraw-Hill, New Delhi, 2007.

Zeithaml, Valarie A. and Mary J. Bitner, *Services Marketing, Integrating Customer Focus Across the Firm*, Tata McGraw-Hill, New Delhi, 2006.

Axis Softech, http://www.axissoftech.com, last accessed on 29 October 2011.

BNG Infotech, http://www.bng.co.in, last accessed on 29 October 2011.

India Brand Equity Foundation, http://www.ibef.org/industry/insurance_industry.aspx, last accessed on 29 October 2011.

National portal of India, http://business.gov.in/outerwin.php, last accessed on 29 October 2011.

'Service sector', http://indiabudget.nic.in/es2010-11/echap-10.pdf, last accessed on 26 October 2011.

http://info.shine.com/Industry-Information/Construction-and-Real-Estate/855.aspx, last accessed on 29 October 2011.

http://info.shine.com/Industry-Information/Construction-and-Real-Estate/855.aspx, last accessed on 7 November 2011.

http://rndinfo.com/exclusivehealthcare.html, last accessed on 30 October 2011.

http://www.oracle.com/us/industries/financial-services/banking/index.html, last accessed on 31 October 2011.

www.powerbrainsoftware.com, last accessed on 31 December 2012.

CASE STUDY

ICICI Lombard: Insures Responsive Service with IT

Using state-of-the-art insurance applications, ICICI Lombard General Insurance Company Limited, a leading private sector player in the field of non-life insurance, is meeting the challenges faced by today's' general insurance sector. It has not only satisfied customers by providing hassle-free, efficient, and improved services, but has also gained the kind of technological edge it requires to face the competitive world. Initially, the products used to be the deal clinchers for companies. However, today, with the boundaries of the global market space converging, efficient delivery of services has become the USP. The spotlights have focussed on service delivery while efficiency is the key word. Insurance is no exception to this. However, the redundancy and duplication of processes involved in the insurance sector can mar the ultimate delivery experience.

Industry

ICICI Lombard is a 74:26 joint venture between ICICI Bank Limited and the Canada-based $26 billion Fairfax Financial Holdings Limited. ICICI Bank is India's second largest bank and ICICI Lombard is India's largest private sector general insurance company with its corporate office in Mumbai. ICICI Lombard's major categories of products and services include health insurance, motor insurance, home insurance, travel insurance, and personal accident insurance.

ICICI Lombard GIC Ltd is the largest private sector general insurance company in India with a gross written premium (GWP) of ₹36,948 million for the year ended 31 March 2010. The company has issued over 44 lakh policies, settled over 62 lakh claims, and has a claim disposal ratio of 96% (percentage of claims settled against claims reported) as on 31 March 2010. The company has 4634 employees and 350 branches, as on 31 March 2010.

Pain Points

ICICI Lombard had a problem. The company's distribution network spans 65 locations in India and connectivity was never simple. As information access is the key to delivering customized insurance policies, the company needed a system that would give its employees access and smoothen the policy management process.

For the past few years, the company's agents have been initiating critical daily tasks by contacting company representatives at the insurer's head office. This led to duplication of effort, which made the processes increasingly inefficient and burdensome with the rise in sales volume. They realized that integrating and streamlining policy application and documentation processes would make operations less strenuous and reduce administrative overheads.

They envisioned a solution that would provide their agents direct, real-time access to ERP applications to drive sale and support of the policies and save on time and cost.

They intended to remove the duplication of processes. 'With everyone involved in preparing, printing, mailing, storing, and retrieving policy documents and always in several sets of duplicates, it is easy to see how costly and time-consuming the process is', maintained a senior manager in the company.

Approach

To address the current and future business growth, ICICI Lombard was searching for a core insurance solution. After an extensive review of the existing products, ICICI Lombard chose CMC for the total solution of its insurance business. GENISYS Configurator, one of the products developed by CMC, was made available to ICICI Lombard. It was further customized to suit ICICI Lombard's requirements, with specific reference to legal and statutory needs. Furthermore, CMC's ability to provide a fully integrated system came handy for ICICI Lombard to create a computerized system and meet present and future challenges.

Solution

GENISYS Configurator is a suite of components that addresses the needs of a comprehensive insurance system. Configurator is available as a product, with its entire suite of components serving the needs of a typical insurance organization, or as individual components based on specific organizational needs. After much deliberation, the application provider delivered a browser-based transaction application that established a unified, service-oriented process to quote and issue insurance policies. This web-based quoting engine is designed to maximize flexibility and render ease of integration. It is also a robust marketing tool that is equipped with a dynamic and user-friendly interface. For each policy, the solution creates a PDF containing insurance details, which is automatically attached to the policy with descriptions and dates. This delivers a 95% saving in time and effort to the management, underwriters, claimants, as well as external users.

Configurator components can be customized to suit the specific practices of any organization. Configurator allows users to rapidly and easily define new insurance products, make changes to existing products, and establish rules that govern the product's behaviour. Configurator can integrate seamlessly with any back office system for a more efficient new business process. The system can be interfaced with a multitude of new-age delivery channels. The open framework provides immense scalability and allows easy integration to external systems. GENISYS Configurator went live in ICICI Lombard in May 2006.

The following are some of the fundamental features of the solution implemented:

- Any time, anywhere insurance through browser
- Product definition engine
- Tariff definition engine
- Business rule builder
- Automatic premium computation
- Quotation generation
- Endorsement
- Renewal notice
- Changes through parameters
- Backup/Recovery utilities
- Session and transaction log
- Security at all levels
- Audit trail at all levels
- Web-enabled policies, web-enabled queries, etc.
- Flexible MIS reports/queries
- Easy introduction of new products/services at the branch office level

Benefits

The policy management system rendered many benefits. The solution has allowed the client to handle his core business online and the robust architecture has improved the productivity and lowered the costs. It has consolidated various systems into a single homogenous entity improving manageability, reducing maintenance cost, and ensuring lesser downtime. The solution has established a single database for all the data residing in contrasting systems. The access to this data has been enhanced rendering higher customer service levels and reduced customer query response times. The solution is a pan-country application and has standardized the administration process for clients across the country. It has automated manual tasks, thereby delivering significant efficiency benefits in operations. The solution has delivered transparent and seamless flow of data between databases belonging to various modules.

Improved business efficiency is translating into faster closing of sales and higher customer retention. The new infrastructure means that customers can be serviced faster, and that all policy-related issues can be monitored and tracked at any point. Discrepancies can be corrected immediately. Citrix helped the client in efficient product and service delivery, and consequently they have got the desired edge in today's competitive arena.

The solution lets employees access products and policy information using existing hardware; even dial-up connections are good enough. At present, over 800 users access modules such as Premia (ERP), Talisma (CRM), and Final 10 (insurance accounting system). Operationally, ICICI Lombard has accrued significant savings, which have been made possible by the solution providing application access from 65 locations. With the thin-client-fat-server model adopted by the company, only the application running on the head office server needs to be updated. The company estimates huge annual savings due to deployment of these solutions.

Discussion Questions

1. Examine the requirements of an insurance company and figure out why a generic ERP like SAP cannot suit the purpose of this sector?
2. What are the various modules of a comprehensive insurance information management system? Mention the functionalities offered by each of them.
3. What are the benefits derived by the ICICI Lombard management by implementing the insurance application across the organization?

Sources:
'ICICI Lombard's simple solutions', *Express Computers*, January 2005, http://www.expresscomputeronline.com/20050117/management01.shtml, last accessed on 7 November 2011.
http://www.cmcltd.com/case_studies/PDF/CaseStudyICICI.pdf, last accessed on 7 November 2011.
https://www.icicilombard.com/about-us/why-icici.html, last accessed on 7 November 2011.
https://www.icicilombard.com/default.cms?&gclid=CPKh25rxo6wCFU0b6woddAt81Q, last accessed on 7 November 2011.

11

E-commerce

> On the Internet, the barriers of time, distance, and form are broken down, and businesses are able to transact the sale of goods and services 24 hours a day, 7 days a week, 365 days a year with consumers, all over the world. In certain cases, it is even possible to convert a physical good (CD, packaged software, newspaper) to a virtual good (MP3 audio, downloadable software, information in HTML format).
>
> —FAISAL HOQUE

LEARNING OBJECTIVES

After studying this chapter, you will be able to

- define e-commerce
- understand the world wide web (WWW) and its elements
- develop new Internet business models
- differentiate among the categories of e-commerce
- appreciate the essentials of e-commerce
- explain electronic payment systems as an important component in e-commerce
- appreciate the trends and challenges in e-commerce
- describe the e-commerce scenario in India

EXHIBIT 11.1

India: The Second Coming of E-commerce

The estimated size of the e-commerce market in India in 2011 was ₹50,000 crore, up from ₹8145 crore in 2007. The value of total early-stage funding received by the e-commerce start-ups is approximately ₹400 crore. As per an Internet and Mobile Association of India (IAMAI) estimate, around 200 consumer e-commerce start-ups have come up during 2009–11.

Many e-commerce sites in India started way back in 1999, but many of them could not survive the 'dot-com bubble burst' of 2001. After about a decade, with the second wave of e-commerce in India rolling, Indian Internet-driven companies seem to have learnt from their experiences and have evolved in their approach to online business models. Many companies of the 1999 era could not survive until 2011, but those who did have certainly set high benchmarks for the newbies.

'When we started selling online in 1999', says K. Vaitheeswaran, founder and chief executive officer of Indiaplaza, 'the total Internet population in India was three million, and the number of people who were shopping online was just a few thousands. The market was too small. Today, with about 70 million Internet users in India, the market is ready.' He should know. His is probably the only pure-play e-commerce company that has survived all these years. While the user base has increased, people have also got used to the Internet as a medium and are using it for multiple reasons. Shopping is just yet another way of making use of it. 'When you use a medium for multiple reasons, it becomes a part of your life', says Pearl Uppal, co-founder and chief executive officer (CEO), Fashion and You.

The travel segment of e-commerce always enjoyed an upper hand with easy-to-deliver products and instant gratification for buyers. Mukesh Bansal, CEO, Myntra.com feels that due to the proliferation of the travel segment, the comfort level of people in making online payments increased significantly and they were made ready for the next level of online shopping, not just for tickets but for other products as well. Today, the growth in the e-commerce market is driven by the need of urban India to save time. Many funding companies have started putting their money and trust in start-ups, thus opening ways for many zealous entrepreneurs to start their Internet businesses. According to Kunal Bahl, CEO and founder, Jasper (SnapDeal.com), with matured credit card penetration, increase in Internet penetration, increase in people's trust on the Internet,

availability of more online options, and with lives becoming busier, the recent years have seen a resurgence of e-commerce in India. The online non-travel industry can be categorized as follows: e-tailing, comprising online retailers and online auctions; online classifieds comprising online jobs, matrimony, property, automobile and general classifieds; and paid content subscription and digital downloads comprising research, articles, exclusive videos, and more. The top categories according to investors are travel, classifieds, group buying, auto sales, and luxury brands.

According to Mehul Gupta, assistant vice-president, IAMAI, online travel, which includes booking rail and air tickets, hotel accommodations and tour packages comprised 70% of the whole pie. E-tailing, which includes durable products—electronic items, home and kitchen appliances as well as personal items such as apparels and jewellery—was 13%.

Transactions for financial services such as insurance payments and renewals and trading accounts amounted to 9%, and downloading mobile and digital content was 2% of the overall share. Other online services such as classifieds (jobs, matrimonial, cars, real estate, and others), online food delivery and buying movie tickets and DVD rentals comprised 6% of the overall market.

The online travel industry has a strong government presence with the website of the Indian railways, www.irctc.com, being its most successful initiative. Some equally successful private players are Makemytrip, Cleartrip, Yatra, etc. After the success of these initiatives, these travel sites are now expanding their portfolio of services to add hotel bookings and holiday packages as well. A decade ago, travel agents had a better say when it came to selling travel solutions. However, the intense competition among online travel portals and various hospitality websites have reduced intermediary commission rates, thus offering more economic value to online transactions.

The changing lifestyle and mindset of the Indian customer has led to a spur in the e-retail industry. Retailers also see huge business opportunities as they can cater to consumers across geographies, no operational timings, unlimited shelf space, and almost zero infrastructure. Companies such as Snapdeal, Infibeam, Deals and You, Futurebazaar, and many more are great examples. In addition to this, online fashion retail is becoming an emerging

(Contd)

Exhibit 11.1 (Contd)

trend in this segment with companies such as Fashion and You, 99labels, and many others.

As long as people keep hunting for *naukri* (employment), *sathi* (life partners), and *makaan* (housing), the online classified segment of e-commerce will keep doing business consistently. This segment can be broadly divided into three sectors—jobs, matrimonial, and real estate. The business of this segment has been recognized as one of the strongest in the non-travel category of e-commerce. Naukri.com, shaadi.com, jeevansathi.com, bharatmatrimony.com, 99acres.com, makaan.com, indiaproperty.com, etc., are some of the better known names in this arena.

Free online advertising has changed the rules of the game. The emergence of free online classifieds in the industry has provided a means for business owners to save up on advertising efforts. By posting advertisements on the Internet, business owners have been able to break physical and distance barriers and reach the millions of diverse consumers across the globe. As they are able to showcase their products to a wide range of consumers,

it enables business owners to gather more patrons and subsequently, increase their return on investment. Online classifieds in the Internet are not only useful for selling goods and services, but can also be utilized in gathering a labour force and for identifying people who are qualified in providing precisely what a business owner needs. For instance, travel alone accounted for more than $4 billion in revenue last year. According to another report, out of the ₹9000 crore transacted in e-commerce in India, ₹5500 crore was spent on buying travel tickets alone.

Interestingly, an eBay India census 2010 report announced that out of their 2.5 million users, in the last one year, nearly a third came from rural locations. While New Delhi is the leading e-commerce city, Mumbai and Jaipur follow, and Maharashtra as a state tops the list.

Source:
Manoah, Drishti D., 'The second coming of e-commerce', *Data Quest*, www.dqindia.ciol.com, last accessed on 16 February 2011 (Reprinted with permission).

Websites such as naukri.com, myntra.com, shaadi.com, makemytrip.com, snapdeal.com, and 99acres.com are new business models that emerged after the advent of the world wide web (WWW). Earlier, these services were provided by traditional consultants or middlemen. Even traditional businesses such as retailing assumed new dimensions with the introduction of virtual stores. These stores either support existing businesses or are launched as new business models altogether. E-commerce initiatives such as Flipkart.com, SnapDeal, YouTube, GettyImages, and iTunes are new business models. Traditional business activities involving physical channels of buying and distribution are now supported by web-based e-commerce activities. Exhibit 11.1 illustrates the enormous scope and potential of e-commerce businesses in India.

E-COMMERCE

E-commerce refers to the use of the Internet and the web to transact business deals. It involves transactions between two organizations or individuals over the Internet. E-commerce not only involves the buying and selling of goods and services, but also the entire online process of developing, marketing, selling, delivering, servicing, and paying online. E-commerce has also evolved as a tool for strategic business planning and competitive advantage. According to Kalakota (1997), e-commerce is changing the shape of competition, the speed of action, and the streamlining of interactions, products, and payments from customers to companies and from companies to suppliers.

E-commerce is a modern business methodology that uses the electronic media and is an effort towards cost cutting, quality improvement, and increasing speed of services. Thus, e-commerce of any nature involves complete transaction processing, except physical movement of goods, over the Internet.

E-commerce began in 1995 when one of the first Internet portals, Netscape.com, accepted the first advertisements from corporations and thus, popularized the idea that the web can be a new medium for advertisements and publicity.

E-commerce processes use the WWW for conducting all business activities. Before we discuss e-commerce further, we will have to make our fundamentals about the web clear.

WORLD WIDE WEB

The phenomenon of Internet-based transactions cannot be understood without understanding the WWW, which is the backbone of modern e-commerce. The web began in 1989 when Tim Berners-Lee from the European Laboratory for Particle Physics proposed the web project for sharing of information among its members. The WWW is a system with universally accepted standards (protocols) for storing, retrieving, formatting, and displaying information using a client–server architecture. In client–server architecture, the web servers store and retrieve information, and manage data, applications, and security. The client is the interface between the user and the web server and displays the information through a core browser or application. For example, yahoomail, gmail, etc., use web servers to store e-mail data, run the e-mail management application, and provide security to our e-mail data. The computer terminal on which we work is a client of the web server, which functions as an interface between the user and the web server.

The web is quite distinct from the Internet. While the Internet is a network of networks, the web is a global information sharing architecture that integrates information stored on this network. Software is the foundation on which the web facilitates navigation and publishing of information in a particular format called a web page. Web pages and their contents stored on web servers are delivered by the Internet. Figure 11.1 displays the web architecture.

The world wide web works around the following important concepts:

- Uniform resource locator (URL)
- Hypertext transfer protocol (HTTP)
- Hypertext mark-up language (HTML)
- Common gateway interface (CGI)

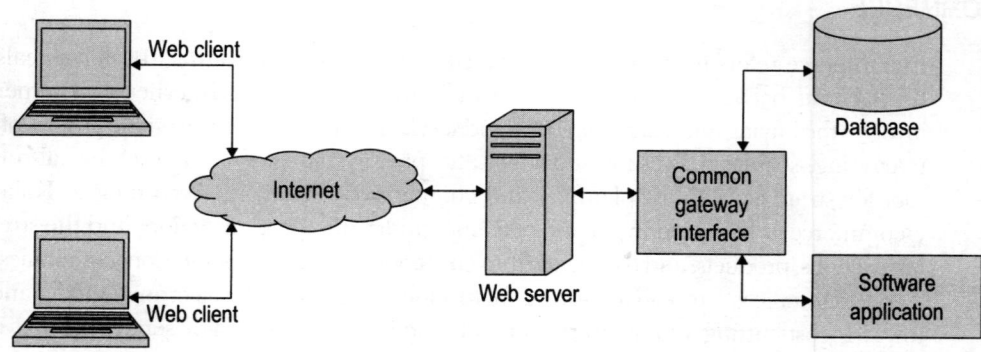

Fig. 11.1 Web architecture

Uniform Resource Locator

There are millions and trillions of computers connected to the Internet. Finding a file on the Internet would be impossible if there was no structured addressing system. The addressing scheme, known as uniform resource locator, makes hypermedia publishing possible, despite the existence of different protocols. Hypermedia refers to documents containing multiple forms of media such as text, graphics, video, and sound that can be searched like hypertext. Hypermedia consists of documents and links. A link or a pointer in one document indicates further linkages to another document. This concept is called hypertext. Hypermedia has the ability to use several media in a single document for display through the browser.

The documents that the browser displays are hypertext that contain pointers to other documents. The pointer is implemented using a concept that is central to all web browsers called uniform resource locator (URL). A URL marks the unique location on the Internet where a file can be found. A URL is also known as a web address.

URLs use a perfectly consistent pattern. The web address consists of three parts differentiated with a dot (.). The first part gives the name of the resource, the second part gives the name of the server, and the third part gives the full file name of the resource.

For example, http://www.delhiuniversity.com/mbacourse.htm is a complete web address (also known as domain name), which has three distinct parts.

http://www	resource (access method)
delhiuniversity.com	server name (location)
mbacourse.html	file name, which has details of products

In this example, delhiuniversity.com represents a domain name. The domain name identifies a unique node on the Internet and corresponds to a unique four-part numeric-only IP (Internet protocol) address. For example, delhiuniversity.com may represent the IP address 192.168.95.22.

In all protocols, the right slash (/) is reserved and used to represent hierarchical spaces.

URLs are important components of the Internet architecture. They facilitate easy search in locating an object on the Internet. Their working is independent of the type of server, network topology, and operating system.

Hypertext Transfer Protocol

Hypertext transfer protocol (HTTP) is a communication standard used to transfer pages on the web. HTTP is a language or a network protocol used by client browsers and servers on the Internet. Kalakota (1997) simplifies HTTP as a 'simple request/response protocol that is currently run over TCP and is the basis of the WWW. In short, HTTP is a protocol for transferring information efficiently between the requesting client and the server'.

HTTP can transfer multimedia data such as text, images, or sounds which are all in HTML formats. HTML refers to hypertext mark-up language, which is a common language that is used to interchange documents on the web. This forms the basic fabric of the web. While communicating, the client sends a list of formats it can accept and the server sends data in any of the formats in which it can produce the data. Hence, it uses and accepts formats of different types without any standardization.

The web handles all kinds of digital communication, and links computers and networks across the globe. A web page can contain text, graphics, animation, audio, video, images, or programs.

Hypertext Mark-up Language

We surf the Internet by clicking on links provided on web pages. These pages have been created using standards called Hypertext mark-up language (HTML). The web uses a graphical user interface (GUI) for easy and aesthetic viewing and HTML supports this interface. HTML is a language that every web client is required to understand. It is used for creating hypertext documents containing text, graphics, sounds, images, etc. HTML uses tags to specify how data of varying nature is placed on a document. The beauty of the language lies in its ability to club every type of data in the page—text, data, hypermedia, graphics, or sound. HTML formats documents and incorporates dynamic links to other documents stored in the same or remote computers.

XML, an abbreviation for extensible mark-up language, is a further development over HTML. While HTML only determines how text and images are displayed on a document, XML further specifies the meaning or detail of the data on the pages. Browsers such as Internet Explorer, Netscape, Google Chrome, and Firefox are programmed according to HTML standards, which are universally accepted.

Common Gateway Interface

Common gateway interface (CGI) is a standard interface between web servers and the applications. When an application runs on a client, the browser needs to fetch data from other servers. Server scripts are written to reach these servers, which obtain the data and gives it to the browser to process further. The scripts are written in many languages that conform to CGI standards. CGI is also used to integrate databases with the web; due to the integration capability of CGI to get data from other non-web-server databases, the web offers a plethora of business applications.

NEW INTERNET BUSINESS MODELS

With the advent of the Internet, commerce has undergone a revolutionary change. There are many new business models coming up and many old ones are no longer viable. The new Internet-based business models use IT and the web for value addition to the existing products and services or to provide a foundation for new products and services. These business models use the rich communication capabilities of the Internet. The new Internet-based businesses can be grouped under heads such as information portals, social networking, digital content distribution, entertainment, trade services, and classified services.

Table 11.1 describes some of the most important Internet-based business models that have emerged during the recent past.

Information Portals

Many e-commerce businesses are based on the Internet's rich communication and interactive capabilities. Yahoo!, Gmail, Hotmail, Indiatimes, Rediffmail, etc., use strong communication capabilities and earn their revenue from huge advertisements on their sites. According to Laudon

Table 11.1   Internet business models and examples

Category	Description	Revenue model	Examples
Portals	Entry point to the web, provide general information and services such as news and e-mail	Advertisement	Rediffmail.com, yahoo.com, msn.com, google.com
Virtual storefronts	Sells physical goods directly to consumers and individual business owners	Sales of products	Flipkart.com, indiatimes.com, amazon.com, indiaplaza.com, futurebazaar.com
Information brokers	Provide product, pricing, and availability information to consumers	Advertisement, commission from trading	99acres.com, naaptol.com, justdial.com, fundoodata.com, magicbricks.com
Content providers	Provide digital content such as digital news, music, photos, or video over the web	Sale of digital contents, advertisements	Gettyimages.com, iTunes.com, musicindiaonline.com, musictoday.in
Online marketplace	Provide online environments where buyers meet sellers to buy products, provide auctions, offer products	Transaction fee	Sharekhan.com, eBay.com, bolijeeto.com, nilaami.in
Social networking sites	Provide online meeting places for people with matching interests	Paid subscription, advertising	Linkedin.com, myspace.com, facebook.com, tagged.com
Service providers	Provide data, photo and video sharing, and user generated data contents	Subscription-based fee, advertising	Naukri.com, jeevansathi.com, youtube.com, google maps
Transaction brokers	Process online sales transactions for a customer and provide information on rates	Fee for each transaction	Irctc.co.in, makemytrip.com, yatra.com, sharekhan.com

(2010), the web's information resources are so vast and rich that portals have emerged as Internet business models to help individuals and organizations locate information more efficiently. Sites such as Yahoo! provide personalized, integrated information for a variety of sources. Besides functioning as a search engine, it provides news, sports, weather, telephone directories, maps, games, shopping, e-mail, chat, discussion boards, etc. These Internet-based businesses place pop-ups and banner ads on their websites. Such businesses provide free e-mail and search engine services. If they start charging for e-mail storage box beyond a particular size, their revenue will increase to gigantic proportions. However, there are strategic compulsions that restrict them from doing so.

Google is the largest search engine in the world; however, there are regional search engines doing fantastic business. For example, Navet, a Korean search engine service provider, launched in 2001, has 74% of the search page views in Korea. Local search engines are also available in China and Japan.

Social Networking

All technological advancements have been brought about for meeting individual needs. Social groups have been created after the invention of the Internet. For the first time in history, technology has served a social aspect. The Internet has created online communities, where people with similar interests are able to communicate with each other from different locations. The source of revenue for these communities and business portals comes from providing data to target customers and the placement of banners and pop-up advertisements on their websites.

Social networking sites are online communities that have become extremely popular. Social networking is the practice of expanding one's business or social contacts by making connections through individuals. These sites link people through business, interest groups, or friends. For example, LinkedIn focuses on professional and job networking; Facebook, Friendster, MySpace, and Twitter attract people who are interested in enlarging their friend circles. Social networking sites such as Tagged are fun sites and focus on online games.

According to Keith Hampton (2011), today, almost every Internet user is a member of at least one social networking site. These sites encourage members to reveal a great deal of information about them and exchange the same with other members. Businesses harness this information for carefully targeted sales promotion and personal interaction with potential customers.

Digital Content

The web offers great business opportunities for products and services that can be digitized. Besides delivering movies, music, and games, there are many businesses delivering online news, documents, etc. Applications such as GoogleDocs, Live Documents, Office Live Workspace, and HyperOffice provide functions to create, manage, and store documents online. There are sites such as ViewdocsOnline, Contracts.org.in, and Netlawman.co.in that provide formats of various documents including legal agreements, contracts, etc., for a fee. In addition to their regular newspapers in print form, media houses also provide digital news through their websites (e.g., timesofindia.com and hindustantimes.com).

Entertainment

The Internet revolution has had a great impact on the entertainment industry consisting of television, movies, music, and radio. Internet-based new business models, which deliver entertainment in digital form, have come up. Raaga.com, bollywoodmusic, musictoday.in, youtube, iTunes, musicindiaonline, etc., are e-commerce business models that deliver music online. Similarly, there are gaming sites such as zapak.com, ibibo.com, games.com, and pcgames4fun. com that attract online players.

Some radio channels such as npr.com, planetradiocity, hindiradios, and fever are also available on the web for online listening. Movies-on-demand is a new concept that has been popularized by the web. There are websites such as watchmoviesindia.com, bollyclips.com, netflix.com, amazon.com, movielink.com, bharatmovies.com, and easymoviesIndia.com in this category of e-commerce. Apple's iTunes music services have inspired a new form of digital content delivery called podcasting. Podcasting is a method of publishing audio broadcasts via the Internet, allowing subscribers to download audio files.

Trade Services

Trade services are online directories and a marketplace for buyers and sellers. These e-commerce businesses provide their services at a subscription fee. The sellers' product details, company profiles, etc., are hosted on a yearly basis. In India, there are trade directories (e-trade service marketplace) such as tradeindia.com, justdial.com, sulekha.com, and fundoodata.com. Alibaba is China's leading e-commerce company, operating the world's largest online marketplace for both international and domestic trade.

Classified Services

E-commerce businesses related to classified services hold a great future in India. Earlier, these services were offered by middlemen called agents or brokers. E-commerce has opened a large avenue for operators in the digital world. E-commerce sites such as naukri.com, monsterindia. com, timesjobs.com, shine.com, and jobsahead.com are a marketplace for employers and job seekers. Jeevansathi.com, shaadi.com, bharatmatrimony.com, vivaah.com, mangaljodi.com, lifepartnerIndia.com, etc., are e-commerce portals that are flourishing because of the matrimonial business. Similarly, there are many e-commerce portals for property trade and renting such as 99acres.com, magicbricks.com, indiaproperty.com, and makaan.com. All these businesses are very successful as these are based on a revenue model and charge a small fee for providing job-, matrimonial-, and property-related information.

CATEGORIES OF E-COMMERCE

The most popular way of categorizing e-commerce is on the basis of the nature of participants in the trade. Based on this, e-commerce is classified into three major categories, called business-to-consumer (B2C) e-commerce, business-to-business (B2B) e-commerce, and consumer-to-consumer (C2C) e-commerce.

Business-to-consumer E-commerce

Business-to-consumer e-commerce involves retailing products and services to individual consumers. Selling and buying of goods and services between an organization and the end consumer is known as B2C e-commerce. There are millions of organizations worldwide that have established e-commerce portals as an extension of their present retail businesses. Web portals like amazon.com are dedicated businesses selling goods through the web. In India, crossword. com, firstandsecond.com, indiatimes.com, makemytrip.com, indiaproperty.com, magicbricks. com, naukri.com, etc., are examples of B2C electronic storefronts selling goods and services.

Business-to-business E-commerce

Business-to-business e-commerce involves buying and selling of goods and services between two organizations. Organizational procurement systems, tendering, e-procurement portals, etc., are examples of B2B commerce. Most organizations today, establish portals through which their trading partners can place orders for goods and services offered by the organization. ITC's e-chaupal.com is an initiative that disseminates information and knowledge to farmers and helps them sell their produce at the latest market price. There are corporate sites such as http://tenders. ongc.co.in, https://www.indianoiltenders.com, and so on, which belong to the B2B category of e-commerce.

Consumer-to-consumer E-commerce

Consumer-to-consumer e-commerce involves selling of goods and services by a consumer to another consumer. Web auction sites such as eBay, winningbids.com, bidjeeto.com, and starbid.

com are examples of C2C commerce, where a consumer can sell his new or used goods to another consumer. 99acres.com offers services for individuals and organizations to display property for sale and rentals. Similarly, carwale.com, cartradeindia.com, secondhandmall.com, and eBay.com are C2C e-commerce sites for selling used cars, old gadgets, etc.

ESSENTIALS OF E-COMMERCE

There are certain essential components for an electronic business to be successful. We must consider these components well in advance before setting up an electronic storefront. The essentials of e-commerce processes for successful operation and management are illustrated in Fig. 11.2.

Right Revenue Model

The long-term continuity and sustainability of businesses, brick or click, are dependent on the revenue model. For any business, electronic or otherwise, to sustain in the competitive marketplace, its capability to generate revenue and profits is of utmost importance. Many e-commerce initiatives failed during the infamous 'dot-com bubble burst' of 2000–2001 because of inappropriate revenue models. The hype about making millions through Internet businesses was based on unrealistic and unconvincing models. The main targeted revenue was through selling advertisements on the Internet. Millions of dot-com companies chased a few advertising funds. The result was, only a few companies such as Yahoo!, Google, Hotmail, e-Bay, Indiatimes, and Rediff generated some revenue, and the rest were sheer failures. Most of them shut shop within a few months. Only e-businesses focusing on selling goods and services such as eBay, Amazon, Indiamart, Indiaplaza, Ferns N Petals, and Tradeindia succeeded.

We have seen in Exhibit 11.1 that online shopping habits, in India as well as the globe, are on the rise. Over one-third online Indians (population that is online/uses websites for purchase) buy airline tickets over the Internet. The most successful e-commerce business models are travel ticketing, classified services such as matrimonial, employment, and property rentals. Books, music, and electronic goods are the most popular commodities on the Internet. Goods and services that do not require a personal touch and feel but provide great value if bought through the Internet are the most sought after.

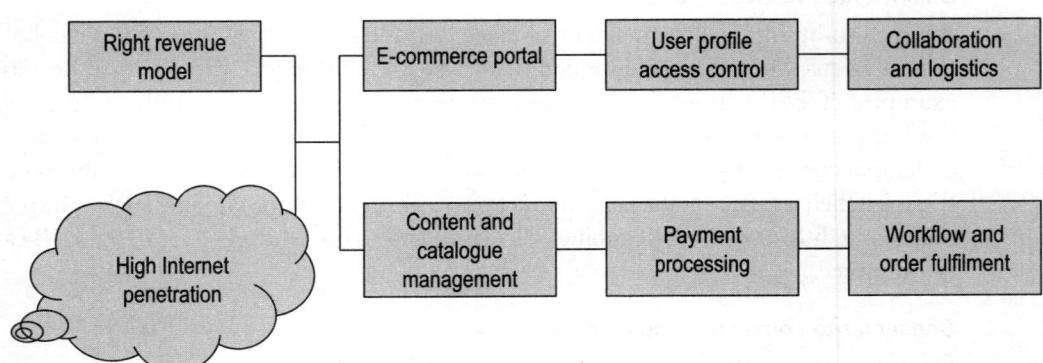

Fig. 11.2 Essential components and processes for a successful e-commerce business

High Penetration of Internet

For any e-commerce business to be successful, the penetration of computers and the Internet in that society must be very high. People should have the habit of browsing through the Internet for some of their tasks or for entertainment. They can go shopping, look for solutions, collect information, seek entertainment, and undertake knowledge enhancement activities, all on the Internet. These Internet habits are going to drive online shopping. Besides increasing trade and commerce, the Internet is going to be the enabler of social advancement and justice through knowledge and information dissemination.

We are able to see a remarkable growth in online shopping activities in India. Exhibit 11.1 shows that the online population in India increased from 3 million in 1999 to 70 million in 2011. This growth pattern is paving the way for more e-commerce businesses in India. There are four key drivers for online shopping catching up in India:

- Internet and increased personal computer penetration, aided by falling prices of computers
- Growth of personal computer penetration (48% in June 2011)
- India's mushrooming middle class, with growing purchasing power and limited personal time
- Increasing usage of credit and debit cards for online purchases
- Growing young population, which spends significant time online

E-commerce Portals

The web pages through which e-commerce transactions are accomplished are specialized software. These web pages are aesthetically designed, look attractive, and are also known as e-commerce portals. These software applications are now readily available for running e-commerce businesses. The applications are installed on web servers that are connected to the Internet through a public IP address. E-commerce sites are dynamic in nature. In a dynamic web page, the information regularly changes as it interacts with the customer or the viewer.

For example, an e-commerce website selling books would display the availability of a particular book in the store. If in the next moment, the last copy of the book is sold, the site would display that the book is not available or out of stock. According to Joshi (2009), e-commerce portals include the following:

- Setting up electronic storefronts and catalogues to display products and pricing information
- Designing shopping carts so that customers can select and buy items
- Making an e-payment collection system and securing the site with international authenticating agencies such as VeriSign and Norton Secured
- Connecting with the back office ERP servers and updating stock availability on the site

The e-commerce website must be thoroughly optimized by various search engines so that customers can find the products and services easily. Similarly, there has to be an internal search engine that searches for products in the required category and price range, and other parameters supplied by the visiting customer.

Content and Catalogue Management

E-commerce portals are very complex and have hundreds of pages that are composed of data in the form of text, graphics, images, and sound. The contents of these pages are dynamic in nature and frequently change depending on environmental factors such as type of products, customers, prices, and requests by visitors. Even the static contents need updating from time to time due to changes in the company profile and modification in product or contact information. These changes are carried out offline and the contents are frequently updated so that the site remains up and running. In the dynamic pages, the organization may need to frequently change the profiles, product prices, or any other information related to the organization or the products frequently. The content management tool available in the market helps in making those changes. Thus, content management tools provide a structured and easy approach to change the contents, whenever needed.

According to O'Brien (2007), the content management software helps e-commerce companies develop, generate, deliver, update, and archive text data and multimedia information on e-commerce websites. The e-commerce contents include e-catalogues, which display product information. These catalogues are multimedia databases of products with prices and probably an image and available inventory of the product. Nowadays, there are content and catalogue management tools available in the market, which are used by many e-commerce companies.

The content management tools also include product configuration processes that support customer self-service and customization functions. For example, Dell and Cisco e-commerce sites use tools to support build-to-order and customization of products. The e-commerce portal includes a shopping cart function, which stores the goods selected by the customers till the time the customer makes a checkout.

User Profiles and Security

Most e-commerce portals ask first-time visitors to register and create their profiles, and then assign passwords to them. The websites start profiling the customer by gathering information about them—their website behaviour and choices, tastes, and preferences. These profiles are built on the basis of user registration, tracking cookies, and feedback. Later, the profiles are used to recognize them as individuals. The websites provide users a personalized view of the contents, and offer product recommendations and advertisements. For example, makemytrip.com displays the frequently travelled sectors and offers discounts based on the registered user profile.

Some e-commerce portals maintain security and allow further navigation only to registered customers who have been assigned passwords. According to O'Brien (2007), e-commerce processes must establish mutual trust and secure access between the parties in an e-commerce transaction by authenticating users, authorizing access, and enforcing security features. The registered user is given access to only the relevant portion of the site, prohibiting access to administration, restricted data, and other people's account information.

Workflow and Order Fulfilment

The order that has been received at the e-commerce site is retrieved at the back office for processing and fulfilment. Most e-commerce applications trigger an event notification to the back office system regarding a customer's website access, registration, payment, and delivery processes. An efficient back office order processing application supports the e-commerce portal's business activities. An event notification software works with a workflow application to monitor all e-commerce processes and records events.

The e-commerce organizations work on a workflow management software to automate the processes and perform order processing and distribution activities. The e-business workflow systems for enterprise collaboration helps employees collaborate to perform structured tasks within the knowledge-based processes. For example, the processes may involve a sequence of tasks such as order acknowledgement, order entry, authorization, dispatch advice, procurement advice, physical pick-list, inspection, billing, documentation, and dispatch.

Collaboration and Logistics

Physical distribution of goods is a serious challenge for e-commerce businesses. It requires collaboration arrangements and trading services with suppliers, customers, and logistic providers. Similarly, e-commerce companies may face the problems of shipping large quantities or perishable goods to customers spread over a large geographical area. E-commerce organizations rely on collaborating with suppliers for providing logistic arrangements to reach the customer. The essential collaboration among trading partners in e-commerce may be provided by Internet-based trading services.

For example, Ferns N Petals, an India-based online supplier of flowers, has a B2B trading arrangement with suppliers for supply of flowers to their customers all over the globe. This is why some of the goods have found favour with both e-retailers and consumers, and others have not. Services like e-ticketing, and classified services such as job-portals and matrimonial services are quite popular and make good business sense.

Fulfilment of orders via the Internet poses challenges because of e-commerce's global reach, governmental, and societal implications. For instance, as Exhibit 11.2 describes, Myntra, the e-commerce organization gets about 1000 orders per day. The orders might come from any part of the country, big or small. To be able to ship all products effectively and keep customers satisfied, they require a very sophisticated logistic infrastructure. This is why they employ people with a deep knowledge of the supply chain, either from the retail or logistics background.

EXHIBIT 11.2
E-commerce: Issue of Online Payments

The online travel industry with successful e-commerce portals such as IRCTC, Makemytrip, Cleartrip, and Yatra has induced buyers to transact and pay online and has thus paved the way for other e-commerce transactions.

Meanwhile, urban India is slowly but surely getting comfortable with using credit cards and other online payment mechanisms. There may be a problem with resolution of complaints, especially in case of wrong or delayed deliveries. That is why most e-tailers today focus on customer care, while many others are trying to personalize each customer experience and create real consumer-centric promotions.

Today, a lot of focus is on building a strong back-end team. 'We get about 1000 orders per day and orders might come from any part of the country, big or small. To be able to ship all products effectively and keep customers satisfied, we require a very sophisticated logistic infrastructure, which is why we employ people with deep knowledge of the supply chain, either from retail or logistics background,' says Mukesh Bansal, chief executive officer (CEO), Myntra.com, who had a workforce of around 150 people as of January 2011. Kunal Bahl of SnapDeal says that his strong and capable IT team plays a major part in the success of his company of 300 employees.

Besides recognizing and treating the customer as king, it is important to ensure the company's presence on recognized shopping comparison sites. Many people visit these sites to check where the company stands and

(Contd)

Exhibit 11.2 (Contd)

read the product reviews. All e-retailers agree that nothing authenticates their offering to an undecided customer like a good product review.

A web portal without an online payment facility does not become commerce, but simply a directory of services. Online payment service providers in India are, however, trying to provide sustained support by creating payment access to millions of consumers who do not have appropriate payment options. According to Naveen Surya, managing director, Itz Cash Card, there is a large percentage of consumers who do not have access to debit/credit cards unless they have acquired prepaid cards from online payment service providers.

About 25% growth has taken place over the past year in average transaction volumes for the online payment business. According to Bikramjit Sen, CEO, TechProcess Solutions, their online payment gateway is integrated with over 500 of India's leading entities (from sectors such as utility, insurance, Internet service providers (ISPs), direct to home (DTH), telecom/mobile, e-shopping, flowers and fruits delivery, eateries, educations, and charity) and 25 of India's leading public sector, private, and foreign banks to effect online payments through net banking.

In addition to changing demographic profiles and increasing consumer awareness, such online payment service providers can help bridge the gap between the service provider, customers, and payment channels with their customized, secure, and relevant e-commerce solutions, and are largely instrumental in the turnaround and growth in e-commerce.

Source:
Manoah, Drishti D., 'The second coming of e-commerce', *Data Quest*, www.dqindia.ciol.com, last accessed on 16 February 2011 (Reprinted with permission).

E-PAYMENT SYSTEMS

Exhibit 11.2 illustrates how organizations are building alternative payment systems such as 'Itz Cash' to support e-commerce. A change in banking habits and the proliferation of credit and debit cards are required for e-commerce to flourish. Cash and cheques are not suitable for e-commerce transactions. There are many accepted alternatives such as credit cards, debit cards, net banking payments, electronic fund transfers, prepaid cash cards, and electronic bill payment options. Figure 11.3 displays a secure e-payment system with many payment alternatives.

The sudden rise in usage of online banking and credit cards, backed by the aggressive push by consumer banking majors in India, has helped break down many of the earlier apprehensions about card ownership and usage. As ownership of credit cards grows, a large proportion of online shoppers are likely to use credit cards for B2C e-commerce transactions. Indians make a relatively high number of purchases using credit cards, higher than the global average.

Many B2B e-commerce systems rely on a more complex system of electronic fund transfers, which may include net banking, electronic bill payment system, or electronic cash. The electronic fund transfer systems use a variety of information technologies to capture and process money and credit transfers between the bank and businesses and their customers. Web-based payment services such as PayPal and BillPoint for cash transfers and bill payments are very popular forms of online e-payment systems.

Securing Electronic Payments

Besides good electronic payment habits of the customers, establishing a reliable and secured e-payment mechanism on the e-commerce portal is crucial. People are still wary of using credit or debit cards on the Internet because the card information is vulnerable to tracking by network sniffers, tracking cookies, and spyware software. There is a possibility of misuse as well. Therefore,

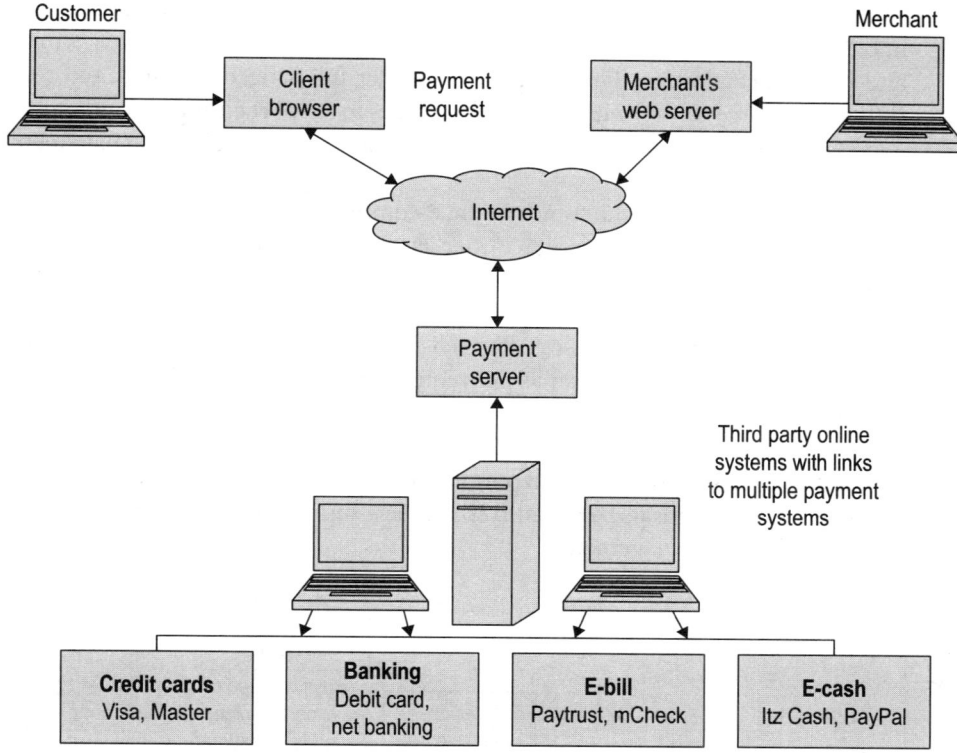

Fig. 11.3 Example of a secure e-payment system with many payment alternatives

the payment mechanism must be secured using secure sockets layer (SSL) authentication by security agencies such as VeriSign and Norton Secured. This authentication gives confidence to the customers and they are assured that their credit card number is not being misused. SSL technology, developed by Netscape Communication, automatically encrypts data passing between the client's web browser and the merchant's server. With this security, the transaction partners can begin a secure session that guarantees message privacy and message integrity. We will discuss Internet security in detail in Chapter 17.

According to Morgan (1999), secure electronic transaction or SET, a standard for e-payment security, uses the digital wallet approach. In this method, software encrypts a digital envelope of digital certificates specifying the payment details for each transaction. SET has been supported by Visa, MasterCard, IBM, Microsoft, Netscape, and other companies. Therefore, a system like SET may become the standard for secure e-payments on the Internet.

TRENDS IN E-COMMERCE

From an electronic storage of corporate profiles, brochures, and product catalogues to online trading and e-business empowerment, e-commerce has come a long way. According to O'Brien (2007), e-commerce is changing how companies do business both internally and externally with their customers, suppliers, and other business partners. With e-commerce gaining maturity in the world of business, its applications have gone through several major changes. For example, initially in B2C e-commerce, websites were used to store electronic documents such as multimedia profiles and product catalogues. Then, it moved to offer full-fledged products and services. Similarly, B2B e-commerce started with corporate websites to support customers and moved on to intranet and extranet and supported greater initiatives such as supply chain management and customer relationship management.

Figure 11.4 illustrates the trends in the e-commerce space.

As we see, the B2C e-commerce market changed from e-catalogue storage to interactive marketing capabilities, which provided a personalized shopping experience to users. Then, it moved on to an integrated web store where the customer could have a better shopping experience. Further, e-commerce businesses offer self-service stores where customers can configure and customize products and services as per requirements.

B2B e-commerce initially offered customers self-service portals, which quickly changed to procurement automation and connected partners through extranets and information exchanges. Then, the business moved to a B2B portal where the partners could buy, sell, exchange, or conduct auctions. These trends in B2C and B2B markets supported customer relationship management and supply chain management.

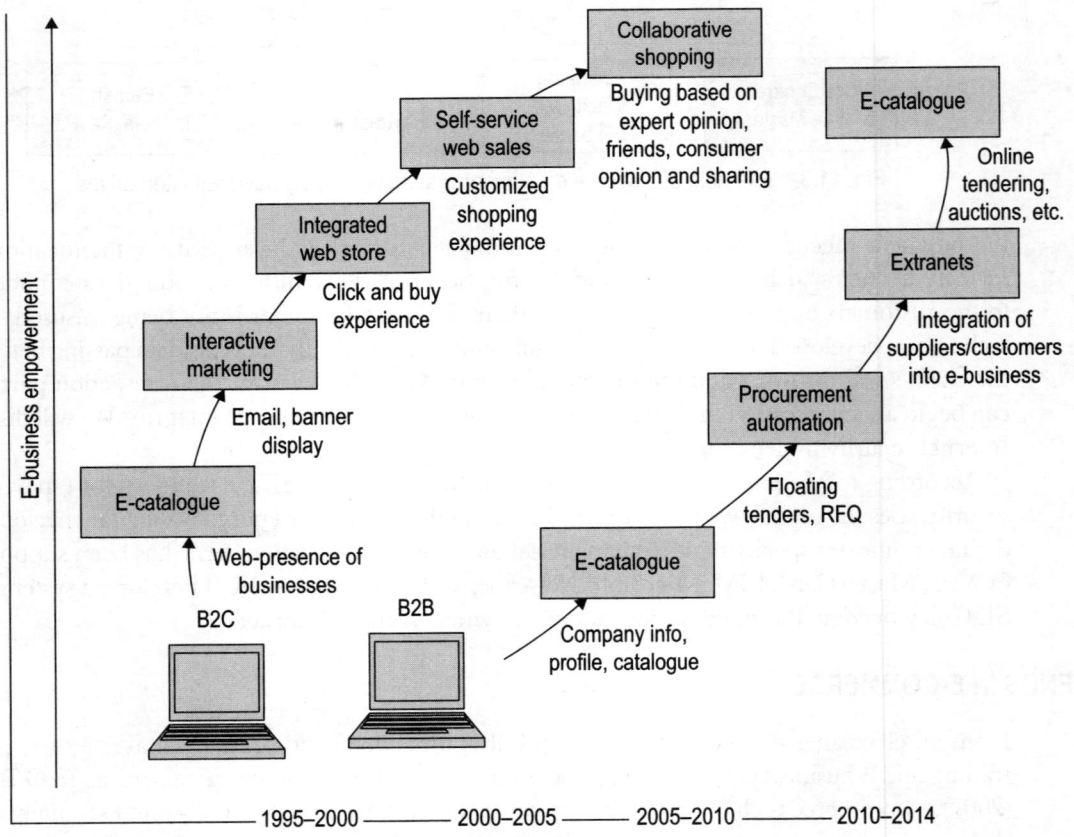

Fig. 11.4 Trends in e-commerce

CHALLENGES OF E-COMMERCE

Shoppers Stop's e-commerce initiative (Exhibit 11.3) is seen by the company as an extension of the current retailing business. The vice-president is of the view that e-commerce retailing is comparatively a new concept in India. The company faced many challenges. The lack of maturity

---

EXHIBIT 11.3

Shoppers Stop: The E-commerce Initiative with Deliveries across India

Vivek Mathur, vice-president, corporate planning and e-commerce, Shoppers Stop Ltd, explains his e-commerce initiatives and deliveries in an interview on 1 July 2011.

You led the online store of Shoppers Stop in 2008. What were the initial challenges you faced as an entrant to the online platform?

For the last three years, I have been involved in the e-commerce initiative of Shoppers Stop, which is very challenging as it is yet a new concept in India. Already, we have a very strong physical presence; so our challenges were unlike start-ups. There was availability of management, vendor base, large assortment of products, etc. Our primary challenge was technology selection—choosing and managing technology. We have launched our e-store with delivery across major cities in India. The portal, Shoppersstop.com, retails all the products, including apparel, cosmetics, and accessories, available at Shoppers Stop stores.

You have initiated the online version of Shoppers Stop. How is the online performance of Shoppers Stop in terms of sales, traffic, and traction?

We are growing significantly in terms of traffic, sales, and traction. We are achieving all our objectives. Our website offers a user experience that is probably among one of the best in India. We get a fair amount of traffic and around 4,00,000 people are visiting the website every month. On the sales front, our performance is in compliance with our target, but I cannot share the exact figures.

How do you see the shift of urban customers (including tier 2 and 3 cities) from the offline to online medium and what is the potential of the shift at present and in the future?

Although online retail in India is still in the early stage, it is catching up with urban customers. However, there are reasons for the slow shift—low PC and Internet penetration. As of now, broadband access is expensive. The second

reason is that less number of people are using credit and debit cards. The condition is similar to what malls had faced in their early stage. Then, people were quite apprehensive about it; however, now it fits and gels well with the same people who denounced it once. The shift will definitely happen in the time to come as online shopping has a lot of advantages such as convenience, cost effectiveness, and time saving. Look at China's overall e-tail market size; it is expected to be neck to neck with the US in the next two to three years. Similarly, it will also grow in India.

Nowadays, the online medium is largely seen as a platform for promoting and enhancing brand images by retailers, and not for sales. Do you think this is the right strategy and why?

It is definitely happening. At this stage, Indian market and consumers are not yet ready for online retail. However, people are using online media to select the products as it offers a wide range of options with a chance to compare the merchandise provided by different retailers in the same product category. I do not think it is a strategy from a retailer's point of view. A website has great impact on offline businesses; customers access brands and their products on websites and then, buy it from the brand's brick and mortar outlets. We are not looking at the site as a separate business. It is an extension of our brand, which has a strong presence in the physical retail segment. We want to create the same experience for our customers online.

There are a lot of complaints from customers shopping at your site. What are you doing to address this issue?

In the beginning we were getting complaints but the number was not large, and in contrast with other retailers, its proportion is far lesser. The first step towards it is an acknowledgment of getting complaints in itself; nevertheless, it is our priority to respond to a customer's complaints in the shortest possible time through our state-of-the-art

(Contd)

Exhibit 11.3 (Contd)

customer support system. Apart from this, we have a return policy for merchandise where unsatisfied customers replace them or take their money back. As far as shipment of goods is concerned, we hardly suffer as we have a stock of every merchandise that Shoppers Stop showcases on its website. Meanwhile, if you look at the overall logistic scenario for online retail in India, undoubtedly, there is room for development.

You are leading the corporate strategy of Shoppers Stop; tell us what has been planned for the future of Shoppers Stop through online medium?
Our main focus is to build a multi-channel capacity. So far, I have said that online retail in India is small; consequently, our main effort is to build a linkage between offline and online models. There are lots of exercises going on in that direction. Customers' needs are fast changing and we need to recognize this change and align our capabilities accordingly. For example, a buyer has seen something at Shoppers Stop's offline store but later if he/she wants to purchase it online, we must have a proper channel to facilitate the customer's desire.

According to you, what is the most difficult part of running an online store at present?
Let us look at this from a retailer's point of view—it is very difficult to know a customer's behaviour. However, Shoppers Stop is using different analytics to understand the customer's changing behaviour. By using these analytics, we have been able to track and monitor the activities and the changing purchasing pattern of consumers. Beside this, retailers should stress towards weaving different channels into a single thread, especially if they have a multi-channel business model.

The e-commerce solution used by the retail chain has been developed by Novator, the Toronto-based online retail service provider. Two years ago, Novator opened a delivery office in Mumbai to support e-retailing opportunities. Novator offers a complete outsourced e-commerce solution incorporating Virtual Retailer, a fully integrated multi-channel platform. Novator's solution includes strategy, design, deployment, hosting, and monitoring with ongoing e-retail services and support.

Sources:
Adapted from an interview of Vivek Mathur, vice-president–e-commerce, Shoppers Stop, http://www.iamwire.com/2011/07/305/, last accessed on 1 July 2011.
'Shoppers Stop in e-commerce; launches website', published on 9 July 2008, http://www.indiaretailing.com/News.aspx?Topic=1&Id=2169, last accessed on 11 April 2012.
'Shoppers Stop launches online store with delivery across cities in India', published on 18 September 2008, http://www.alootechie.com/news/shoppers-stop-launches-online-store-with-delivery-across-cities-in-india, last accessed on 11 April 2012.

of the online customer, availability of right and trained manpower, and selection and evaluation of e-commerce solutions are cited as some of the challenges the large retail giant faced. Although e-commerce offers a lot of new business opportunities, it also poses many challenges. Besides many challenges in e-commerce application development, order fulfilment and logistics, and online payment processing, the following are some of the other challenges we need to discuss.

Unproven Business Models

In the formative years of the dot-com era, most businesses on the Internet were experiments in new areas and did not provide enduring sources of profit. This was the primary reason for closing down more than 90% of the pure e-commerce companies during the beginning of this century. Today, the surviving dot-com businesses have matured to a great extent. However, some of the businesses are at the experimental level and do not guarantee regular revenue. Portals that disseminate information and only rely on advertisement revenue may not be sustainable (barring a few such as Yahoo! and MSN) in the long run.

For example, there are many portals offering information on health and wellness. They have nothing to sell in particular, but only rely on advertisements by pharmaceutical companies and doctors. They need to reassess their business model. Thus, the products or services any e-commerce organization chooses to offer must be e-commerce friendly. Products that require touch and feel before buying, products that are not available in standard packaging and brands, etc., may not be suitable for e-commerce.

Requirement to Change Business Processes

The process of procurement, storage, and logistics is different in e-commerce and has changed from the traditional brick-store businesses. The e-commerce organization has to carefully redesign and integrate various processes to suit the new electronic business. Traditional sections of departments and management hierarchy may pose hindrances and bottlenecks in the process of order processing and shipments.

For example, traditional businesses may require goods to be present at the warehouse and inspected before being shipped to the customer. However, in electronic retail, shipping of flowers to a customer in Chennai from New Delhi would not be possible. The e-retailer would collaborate with a local supplier in Chennai, who is instructed to deliver a bouquet to a customer in that city. This would require bypassing certain business rules and may call for mutual trust with the local supplier. It would require business confidence that the supplier would deliver the required product in good quantity and perfect quality. Merchandise planning and demand analysis is also difficult in electronic retail, as compared to traditional retail businesses.

Channel Conflicts

Companies selling via the Internet as well as brick stores may find their interests conflicting at many places. In electronic storefront orders, the goods directly reach the end consumer; distributors and sellers may feel a threat to their existence. Most of the time, it is seen that retailers tend to reduce prices in an e-store. The sale at the brick store may drop because the retailer may tend to sell more on the Internet as a result of reduction in prices. The e-commerce business tends to keep the prices low because there are fewer overheads in administration and inventory carrying costs. The other reason for selling more at the electronic storefront is that retailers reduce prices in slack seasons and increase prices in peak hours. This can be efficiently managed over the Internet.

Some examples are prices of airlines and hotels. Their prices are low if the booking is done via the Internet. This is because, if some seats of an airline go empty or rooms remain vacant, they are not contributing towards revenue generation. By offering the seats or rooms at a lesser price, they will at least bear the marginal costs.

Legal Issues

Proper laws governing Internet-based transactions have not yet evolved fully in India. Applicability, authenticity, and validity of e-mails, digital signatures, application of copyright laws, etc., are being evaluated by various government authorities. Electronic mails, purchase orders, bills, and other electronic documents must be recognized as valid and tenable in a court of law as an impetus to e-commerce business. Of late, e-mails and digital signatures are being recognized as valid proofs for any legal purpose. Value added tax (VAT) is yet another area that creates problems. As taxes are levied and shared by multiple government agencies at the local, state, or central level, there are no clear rules to guide retailers on the same. In e-commerce transactions, the place of billing, the place of dispatch of goods, and the place of delivery differ. If these three places fall in different jurisdictions, levy and submission of taxes would be an issue. A uniform goods and service tax (GST) would take care of it once it is implemented fully.

Security and Privacy

Security is one of the major challenges in the digital world. Despite security arrangements such as passwords, encryption, and firewalls, we occasionally come across news of website hacking, data pilferage, etc. As it is present on a public domain, the Internet is more susceptible to unauthorized peeping. People are wary of divulging credit card-related information and personal details on the Internet because it can be tracked and then misused. Cybercriminals exploit the weaknesses and vulnerabilities in the Internet and often intrude into computer systems, retrieving passwords and banking information. Similarly, the security of an online e-payment system is a major concern, despite erecting sufficient security layers by the e-commerce business organizations.

E-COMMERCE SCENARIO IN INDIA

The 2011 research by the Internet and Mobile Association of India (IAMAI) and IMRB reports has pegged the e-commerce market at around ₹50,000 crore. The report seems bullish on India's growth in e-commerce services, and the amount is a mind-boggling sum for a country like India, which is still mostly rural. No wonder then that capital is chasing entrepreneurs and we may have India's first billion dollar Internet company. Exhibit 11.1 shows how e-commerce businesses are gaining momentum again. With the surge in PC penetration, Internet awareness, and computer literacy, people are using the Internet, more as an enabler and facilitator of tasks rather than for mere messaging and entertainment. The characteristics of the Indian e-commerce scenario are summarized as follows:

- Travel industry spending still dominates, while other services continue to lag.
- Digital downloads is a new and growing category of online expenditure in India.
- E-commerce still remains a small part of the online activities of Indian net users.
- Air tickets continue to dominate the travel commerce business.
- Online shopping is pretty much dominated by electronic goods and peripherals.
- The increase in finance-related transactions is heartening; it shows a growing trust and convenience of e-commerce for the upper middle class.
- There are many start-ups in other online segments but the result is still elusive.
- Credit cards and debit cards dominate payment options; offline methods such as cash on delivery and cash cards are catching up.
- Trust still remains a huge obstacle in online purchases. Online retailers have to come up with a strategy for creating trust.

In India, the relationship between the Internet and e-commerce has crossed the nascent stage. According to recent estimates, there were 121 million Internet users in December 2011, out of which 97 million were active users. The e-commerce market, which was ₹19,688 crore at the end of 2009, grew to a whopping ₹46,500 crore in December 2011.

The online travel market consists of 81% of the total e-commerce market, estimated at ₹38,000 in December 2011. Another area that has shown significant growth is the financial services market, which is around 8% of the total e-commerce market, such as online insurance payments and transactions through trading accounts, which grew from ₹1540 crore to an estimated ₹2700 crore by December 2011.

Digital downloads have been gaining momentum and were expected to grow to ₹1100 crore by the end of 2011. E-tailing, which includes purchases of durable products such as electronic items, home and kitchen appliances, as well as personal items such as apparel and jewellery, constitutes 8% of the overall e-commerce market in the country. This sector was expected to grow by 62% and touch ₹2700 crore (*Economic Times*, 11 March 2011).

Business Potential of Various Segments

Based on the revenue generated, e-commerce activities can be grouped under the following major groups as illustrated in Table 11.2.

Thus, the Internet audience is expected to accumulate 121 million users by 2013 and possess unlimited shelf space. It is not bound by operational timings and geographical boundaries, encourages credit card usage, and facilitates flexible banking hours, at a comparatively minuscule cost.

Table 11.2   E-commerce categories with revenue estimates

Category	Description	Revenue in December 2011	Revenue in 2007–2008
Travels	Air tickets, rail tickets, hotel booking	₹38,000 crore	₹7200 crore
Classifieds	Job, matrimonial, property, dating	₹3400 crore	₹820 crore
Financial services	Insurance, share-trading	₹2700 crore	₹900 crore
E-tailing	Shopping of consumer goods	₹2700 crore	₹1105 crore
Digital downloads	Downloading of songs, movies, pictures, etc.	₹1100 crore	Not available

SUMMARY

Electronic commerce refers to the use of the Internet and the web to transact business deals. It involves transactions between two organizations or individuals over a public network called the Internet. E-commerce runs via the world wide web (WWW). The WWW is the backbone of modern e-commerce. It is a system with universally accepted standards (protocols) for storing, retrieving, formatting, and displaying information using a client–server architecture.

WWW works around important concepts such as uniform resource locator (URL), hypertext transfer protocol (HTTP), hypertext mark-up language (HTML), and common gateway interface (CGI). The web addressing scheme, known as URL, makes hypermedia publishing possible despite many different protocols. A URL marks the unique location on the Internet where a file can be found. Hypertext transfer protocol is a communication standard used to transfer pages on the web. The language in which web pages are created is using a standard called HTML. It is used for creating hypertext documents containing text, graphics, sounds, images, etc. XML, an abbreviation for extensible mark-up language, is a further development over HTML. Common gateway interface

(CGI) is a standard interface between web servers and the applications

The new Internet-based business models use IT and the web for value addition to the existing products and services or provide the foundation for new products and services. These new Internet businesses are based on the Internet's many capabilities like communication, etc. The new e-commerce businesses can be grouped as information portals, social networking, digital service, entertainment, trade services, classified services, etc.

The most popular way of categorizing e-commerce is on the basis of the nature of participants in the trade. Based on this, e-commerce is classified into three major categories, called business-to-consumer (B2C) e-commerce, business-to-business (B2B) e-commerce, and consumer-to-consumer (C2C) e-commerce.

There are certain essential components for an electronic business to be successful. The essentials of e-commerce processes for successful operations and management are the right revenue model, high Internet penetration, an e-commerce portal, content and catalogue management, workflow management, collaboration and logistics, and e-payment processing.

E-commerce requires alternative payment systems. There are many accepted alternatives such as credit cards, debit cards, net banking payments, electronic fund transfers, prepaid cash cards, and electronic bill payment options. Establishing an e-payment mechanism that is reliable and secure on the e-commerce portal is crucial.

From an electronic storage of corporate profiles, brochures, and product catalogues to online trading and e-business empowerment, e-commerce has come a long way. E-commerce is redefining businesses and how they deal with their customers, suppliers, and other business partners.

Besides many challenges in e-commerce application development, order fulfilment and logistics, and online payment processing, there are challenges in the form of unproven business models, business process change requirements, channel conflicts, legal issues, security and privacy, etc.

The latest research (by IAMAI and IMRB) reports value the e-commerce market at around ₹50,000 crore by the end of 2011. The report seems highly optimistic for a country like India, which is still mostly rural. The online travel market tops the e-commerce market at an estimated ₹38,000 in December 2011, followed by classified services at ₹3400 crore, financial services at ₹2700 crore, and e-tailing at ₹2700 crore.

KEY TERMS

Business-to-business (B2B) e-commerce A form of e-commerce that involves buying and selling of goods and services between two organizations on the Internet.

Business-to-consumer (B2C) e-commerce A form of e-commerce that involves retailing products and services to individual consumers.

Consumer-to-consumer (C2C) e-commerce A form of e-commerce that involves consumer to consumer transaction over the Internet.

Common gateway interface (CGI) A standard interface between web servers and the applications.

Content management A process that provides a structured and easy approach to change the contents, usually with a tool, whenever needed.

Digital contents Contents on a website such as news, movies, and music that are traded online.

Digital wallet An electronic smart card system that can be used for making payments.

Domain name A particular web address represented by an Internet protocol (IP) address.

Dynamic website A website that changes its contents in the next refresh to show the latest information such as prices, temperature, and score board.

E-commerce Use of the Internet and the web to transact business deals.

Electronic fund transfer Processes and technologies to capture and process money and credit transfers between the bank and businesses.

Electronic storefront A virtual shop that is engaged in trading and e-commerce.

Hypermedia Documents containing multiple forms of media such as text, graphics, video, and sound that can be searched like hypertext.

Hypertext A text in electronic form that has been indexed and linked by creating tags so that it can be searched.

Podcasting A method of publishing audio broadcasts via the Internet, allowing subscribers to download audio files onto their personal computer.

Portal An entry point to web pages that provide information, news, e-mail services, etc.

Secure electronic transaction (SET) A software encrypted digital envelop of digital certificates specifying the payment details for each transaction.

Secure sockets layer (SSL) An encryption method for websites that makes them highly secured.

Server scripts Small programs written to reach web servers, which obtains the data and gives it to the browser to process further.

Social networking A concept that links people who are like-minded and interested in similar subjects.

Static websites Web portals that do not change over a long period of time and generally display company information.

Trade services Online directories and a marketplace for buyers and sellers.

Uniform resource locator (URL) The addressing scheme for servers on the Internet.

User profiling Gathering information about web users, their website behaviour and choices, tastes, and preferences.

Workflow management A software to automate work processes and perform order processing and distribution activities.

World wide web (WWW) A system with universally accepted standards (protocols) for storing, retrieving, formatting, and displaying information using the Internet.

Extensible mark-up language (XML) A further development over HTML for web programming.

CONCEPT REVIEW QUESTIONS

1. What do you understand by e-commerce? Distinguish between pure e-commerce and click-n-brick e-commerce.
2. What is the world wide web? Explain URL, HTML, and CGI.
3. What do you understand by a protocol? On which protocol does the Internet work?
4. How has Internet technology changed business models? Describe any four Internet business models for e-commerce.
5. What are the various types of e-commerce and how has e-commerce changed consumer retailing and business-to-business transactions?
6. What are the essentials of e-commerce? Explain six essentials with examples.
7. What is electronic funds transfer? Describe suitable payment mechanisms for e-commerce businesses.
8. What are the various e-commerce businesses and technological trends?
9. What are the challenges faced by e-commerce businesses today?
10. What does the latest research on the buying habits of Internet users in India indicate?
11. What are the best products to sell through e-tailing?

CRITICAL THINKING QUESTIONS

1. 'The Internet may not make the brick-and-mortar business obsolete, but they will have to change their business models to achieve strategic advantages.' Do you agree with this statement? Why or why not?
2. Nowadays, the online medium is largely seen as a platform for promoting and enhancing brand image by retailers, and not for sales. Do you think this is the right strategy and why?
3. Many e-commerce business failures in the beginning of the last decade were termed 'dot-com burst'. Do your research and find out what could be the reason for such failures.

MIS DEVELOPMENT

Most B2C e-commerce ventures take the form of a retail business portal on the WWW. Whether a huge retail web store like Amazon.com or a small speciality online retailer, their primary focus is to develop, operate, and manage the website successfully. Soon after successfully completing your MBA degree, you decide to become an e-entrepreneur.

Exercise

1. Select a product or service that you want to deal in. Make a detailed plan to develop an e-commerce portal accordingly.

2. Check out the B2C e-commerce sites that match your products and style on the Internet. Make a list of such sites that appeal to you.
3. Develop a blueprint of activities that you will perform.
4. A portal development involves several steps. Carry out these activities within the following framework:
   (a) Develop an e-commerce portal: Build and promote
   (b) Serve your customers: Services, transactions, and support
   (c) Manage the portal: Manage, operate, and protect

REFERENCES

Gorden, Davis and Margethe Olson, *Management Information Systems*, The McGraw-Hill Book Company, Singapore, 1996.

Hoque, Faisal, *E-Enterprise: Business Models, Architecture and Components*, Cambridge University Press, Cambridge, UK, 2000.

Jawadekar, Waman S., *Management Information Systems*, *Text and Cases*, Tata McGraw-Hill, New Delhi, 2008.

Joshi, Girdhar, *Information Technology for Retail*, Oxford University Press, New Delhi, 2009.

Kalakota, Ravi and Andrew B. Whinston, *Electronic Commerce: A Manager's Guide*, Addison-Wesley, Boston, 1997.

Kalakota, Ravi and Marcia Robinson, *E-Business: Roadmap for Success*, Addison-Wesley, Boston, 1999.

Laudon, Ken, Jane Laudon, and Rajanish Dass, *Management Information System*, Pearson Education, Singapore, 2010.

Morgan, Cynthia, 'Dead set against SET?', *Computerworld*, International Data Group, Massachusetts, 29 March 1999.

O'Brien, James, George M. Marakas, and Ramesh Behl, *Management Information Systems*, Tata McGraw-Hill, New Delhi, 2007.

Hampton, Keith, Lauren Sessions Goulet, Lee Rainie, Kristen Purcell, 'Social networking sites and our lives', 16 June 2011, http://www.pewinternet.org/Reports/2011/Technology-and-social-networks/Part-2.aspx?view=all, last accessed on 21 November 2011.

http://articles.economictimes.indiatimes.com/2011-03-21/news/29171192_1_online-travel-market-e-commerce-travel-insurance, last accessed on 11 March 2011.

www.iamai.in, last accessed on 11 March 2011.

CASE STUDY

SnapDeal.com: An E-commerce Entrepreneurial Saga

Kunal Bahl, co-founder and chief executive officer, Snap-Deal.com, is considered the poster boy of daily deals e-commerce business in India. In an interview, he shares his story about the journey of SnapDeal, its way forward, and the present scenario of the e-commerce market in India.

How did SnapDeal come into existence? What made you initiate the business plan?

The idea struck me when I came across an advertisement in Entertainment Publications (a priced discount coupon booklet on apparel, food, movies, and gizmos), selling over 10 million copies a year across 156 cities in the US to consumers who see it as a great bargain. This is because they recover the cost of the booklet within the first few transactions itself. The concept of coupons has, of course, been extremely successful in the US, with over 400 billion coupons released every year.

With an increased disposable income in India, rising Internet penetration, and willingness of retailers to use the Internet as a channel for customer acquisition, there was a very large untapped market. We realized that small business owners had the potential of changing the landscape of local merchant e-commerce in India. Thus, SnapDeal was born in February 2010. There are approximately 90 million Internet users in India. A substantial number of these users would be shopping online for various products and services. We were sure, that given the attractiveness of the SnapDeal platform, we would be able to attract these customers to buy goods and services through our e-coupons.

When SnapDeal started, what were your prime focus areas?

In just 15 months' time, the business continued to grow at around 50–60% month on month. Most of that happened as we were focused on getting or doing three things very correctly. Our prime focus was to create an excellent customer experience on the website. Secondly, when we started out, people said that the daily deals model has low barriers to entry. However, soon after we started out, we realized that the biggest barrier in this business is to build your brand. Presently, we have reached a point where in India, whenever a consumer thinks deals, they think SnapDeal. Achieving this status was not easy. Our vision for SnapDeal is that it needs to be participating in consumer's lives everyday. Customers write in to us to say that when they get to office in the morning, before they check Facebook, they check SnapDeal. To us, even if there are 50 people out there who are doing this right now, we know that if we maintain the trajectory of our progress and customer centricity, we will have 5 million people doing that eventually every day.

What was the idea behind SnapDeal? How has the experience been so far?

In September 2011, about a year and a half of our starting the offline couponing business, a couple of small retailers approached us and discussed the idea of starting the service on the Internet. It struck us that when a small merchant is saying that the Internet is working for him as a means of customer acquisition, this must be a watershed moment in the evolution of local advertising and e-commerce in India. At that time, content companies sold impressions on the Internet through banner ads and typically fleeced smaller advertisers into paying them clicks-per-month (CPM) rates with no conversions to offline sales. Hence, those small merchants told us that if we did something on the Internet, they were ready to do it with us, and then there was no looking back for us.

However, we did not know anything about the Internet and spent a lot of time understanding the medium. We also invested a lot of effort in selecting and registering the domain name. Initially, we did not even have the .com domain and when SnapDeal launched, it was SnapDeal.in. We bought the .com three months later for $3000 and we thought that was a lot of money. At that time, our website was really shabby; however, over a period of time, we improved and built an excellent technology team, who, in turn re-built the entire platform. It would be fair to say that SnapDeal as a technology platform is one of the most robust sites in India that supports over 1.2 million visitors every day and still loads in less than one second.

We gradually saw our traffic growing and around September 2010, we decided to take the brand to the next level and hence, planned to go on television (TV). We planned our media in such a manner that we were actually able to track our return on investment (ROI) and this resulted in us getting a disproportionate ROI from the campaign. Thus, doing TV was a net positive investment for us.

How would you differentiate your products/services?
SnapDeal is an online discount deals platform for products and services ranging from dining and travel to movies, spa, gadgets, and luxury products across 50 cities in India. Consumers can buy the deals online and redeem the deal at a merchant location by showing the voucher or in the case of a product deal, the product gets shipped directly to the consumer's home.

Since its inception, SnapDeal.com has been into innovation and creation. This is evident in the number of retailers that we work with across the country, the categories that are showcased on the site, the unique option pricing model that we follow, and the customer-centric focus that we have in everything we do. Due to our ongoing efforts, SnapDeal now has over a 70% market share in India. We are also unique from the perspective of offering deals across multiple categories—restaurants, spas, and other local merchants, but also branded products such as perfumes, watches, bags, sunglasses, and mobile phones, among others, at great prices as well.

What was the initial range of products or deals? Do you plan to introduce further verticals to your business?
We constantly innovate on the products and services that are showcased on the platform. Currently, there are three broad verticals—branded products and accessories, travel, and lifestyle services. Within each of these verticals, there are sub-categories, which deal with a variety of products and services ranging from electronics to dining, health and beauty, entertainment, etc. Going forward, the idea is to keep innovating and offer customers a wide array of choices.

It is due to these innovations that we have been able to grow to eight million subscribers in a short span, and we continue to grow at the rate of one new subscriber every passing second. We are currently amongst the top 20 most visited websites in the country, and are rated the leading e-commerce company as per the Dataquest/Sapient consumer survey 2011.

What were your initial challenges?
One of the initial challenges was to hire people so that we can expand rapidly. We started operations from a residential area, which made it extremely difficult to hire people. Prospective employees did not turn up for interviews. We did not have good technology talent when we started, and that proved to be a big challenge given we were building an e-commerce platform. However, we were able to weather many of these challenges of attracting bright, talented professionals, and today, we have a team of more than 400 talented professionals in our organization across the country, which is expected to grow to 700 team members by the end of 2011. One of the most difficult tasks was convincing investors to fund our venture. We approached 15 venture capitalists and managed to get funds from just one. While some investors liked our idea, they believed that the Indian market would not embrace it. One investor rejected my proposal within five minutes of presenting it. His reasoning was customers did not want coupons as they loved to haggle personally.

Pursuing retailers was another big challenge because they were averse to trying something new. To them, we were just sales guys, not dissimilar to the ones they met every day. Rohit Bansal, (co-founder of Snapdeal) and I would often sit outside restaurants for hours to meet the managers. Over a period of time, we have expanded to a large number of cities and categories, including travel and products.

How did you build the human resource pool at the initial stage and what is your functional hierarchy?
It was not easy to find the right people for the right kind of role. And being a start-up, that was the most important element of building a successful firm. Having a good assessment process did help our cause. Our company is streamlined into various departments that handle specific roles. This include business development, logistics, inventory sourcing, content, production, technology, online

and offline marketing, human resources, accounts, and customer support teams, among others.

What is your target group?

Given the wide array of products and services that are on offer across various cities and various categories, our target audience is within the age group of 18–40 years. This includes students and first-time jobbers to the mid- and top-level management. A tattoo deal has wide acceptance among the younger age groups, whereas an attractive travel package to Bhutan or Kuala Lumpur draws the attention of those who are slightly older.

Given the inherent attractiveness of the platform, any customer who is aware of it, generally subscribes to the services. The challenge is to retain her and ensure a seamless experience, to ensure that she comes back to the website. A constant feedback process through various channels also ensures that we get the right set of clients for our customers.

Did you have any financial assistance while starting out? What is your revenue generating model?

Our first angel investment was ₹40 lakhs (in equal amounts) that my co-founder, Rohit Bansal, and I had put from the savings. In December 2010, we raised $12 million from two private equity players. This time, we had the choice of selecting among five investors who were eager to finance Snapdeal. Snapdeal has overcome various challenges to be where it stands today. We will continue to scale our business efficiently and aggressively and innovate with new marketing initiatives.

We charge a marketing fee of 20–30% from the merchant, on every voucher sold through the platform. It is a free-of-cost service to the end customer. When we started, our initial target was to sell 100 deals per day; however, within six to nine months, we were selling over 1000 deals per day. Today, the site is ranked twenty second in terms of traffic and was rated the leading e-commerce site in terms of traction by the Dataquest/Sapient Nitro E-commerce Survey 2011. By the end of 2011, Snapdeal will have a turnover of over ₹100 crore.

What kind of after-sales services do you provide to your customers?

Customer satisfaction is our primary goal. We try and ensure that each and every customer has a seamless experience after buying goods and services from our website. We also request feedback from our customers, and we strive to never leave a customer dissatisfied with our services. We have a 'no questions asked' refund policy in case any of the customers is unhappy for whatever reason.

We ensure that the customer gets attention from the merchant. The merchant has to work with a customer-centric value. We need to bridge the gap between expectations and delivery. One way to bridge the gap can be ensuring through training and education that the merchants and their staff treat the consumers well. Finally, if there is an issue with the customer, then there should be a 'no questions asked' money back guarantee. In case there is a merchant who is a repeat offender, for whatever reason, we make sure that the merchant is blacklisted. Hence, in our case, such things happen with less than 5% of the deals we sell and this is because of the checks that we perform time and again with solid back end processes.

Are you optimistic about the growth of e-commerce? What do you have to say about Indian consumers' online habits?

India's e-commerce industry is experiencing a spurt in growth in sectors such as online travel, e-retailing, daily deals, jobs, and matrimony. Though the growth in all of these sectors has been more than expected in the recent past, there is a lot more potential, which is waiting to be tapped.

Highly concentrated urban areas with very high literacy rates, a vast rural population with a fast increasing literacy rate, a rapidly growing Internet user base, technology advancement and adoption, and such other factors make India a dream destination for e-commerce players. The consumer behaviour has definitely changed and there are a lot of reasons for the same. The Internet allows you to do so many things that the interest and confidence of the consumers to buy online has increased. That is probably the reason why India is the fastest growing market for Facebook. There is significantly and increased propensity among consumers to buy things online and that propensity is different among consumers in Tier I and Tier II cities. For Tier I consumers, e-commerce means convenience because cities are large and there is too much traffic and too little time. In smaller cities, e-commerce helps them meet their aspirations. For instance, today if we are selling Reebok sunglasses, we are providing people in Guntur an access to these products and also at a deep discount.

Speaking about the overall e-commerce market in India, right now we are seeing a lot verticalization taking place. Do you think verticalization is the way to go for Indian e-commerce players?

I do not think so, because in India, everyone will try to do everything and try to become an Amazon. Presently, the market is divided; from an e-commerce format standpoint, into catalogue e-retailers and people like us, who feature limited, deal oriented, inventory. In our view when multiple companies sell the same stuff at the same time, while there is differentiation on service quality, eventually there is margin erosion. Hence, we like our strategy of value based pricing of unique inventory across categories as it helps to sustain significantly higher margins; we pick what we want to sell, given we are an impulse-based commerce platform.

What are your expansion plans? Where do you see SnapDeal five years from now?

We are currently competing with ourselves; the question of how to grow faster is the one that keeps us up at night. We continue to rapidly grow our footprint across India and by end of 2011 we plan to extend our footprint to 100 cities. In addition to the aggressive organic growth plans, SnapDeal is on the lookout for small-sized acquisitions and we have a target to seal two deals in the range of USD 1 million each in the next three to six months. We are looking at small companies that are riding on innovations and great ideas.

In the next couple of quarters, we will become a strong player in the products space as well. We started product deals a couple of months back and the day we started, our vendors (who also supply to all e-commerce companies in India) told us that they have never seen such volumes from an e-commerce company in such short periods of time. The beauty is that we are not even doing COD (cash on delivery) yet, which accounts for up to 80% sales for many Indian e-commerce companies. We are targeting to cross ₹100 crore of revenue by fiscal year 2011 and a lot of this will come from deals, with products and travel being a part of it.

Discussion Questions

1. What are the reasons for the success of SnapDeal in a very short span of time?
2. What were the challenges faced by the promoters of SnapDeal and how did they overcome them?
3. Going by the experience of SnapDeal, do you still think that the Indian e-commerce market is immature?
4. What lessons do your learn from this case regarding development of a successful e-commerce business?

Sources:
'Digital marketing: Snapdeal—An entrepreneurial saga', http://dqindia.ciol.com/content/top_stories/2011/111051001.asp, last accessed on 16 August 2011.
'Today, when consumers think deals, they think SnapDeal!', http://www.alootechie.com/interviews/when-consumers-think-deals-they-think-snapdeal, 31 May 2011, last accessed on 17 November 2011.
http://www.bizxchange.in/u47/S-6P-6A-2011081620110816165 3176908ae33292T-1N-/Success-Story.html, last accessed on 16 August 2011.

12

Decision Support Systems

Decision support systems couple the intellectual resources of individuals with the capabilities of the computer to improve the quality of decisions. It is a computer-based support system for management decision-makers who deal with semi-structured problem. Note that the term decision support system, like management information system and other terms in the field of management support systems (MSS), is a content-free expression; that is, it means different things to different people. Therefore, there is no universally accepted definition of DSS.

—Efraim Turban

LEARNING OBJECTIVES

After studying this chapter, you will be able to

- define decision-making
- appreciate the business value of improved decision-making
- differentiate between types of decisions
- know the methods of selecting decision alternatives
- get acquainted with the concepts of a decision support system (DSS)
- appreciate DSS trends
- get a view of business analytics (BA) and business intelligence (BI)
- understand BI tools such as OLAP, GIS, and DVS
- know how to use DSS with modelling tools
- use data mining for DSS
- understand executive support systems (ESS)

EXHIBIT 12.1

Mahindra Finance: Improving Decisions by Using Business Intelligence Tools

Mahindra and Mahindra Financial Services Limited (MMFSL) is one of India's leading non-banking finance companies (NBFC). A ₹15,000-crore group, MMFSL's rural financing is considered as the cornerstone of poverty reduction, rural development, and inclusive growth in many parts of the country. With loans to over 15,50,000 customers belonging to the low-income groups, MMFSL has proved to be a catalyst in helping rural India surge ahead in a big way. Since 1945, the Mahindra Group, employing more than 8700 employees, has remained partners in the progress of rural India through both growth and turbulence.

Mahindra Finance has increasingly leveraged IT to drive operational efficiency and improve decision-making. The use of business intelligence (BI) tools enabled the management to attain greater customer insights and undertake strategic planning.

Need for BI

Managing a huge customer base of around 1.5 million with equally increasing transactions required an MIS reporting and data analysis solution, which generated and scheduled reports, helping the management track performance and day-to-day operations. BI was considered an appropriate tool to collect the required information to be observed in real time. This is expected to help realize productivity gains.

Challenges

As the top management's expectations were huge, the challenges were immense for Suresh Shanmugam, Head, Business IT Solutions. BI was supposed to project a clear picture, to define the corporate strategy, and to drive profitability for the company. 'The top management understands that data they received through the system would enable them to understand the market pulse, identify strengths and weaknesses, while measuring the progress of the company from time to time', says Shanmugam. An automated e-mail was of prime importance. While the IT team had initiated an SMS solution, it was restricted to providing only the summary and not the details. The details were sought as part of spreadsheet-driven reports.

Solution

Since BI as a technology is still in its nascent stages, the selection of the right technology was the toughest of all tasks for the IT head. The market is invaded by a plethora of solutions, with each vendor vouching to have the best solution. After a detailed evaluation process, MMFSL went ahead to deploy 1KEY Scheduler and multidimensional data analysis tool from MAIA Intelligence. The budget not being a constraint for MMFSL, the amount allocated for BI was to the tune of ₹50 lakhs.

The team found that the 1KEY Touch BI tool possessed the ability to create a single dashboard using reports from disparate systems. Besides other specified prerequisites, this is an added advantage. The business agility feature enabled operational managers to monitor productivity on a real-time basis and make tactical decisions on resources allocated within the team as well as across zonal teams, which was hitherto done based on backdated information. The management was not convinced about investing in technology during such cash crunch times. The IT team took a decision to do a proof of concept (PoC) to generate reports from various businesses and back-office applications, which could help understand the data in terms of sales collection. The outcome of this had a positive impact on the management.

Implementation Plan

Implementing 1KEY BI was done with certain objectives in mind, which included, providing business users with clear opportunities to improve their business performance through information delivery. The information was reflective of the business communities' processes and their outcomes and provides appropriate levels of formatting, timeliness, history, detail, and quality as per the project specifications. As per the plan, MMFSL hired two professionals, one with technical knowledge to implement, and the other to impart training to the business users and IT software group. During the implementation process, certain requirements of reports got easily resolved, while a few were complex and time-consuming. It was done in a phased manner to observe the impact and consequences thereof. The project team delivered the best through 1KEY Scheduler where mass mailing was made possible to convert the information into reports.

Business Benefits

According to Shanmugam, the success of the existing 1KEY BI implementation boosted their confidence to procure the newly launched 1KEY Touch. This was an

(Contd)

Exhibit 12.1 (Contd)

interactive dashboard based on the rich Internet application (RIA) technology. Implementation of 1KEY has resulted in 30–35% productivity improvement at the IT level in terms of meeting the users' reporting analysis needs. 'We observed 20–25% productivity increase at the business user level due to the user-friendly interface of the solutions and its capability to provide on the fly ad hoc reporting analysis', says Shanmugam. Some of the other advantages that MMFSL saw were faster decision-making owing to the interactive graphics, gauges, and filters, and deeper insights into the business user pay out scenarios. Shanmugam intends to implement BI at the finance level in 2012.

Sources:
Adapted from a case study, 'Mahindra and Mahindra Financial Services Ltd', http://www.maia-intelligence.com/pdf/MMFSL-ITNext-Oct-11.pdf, last accessed on 12 December 2011.
'Enlightening with intelligence—ITNEXT', www.itnext.in/content/enlightening-intelligence.html, last accessed on 12 December 2011.
'Mahindra Finance gains comprehensive insights using BI', http://www.blog.maia-intelligence.com/mahindra-finance-gains-comprehensiv, last accessed on 12 December 2011.
http://www.issuu.com/itnext/docs/it_next_october_2011
http://www.mahindrafinance.com/aboutus.aspx, last accessed on 12 December 2011.

MMFSL opted to implement a BI tool to extract data from various legacy and enterprise solutions to improve decision-making and bring in efficiency in operations (Exhibit 12.1). The powerful dashboards provided by the 1KEY BI tool helped managers improve decision-making. This resulted in a 30–35% productivity improvement at the IT level in terms of meeting the users' reporting analysis needs. The initiative helped senior managers work with a user-friendly interface for software with graphical representation of data. The managers were able to improve decision-making with the on the fly ad hoc reporting analysis.

Thus, organizations need information systems that can support the diverse needs of decision support and information management by their business managers. In this chapter, we will briefly discuss decision-making, the value of improved decision-making, and how various decision alternatives are arrived at. We will discuss at length the decision support tools, analytics, and information systems used by managers to meet their professional requirements of decision-making. We will concentrate on how IT has significantly strengthened the role that information systems play in supporting decision-making activities in the modern organization.

DECISION-MAKING

A decision is a choice out of several alternatives available to the decision-maker to achieve some objective at a given point of time. Decision-making is a process of selecting an optimum or the most suitable alternative from a number of alternatives. Thus, a decision is an outcome or the end-result, while decision-making is a process. Organizational decision-making is a complex process, especially at the higher echelons of management. Such complexity is the result of factors such as knowledge of decision variables, job responsibility, feasibility of the decision outcome, ethical and moral values of the decision-makers, and the probable impact on business. Similarly, the personal values of the decision-maker play a very important role in organizational decision-making. Sometimes a sound business decision may clash with the personal values and ethics of the decision-maker.

The role of a decision support system in the process of decision-making is to provide facts and figures so that decision-making in a business is improved.

Business Value of Improved Decision-making

A business decision represents a course of action selected from a number of possible alternatives. In order to achieve certain objectives, a number of decisions are made in the process of carrying out businesses. Right, timely, and improved decisions are necessary for the survival of a business. Earlier, business decisions were made by the managers; however, now with the availability of information, decisions are made at all hierarchical levels of an organization. According to Laudon (2010), decisions are made at all levels of the firm and some of these decisions are common, routine, and numerous. Although the value of improving any single decision may be small, improving hundreds or thousands of 'small' decisions adds up to a large value for the business annually.

Table 12.1 estimates the business value of some of the important but improved decisions made in the day-to-day operations of D. B. Engineering Pvt. Ltd, a small and medium enterprise (SME), having around ₹100 million as turnover. It illustrates some of the key decisions made by the managers of the company, where the new system of improvement may improve the quality of decisions. The table provides selected estimates of approximate value in terms of cost savings, interest calculation, and missed opportunity costs.

Types of Decisions

Managers in the organization make a range of decisions in their routine and non-routine job activities. The types of decisions are based on the decision activities at the organizational levels. Various decisions are made at different levels of the organization. Some decisions are based on predefined rules and form part of the standard operating procedures (SOPs) of the organization. There are many decisions where the outcome is not known or uncertain. Based on the nature of the decisions, the nature of development of alternatives and choices vary. This also affects the design of the information system to support the decision-making process. Thus, decisions can be classified on three counts:

- Purpose of decision-making
- Level of programmability
- Knowledge of outcome

Purpose of Decision-making

We have discussed earlier that a management is classified into different levels such as executive, strategic, managerial, knowledge, and operational. Based on these management functions,

Table 12.1 Examples of the business value of improved decisions

Basic strategies	Decision-maker	Number of annual decisions	Value of a right decision	Annual value
Follow-up with customers for repeat order	Sales manager	12	₹100,000	₹1,200,000
Selection of vendor with the lowest price quotation	Purchase manager	6	₹75,000	₹450,000
Decision on raw material inventory level	Store manager	300	₹5000	₹1,500,000
Production scheduling	Production manager	150	₹6000	₹900,000
Manufacturing machinery maintenance and upkeep	Plant manager	12	₹50,000	₹600,000
Timely order confirmation and execution	Account manager	24	₹50,000	₹1,200,000
Timely debt follow-up and recovery	Finance executive	36	₹5000	₹180,000
Funds management	Finance manager	12	₹5000	₹60,000

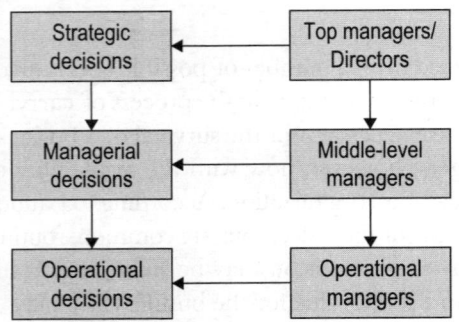

Fig.12.1   Decision-making at different levels of management

Anthony (1965) has categorized organizational decisions into three categories—strategic planning decisions, management control decisions, and operational control decisions. Figure 12.1 illustrates decision-making at different levels of management.

Strategic planning decisions   These decisions are targeted at achieving organizational objectives, resources, and long-term policies. The top management takes such decisions that are usually long-term in nature and involve large investments. The decision to shift the manufacturing unit from one zone to another, the decision to enter or exit from a new market, etc., are strategic planning decisions.

Managerial control decisions   These decisions are concerned with the issues of smooth and effective implementation of policies. These decisions are taken by managers at the middle-level management. Such decisions ensure that the organizational resources are utilized in an optimum manner. These decisions are related to evaluating and choosing new products and services, deciding on the right product mix, and communicating new ideas across and beyond the organization. The decision to start or stop a marketing campaign, the decision to create and approve an expenditure budget, etc., fall in this category of decision-making.

Canara Bank's decision to implement the core banking solution in some of its regional rural banks was taken with the aim of exercising managerial control over the banks and to provide customers with an advanced banking experience, as illustrated in Exhibit 12.2.

Operational control decisions   These decisions are made to ensure that the day-to-day work is carried out in an efficient manner. These decisions are taken by the operation-level managers and deal with the routine operations of the organization. Decisions related to production scheduling,

---

EXHIBIT 12.2

Canara Bank: Implementing IT Solutions for Rural Bank Initiative

Canara Bank has partnered with Wipro Infotech, the provider of IT and business transformation services to drive its regional rural bank (RRB) initiative. The contract is aimed at providing a technology-driven, core banking solution for three of Canara Bank's sponsored regional rural banks—Pragathi Gramin Bank (Karnataka), South Malabar Gramin Bank (Kerala), and Shreya Gramin Bank (Uttar Pradesh).

'Wipro plans to deliver extremely robust, scalable and flexible centralized core banking solution aligned with the corporate mission, strategy and business plan of the regional rural banks', remarked Anand Sankaran, Senior Vice President, Wipro Infotech. The project aims to integrate around 900 branches and offices in a phased manner, which include branches, extension counters, service units, head offices, regional offices, training centres, other back offices, data centres, disaster recovery centres, project offices which would also operate as the data centre monitoring unit, and a network operations centre (NOC). Wipro, with its practices in governance, process excellence, and integrated service delivery, will deliver business-IT alignment by deploying and implementing the core banking solution and the identified delivery channels. The company

(Contd)

Exhibit 12.2 (Contd)

will also set up a 24-hour centralized helpdesk facility for the project, covering applications, data centres, networks, security, and end-user systems.

This decision of Canara bank highlights the customer-centric approach to its regional rural banks. With this implementation, the rural banks will also be in compliance with statutory and regulatory requirements including MIS.

Sources:
'Canara Bank implements CBS', www.oracle.com/us/industries/financial-services/045530.pdf, last accessed on 22 November 2011.
'Wipro to provide IT solution for Canara's regional rural banks', www.biztech2.com, 11 March 2011, last accessed on 22 August 2011.
http://www.domain-b.com/finance/banks/canara_bank/2004 1009_computerised.htm, last accessed on 22 August 2011.

purchasing, and inventory are part of operation control decisions. These include decisions to increase or decrease inventory levels, to control the credit limit of customers, to offer special discounts to customers, etc.

Table 12.2 shows the various management levels and the types of decisions taken by them. You can see that at the operation level, the decisions are routine, while at the strategic level, the decisions are related to long-term goals and policies.

Level of Programmability

Based on the level of programmability, decisions made at all management levels can further be classified into programmed or non-programmed decisions. What Simon (1965) called as programmed and non-programmed decisions, Gorry (1971) named as structured and unstructured decisions. This classification is based on the nature of rules applicability in decision-making processes.

Structured/Programmed decisions   Structured or programmed decisions are well defined, rule-based, and have some SOPs, which may be used to arrive at a decision. These decisions are repetitive, routine, and involve a definite and well-defined decision-making process. These are also called programmed decisions because certain rules, methods, and guidelines can be

Table 12.2   Decisions at various levels of management in the organization

Management level	Examples of business decisions
Strategic	• Do we need to start a new business line?
	• Can we go for overseas markets and export our products?
	• Should we relocate our factory to a new SEZ?
Management	• Do we need to change processes to minimize production wastage?
	• By how much should the budget increase to accommodate the extra expenditure?
	• Is it necessary to create a new post in the sales hierarchy for a senior regional manager?
Knowledge	• Do we introduce new designs of the products?
	• Is it necessary to start a new advertising campaign highlighting the new features in the product?
	• Should we switch over to new office tool MS-365?
Operational	• Must we stop further purchases till the existing inventory lasts?
	• Can we send soft copies of bills to clients in place of paper ones?
	• Should we increase the reminder frequency for outstanding bills?

applied to develop alternatives. Simply put, if you can apply a rule when deciding what to do, it is a structured decision. MIS can be developed to engineer such rules and help the management take the right decisions. Sometimes, the system itself plays the role of a decision-maker, based on certain rules and methods.

For example, the system can be designed to stop order acceptance if more than the permitted level of payment is outstanding with the customer. This is purely a programmed decision. In addition, such decisions can be analysed, their effectiveness evaluated from time to time, and the rules changed to improve the system.

Modern techniques for making such decisions involve tools that include operation research, mathematical analysis, modelling and simulation, etc.

Unstructured/Non-programmed decisions   Decisions that are not well-defined and have no SOP are known as unstructured or non-programmed decisions. Unstructured decisions cannot be programmed and are thus called non-programmed decisions. These kinds of decisions are not very frequent but their stakes are bigger. This is one reason why such decisions are taken by senior-level managers. According to Gorry (1971), the unstructured decisions are the ones in which the decision-maker must provide judgment, evaluation, and insights into the problem definition. Each of these decisions is novel, important, and non-routine, and there is no well understood and agreed procedure for making them. Most often, the unstructured decisions are solved through judgement, intuition, and rule of thumb. Management information systems can help managers in such situations in a limited manner by identifying problems and providing relevant inputs.

For example, the decision to relocate the manufacturing unit to a new state or new economic zone can be supported by information about tax holidays, availability of raw material and manpower resources, saving on excise duty, etc., in the new zone.

Modern tools for unstructured decision-making include specialized data analysis applications, heuristic techniques, etc. Most of the decisions in the real world are either structured or unstructured. However, the decisions that do not fall in either of these two categories can be termed as semi-structured decisions.

Knowledge of Outcomes

Another approach of classifying decisions is based on the knowledge of the result of the decision. The result refers to the outcome of the decision once it is made and implemented. These are based on the degree of knowledge about the outcome of the decision. If the outcome is supposed to be certain, there is little risk involved. Therefore, the decision-making process is simple and based on certain rules. On the contrary, if the manager is not sure of the outcome of the decision, the decision is under high risk and the process is unstructured. On this basis, decision-making can be classified into three categories—decision under certainty, decision under risk, and decision under uncertainty.

Decision under certainty   Decision-making under certainty happens when the outcome of each alternative is known. This theory assumes that there is only one outcome for each alternative. In such a case, the decision-maker chooses the alternative with the optimum result. In this case, there is supposed to be little or no risk at all. For example, if a 5% reduction in the price of a product has a definite outcome of a 5% increase in sales, the decision to reduce the price would be termed a decision under certainty.

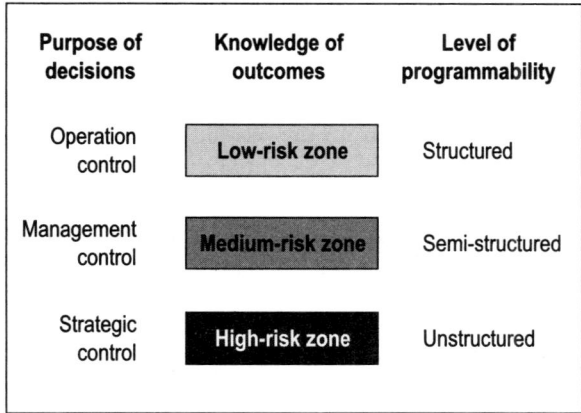

Fig. 12.2   Grid showing various types of decisions
and the risks they involve

Decision under risk   Decision-making under risk is carried out when there is a possibility of multiple outcomes for each alternative and a probability of occurrence can be attached to each outcome. In such cases, instead of optimizing the alternative, the manager optimizes the probable outcome. For example, if the manager has to make a choice between two actions, one offering a 5% probability of ₹2,00,000 profit and the other an 80% probability of profit of ₹20,000, the rational manager will choose the second alternative because it gives a higher expected value.

$$\text{Outcome} \times \text{Profitability} = \text{Expected value}$$
$$Alt1: 2,00,000 \times 0.05 = 10,000$$
$$Alt2: 20,000 \times 0.80 = 16,000$$

Decision under uncertainty   Decision-making under uncertainty takes place when there are a number of outcomes for each alternative and the probabilities of their occurrences are not known. The basic difference between decisions under risk and uncertainty is that in the case of the former, the probability is known, whereas in the case of the latter, it is not known. In this case, different methods are used, including treating each alternative with the same probability. For example, if the impact of various media advertising campaigns is not known, and the manager has to take a decision as to which media to choose, it would be a decision under uncertainty.

Figure 12.2 illustrates the various types of decisions and the risks they involve.

METHODS FOR DECIDING DECISION ALTERNATIVES

A decision-maker may use various methods to choose from several alternatives. The methods are primarily search processes to select the best alternative, which satisfies the maximum number of conditions. These methods assume that all alternatives are known to the decision-maker. We will discuss the following three methods for the selection of decision alternatives:

- Pay-off analysis
- Decision tree analysis
- Optimization techniques

Pay-off Analysis

When all the alternatives and their outcomes are not known (i.e., decision-making under risk and uncertainty), the decision is made applying the pay-off analysis. In the decision-making process, the manager chooses from the alternatives and calls the alternative his/her 'strategy' to achieve a goal or an objective. There are certain factors that affect the outcome of different strategies. It is assumed that these factors or conditions, also known as 'states of nature', are beyond the control of the decision-maker. The strategy, along with the conditions, determines the degree to which the goal is actually achieved. Thus, the achievement of the goal is measured in terms of pay-off.

In order to reach a conclusion, a pay-off matrix is constructed where the rows show the alternatives and the columns show the conditions or the states of nature with the probability of occurrence. Each cell (row and column) is an intersection of a strategy and a state of nature, and contains the pay-off. If the state of nature is known with certainty, the decision-maker selects the strategy that provides him the highest pay-off. Table 12.3 illustrates a typical pay-off matrix.

Let us understand the pay-off matrix with the help of an example. Datex Infocomm, a New Delhi-based uninterruptible power supply (UPS) manufacturer, faces stiff competition from its international competitors and the market seems stagnant. The management of Datex decides to change the price and ponders on the following three alternatives:

- Increase the price
- Decrease the price
- No change in price

There are three states of nature that affect the pay-off from each strategy.

- Competitor increases price
- Competitor does not act, maintains status quo
- Competitor decreases price

The various pay-offs (profit or loss) from the combination of strategy and conditions are given in the pay-off matrix in Table 12.4.

This matrix shows strategies that the company can adopt. The table also shows the states of nature with their probabilities of occurrence as well. These probabilities represent the likelihood of occurrence of the specific states of nature, either based on historical data or on the basis of personal judgment of the decision-maker. It is assumed that if Datex does not change the price and competition also does not change the price, Datex's gain is '5'. This is the status quo situation. If the price is changed by the company and the competitor responds by doing the same, the decision-maker evaluates the situation and calculates the expected value (EV). The decision is

Table 12.3 Pay-off matrix

		States of nature		
Strategies	N1	N2	N3	N4
S1				
S2		A		
		(pay-off)		
S3				

Table 12.4 Pay-off matrix

Decision alternatives (strategy)	States of nature			
	Increase 0.50	Decrease 0.20	No change 0.30	Expected value
Increase the price (S1)	5	3	7	5.20
Decrease the price (S2)	10	5	12	9.60
No change in the price (S3)	8	8	5	6.10

taken by choosing the decision alternative that has the maximum expected value of outcome. The expected values are calculated as follows:

$$\text{Expected value of strategy} = \text{Pay-off} \times \text{states of nature (1)} + \text{pay-off} \times \text{states of nature (2)} +$$
$$\text{pay-off} \times \text{states of nature (3)}$$
$$\text{EV of S1} = (5 \times 0.50) + (3 \times 0.20) + (7 \times 0.30)$$
$$= 2.50 + 0.60 + 2.10 = 5.20$$
$$\text{EV of S2} = (10 \times 0.50) + (5 \times 0.20) + (12 \times 0.30)$$
$$= 5.00 + 1.00 + 3.60 = 9.60$$
$$\text{EV of S3} = (8 \times 0.50) + (8 \times 0.20) + (5 \times 0.30)$$
$$= 4.00 + 1.60 + 1.50 = 7.10$$

The maximum expected value (gain) is found in strategy number two, that is, decrease the price. Thus, the decision-maker will select this strategy.

Decision Tree Analysis

A decision tree is a graphical representation of the sequence of decisions and actions based on various conditions applied during decision-making. The analysis of variables resembles a tree with its branches, and hence is called decision tree analysis.

We will explain the decision tree analysis with the help of the following example. Drugfarm Laboratories Ltd manufactures pharmaceutical products and is evaluating the options of marketing these products. The company has the choice of appointing its own medical representatives (MR) or selling the product through wholesales agents throughout the country. Based on these two modes of distribution, the company may have high or low market penetration and gains as shown in Table 12.5 and Fig. 12.3. The probabilities and net gains may be as follows:

$$\text{Expected pay-off for MR channel: } (0.60 \times 120) + (0.40 \times 80) = 104$$
$$\text{Expected pay-off for sales agents: } (0.70 \times 100) + (0.30 \times 60) = 88$$

The problem that the management of Drugfarm Laboratories faces is the selection of the distribution channel to be followed. Based on the aforementioned decision analysis, the management will obviously choose the channel that gives them maximum returns. The decision tree approach is useful when the management visualizes a series of decisions having alternative paths with associated probabilities.

Optimization Techniques

Operation research (OR) provides a plethora of optimization techniques that are used for decision-making. Operation research is a discipline that deals with the application of advanced analytical methods to help make better decisions. These techniques assume that all alternatives and their outcomes are known to the decision maker. Some of these techniques are linear

Table 12.5 Channel alternatives of Drugfarm Lab

Channel	High penetration	Net gains	Low penetration	Net gains
MR channel	0.60	₹120	0.40	₹80
Sales agents	0.70	₹100	0.30	₹60

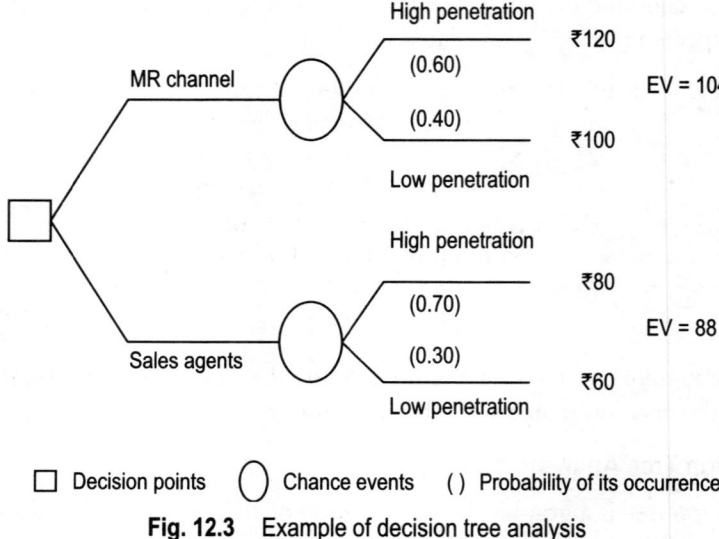

Fig. 12.3   Example of decision tree analysis

programming, integer programming, dynamic programming, queuing models, inventory models, capital budgeting, etc.

These techniques are part of operation research, which you may have already studied. We will not discuss these techniques in this text.

DECISION SUPPORT SYSTEM CONCEPTS

Having discussed the concept of decision-making and choosing from decision alternatives, we can discuss how decision support systems (DSS) are designed to help managers make decisions. DSS combine data and sophisticated data analysis models to support non-routine decision-making. Keen (1978) provides a classical definition—'Decision support systems couple the intellectual resources of individuals with the capabilities of the computer to improve the quality of decisions. It is a computer-based support system for management decision-makers who deal with semi-structured problems.' Thus, we can say that DSS are computer-based information systems that provide interactive information support to managers during the decision-making process. DSS use analytical models, a variety of databases, the decision-maker's insights and judgments, and an interactive, computer-based modelling process to support the making of semi-structured business decisions.

For example, the sales manager at Brainsoft India Inc. uses MIS to derive various sales reports such as monthly and quarterly sales comparisons, sales according to product, segment, salespersons, or geographical area, and so on. These are simple periodical and exception reports. On the other hand, a DSS is also capable of showing the effects on sales performance, based on factors such as promotional expenses or increase/decrease in a salesperson's initiative. Table 12.6 compares the information and decision support capabilities of MIS and DSS.

Components

Decision support systems rely on model-driven and data-driven systems. They use analytical models and buried legacy data as system resources. Buried legacy data refers to the data accumulated over

Table 12.6   Comparison between MIS and DSS in their decision support capabilities

Parameter	MIS	DSS
Scope	Basic form of management information	Advanced form of MIS
Capability	Provides information regarding performance of the business	Provides information regarding a specific problem or opportunity in decision-making
Information frequency	Periodic, demand-based, exception, and pre-specified reports	Specialized reports, and interactive inquiries and responses
Information format	Pre-specified reports and fixed format reports	Ad hoc, flexible, and adoptable reports
Processing methodology	Information generated by extraction of business data	Information produced by analytical modelling of business data
Purpose of information	Operates solely on operational efficiency	Helps in making effective decisions
Communication	Allows communication between managers from different areas in a business organization	Concerned with leadership and senior management in an organization, providing effective judgment support
Information flow	Allows flow of information in both upward and downward directions	Allows flow of information in only an upward direction
Examples of information	Sales orders, production scheduling, weekly sales reports, monthly budget variation	New business initiatives, plant relocation, company reorganization, mergers, acquisitions, etc.
Usage by	Usually middle and senior management	Usually senior and top management

a period of time through various data entries and reporting software used by the organization. This data is extracted with the help of applications such as data mining and online transaction processing tools. As such, the components of DSS are databases, DSS software tools, and models.

The DSS database is a collection of current or historical data from a variety of applications. The database could be separate data from various legacy applications or a massive database, which is updated by transaction processing systems and enterprise applications. Usually the DSS database is extracted from various databases to apply analytical methods, so that this process does not interfere with transaction processing and operations.

The DSS software tools contain systems that are used for data analysis. These tools are data mining tools, online analytical processing (OLAP) tools, etc. Besides these, there can be mathematical and analytical models available to the user for applying what-if analysis, sensitivity analysis, etc. Laudon (2010) defines a model as an abstract representation that illustrates the components or relationships of a phenomenon. A model may be a physical model (e.g., a model aeroplane), a mathematical model (e.g., an equation), or a verbal model (e.g., a description of a procedure for writing an order).

There are various models such as statistical models, forecasting models, and sensitivity analysis models that can be applied to the historical data of the organization. These models help establish a trend and thus support organizational decision-making.

Decision Support Trends

We discussed in Chapter 1 that the primary use of IT in information systems has been to support business managers with data and information that would help them make efficient and effective decisions during the course of managing the business. According to Gantz (1999), during the 1990s, both academic researchers and business practitioners began reporting that the traditional managerial focus originating in classic MIS (1960s), DSS (1970s), and executive information systems (EIS, 1980s) was expanding. The fast pace of new information technologies such as PC hardware and software suites, client–server networks, and networked PC versions of DSS/EIS software made decision support available to the lower levels of management, as well as non-managerial individuals, and self-directed teams of business professionals.

According to Kalakota (2001), this trend has been accelerated with the dramatic growth of the Internet, intranets, and extranets that network companies and their stakeholders. The e-business and e-commerce initiatives that are being implemented by many companies are also expanding the information and decision support uses and expectations of a company's employees, managers, customers, suppliers, and other business partners.

The availability and demand for high-end information paved the way for more sophisticated analytical tools like BI tools for decision support. We will discuss BI in more detail in this chapter.

BUSINESS ANALYTICS AND BUSINESS INTELLIGENCE

Business analytics (BA) can answer questions such as why is this happening, what if these trends continue, and what will happen next. In other words, querying, reporting, analytical processing, and alert tools can answer questions such as what happened, how many, how often, where the problem is, and what actions are needed. Therefore, business analytics refers to the skills, technologies, applications, and practices for continuous iterative exploration and investigation of past business performances to gain insight and drive business planning. Business analytics focuses on developing new insights and understanding business performance, based on data and statistical methods. In contrast, BI traditionally focuses on using a consistent set of metrics to measure past performance and guide business planning, which is also based on data and statistical methods. According to Turban (2005), BI involves acquiring data and information (and perhaps, even knowledge) from a wide variety of sources and utilizing them in decision-making. Technically, BA adds an additional dimension to BI—models and solution methods.

Business analytics makes extensive use of data, statistical and quantitative analysis, explanatory and predictive modelling, and fact-based management to drive decision-making. Businesses are open to any kind of analytics; however, domains such as retail sales, financial services, risk and credit, marketing, collections, fraud, pricing, supply chain, and transportation analytics are widely popular. Table 12.7 displays a list of some of the popular BI software.

Online Analytical Processing

In today's competitive and challenging world of business, managers demand information and answers to complex business queries. The information systems have invented many such tools to answer those queries. One of these tools is online analytical processing.

Online analytical processing, or OLAP as it is popularly called, is an approach to swiftly answer multidimensional analytical queries. OLAP is part of a broader category of BI, which also encompasses relational reporting and data mining. Typical applications of OLAP include business reporting for sales, marketing, management reporting, business process management (BPM), budgeting and forecasting, financial reporting, etc. Business process management is an approach that considers processes to be strategic assets of an organization that must be understood, managed, and improved to deliver value added products and services to clients.

Table 12.7   Popular BI software tools

BI tool	Offered by	Web address
1KEY AGILE	MAIA Intelligence	http://www.maia-intelligence.com/agile.htm
WebFOCUS	Information Builders	http://www.informationbuilders.com/business-intelligence
Oracle EPM, BI tools, Oracle Exalytics	Oracle Corp.	http://www.oracle.com/us/solutions/ent-performance-bi/index.html
IBM Congnos® Business Intelligence	IBM	http://www-01.ibm.com/software/analytics/business-intelligence.html
SAS Business Intelligence	SAS	http://www.sas.com/technologies/bi/
Microsoft Business Intelligence	Microsoft	http://www.microsoft.com/BI/en-us/pages/home.aspx
Elegant J BI Tools	Elegantj	http://www.elegantjbi.com/
BodhTree Business Intelligence	BodhTree BI Consulting Services	http://www.bodhtree.com/business-intelligence.php
TechAxes BI	TechAxes	http://www.techaxes.com/

According to O'Brien (2007), OLAP enables managers and analysts to interactively examine and manipulate large amounts of detailed and consolidated data from many perspectives. OLAP involves analysing complex relationships among thousands or even millions of data items stored in data marts, data warehouses, and other multidimensional databases to discover patterns, trends, and exception conditions.

For example, Pidilite Industries uses BI tools to make pricing decisions in the industry where the cost of raw material is dynamic and constantly changing.

As OLAP systems work online on real-time basis, sometimes, dedicated OLAP servers are recommended so that the real-time enterprise data is not disturbed during processing. In this case, the data is retrieved from corporate databases and stored in an OLAP multidimensional database for retrieval by front-end users (as shown in Fig. 12.4).

OLAP involves several operations including data consolidation, drill-down, and slicing and dicing.

Consolidation   Consolidation involves the aggregation of data. This process consolidates various kinds of data and provides analytical figures as per the query. For example, we can consolidate sales data for various sales offices, regions, zones, and countries.

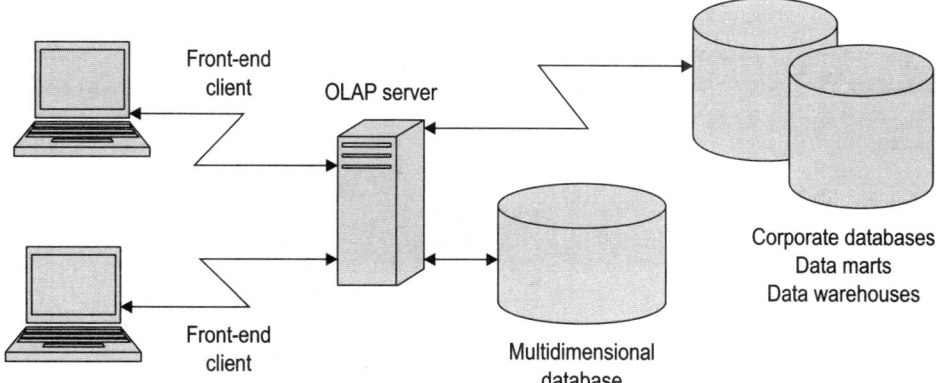

Fig. 12.4   OLAP may involve specialized OLAP servers

Drill-down   Drill down refers to the ability of the software to dig into the database and excavate data up to the most detailed level. For example, the financial data may be drilled down to monthly, weekly, daily, or per transaction levels.

Slicing and dicing   Slicing and dicing refers to the ability to look at the database from different angles. For example, one slice of the sales data of a garment retailing business may show product style-based sales figures for a month, while the other slice may show size or colour-based sales figures, as shown in Fig. 12.5.

Geographic Information Systems and Data Visualization Systems

Geographic information systems (GIS) and data visualization systems (DVS) are special forms of DSS that make the presentation of data easier to use, decipher, and act on. These forms of DSS present the data in the form of graphics, charts, tables, maps, digital images, animation, and three-dimensional presentations.

A geographic information system is a DSS that uses geographic databases to construct and display maps. The data, which is in the form of digitized maps, is used for planning and decision-making. GIS have modelling capabilities, which managers use to change data and revise business scenarios to arrive at a better solution. For example, retail companies and banks use GIS for finding better and profitable store locations and ATMs. Globally, companies such as Levi Strauss and

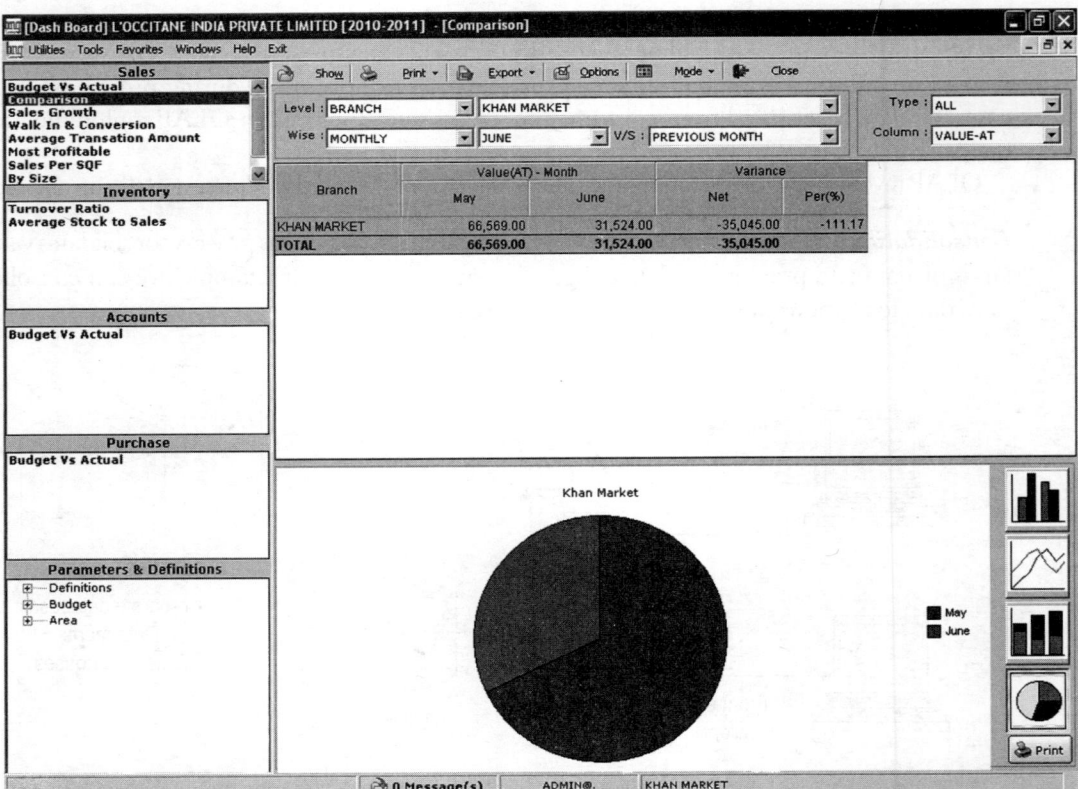

Fig. 12.5   OLAP tools' ability to generate information with different viewpoints [BNG Infotech, www.bng.co.in]

Federal Express use GIS packages (MapInfo, Atlas GIS) for GIS applications. Various government agencies use GIS for viewing and assessing floods, forest fires, earthquake damages, etc. Google Maps display geographical information.

Graphics, charts, maps, etc., are all results of data visualization technologies. Data visualization tools help users see patterns and relationships in large amounts of data in the form of graphs that would be difficult to decipher if presented in traditional text formats. Some DVS tools offer interactive facility where the user can change the data and see the effects on the results.

USING DECISION SUPPORT SYSTEMS

Decision support systems involve the use of many types of analytical modelling—what-if analysis, sensitivity analysis, goal-seeking analysis, optimization, and data mining. Modelling is a key element in most DSS/BI. There are many software tools available; they are developed in programming languages that can work on disparate databases and generate DSS. We will briefly discuss popular modelling techniques for getting familiar with the important concepts as they relate to BI and DSS. Next, the modelling concept is described using electronic spreadsheets. The basic types of analytical modelling techniques and their purposes are explained with examples in Table 12.8.

Modelling with Spreadsheets

Spreadsheets were initially developed for personal computers; however, now they also run on larger systems. The spreadsheet framework is the basis for multidimensional OLAP tools. According to Alan Whitehouse (2011), Excel spreadsheets are the most popular and widely used tools for data analysis. According to Turban (2005), with their strength and flexibility, spreadsheet packages were quickly recognized as easy-to-use implementation software for the development of a wide range of applications in business, engineering, mathematics, and science. As spreadsheet packages evolved, add-ins were developed for structuring and solving specific model classes.

Spreadsheets offer many powerful financial, statistical, mathematical, and other functions. Modelling types that spreadsheets can handle are the what-if analysis and goal-seeking analysis. They are programmable with macros as well. In what-if analysis, we can promptly see the result

Table 12.8   Basic types of modelling analysis explained with examples

Types of modelling	Activities	Example (to determine relationship between advertising and sales)
What-if analysis	What-if analysis begins with a set of conditions and determines their result.	What would happen to sales if advertising expenses were reduced by 25%?
Sensitivity analysis	Sensitivity analysis is carried out to see the impact of repeated change in one variable.	If advertising budget is repeatedly reduced by ₹10,000, what will its impact on sales be?
Goal-seeking analysis	Goal-seeking analysis begins with a desired result and determines the conditions that will produce it.	By how much should advertising increase to achieve sales worth ₹10 million?
Optimization analysis	Optimization analysis helps find an optimum value for selected variables that work within certain constraints.	To achieve a sales target of ₹10 million, how much (from a budget of ₹5, 00,000) should be allotted to advertising in trade journals and search engines?

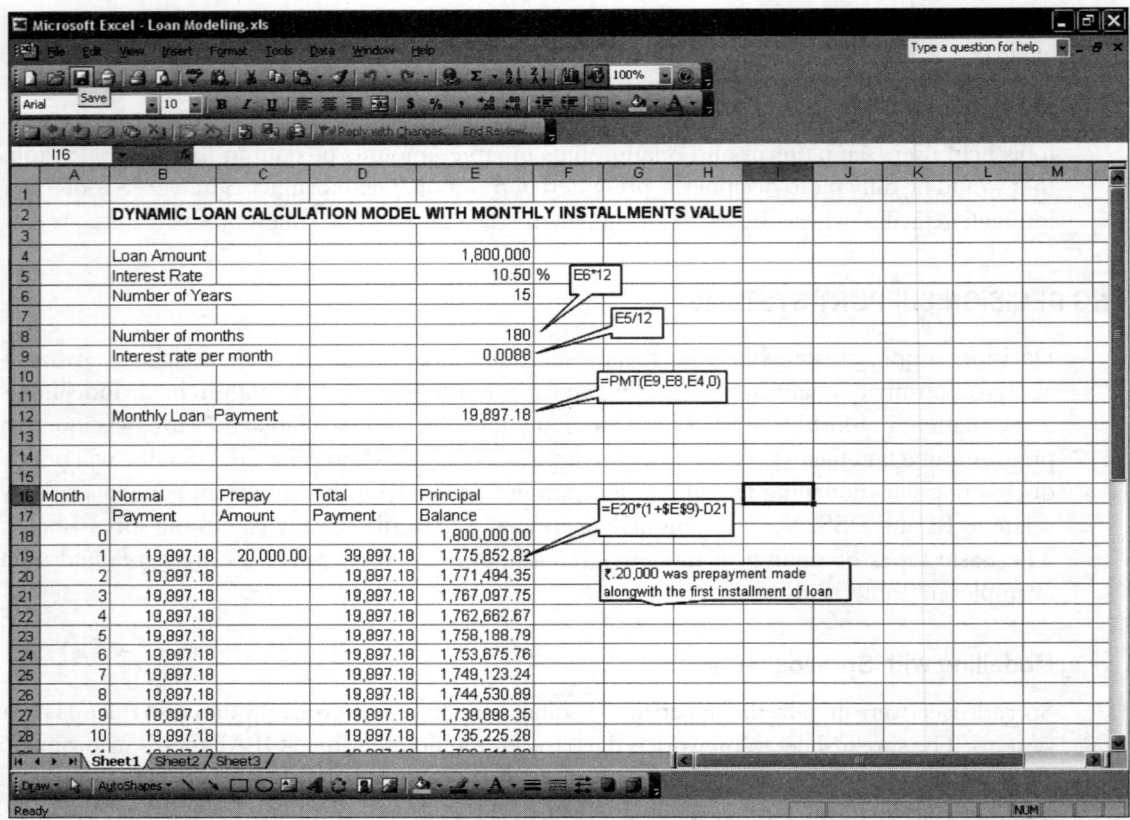

Fig. 12.6 MS Excel spreadsheet-based dynamic model of loan repayment

when a cell value is changed. Figure 12.6 explains how a loan's monthly instalments change, by changing the rate of interest or the principal amount.

What-if Analysis

In what-if analysis, the user makes changes to one or more variables or relationship and observes the resultant changes in the value of other variables. What-if analysis is structured as 'what will happen to the solution if an input variable or a parameter value is changed?' For example, what will happen to the sales if the advertising budget is increased by 20%? Or, what will happen to the net profit, if revenues increase by 10% and distribution costs increase by 15%?

Like spreadsheets, the what-if analysis modelling software provides an appropriate user interface. Users can ask the computer to model these questions and get immediate answers. They can perform multiple cases and thereby change the percentage or any other data in the question.

Figure 12.7 shows a spreadsheet example of a what-if analysis for a cash flow problem. The manager can change the value of the variable (sales per unit or revenue per unit) and immediately see the changes in variable costs and net profit. With a 10% increase in revenue and a 12% increase in variable costs, every subsequent quarter, the net profit rose to ₹3,52,199 in Q4 from ₹2,20,000 in Q1.

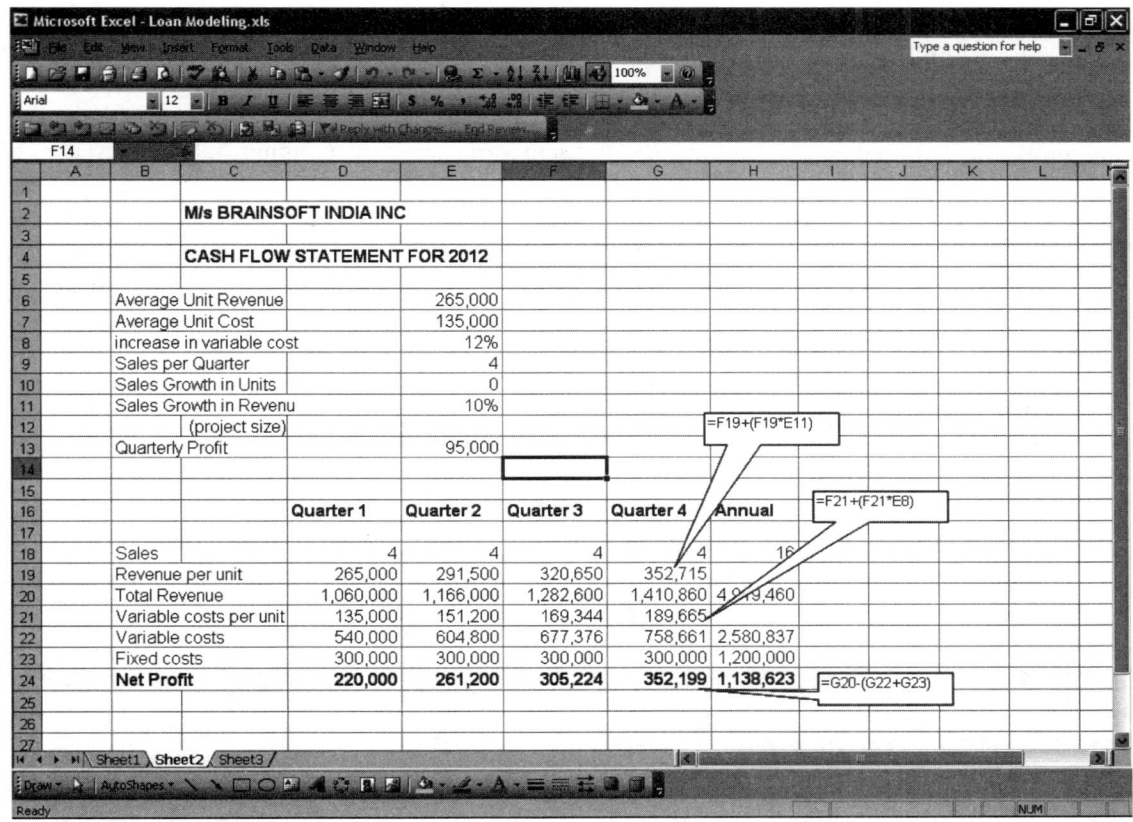

Fig. 12.7 Example of what-if analysis using a spreadsheet

Sensitivity Analysis

Sensitivity analysis is similar to the what-if analysis. In sensitivity analysis, the value of only one variable is changed repeatedly and the resulting changes in other variables are observed. According to O'Brien (2007), sensitivity analysis is really a case of what-if analysis involving repeated changes to only one variable at a time. Typically, sensitivity analysis is used when decision-makers are uncertain about the assumptions made in estimating the value of certain key variables. The change in the value of a variable is carried out on a trial-and-error approach. The input variable is changed until the desired result is achieved. What-if analysis and goal-seeking analysis are two such approaches to problem solving.

However, there are software solutions available for automatic sensitivity analyses. These software systems report the range within which a certain input variable or parameter value can vary without making any significant impact on the proposed solution. Automatic sensitivity analysis is powerful because of its ability to establish ranges and limits very quickly.

Goal-seeking Analysis

In goal-seeking analysis, we set the goal first and then change the input variables. Goal-seeking analysis calculates the values of the inputs necessary to achieve the desired level of output (goal). It proposes a backward solution approach. Goal-seeking analysis answers questions of the following type: what is the annual R&D budget needed for an annual growth rate of 40% in the next two years? How many support engineers will be needed to implement projects within stipulated time limit?

Goal-seeking analyses are suitable for applications like determining break-even analysis. This involves determining the value of the decision variables (e.g., minimum sales or revenue) to achieve a no-loss situation.

An example of goal-seeking analysis is shown in Fig. 12.8. Chetna Marketing sets a goal of achieving break-even point in the first quarter of the following year of operations. Given the initial sales revenue, profit of margins, and fixed cost, you can change the desired increase in sales variable till the time the net profit is either zero or a positive value. You can see that to achieve this goal, the company will need a sales growth of at least 41% each quarter.

Optimization Analysis

Optimization analysis is a more complex form of goal-seeking analysis. Instead of setting a specific target value for a variable, the goal is to find the optimum value for one or more target variables, within the constraints. In this case, one or more variables are repeatedly changed until the best value for the target variables are determined. For example, we can find the optimum profit by making changes in various revenue sources or expenditure outlets. Changes to these heads will be subject to constraints such as plant capacity, available finances, and market share determined

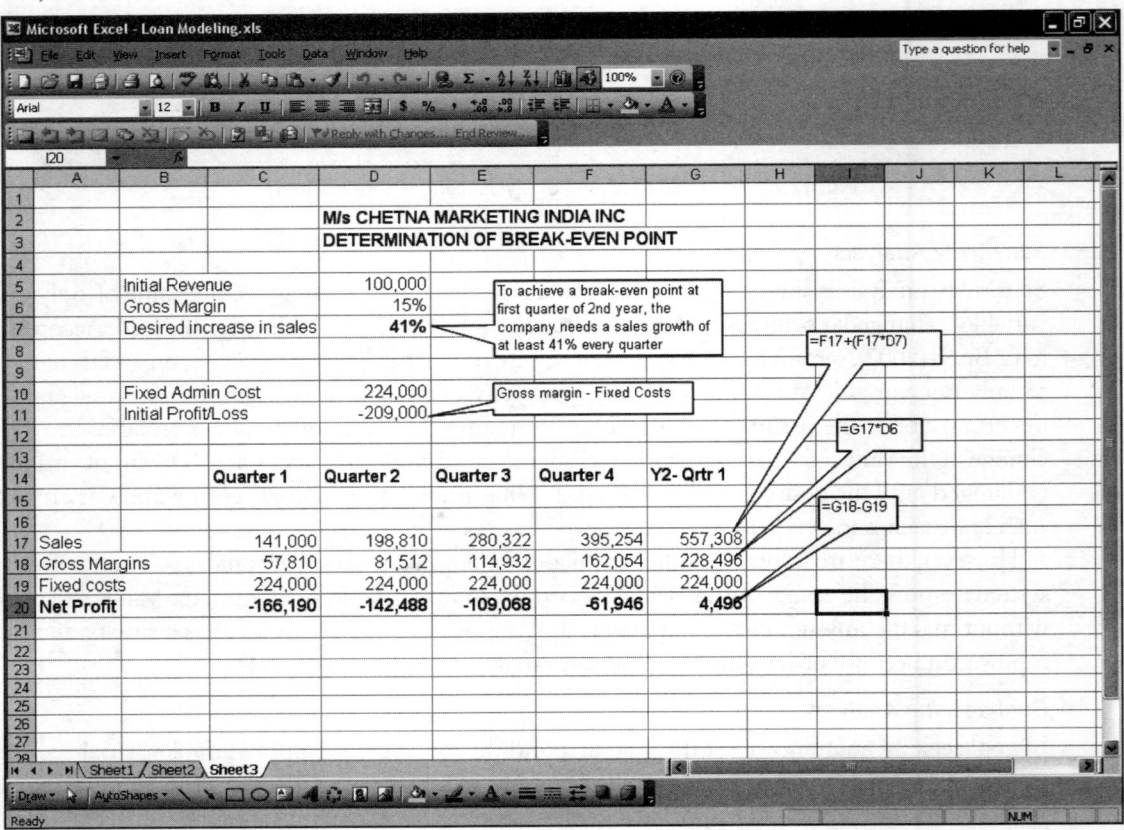

Fig. 12.8 Example of goal-seeking analysis using spreadsheets

by the competitive forces. Optimization can be accomplished by using software tools like Solver in MS Excel and other linear programming tools that offer optimization techniques.

Data Mining for Decision Support

We discussed data mining in Chapter 6 as a tool for organizing and managing data resources of an organization. The primary objective of data mining is to provide decision support to managers. This is also known as knowledge discovery. According to O'Brien (2007), data mining software analyses the vast stores of historical business data that have been prepared for analysis in corporate data warehouses, and tries to discover patterns, trends, and correlations hidden in the data that can help a company improve its business performance.

Data mining is used by business managers for decision support while determining buying patterns, analysing customer tastes and preferences, and identifying redundant costs, hidden profitable relationships and opportunities, unprofitable product lines, etc. For example, organizations use data mining to find the impact of marketing schemes, discover ways to reach untapped profitable customers, etc.

Exhibit 12.3 describes how Bharti Airtel mines data to find key customers in their social networks and gains a competitive advantage by retaining them.

EXHIBIT 12.3

Bharti Airtel: Mining Social Networks for Decision Support

Telecom operators naturally prize mobile phone subscribers who spend a lot on call charges. However, in reality, thriftier customers are more valuable. Known as 'influencers', these subscribers frequently persuade their friends, family, and colleagues to follow them when they switch to a rival operator. The trick, then, is to identify such trendsetting subscribers and keep them on board with special discounts and promotions. People at higher rungs of an organization or society often receive quick callbacks, do not worry about calling other people late at night, and tend to get more calls at times when social events are most often organized, for example, Friday afternoons. Influential customers also reveal their clout by making long-duration calls, while the calls they receive are generally of a short duration.

Companies can spot these influencers and work out several techniques with them, by crunching vast quantities of calling data with sophisticated 'network analysis' software. Instead of looking at the call records of a single customer at a time, it looks at customers within the context of their social network. The ability to retain customers is particularly important in hyper-competitive markets, for, example, India. According to Amrita Gangotra, the firm's director for information technology, Bharti Airtel is India's biggest mobile operator, handles over three billion calls a day, and has greatly reduced customer defections by deploying the software.

Data mining on usage patterns helps create innovative promotions for specific users. Even credit card companies are using data mining for high usage customers and targeted promotions. The market for such software is booming. By one estimate, there are more than 100 packages for network analysis, also known as link analysis or predictive analysis. The raw data used may extend far beyond phone records to encompass information available from private and governmental entities, and Internet sources like Facebook. IBM, the supplier of the system used by Bharti Airtel, says its annual sales of such software, now growing at double-digit rates, will exceed $15 billion by 2015. In the past five years, IBM has spent more than $11 billion buying the makers of network-analysis software. Gartner, a market-research firm, ranks the technology at number two in its list of strategic business operations meriting significant investment this year.

Adoption is being driven by the availability of more sources of information and by the fact that network-analysis software is becoming easier to use. According to Mark Ramsey, the firm's head of business analytics for Eastern Europe, the Middle East, and Africa, a decade ago, IBM employed experts holding PhDs in mathematics to study

(Contd)

Exhibit 12.3 (Contd)

social networks. Today, college graduates can operate analysis software and handle enormous quantities of data. Bharti Airtel employs only about 100 analysts to keep tabs on its 135 million subscribers.

Companies have long mined their data to improve sales and productivity. However, broadening data mining to include analysis of social networks makes new things possible. Data mining techniques are also used to extract information on customer behaviour patterns. Airtel Vodafone's customer-facing personnel are able to input the information they collect on a daily basis, so that it is integrated with data already stored in the warehouse. This data is subsequently combined and converted into information structures for enquiries.

Sources:
'Mining social network', *The Economist*, 2 September 2010, http://www.economist.com/node/16910031, last accessed on 15 December 2011.
Presentations by Vijay Srinivasan, COO, Bharti Airtel, 'Sybase develops business intelligence for Airtel Vodaphone data warehouse', http://www.sybase.com/detail?id=1012492, last accessed on 15 December 2011.

EXECUTIVE SUPPORT SYSTEMS

As introduced in Chapter 1, executive support systems (ESS) are usually meant for the top executives of an organization and they combine many features of MIS and DSS. Thus, the first objective of executive information systems is to provide top executives with prompt and easy access to information about the organization's critical success factors. These are key factors that are critical to achieving an organization's strategic objectives. For example, for an e-commerce portal like Timesdeals.com, its reach and attraction to the target audience would be critical for its success and failure. Therefore, the management of the portal would be interested in information such as who (demographic details) surfs the site, whether they get the necessary motivation to register and acquire deals, and what is the traffic flow at competitors' portals.

Executive support systems are no longer the prerogative of the top executives, as ESS is now being used by managers at all levels and decision-makers in the organization. The other names for ESS are executive information systems and enterprise information systems.

Features

The ESS provides information in the form of summary, charts, and graphs, as suited to the top management's preferences. The ESS tries to avoid the problem of data overload by filtering the data and presenting it in a graphical or dashboard format. ESS has the ability to drill-down, which is a method of moving from the summary data to the lower levels of a transaction voucher.

Laudon (2010) argues that a major challenge of ESS has been to integrate data from systems designed for very different purposes so that the senior executives are able to review organizational performance from a firm-wide perspective. Nowadays, ESS rely on data generated by the organizations' existing enterprise applications such as enterprise resource planning, supply chain management, and customer relationship management.

SUMMARY

Decision-making is the process of selecting an optimum or the most suitable alternative from a number of alternatives. Decision is the outcome or end-result, while decision-making is a process. The types of decisions are based on the decisional activities at the organizational levels. Based on these management functions, decision can be classified on three counts: purpose of decision-making, level of programmability, and knowledge of outcome.

Organizational decisions are grouped into three categories—strategic planning decisions, management control decisions, and operational control decisions. Based on the level of programmability, decisions made at all management levels can further be classified into programmed or non-programmed decisions. On the basis of knowledge of the outcome, decision-making can be again classified into three categories—decision under certainty, decision under risk, and decision under uncertainty. A decision-maker may use various methods to choose from several alternatives. The methods are primarily search processes to select the best alternative that satisfies maximum conditions. There are three methods of selecting decision alternatives. These methods are pay-off analysis, decision tree analysis, and optimization techniques.

Decision support systems are designed to help managers take decisions. DSS are computer-based information systems that provide interactive information support to managers during the decision-making process. The components of DSS are databases, DSS software tools, and models. The primary use of IT in information systems has been to support business managers with data and information to help them make efficient and effective decisions during the course of managing the business. The availability and demand for high-end information paved the way for more sophisticated analytical tools for decision support, like business intelligence (BI) tools.

Business analytics refers to the skills, technologies, applications, and practices for continuous iterative exploration and investigation into past business performances to gain insight and drive business planning. BI involves acquiring data and information, and even knowledge, from a wide variety of sources and utilizing them in decision-making. Online analytical processing (OLAP), is an approach to swiftly answer multidimensional analytical queries. It is part of a broader category of BI, which also encompasses relational reporting and data mining. Geographic information systems (GIS) and data visualization systems (DVS) are special forms of DSS that present data in the form of graphics, charts, tables, maps, digital images, animation, and three-dimensional presentations. These forms make data easier to use, decipher, and act on.

DSS involves the use of analytical modelling such as what-if analysis, sensitivity analysis, goal-seeking analysis, optimization, and data mining. Modelling is a key element in most DSS/BI. The spreadsheet framework is the basis for multidimensional OLAP tools. Spreadsheets offer many powerful financial, statistical, mathematical, and other functions. In what-if analysis, the user makes changes to one or more variables or relationship and observes the resultant changes in the value of other variables. In sensitivity analysis, the value of only one variable is changed repeatedly and the resulting changes on other variables are observed. Goal-seeking analysis calculates the values of the inputs needed to achieve a desired level of output. Optimization analysis is a more complex form of goal-seeking analysis. Instead of setting a specific target value for a variable, the goal is to find the optimum value for one or more target variables, within the constraints. Data mining is used by business managers for decision support in the area of determining buying patterns, customer tastes and preferences, identifying redundant costs, hidden profitable relationships and opportunities, unprofitable product lines, etc.

The first objective of executive information systems (EIS) is to provide top executives with prompt and easy access to information about the organization's critical success factors. The executive support systems are no longer the prerogative of only the top executives, as ESS is being used by all types of managers and decision-makers in the organization.

KEY TERMS

Business analytics (BA)   The skills, technologies, applications, and practices for continuous iterative exploration and investigation of past business performances to gain insight and drive business planning.

Business intelligence (BI)   Acquiring data and information, and even knowledge, from a wide variety of sources and utilizing them in decision-making.

Business process management   An approach that considers processes to be strategic assets of an organization that must be understood, managed, and improved to deliver value-added products and services to clients.

Data mining   Digging through corporate data warehouses and discovering patterns, trends, and correlations hidden in the data.

Data visualization systems (DVS)   A special form of DSS that present data in a format, which is easier to use, decipher, and act on.

Data-driven DSS   DSS that rely on data for decision support.

Decision support systems   Computer-based information systems that provide interactive information support to managers during the decision-making process.

Decision tree analysis A graphical representation of sequence of decisions and actions based on various conditions applied during decision-making.

Drill-down The ability of the software to dig into the database and excavate data up to the most detailed level.

Executive support systems (ESS) Provide top executives with prompt and easy access to information about the organization's critical success factors.

Geographic information systems (GIS) is a decision support system that uses geographic databases to construct and display maps.

Goal-seeking analysis Calculates the values of the inputs necessary to achieve the desired level of output (goal).

Model-driven DSS DSS that relies on mathematical models for decision support.

Online analytical processing An approach to swiftly answer multidimensional analytical queries.

Optimization analysis The goal to find the optimum value

for one or more target variables, within constraints.

Optimization technique Operation research techniques used for decision-making that assume all alternatives and their outcomes are known to the decision-maker.

Pay-off analysis The strategy along with the conditions that determine the degree to which the goal is actually achieved in decision-making.

Pay-off matrix The method of decision-making where the state of nature is known with certainty and the decision-maker selects the strategy that provides him the highest pay-off.

Sensitivity analysis The value of only one variable is changed repeatedly and the resulting changes on other variables are observed.

Slicing and dicing The ability to look at the database from different angles

What-if analysis The user makes changes to one or more variables or relationship and observes the resultant changes in the value of other variables.

CONCEPT REVIEW QUESTIONS

1. What is decision-making? How can improved decision-making bring in efficiency and increase revenue generation in an organization?
2. Enumerate the various basis of classifying decisions. Explain structured and unstructured decisions with the help of examples.
3. What are the different models of decision-making? Explain each with an example.
4. Which are the methods of deciding decision alternatives? Give the advantages and disadvantages of each of them.
5. How do information systems support the activities of managers and management in decision-making?
6. What are the components of decision support systems? What trends do you observe in the DSS arena?
7. What do you understand by business intelligence? Enumerate the various tools available for business decision-making.
8. What is analytical modelling? Explain the analytical models available as decision support systems.
9. What is the difference between what-if analysis and sensitivity analysis?
10. How do you differentiate between goal-seeking analysis and optimization analysis?

CRITICAL THINKING QUESTIONS

1. All models of decision-making assume that the decision-maker knows all the possible alternatives and their outcomes. However, in real-life there are many situations where both are not known. Examine this statement and fortify your answers with examples.
2. Assume that you, as a manager of your company, have to take the following decisions. Identify the activities that will precede decision-making and classify the decisions.
   (a) Appoint a chief accounts officer to take control

of finances and accounting.
   (b) Purchase machinery for your new manufacturing unit.
   (c) Start an advertising campaign in visual and print media.
   (d) Introduce a new product in the market.
3. Companies appear to believe that business intelligence is a 'business issue' and not a 'technology issue'. Do you agree with this statement? Why or why not?

4. 'Executive support systems are no longer the pre-rogative of the top executives, as ESS is being used by all types of managers and decision-makers in the organization'. Critically examine this statement.

MIS DEVELOPMENT

Mascot Foods Pvt. Ltd is a Noida-based company that is into manufacturing of various packaged food including biscuits and other bakery products. The company has around 25 products that are packaged in more than 100 ways. The company mainly distributes its products in North India, in the states of Uttar Pradesh, Uttarakhand, Himachal Pradesh, Punjab, and Haryana. The company set up its manufacturing unit around 12 years back. It uses agricultural produce as the main raw material for its products. The main raw materials are wheat flour, sugar, eggs, preservatives, and additional flavours. The input costs vary with the availability of farm products, which in turn, are a result of crop production and dependent on rainfall during the previous year. Besides the raw material costs, labour management is another factor that the company has to take care. Looking at the seasonal variations in raw material availability, the company has to maintain enough buffer stocks.

The company distributes its products through a net-work of dealers and distributors. They have appointed distributors in all the major zones they operate in. Further, the distributors supply goods to the dealers in every city. The dealers approach retailers in towns and villages. Thus, the products of the company reach thousands of retailers in the area they are operating in.

To create demand and awareness about its products, the company regularly launches advertising campaigns in the visual and print media. The marketing manager has to be careful in choosing the most effective media, given the limited regional area for their market. Besides the publicity, the marketing manager also resorts to dis-counts, freebies, and attractive schemes for retailers, so that the retailers push the products' sales from their ends.

The company's sales have been almost stagnant for the last three years. Thus, the top management is exploring the option of increasing reach by marketing their products in other parts of the country, especially the central and eastern states. Given the geography and demand in this area, the top managers are of the view that the present production capacity would not suffice to meet the demand. To meet future demands, the company will have to increase its production capacity, probably by putting up a new manufacturing unit in some other region. The company management was aware that some of the new states were offering tax-free zones for attract-ing industries in those states.

Exercise

Identify the various decisions that the management of a company makes during the course of running the business. Classify these decisions on the basis of their type—purpose of decision, level of outcome, and pro-grammability. Figure out the numerous activities that may precede the decisions.

REFERENCES

Anthony, Robert B., *Planning and Control Systems: A Framework for Analysis*, Division of Research, Harvard University, Boston, 1965.

Gantz, John, 'The new world of enterprise reporting is here', *Computerworld*, 1 February 1999.

Gorry, G. Anthony and Michael S. Scott Morton: 'A frame-work for management information systems', *Management Review*, 1971.

Jaiswal, Mahadeo and Monika Mittal, *Management Information Systems*, Oxford University Press, New Delhi, 2004.

Jawadekar, Waman S., *Management Information Systems: Text and Cases*, Tata McGraw-Hill, New Delhi, 2008.

Kalakota, Ravi and Marcia Robinson, *E-business 2.0: Roadmap for Success*, Addison-Wesley, Reading, 2001.

Keen, Peter and Michael Scott Morton, *Decision Support Sys-tems: An Organizational Perspective*, Addison-Wesley Publishing Company, Reading, 1978.

Kenneth, Laudon, Jane Laudon, and Rajanish Dass, *Man-agement Information Systems*, Pearson Education, Singapore, 2010.

Kotter, John T., 'What Effective General Managers Really Do', *Harvard Business Review*, November–December 1982.

O'Brien, James A., George M. Marakas, and Behl, *Management Information Systems*, Tata McGraw-Hill, New Delhi, 2007.

Simon, Herber A., *The New Science of Management Decisions*, Harper & Row, New York, 1960.

Simon, Herber A., *Top Management Planning*, The Macmillan Company, 1965.

Turban, Efraim, Jay E. Aronson, and Ting-Peng Liang, *Decision Support Systems and Intelligent Systems*, Pearson Education, Singapore, 2005.

http://alanwhitehouse.wordpress.com/2011/04/07/the-microsoft-business-intelligence-stack-cheat-sheet, last accessed on 9 January 2013.

CASE STUDY

CEAT: Exploring New Terrain in Decision Support with BI Tools

A comprehensive BI application addresses data analysis and business reporting for smooth decision-making at CEAT. The BI tools that are used connect various applications like SAP and other non-SAP applications in CRM, production, finance, sales, distribution, and marketing data. Excerpts from an interview with Niranjan Bhalivade, chief information officer, CEAT Ltd, are given here.

Tell us something about the business of CEAT.
CEAT, beginning its operations in India in 1958, is a leading manufacturer of automobile tyres in India, and one of the most recognized brands in the country. The company also exports a range of tyres to over 130 countries. CEAT has a wide distribution network of over 3500 dealers, 37 regional offices and more than 136 C & F agents. The company's manufacturing plants are located in Mumbai, Nasik and Halol. CEAT manufactures the largest range of tyres in the industry, which incorporate both cross-ply and radial technology. The range of tyres cover virtually all user segments—from giant earthmovers to specialty tyres for scooters and motorcycles. The company also markets tubes and flaps. The company has achieved a turnover of ₹3500 crore and is headquartered in Mumbai.

What kind of business applications and IT infrastructure are currently in use at your company?
We are using enterprise application SAP and a customized CRM application. The databases are Oracle and MS SQL, the data warehouse is based on SQL Server 2008. Lately, we have procured a BI tool, 1KEY BI from Maia Intelligence.

Can you describe the initiative and the solution you deployed?
The comprehensive BI application addresses data analysis and MIS reporting needs of CEAT by connecting SAP and non-SAP CRM data from across multiple areas of business, namely production, finance, sales, and distribution.

What was the IT or business challenge faced that led you to this project?
Business users, key personnel, managers, and top management at CEAT wanted information visibility on the web. Territory managers were not able to see entire report in a single sheet. Before going to a dealer, they were doing a lot of manual homework. They were not getting correct data during discussions with the dealer. Adhering to continuous report requests from business users was becoming a challenge as generation of SAP reports required lot of effort and time.

What IT strategy was planned to overcome these business challenges?
A web-based BI tool that was easy to reach out to users was being looked upon as the solution to cater to the challenges faced. BI tool would help my team to pay one-time attention to develop reports and thereon business users could easily do their own analysis as the way they want and in the required format. BI tool could help us easily deploy reports, give its access to the business users and no longer need to manually prepare on a spreadsheet.

What was the evaluation process and why did you choose a particular vendor?
Prior to selecting 1KEY BI, we evaluated BI tools based on various parameters such as ease of use, cost effectiveness, dashboards availability, anywhere access through the web, reach in large user base, empower the business users to build their own reports from the base cube and be able to slice and dice the info for further analysis. CEAT selected 1KEY BI because it provided us with far more than just trending and reporting. It gave us a higher level of BI capabilities that integrated easily with our existing production and control systems data from SAP and non-SAP data; provided deep insight into our batch processes; facilitated information-sharing among our production and supervisory staff so they could better monitor production in their appropriate contexts; was cost-effective with low TCO and having a dashboard feature.

Can you explain the plan and roll-out of the project?
The initial plan was to develop reports for one department at a time so that we could provide all kind of reports required. In the process, we ensured that the quality and performance is not degraded anywhere. We also released the tool for identified MIS users only along with a basic

(Contd)

training session. The implementation process began in April 2010 and went on for six months to develop the initial requirements collected from different departments with the team of two BI consultants from Paramatrix and one project manager from MAIA Intelligence. SAP data was pulled using SQL Server's SSIS and Microsoft BizTalk and reports created on 1KEY. Four people from CEAT's IT team, two each from sales and distribution, and finance were involved as member of the core implementing team. The entire set-up including the development (of reports) and support is now managed by the IT team of CEAT.

What was the role of the partner as a value addition in the implementation of this project?

The support by the vendor—MAIA Intelligence, has been excellent. They have trained the IT team at CEAT on development and administrative support perspective. Later on, the in-house team took over the development for upcoming requirements from business users side. The service of vendor company helped CEAT gain greater insight into product and producer effectiveness and support better analysis and decision-making. The BI consultants helped the company develop a roadmap to align BI processes and technology with its business strategy.

What were the measurable benefits post implementation?

Life is now very much productive for CEAT with 1KEY BI. The company completed the project much ahead of the deadline and found 1KEY a highly integrated BI with faster implementation and more efficient. BI has now become the primary source of information at CEAT. This BI project helped CEAT gain fast and accurate insight with access from hard-to-reach SAP data to solve complex business problems, react quickly to changing market trends, improve financial exposures, drive change, gain real-time insight into customer and market trends. Users at CEAT now use pre-configured reports, with powerful ad hoc capabilities and interactive visual analytics. BI now allows CEAT to easily extend to include a wide range of data elements and sources. Through easy-to-use interactive graphics, gauges, and filters, business users can play out scenarios, explore potential outcomes and gain a deeper insight that can help you reach decisions faster—and they do not have to be a technology expert or know how to construct complex queries to do so. BI helps CEAT extract SAP data from across the domains to gain a consolidated view of information from a wide variety of sources across the enterprise.

What was something indigenous or radically different about the project or initiative?

The IT team at CEAT is excited about the efficiencies they are realizing by standardizing on for enterprise monitoring, reporting, and analysis. BI project was cost effective and hence has turned to form a great value proposition for CEAT. We are very much confident to achieve ROI within the very first year of implementation of BI.

Business user's acceptance is a key measure for the success of any project. A quote from the key business user of the project on the solution deployed?

With BI, business users at CEAT can now access enterprise-wide ERP and CRM data quickly and reliably, thereby, allowing business users to gain accurate insight into information and proactively respond to rapidly changing conditions. 1KEY BI fits the needs of our growing business with its dynamic, cutting-edge features. and the scalability to keep our growing user base apprised of business performance. Around 100 to 150 real-time reports are being used by CEAT to monitor the business numbers, track productivity, schedule resources based on volumes and manpower rooster from BI.

How successful would you rate the implementation of BI tools in your organization?

This truly is an extraordinary success story. BI is the major element that enabled everything to happen. It is not the only important reason for all that happens at CEAT, but it is an important factor in our success, and we couldn't have gotten these amazing results without it. BI is a critical enabling tool for us. But the success of this BI project is no less than an achievement in itself especially for us, the IT team. The agility of developing a report on BI has helped quickly respond to the reporting needs from users giving us a peace of mind and simultaneously it has also empowered business users to do on-the-fly slicing and dicing, drill-down of information for ad-hoc analysis in variety of report formats with ease on a daily basis.

Our people have responded well to the possibilities they see in 1KEY. It's intuitively easy to use, so they can easily leverage it to their own application needs. Any authorized person will be able to pull up trends in the dashboards and use that information for any application needs they may have. They won't have to ask IT for help and they won't need to ask us for data.

(Contd)

Something you would like to share with your fellow CIOs.

Information is said to be the most important resource for managers and decision makers. Nowadays, the difficulty is not in getting the information but rather how to select the relevant information from the abundance of data and information. BI gives single source for critical information throughout the organization, so one can spend less time debating data and more energy making critical decisions.

Final words on industry-wide adoption of this type of project.

Successful business management consists of managing information from across multiple areas of the business.

Discussion Questions

1. What were the challenges that CEAT faced before deciding on a decision support system?
2. How did CEAT benefit from using BI tools? Has decision-making really improved?
3. What kind of business analytics are required by the CEAT management for decision support using this BI tool?
4. Find out the various BI tools providers in India and compare the functionalities provided by them with the 1KEY BI tool used by CEAT in this case.

Sources:

'A case study of fortnight' based on an interview of Niranjan Bhalivade, CIO, CEAT Limited, http://www.cioklub.com/case_study_364.php?cioid=364&ciofeaflg=casestudy, last accessed on 9 January 2013.

Case study at www.maia-intelligence.com, last accessed on 16 December 2011.

http://www.ceat.in/newsite/aboutus/ceat-company-overview.asp, last accessed on 20 December 2011.

http://pcquest.ciol.com/content/contentimplementation2011/2011/111061009.asp, last accessed on 15 December 2011.

13

Knowledge Management and Intelligent Systems

Companies today live in knowledge ecologies where one company feeds knowledge into another. What counts is a networked approach to KM, involving internal as well as external parties. The logic behind this is as simple as it is compelling: if you cut off the outflow of knowledge, you will also cut off the inflow. We believe, therefore, that the firm's openness to external experts and the sharing of ideas within a broad network will be a key driver for maintaining competitive success.

–THOMAS DAVENPORT

LEARNING OBJECTIVES

After studying this chapter, you will be able to

- understand knowledge management (KM) and knowledge management systems
- appreciate the business value of knowledge management
- explain the various knowledge management initiatives
- define the knowledge management categories
- understand the challenges of knowledge management
- illustrate artificial intelligence (AI) and appreciate its role in decision support systems (DSS)
- describe expert systems, neural networks, fuzzy logic, genetic algorithm, and intelligent agents

EXHIBIT 13.1

IndusInd Bank, Siemens, and BlueCoat Excel in Knowledge Management

IndusInd Bank Ltd received the prestigious 'Best Use of Technology in E-learning Initiatives 2010' award in the private bank category from the Indian Banks' Association (IBA) on Tuesday, 2 March 2011.

The bank was awarded for the use of knowledge management (KM) technologies for internal knowledge sharing and e-learning with effective measurement and monitoring of training initiatives. Paul Abraham, chief operations officer (COO), IndusInd Bank, said, 'The effective use of technology is one of the important drivers of growth for our Bank. Training is an effective tool, which is important for creating a productive work force, and adoption of this channel is a great, low cost/high coverage initiative for us. We have also put in place a robust risk management system for providing better and secured customer service. This recognition is of great encouragement to all our employees'.

IndusInd Bank, which commenced its operations in 1994, caters to the needs of both consumer and corporate customers. It has a robust technology platform supporting multi-channel delivery capabilities. The Bank believes in driving its business through technology.

Awards recognize organizations that are leaders in creating organizational intellectual capital and value through the transformation of knowledge into world-class products, services, and solutions.

The knowledge management effort at IndusInd Bank deepens employee interaction through rich social engagement. The KM system at the Bank is a collaborative environment that incorporates the shared knowledge and content created by its employees, partners, and customers with an advanced knowledge base tool and automated content integration. The social collaboration features of the platform help companies improve access to organization-wide expertise, generate ideas, and accelerate innovation. The KM initiative is designed to help the organization manage and execute the numerous ideas and suggestions of its workforce, resulting in solutions, higher productivity, and faster response and delivery times.

Siemens appreciated the value of knowledge management, as early as 1999, when the central management of the company created an organizational unit that would be responsible for worldwide deployment of knowledge management. At the heart of Siemens' technical solution to KM is a website called ShareNet, which combines elements of a database repository, a chat room, and a search engine. Online entry forms allow employees to store information they think might be useful to colleagues. Other employees are able to search the repository, browse according to topics, and contact authors for more information on the subject using the available communication channels.

Knowledge management at Siemens began in a bottom-up manner via various mid-level initiatives in communities of practice and bodies of knowledge. The managers of these initiatives formed a semi-official community of practice. This was followed by a corporate knowledge function that officially supported and coordinated these various initiatives, via the creation of the corporate KM (CKM) office in 1999.

KM implementation at Siemens involved establishing a network to collect, categorize, and share information using databases and intranets. However, the major challenges were cultural change and human interfaces.

Mumbai-based BlueCoat Systems Inc., a vendor of application delivery networking solutions, has launched an advanced KM system designed to provide on-premise technical and service engineers with a means to search and access technical, solution and product content, required to realize the full potential of its Blue Coat product line, regardless of its location or format.

A part of the ongoing investment by Blue Coat in its service and support capabilities, the KM system enhances the Blue Touch online portal by providing a single customizable search tool across all technical documentation, support solutions, customer forums, alerts, and other sources, and enables customers to quickly find accurate and intuitive answers to their support questions. An online portal provides users with a channel for downloading the latest software and documentation, or to search security advisories, submit and track service requests, and license or activate products.

'Over the last 12 months, Blue Coat has made significant investments in its service and support organization to provide its customers with the tools, knowledge and expertise they need to support strategic deployments,' said Grant Gordon, senior vice-president, Global Service and Support at Blue Coat Systems. The KM system is integral to this initiative and unifies the vast reserve of technical knowledge and expertise that the company maintains in multiple locations.

(Contd)

Exhibit 13.1 (Contd)

Sources:

Blue Coat Enhances Knowledge Management System, http://www.ciol.com/News/News-Reports/Blue-Coat-enhances-Knowledge-Management-System/28709122875/0/, published on 28 July 2009, last accessed on 16 March 2012.

Davenport, Thomas, *Knowledge Management Case Book: Siemens Best Practices,* 2003.

'IndusInd Bank bags the IBA award', http://www.ciol.com/Enterprise/BFSI/News-Reports/IndusInd-Bank-bags-the-IBA-award/147572/0/, published on 10 March 2011, last accessed on 16 March 2012.

'IndusInd Bank bags the IBA award for 'Best Use of Technology in E-learning-2010', http://www.business-standard.com/india/news/indusind-bank-bagsiba-award-for-best-usetechnology-in-e-learning-2010/427881/, last accessed on 16 March 2012.

'MindTree launches KM solutions', www.ciol.com/EC-Manufacturing/News-Reports/MindTree-launches-knowledge-management-solution/9709122114/, last accessed on 16 March 2012.

Santosus, Megan, 'How Siemens keep KM blooming,' February 2003, http://www.cio.com, last accessed on 16 March 2012.

http://www.moneycontrol.com/stocks/stock_market/corp_notices.php?autono=416686, last accessed on 16 March 2012.

The initiatives of IndusInd Bank, Siemens, and BlueCoat given in Exhibit 13.1 explain the concept of knowledge management. The knowledge management system at IndusInd Bank facilitates a collaborative environment by using an advanced knowledge base tool and automated content integration. At Siemens, the social collaboration features of the platform help companies improve access to organization-wide expertise, generate ideas, and accelerate innovation. At BlueCoat, the knowledge management initiative is designed to help the organization manage and execute the numerous ideas and suggestions of its workforce, resulting in solutions, higher productivity, and faster response and delivery time. The knowledge management effort unifies the vast reserve of technical knowledge and expertise that BlueCoat uses at various locations.

In this chapter, we will explain what knowledge management systems are, learn to appreciate various initiatives in this direction, and discuss knowledge-based intelligent systems used in management information systems (MIS).

KNOWLEDGE MANAGEMENT

In an organization, knowledge is an outcome of research, development, and organizational experiences. It is accumulated in the process of business delivery. Knowledge comprises one's experience. The insights and experiences comprising knowledge are embodied either in individuals or in the form of business processes. Thus, knowledge frequently takes the form of the best practices, policies, and business solutions at the project as well as enterprise level of the organization.

KM is the process through which organizations generate value from their intellectual and knowledge-based assets. Most often, generating value from such assets involves creating a knowledge repository, systematizing what employees, partners, and customers know, and sharing that information among employees, departments, and even with other companies in an effort to devise the best practices.

It is thus a process of organizational learning and problem-solving. Though KM is often facilitated by IT, technology in itself is not knowledge management.

Knowledge Management Systems

Knowledge management systems help organizations identify, select, organize, disseminate, and transfer important information and expertise that are part of organizational experience and were hitherto unstructured. According to Turban (2005), knowledge management is more a methodology applied to business practices than a technology or a product. Nevertheless, IT is crucial to the success of every KM system. IT enables knowledge management by providing the enterprise architecture upon which it is built. Knowledge management systems are developed using three sets of technologies—communication, collaboration, and storage and retrieval.

According to O'Brien (2007), many times, enterprise knowledge portals play an essential role in helping companies use their intranets as KM systems to share and disseminate knowledge and support decision-making by managers and business professionals. KM has become an important theme in many organizations, as it is realized that much of the business organization's value depends on its ability to create and manage a knowledge base. The set of rules that model human knowledge are collectively called *knowledge base*.

The forces that drive knowledge management are internal as well as external. KM as a system covers the process of knowledge creation and acquisition from internal processes and the external world. The collected knowledge is incorporated in organizational policies and procedures, and then disseminated to the stakeholders. The complete knowledge acquisition and storage processes are depicted in Fig. 13.1.

Business Value

In today's information-driven economy, companies uncover most of the opportunities, and ultimately derive the maximum value, from intellectual rather than physical assets. To get the maximum value from a company's intellectual assets, knowledge management practitioners maintain that knowledge must be shared and must serve as the foundation for collaboration. According to Agarwal (2010), today, organizations have realized that knowledge is a strategic resource that gives them a sustainable competitive advantage and helps them achieve their long-term goals. The realization that knowledge is the key driver behind organizational success comes from the need to respond to global and increasingly competitive markets, sophisticated and demanding stakeholders, and rapid technological changes. It is knowledge that helps organizations deal with these challenges effectively.

Knowledge has become so imperative that it is treated at par with business assets such as buildings and machinery. The knowledge of delivering services and products efficiently and effectively to better competition, is what gaining a strategic advantage is all about. Delivering something better than the competitor is the core competency of an organization. With the realization that knowledge is their core competency, organizations are now attempting to manage it in a more systematic and effective way, using the latest advances in computer and information technologies.

For example, the knowledge of better construction and land acquisition techniques was a core competency for DLF and made the company one of the major real estate owners in the national capital region.

Initiatives

A survey of European firms by KPMG (an international audit and accounting consultant) in 1998 found that almost half the companies reported having suffered a significant setback from losing key employees. It is also observed that much of the knowledge needed to perform a task

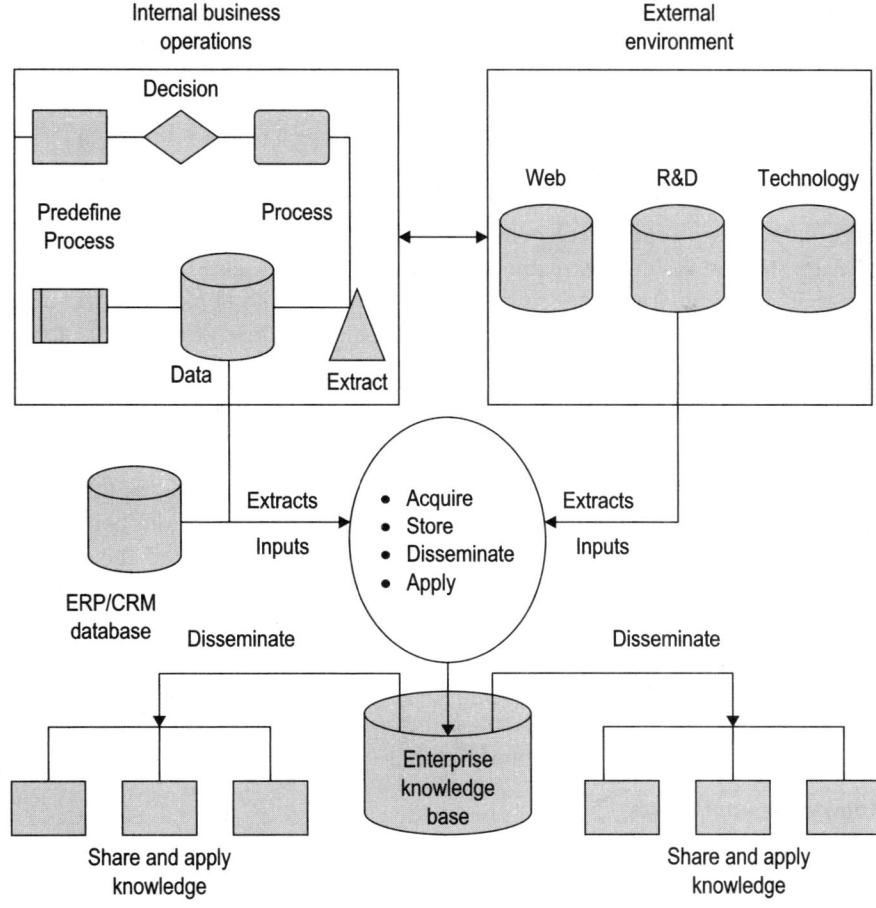

Fig. 13.1   Knowledge acquisition and storage process in an organization

is within the organization, but finding it is a challenge. Davenport (1998) has suggested that a knowledge management system has one of three aims: (a) to make knowledge visible, mainly through maps, yellow pages, and hypertext, (b) to develop a knowledge-intensive culture, or (c) to build a knowledge infrastructure. These objectives are not mutually exclusive, and firms may attempt all the three as part of a knowledge management initiative.

There are several activities that are carried out during the knowledge management process. These include identification, creation, storage, transfer, sharing, seeking, sourcing, and usage of knowledge. The knowledge flow in an organization necessarily involves four steps—knowledge acquisition, storage, dissemination, and application—as illustrated in Fig. 13.1.

Knowledge Acquisition

Knowledge acquisition is a process of knowledge identification and generation of new insights, ideas, and routines. Earlier, knowledge management involved building corporate repositories of documents, reports, presentations, and manuals of organizational practices. Now, these efforts have been extended to include unstructured documents such as e-mails, text documents, and contributions by individuals. New knowledge is also created by discovering patterns and hidden facts in corporate data. Organizations' transaction processing data also provides information about sales, customers, vendors, etc.

Knowledge Storage

Storage of knowledge involves creation of a database or central repository. Documents management systems that digitize, index, and tag documents to a systematic framework are large databases of stored collection of documents. Expert systems, which are widely used as decision support systems (explained later in this chapter), also help in preserving the knowledge that is acquired by organizations during processes and developing cultures in their lifetime. The advancement in IT has opened new avenues in enterprise portals and intranet-based systems as repositories of knowledge. For example, an organization can motivate its employees to share their experiences, suggest new solutions, and share new breakthroughs on the corporate portal or intranet.

Knowledge Dissemination

Knowledge that is not shared is of no use to anybody. Organizations benefit from the knowledge repositories only when the knowledge is shared and is available to the person in need of it for making the right and effective decisions. Though knowledge is treated as private and confidential by individuals, the management should reward sharing of knowledge for the benefit of the entire organization. According to Laudon (2010), portal, e-mail, instant messaging, wikis, social networks, and search engines have added to an existing array of collaboration technologies and office systems for sharing calendars, documents, data, and graphics. Corporate portals and intranets are supposed to be the best repositories of a knowledge base that is shared by everyone in the organization.

Knowledge Application

Knowledge is used after seeking or sourcing it from the organizations' knowledge repository. Knowledge that is not shared and applied to the practical problems in the organization does not add any business value. To generate better return on investments, organizations should consider knowledge as an indispensable part of the management decision-making process.

Categories

The challenge of a KM system is to identify and integrate all the components to meet the knowledge management needs of the organization. The knowledge base is developed using networked technologies, enterprise databases, content management systems, work systems, and by analytical tools to discover patterns. All these activities can be clubbed together into three broad categories—enterprise knowledge portals, knowledge work systems, and intelligent techniques—as illustrated in Table 13.1.

Enterprise knowledge portals are general-purpose company-wide efforts to collect, store, share, and apply knowledge in the organization. Knowledge portals are the doorways to many KM systems. These systems include the knowledge base in the enterprise solutions, content management systems, portals, search engines, and collaboration tools such as e-mails, wikis, electronic document management systems, and learning systems within the organization. There are a number of tools and systems being offered by various vendors as ready-to-use applications for knowledge management. Table 13.2 presents a detailed comparison of these tools.

Table. 13.1   Categories of knowledge management systems with examples

Categories of KMS	Description	IT tools for KM	Purpose
Enterprise knowledge portals	General-purpose enterprise portals, content management systems, collaboration tools, and knowledge network systems	Collaboration tools such as Lotus Notes, wikis, file sharing, chat-forums, workflow systems, newsletters, documents management, employee directories, storage of best practices, SOPs, and FAQs	Knowledge building and sharing
Knowledge work systems	Specialized tools for knowledge workers such as engineers and doctors	Computer-aided design (CAD) tools, computer-aided manufacturing (CAM) tools, 3D visualization, analysers, and virtual reality tools	Knowledge-work delivery
Intelligent techniques	Artificial intelligence tools for discovering patterns by data analysis	Data mining, OLAP, neural networks, fuzzy logic, genetic algorithms, and expert systems	Discovering knowledge by analysis

Table 13.2   KM tools offered by international vendors

Knowledge management category	Description	Products
Collaborative computing tools	Groupware are used to enhance tacit knowledge and provide enterprise-wide collaborative environment	Lotus Notes/Domino, MeetingPlace, QuickPlace, eRoom, PlaceWare
Enterprise knowledge portals	Evolved from expert information systems (EIS) and group-support system, combine data integration, reporting mechanism, and collaboration	IBM/Lotus, Knowmadic, OpenText, Autonomy, Brio, Microsoft, Oracle, Dataware, Epicentric
Electronic document management	Electronic document management proposes documents on electronic form as the collaborative focus of work. Used as knowledge repository, content management tools	OmniDocs by Newgen, DocuShare by Xerox, Lotus Notes by IBM, Enterprise Work Management by Eastman
Knowledge management suites	Out-of-the-box packages to combine communication, collaboration, and storage technology into one	IBM/Lotus, QuickPlace, Sametime, KnowledgeX

Organizations use specialized software tools such as computer-aided design (CAD), computer-aided manufacturing, and three dimensional visualization tools. These tools and systems are used by knowledge workers such as scientists, engineers, and doctors. These activities can be grouped as *knowledge work systems*.

Intelligent techniques such as data mining, expert systems, neural networks, genetic algorithm, fuzzy logic, and intelligent agents are used to discover knowledge. Though KM systems typically do not involve running models to solve problems, they provide help in solving problems by applying knowledge. Hence, intelligent techniques can be useful in gaining knowledge and business insights.

CHALLENGES

There is no universally accepted definition of KM, just as there is no agreement as to what constitutes knowledge in the first place. For different people, knowledge management means different things. For this reason, KM poses challenges in the form of getting employees to collaborate and share ideas, maintaining and updating the knowledge base, and dealing with the data deluge that is created as a consequence of stakeholders' participation in knowledge base creation.

Getting Employees on Board

Knowledge management is a collaborative effort. The major problem that occurs in KM is getting employees to participate in the knowledge-building process. In an environment where an individual's knowledge is valued and rewarded, establishing a culture that recognizes tacit knowledge and encourages employees to share it is critical. The importance of selling the KM concept to employees should not be underestimated. KM is a process in which employees are asked to share their knowledge and experience—the very traits that make them valuable as individuals. To encourage people to participate in this effort, an organization has to inculcate knowledge collection and dissemination into employees' everyday jobs. It should be as easy and natural for employees to participate in the knowledge base building process as performing their daily routine jobs.

Updating Knowledge Base

Organizational experience and knowledge change with time. As with many physical assets, the value of knowledge can erode over time. As knowledge is outdated fast, the content in a KM programme should be constantly updated by adding new knowledge and experience by employees, and research outcomes to the knowledge base. The knowledge may become irrelevant with passing time; new knowledge and experience must be added to the system. Therefore, knowledge management is a constantly evolving business practice. Exhibit 13.2 illustrates how Wipro continuously strived for its KM initiatives and received the KM Reality award in 2002 for the same.

As illustrated in the opening exhibit, BlueCoat constantly updates its technical expertise and experience to the KM system to help its employees and customers.

EXHIBIT 13.2

Wipro: How a Knowledge Management Vision Became a Reality

Wipro Technologies' KM initiative has its roots in a quality assurance system that the company developed over a decade. Wipro's efforts in building and maintaining a successful corporate-wide KM programme was rewarded by KM Reality Magazine in 2002.

As part of its approach to KM, Wipro has successfully used its inherent strengths in people and processes to evolve an IT-enabled framework cutting across the boundaries of culture, content, communities, and business processes. Wipro's initiatives such as Six Sigma, PCMM, and CMMi are added to the central knowledge management repository on a continuous basis.

Wipro Technologies is the technology services division of Wipro Ltd, which was founded in 1945 and manufactured a variety of consumer and electronics products. In 1980, Wipro Ltd entered the information technology field. Head quartered in Bengaluru, Wipro Technologies now serves more than 300 clients, including companies such as Cisco, Sony, IBM, and Ericsson. About half of its work is in enterprise IT development, in which Wipro helps companies run their IT systems, and the other half is engineering work involving the design of software products.

Wipro attributes its record of completing over 90% of projects on time (compared to the industry average of 55%) to the Six Sigma programme. It also cites a significant defect reduction and a failure rate of only 1% in its hardware business. Wipro also offers Six Sigma consulting services to companies that need to implement their own programmes. For example, a multinational chemical company wanted to improve the quality of its products, reducing the number of defects detected after delivery. It engaged Wipro to provide a set of web-based interactive technical support tools to reduce defects.

(Contd)

Exhibit 13.2 (Contd)

The process of capturing and disseminating information has continued to grow in the company. Wipro uses SharePoint from Microsoft for its document repository, which is accessible to everyone. Learning is an ongoing process, supported by readily available information and structured learning.

'Sometimes, there is work to be done on knowledge to convert it to a form in which it can be absorbed', says Sambuddha Deb, chief quality officer, Wipro Technologies. 'We use a variety of computer-based training tools, and also turn to outside developers.'

The company also supports centres of excellence (CoEs) in which people learn and create new knowledge and propagate knowledge throughout the enterprise. The CoEs have a number of different focus areas, including telecom, e-commerce, enterprise application services, and embedded solutions. In addition to generating new patents and reusable components and services, the CoEs also provide a forum for Wipro staff to develop their expertise.

Praising Wipro's KM initiative, Hugh McKellar, KM World's executive editor said, 'In many organizations, knowledge management is just rhetoric. The KM Reality award recognizes an organization in which knowledge management is a positive reality.'

According to Deb, 'Having a unified framework has helped build a cohesive knowledge base across the company accessible to the entire user community in Wipro. Winning this award is a validation of our approach to collaboration and knowledge management at Wipro.'

Wipro has started providing end-to-end collaboration and knowledge management services, including KM application development for knowledge portals, expertise management systems, knowledge repositories, and executive dashboards to global corporate enterprises through a unique blend of domain knowledge, technology expertise, and process excellence.

'As the recipient of Year 2002 KM Reality award, Wipro is an organization demonstrating leadership in the implementation of knowledge management practices and processes by realising measurable business benefits. Wipro as the winner of the KM Reality award consistently delivered on the expectation of knowledge management,' Deb added.

Sources:
Lamont, Judith, 'Behind the scenes at Wipro: How a KM vision became reality', http://www.kmworld.com/Articles/Editorial/Feature/Behind-the-scenes-at-Wipro-How-a-KM-vision-became-reality-9485.aspx, last accessed on 17 March 2012.
'Wipro bags KM Reality Award for knowledge management', http://www.domain-b.com/companies/companies_w/wipro/20021119_km_reality.html, last accessed on 19 November 2002.

Data Deluge

Participation by employees, customers, and suppliers in an unguided and moderated manner may lead to contradiction and confusion with regard to vast amounts of data. Therefore, organizations need to detect information overload diligently. Quantity rarely equals quality, and knowledge management is no exception. Thus, the primary task of a KM system is to identify and disseminate knowledge gems from a sea of information. For example, at the macro level, wikis are the perfect example of collaborative KM. The inputs by various participants must be examined before publishing.

The knowledge-based decision support system (DSS) can enhance the decision support capabilities by not only providing tools for decision-making, but also by enhancing various computerized decision support systems. Artificial intelligence, expert systems, neural networks, fuzzy logic systems, genetic algorithms, and intelligent agents are some such knowledge-based DSS. We will discuss the essentials of these techniques in the following sections.

ARTIFICIAL INTELLIGENCE

Artificial intelligence (AI) refers to replicating the thought process of humans into machines like computers. AI is the behaviour of a machine, which if performed by humans, would be called intelligent. Rich (1991) defines AI as 'the study of how to make computers do things at which, at

Table 13.3 Examples of commercial applications of artificial intelligence

Decision support
- Use of expert knowledge to attain high-level decision performance
- Intelligent work environment that explains complex engineering design and decision-making
- Situation assessment and resource allocation software used in airlines, airports, and logistic centres

Manufacturing and hazardous work
- Robotics for manufacturing in hazardous processes
- Machine vision inspection systems for gauging, guiding, identifying, and inspecting products

Information management
- AI-based Internet systems that retrieve information

- Natural language technology to retrieve any sort of online information such as text, pictures, videos, maps, and audio clips in response to the English language
- Data mining for marketing trend analysis, financial forecasting, etc.

Speech and language processing
- Voice and speech recognition technology are being used in call centres
- Computer users can interact with computers in their local/native languages
- Automatic translation is possible with AI
- Human computer interface that can understand spoken language and gestures and facilitate problem-solving

the moment, people are better.' According to O'Brien, (2007), the objective of AI is to develop computers that can simulate the ability to think, as well as see, hear, walk, talk, and feel. A major thrust of AI is the simulation of computer functions normally associated with human intelligence, such as reasoning, learning, and problem-solving.

AI technologies are being used in a variety of ways to improve business decisions. According to Winston (1997), AI-enabled applications are involved in information distribution and retrieval, database mining, product design, manufacturing, inspection, training, user support, surgical planning, resource scheduling, and complex resource management. Table 13.3 illustrates some of the commercial applications of AI.

In the context of decision support and MIS, artificial intelligence methods and tools are embedded in a number of KM systems. AI methods can assist in identifying expertise, eliciting knowledge automatically, interfacing through natural language processing, and conducting smart search through intelligent agents.

Commercial Applications

AI is extensively used in the fields of science, medicine, and education. It is also gaining popularity in commercial and business applications. AI is being used for decision support and information management to carry out hazardous manufacturing jobs and language and speech processing.

EXPERT SYSTEMS

When an organization comes across a complex problem, it often turns to an expert for advice. The expert is supposed to have specific knowledge and experience in the problem area and should be aware of the alternatives, chances of success, and costs and benefits to the organization. For more structured problems, organizations use computer-based expert systems.

Expert systems are the most popular and widely-used application of AI in business. Expert systems are knowledge-based information systems that use expert knowledge in a specific and limited domain in business decision-making. Expert systems provide answers to questions in very specific problem areas by inferring conclusions like how a human expert would from the set of rules defined in the software. Expert systems offer applications in taxation, credit analysis, equipment maintenance, fault diagnosis, etc., as a tool to improve productivity and quality.

Laudon (2010) argues that expert systems lack the breadth of knowledge and the understanding of fundamental principles of a human expert. They typically perform very limited tasks, which can also be performed by professionals in a few minutes or hours, such as diagnosing a malfunctioning machine or determining whether credit should be granted for a loan.

However, later generation expert systems are more flexible in adopting multiple knowledge and reasoning methods. They may integrate neural networks with rule-based inferences to achieve higher decision performance.

Components

Expert systems involve three components—knowledge base, inference engine, and user interface. These systems use if-then rules to represent and store their knowledge and can apply reasoning methods to solve a problem. The set of rules that model human knowledge are collectively called knowledge base. These set of rules are nested in the software program to be used for decision-making. Figure 13.2 illustrates an example of how rules are embedded in a software program.

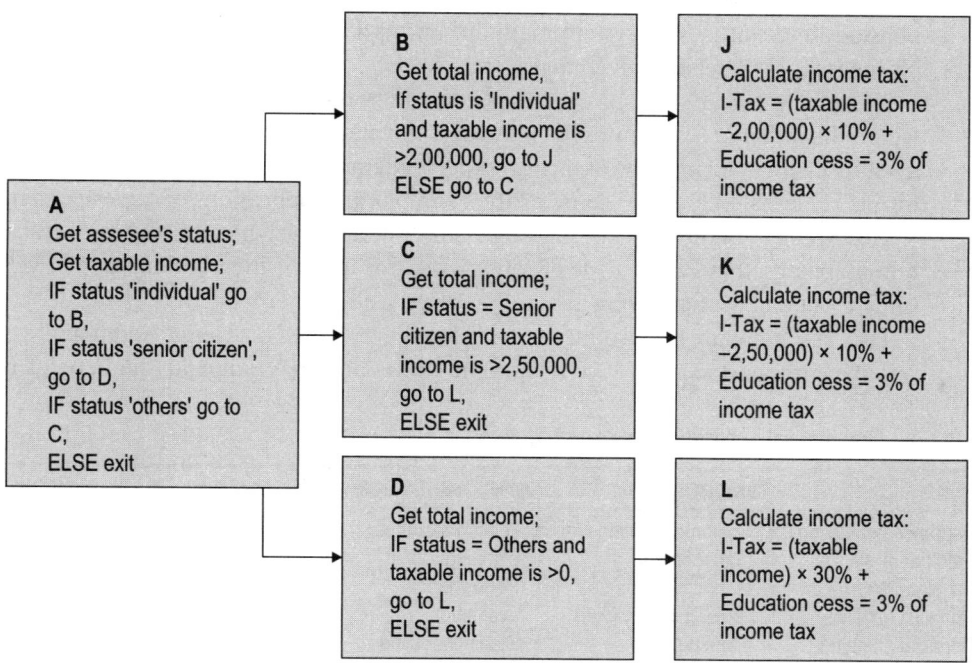

Fig. 13.2   Defining rules in a simple income tax calculation expert system
for an individual salaried person

The method used to search through the knowledge base is called inference engine. This is known as the control structure or the rule interpreter. The inference engine is essentially a software program that processes knowledge such as rules and facts, related to a problem.

Expert systems contain a language processor for problem-oriented communication between the user and the computer. This user interface establishes communication in the natural language with the user in the form of questions, forms, menus, and graphs.

Applications

Expert systems have been applied in many business and technological areas to support decision-making. They provide a number of benefits to businesses such as improved decisions, reduced errors, decreased costs, and higher levels of quality and service. Expert systems have been used by banks and lending companies. They are built with the capability to analyse credit records of customers and assess the value. Similarly, rules in the knowledge base can also help assess the risk and risk management policies.

Expert systems have been used in customer support, finance, marketing, human resource management, manufacturing, vendor evaluation, etc. For example, Logitech, one of the world's largest manufacturers of mouse and web cameras, uses expert systems for customer support. The web-based software emulates the way a human would interact with a customer, allows the user to ask questions or describe problems in the natural language, and carries on an intelligent conversation with the user and provides an accurate answer.

Nestlé Food Corporation has deployed an expert system that provides information on employee pension fund status. The system maintains an updated knowledge base to give the user advice on the impact of regulation changes, etc.

In India, there are web-based self-assessment and income tax return filing systems available, where the individual can enter the required information and the system calculates tax, generates a self-assessment form to the user as an expert system (similar to http://www.taxsmile.com/index.html). Table 13.4 illustrates some of the examples of applications of expert systems.

According to Laudon (2010), although expert systems lack the robust and general intelligence of human beings, they can provide benefits to organizations if their limitations are well understood. Only certain classes of problems can be solved using expert systems.

Expert systems are useful only in solving highly structured problems. Additionally, expert systems require large and expensive development efforts and may outgrow the benefits of using such

Table 13.4   Commercial applications of expert systems

Finance	Marketing	Human Resource	Manufacturing	Procurement
• Insurance evaluation • Credit analysis • Tax planning • Financial analysis • Financial planning • Performance evaluation	• Customer relationship management • Market analysis • Product and market planning	• Human resource planning • Performance evaluation • Staff scheduling • Pension management • Legal advising	• Production planning • Quality management • Product design • Equipment maintenance and repair	• Vendor evaluation • Vendor relationship • Equipment selection

expert systems. Many times, the rules used in expert systems continually change and maintaining the systems become very expensive for the organization.

NEURAL NETWORKS

We earlier discussed that expert systems help in decision-making if the problem is well structured, and use explicit data, information, or knowledge stored in a computer system. However, in a complex real-life situation, managers take decisions based on partial, incomplete, or sometimes even inaccurate information. Such situations occur in a rapidly changing environment. Therefore, decision-makers rely on their experience of handling similar situations. They recall their experiences and suggest solutions for which the exact replica is not available. When this approach to problem-solving is applied by a computer system, it is called artificial neural networks.

Neural networks are so called because these systems are modelled after the brain's mesh like a network of interconnected processing elements, the neuron cells. Neural networks discover knowledge by using hardware and software that simulate the processing pattern of the biological brain. They 'learn' from the data they process. They use large amounts of data and find patterns and relationships that would be too complicated and difficult for a human being to analyse. According to Botchner (1997), the more data examples a neural network receives as input, the better it can learn to duplicate the results of the examples it processes.

According to Turban (2005), neural computing uses a pattern-recognition approach to problem-solving, and it has been employed successfully in many business applications. Neural network applications in medicine, science, and business address problems in pattern classification, prediction, financial analysis, and control and optimization. Medical science finds great use of neural networks for screening patients for coronary artery diseases, epilepsy, etc., and carrying out pattern recognition of pathology images.

In the business world, the financial industry uses neural networks to discern patterns in vast pools of data that might help predict the performance of equities, corporate bond ratings, corporate bankruptcies, etc.

Neural networks need training by feeding various types of data and posing questions so that they can establish a pattern. Surprisingly, neural networks may not reach the same conclusion for a problem when it is posed to the system the next time. They cannot guarantee a certain conclusive result every time a problem is given. This is because such networks are sensitive and the relationship they establish in the pool of data may change. Therefore, neural networks are mostly used as a support to human decision-making and not as a substitute for it.

FUZZY LOGIC SYSTEMS

Fuzzy logic is an advance DSS. It approaches problems the way people handle them. According to O'Brien (2007), fuzzy logic is a method of reasoning that resembles human reasoning as it allows for approximate value and inferences (fuzzy logic), and incomplete and ambiguous data (fuzzy data), instead of relying only on crisp data, such as binary (yes/no) choices.

For example, we say the temperature is hot, cold, or warm; or a company is large, medium, or small. What makes a company medium? Can we say one million or a lesser turnover makes the company medium? These categories represent a range of values. These imprecisions can

EXHIBIT 13.3

Fuzzy Logic: The Social Impact

According to James Douglas, chairman and founder of the London-based executive search firm, EMA Partners International, India is where the opportunity lies. He visited India and presented his views about Indian managers. What about Indian managers? How do they compare with their global counterparts? He points out that there are certain characteristics about Indian managers—they are entrepreneurial and have the ability and preparedness to do new things and not be boxed in. On the other hand, too many of the Western managers play safe when times are tough.

'India operates on fuzzy logic and there is ambiguity in the way people do things, so Indians are able to cope with ambiguity better. In a European environment, managers are unwilling to cope with situations when things go wrong. If you have been working in a growth situation and then you hit the brick wall, people surrender; so, I think the ability to

think on their feet and cope with the uncertainty of the future has given me a positive impression of Indian managers. Indians working outside of India have turned around tough situations in a different cultural situation,' he says. Around 10 years ago, it was pretty difficult to find an Indian chief executive officer (CEO) in a western country; however, today there are a number of major corporations, which have appointed senior Indian executives and the trend is likely to grow, says Douglas confidently. That is something even most management gurus talk about.

Source:
'India's fuzzy logic helps Indians cope with ambiguity better', *The Times of India*, 19 November 2011, http://timesofindia. indiatimes.com/business/india-business/Indias-fuzzy-logic-helps-Indians-cope-with-ambiguity-better/articleshow/ 10791874.cms, last accessed on 18 December 2011.

be handled mathematically in a precise way to assist decision-makers in solving problems with imprecise statements for their inputs.

Fuzzy logic is a rule-based AI that can represent such ambiguity by creating rules that use approximate or subjective values. Organizations can develop software using individual knowledge wherever there is linguistic ambiguity. For example, rules can be defined to categorize a company into small if the turnover is below 10 million, medium between 10 to 50 million, and large if more than 50 million.

Fuzzy logic finds applications in fraud detection in medical claims processed by healthcare providers in the US. Exhibit 13.3 talks about the impact of fuzzy logic.

GENETIC ALGORITHMS

Genetic algorithms are also an advanced form of AI. They are inspired by the Darwinian Theory (survival of the fittest) and solve problems in an evolutionary manner. They mimic the process of evolution and search for an increasingly better solution by using techniques such as randomization and mathematical functions like algorithms.

Genetic algorithms are useful for solving problems that are dynamic and complex in nature, involving thousands of possible solutions. The technique evaluates all possible solutions and suggests the best optimal solution. It is useful for problems where the range of possible solutions can be represented genetically and criteria can be defined for evaluating the fitness. Genetic algorithms are capable of evaluating many solution alternatives at a very high speed.

According to Goldberg (1994), genetic algorithms were first used to simulate millions of years in biological, geological, and ecosystem evolution in just a few minutes on a computer. Now, genetic algorithm software is being used to model a variety of scientific, technical, and business processes.

Hindustan Aeronautics in Bengaluru uses genetic algorithms for DSS in designing products.

INTELLIGENT AGENTS

Intelligent agents are gaining popularity as tools of artificial intelligence to perform certain predefined tasks for the users. According to Laudon (2010), intelligence agents are software programs that work in the background without direct human intervention to carry out specific, repetitive, and predictable tasks for an individual user, business process, or software application.

Most intelligent agents include expert systems or another intelligent component to perform a predefined task. The agent applies a limited built-in or learned knowledge base to accomplish tasks or take decisions on the user's behalf. For example, an intelligent agent can delete junk mails, schedule appointments, or suggest a pen of your preference when you buy a diary online on an e-commerce portal. Applications of intelligent agents include finding pattern in consumer behaviour, stock market analysis, supply chain, etc.

There are many built-in intelligent agents available in today's operating systems, office productivity tools, e-mail systems, mobile computing systems, etc. The wizards in MS-Office are built-in intelligent tools that can analyse how an end-user is using the software package and offer their suggestions on various usages.

SGC Logistics Ltd, a New Delhi-based logistic firm, implemented an offline desktop application for its freight transportation management. The software runs independently in branches and works on a distributed database at each site of implementation, including the head office. An intelligent agent, developed by BNG Infotech, called 'Static IP Agent', resides in the applications in the branches. At a certain frequency, the Agent looks for Internet connectivity and tries to connect to the desired database server (based on the IP identity). If the Internet connection is working, it pushes the branch data into the server and pulls the relevant information for the branch. This is done without the knowledge of the users at both the sites.

These tools of AI for DSS help managers in decision-making. These concepts and ideas may be developed in different areas and may be applied to different domains.

SUMMARY

Knowledge management (KM) is the process through which organizations generate value from their intellectual and knowledge-based assets. KM systems help organizations identify, select, organize, disseminate, and transfer important information and expertise that are part of organizational experience and were hitherto unstructured in the organization.

Knowledge has become so imperative that it is treated as a kind of business asset such as buildings and machinery. To get the most value from a company's intellectual assets, knowledge must be shared and serve as the foundation for collaboration.

The knowledge flow in the organization necessarily involves four steps—knowledge acquisition, storage, dissemination, and application. The knowledge base is developed using networked technologies, enterprise databases, content management systems, work systems, and by analytical tools to discover patterns. All these activities can be clubbed together into three broad categories—enterprise-wide KM systems, knowledge work systems, and intelligent techniques.

KM poses challenges in the form of getting employees to collaborate and share ideas, maintaining and updating the knowledge base, and dealing with the data deluge that is created as a consequence of stakeholders' participation in knowledge base creation.

Artificial intelligence (AI) involves replicating the thought process of humans in machines like computers. A major thrust of AI is the simulation of computer functions normally associated with human intelligence, such as reasoning, learning, and problem-solving.

Expert systems are the most popular and widely-used applications of AI in business. Expert systems are knowledge-based information systems that use expert knowledge in a specific and limited domain in business decision-making. The expert systems involve three components—knowledge base, inference engine, and user interface. Expert systems have been used in customer support, finance, marketing, human resource management, manufacturing, vendor evaluation, etc.

Often, managers make decisions out of incomplete information or partial data; hence, they recall their experiences and suggest solutions for which the exact replica is not available. When this approach to problem-solving is applied by a computer system, it is called an artificial neural network. Neural computing uses a pattern-recognition approach to problem-solving, and they have been employed successfully in many business applications.

Fuzzy logic is a method of reasoning that resembles human reasoning as it allows for approximate value and inferences (fuzzy logic), and incomplete and ambiguous data

(fuzzy data) instead of relying only on crisp data like binary (yes/no) choices. Fuzzy logic is a rule-based AI that can represent such ambiguity by creating rules that use approximate or subjective values.

Genetic algorithms are also an advanced form of AI that solve problems in an evolutionary manner. They mimic the process of evolution and search for an increasingly better solution by using techniques like randomization and other mathematical functions like algorithms.

Intelligent agents are gaining popularity as tools of AI to perform certain predefined tasks for the users. Intelligence agents act as software programs that work in the background without direct human intervention to carry out specific, repetitive, and predictable tasks for an individual user, a business process, or a software application.

KEY TERMS

Artificial intelligence (AI) A technology for replicating the thought process of humans in machines like computers.

Cognitive science An area of artificial intelligence that researches how the human brain works and applies the findings to a computer-based system design.

Collaboration tools Systems that help create and share documents by a group of people.

Content management systems Systems to create, use, and share contents in an enterprise knowledge portal.

Enterprise knowledge portals General-purpose company-wide efforts to collect, store, share, and apply knowledge in the organization.

Expert systems Knowledge-based information systems that use expert knowledge in a specific and limited domain in business decision-making.

Fuzzy logic A method of reasoning that resembles human reasoning since it allows for approximate values and inferences.

Genetic algorithm Systems that mimic the process of evolution and search for an increasingly better solution by using techniques like randomization and other mathematical functions.

Inference engine A method used to search through the knowledge base.

Intelligent agents Software programs that work in the background without direct human intervention to carry out specific tasks.

Intelligent techniques Tools for discovering patterns and applying knowledge to discrete decisions and knowledge domains.

Knowledge base A set of rules that model human knowledge.

Knowledge management systems IT-enabled systems that help organizations to identify, select, organize, disseminate, and transfer important information and expertise.

Knowledge work systems Specialized workstations and tools for knowledge workers like engineers to create and discover knowledge.

Neural networks Use of hardware and software to simulate the processing pattern of the biological brain.

Robotic applications Applications using machines with computer intelligence and human-like physical capabilities.

Strategic resource A resource that gives an organization a sustainable competitive advantage.

CONCEPT REVIEW QUESTIONS

1. What is knowledge management? Define the role of knowledge management systems in business.
2. What are the various stages in knowledge management in a business organization?
3. What are the various ways by which knowledge is

created or used for business decision-making?
4. What are the challenges of knowledge management systems?
5. Discuss the various ways in which knowledge management systems could help organizations with

manufacturing and production systems.

6. What do you understand by artificial intelligence (AI)? Given examples of AI in business.

7. How do expert systems help business managers in decision-making?

8. Define and explain the following tools of knowledge

management that help in management information systems:

(a) Neural networks

(b) Fuzzy logic

(c) Genetic algorithm

(d) Intelligent agents

CRITICAL THINKING QUESTIONS

1. Why is it difficult to capture and manage knowledge in a business organization?

2. 'Knowledge management is a process of generating value from knowledge-based assets. It has nothing to do with IT.' Discuss this statement with suitable

examples.

3. What are some of the limitations you see in the use of AI technologies such as expert systems, genetic algorithms, and intelligent agents?

MIS DEVELOPMENT

Naaptol.com is an Indian e-commerce site that helps in comparing and selling goods online. Promoting itself as a 'knowledge store', the company was established in January 2008 and is the first comparison-based social shopping portal of India. From consumer goods to laptops, mobiles to clothes, books to kitchenware, liquid crystal display (LCD) TVs to gifts, jewellery to home appliances and a lot more, can be found with the latest deals and at the lowest prices. By visiting the website of this store, you will find thousands of exciting offers. The site helps one compare prices and shop online for cameras, mobiles, laptops, bikes, and cars. At the click of the mouse, you can compare various products, find

stores, and click interesting deals.

Exercise

1. Log in to this website and find out how products, their prices, and qualities can be compared. Study the reviews and find out how valid or invalid those reviews are for any category of products.

2. Would it be justified to call naaptol.com a web-based decision support system for retail consumers? Why or why not?

3. Find out similar e-commerce sites and compile a list while comparing the features offered by them.

REFERENCES

Agrawal, Dr Anand Mohan, 'Knowledge management in higher technical institutes', www.iamot.org/conference/index.php/ocs/4/paper/viewFile/982/405, last accessed on 16 December 2011.

Botchner, Ed, 'Data mining: Plumbing the depths of corporate databases', *Computerworld*, 21 April 1997.

Davenport, Thomas H. and Gilbert Probst, *Knowledge Management Case Book: Siemens Best Practices*, John Wiley & Sons, New York, 2002.

Davenport, Thomas H. and Larry Prusak, *Working Knowledge: How Organizations Manage What they Know*, Harvard Business School Press, Boston, 2000.

Gantz, John, 'The new world of enterprise reporting is here', *Computerworld*, 1 February 1999.

Goldberg, David, 'Genetic and evolutionary algorithms come

of age', *Communication of ACM*, 1994.

Jaiswal, Mahadeo and Monika Mittal, *Management Information Systems*, Oxford University Press, New Delhi, 2004.

Jawadekar, Waman S., *Management Information Systems, Text and Cases*, Tata McGraw-Hill, New Delhi, 2008.

Kalakota, Ravi and Marcia Robinson, *E-business 2.0: Roadmap for Success*, Addison-Wesley, Reading, 2001.

Laudon, Ken, Jane Laudon, and RajanishDass, *Management Information Systems*, Pearson Education, Singapore, 2010.

O'Brien, James A., George M. Marakas, and Ramesh Behl, *Management Information Systems*, Tata McGraw-Hill, New Delhi, 2007.

Rich, Elaine and Kevin Knight, *Artificial Intelligence*, McGraw-Hill, New York, 1991.

Turban, Efraim, Jay E. Ronson, and Ling-Peng Liang, *Decision*

Support Systems and Intelligent Systems, Pearson Education, Singapore, 2005.

Winston, Patrick, 'Rethinking artificial intelligence', Massachusetts Institute of Technology, September, 1997.

http://alanwhitehouse.wordpress.com/2011/04/07/the-microsoft-business-intelligence-stack-cheat-sheet/, last accessed on 15 December 2011.

CASE STUDY

Siemens: Raising the Benchmark in Knowledge Management

Siemens has been renowned for its excellence in implementing KM since 1999, as seen by the global recognition of its outstanding performance in delivering a knowledge-driven culture and maximizing enterprise intellectual capital. Given the networked nature of MNCs like Siemens, there are different applications of knowledge that do not apply to single-site companies. The notion of knowledge transfer, for example, is far more intricate within MNCs as opposed to non-MNCs. Within MNCs, flow of knowledge is convoluted due to multiple organization layers, dispersed geographical locations, and diverse cultural values.

Organizational Background

Siemens AG is a German multinational conglomerate headquartered in Munich, Germany. It is the largest Europe-based electronics and electrical engineering company. Siemens is an integrated technology company with activities grouped in the fields of industry, energy, healthcare, equity investments, IT solutions and services, and financial services (SFS). Siemens and its subsidiaries employ approximately 3,60,000 people across nearly 190 countries in Europe, Africa, Middle East, Americas, Asia, and Australia. The giant reported global revenue of approximately €71 billion in 2011.

Due to the company's worldwide operations, responsibilities and managerial roles were organized into different regions. Corporate governance was looked after by a managing board that was responsible for conducting top management activities across different divisions worldwide. The reporting structure followed a decentralized structure, which meant that each division was independent from other divisions in terms of managerial and operational roles although sharing a similar reporting structure towards headquarters.

Knowledge Management Initiatives

As also highlighted in Exhibit 13.1, knowledge management at Siemens began in a bottom-up manner via various mid-level initiatives. Managers of these initiatives themselves formed a semi-official community of practice. This was then followed by a corporate knowledge function, which officially supported and coordinated these various initiatives via the creation of the corporate KM (CKM) office in 1999.

Siemens appreciated the value of KM in creating an organizational unit that would be responsible for worldwide deployment of KM. At the heart of Siemens' technical solution to knowledge management is a website called ShareNet, which combines elements of a database repository, a chat room, and a search engine. Online entry forms allow employees to store information that they think might be useful to colleagues. Other employees are able to search the repository, browse by topics, and then contact the authors for more information on the subject using the available communication channels.

Increasingly, information is either a part of or an important facilitator of Siemens' diverse businesses. As knowledge management is greatly enhanced by the effective use of IT, it is not surprising that Siemens was a relatively early and enthusiastic adopter of KM. The IT-driven nature of the company's businesses also provides a strong motivation to manage knowledge effectively. One attribute of these technologies is that they change very rapidly; keeping up with various computing and communications technologies is much easier when a company has a system for rapidly circulating new knowledge.

Another innovative knowledge management practice comes from Siemens' German sales unit and was called knowledge networking service (KNS). The objective of knowledge networking is to 'create a living network of knowledge amongst all employees'. The key requisites for KNS are a mix of high-tech and high-touch networking, encouraging voluntary participation, and creating a mix of interdisciplinary backgrounds.

Siemens industrial services has its presence in over 70 countries and employs 22,000 people. It uses a knowledge-sharing tool called 'know-how exchange' to connect experts, employees and their diverse project experiences. Areas of expertise here include engineering layouts, project structures, plant building, and contract negotiation for automotive and textile plants. A search interface called 'knowledge spider' has been developed, searching across people, teams, events, and activities. The KM initiative is actively promoted via in-house magazines and public relations campaigns.

The knowledge areas covered include financing, planning, engineering, and operation. This helps sales staff devise customized telecom solutions using existing service packages, business plans, and profitability paths. ShareNet helps tap and share local innovation in different parts of the world via project debriefings, manuals, codified databases, structured questionnaires, chat rooms, and hot lines. Technically based on OpenText's LiveLink, it is used by 7000 sales and marketing staff.

Knowledge Management Strategy Development

From a KM strategy development perspective, the initial phase of KM in Siemens saw a strong focus on knowledge reuse through sharing the best practices. ShareNet was intended to help find the knowledge and best practices needed and reuse them to perform particular tasks. The basic idea of ShareNet was that knowledge created somewhere in the world should be made available for global reuse. ShareNet intends to network all local solution efforts to facilitate cooperative global learning, local reuse of global best practices, and the creation of global solution competences.

From 2008, Siemens has included the development of enterprise social software as part of its knowledge management strategy development. This development was driven by external factors like the growing informal use of social networking tools within the communities. This emerging adoption of social software in Siemens showed the transition in Siemens knowledge management, from primarily connecting people to content, to currently including connecting people to people.

The CKM office held an international meeting in Munich in May 2000, drawing over 200 managers and KM practitioners to formally reflect on the company's KM strategy via the CKM Council and CKM TaskForce. Moving beyond a loose association of KM followers, the company now has formal support, constancy, transparency and a joint approach for KM practices.

Organizational Culture

There can be numerous barriers to sharing knowledge in a company—personal (lack of time or confidence), collective (in-house competition), structural (poor IT infrastructure), or political (lack of openness). Siemens did have its share. Siemens overcame these obstacles by building a knowledge base organizational culture and adopted various motivational methods.

As part of building the organizational culture, several incentive schemes were introduced, both financial and non-financial, to encourage high user participation in using ShareNet from around the period of 1999–2003. Among these was bonus-on-top, which entailed financial bonus and reward schemes in the form of mileage. Employees were motivated in India by offering incentives in forms of gifts for their personal benefit. Likewise, China witnessed cultural bias in terms of participation when English language was found as a barrier to sharing knowledge and caused a low level of participation. The employees in China were reluctant to participate freely due to their traditional beliefs.

In terms of participation within ShareNet, different motivational factors emerged. While financial incentives culturally remained the strong motivation factor in India, they were not perceived as equal in China. The ShareNet users in China felt that the material rewards were not the main driver to participate, particularly when referring to the spare time they needed to spend for making contributions. Instead, recognition and demonstrated capability were the more important motivational factors.

Risk Management

Risk management was done while developing ShareNet by accepting inputs from subsidiaries. It also involved ensuring buy-in and quality contribution within the user base. The incorporation of content editors, ShareNet managers in local subsidiaries and ShareNet consultants in the headquarters, were attempts to mitigate risks specific to quality assurance. Different incentive schemes throughout different periods of time indicated the versatility of Siemens' approach in managing risks related to functional KM systems.

Siemens' best practice sharing initiatives try to overcome risks by connecting people, incentivizing, designing a topic structure for relevant experience, providing content support for editing and structuring of experiences, and finally through a cascaded communication strategy comprising divisional workshops, posters, postcards, flyers and even matchboxes with the KM Intranet URL. Siemens also has an office of best practices like CKM, which plays an active role in implementation of the concept.

Success Factors

Its success is due to leadership support (from the ShareNet Committee that includes local and global representatives), organizational support (global editor, regional contributors, training bootcamps), motivation system (ShareNet 'shares' for contributions that can be exchanged for equipment or conference fees), organizational culture (promoting sharing with messages like 'Unlike in school, copying is not only allowed – it is required'), and quantifiable benefits (e.g., cost saving by reuse of tenders, increased revenues by competing faster, and alignment with customer needs by spotting worldwide trends).

Employees were encouraged to take part in this exchange and develop a sense of personal responsibility for their participation, so as to create a win-win situation for all. The exchange has a growing number of entries of references, tools, products, customers, industry sectors, and technologies. Know-how transfer has been integrated into standard business processes to enable an employee to learn from others' experiences.

An editorial team helps manage a 'Knowledge and More' personal account statement for employees. Employees receive points for submitting business tips used by call centres and other service staff; these points can be tallied and converted into prizes. All staff are trained on how to use the KM Intranet, through an 'intranet driving license.' They are also sensitized to use it regularly. Knowledge is shared internally and with IBM, Toshiba, Motorola, NEC, Nokia, and Sony. The primary aim for such cooperation and network formation include sharing of risk and development costs, and reducing time to market. The KM initiative uses communities of practice (including NetMeeting and face-to-face get-togethers) to interconnect experts across restructured divisions and different locations, swiftly integrate new employees, and reduce redundancies at different sites.

Discussion Questions

1. What were the KM initiatives taken by Siemens?
2. What did Siemens do to create a knowledge culture in the organization globally?
3. How were the risks of failure of KM mitigated by Siemens?
4. KM is not just use and application of IT and enterprise solutions. Discuss this statement in the light of the Siemens case.

Sources:

Ardianto, Danny and Kerry Tanner (2011). 'Knowledge management governance in multinational companies: A case study of Siemens', PACIS Proceedings.

MacCormack, A., Herman, K., and Volpel, S. (2002), Siemens ShareNet: Building a knowledge network, last accessed on 17 April 2010.

Santosus, Megan, 'Knowledge management: How Siemens keep KM blooming', http://cio.co.nz/cio.nsf/tech/knowledge-management-how-siemens-keeps-km-blooming, last accessed on 17 April 2012.

Thomas, Davenport and Gilbert Probst, '*Knowledge Management Case Book: Siemens Best Practices*', John Wiley/Publicus Corporate Publishing, 2002, Review by Madanmohan Rao at http://www.techsparks.com/Knowledge-Management-Case-Book-Siemens-Best-Practices, last accessed on 17 April 2012.

http://mis.dankook.ac.kr/jchoi/teaching/kms/resource/Siemens ShareNetHBScase.pdf, last accessed on 19 March 2012.

http://www.siemens.com/entry/cc/en, last accessed on 19 March 2012.

14

Mobile Computing and M-commerce

> ❛ *Mobile is a new paradigm for businesses, as it emerges as a powerful sales channel and marketing medium which these businesses must strategize and plan for. With the proliferation of data services, the mobile is slowly going to take on bigger roles in all aspects of businesses and also inevitably the consumers' lives the world over. One is slowly reaching a point where developing a viable mobile strategy is becoming an imperative for small and large businesses for their long-term growth and sustenance.* ❜
>
> –VISHAL SINGHAL

LEARNING OBJECTIVES

After studying this chapter, you will be able to

- appreciate emerging mobile digital platforms
- define mobile computing
- understand the functioning of cellular systems
- know about cellular network standards
- define mobile data networks
- comprehend mobile computing services
- understand the concept and challenges of m-commerce
- understand the applications of m-commerce

EXHIBIT 14.1

Standard Chartered Bank Makes Mobile Banking a Breeze

When Standard Chartered, the London-headquartered bank, took a conscious decision to move over to the iPhone platform in May 2010, the device was nowhere close to be seen as an element of the enterprise IT environment. However, the growing proliferation of the iPhone among employees and the foresight of the chief information officer and other top management into the iPhone's enterprise capabilities triggered off one of the landmark tech implementations in recent years.

Standard Chartered Bank is India's largest international bank with 94 branches in 37 cities, a combined customer base of around two million retail customers and more than 2000 corporate and institutional relationships. Its key businesses comprise consumer banking, including deposits, loans, wealth management, private banking, SME banking, and wholesale banking, which includes cash transaction banking, treasury, corporate finance, and custody services.

In June 2011, Standard Chartered announced the launch of an innovative mobile banking application called Standard Chartered 'Breeze'. The product gives customers greater ease of use and a higher degree of convenience through an intuitive, design-rich interface.

Breeze has been developed based on extensive consumer research and is uniquely designed to take the mobile banking industry by storm. Standard Chartered is one of the first players in India to deliver a comprehensive and rich mobile offering, compatible on over 700 handsets. With these handsets supported from rich mobile experiences on Android, Blackberry, and iPhone to the most basic Nokia devices, this represents possibly the richest and the most comprehensive mobile banking experience in India. iPhone will be the newest addition to the suite offering the first bespoke mobile banking application in India.

Standard Chartered Breeze has been designed keeping the consumers' mobility needs in mind. Customers can access Breeze with their existing online username and password, eliminating the need for multiple passwords and making the offering both secure and convenient. Some unique features to highlight are as follows:

- View bank and credit card accounts
- Transfer funds to other banks in India
- Pay utility bills—offering over 100 billers across the country

- ATM locator—locate the nearest SCB branch/ATM
- M-commerce
  - top up a pre-paid mobile phone (across all networks)
  - choose a cinema, seats, and buy tickets
  - find, book, and pay for airline tickets

Matthew Norris, chief information officer, India and South Asia, Standard Chartered Bank, said, 'Breeze is a comprehensive banking platform that enables our customer to personalize how they see, move and manage their money with incredible ease. This new application by Standard Chartered will serve as a key customer touch point that complements the Bank's physical branch network.'

Aman Narain, group head of remote banking, Standard Chartered Bank, commented, 'Breeze is intuitive, easy-to-use, and most importantly secure. It has been designed by a group of people who are truly passionate about creating great experiences for our customers and we are delighted that they will now be able to access and manage their money from their mobile phones, wherever they are, whenever they want.'

Rajashree Nambiar, general manager, distribution, India, said, 'With mobile phones becoming an integral part of our lives, Breeze will provide a safe, secure, and personalized service delivery channel for the bank to reach out to our customer.'

The Breeze application was built for Android devices using Adobe Creative Suite® and Platform technologies including Flex®, Adobe Flash Builder™, and Adobe AIR® 2.5. All other instances of Breeze and associated m-commerce were built in partnership with Monitise, the leader in mobile applications.

Sources:

'Apple iPhone soon to be work mobile for Standard Chartered Bank', http://www.silicon.com/technology/mobile/2010/05/18/apple-iphone-soon-to-be-work-mobile-for-standard-chartered-bank-staff-39745826/, last accessed on 21 December 2011.

Press Release 'Standard Chartered makes mobile banking a breeze', http://www.standardchartered.co.in/media-centre/pdf/2011_2_june_Standard_Chartered_Breeze.pdf, last accessed on 21 December 2011.

Raval, Abhishek, 'StanChart to bank on iPhone', http://biztech2.in.com/casestudies/mobility/stanchart-to-bank-on-iphone/114842/0, last accessed on 15 November 2011.

Standard Chartered Bank's initiatives (Exhibit 14.1) to offer banking services on the mobile platform is targeted as a new generation, safe, secure, and personalized service delivery channel to the customer. With this initiative, the bank is able to serve its customers more effectively. However, more than a case of effectively leveraging enterprise mobility, Standard Chartered Bank's implementation of the mobile platform is a case study in how enterprises can optimally leverage consumer technology to drive up employee productivity.

In this chapter, we are going to discuss the emerging mobile computing technologies, applications, and trends. Our discussion will encompass the technology, services, and its efficient use in mobile commerce (m-commerce) and hence, management information systems.

EMERGING MOBILE DIGITAL PLATFORM

Across the world, the growth of mobile telephony has been astounding. In India, the growth of mobile usage has been phenomenal because of sharply declining prices, availability of technology, and reliable services. Within a decade, India has reached more than 873.61 million subscribers (TRAI data till September 2011) and they are increasing every month. Corporate business strategists and planners find this channel highly efficient, cost-effective, and an effective way of marketing goods and services.

According to Laudon (2010), as computing increasingly takes place over the network, new mobile digital computing platforms have emerged. Communication devices like cell phones and smartphones such as BlackBerry and iPhone have taken over many of the functions of hand-held computers, including transmission of data, web-surfing, transmission of e-mail and instant messages, display of digital content, and exchange of data with internal corporate systems.

Mobile phones have rapidly become such an essential and integral part of our daily lives that we prefer to carry out interpersonal communication such as e-mail exchange and messaging through them. Business managers and decision-makers are increasingly using these devices to coordinate work and communicate with employees.

MOBILE COMPUTING

Mobile computing refers to the use of a variety of wireless devices (laptops, mobile phones, tablets, etc.) that offer mobility to allow people to connect to the Internet, providing wireless transmission to access data and information from whichever location they may be in. Mobile computing is a form of human–computer interaction by which a computer is expected to be on the move during normal usage. Mobile computing involves mobile hardware, software, and wireless communication. In an organizational context, the concept of using mobile devices while on the move and still remaining connected with the enterprise information systems is called mobile computing.

Terms such as mobile, ubiquitous, nomadic, and pervasive are used by researchers to refer to computing that uses small portable devices and wireless communication networks. Mobile computing allows the mobile workforce to access a full range of corporate services and information from anywhere, at any time.

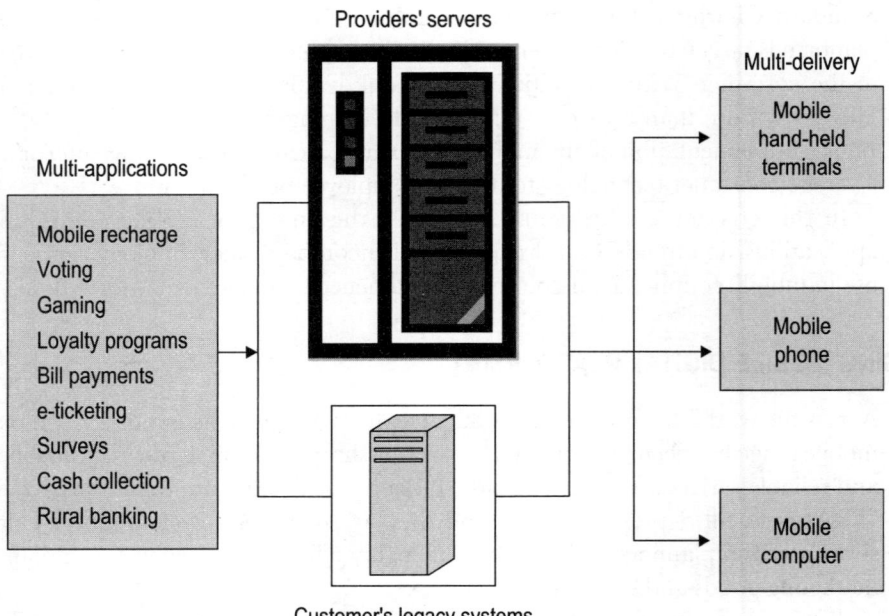

Fig. 14.1   Convergence of multimedia into mobile computing

In the present day mobile computing scenario, the ubiquitous new-age mobile phones offer enormous capabilities—computing, communication, entertainment, and connectivity. This can be called convergence of multimedia in the new-age smartphones (as shown in Fig. 14.1).

Mobile networks are struggling with the sudden explosion in data consumption, driven primarily by video-centric applications on high-end portable devices such as smartphones and tablets. Video-centric applications include the use of images, graphics, and movies on mobile phones. Networks have been choked like never before, leading to embarrassing network outages. Mobile data continues to grow at a phenomenal rate in countries that have already deployed data-centric 3G networks. For example, AT & T has noted a data growth of over 5000% in just three years from 2009 to 2012. Most of this growth is attributed to high bandwidth video-related services such as video chat, IP TV, and access to video content over Internet sites (YouTube and Netflix). The continued price pressure on data rates, along with an unprecedented growth in demand, has created a major challenge for operators around the world.

Mobile Operating Systems

Similar to personal computers, a smartphone requires an operating system to run and play various applications. An operating system for mobiles is known as mobile OS. A mobile OS is the operating system that controls a smartphone, tablet, personal digital assistant (PDA), or any other mobile device. Modern mobile operating systems combine the features of a personal computer operating system with touch screen, cellular, Bluetooth, Wi-Fi, GPS mobile navigation, photo and video camera, speech recognition, voice recorder, music player, etc.

Unlike the PC market, there are many operating systems available for the new generation mobile phones. This is because the manufacturers of mobile phones and their applications came up with a compatible OS. For example, BlackBerry OS was launched in 1999 by Research in Motion (RIM) for BlackBerry phones and Microsoft launched Windows Mobile (Win CE) OS for mobiles.

Androids, BlackBerry, iOS, Windows Phone, Series40, WebOS, etc., are presently the most sought-after mobile operating systems. There are thousands of applications offered for phones supported by these operating systems. We will discuss them briefly.

Android Android, an open source Linux-based OS, comes from Google. It is supported by major hardware vendors and software developers such as Intel, HTC, Samsung, eBay, and Motorola. It was developed in 2005 but appeared in phones in 2008. Android supports Google Docs, apps for business, calendar, and gmail.

BlackBerry BlackBerry OS is proprietary in nature. This OS focuses on easy operation and was originally designed for mobile users in business. Recently, it has seen a surge in third-party applications and has been improved to offer full multimedia support. BlackBerry supports applications that include BlackBerry mobile conferencing and BlackBerry exchange server.

iOS With the birth of Apple's iPhone in June 2007, the iPhone OS was born. iPhone OS was later renamed to iOS to match iPhone, iPad, and other offerings from Apple. Apple's productivity suite—iWork—is available for iPhone.

Windows Phone After Windows Mobile, Microsoft launched Windows Phone in February 2010. The new mobile OS includes a completely new over-hauled user interface and also integrates with many other non-Microsoft services such as Facebook and Google accounts. Windows Phone 7 supports Microsoft Office Mobile that includes Outlook, Word, Excel, and PowerPoint.

Symbian The Symbian OS from Nokia is an open source OS. Symbian has the largest smartphone share in most markets worldwide. Symbian has a strong presence in Japan due to its association with NTT DOCOMO. It has been used by many major handset manufacturers, including BenQ, Fujitsu, LG, Mitsubishi, Motorola, Nokia, Samsung, Sharp, and Sony Ericsson. Currently, Symbian-based devices are being made by Fujitsu, Nokia, Samsung, Sharp, and Sony Ericsson.

According to Brent Rose (2011), the four heavyweights—Android, BlackBerry, iOS, and Windows Phone 7—are going to rule, as Symbian is on the fast track to extinction, and WebOS (found on Palm and some HP devices) is a minor player.

Table 14.1 gives a comparative chart of prominent mobile operating systems.

Table 14.1 Comparison between various mobile operating systems

Mobile OS/Feature	Android	BlackBerry	iOS	Windows Phone	Symbian
Company	Google	RIM	Apple	Microsoft	Nokia
OS family	Linux	Mobile OS	Darwin	Windows CE/NT	Mobile OS
Programmed In	C, C++, Java	Java	C, C++	C, C++, .Net	C++
Licencing	Open source	Proprietary	Proprietary	Proprietary	Public licence
Free apps available	3,00,000	30,000	3,80,000	18,000	–

CELLULAR SYSTEMS

Cellular telephony provides stable communication between two moving objects or a mobile and stationary object. The service provider locates and tracks a caller and assigns a channel to the call. Both the instruments sending and receiving the call use this channel for communication. The signal is transferred from channel to channel (one cell to another cell, as shown in Fig. 14.2) if the caller moves from one range to another. To facilitate smooth transmission, the entire range is divided into cells. Each cell contains mobile towers and each tower has an antenna, which is controlled by a service provider office called mobile telephone switching office (MTSO). MTSO performs the following tasks: coordinating communications, connecting calls, recording call information, and billing subscribers.

The size of the cell is based on the geographical coverage required and the population of the area. The basic range is from 1–10 kilometres. However, if the population of the area is dense, the cell size is reduced to accommodate the traffic. Figure 14.2 illustrates the functioning of a cellular system.

According to Laudon (2010), cell phones and smartphones have become all-purpose devices for digital data transmission. In addition to voice communication, mobile phones are now used for transmitting text, e-mail messages, and instant messaging, clicking digital photos, playing music and games, surfing the web, and even for transmitting and receiving corporate data. It is expected that within a few years, new generation mobile processors and faster mobile networks will enable phones to perform most of the functions of a personal computer.

Cellular Network Standards

There are mainly two international standards for digital cellular service—GSM and CDMA. The global system for mobile communications (GSM) was developed by the European Telecommunication Standards Institute to describe the second generation (2G) of digital cellular networks (the first being, analogue technology). It has the major advantage of international

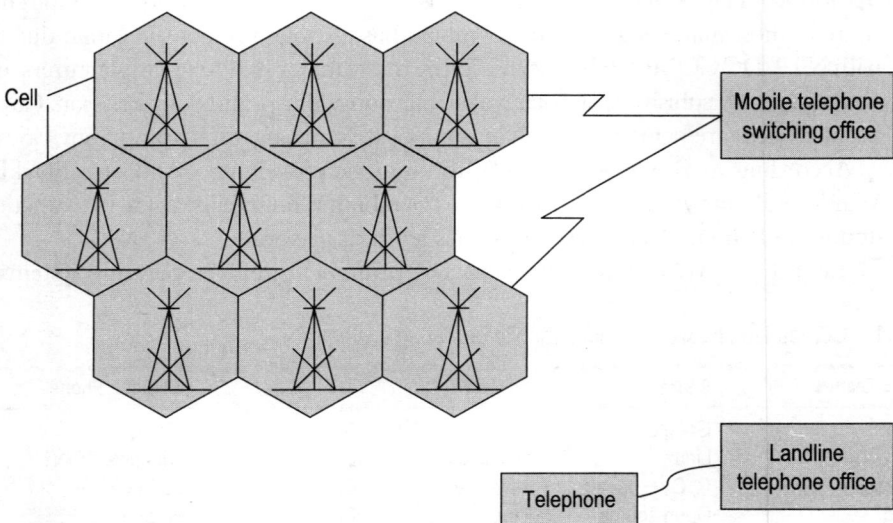

Fig. 14.2   Cellular communication system

roaming capability. In India, GSM networks are commonly used. However, there is a competing technology called code division multiple access (CDMA), which is regarded as a cheaper technology, more efficient in terms of use of spectrum, and provides higher quality throughput of voice and data. In India, Airtel, Idea, Vodafone, etc., provide their services on a GSM network, while CDMA was introduced by Reliance Communications.

The first and second generations of mobile technology were designed for voice and text transmission. The powerful third generation (3G) networks have been designed keeping in mind, transmission of voice, Internet, video, and television, all in a mobile environment. This will be possible only with a very high transmission rate. The proposed transmission speed ranges from 144 Kbps to 2 Mbps. This makes 3G networks suitable for wireless broadband Internet access. Countries such as Japan (NTT DOCOMO launched 3G as early as October 2001), South Korea, Taiwan, Hong Kong, Singapore, New Zealand, UK, and Italy are widely using 3G networks. Countries such as Philippines, Jordan, and Iran are late entrants in this segment. India launched the 3G spectrum in 2009, with MTNL and BSNL launching the services during the initial phase.

The next generation of wireless communication, termed as 4G, will be entirely based on packet-switch transmission technology and capable of providing speed between 1 Mbps and 1 Gbps. It will be high on standards and quality of transmission of voice, data, and multimedia files. WiMax is another technology marketed as 4G, which we discussed in Chapter 7.

Cellular Telephony

Cellular telephony is a radio-based system that works over a certain radio frequency (RF). Cellular telephones work by using radio waves to communicate with radio towers placed within

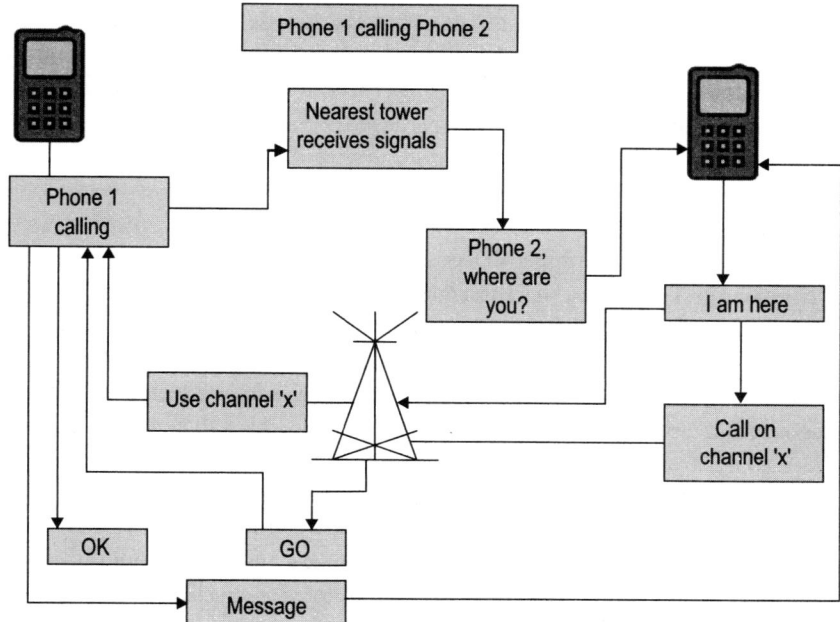

Fig. 14.3   Steps in a mobile communication

adjacent geographical areas. These areas are called cells. When making a call, the handset sends a message to the nearest tower, which in turn sends it further to the next tower. This process is repeated till the phone on which the call is made is located. This is called a handshake between the handsets. A telephone message is transmitted to the local cell by the mobile handset. Following this, it is transmitted to the next antenna, which is placed atop mobile towers. Therefore, the message moves from cell to cell, until it reaches the cell of its destination, where it is transmitted to the receiving mobile handset. The mobile office find outs the location of the receiving mobile set, and sends the signal back to the tower, which is fitted with a transceiver (for receiving and transmitting signals). As the cellular signal travels from one cell to another, a computer that monitors signals from the cell switches the conversation to a radio channel assigned to the next cell (Joshi, 2009).

As illustrated in Fig. 14.3, before assigning a channel for communication, there are at least seven signalled communications between the tower and the communicating mobile handsets.

MOBILE DATA NETWORKS

Wireless networks explicitly designed for two-way transmission of data files are called mobile data networks. These radio-based networks transmit data to and from hand-held computers. Another type of mobile data network is based on a series of radio towers constructed specifically to transmit text and data. Most wireless data schemes use 'packet' technique for transferring data. Packet radio is a communication method that transmits packets of data over a network via RF signals. This technology is called general packet ratio service (GPRS). In this system, the transceiver known as an RF modem, breaks down the data into 128-byte packets. The data contains the addressee's information. Then, these packets are released in the air for transmission. They are read by radio towers and then transmitted to the designated addressee. Each packet is sequentially numbered. At the receiving end, they are reassembled in the proper sequence. If a packet is not received in good condition, the receiver asks the sender to resend the packet, while continuing the receiving and transmission process.

WIRELESS WEB

Smartphones, tablets, laptops, PDAs, and other portal communications devices have paved the way for wireless access to the Internet. These devices play the role of a very thin client in the wireless network. Thin clients are computer devices that do not need a hard disk and its operating system. According to O'Brien (2007), agreement on a standard wireless application protocol (WAP) has encouraged the development of many wireless web applications and services. The telecommunications industry continues to work on third generation (3G) wireless technologies, whose goal is to raise wireless transmission speeds to enable streaming of video and multimedia applications on mobile devices.

For example, smartphones can send and receive e-mail and provide access to web pages, which are custom-designed to support mobile technology and mobile operating systems.

Figure 14.4 illustrates the WAP. According to Messerschmitt (1999), WAP standards specify how web pages in HTML or XML are translated into wireless mark-up language (WML) by filter software and pre-processed by proxy software to prepare web pages for wireless transmission from a web server to a web-enabled wireless device. Filter software are programs that are used to

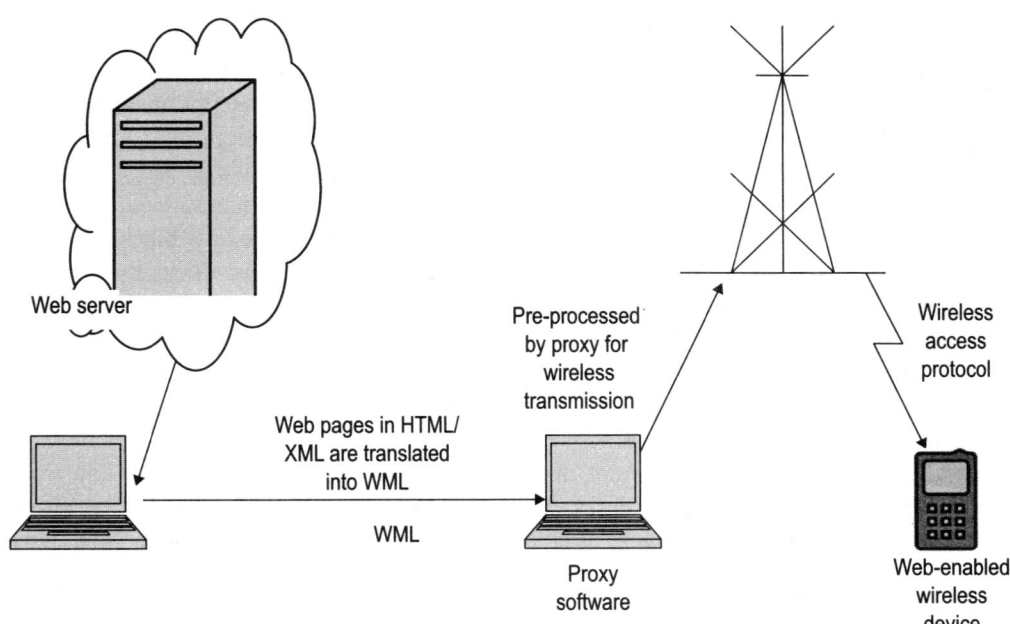

Fig. 14.4   Wireless application protocol for wireless Internet services and mobile devices

process data streams and sort the required data. For example, Find, Sort, etc., are filter commands used in Windows OS. Similarly, proxy software are programs that work on behalf of hardware or any other software to carry out a function.

MOBILE COMPUTING SERVICES

The reach and power of mobile computing is enormous. The power of mobile computing will be realized when appropriate applications are available for performing services over the mobile phone. As discussed in the previous section, presently, mobile phones have taken over many functions of hand-held computers—transmission of data, surfing the web, transmission of e-mail and instant messages, display of digital content, and exchange of data with internal corporate systems. However, with the advancement and availability of newer and faster networks, there will be many more services on offer.

According to Saxena (2009), the next paradigm shift that will take place will be indexed to the widespread provisioning of high-speed, over-the-air (OTA) networks—WiMax, 3G, and, 4G. Mobile phone usage will no longer be 'bucketed' into voice or data buckets with a host of confusing monthly plans or access costs. The list of innovative uses that are currently in development and which will be introduced to mobile users are well beyond the scope of this chapter. However, the ongoing trends illustrate ubiquitous computing capabilities coming soon to the pint-sized gadget called cell phone.

Services Offered

The various services offered by mobile computing in the arena of management support systems and data services can be grouped under the following broad categories:

Mobile Workforce

With the advent of mobile telecommunication, the need for physical space has vanished. For a cabled telephone connection, one had to at least reach the telephone equipment, but mobile telephony has removed even that constraint. Business organizations may find it useful to mobile-enable their workforce. This could mean selecting the right mobile offerings and mobile solutions for particular workforce units. The idea is to increase the efficiency, reach, and productivity of the workforce and provide them with mobile tools such as tablets, Blackberry, palmtops, and other hand-held terminals to help them perform their jobs more efficiently. A mobile workforce is able to operate in real time, fulfil customer needs at peak and off-peak hours, and provide and get business support where and when needed.

For example, Birla 3M has equipped its sales force with mobile terminals. The field sales executive books orders at various distributors premises and the information is instantly sent to the central server for processing.

An important requirement of the mobile computing environment is to allow workers to be as effective as they are at their desks, even at remote locations, and be connected with the network. Connecting through mobile is as efficient as connecting through the local area network.

Remote Data Access

Organizations need to recognize which of their business segments are amenable to the mobile world. This could include all aspects of a firm—marketing, advertising, sales force automation, customer care, sales and support, and summary information portals for the senior management. Having determined which segments need a mobile strategy, the firms need to decide on the solutions that are necessary to provide a robust mobile strategy for each segment.

With the right application in place, mobile phones can give access to data and information over the enterprise network. For example, sales executives can transmit their orders and customer feedback to the corporate server. A retail manager can know his daily sales figures through his mobile phone. Banks send transaction alerts and balances to their customers on cell phones. There are many areas of application where mobile devices can be put to the best use.

Organizations must integrate their IT and business infrastructure with mobile technology domains. This could mean development of custom mobile websites or integration with off-the-shelf mobile portals such as Yahoo mobile, MSN mobile, and Google mobile.

Mobile Banking

Exhibits 14.2 illustrates how HDFC and State Bank of India are vying with each other to introduce mobile banking solutions and provide more responsive customer service. Banking is a huge area for mobile business. This facilitates the use of mobile devices as banking front ends for executing all sorts of financial and payment transactions. The services include managing accounts, checking balances, and transferring funds. Bill payments over mobile phone is another compelling idea and consumers can manage their financial life on the go, thereby conserving precious time for doing more in life.

Banks keep in touch with customers by sending transaction alerts, cheque bouncing messages, or electronic clearance service (ECS) messages so that customers are aware of the position of their funds.

Mobile Advertising and Marketing

Mobile advertising and marketing is a new and exciting domain, which many organizations have started realizing. Organizations need to determine a strategy to use the mobile as a powerful

EXHIBIT 14.2

HDFC and SBI Enthral Customers with Mobile Initiatives

HDFC Bank and State Bank of India (SBI) have launched mobile banking applications. These applications are handset-specific and can be downloaded on Java-enabled handsets. The banks have uploaded these applications on their websites and their customers can download them free of charge. If GPRS is activated on a mobile connection, one can enter their mobile number to get the link for downloading the State Bank Freedom mobile banking application directly on a mobile handset.

HDFC Bank provides a full suite of MobileBanking and Payment Services, including fund transfer facility. One can transfer funds to any HDFC Bank account or any visa card (debit or credit) within India using 'ngpay', which offers the following services:

Movie ticket booking   One can book movie tickets at Fame Cinemas, INOX Cinemas, Fun Cinemas, Filmsn Tickets, etc., and search for shows, select/view seats, and pay for tickets.

Book travel tickets   One can plan journeys through IRCTC, Kingfisher Airlines, MakeMyTrip, Yatra, redBus, Ticketvala, Savaari, etc.

Shopping   One can send flowers and gifts, purchase books, and much more through Ferns N Petals, Gifts 360, Landmark, Archies, FutureBazaar, Asian Sky Shop, etc.

Banks are now endeavouring to simplify the world of banking for their customers. One can now request for cheque books, stop cheques, request demand drafts, access account statements, and do more from any place through a mobile phone.

Sources:
http://www.hdfcbank.com/personal/payments/ngpay/ngpay.htm, last accessed on 28 January 2013.
http://mobile.prepaidsbi.com/sbidownloader/populate.action, last accessed on 2 January 2012.

advertisement medium. The mobile is penetrating a large section of the population globally, and is overtaking the Internet in terms of its reach and scale. It is fast becoming the best way to reach a mass audience for communicating and marketing a firm's products and services. Organizations can develop a powerful brand name in the mobile arena. They need to clearly state how their business is relevant to the mobile users' world and how they can leverage the latest marketing channel—the mobile device—to reach their customers, partners, and suppliers.

Yahoo!, MSN, Google, etc., display advertisements on their mobile home page. Mobile service providers (Airtel, Idea, Vodafone, Reliance, Tata Indicom, etc.) promote their businesses by continuous messaging campaigns. SnapDeal.com, Jabong.com, etc., send mobile messages about attractive deals within a geographical area. Most of the reality shows on Indian television promote the use of SMS and make big money. The cost of such commercial messages is higher and the money is distributed among the telecom company and programme managers.

Customer Relationship Management

Mobile technology has the potential to offer the best strategy for customer relationship management (CRM) and customer satisfaction by keeping in touch with the customer. It provides a strategic advantage by offering a customer-centric system in mobiles. Organizations have realized this potential and started enthralling the customer.

For example, airline companies, IRCTC, etc., send instant messages to their customers regarding booking and cancellation of travel tickets. MakeMyTrip.com goes a step further in customer service by sending messages about waiting list status, ticket confirmation, etc.

Mobile service providers like Airtel send messages to the customer regarding bill generation, payment receipts, etc. There are many more examples from other sectors, too. Nisarg Roadlines in

EXHIBIT 14.3

Mobile Computing: The Future Scene, Not Science Fiction

Picture this. You get off the plane in New Delhi, and turn on your cell phone. Based on your personal profile, you get on your mobile the following:

- All your e-mails from the corporate server and Internet service provider
- Instant access to your savings accounts; checking account balances, recent credit card purchases, the current value of your stock portfolio; and the ability to transfer funds, purchase stocks, and pay bills
- The weather forecast for your three-day trip to New Delhi
- A map of your hotel's location in Connaught Place, with all ATMs of your bank listed
- A list of all Indian restaurants within a five-mile radius of the hotel
- News headlines in your specific area of interest
- A list of book and computer stores in the area that are offering special sales
- You call your friend in New Delhi for a candlelight dinner at the best restaurant 'somewhere' in the vicinity of the Metro Station at Rajiv Chowk, and receive step-by-step directions to the location of your friend's phone

Wishful thinking? Science fiction? No. A lot of this information is already available over wireless networks. The rest could be available soon. A new business model is emerging with the integration of wireless networks, data communications, and e-commerce to create wireless commerce or m-commerce.

Source:
'M-Commerce: The war has begun!', *Silicon India*, December 2000, http://www.siliconindia.com/magazine_articles/MCommerce_The_War_Has_Begun-GOH437271046.html, last accessed on 22 December 2011.

Mumbai sends instant messages on customers' mobile phones when their consignment is dispatched from the booking point and also when it arrives at the destination station. Meru, a rent-a-car travel operator in Mumbai, sends a confirmation message to the customers' mobile phones with car and driver details when a booking is made online or offline. At the same time, the client's details and pickup and drop points are messaged to the driver.

Location-based Services

Mobile telephony has brought about a revolution in the field of digital mapping and location-based services. According to Saxena (2009), the widespread integration of GPS chipsets, along with significantly improved digital mapping information, will vastly improve the usability and adoption of location-based services. There are already services such as Verizon's VZ Navigator, which enable users to locate nearby petrol pumps, ATMs, restaurants, cinemas, etc. Imagine landing in Paris and using your mobile phone to locate directions to the Louvre and then to a fabulous Indian restaurant for dinner in the evening—all from wherever you happen to be in the city at that moment. Exhibit 14.3 illustrates what mobile technology can do for us.

M-COMMERCE

Mobile commerce (M-commerce) refers to conducting business transactions over mobile data network using mobile hand-held terminals such as mobile phones, PDAs, or palmtops. According to Laudon (2002), 'the use of wireless devices such as cell phones or hand-held digital information appliances, to conduct e-commerce transactions over the Internet is called m-commerce'. While all e-commerce transactions are conducted over wired networks, m-commerce transactions are transacted through mobile hand-held devices such as cell phones, smartphones, PDAs, and other digital devices. These devices can connect to the server through a wireless communication technology—GPRS or CDMA. They can then be used to send or receive information or perform an m-commerce transaction.

According to Tandon (2011), there has been tremendous growth in wireless technology in the last decade. This advancement has changed how people do business in an m-commerce environment. For creating a more secure and flexible m-commerce infrastructure so as to meet the new demands, we need to leverage new technologies such as 3G, Bluetooth, and enhanced data rates for global evolution (EDGE) and at the same time, utilize older ones such as WAP, GSM, and GPRS. M-commerce offers the possibility of an entirely new level of financial flexibility, taking advantage of both social and technological developments.

According to Singhal (2008), m-commerce is expected to shoot up from a $2 billion worldwide business in 2007 to a $21 billion business in 2011. This will take away a substantial portion of revenue from the traditional brick and mortar and even online commerce avenues, and bring in revenue to the mobile world. Firms need to decide if their products and services can be marketed and sold via m-commerce channels. Once they pin down the necessity for m-commerce and the particular products and services that need to be sold via mobile channels, firms must choose an appropriate m-commerce solution.

For example, Amazon and e-bay already have mobile portals working on mobile phones. M-commerce enablers can help firms create custom mobile-optimized commerce websites. Firms can implement mobile coupon solutions using a variety of technology providers. If firms do not plan and strategize m-commerce options, they risk losing out to more nimble competitors who adopt this new channel faster. As it stands today, it is possible that m-commerce will prove to be a disruptive channel in the consumer shopping arena, and will quite likely create a similar impact that the Internet created on consumer buying patterns. The focus is always the consumer, who wants control over the timing, content, and format of shopping. Mobile technology opens up these aspects of shopping and empowers the consumer to make decisions in real time, any time, and anywhere.

Singhal (2008) argues that with the proliferation of consumer-oriented devices like iPhone and the entry of Google Android operating system, a proliferation of m-commerce websites is a natural phenomenon, which one expects in the near future. Just as in the case of an e-commerce shopping webfront, each company needs to develop a mobile storefront. The technology and device variance, which exists in mobiles, presents a challenge to any firm trying to develop a mobile storefront. Firms must account for the myriad variety of presently available mobile devices and operating systems, which may access mobile storefronts as well as those that are in the offing.

According to Turban (2005), the two main characteristics driving the interest in m-commerce are mobility and reachability. Mobility implies that Internet access travels with the customer, that is, the customer always has access to the Internet. M-commerce is appealing because wireless connectivity offers customers information from any location. Reachability means that people can be contacted any time, which is seen as a convenience of modern life.

M-commerce Applications

The ability to connect with mobile networks and corporate data servers opens up a number of avenues for usage of mobile hand-held terminals in business. Mobile hand-held terminals function in a similar manner to mobile phones; however, mobile hand-held terminals are loaded with input and output attachments such as printers, barcode scanners, and GPRS modems. These attachments help the user with instant receipt generation or barcode scanning while on the field.

There can be hundreds of applications in m-commerce for such mobile devices. The following sections discuss the most popular and major applications.

Sales Force Automation

Mobile devices and applications offer great business value for sales force automation. Sales personnel engaged in field sales—dealer-sales, medical representatives—can use mobile devices for taking orders. The device works with a simple application that has customer code, product code, salesperson's ID, and the quantity ordered. Once the salesperson enters this data in the device and presses the 'send' button, the data is transmitted to the server through the GPRS modem integrated in the mobile device. The order is instantly available at the distribution warehouse for processing. The sales force mobile applications help increase efficiency of the management system support. The devices can be directly linked with enterprise applications and the available inventory can be transmitted back to the mobiles.

For example, Pidilite Industries mobile enabled its information system by providing mobiles to the sales force, which were integrated with the SAP systems for sales and inventory information to the field staff (see Exhibit 14.4).

EXHIBIT 14.4

Pidilite Mobile-enables its Information System

Pidilite Industries Ltd implemented the SAP ERP system in 2001 to support its growing business operations. Although this streamlined information flow and availability within Pidilite Industries, it did not solve the needs of its large network of channel partners spread across India. They still had to make phone calls to the Pidilite factory or office to get updated sales-related information (namely, product price, stock availability, etc.). The channel partners needed updated information on orders, account status, etc.

In its endeavour to provide responsive service to partners, Pidilite decided to mobile-enable its enterprise information. ValueFirst was invited to provide an effective solution. The system requirements outlined by Pidilite were as follows:

- *24×7 information flow*: Availability of information to its mobile sales force, channel partners, and management team on sending SMS from their mobile phones
- *Communication with SAP*: Capability of communicating with SAP database to extract data from various tables and perform computations based on this data to calculate the required information
- *Plug and play*: A scalable, click, and deploy solution that would allow new processes (as and when they occur) to be configured easily and quickly

- *Easy format*: Information presentation in configurable format
- *Security*: Secure solution that would not compromise on the confidentiality of the information and information access based on user access rights
- *Automatic reporting*: Scheduled broadcasting of daily business reports to the management team and dealers related to invoices and payments
- *Automatic scheduling*: Scheduled and automated alerts to dealers regarding invoices and payments
- *Monitoring*: Logs to monitor to whom it is being broadcasted

The quickly implemented solution allows dealers/distributors of Pidilite to retrieve prices, stock availability, order status, order-booking summary, account status, etc.

Methodology   Sending a simple SMS query. The queries received by a mobile-solution are processed and the requested information is sent back within a few seconds as an SMS to the user's mobile phone.

Source:
http://www.pidilite.com/?m2=5#cat10, last accessed on 18 October 2011.
http://www.slideshare.net/manishraj82/value-first-bpcl, last accessed on 18 October 2011.

Inventory Management

Mobile devices find great applications in warehouse management. In large warehouses, it is not possible to take the computer-attached barcode scanner to every corner of the warehouse. Mobile devices attached with a barcode scanner fulfil this requirement. Whenever a product is removed from the warehouse, it is scanned using the scanner attached to the mobile device. The scanner captures the product barcode and stores the data in the mobile hand-held device. On connecting with the server, the data is updated in the enterprise inventory system.

Bus Ticketing

Many state public transport corporations such as Uttrakhand roadways, Gujarat state road transport, Karnataka state road transport corporation (see case study at the end of the chapter), and BEST in Mumbai have started using mobile electronic ticketing systems. The mobile devices are loaded with an application and a thermal receipt printer. The application has the bus route number and names of stations/stops falling within the route, distance between stations, and fare chart for the entire route. The bus conductor fills in a ticket for the passenger and prints it on a thermal or dot matrix printer, integrated with the device. The data of the complete route is stored in the device. If the device is GPRS-enabled, this data is transmitted online to the bus operator's central server. Otherwise, the conductor can download the data on the server using a cable. The application running on the server analyses the route data and produces reports on route profitability, time taken between different routes, and passenger load on the bus. This helps the management plug loopholes and take corrective action, wherever required.

Restaurant Billing

Waiters in restaurants use mobile devices for taking orders from customers. The order is transmitted to the main restaurant server and a kitchen order ticket (KOT) is printed on the kitchen printer. It saves a lot of time as the waiter does not have to take the order manually and then enter it in the computer. Once the order is placed, served, and completed, the information is transmitted to the billing server. A bill is created against the KOT and settled. The bill is printed on a normal printer connected to a computer, thus completing the transaction. Mobile terminals with waiters are popular in Japan.

Parking Lot Ticketing

Mobile hand-held terminals have become very popular in the time management for parking. With digital terminals, one can enter the in-time and out-time of a vehicle and print a parking ticket. A suitable application in the terminal and price database calculates the amount one has to pay for the parking. These terminals invariably come with integrated thermal printers.

Electricity Bill Generation

The process of electricity billing is a complex, time-consuming process. The meter reader personally visits houses, notes down the meter reading, submits the reading to the data processing department (which is then entered into the systems), after which bills are generated. These bills are then delivered to the house owners for them to make the payments to the electricity distribution company. This process takes up to two months time. If mobile computing devices are used, the time taken for this process can be brought down to two minutes for each household. With a suitable application in place, the customers' previous reading can be downloaded on to the hand-held terminals for a particular route, from the server at the electricity distributor company office. The meter reader can go to the household with this device in hand and enter the current meter reading into it. The device calculates the bill value and prints the bill on an integrated printer. The reader can collect the cash or cheque from the consumer then and there and print a receipt for the same. Back in the office, the data can be uploaded on to the server. In just one visit, the entire process is completed, which would save the consumer a lot of time and also generate more revenue to the electricity distribution company.

Municipal House Tax Collection

Similar to an electricity billing system, the municipality can set up servers and mobile applications. The data of each route, residential blocks, and houses can be downloaded in the mobile terminal. A comprehensive application with rich features in the device can also calculate house tax based on certain inputs—location, property usage, area of the land, built-up area, number of floors. If the municipality server already has all the information related to houses, it can simply be downloaded to the terminal. On visiting the household, the officials can collect taxes and generate a receipt. This can help the consumer save time and there would be much more tax compliance.

Micro Rural Banking

Cash collection is an issue with banks at far-off rural areas, where setting up of a branch may not be a viable business proposition. Small traders, labourers, hawkers, and kiosk operators do not have enough motivation and time for banking. If banks designate collection centres at city corners and authorize them to collect the cash through these terminals, much of the problem would be solved. These terminals can connect with the bank's data server through the GPRS or CDMA technology. The mobile device generates a receipt for each depositor and the bank server updates the account online. In the same way, these centres can be authorized to disburse cash. Any retailer, PCO operator, or mobile services operator can provide this service as an add-on to their regular business, which would be a great revenue-generator for them. The mobile technologies not only provide ease and comfort in banking transactions systems, but also generate new areas of businesses, increasing employment and inculcating banking habits in the underprivileged section of society.

Mobile Prepaid Recharge

Earlier, prepaid mobile recharging was done by buying a paper coupon and then dialling the code obtained after scratching the coupon. This business is now fully taken over by mobile phones themselves. A designated number is dialled from any mobile phone (probably a dealer's) after entering the phone number and recharge value of another prepaid mobile. The server updates the mobile with the value and sends an instant message. The money is paid to the dealer in cash.

Bill Payment Terminals

The bill payment service is the most used, appreciated, and widely present utility aspect in the m-commerce arena. Most of us must have seen these terminals working at a number of retail outlets that collect payments for utility bills such as electricity, water, and telephone. Bill payment terminals use both, land telecommunication lines as well as wireless technology, available in mobile hand-held terminals. 'Easy Bill' by Hero Services is the most widely used service in this arena. Bill payment services have reduced the burden on customers and have opened new business avenues.

Credit Card Payment Processing

You must have seen credit card swiping machines at petrol pumps and other retail outlets. Mobile hand-held terminals with similar functions are substitutes for the dial-up modem-based devices. The most conventional utility of hand-held terminals with dial-up modems is for credit card payment processing at a retail outlet. The mobile terminal connects with the server through the wireless channel, instead of the cabled line as in the conventional process. The mobile terminals promise payment processing practically at any place (a golf course, in a train, or a cricket stadium).

Gaming and Lottery

Games are gaining popularity with the grown-ups. Mobile devices can be used for playing online games and taking part in lotteries. When the mobile device connects with the server with a request for a game, a random number is generated by the server. The number is transmitted back to the mobile device within seconds. If the mobile device has a receipt printer attached to it, it prints the ticket. In such types of online lotteries, the draw is done on an hourly or half-hourly basis. The winning numbers are also communicated to the device. Thus, the winner instantly claims his reward in cash from the game operator.

Challenges of M-commerce

The implementation of m-commerce requires a multitude of infrastructure—hardware, software, and wireless transmission media. There are issues related to hardware compatibility, software availability, insufficient bandwidth, lack of standard protocols, cost of licenses, etc. Several m-commerce issues relating to security, bandwidth, and business have been discussed to meet the challenges of future commerce using mobile wireless technology. According to Tandon (2011), 'the present state of m-computing is not stable or matured. There are some bewildering structural problems, such as the lack of coherence and stability in standards and protocols in the mobile world, bottleneck in network, and the cascade of hardware and software options. However, the present problem is not of a new kind. The emerging wireless Internet, today, looks very much like the wired Internet did five years ago. The road ahead in this field is yet to take a definite shape'.

Hardware compatibility   Hand-held and phone devices differ from desktop and laptop computers in several ways. They generally have smaller screen sizes and limited input capabilities. Many hand-held devices display only a few lines of text and do not have traditional keyboards. Larger screens and the use of colour can enhance usability but at the expense of battery life. With the introduction of iPhone, BlackBerry, and other smartphones, vendors are trying to bring in both features in their designs, namely, large coloured screens and longer battery life.

Software availability   The software in both operating systems and m-commerce applications, needs drastic upgradation to suit the demanding world of mobile computing. All mobile phones are not capable of running operating systems such as WinCE and Android. M-commerce will experience a sea change once phones with operating system capabilities become abundantly available. Larger applications would require databases to be ported on mobile devices. Thus, compatible databases from database management systems vendors (Oracle and Microsoft) should be available for mobile devices. Applications developed on J2ME (mobile compatible Java language) etc., would enrich new m-commerce.

Suitability of bandwidth   As the demand for bandwidth increases for new and existing network applications, service providers may face a scarcity of bandwidth in the near future. This problem may be partially tackled by the reuse of frequencies. Different standards such as Bluetooth and IEEE 802.11 may recommend using the same frequency range and that may cause interference. One type of interference occurs when a channel employing frequency-hopping interrupts another channel and consumes the latter channel's frequency. It remains to be seen if such interference becomes a problem.

Lack of standard security protocols   Currently, only a few wireless communication protocols offer encryption of the transmission. In the security models of protocols that do have security encryption like WAP, transmission security weaknesses have been identified in the current set of protocols.

The mobile Internet channel has opened up possibilities that businesses could only once dream of. There is a big gap between what technology can do today and what the consumer has been led to expect. The good news is that slow transmission speed, difficult user interfaces, and high costs—some of the causes of frustration among consumers—are being addressed by operators and equipment manufacturers. M-commerce players will need to move fast to improve user interface and offer innovative pricing structures.

SUMMARY

In India, the growth of mobile usage has been phenomenal because of a sharp decline in prices, availability of technology, and reliable services. Computing is increasingly taking place over the network and new mobile digital computing platforms have emerged. Communication devices such as cell phones and smartphones such as the BlackBerry and iPhone have taken on many functions of hand-held computers, including transmitting data, surfing the web, transmitting e-mail and instant messages, displaying digital content, and exchanging data with internal corporate systems.

Mobile computing refers to the use of a variety of wireless devices such as laptops and mobile phones that offer mobility in allowing people to connect to the Internet, providing wireless transmission to access data and information irrespective of location. Cellular telephony provides stable communication between two moving objects, or a mobile and stationary object.

There are mainly two international standards for digital cellular service. These are GSM and CDMA. The global system for mobile communications (GSM) is an European standard. Code division multiple access (CDMA), regarded as a cheaper technology, is more efficient in terms of use of spectrum, and provides higher quality throughput of voice and data.

Cellular telephony is a radio-based system that works over a certain radio frequency (RF). Cellular telephones work by using radio waves to communicate with radio towers placed within adjacent geographical areas called cells. Wireless networks explicitly designed for two-way transmission of data files are called mobile data networks. These radio-based networks transmit data to and from hand-held computers. Smart mobile phones such as Smartphone, BlackBerry, pagers, PDAs, and other portal communications devices have paved the way for wireless access to the Internet.

Presently, mobile phones have taken over many functions of hand-held computers, including transmitting data, e-mails, and instant messages, surfing the web, displaying digital content, and exchanging data with internal corporate systems. The various services offered by mobile computing in the arena of management support systems and data services are grouped under heads such as mobile workforce, remote data access, mobile banking, mobile advertising and marketing, customer relationship management, and location-based services.

Mobile commerce or m-commerce refers to conducting

business transactions over a mobile data network using mobile hand-held terminals such as mobile phones, PDAs, or palmtops. The two main characteristics driving the interest in m-commerce are mobility and reachability. The ability to connect with mobile networks and corporate data servers has opened many avenues for the usage of mobile hand-held terminals in business. Sales force automation, inventory management, bus ticketing, restaurant billing, parking lot ticketing, electricity bill generation, municipality tax collection, rural banking, mobile pre-paid recharge, bill payment terminals, credit card payment processing, gaming and lotteries, etc., are a few areas where mobile-based applications are used.

The implementation of m-commerce requires a multitude of infrastructure such as hardware, software, and wireless transmission media. There are many challenges to m-commerce related to hardware compatibility, software availability, insufficient bandwidth, lack of standard protocols, cost of licenses, etc.

KEY TERMS

3G networks   Third generation networks for mobile communication that offer high speed.

Code division multiple access (CDMA)   Uses a specialized code as the basis of channelling and is regarded as a cheaper technology.

Cellular network standards   Communication standards used for mobile communication.

Cellular telephony   Communication between two moving objects, or one mobile and another stationary object.

Enhanced data rates for global evolution (EDGE)   A new generation mobile technology.

General packet ratio service (GPRS)   A technique for transferring data over mobile networks.

Global system for mobile communications (GSM)   International standard for digital cellular service.

M-commerce   Conducting business transactions over mobile data networks using mobile hand-held terminals such as mobile phones, PDAs, or palmtops.

Mobile digital computing   The use of wireless devices such as laptops and mobile phones that offer mobility in allowing people to connect to the Internet, and providing wireless transmission to access data and information from various locations.

Over-the-air (OTA) networks   Refers to wireless communication.

Radio frequency   Radio waves used to carry data.

Wireless application protocols (WAP)   Specifies how web pages in HTML or XML are translated to wireless mark-up languages.

Wireless networks   Networks that are designed for two-way transmission of data files on wireless media.

Wireless web   The way for wireless access to the Internet through portal communications devices, for example, smartphone, BlackBerry, and PDA.

Wireless mark-up language (WML)   Used for mobile technology applications.

CONCEPT REVIEW QUESTIONS

1. What do you understand by mobile computing?
2. What are the various mobile operating systems and how are they advantageous to a mobile user?
3. What are cellular systems? Explain the functioning of cellular telephony.
4. How do mobile data networks function? Explain wireless web.
5. What are the various mobile computing services?
   Explain with examples.
6. Explain m-commerce. What is the future of m-commerce in India?
7. What is the utility of mobile hand-held devices in various m-commerce applications?
8. What are the challenges faced by organizations in conducting m-commerce?

CRITICAL THINKING QUESTIONS

1. 'M-commerce is nothing but e-commerce performed through mobile phones'. Explain with suitable examples.

2. 'E-commerce will die an early death, as the business will switch over to m-commerce'. Do you agree with this statement? Why or why not?

3. The applications of mobile hand-held terminals seem so large and wide. Despite this, various sectors, including the government, have not been very keen in implementing such mobile applications. Why is it so?

MIS DEVELOPMENT

eBay has been the standout leader in m-commerce with the iPhone applications they launched in 2008, and the Blackberry and Android applications launched in 2009 and 2010 respectively. In 2009, the company saw more than $600 million dollars in goods sold via mobile applications, which was a 200% increase from 2008. The launch of their app notified bidders with push alerts and SMS notifications when they had been outbid, and allowed them to cast another attempt or keep track of ending auctions. According to eBay (Marcus, Stephanie, 22 January 2010, http://mashable.com/2010/07/22/2010-mobile-commerce-trends/), one item is purchased every two seconds using the eBay mobile app, with apparel, auto parts, cell phones/accessories, sporting goods, and collectibles ranking as the top five categories of purchased items.

Exercise
Dig the Internet further for m-commerce applications. What do you observe? What are the other applications that have not been discussed in this chapter? Find out trends in m-commerce applications and acceptability. What are people buying more with their mobiles? What kinds of applications are being developed by mobile hardware and software vendors?

REFERENCES

Davis, Gorden and Margethe Olson, *Management Information Systems*, McGraw-Hill, Singapore, 1996.

Joshi, Girdhar, *Information Technology for Retail*, Oxford University Press, New Delhi, 2009.

Laudon, Ken, Jane Laudon, and Rajanish Dass, *Management Information System*, Pearson Education, Singapore, 2010.

Laudon, Kenneth and Jane Laudon, *Management Information System*, Pearson Education, Singapore, 2002.

Marcus, Stephanie, 'Top 5 Mobile commerce trends', http://mashable.com/2010/07/22/2010-mobile-commerce-trends, 22 January 2010, last accessed on 25 December 2011.

Messerschmitt, David, *Network Applications: A Guide to the New Computing Infrastructure*, Morgan Kaufmann, San Francisco, 1999.

O'Brien, James A., George M. Marakas, and Ramesh Behl, *Management Information Systems*, Tata McGraw-Hill, New Delhi, 2007.

Rose Brent, 'Mobile OS showdown', PC World, June 2011, http://www.pcworld.com/businesscenter/article/229173/mobile_os_showdown_android_blackberry_ios_and_windows_phone_7.html, last accessed on 25 August 2012.

Saxena, Sankalp, 'Mobile phones: The convergent device for ubiquitous computing', http://www.siliconindia.com/magazine_articles/REGK707043917.html, 1 April 2009, last accessed on 25 December 2011.

Singhal, Vishal, 'Mobile strategy—The new corporate imperative', http://www.siliconindia.com/magazine_articles/Mobile_Strategy__The_New_Corporate_Imperative-DMKZ462464795.html, last accessed on 21 December 2011.

TRAI, http://trak.in/Tags/Business/mobile-subscribers-in-india/, last accessed on 28 January 2013.

Tandon, Ravi, Swarup Mandal, and Debashis Saha, 'M-commerce—Issues and challenges', a case paper, http://www.hipc.org/hipc2003/HiPC03Posters/m-commerce.pdf, last accessed on 24 December 2011.

Turban, Efraim, Jay E. Ronson, and Ting-Peng Liang, *Decision Support Systems & Intelligent Systems*, Pearson Education, Singapore, 2005.

www.telserra.com, last accessed on 30 January 2013.

CASE STUDY

KSRTC: Going Mobile in Bus Ticketing

The Karnataka state road transport corporation (KSRTC) has become the first state transport undertaking (STU) to introduce URL-based mobile booking application. Tickets can be now be booked in a single hand, while enjoying a cup of tea in the other. There is no need to download or request any additional application to book the tickets on your mobile phone. Simply access the URL, ksrtc.in/mobile from a GPRS-enabled handset and book your ticket within two minutes. Enjoy the best user-friendly GUI that has been developed for mobile booking-savvy users.

KRSTC—The Forward-looking State Transport Undertaking

KSRTC was established in 1961 and operates 6463 schedules, covering 2.22 million kms and carries 2.4 million passengers every day. KSRTC is the most preferred transport service of the people of Karnataka and neighbouring states. It is the first STU in India to implement a web-based online reservation system called AWATAR (anywhere anytime advanced reservation). KSRTC was the first STU to launch e-booking and mobile booking using credit/debit cards. KSRTC has won several national and international awards for its transport, IT, and environmental initiatives.

Mobile Leap Forward

Booking bus tickets just become easier. On 15 October 2009, KSRTC launched the mobile ticket booking service. Passengers can use this service to book tickets in buses ranging from the Karnataka *saarige* to the luxury *Airavat* volvos. Addressing the media, transport minister, R Ashok, said, 'KSRTC is making use of information technology to provide improvised facilities and services to commuters. Travellers can make use of this through the 'ngpay' application.'

To book tickets on the mobile, customers need to first download the 'ngpay' application on their mobile. For this, they first need to SMS 'KSRTC' to a given number from a GPRS-enabled mobile, following which, they can download the 'ngpay' application. After following the registration formalities, customers can choose the service of their choice, choose seat numbers, and also specify a pick-up point. Following this, they can make the payment through a secure gateway using either credit or debit cards, bank accounts, or cash cards.

Once the transaction is complete, a PNR number will be generated and sent as an SMS. An e-ticket will be sent to the customer via e-mail. In case a customer does not have an e-mail id, the PNR number can be shown at any of the KSRTC reservation counters to generate the ticket.

Web-based Mobile Online Booking

Later, in May 2011, KSRTC went one step ahead to reach and serve its esteemed and valued passengers by introducing web-based mobile booking application.

The user has to just register once with the operator for both e-ticketing and m-ticketing. As part of its go-green initiatives, KSRTC has become the first transport entity in the country to offer paperless ticket travel. A passenger who books an e-ticket or m-ticket (mobile booking) need not get a printout of the ticket. Instead, he/she can now show the ticket details received on his/her mobile along with a proof of his/her identity to the conductor on the bus. 'We have taken a decision in principle to permit mobile tickets (on KSRTC buses). We are now checking whether this information has gone down well with the conductors. This facility will definitely be useful to passengers,' said Gaurav Gupta, managing director, KSRTC, in an interview to The Hindu.

As the passenger had to show the identity card along with the mobile ticket while boarding the bus, there would be lesser chances of impersonation, he noted.

When the passenger books an e-ticket or m-ticket, a system-generated ticket will be sent to the registered mobile number of that passenger. The soft copy of the ticket comprises details about the originating and destination places, name of the passenger/s, trip code, PNR number, date of journey, departure time, seat number/s, class of service, boarding point, and platform number.

With KSRTC deciding to permit m-tickets on board, the passenger is relieved of the burden of getting the ticket printed. Even while on the move, one can book a ticket and later hop on to a KSRTC service without making the effort to locate a cyber café to get a printout of the ticket.

Besides making booking of tickets a hassle-free experience, KSRTC has made the process of cancellation of tickets also equally hassle-free. Cancellation is now possible through the web portal or mobile portal.

On an average, 5000–6000 e-tickets are booked every day and if every passenger prefers to use an m-ticket, it would translate to huge savings with regard to paper consumption. Although KSTRC allows e-booking and m-booking of tickets using credit/debit cards and Internet banking accounts of some banks, it does not store any data of the customers relating to their transactions. Once the passenger blocks a seat or seats and proceeds for payment, the transactions are carried out through a secured connection directly with the bank.

'This will be one of the most people-friendly policies KSRTC has come up with. It saves a lot of effort for us. With new cell phones and fast Internet connection, this will prove to be a real advantage', said a regular passenger of KSRTC.

Buoyed by the success of the project, KSRTC has launched a website too. 'Earlier, people could book using their mobiles; however, they had to take a printout of the ticket before the journey. Now, we have sent circulars to all the conductors directing them to accept the tickets on mobile phones on production of any ID card,' said Channabasappa, chief manager, commuter relations, KSRTC.

'The mobile website is user-friendly. It does not have too many functions so it opens fast and booking on this too is much faster. Even choosing the destinations and the dates is much easier', said another commuter.

'It is extremely convenient and seems to have a pretty simple interface. It is good that it only asks you for basic details. The only drawback is that you have to register using a computer before being able to access this on your phone,' said yet another happy customer.

With the emergence of new technologies in the market, KSRTC is planning on making mobile-specific applications. 'One of our target groups is youngsters of the city, who are tech-savvy. We are planning on creating specific applications for Blackberries, iPhones, etc.', said Gupta.

Discussion Questions

1. The mobile ticketing initiative by KSRTC has not only created a customer-centric business environment but also helped the organization gain strategic advantages. Discuss.

2. Search the web and find out which other government or state owned public transport organizations are as tech savvy as KSRTC and have taken initiatives in this direction.

3. Find out the applications of mobile-based technology and systems in other areas of e-governance, besides the areas already discussed in this chapter.

Sources:

Dev, Arun, 'Travel on a KSRTC bus via SMS', 2 June 2011, http://articles.timesofindia.indiatimes.com/2011-06-02/bangalore/29612821_1_ksrtc, last accessed on 28 January 2013.

'KSRTC goes mobile for bus tickets', 16 October 2009, http://www.dnaindia.com/bangalore/report_ksrtc-goes-mobile-for-bus-tickets_1299583, last accessed on 28 January 2013.

'KSRTC offers paperless ticket travel', 20 June 2011, http://www.hindu.com/2011/06/20/stories/2011062052550500.htm, last accessed on 23 December 2011

http://www.ksrtc.in/wap/aboutus.htm, last accessed on 23 December 2011.

http://www.ksrtc.in/site/mobile-booking, last accessed on 23 December 2011.

Part IV

Development of MIS

- Information Systems Planning and Development

- Implementing Information Systems

Information Systems Planning and Development

> *Betting on new IT innovations can mean betting the future of the company. Leading-edge firms are sometimes said to be on the 'bleeding edge'. Almost any business executive is aware of disastrous projects that had to be written off, often after large cost overruns, because the promised new systems simply did not work.*
>
> —Peter Keen

LEARNING OBJECTIVES

After studying this chapter, you will be able to

- understand the significance of information system (IS) planning
- compare the various components of IS planning
- get acquainted with IS planning methodologies
- define the system development life cycle (SDLC)
- explain the role of feasibility study in system development
- gain expertise in system analysis
- comprehend the methods of system design
- describe other development functions such as construction, testing, implementation, and maintenance
- understand why prototyping is required
- appreciate modern system development approaches such as rapid application development (RAD), object-oriented system development (OOSD), and computer-aided software engineering (CASE) tools
- throw light on the need for outsourcing and application software packages

EXHIBIT 15.1

D.B. Engineering: Aligning IT Plans with Business Plans

D.B. Engineering (P) Ltd, the brand owners of Atlas Knives, realized early that long-term business plans must be supported by equally strong and realistic information system (IS) plans. The company developed its IT-based business strategy while developing enterprise software solution for all operations.

D.B. Engineering is one of the largest manufacturers of cutting tools in India. Since the company's inception in 1951, it has treaded a path dedicated to producing world-class industrial machine knives and blades. This has been achieved by innovation in products through constant research and development (R&D) and by bringing in the latest technology, computer numerical control (CNC) machines, and in-house latest heat treatment techniques. The company has its corporate office in New Delhi and has five manufacturing units in the national capital region (NCR), and employs over 600 trained technicians. It has modern manufacturing facilities, a quality assurance system, and well-equipped R&D facilities. Supported by enterprise resource planning (ERP) and information management systems across all units, the company serves its customers with ever increasing satisfaction. The company has a proven range of cutting tools for metal, paper, printing, packaging, plastic, wood, rubber, etc. These products have become a benchmark under the brand, Atlas knives.

IT Strategy

The IS requirement of the management became more demanding with growing business operations. The company chalked out a plan for IS development that could serve all the functions and cater to the needs of at least the next decade. Given the peculiar requirements of the blades industry, a custom-build solution was worked on. The company invited BNG Infotech for the development of an IS plan and solution. The vendor advised to develop a solution on the latest web and Windows platform and relational database management system (RDBMS) databases.

The solution was custom-built and carried the full software development life cycle approach. The requirement analysis was done by conducting a number of meetings with the users and management. The study, review, and approval of user requirement documentation took around three months. Based on the user requirement analysis, the system was then designed by the technical team.

The solutions were designed and developed for key areas of the company's business such as purchase management, order processing, sales, stores and inventory, manufacturing, accounts, and sales force automation. Order management was one of the critical areas, as the company received a number of small and large orders that go through a long process of order confirmation, engineering designing, costing, job-order initiation, etc.

Once the prototype was developed and tested, the solution was put for final integration, testing, and implementation. The critical module of order processing was first tested and implemented. The order management was integrated with the e-commerce portal of the company, wherein the company received enquiries and orders for its products. Later, the core modules of purchase, sales, inventory, production, and finance were implemented in one major unit and corporate office that went live within the next six months. The employees were rewarded for re-entering three months data in the new system just to check the accuracy and robustness of the system. Later, the system was rolled out to other manufacturing units and sales offices.

The task force consisting of functional heads, an IT manager, and the managing director, monitored and steered the process of project management.

Sources:
Author's interactions during system development.
http://www.atlasknives.com/aboutus.htm, last accessed on 27 December 2011.

D.B. Engineering's initiative to align its information system (IS) plan with the business plan illustrates the importance of IT to gain a strategic advantage and for business sustenance (Exhibit 15.1). The experience of the company illustrates some of the steps required to design and develop a new IS. Developing a new IS entailed analysing the users' requirements, identifying problem areas in the existing systems used by the organization, selecting appropriate technology and tools, and redesigning business processes. The management of the company had to monitor the system development project.

In this chapter, we will discuss organizational planning with respect to the use of IS, all the aspects of a system development life cycle (SDLC) such as feasibility study, system analysis, design, development, and prototyping. We will also discuss alternative methods of system development and acquisition.

INFORMATION SYSTEMS PLANNING

According to Keen (1991), 'Betting on new IT innovations can mean betting the future of the company'. Therefore, any unplanned or miscalculated steps in IS building process can have a far-reaching impact on the existence and sustainability of the business organization. The fundamental business objectives of customer satisfaction, profitability, and sustenance can be achieved by aligning IT goals with business objectives.

IS planning is the process of deciding the objectives for organizational computing and identifying computer applications to achieve them. According to O'Brien (2007), the business/IT planning process focuses on discovering innovative approaches to satisfying a company's customer and business value goals. This planning process leads to the development of strategies and business models for new e-business and e-commerce platforms, processes, products, and services. Following this, a company can develop IT strategies and IT architecture that supports building and implementing their newly planned business applications.

The IS planning process involves the following:

- Identifying the status of IS in the organization
- Evaluating various applications in the organizational IS
- Establishing a priority ranking for these applications
- Determining the best IS architecture for top priority applications

Components

The following are the components of IS planning. These steps are followed while planning and developing IS strategies in the organization.

- IS strategy development
- IS technology architecture
- IS resource management

Figure 15.1 illustrates how business objectives and values drive IS strategies as well as applications development and implementation.

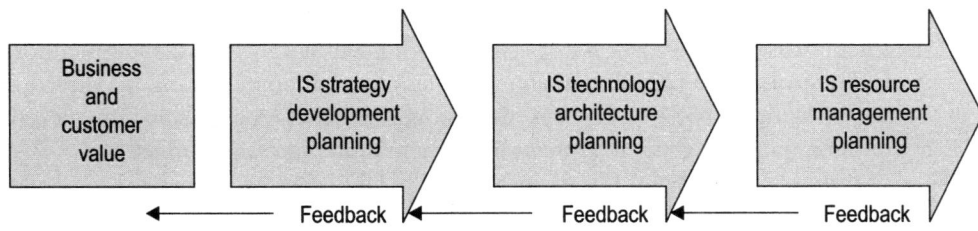

Fig. 15.1   Aligning business objectives and values with IS strategies

Information Systems Strategy Development

This involves developing IS/IT strategies that support the long-term objectives of companies. IS strategies support and align with business strategies. Strategists use IT to create customer centric e-business systems as a step towards strategy development. According to De Gues (1997), companies need a strategic framework that can bridge the gap between simply connecting to the Internet and harnessing its power for a competitive advantage. The most valuable Internet applications allow companies to transcend communication barriers and establish connections that will enhance productivity, stimulate innovative development, and improve customer relations.

Information Systems Technology Architecture

IS technology architecture planning succeeds IS strategy development. This involves choosing the right technology architecture and applications that support IS, business strategies, and e-business initiatives (selection and implementation of customer relationship management (CRM) to support customer-focused business). If an IS strategy aims at the creation of an e-commerce business channel, the IS technology must support planning for parallel distribution channels through web and related technologies.

Information Systems Resource Management

IS technology architecture is succeeded by an IS resource management initiative. IS resource management involves planning and developing strategic plans for creating, managing, or outsourcing an organization's IT resources. IT resources include hardware, software, data, network, and people resources. For example, the planning for e-commerce business channel calls for procurement and commissioning of web servers, development of e-commerce applications, content and catalogue management, establishment of payment gateway, and ensuring security of data, application, and payment processing through a bank.

Planning Methodologies

Organizations generally apply one or a number of methodologies to perform the IS planning. The three popular methodologies include business systems planning (BSP), strategic systems planning (SSP), and information engineering (IE).

Business Systems Planning

Business systems planning (BSP), first developed by IBM, involves top-down planning with bottom-up implementation strategy. In this methodology, a firm identifies its business mission, objectives, and functions, and analyses how these objectives determineits business processes. In this approach, the strategic systems are incorporated into top-level planning, which contains a statement of corporate goals and specifies how IT will support the achievement of those goals. According to Laudon (2010), the plan serves as a road map indicating the direction of systems development (the purpose of the plan), the rationale, current systems/situations, new developments to consider, the management strategy, implementation plan, and budget.

For example, when Solus Group in New Delhi launched the hypermarket format for its retail chain, the company's business plan defined and specified how IT will support its goal of being a well-known brand in the hypermarket segment.

Business systems planning emphasizes top management commitment and executive involvement in the planning process. Top executive sponsorship of the project is perceived to be critical.

Strategic Systems Planning

Strategic systems planning (SSP) determines the overall direction of systems development. It defines a business function model by analysing major functional areas. An IS architecture identifies new systems and their implementation schedule. Strategic planning calls for evaluating various Internet technologies, e-business, and e-commerce applications that can be used in the organization as a tool for gaining a strategic advantage.

For example, Anna University of Technology, Coimbatore, analysed and appreciated the fact that the foolproof conduct of the examination system was a strategic step. The University planned to implement IntelliEXAMS, the software suite from Mindlogicx, Bengaluru, that would manage the examination process by diligently handling the complete life cycle starting from online registration of candidates to printing of marksheets.

Information Engineering

The information engineering (IE) method of IS planning was developed by James Martin (1982). IE is a methodology that is used to build an IT architecture to plan, analyse, design, and implement applications for an enterprise. According to Lederer (1988), IE provides techniques for building enterprise, data, and process models. These form a comprehensive knowledge base, which then creates and maintains information systems. IE is considered a more technically oriented approach than other IS planning methodologies.

In conjunction with information engineering, Martin (1982) advocates the use of critical success factors (CSFs) technique for identifying issues considered by business executives as the most vital for the success of their organization. According to Rockart (1979), the critical success factor approach argues that an organization's information requirements are determined by a limited number of critical success factors as perceived by the managers. If these goals can be attained, the success of the firm or organization is assured.

According to Laudon (2010), the principal method used in CSF analysis is personal interviews. Three or four interviews are conducted with a number of top managers identifying their goals and the resulting CSFs. These personal CSFs are aggregated to develop a picture of the firm's CSFs. Later, systems are built to deliver information on these CSFs.

The CSFs vary from organization to organization, and are shaped by the individuals and environment in which they operate. For example, CSFs for a retail outlet may be its location, the assortment of goods, discounts offered, and promotional activities undertaken. Thus, IS planning must provide necessary information to meet the desired goals.

SYSTEM DEVELOPMENT LIFE CYCLE

A system development process goes through a series of decisions, actions, feedback, and reviews as per the IS plan. System development is a structured kind of problem-solving approach with distinct activities. When these activities are performed in a systematic and cyclic way, they are together called the system development life cycle. SDLC is a mechanism that ensures that only IS that meet the established requirements of the organization are developed. According to Jaiswal (2004), these methodologies impose various degrees of discipline on the software development process with the goal of making the process more efficient and predictable. The term system development life cycle signifies that

• the approach deals with all aspects of the system, that is, hardware, networking, system software, application software, database, and human efforts involved;
• there are reviews that check the product, processes, and usage against the plan; and
• the process is cyclical, that is, each version of the system becomes part of the environment, and the next version is developed.

An SDLC involves (a) feasibility study, (b) system analysis, (c) system design, (d) system construction, (e) testing and evaluation, (f) system implementation, and (g) maintenance.

Figure 15.2 illustrates an SDLC. It is obvious from the figure why it is also called a waterfall approach of system development. These seven steps of the cycle are based on the stages of the system approach. In this approach, we can recycle to any previous step, in case any modification or rework is required.

This SDLC methodology is closely linked to what is popularly known as structured system analysis and design (SSAD). The structured approach refers to the fact that the techniques are done step by step, with each step building on the previous one. These methodologies are top-down, progressing from the highest to the lowest, and from abstract to a detailed one. Table 15.1 illustrates the SSAD steps undertaken in the development of a system with the outcomes they offer.

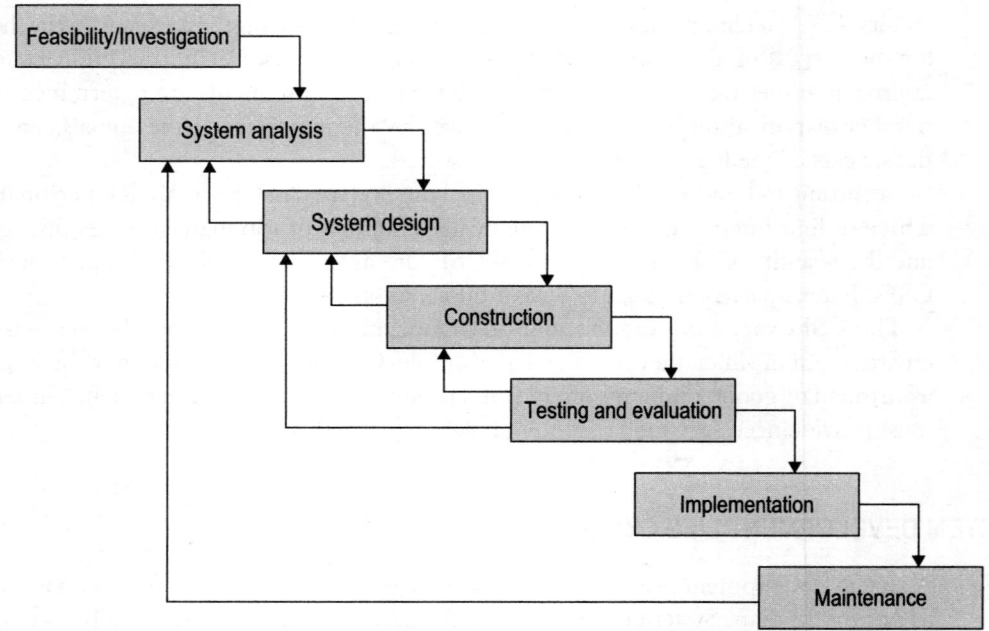

Fig. 15.2   Waterfall model of system development life cycle

Table 15.1   Structured system analysis and design outcomes

SDLC phase	Description	Deliverables
Feasibility study	Conduct feasibility study to see the viability of the new IS and undertake cost–benefit analysis	Feasibility report
System analysis	Analyse information needs of employees, customers, and vendors, document system requirements and understand how the present system works	Specifications of the present systems
System design	Determine specifications for hardware, software, people, network, and data resources, and define product specifications that will meet the information requirements as analysed	Specifications of the proposed systems
System construction	Actual programming or coding as per the system study and design documents, user manual, and other documents development	Programs, documentation, and user manuals
Testing and evaluation	Test, verify, and validate the systems—hardware, software, and products just built	Test reports and evaluation results
System implementation	Hand over the system to users, adapt a new business information system, and provide handholding support and training to users	System going live and feedback
Maintenance	Upkeep and maintain the system, resolve issues and troubleshoot, and conduct periodical reviews to monitor, evaluate, and modify as per the organization's needs	Feedback, updates, and new versions

Feasibility Study

A feasibility study is the first step in the process of system development. Since system development processes are complex, costly, and time consuming, it calls for a preliminary study to assess the major information requirements, resource requirements, costs, benefits, and feasibility of the proposed systems. The feasibility study is jointly done by business professionals and IS specialists before the actual system analysis and design is carried out. The team presents a document called feasibility study report, which outlines the preliminary specifications, modules, and development plan to the management for its approval.

In the feasibility study, the team presents various aspects of feasibility in the organization, such as organizational, economic, technical, and operational (O'Brien, 2007), as illustrated in Table 15.2.

Table 15.2   Factors assessed in a feasibility report

Organizational feasibility	Economic feasibility
1. Is the organization's environment conducive for a system change today? 2. How well does the proposed system support the business objectives and priorities of the organization?	1. What is the budget needed for this project? 2. How much cost will be saved after the project is completed? 3. Will there be any increased revenue? 4. What will the decreased investment requirements be? 5. Will this lead to increased profits?

Technical feasibility	Operational feasibility
1. What kind of hardware, software, and network capabilities are required? 2. Are we going in for the latest development tools and technologies? 3. Are these resources available?	1. Will this system be acceptable to employees, customers, and suppliers? 2. Is the management committed to this IS project, is full support available? 3. Does this IS meet government and other statutory requirements?

EXHIBIT 15.2

Chetna Logistics: A Case of Operational Difficulty

Chetna Logistics is a New Delhi-based transportation and warehousing company. Faisal Khan, the energetic young director of the company, is computer savvy and always thinks about being ahead of the competition. As logistics and transportation is a multi-location business activity, the company maintains around 20 branches across the country. The company has been using a desktop application for the last 10 years.

As terms such as online, real-time, Internet-based, and web-based became buzzwords in the business world, Khan proposed and got an online web-based information system developed for its operations. As logistics business requires connectivity and real-time data at all branches, (i.e., the data should move faster than the trucks), the deployment of an online web-based solution was the right decision. The system development went through the complete process of SDLC. Finally, the system was tested and deployed within the stipulated time and cost guidelines.

When the system was put to operation, the users, who were accustomed to a desktop application, found the web layout a bit difficult. The input screens, the navigation, and the submission processes were unfamiliar. The 'enter' key found a replacement with 'tab' key, the 'save' button found a replacement by 'submit' button, amongst others. When a lengthy 'consignment' input form was filled with data and submitted for saving, the connection to the server was broken. This could be attributed to the Internet or bandwidth issues. The users felt that productivity was down by 50%. The management, the technicians, and the users struggled for six months to improve and get acclimatized with the new IS, but without any result. Finally, Khan ordered that the system be shutdown and switched over to the good old desktop version of the application.

(Hypothetical example based on author's personal experience.)

Organizational feasibility answers the question as to how well the proposed system supports the strategic business priorities of the organization. It is about how well prepared the organization is for the new proposed IS. Economic feasibility is concerned with the budgetary outlay for the project, cost savings, and profit enhancements as a result of the implementation of this new IS. For example, if the proposed total cost of development and operation of information systems is higher than the savings and benefits, the management will not approve the budget expenses.

Technical feasibility involves estimation of hardware, software, and network capabilities required for running the new IS. For example, if the proposed system requires a leased broadband telecommunication line, while at the rural manufacturing unit of the company, no telecom operator provides the same, the project is said to be not feasible technically. Operational feasibility is about the willingness and ability of the management, employees, customers, and other stakeholders to use and support the proposed IS. For example, if the employees find the software difficult to use, they will resist the same, and the project will not be operationally feasible. Exhibit 15.2 illustrates how Chetna Logistics retrograded from the latest web-based IS to a desktop application because of operational difficulty.

System Analysis

System analysis is the in-depth study of end-user information requirements that form the basis for system design and product specifications. System analysis consists of identifying and defining the problems, identifying its causes, specifying the solutions, and identifying the information requirements that must be satisfied by the proposed solution. According to O'Brien (2007), a system analysis traditionally involves a detailed study of the following:

- The information needs of a company and end users
- The activities, resources, and products of one or more of the present IS being used, if any
- The IS capabilities required to meet an organization's information needs

The system analysis is a study of the organization, the users, the organization's environment, the existing systems, and the functional requirements at the user level.

Organizational Analysis

The study of the organization is called organizational analysis. This involves understanding of the organization's environment, its management structure, its people, its business activities, and its present IS. The team must know the end-users who will be affected by the proposed IS.

Analysis of the existing systems is part of the system analysis. The analyst analyses how the system uses hardware, operating systems, database management systems, network, and human resources. The various input, output, processing systems, and their outcomes and impact on the IS are analysed. At this stage, the analyst figures out the shortcomings, lacunae, and problem areas in the system that need to be taken care of in the new proposed IS.

For example, a team developing production planning and control systems for an organization in sheet metal forging must know the company, its people, the business activities, and the existing software system, in order to develop a trouble-free information system. Exhibit 15.3 illustrates

EXHIBIT 15.3

D.B. Engineering: The System Analysis and Design Process

D.B. Engineering was an advanced user of information systems, though it was using desperate applications that were developed over a period of time and hardly communicated with each other in terms of data transfer, job-work management, order costing, accounting, etc. However, some of the processes were not computerized. There were five manufacturing units scattered over New Delhi and Noida. Before handing over the system development project to BNG Infotech, an internal team of two managers conducted a feasibility study and made rough calculations of costs and time estimations. The team led by Akashdeep Gupta, system manager, and Satyendra Kumar, sales manager, sized up the hardware, the system software, the network resources, and manpower requirements. It also did costing for the project, which included a leased line for the corporate office in Delhi connecting the manufacturing units in Noida.

The system analysis team comprising two system analysts from BNG Infotech and the system manager from D.B. Engineering conducted requirement analysis for every process. The system analysis involved conducting a number of meetings with the users and management. The existing computerized departments and processes were analysed and the pain areas were detected. The process, which was not using any IS, posed challenges because many times, the users were unaware of what they needed.

It was observed by the analyst team that the real method of correct system analysis was by ascertaining the output or reports in each process. The output was derived from the input data in document format. The outputs for each major process were drawn in Excel and sent to users for their suggestions and observations. Once the output was finalized, the input and procedures were designed by the designers. Data flow diagrams and process flow charts were created. The designing process culminated with specifications for each function in the business process.

The entire collection of system analysis, design, and specifications found place in a document called system study and analysis document (SSAD). This document was reviewed, modified, and then approved by the management of D.B. Engineering, which formed the basis for system development.

(Example based on author's personal experience.)

how a system study is carried out for developing a new solution for an existing user organization in the manufacturing segment.

Requirement Analysis

The most difficult task of system analysis is to define the specific information requirements. Laudon (2010) opines that at the most basic level, the information requirements of a new system involve identifying who needs what information, where, when, and how. Requirement analysis carefully defines the objectives of the new or modified system and develops a detailed description of the functions that the new system must perform. As per one estimate, 60% of the IS projects fail because of faulty requirement analysis. Such systems either fail to deliver the results or are discarded by users because of inefficient performances.

Functional requirement analysis is usually done by system analysts along with end-users. At the analysis stage, requirements are not tied together with IS resources such as hardware, software, data, network, or people. This is taken care of later in the design stage.

System Design

System analysis dictates what a system should do to meet the information requirements of an organization; the system design answers how the system will accomplish this objective. System design encompasses all the design activities that generate system specifications meeting the functional requirements that were developed during the system analysis process.

The system design process follows a structured system analysis and design approach, which is a step-by-step method of system design. In this process, a relationship is established between the systems components and flow of data between them. This tool for representing a system's component processes and the flow of data between them is called data flow diagram (DFD). According to Laudon (2010), the DFD offers a logical graphic model of information flow, portioning a system into modules that show manageable levels of detail. It rigorously specifies the processes or transformations that occur in each module and the interfaces that exist between different processes.

In the process design framework, a broader logical model of the process is defined in the DFD as illustrated in Fig. 15.3. This simple DFD shows that a customer places an order, which is validated with the customer database. In the second process of customer order acceptance, the order is checked with pre-existing product and price databases. The accepted order data is maintained in the 'accepted order database'. Finally, the accepted order is printed in the third process and placed with the customer.

System design consists of three activities—user interface design, database design, and process design—as displayed in Fig. 15.4.

All the three designing activities result in specifications for user interface methods, database structures, and processing and control procedures.

User Interface Design

A user interface design consists of input forms, output forms, reports, and dialogue designs. As user interface is the bridge between the business users and their computer application, it has to be designed in the most appealing, aesthetic, ergonomic, efficient, and user-friendly manner. According to Jawadekar (2007), in this phase, the designer's task is to identify those data items that will be an input to the system. The designer finds a linkage to the input data from the output.

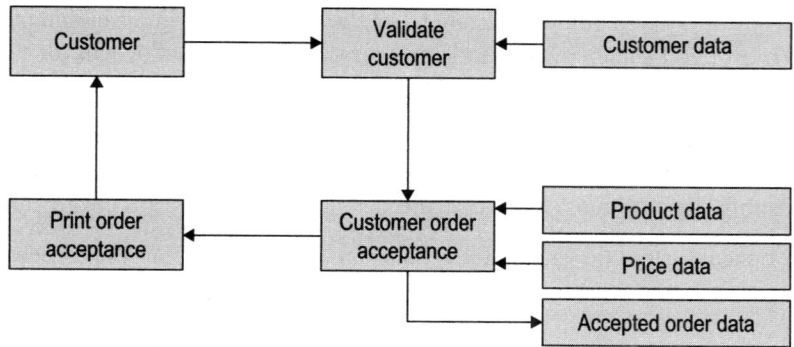

Fig. 15.3 Data flow diagrams illustrating logical model of the process

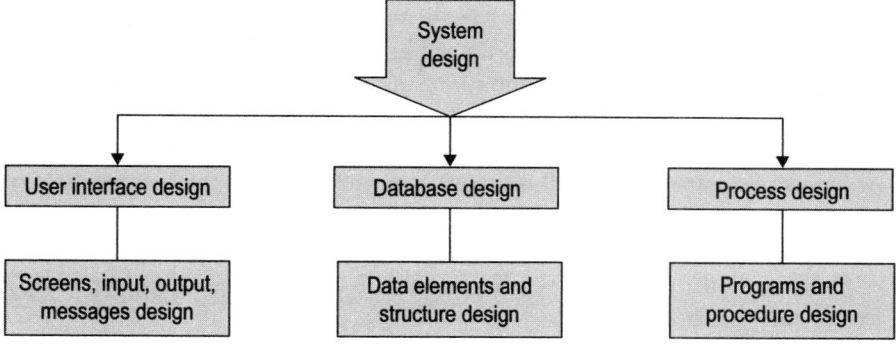

Fig. 15.4 System design involves user interface, database, and process design

The output design requires presenting the information on display as well as in a printing format. A good layout improves the utility of the information reports by highlighting the areas of concern where the attention of the management and its response is required immediately.

User interface design also involves designing dialogues between a computer and the user. These dialogues are displayed during data entry or report generation as messages.

Database Design

In this process, the designer designs the structure of the database, which is based on the input and output data design. The data items are first defined at the atomic level and then specifications are defined for each data item. The specification is expressed in terms of length, nature, type, attribute, condition, validity, etc., of a data item.

For example, the data can be an item having twelve characters, presented in numeric value having two decimal places, or a value where an input will have to be compulsorily keyed in. We discussed database designing in Chapter 6.

Process Design

The process design specifies how the computer system will function from data entry to the output stage. The procedure indicates the logic of data processing and the flow of control from the start to the end of the process. The process design is supported by flow charts for each process. The flow charts of the system guide the analyst and the programmer in developing the system. Jawadekar (2007) proposes the following guidelines for drawing system flow charts:

- Identify the start and end of the system.
- Identify the inputs in terms of the data and documents entering the system, in their logical order. Determine the transactions and the master files in the system.
- Identify the output at each stage and decide the media for processing and storage.

A typical system flow chart for a material requirement planning process in a manufacturing set-up is illustrated in Fig. 15.5.

Construction

The construction stage is also known as the programming or coding stage. In this stage of system development, the system specifications that were prepared during the design stage are translated into software programs. The programming is executed by technically trained personnel. Today, most organizations outsource the programming part or opt for a ready-made software package that meets their maximum requirements. There are obvious advantages of doing this. The standard software packages from established vendors are built as per the best practices of the industry and they offer far more features, flexibility, adaptability, and are robust in performance. For example, most of the companies prefer enterprise solutions such as SAP, Oracle, Ramco, and Finnacle.

Construction or development of systems is either done using the SDLC method or the prototyping method.

System Development Life Cycle

System development life cycle is a traditional approach of system development that takes care of all the development phases covering feasibility study, system analysis, system design, coding, implementation, testing, and maintenance. The traditional SDLC approach is a phased approach to system building that divides system development into formal stages as already discussed. This approach is still used for building large complex systems that require formal requirement analysis, predefined specifications, and control over system building processes.

The programmer in the coding process invariably refers to the entire system design documents and develops and debugs programs as per the feedback received from the design and testing processes. The system is used only when the entire application has been developed.

However, this approach, which is predominantly a 'waterfall approach', suggests that the new task can be taken up only once the old one is completed. It does not offer flexibility and agility in the development process. As such, this approach can be costly, time-consuming, and rigid. IT specialists thus propose an alternative method called prototyping.

Prototyping

Prototyping is the rapid development and testing of working models or prototypes of new systems in an interactive process that can be used by both IT specialists and business managers. According to O'Brien (2007), prototyping, as a development tool, makes the development process faster and easier, especially for projects where end-user requirements are hard to define. Prototyping

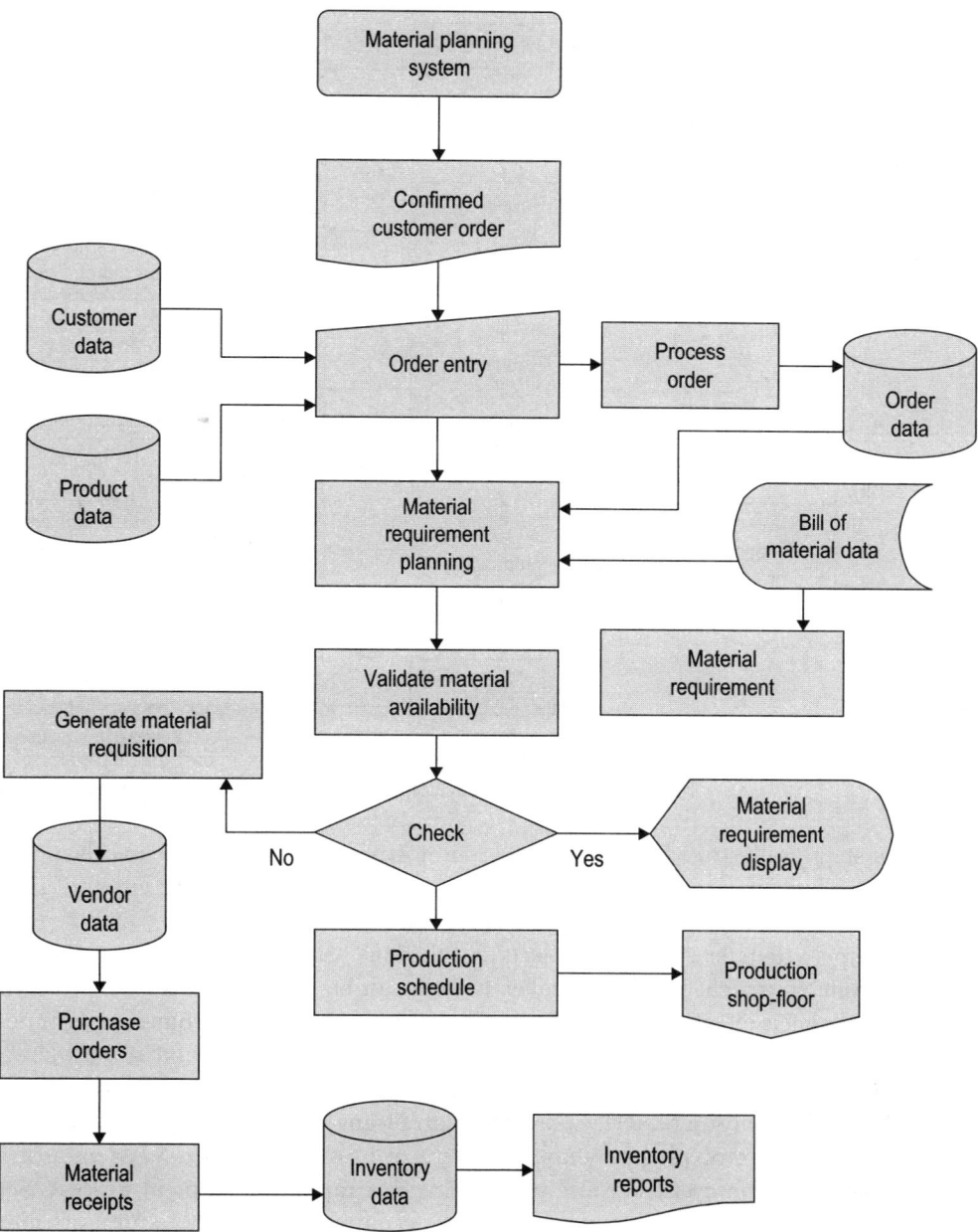

Fig. 15.5   Typical flow chart for material requirement planning process

has opened up application development to end-users because it simplifies and accelerates system design.

Prototyping is a repetitive and interactive process that combines the steps of the traditional software development life cycle. Prototyping is done for a small part of the system and is put to use for evaluation before the entire system is constructed. The process can be broken down into

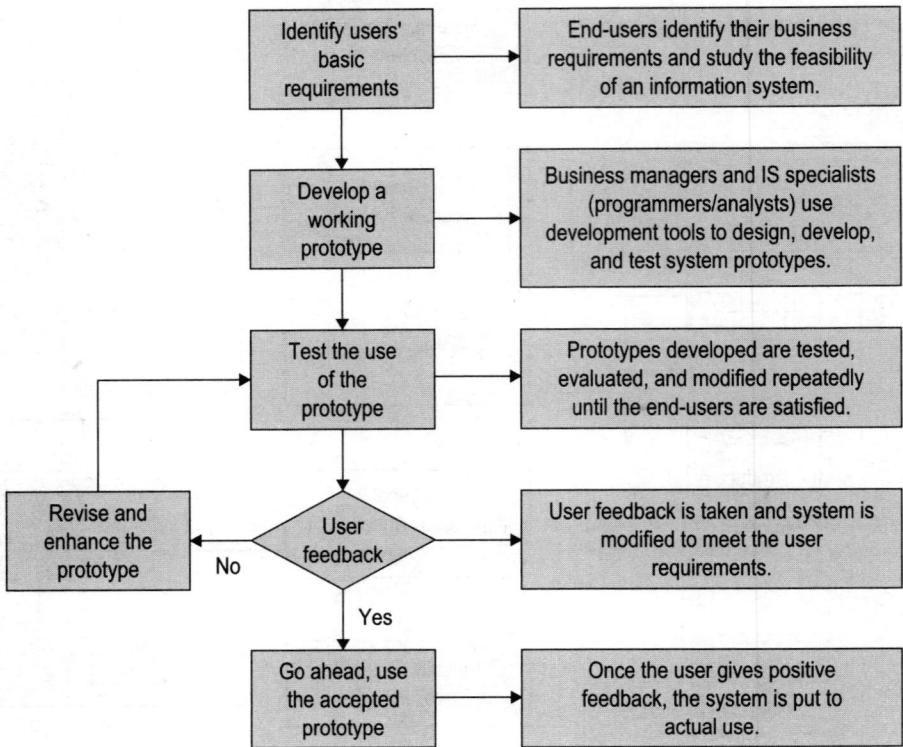

Fig. 15.6   Information systems development using prototyping

four steps as illustrated in Fig. 15.6. As a prototype can be developed quickly and inexpensively, systems builders can go through several changes, repeating the steps to refine and enhance the prototype before arriving at the final operational model.

Large system development projects are still done with the conventional software development life cycle approach; however, smaller systems can be developed with the prototype approach. Prototyping is most useful when there is some uncertainty about requirements or design. Usually prototyping encourages user participation during development and is the right approach for end-use interface design, in which the screens for input and output, web pages, and reports are created. The end-user interface design is part of any system development process.

However, prototyping may not produce as robust and polished a system as in the software development life cycle, because prototyping is a rapid development process. Some of these hastily constructed systems may not easily accommodate the data and users in case of large organizations.

System Development Approaches

Worldwide, businesses encounter frequent changes due to environmental changes and competitive forces, and have to respond to new opportunities and challenges posed by globalization. Organizations look for alternative methods of system development that are shorter, more informal, and adaptive in the new digital age. This has resulted in new fast-cycle and technology-enabled techniques such as rapid application development (RAD), object-oriented system development (OOSD), and computer-aided software engineering (CASE) to emerge.

Rapid application development   Rapid application development (RAD) refers to the process of creating workable systems in a very short period of time. This is an application development method with a goal to meet tight time schedules. RAD is a methodology for compressing the analysis, design, coding, and testing phases into a series of short, iterative development cycles. Prototyping is a common approach used in RAD.

RAD is often used in conjunction with object-oriented programming. RAD tools provide ease and versatility of computer-aided software engineering tools for user interface development and for preparing reusable codes. Typically, RAD programs include wizards for easy application generation, graphical user interface (GUI) development, object libraries that can be easily integrated into applications, groupware for managing team development, prototyping and debugging utilities, and so on.

RAD allows building systems just by reusing the pre-built components stored in the object libraries. For example, when developing a sales billing system, the programmer can use pre-built programs such as date function, tax calculation, and discount calculation.

The SDLC approach uses the sequential method of development, that is, only after completion of the first step, the second is worked upon. However, in RAD, the development process need not be sequential, and the important parts of the system can be developed simultaneously. Figure 15.7 illustrates and compares the traditional development and the RAD techniques.

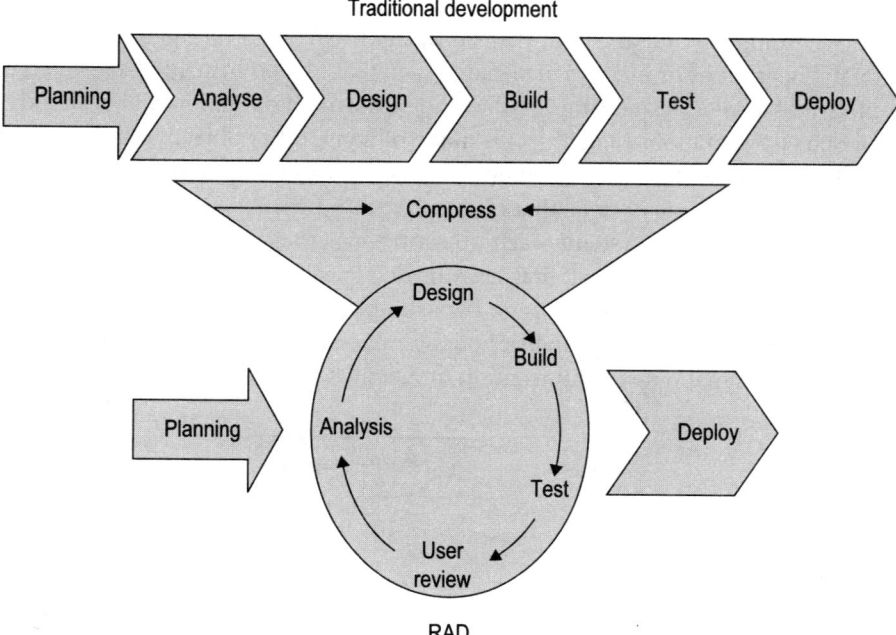

Fig. 15.7   Traditional system development process compared with rapid application development [Jaiswal (2004)]

Some of the fourth generation development tools such as Visual Basic, Delphi, and PowerBuilder offer a RAD development platform. Visual Basic is known for its pioneering role in creating a visual programming environment with the capability to drag-and-drop objects for developing programs. The user-friendliness of Visual Basic makes it one of the most popular RAD tools in the application development industry.

This leads to agile development and component-based development processes. Agile development refers to the rapid delivery of working software by breaking a large project into a series of small sub-projects. A distinct team works on each sub-project taking care of the complete SDLC. The systems are then joined together and the rectifications take place in the next iteration. Agile methods emphasize face-to-face communication over written documents, encouraging people to collaborate and make decisions quickly and effectively.

Component-based development is a technique of further expediting software creation. In this technique, smaller software components are reassembled to create larger business systems. For example, software components such as online ordering, payment gateway, inventory calculation, shopping carts, and catalogues, which are commercially available in the market are combined and integrated to build e-commerce sites.

Object-oriented system development　The conventional approach requires the system to be viewed in terms of data and functions and is designed in the form of document definition, file format, and record definition either as a master or transaction process. In object-oriented system development (OOSD), the view is changed to an object. The object combines the data and the specific process that operates on that data. OOSD is a software engineering approach that models a system as a group of interacting objects.

According to Laudon (2010), data encapsulated in an object can be accessed and modified only by the operations or methods associated with that object. Instead of passing data to procedures, programs send a message for an object to perform an operation that is already embedded in it. In object-orientation, each object is made of some other objects, which may have a relation to each other. Therefore, it is based on the concepts of class and inheritance. Objects belonging to one class have the feature of that class.

In object oriented systems, each object belongs to a 'class'. An object that belongs to a class is called an 'inheritance' of that class having specific value and status. An object inherits the properties of the class it belongs to. For example, as illustrated in Fig. 15.8, the customer's name is an object that inherits properties of the class customer order. Similarly, customer order is an object that is made up of information inputs such as customer address, customer VAT number,

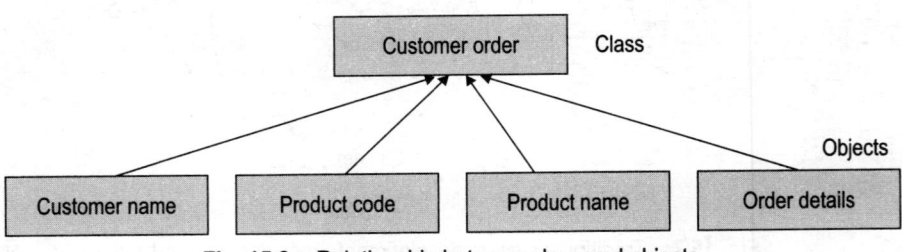

Fig. 15.8　Relationship between class and objects

product code, product name, order quantity, delivery date, payment terms, mode of transport, and bill discounts. These inputs are viewed as objects in themselves.

OOSD facilitates reuse of classes that are already available in the library of reusable software objects and allows adding new objects created during the designing process. Since the objects are reusable, the object-oriented development drastically reduces the time and cost of writing software because organizations can reuse the objects already created as building blocks for other applications.

Computer-aided software engineering   Computer-aided software engineering (CASE) is another approach to develop systems in a much faster mode. The term, CASE, refers to the technique used for the automated development of software. CASE functions include analysis, design, and programming. CASE tools automate methods for designing, documenting, and producing a structured computer code in the desired programming language.

CASE tools support the complete system development process activities such as requirement engineering, design, program development, and testing. Therefore, CASE tools include design editors, data dictionaries, compilers, debuggers, system building tools, etc.

According to Laudon (2010), CASE tools try to increase productivity and quality by doing the following:

- Enforce a standard development methodology and design discipline.
- Improve communication between users and the technical specialist.
- Organize and correlate design components and provide rapid access to them using a design repository.
- Automate tedious and error-prone portions of analysis and design.
- Automate code generation and testing and control rollout.

CASE tools maintain an information repository that includes data flow diagrams, flow charges, structure charts, entity relationship diagrams, data definitions, specifications, screen layouts, report formats, and test results. For a successful CASE, the development method needs organizational discipline for adhering to programming standards and automating code generation.

Testing and Evaluation

Software development can be made successful through testing and evaluation of the system. The testing is done to ascertain whether the system produces the right results, is bug free, and is made as per the system specifications produced during system design. In the modern agile form of software development, systems are technically tested by a qualified testing team during program development using various automated tools such as WinRunner, LoadRunner, LoadStorm, QARun, WebLoad, and Team Test, which ensure product quality and efficiency. Similarly, there are numerous testing techniques, approaches, and methodologies applied by the test engineers.

WinRunner is a functional graphical user interface (GUI) testing tool from Hewlett-Packard (HP). This is the most popular tool for testing software for its GUI. It tests, verifies, and replays user interactions and identifies mistakes in the software function. The software has now been upgraded as FT11 (functional testing) by HP. LoadRunner also comes from the HP stable and is used for testing programs for system behaviour performance. HP LoadRunner can simulate hundreds or thousands of concurrent users to put the application through the rigors of real-life user loads, while collecting information from key infrastructure components (web servers, database servers, etc.). The results can then be analysed in detail to explore the reasons for a particular behaviour. QARun is also a functional testing tool developed and marketed by Compuware and is used for quality testing of software. IBM Rational TeamTest is another high-end tool for testing the functional integrity of a software. LoadStorm, from CustomerCentrix, is used for load testing. Load testing of an application involves creation of heavy user traffic and measuring its response. The tool also improves the performance of applications to meet the required standards.

Testing Approaches

As a user-organization, a company can conduct testing on its in-house developed systems, as well as an outsourced application development. A well thought-out testing plan must be presented before the testing activity takes place. The IS can be tested using the following three methods:

- Unit testing
- System testing
- Acceptance testing

Unit testing   Unit testing is a test that is often automated and validates that individual units of a source code are working properly. A unit is the smallest testable part of an application. In procedural programming, a unit may be an individual program, function, procedure, etc., and is also known as component testing. It verifies a specific section of the program, usually at the function level. It tests each program separately. The main objective of this testing is to ensure that the programs are error free. With unit testing, the errors are located in the program and then handed over to the programmer for rectification in the program.

System testing   System testing of software or hardware refers to the testing that is conducted on a complete, integrated system to evaluate the system's compliance with its specified requirements. System testers need not have knowledge of the inner design of the software code or logic in the hardware design. System testing is done to test the functioning of the IS as a whole. The purpose of integration testing is to detect inconsistencies between the software units that are integrated or between any of the hardware assemblies. According to Laudon (2010), system testing tries to determine whether discrete modules will function together as planned and whether discrepancies exist between the way the system actually works and the way it was conceived. In this testing approach, performance time, peak loads, capacity for file storage, etc., are tested.

System testing includes GUI testing, system performance testing, compatibility testing, usability testing, exception handling, load testing, stress testing, security testing, scalability testing, etc.

Acceptance testing   Acceptance testing ensures that the system is ready for deployment. Acceptance testing is usually performed by the customer, often in their test environment, on their own hardware. This is also known as user acceptance testing (UAT). Acceptance testing may be performed as part of the hand-off process between any two phases of development. Acceptance tests ensure completeness of the project in all respects. The user compares the delivered system with the original specifications and passes it for actual usage.

Implementation

Once a new IS has been designed, developed, and tested, it must be implemented and maintained to keep the system operating smoothly in the organization. The system implementation stage involves hardware and software acquisition, conversion, data migration, training, etc. There are various strategies used for system implementation. The implementation roll-out strategies are the big bang strategy, pilot strategy, phased approach strategy, and parallel strategy.

These challenges, strategies, and approaches have been discussed in detail in Chapter 16.

Maintenance

Maintenance of the system is an ongoing process and involves continuous debugging, improvizing, optimizing, processing speed efficiency, updating new requirements, and updating hardware, software, and documentation.

Whether an in-house development or outsourced application, maintenance is essential. Most organizations build their own IT initiatives to take care of the maintenance part. Usually, the outsourced packaged software is maintained by the vendor and updated in the form of version change. We will discuss the IT organization in Chapter 19.

According to Laudon (2010), approximately 20% of the time devoted to maintenance is used for debugging or correcting emergency production problems. Another 20% is concerned with changes in data, files, reports, hardware, or system software. However, 60% of all maintenance work consists of making user enhancements, improving documentation, and recoding system components for greater processing efficiency. The amount of work in the third category of maintenance problems could be reduced significantly through better systems analysis and design practices.

Outsourcing Application Software Packages

Exhibit 15.4 illustrates how organizations such as Nippo Batteries opt for outsourcing of IS development and implementation of projects. As the best IS are available in the form of universally accepted enterprise resource planning software, organizations seldom go in for the complex, time-consuming, risk-bearing, and trial-and-error system of in-house application development.

Therefore, organizations prefer purchasing software from a vendor, rent a software solution from an application software provider, or outsource the development of an application to an outside developer.

Application Software Packages

With the popularity of personal computers in business, many generalized software packages were developed and marketed for functions such as accounting, inventory, human resource, and production. These standard software packages fulfil the requirements of most of the organizations. For example, Tally, Busy, Miracle, Fact, QuickBooks, etc. are standard packages for general trading accounting. SAP, MfgPro, Oracle Financial, Accpac, MS-Dynamics, etc., are enterprise-level business management software that cater to most organizational functions.

According to Laudon (2010), if a software package can fulfil most of the organization's requirements, the company does not have to write its own software. The company can save time

EXHIBIT 15.4

Nippo Batteries: Outsourcing Application Package to Microsoft-NAV

Nippo Batteries Co. Ltd is a household name in India for the 'Nippo' brand of batteries. The company deals with a variety of products such as batteries, compact fluorescent lamps, power stations, torches, and emergency power. Since its inception in 1972, the Chennai-headquartered Nippo has been providing millions of its customers with quality and performance that is second to none.

During the development of IS to meet the organization's requirements, Nippo Batteries thought it worthwhile to outsource an established and robust application package from Microsoft—Dynamics Navision 2009. The enterprise software was procured for around 42 users on a system base of 90 throughout the country. The system runs on IBM servers and desktop and uses SQL server as a relational database management system.

Nippo was earlier using a home-grown information system, which did not have a mature manufacturing module that could assist in workflow and work-in-progress computations. Though the legacy system developed over a period of time, it never offered flexibility and efficiency, and critical reports like downtime of the machines were calculated manually. The main reason for opting for Dynamics was its manufacturing module, workflow, and work-in-process (WIP) costing features. The company evaluated SAP and Oracle E-Business Suite but found MS-Dynamics to be cost effective. The team, headed by the IT manager, identified the constraints that were involved in the ERP system and educated the end-users accordingly.

Nippo availed expert guidelines from Blue Star Info-Tech, one of the implementers of MS-Dynamics. Their expertise on MS-Dynamics reduced the time period of migrating to the new system.

However, after migrating to the new MS-Dynamics NAV, they are able to calculate downtime on a daily basis, identify reasons for the downtime, and take preventive action. This improved their daily production, thereby, reducing the inventory cost to a great extent. The company took the wise decision of bringing about only a low level of customization. They managed to use the application as it was and to acquire the best business practices, they fine-tuned their process flow change accordingly.

The IT manager of the company makes it amply clear by saying, 'Be clear of the company business goals and align IT with your business goals. Make sure your IT department is agile. Be clear with what you expect from ERP. Adapt the ERP without much of customization. Be sure of various business processes involved and how ERP fulfil those.'

Sources:
http://www.cioklub.com/case_study_1056.php?cioid=1056&ciofe aflg=casestudy, last accessed on 27 December 2011.
http://www.msdynamicnavblog.blogspot.com/2011_03_12_ archive.html, last accessed on 27 December 2011.
http://www.nippobatteries.com/html/index.asp, last accessed on 27 December 2011.

and money by using the pre-written, pre-designed, pre-tested software programs from the package. Package vendors supply most of the ongoing maintenance and support for the system, including enhancements to keep the system in line with ongoing technical and business developments.

In a generic software package adaptation, the customization needs to be kept at a bare minimum. Customization means modifying a software package to meet the organization's unique requirements without destroying the integrity and shaking the architecture of the package software. A great deal of customization is expensive, time-consuming, and it nullifies the advantages of package software, a view also expressed by the Nippo Batteries management, as illustrated in Exhibit 15.4.

When an organization opts for a standard software package for adaptation for development of its own system, the system evaluation is done in the system analysis stage. The important evaluation criteria include functions offered by the package, flexibility, user friendliness, hardware, software, network resource requirement, installation and maintenance, cost of package, and industry references provided by the vendor. These evaluation criteria have been discussed in Chapter 16.

Outsourcing Development Services

For most organizations, it is not viable to develop an application in-house, as creating and maintaining an IT department with system analysts, business analysts, system designers, programmers, test engineers, etc., is an expensive affair. Moreover, retaining IT staff in non-IT companies is difficult.

Organizations can outsource the development, designing, and maintenance of the system to an external organization that specializes in providing these services. The outsourcing concept is very popular because these outsourced firms are supposed to possess skills, resources, and expertise and can deliver quality products and services at a very competitive price. Therefore, they are very cost-effective, compared to the in-house development. Companies can also subscribe to the services of hardware, software, and other resources that have been popular, such as cloud computing and software as a service (SaaS) concept.

For example, developing an application to meet the IS requirements of a small-medium business (SMB) would require 10–12 IT specialists for two to three years. Instead, a SME ERP such as SAP Business One would take five to six months for implementation. Table 15.3 shows a comparison of total cost of operations (TCO) for a period of 10 years for both in-house development and outsourcing generic application.

Thus, an organization can decide whether to go for in-house development, outsource the development processes, or procure a standard ready-to-use software package.

Table 15.3   Approximate costs comparison of in-house development efforts and package application implementation

Cost of in-house development	Amount (₹)	Cost of purchasing and implementing a standard mid-segment ERP	Amount (₹)
1. Salaries of 12 IT specialists (team leader, analysts, designers, programmers, and testers) for development @ ₹6,00,000 per person per annum for three years	2,16,00,000	1. SAP B1 Product with sales, purchase, inventory, accounting, finance, manufacturing planning modules and user license cost for 50 users license	30,00,000
2. Salaries of 2 IT specialists (manager, programmer) for maintenance @ ₹600,000 per person per annum for 10 years	1,20,00,000	2. Implementation cost for 50 users 3. Maintenance cost for 10 years @30% of product cost per annum	10,00,000 90,00,000
Total	**3,26,00,000**	**Total**	**1,30,00,000**

SUMMARY

Information systems planning is the process of deciding the objectives for organizational computing and identifying potential computer applications that the organization should implement. Information system planning has three components—IS strategy development, IS technology architecture, and IS resource management. Organizations generally apply one or a number of methodologies in order to perform the information system planning. Three popular methodologies include business systems planning (BSP), strategic systems planning (SSP), and information engineering (IE).

The business system plan serves as a road map, indicating the direction of systems development (the purpose of the plan), the rationale, the current systems/situations, new developments to consider, the management strategy, implementation plan, and budget. Critical success factors (CSF) technique must be used for identifying issues considered by business executives as most vital for the success of their organization.

System development is a structured kind of problem-solving approach with distinct activities. These activities, when performed in a systematic and cyclic way, are called system development life cycle (SDLC). This SDLC methodology is closely linked to what is popularly known as structured system analysis and design (SSAD). The structured approach refers to the fact that the techniques are step by step, with each step building on the previous one. SDLC involves (a) feasibility study, (b) system analysis, (c) system design, (d) system construction, (e) testing and evaluation, (f) system implementation, and (g) maintenance.

System analysis is the in-depth study of end-user information requirements, which forms the basis for system design and product specifications. System analysis consists of identifying and defining the problems, identifying its causes, specifying the solutions, and identifying the information requirements that must be satisfied by the proposed solution. System design encompasses the design activities that generate system specifications meeting the functional requirements that were developed during the system analysis process. System design consists of three activities: user interface design, data structure design, and process design.

Prototyping is the rapid development and testing of working models or prototypes of new systems in an interactive process that can be used by both IT specialists and business managers. Prototyping is a repetitive and interactive process that combines steps of the traditional system.

New, shorter, more informal, and adaptive fast-cycle and technology-enabled techniques such as rapid application development (RAD), object-oriented system development (OOSD), and computer-aided software engineering (CASE) have emerged as the new approaches to development. RAD is a methodology for compressing the analysis, design, coding, and testing phases into a series of short and iterative development cycles. Object-oriented analysis and design (OOAD) is a software engineering approach that models a system as a group of interacting objects. The term, CASE, refers to the technique used for the automated development of software. CASE functions include analysis, design, and programming. The tools automate methods for designing, documenting, and producing a structured computer code in the desired programming language.

System testing is done to ascertain whether the system produces the right results, is bug free, and made as per the system specifications produced during system design. In the modern agile form of software development, systems are technically tested by a qualified testing team during program development using various automated tools. Some of the tools used are WinRunner, LoadRunner, Rational TeamTest, QATest, etc. There are hundreds of methods of system testing. All these methods are consolidated in three types of tests viz., unit testing, system testing, and acceptance testing.

Post testing, systems are implemented and maintained to keep the system operating smoothly in the organization. The system implementation stage involves hardware and software acquisition, conversion, data migration, training, etc. Maintenance of the system is an ongoing process and involves continuous debugging, improvizing, optimizing, processing speed efficiency, updating new requirements, and updating hardware, software, and documentation.

Due to complexity and the time-consuming nature of software development, organizations prefer purchasing a software form a vendor, rent a software solution from an application software provider, or outsource the development of an application to an outside developer.

KEY TERMS

Acceptance testing   A test to ensure that the system is ready for deployment.

Agile development   Rapid delivery of working software by breaking a large project into a series of small sub-projects.

Business systems planning (BSP)   Identifying a business mission, objectives, and functions, and how these objectives determine business processes.

Component-based development   A technique of expediting software creation in which smaller software components are reassembled to create larger business systems.

Computer-aided software engineering (CASE)   A technique used for automated development of software including system study, analysis, and coding.

Critical success factors (CSF)   A small number of key factors that executives consider critical to the success of the enterprise.

Data structure design   Defining a database structure with data item attributes.

Dataflow diagram (DFD)   A diagram that involves a logical graphic model of information flow, and portioning a system into modules that show manageable levels of detail.

Economic feasibility   A study of budgetary outlays, cost savings, and profit enhancements as a result of the implementation of new IS.

Feasibility study   A preliminary study to assess the major information and resource requirements, and costs, benefits, and feasibility of the proposed systems.

Flowchart   A graphical representation in which symbols are used to represent operations, data, flow, logic, equipment, etc. It illustrates the structure and sequence of operations, and components and flow of IS.

Information engineering (IE)   A technical approach used to build an IT architecture to plan, analyse, design, and implement applications.

Information systems planning   The process of deciding the objectives for organizational computing and identifying potential computer applications that the organization should implement.

IS resource management   Developing strategic plans for creating, managing, or outsourcing an organization's IT resources.

IS strategy development   Developing IS/IT strategies that support an organization's long-term objectives.

IS technology architecture   Choosing the right technology architecture and applications that support IS and business strategy and e-business initiatives.

Object-oriented system development (OOSD)   A software engineering approach that models a system as a group of interacting objects.

Operational feasibility   Willingness and ability of the management, employees, customers, and other stakeholders to use and support the proposed IS.

Organizational analysis   Understanding of the organization's environment, management structure, people, and business activities, for new IS.

Organizational feasibility   Preparedness of the organization for the proposed IS.

Process design   Specifying how the computer system will function from data entry to the output stage.

Prototyping   The rapid development and testing of working models or prototypes of new systems in an interactive process that can be used by both IT specialists and business managers.

Rapid application development (RAD)   The process of creating workable systems in a very short period of time.

Requirement analysis   Defining the objectives of a new system and developing a detailed description of the functions that this system must perform.

Strategic systems planning (SSP)   Defines a business function model by analysing the major functional areas.

Structured system analysis and design (SSAD)   A step-by-step method of system design that involves establishing a relationship between the components of a system and the flow of data between them.

System analysis   An in-depth study of end-user information requirements, which forms the basis for system design and product specifications.

System construction   Actual development and writing of programs using a programming language.

System design   Deciding how a proposed IS will meet the information needs of end-users, including logical and physical design activities, interface, data, and process design activities.

System development life cycle (SDLC)   A series of decisions, actions, feedback, and reviews in the IS development plan.

System implementation   Handing over the system to users, adopting new business IS, providing handholding support and training to users.

System maintenance   An ongoing process that involves continuous debugging, improvizing, optimizing, processing speed efficiency, updating new requirements, and updating hardware, software, and documentation.

System testing   Testing the functioning of the IS as a whole.

Technical feasibility   Estimation of hardware, software, and network capabilities required for running the new IS.

Unit testing   Verifying a specific section of the program, usually at the function level.

User interface design   Designing input forms, output forms, reports, and dialogues in a system design process.

CONCEPT REVIEW QUESTIONS

1. What is information system (IS) planning? What are the various components of IS planning?
2. Which system methodologies are the most popular? Discuss any three such methodologies.
3. What do you understand by system development life cycle (SDLC)? Enumerate the important stages while giving a brief definition of each of them.
4. What is a feasibility study? What business aspects are taken care of in a feasibility study?
5. What is the objective of system analysis and its role in the information system development process?
6. What is the outcome of a system design? What three activities complete the system design process? Explain a data flow diagram (DFD) and flow charts.
7. What are the various testing methods for a developed system?
8. What is prototyping approach in system development? Why is this approach preferred?
9. What is rapid application development (RAD)? Explain object-oriented system development (OOSD) and computer-aided software engineering (CASE).

CRITICAL THINKING QUESTIONS

1. Why is information system planning necessary for organizational competitive advantage?
2. Software development life cycle approach necessarily follows the structured system analysis and design approach. Explain with examples.
3. Prototyping is a rapid application development process that only takes up a small part of the system at a time. Critically examine this statement.
4. Object-oriented analysis and design (OOAD) and computer-aided software engineering (CASE) tools are approaches to rapid application development (RAD). Comment on this statement.
5. Why do organizations today prefer buying and implementing a software package rather than going in for an in-house system development?

MIS DEVELOPMENT

Your college intends to develop an information system (IS) for the students' online examination. This new examination system is envisioned as an online system that allows users to register, conduct exams, evaluate papers, and process the results.

Exercise

Use the SDLC approach for designing such a system. Carry out a detailed feasibility study encompassing the present examination environment in the college, hardware/server requirements, hosting infrastructure requirements, system software and browsers, network resources such as Internet bandwidth availability and other related requirements. Perform cost estimation for hardware, system software, and server applications. Assess the development and manpower efforts for system requirement analysis, designing, testing, and training in terms of man-months or man-days. Calculate overall costs based on the current average remuneration of IT manpower.

You are expected to carry out a requirement analysis by examining the present examination system, identifying the lacunae, loopholes, and problem areas. Design a system that addresses these problems and offers a dynamic solution to reduce the strain on professors, students, as well as the college staff. Design the system with the help of data flow diagrams and flow charts for each process in the online examination system—registering, conducting, and evaluating.

Draw a blueprint for testing the software once it is developed (supposed to be constructed/developed by the software engineering students of your college or out-sourced to Microsoft). Assess the efforts required to train the invigilators, professors, students, and staff of your college.

REFERENCES

Alter, Steven, *Information Systems-The Foundation of E-business*, Pearson Education, Singapore, 2004.

Davis, Gordon B. and Margrethe Olson, *Management Information Systems*, The McGraw-Hill Book Company, Singapore, 1996.

De Gues, Arie, 'Planning as learning', *Harvard Business Review*, March–April 1997.

Doll, William J., 'Avenues for top management involvement in successful MIS development', *MIS Quarterly*, March 1985.

Jaiswal, Mahadeo and Monika Mittal, *Management Information Systems*, Oxford University Press, New Delhi, 2004.

Jawadekar, Waman S., *Management Information Systems*, Text and Cases, Tata McGraw-Hill, New Delhi, 2008.

Kalakota, Ravi and Marcia Robinson, *E-Business: Roadmap for Success*, Addison-Wesley, MA, 1999.

Keen, Peter G.W., *Shaping the Future: Business Design through Information Technology*, Harvard Business School Press, Boston, 1991.

Laudon, Ken, Jane Laudon, and Rajanish Dass, *Management Information Systems*, Pearson Education, Singapore, 2010.

Lederer, Albert L. and Vijay Sethi, 'Implementation of strategic information systems planning methodologies', *MIS Quarterly*, September 1988, http://zulsidi.tripod.com/pdf/sisp2.pdf, last accessed on 28 December 2011.

Martin, James, *Strategic Data Planning Methodologies*, Prentice-Hall Inc., Englewood Cliffs, 1982.

O'Brien, James A., George M. Marakas, and Ramesh Behl, *Management Information Systems*, Tata McGraw-Hill, New Delhi, 2007.

Rockart, J.F., 'Chief executive define their own data needs', *Harvard Business Review*, March–April 1979.

CASE STUDY

Maruti Udyog: Developing an Automobile Finance System

In its constant endeavour to keep its financing system agile, the management of Maruti Suzuki India Limited (MSIL, formerly Maruti Udyog Limited), dentified the need to leverage the Internet-based enterprise e-commerce applications. An automobile financing system was developed to interact with the dealers as well as alliance partners such as Citicorp Maruti, Maruti Countrywide, ICICI Bank, HDFC Bank, Kotak Mahindra, Sundaram Finance, Bank of Punjab, and IndusInd Bank.

About the Organization

MSIL, a subsidiary of Suzuki Motor Corporation of Japan, is India's largest passenger car company, accounting for a majority of the domestic car market. The journey began in 1985 with the principle of 'Give'—a principle that has been the bedrock of Maruti Suzuki's approach to sustainability. MSIL has strived towards offering high quality, latest technology, and value for money products to its customers. The company has two manufacturing facilities, one each at Gurgaon and Manesar, south of New Delhi, India. Both the facilities have a combined capability to produce over a 1.2 million vehicles annually.

The company plans to expand its manufacturing capacity to 1.75 million by 2013. It offers 14 brands and over 150 variants ranging from people's car, Maruti 800 to the stylish hatchback, Ritz. MSIL is the owner of brands such as Omni, Eeco, Alto, A-star, WagonR, Swift, Zen-Estilo, Gypsy, Grand Vitara, SX4, and Swift DZire. In the fiscal year 2009–10, MSIL became the only Indian company to manufacture and sell one million cars in a year. The company has an employee strength of over 8500, ending March 2012.

Maruti Finance is one of the premium services offered by MSIL to tackle this challenge. It offers competitive financing deals to its customers with the help of a strong dealer and alliance consortium.

Challenge

Managing the huge network of dealers, sales, and financing on a daily basis is not a simple task. The challenge was to track the business movement of sales and finance at the distributor and alliance levels and ensure that business critical data were readily available across the network.

System Developer

Maruti shortlisted the Gurgaon-based Binary Semantics Limited (BSL) as its IT partner for system development.

BSL is a client-centric global software development company offering IT services, consulting services, and knowledge management services across several industry segments such as automobiles, manufacturing, FMCG, technology, insurance, travel, hospitality, and business to business (B2B) publishing. Their global operations spread across USA, Canada, Europe, and India have won over 150 satisfied customers. BSL leverages its strong technology expertise and deep industry knowledge to develop customized solutions and services to fit your needs.

Solution

BSL carried out a feasibility study along with the key members of the user organization to create a B2B application portal that could be accessed across the network and facilitated the overall financing process. The key modules of Maruti automobile finance system are as follows—loan, accounting, master, payout, and reports subsystems.

System Development Methodology

BSL completed the project within a tight time schedule. This was possible as the IT specialist used OOAD methodology. BSL used the RAD technique and reused the pre-built components for various functions available in a generic application. The solution provided by BSL integrated SQL Server 2000 at the back-end with ASP forming the front-end on a robust Microsoft architecture. As the system was to be used across the country, data security was given prime importance and it was deployed on the virtual private network.

Benefits

With the application in place, Maruti dealers serve as a one-stop shop for customers who opt for financing their vehicles. This has helped them achieve a higher degree of customer servicing and satisfaction. Post implementation, the IS helped Maruti in the following ways:

- Facilitate the financing of cars for customers through its dealer network in conjunction with an alliance partner.
- Track the number of cars and customers successfully financed through the network.
- Create a database of prospective customers for future analysis.
- Raise monthly or periodic claims for commission on the

alliance partner for the loan amount sanctioned through the network.

- Maintain the customer history relating to the payments.
- Generate MIS reports from the database.

Project in a nutshell	
Project	: Automobile Finance System
Customer	: Maruti Suzuki India Limited
Application	: B2B
Tools used	: MS SQL Server 2000, ASP, Dream-Weaver, Visual InterDev, MS Visio, XML, ErWin
Platform	: Windows Server 2003
System scope	: Requirement analysis, designing, prototyping, development, testing, and implementation

Discussion Questions

1. What prompted Maruti Suzuki India Limited (MSIL) to outsource the development of the auto finance system? Could a packaged software system meet the requirements?

2. What kinds of system development methodologies were used by Binary Semantics to develop an IS for MSIL? Did this method adhere to the SDLC approach?

3. What was the business case of implementing the IS system? What tangible and intangible benefits did MSIL perceive in this case?

4. Testified by this case, do you think most of the present day IS development is happening through rapid application development (RAD) techniques clubbing together object-oriented analysis and development (OOAD) and computer-aided software engineering (CASE) tools? Find out some other development project done using CASE tools.

Sources:
http://www.binarysemantics.com/casestudies_maruti-finance.htm, last accessed on 2 January 2012.
http://www.binarysemantics.com/About_Us.htm, last accessed on 2 January 2012.
http://www.marutisuzuki.com/about-us.aspx, last accessed on 2 January 2012.

16

Implementing Information Systems

> *Information technology has created a seismic shift in the way companies do business. Just knowing the importance and structure of e-business is not enough. You need to create and implement an action plan that allows you to make the transition from an old business design to a new e-business design... Many companies plan really well, yet few translate strategy into action, even though senior management consistently identifies e-business as an area of great opportunity and one in which the company needs stranger capabilities.*

—Ravi Kalakota and Marcia Robinson

LEARNING OBJECTIVES

After studying this chapter, you will be able to

- understand the planning process in MIS implementation
- know how to set objectives and define key performance indicators
- understand the challenges of implementation
- appreciate the process of hardware and software evaluation
- outline the stages of implementation
- get acquainted with the implementation process and activities
- be able to decide roll-out strategies
- identify the causes for the success and failures of implementation

EXHIBIT 16.1

Anna University Implements Examination Information Systems

Anna University was established as a unitary type of university in Chennai in 1978 with four constituent institutions. In 2002, it was converted into an affiliated university wherein all the government, government-aided. and self-financing engineering colleges in Tamil Nadu, numbering around 102, were affiliated to it.

In December 2008, Anna University completed the implementation of IntelliEXAMS, the examination management suite from Mind logicx Infotech Ltd, Bengaluru. This is an integrated system for automating the entire life cycle of examination management at Anna University. With this, the university would set a new benchmark in the new age examination management system and drive knowledge revolution to its next level by addressing the pain points of the university. This project benefits 75,000 students and 110 colleges across eight districts of Tamil Nadu wherein the university and the colleges are networked through VPN. The intelliEXAMS framework was built as a technology suite and provides solution to universities and institutions as a managed application service (MAS). It is a web-based authoring tool that offers convenience and alacrity and at the same time its hardware-based authentication ensures that the whole process is highly secure and foolproof. IntelliEX-AMS manages the examination process of Anna University, Coimbatore (AU-C) by diligently handling the complete life cycle of their high stake examinations covering online registration of candidates, online scheduling of examinations, examination fee management, internal mark uploading, online hall ticket generation, distributed authoring of question papers, secured question paper delivery, multiple digital evaluation, tracking of students' performance, publishing of results, and printing of mark sheets and certificates. The work flow process integrated in the system provides instant access to the university authorities for effectively managing the whole process in a scientific manner.

Dr Radhakrishnan, vice-chancellor, Anna University, said,'This would herald a new digital trend that showcases the power of information technology in managing examinations virtually in a transparent, efficient, and foolproof manner. By deploying the solution, we have effectively tackled the problems normally associated with the conduct of such examinations and we have put Anna University on the global map. I am sure Anna University would set benchmarking standards for other universities by adapting to the e-governance framework.'

Suresh Elangovan, chief executive officer, Mindlogicx, said, 'We are delighted to be the pioneer in conceiving and implementing India's first integrated e–governance framework for the examination management system (EMS). Our insight of examination management currently followed by universities helped us map the pain points of universities, which we have addressed through intelliEXAMS. The EMS can handle both offline and online examinations even when the question papers are transmitted from the university just a few minutes before the commencement of the examinations. It possesses security features such as a 128-bit encryption and hardware-based authentication; the system deployed here is similar to the one that is being used for online banking or e-commerce transactions. The certificate authentication is done through a standard browser or mobile browser.

As part of implementation, Mindlogicx has set up a network operating centre (NoC) in the university campus and the same is connected to all examination delivery centres across colleges where examinations are conducted. Further, the system enables error-free digital multiple evaluation from the designated central valuation centres, and timely and accurate declaration of results. Other features of the project include providing controlled access to faculties for question bank authoring, remote monitoring of the examination by the administrators, dashboards as decisions support tools, and storage and retrieval of digitized answer scripts for revaluation and re-totalling besides backup and disaster recovery.

Sources:
http://www.autcbe.ac.in/about.aspx, last accessed on 4 January 2012.
http://www.mindlogicx.com/intelliEXAMS.html, last accessed on 4 January 2012.

Anna University's initiative to implement the examination management system helped it to leverage the power of information technology by managing examinations virtually in a transparent, efficient, and foolproof manner (Exhibit 16.1). The university implemented the EMS and obtained the desired results. The IS strategy of the university strengthened the concept of

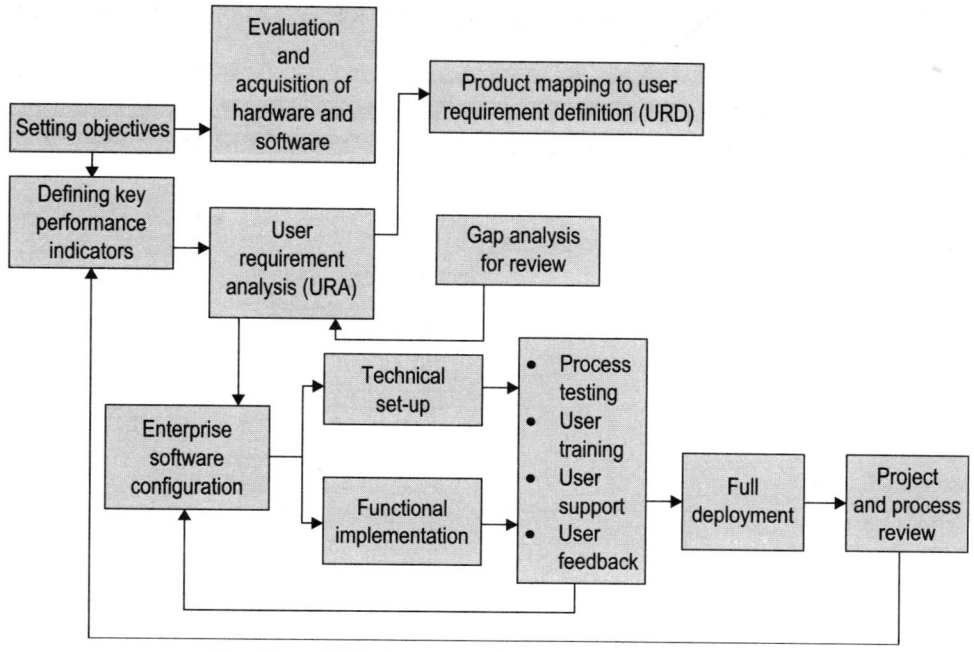

Fig. 16.1   Multi-step approach to system implementation

implementing the best packaged software solutions. The implementation process went through a number of activities, processes, and challenges.

Since the beginning of this century, most of the firms in India have shifted their IS strategy from developing systems in-house to implementing packaged solutions such as ERP (enterprise resource planning), MRP (material requirements planning), and CRM (customer relationship management). In this chapter, we will discuss the various tasks, processes, activities, and challenges involved in information system implementation, which include the packaged software as mentioned earlier.

Implementing MIS is a complex and time-consuming process. Therefore, the implementation should be treated akin to a project management task. Poorly managed projects lead to cost overrun, time delays, and deliver results below expectations, thus resulting in total project failures. As we know, implementing enterprise solutions and business systems is a daunting task and involves risks of failure; therefore, utmost care should be taken in deciding the course of action. MIS implementation involves defining objectives, setting targets and benchmarks, evaluating various hardware and software products, configuring and setting up software, training support and feedback, deciding roll-out strategies, and choosing the right implementation methodology.

Figure 16.1 illustrates the complete implementation processes right from setting objectives to project review.

PLANNING OF IMPLEMENTATION

Implementation of MIS is a complex process and involves various steps. As in any project management, implementation also requires meticulous planning and control measures. In the

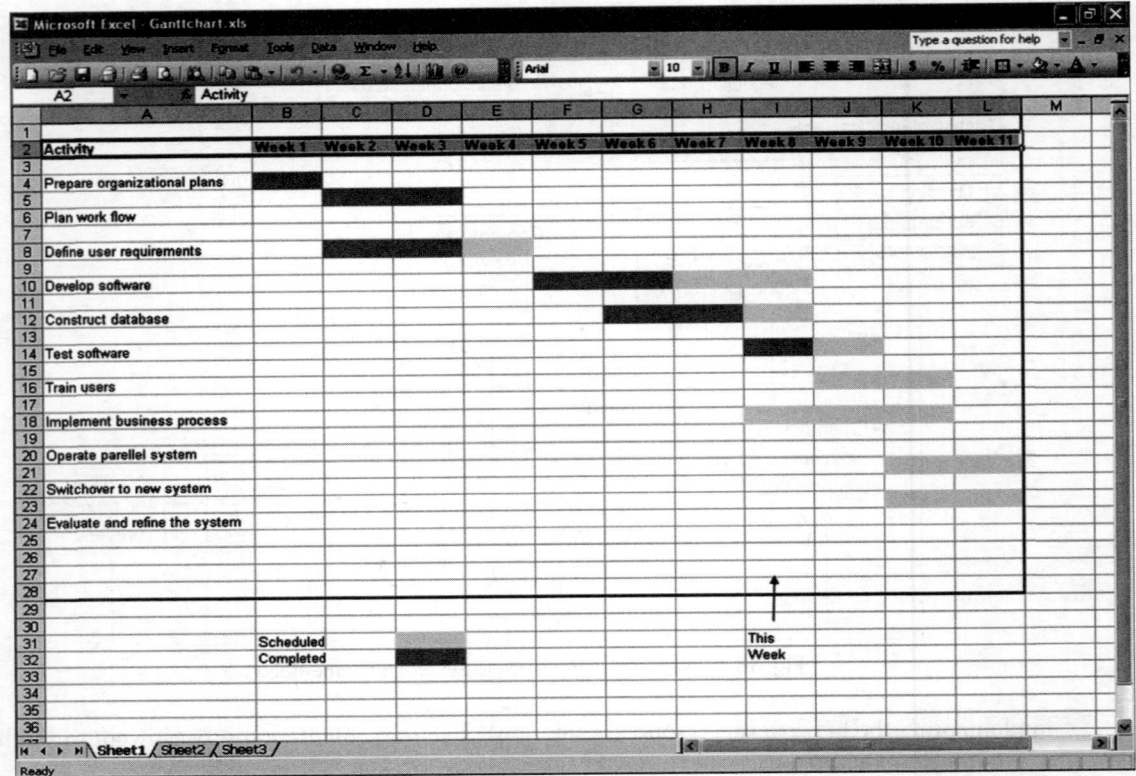

Fig. 16.2 Use of Gantt chart for project review and control

process of implementation, time and cost estimates are obtained. This not only involves selecting and acquiring the right hardware and software, but also setting short-term and long-term goals. The task involved is to define objectives whose performance can be measured once the system is implemented. The management can modify and correct the processes to achieve the desired results. In such projects, some activities are concurrent and some are sequential in nature. To achieve optimum results and efficiency, the project manager should make use of tools, such as Gantt chart (as shown in Fig. 16.2) or network diagrams, which can provide a clear picture of the plan and also a benchmark for review. Prior to implementing a new MIS, the following preparatory exercises need to be done:

- Set objectives.
- Define key performance indicators (KPI).
- Muster organizational support for the new MIS.
- Commit resources.

Set objectives MIS implementation is always preceded by setting clear objectives about organizational aims and targets. Objectives explain what the company wishes to achieve by implementing the MIS. First, broader goals are defined and then these goals are further broken into smaller and measurable objectives. During the course of MIS implementation and review, the results are compared with objectives. For instance, look at the following objectives:

- Create new business opportunities.
- Improve stock control.
- Integrate cross-functional information systems.
- Make the procurement system more efficient.
- Increase employee satisfaction and reduce turnover.
- Develop sales analytics.
- Bring in efficiency in production system.
- Work more closely with partners.
- Improve customer relationship.

One can set objectives as per the company's mission and visions.

Define key performance indicators The objectives of implementing an MIS are broad in their sense and content. These objectives are made more specific and measurable. Therefore, key performance indicators (KPI) are defined. KPIs act as the benchmark for testing the success of an MIS once the solution has been implemented and stabilized in the organization. On successful completion of MIS implementation, the accrued benefits and outcomes are compared with the benchmark. By doing so, one is able to measure the volume and extent of success of the project. Enterprise software by itself offers many inherent benefits, which can be further classified as qualitative or quantitative. A more complete analysis of return can be made by looking at the overall payback that the enterprise software can offer to a company. Enterprise software payback includes not only quantifiable improvements in bottom and top line functionality, but also more qualitative measures such as new business opportunities, improved customer and partner relations, and improved time to market, which lead to faster product development and thus, take it to the market earlier. These factors contribute significantly to the success of a company's information system implementation and use.

Quantify key performance indicators Key performance indicators must be quantified to the maximum extent possible. The benefits in quantitative terms are easy to measure and monitor. Therefore, the benefits of a more efficient transaction processing and unified data models should be quantified. The objective datasheet should have information (as shown in the sample data) illustrated in Exhibit 16.2.

An efficient MIS not only records transactions and prints documents, but also provides results to measure these indicators to give the necessary feedback to the business.

Muster support for ERP implementation Introduction of new MIS or ERP systems brings in change in the functioning of the management. To make the system more responsive, new processes are introduced and rotten processes are discarded. This creates resistance among the employees and management as well. Implementing new information systems also involve large budgetary outlays. Thus, one section of the management may favour such expenses and the other may oppose it. Therefore, it becomes imperative to create a politically conducive environment. The ERP implementation endeavour must be supported by the key employees and stakeholders in the organization. It needs to be understood that a perfect information system is not a driver but

EXHIBIT 16.2

Examples of Key Performance Indicators

- Increase production from _____ to _____ pieces per day.
- Reduce wastage in production from _____ % to _____ % in the future.
- Increase turnover from _____ million to _____ million.
- Reduce inventory from _____ thousand to _____ thousand.
- Reduce inventory carrying cost from _____ thousand to _____ thousand.
- Reduce order delivery average time from _____ days to _____ days.
- Increase number of customers served in a year by _____ %.
- Reduce lead time for a product from _____ days to _____ days.
- Reduce debt outstanding from _____ thousand to _____ thousand per month.

- Reduce payables from _____ thousand to _____ thousand per month.
- Improve collection ratio from _____ to _____ per month
- Reduce rejections at shop floor from _____ to _____ pieces per month.
- Reduce the average time taken in creating one document (e.g., purchase order) from (presently) _____ minutes to (proposed) _____ minutes.
- Reduce the complaint handling time from _____ hours per complaint to _____ hours per complaint.
- Reduce employees' absenteeism from _____ man-days per week to _____ man-days per week.
- Reduce customers' complaints from _____ to _____ (number) per month.

an enabler to business. All the expected benefits cannot be achieved unless business owners are committed to realizing them. The process of identifying KPIs, deciding targets, etc., should be agreed upon by all the process owners. Necessary business initiatives must be in place to achieve these targets. The implementation process has to be closely monitored and guided by the taskforce created for the purpose, which should have representatives from all groups of stakeholders.

Commit resources   All said and done, nothing moves without enough money and power. More often, it is observed that the reason behind failure of implementation of new systems is half-hearted support in terms of mobilization of resources such as time, human resources, and money. The top management's willingness to support new systems is not fully backed by adequate resources. These organizational resources include budgets for buying new systems, hardware, software, databases, etc. Resources, in terms of critical time of key personnel, time of data creators, and testers in the organization, are very important. As per one estimate, 40% of the projects fail because of insufficient system study. Consultants cannot understand organizational processes if they are not given enough time by the internal people. The gap between facts and what is understood by analysts leads to faulty solution delivery.

CHALLENGES OF IMPLEMENTATION

Although ERP systems promise benefits that range from increasing efficiency to transformation of quality, productivity, and profitability in the organization, their implementation can pose some unexpected organizational challenges and changes in its structure and culture. A 1999

Table 16.1 Challenges faced by companies in implementing intranet portals and ERP systems

Intranet enterprise portal	Enterprise resource planning
• Security management	• Overcoming end-user resistance
• Getting employees to use it	• Getting top management support
• Defining purpose and scope of the portal	• Dealing with multiple vendors/service providers
• Ensuring consistent data quality	• Scheduling tasks
• Finding technical expertise	• Integrating legacy systems
• Making it user-friendly	• Data conversion
• Selling project internally within the organization	• Changing mindsets and making people accept new processes
• Upgrading portal on regular basis	• Recruiting and maintaining IT staff
• Freezing requirements	• System upgrade issues
• Organizing data	• Moving to a new platform
• Huge costs outlay	• Business process changes
	• Teamwork coordination
	• Huge costs outlay

Gartner report states that 90% of the Fortune 500 companies have tried to implement ERP at least once. Similarly, a study of Fortune 500 companies found that the average implementation time is more than 23 months and the average total cost of ownership (TCO) is $15 million. About 25% of the cases stated a drop in business performance initially; this lasted three to nine months after the commencement of operations. It is also interesting to know that the software and hardware components of an ERP project represent a small fraction of the TCO. A study conducted by McKinsey & Co. reveals that systems integration and change management represent more than 80% of the TCO of an ERP and the rest is mostly accounted for by hardware and software. These figures are indicative of the challenges faced in the implementation of a new MIS. There are many challenges faced by the organization (as depicted in Table 16.1); however, we will summarize them under end-user resistance, and change management.

End-user resistance As discussed earlier, mustering organizational support from all stakeholders is an inevitable planning exercise for implementing the MIS. If this exercise is not property done, user resistance is increased manifold. As implementing the ERP may involve a change in strategy, processes, technology, and even people, it may generate some resistance from the people affected by it. For example, during the late 1980s and 1990s, there was considerable resistance by employees of public sector banks in India, as banks initiated the processes of computerization. Employees associations resorted to strikes as they anticipated job cuts due to computerization.

The problem of user resistance can be overcome by proper education and training as illustrated in Exhibit 16.3. Users must be involved at every step of planning, development, and implementation of the new MIS.

Change management According to one study, across the world, 35% of all ERP implementation programmes failed to achieve the targeted business benefits mainly because it was taken as an automation programme instead of a change management programme. During the implementation of the new MIS, enterprise-wide structural changes should be managed

EXHIBIT 16.3

D.B. Engineering: User Resistance in SFA Implementation

D.B. Engineering (DBE) is a New Delhi-based engineering company that is into manufacturing of industrial knives and blades. The manufacturing model of the firm is make-to-order for both domestic and export orders. The company's large sales team is always on the move for ensuring sales order booking and customer acquisition. Salesmen were reporting to office in two to three months' time and submitting their tour programmes and travel expenditure bills for reimbursement. However, they used to send customer contact programme on a weekly basis by courier. This process used to delay order confirmation with the customer and thus, there was overall delay in processing and dispatching.

'In this era of cut-throat competition and unpredictable customer behaviour, we cannot afford such delays and loss of revenue. We have decided to implement a web-based sales force automation programme that can take care of sales persons' activities such as tour programme, customer contact, sales order, and even salesmen's expenditure report submission,' opined Deepak Beri, director of DBE.

DBE sourced indigenous SFA software and got some customization done on it as per the company's requirements. The application was hosted on DBE's web server and a two-day training was arranged for all the salesmen at their corporate office in Okhla with immediate effect. Even though a few reservations and doubts were encountered during the session, at the end of the training programme, everybody seemed happy.

Akashdeep Agrawal, systems manager, reported that even after two weeks, there was no data entered in the system. The matter was reported to the vice-president of sales. He decided to call each salesman personally and know the reasons. The reasons seemed bizarre and some of them were as follows:

- The application could not run on his/her browser, he/she needed to load a new browser.
- There were no Internet cafes in his/her region of operations; he had to travel 30 kms.
- The application was too slow and entering all the tour programmes was a lot of work.
- The system did not accept his/her login ID and password.
- Things were still not clear to him/her, maybe he needed more training next month.
- He did not have time during the day; however, at nights, the server may be down.
- He was afraid that other salesmen might see his leads and track his customers.
- The colour scheme in the portal was not too pleasing to the eye.
- The font size was too small and caused stress on the eyes.

Considering the variety of issues faced by the sales team, DBE conducted special training for the global sales team in its head office. Post training, DBE was able to overcome these excuses and the software was implemented successfully.

(Example based on author's personal experience.)

efficiently. This includes people, organization, business processes, and organizational culture. According to Jaiswal (2004), 'a culture with shared values and common aims is conducive to success. Organizations should have a strong corporate identity that is open to change.'

Change occurs at many levels in the organization—strategy, process, people, and technology. The right approach is to manage change at all levels.

EVALUATION OF HARDWARE AND SOFTWARE

Once the post-implementation objectives are set and key performance indicators are quantified, the next important job is to procure the required hardware, software, and services. The process of acquiring the necessary equipment should start once the system study is complete and the task force committee has agreed on the specifications.

Based on the product specifications finalized during the design stage of MIS development, companies either float tenders or present these specifications in a document called request for quotation (RFQ) or request for proposal (RFP). Following this, these documents are presented to various vendors for submission of their prices and terms, which paves the way for a purchase order. The corporate procedure for comparing quotations is based on prices, quality, and terms of delivery and payments. They use a scoring system of evaluation. For each product, evaluation factors are defined and given scores, with a maximum of 10, for example. Then, each competing proposal is given scores based on how well they meet the user specifications.

It is easier to test the performance of hardware as they are available in standard specifications from international manufacturers. However, it is difficult to test the performance of software, which require relevant data and networks. They can be tested with specialized software, benchmark tests, and test data. Benchmarking simulates the processing of a given job on several computers and evaluates their performance. Managers can develop their own evaluation factors for each category of products. Sample evaluation tables are given here for both hardware and software (Tables 16.2 and 16.3).

The summary of evaluation factors in Tables 16.2 and 16.3 are only suggested lists. However, you can develop your own evaluation factors. Moreover, the factors can be different for different types of products such as computers, software, and Internet services. For example, evaluation factors for software may have many more factors than what is given for hardware. Similarly, some factors may not carry much weight, given the complexity of the software; for example, a cheaper software is of no use if it is slow, complicated, full of bugs, and poorly supported by the vendor.

Table 16.2   Sample hardware evaluation factors

Parameters	Hardware evaluation factors	Rating scale	Score
Compatibility	Is the hardware compatible with the company's existing hardware and machines supplied by other vendors?	1–10	
Connectivity	Can it support various networks, LAN, WAN, and the Internet? Does it support Wi-fi technology?	1–10	
Cost	What is the purchase and maintenance cost?	1–10	
Maintenance support	Are maintenance support services available from the manufacturer or local provider for this hardware?	1–10	
Performance	How are the machines rated in speed and capacity?	1–10	
Reliability	Do the machines have control and diagnostic features and the cost of risk mitigation?	1–10	
Scalability	Can it handle the increasing demands and requirements of the organization?	1–10	
Software support	Can they support the latest version of OS or open-source operating systems?	1–10	
Technology	Are the machines built using the latest technology? What is the life expectancy?	1–10	
User-friendliness	Is it user-friendly, safe, and comfortable for users? Overall rating	1–10	

Table 16.3   Sample software evaluation factors

Parameters	Software evaluation factors	Rating scale	Score
Compatibility	Is the software compatible with the company's existing hardware and other software?	1–10	
Connectivity	Can it support various networks, LAN, WAN, and the Internet? Does it support Wi-fi technology?	1–10	
Cost	What is the purchase and maintenance cost?	1–10	
Efficiency	Is the software well-developed, keeping in mind standard coding structures?	1–10	
Flexibility	How easily can the software fit into the company's business processes without much customization?	1–10	
Maintenance support	Are maintenance support services available from the manufacturer or local provider for this hardware?	1–10	
Performance	How is the software rated in efficiency and processing?	1–10	
Quality	Is the software bug free? Which are the known bugs?	1–10	
Reliability	Does the software have control and diagnostic features? What is the cost of risk mitigation?	1–10	
Scalability	Can it handle the increasing demands and requirements in the organization for the next 10 years?	1–10	
Security	How secure is the software from error handling, malfunctions, hacking, and access point of view?	1–10	
Software support	Can it support the latest version of OS or open-source operating systems?	1–10	
Technology	Is the software developed with the latest technology and support Web, mobile, etc.? What is the life expectancy?	1–10	
User-friendliness	Is it user-friendly, safe, and comfortable for users? Overall rating	1–10	

STAGES OF IMPLEMENTATION

Implementation of MIS involves various steps. The pre-implementation steps (discussed in Chapter 13) involve system analysis, system design, and development of software. Partha Chakraborty (1998) describes the four processes in the ERP implementation life cycle as analysis, designing, construction, and implementation. These are illustrated in Fig. 16.3. The final stage of deployment is called implementation.System analysis and design is confined to understanding the users' requirements, analysing them, and converting them into a software system. In case of implementation of standard enterprise solutions, ERP is configured to meet the requirements.

Analysis involves the study, identification, and documentation of business requirements and chalking out a project work plan. It aligns the project with the long-term strategic goals of the enterprise. The existing business process of the organization is studied and documented. Simultaneously, an evaluation of the existing technical infrastructure of the company is carried out. Analysis is done by the most experienced resources that possess vast functional knowledge of the business processes. This is followed by gap analysis, which involves mapping of the existing

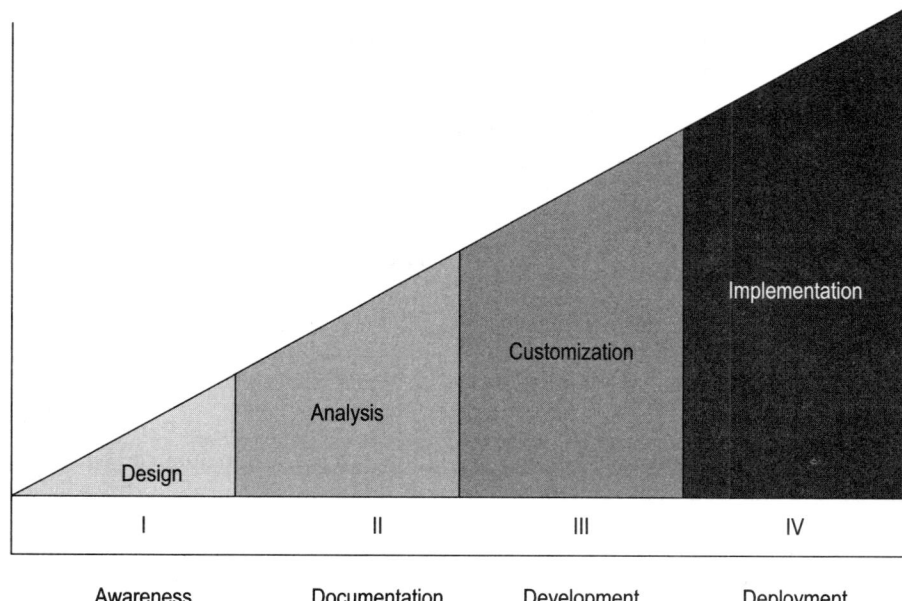

Fig. 16.3   Stages in MIS development and implementation

business processes with the software functionality and the best practices of the industry. The aim is to devise an optimum process that is supported by software and at the same time, ensure that it conforms to the best business practices in the industry. While deciding on the changes, it must be kept in mind that one should not change the basic way in which the software is structured. Indiscriminate customization can lead to system failure or at the least, a system that is impossible to upgrade and maintain.

The design stage starts off with the functional team developing software and database structures. Enterprise software is configured by initially setting the parameters to accommodate various business processes and functions. The gaps or to-be-built findings required by the new system are available in the ready packages. Once the gap analysis is complete, the development team works on designing modules that will enhance the functionalities in the package. Gaps should be as minimal as possible; too many gaps identified at later stages are undoable and hence, may lead to failure of implementation. Instead of incorporating heavy structural changes in the application, business processes may be fit into the system.

In the development phase, the programming team works on customization within the scope of the gap analysis. The team refers to the study documents created during system study and design documents created by the design experts. Program development and testing are two important aspects of the construction phase. Various types of tests such as functional, logical, load, and speed tests are carried out.

IMPLEMENTATION PROCESS

The implementation process in the life cycle of MIS deployment performs the last few critical activities necessary for the system going live. A well thought out process is a road map. It divides

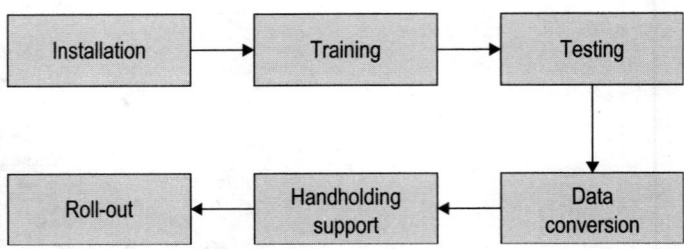

Fig. 16.4   Implementation processes

the entire implementation project into smaller and more manageable groups of activities. The best approach encompasses all the components that go on to provide a complete business solution, rather than merely implementing a software package. Implementation process typically requires a project management effort on the part of the IT and business managers. They must create a project plan, which includes job responsibilities, timelines, and financial budgets. Implementation of a new management information system (MIS) mainly involves the following activities (as shown in Fig. 16.4):

- Installation
- Training
- Testing
- Data conversion
- Handholding support
- Roll-out

Installation   Once the system is ready and tested technically and functionally at the development centre, it is ready for implementation. The first step in this process is the installation of applications on the servers and users' terminals. The database management system is also set up and configured. During this process, the systems managers configure printers, and test LAN and WAN connectivity.

Training   Once the system is installed, it is imperative for the functional team to start conducting end-user training. Users are classified under different groups based on their area of operations or functions they perform. MIS managers design training programmes as per the requirement of the users. The training should be process-driven, that is, each person should be trained on the processes and tasks they do. The users are given training on data entry, report generation, query application, etc. The managers in charge of maintenance of the system are given training on maintenance, backup, restoration of data, day-to-day troubleshooting, etc. Users must be taken into confidence and made aware of the fact that the new MIS system is beneficial to both the organization and its people. The success of MIS implementation depends on how well the users accept the system and use it.

Testing   Testing is done at all stages of design, development, and implementation. System testing involves debugging of software, and testing of website performance and hardware. Subsequent to installation and training, the system should be put through a thorough test on a simulated environment or on live data. This shows the integration of the prototyped system and the custom-developed objects. The functionalities thus created are tested logically and in the light of user requirements. Onsite tests are carried out on live data and changes are made as per the requirements.

Data conversion Today, most organizations use some kind of computer-based information system. Implementation of new information systems involves replacing an old system, its software, and databases. However, the organizations would still need the old data for analysis and reporting. Organizations insist on transferring the old data into the new system. This is called data conversion or data porting. Data porting refers to importing of data from other systems like legacy software to the new ERP. Data migration refers to a change of database because of the change in database management software. For example, earlier, the system might have been using an SQL database; however, the new ERP system works on an Oracle database. Thus, data conversion is one of the essential processes in implementation of the new information system.

Handholding support For large management information systems, mere training is not enough. A technical person with an understanding of design, development, and implementation of the MIS should be available for supporting the user and troubleshooting, in case a need arises. Handholding support involves creation of forms, document design, getting data entry done into the system, helping users in generation of periodical reports, query generation, and modification for generating the required results from the newly developed system. During this period, the team also helps the users with changes and modifications in documents created during development. These documents may either be paper documents or online help available in most of the modern systems.

Roll-out Roll-out refers to the process of switch-over from an old system to the new system being implemented. It is also known as conversion or changeover. The changeover is a very difficult task and requires a meticulous process of conversion. While implementing a new system, the organization may already be using some software. A document may be generated in one process and the connecting document may be in the new system. For example, the purchase department may have raised a purchase order on a vendor sometime back and by the time the goods are received, the new system is in place, in which, the reference of the purchase order is not available for making a goods receipt note. Therefore, the organization may think of various roll-out processes such as parallel running of both systems for a particular duration, a sudden changeover, a phased weeding out of the old one, and adaptation of the new one.

For example, Exhibit 16.4 illustrates how Titan Industries, the owner of 665 retail stores in the country, managed roll-out of retail point-of-sales (POS) software and integrated it with SAP Business One.

EXHIBIT 16.4

Titan Industries: Implementing Retail POS Systems

Titan recently collaborated with its long-time implementation partner, Enteg, to deploy a new point-of-sale (PoS) solution for its retail division.

'The PoS application is a flexible and robust retail management solution integrated with SAP Business One, with precisely managed store operations and a consolidated store. It is an efficient application and has an easy-to-use PoS interface, which is user-friendly and enables quick customer service', remarked C.S. Ramesh, general manager, IT, Titan Industries.

Titan's success story began in 1984 with a joint venture between the Tata Group and the Tamil Nadu Industrial

(Contd)

Exhibit 16.4 (Contd)

Development Corporation. With the launch of Titan quartz watches that sported an international look, Titan Industries transformed the Indian watch market. After Sonata—a value brand of functionally styled watches at affordable prices—Titan Industries reached out to the youth segment with Fastrack. Fastrack was its third brand and was trendy and chic as well. The company has sold 100 million watches world over and manufactures 12 million watches every year. With over 665 retail stores across a carpet area of over 9,24,611 sq. ft., Titan Industries has India's largest retail network. The company has over 317 exclusive 'World of Titan' showrooms and over 50 Fastrack stores. It also has a large network of over 650 after-sales-service centres. Titan Industries is also the largest jewellery retailer in India with over 124 Tanishq boutiques and Zoya stores, over 29 Gold Plus stores. It also sports over 183 Titan Eye+ stores. The company has two exclusive design studios for watches and jewellery.

Titan required a PoS application to carry out retail-transactions in the Retail Eye+ showrooms. Enteg offered to develop a PoS application built on Java platform. The customized solution is used to capture eye power details, which enables quick customer service. It also has an online/offline-enabled application that enables a quick response to changing market requirements with fast implementation of new capabilities.

Titan has been a long time user of SAP ERP solutions. It utilizes SAP Net weaver for its large format of retail operations in stores such as Shopper's Stop and Reliance, to manage its distribution. The company also developed its portal using Netweaver for knowledge management. About a year back, it had partnered with Enteg to create a customized lean retail solution for sales management. Another recent project was an IVR system based on SAP IS Retail, which was a Java-based application developed by Enteg.

Titan has recently expanded into a number of areas as it looks to position itself as a global lifestyle brand. It now operates three separate divisions—eyewear, watches, and jewellery, with the systems all standardized on either Oracle or SAP. 'Our jewellery department is based on Oracle, while the other two are on SAP', informed Ramesh. 'Before selecting any solution, we see if we can standardize the application'.

Apart from this, the company is also conducting pilots for a new BI platform. It is also testing added functionalities such as unified loyalty and workflow management. 'We carry out a number of loyalty services; most are outsourced while one is in-house. With the number of stores we are opening, we feel it makes sense that we consolidate these services for better management', informed Ramesh.

Sources:
Shreshtha, Abhinna, 'Titan industries implements retail management solution', http://www.cxotoday.com/story/titan-industries-implements-retail-management-solution/ 13 January 2011; www.enteg.com/news-events, last accessed on 12 January 2011.

http://www.titan.co.in/corporate, last accessed on 15 January 2012.

APPROACHES TO IMPLEMENTATION ROLL-OUT

There are various methodologies or approaches to system implementation in the organization. A methodology is a tried and tested roadmap to perform a task. Knowing what to do at each step is important; even more important is what follows, so that it can be planned for. A methodology usually makes the difference between success and failure. It chalks out an implementation sequence that best fits an organization. As every organization has its own culture and character, the organization can choose the best roll-out strategy.

While creating a blueprint for ERP implementation, strategies and approaches are decided well in advance. The implementation approach encompasses the sequence in which the ERP package is implemented and rolled out to various business units. The following four approaches are the most popular implementation roll-out choices, as shown in Fig. 16.5:

- Big bang
- Pilot
- Phased
- Parallel

Big bang approach This approach believes in 'do everything in one shot'. This is also known as 'direct' or 'plunge' approach. In the big bang approach, all modules of the system are

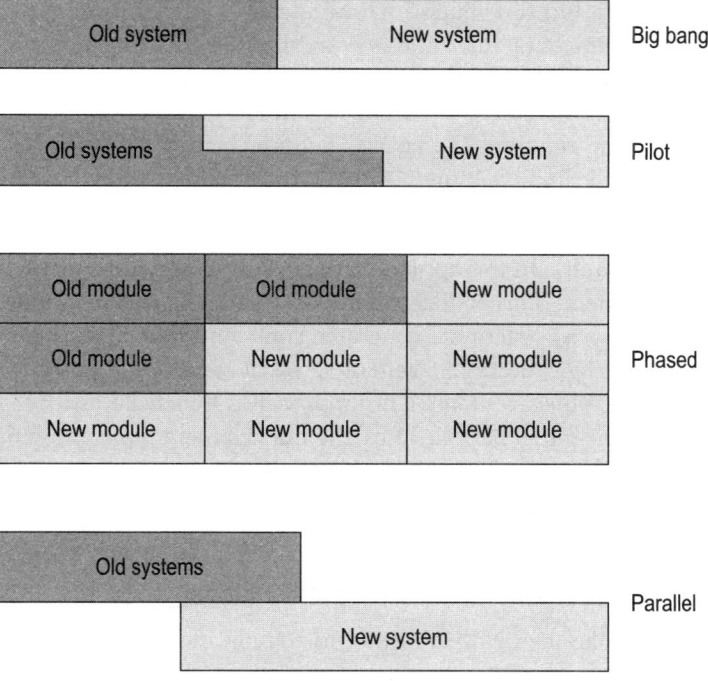

Fig. 16.5   Four major forms of roll-out of new MIS

implemented at one go across all functional departments and business units of the company. This kind of approach has its own positives and negatives. The plus point is that it offers an integrated platform for all departments and all the holes are plugged at once. However, taking up all the modules and functions at one go requires a lot of coordination, human resources, and management willpower. It is very risky as failure in one department may lead to failure in another, or at least the stakeholders may lose confidence.

Pilot approach   In pilot conversion, one department or work unit serves as a test site. Once the pilot is successful, the rest of the implementation is carried out. To overcome the negatives of the big bang approach, the organization treads with caution. In the pilot approach, all modules are implemented across one key department or business unit. It is beneficial as any malfunction or error in the system can be corrected before the system is rolled-out to the entire organization. In this implementation strategy, one business unit is taken up first. Usually, strategists take up the unit that is relatively easy, forthcoming, and where the business processes are relatively systematic. Easy and simple units offer lesser resistance, and lower risks and costs, thus ensuring ERP acceptance and success. The first successful project gives confidence to both—the implementers and the organization. Once it is successful, implementation is rolled-out to the entire organization. It saves on specialized resources as the same expertise can be used in further implementation.

Phased approach   In this approach, the implementation is done in phases. The modules of the systems to be implemented are grouped or segmented. Thus, this is also known as 'modular' approach. One group or segment is taken up at a time for implementation. For example, the marketing, sales, and distribution modules can be grouped together for implementation at a time. The advantages of this approach are that the pace of change in the organization is slow, thus, minimizing resource mobilization in terms of money and human resources. The modular approach is much helpful as it partially combines both, the pilot and big bang approaches. It takes one module at a time and takes the entire chain of users who are involved in this process. For instance, while implementing the marketing module, it will involve the front sales people, the customer relationship people, and the top-level managers.

Parallel approach   In this approach, the new system is implemented and operated in parallel with the old system. This is done till the time the new system is tested and user acceptance is taken. Once the new system has generated confidence among users, the old system is discarded. In this methodology, the results generated by the new systems are compared with the existing one and rectifications are done. This approach is beneficial as there is no dependency on the new system in the initial period. Thus, the management has enough time to check the accuracy and stability of the system. However, this approach is expensive as the organization requires two sets of people to maintain two systems at the same time. Nevertheless, in certain critical areas such as payroll, examinations, airport management, and defence systems, this may be a necessity.

Causes of Success and Failure of Implementation

Since implementation of MIS and enterprise applications involve huge resources in terms of cost, time, and human resources, ensuring their success is of prime importance for the management. A very large number of information systems fail to deliver benefits or solve the problem for which they were built because the process of implementation is not managed properly. Many research findings reveal that more than half the projects fail to achieve their objective and around a third are shelved before completion, as illustrated in Exhibit 16.5.

EXHIBIT 16.5

ERP Implementation: Failure Factors

'The analysis of IT failures can yield great insight and help guide us toward success.'

–Michael Krigsman

There is no shortage of headlines or analyst reports citing ERP implementation debacles and a chilling industry implementation failure rate. There have been published reports from research firms—Gartner, Standish Group, KPMG Canada, Conference Board, Robbins-Gioia Survey—that have been doing surveys on all types of IT projects since 1994. The cost of these failures and overruns are just the tip of the proverbial iceberg. The lost opportunity costs are not measurable but could clearly exceed the out-of-pocket expenses. However, recognizing the repeated causes of failure permits understanding, preventative occurrence, and proactive risk mitigation strategies. Some of the research findings reveal some surprising facts, as mentioned here:

- 51% viewed their ERP implementation as unsuccessful.
- 46% of the participants noted that while their organization had an ERP system in place or was implementing a system, they did not feel their organization understood how to use the system to improve the way they conduct business.
- 56% of survey respondents noted their organization has a program management office (PMO) in place, and of these respondents, only 36% felt their ERP implementation was unsuccessful.
- 55–75% of all projects fail to meet their objectives.
- 31.1% of projects are cancelled before completion.

(Contd)

Exhibit 16.5 (Contd)

- 34% were very 'satisfied'.
- 58% were 'somewhat satisfied'.
- 8% were unhappy with what they got.
- 40% of the projects failed to achieve their business case within one year of going live.
- Over 61% of the projects that were analysed were deemed to have failed.
- Only 16.2% of software projects are completed on time and within the budget.

The following are the prominent among many causes of information systems failure:

- Failed cross-representation agreement on enterprise-wide business processes
- Lack of visible, vocal, and meaningful executive sponsorship.
- Lack of formal and disciplined project management

- Turnover of key staff of a project team
- Inability to identify and mitigate risks or remedy incidents, which ultimately escalate
- Insufficient training
- Troubled user adoption
- Too much software customization
- Project viewed as an 'IT' project, instead as a business project

Sources:
'Cause of IT failures', http://www.erp.asia/erp-failures.asp, last accessed on 5 January 2012.
'The Robbins-Gioia survey (2001)', 'Conference Board survey (2001)', 'The chaos report (1995)', http://www.it-cortex.com/Stat_Failure_Rate.htm, last accessed on 29 January 2013.
http://www.zdnet.com/blog/projectfailures/three-tips-for-studying-it-failure/14861, last accessed on 5 January 2012.

Laudon (2002) cites the following four factors that influence the outcome of MIS implementation:

- The roles of users in the implementation process
- The degree of management support for the implementation effort
- The level of complexity and risk of the implementation project
- The quality of management of the implementation process

The implementation result can be largely determined by the users' role, the degree of management support, the level of complexity and risk in the project, and how the implementation project is managed. The failure or success of an MIS implementation is manifested in the design, costs, operations, and data of the systems, as illustrated in Fig. 16.6. These are the indicators of the outcome of an MIS implementation.

User Involvement and Influence

User involvement is key to the success or failure of an information systems project. Users should be actively involved in all aspects of system design, development, and implementation, so that they can mould the system as per their actual requirement and thus change the results of information system implementation. They will also react positively to the changes if they are involved in the change process. Involvement to any extent and hands-on experience with the system helps users to appreciate the benefits. Users and system professionals have different backgrounds and hence, different approaches to a problem. These differences lead to varied organizational loyalties, problem-solving approaches, and dissimilar vocabularies. Laudon (2002) refers to this phenomenon as 'user–designer communication gap', as illustrated in Table 16.4.

For example, IT specialists look at a problem from a technical point of view and suggest solutions that are elegant, and offer hardware and software efficiency, while users look at a problem from delivery of the end result, effectiveness of the system, and ease of use. Communication problems

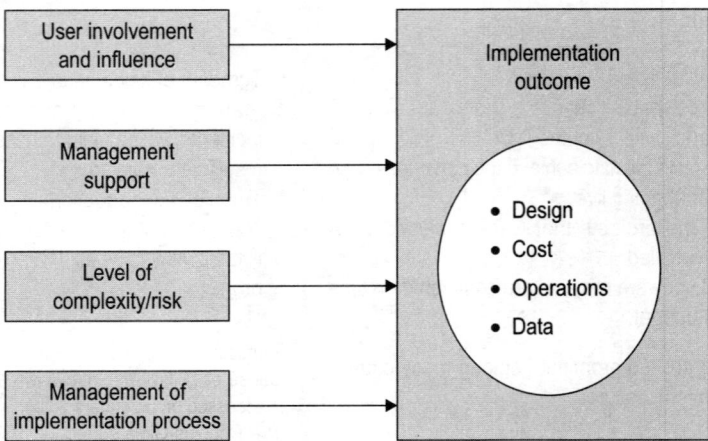

Fig. 16.6   Factors influencing MIS implementation outcome

Table 16.4   Examples of management–user–designer communication gaps

User concerns	Designer concerns	Management concerns
Will the system offer the desired results?	How much memory will this program consume?	Will the system implementation be completed on time?
Will the system run faster on the given operating system on my computer?	How many lines of program codes need to be written to complete the function?	Will the system be completed within the sanctioned budget?
How easily can the system process and print a report?	What is the most efficient way of processing a query for report generation?	Will the system deliver on performance and efficiency?
How much online help will I get when entering data into the system?	How can we reduce the time taken in execution of a particular query?	Would the vendor or developer support the system for a long time?
Will the system enhance my efficiency in performing my duty?	Are we conforming to the latest trends in software writing?	Are we getting the latest in terms of system tools and databases?

among end-users and designers are a major reason why user requirements are not properly incorporated in to the system.

MIS development projects run a very high risk of failure when the gap between the users and designers is very wide and when both the groups follow their respective goals. Users withdraw from the implementation process and the project simply becomes an IT project. One must understand the business value of system implementation. The management and users should treat systems as a major business investment rather than view it as a purely technical project. Even though modern day MIS relies on technology, the primary function of any system is delivering business value. One should remember this point during every aspect of the ERP process, from vendor selection through implementation and going live. It is necessary to always ask—What are the business benefits of this investment? Without defining concrete and specific business benefits, any investment in systems is a waste of money and time.

Management Support and Commitment

According to Michael Krigsman (2010), 'An experienced and committed executive sponsor is an ERP project's best friend. However, the sponsor must genuinely be engaged in the project as an active leader. Active leadership requires time and attention from a senior company executive; ideally, even the CEO should publicly get behind the project.' The executive is the driving force behind the project. If an information system project involves commitment from the senior management, it is more likely to be perceived positively by the users and technicians. They believe that they will get better attention and may be rewarded for successfully implementing such a complex project. Management backing also ensures commitment of resources such as funds and manpower time, which are crucial for the project. William J. Doll (1985) opines that if a manager considers a new system to be of priority, the system is more likely to be treated that way by their subordinates.

Level of Complexity and Risk

The success or failure of a systems project also depends on how complex the project is and the level of risk that it carries. In the parlance of software implementation, the organization must select the least complex and most fit software system. It is easy to get caught up in the technical aspects of software selection; however, as a systems manager, pay close attention to the business results you hope to achieve by implementing this system. The implementing team must discuss this aspect at length with the software vendor, system integrator, and consultants who have been engaged to help with the selection process. They must identify concrete areas in which the new system will make the organization more efficient, profitable, and sensitive to the employees' and customers' needs.

The risk to the project will be more if the project team and system technicians lack the required technical expertise. Therefore, one must ensure that the vendor has successfully implemented similar projects earlier. If the organization's business has uncommon requirements, then, one must try to find a solution that supports vertical industry features and modules that match the organization's requirements, that is, if the solution has a successful implementation record in a similar industry, it is better for the organization. Customization should be as low as possible as unbridled customization can lead to errors and system instability.

The complexity in ERP software is managed through inbuilt system administration and business rules defined in Fig. 16.7. Various generic enterprise resource management software provide a configuration module that enables users to define rules related to their business environment. For example, if the company does not allow feeding of documents on a previous date, the business rules will disable 'allow voucher date change' rule in the configuration module. Thus, the system will strictly adhere to current-date feeds only.

Management of Implementation Process

For ensuring the success of information systems, the implementation itself should be managed properly and efficiently. Effective management starts from the design, development, and selection of technology to the delivery of results. One of the great benefits of a system change is the opportunity to improve business operations. Automating old, inefficient, and dead processes generally makes little sense. It is far better to use implementation as a vehicle to streamline processes, and simplify or improve workflows. This will involve changing how people inside the organization perform their day-to-day work, which is usually one of the most difficult aspects of a system implementation. New information systems are all about transformation and improvement, making change management one of the most important

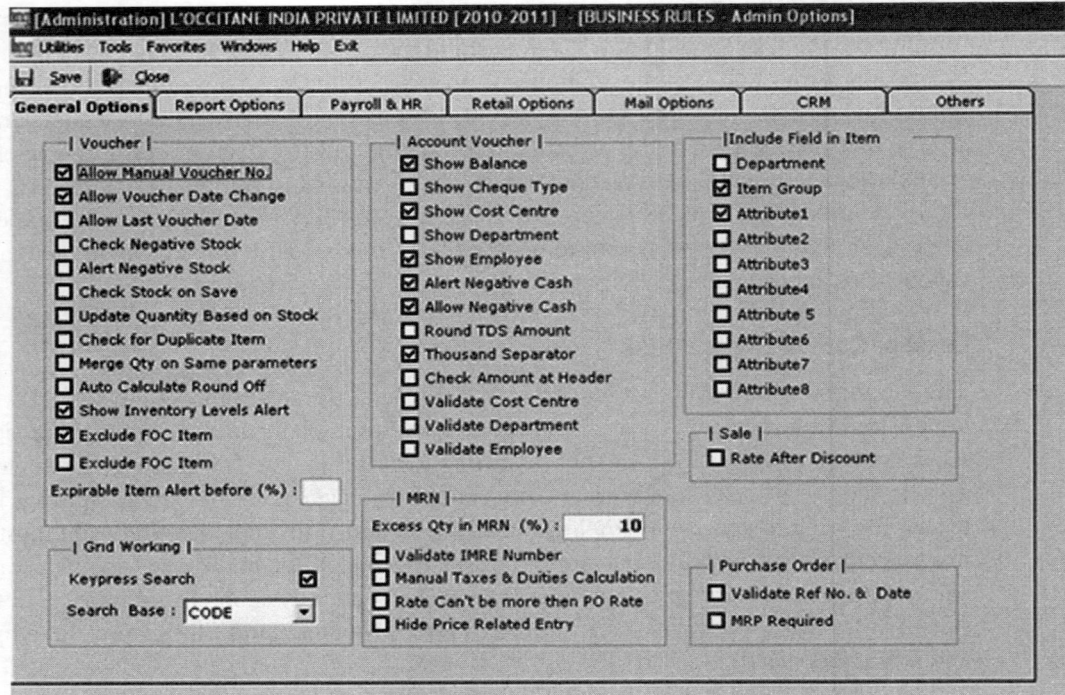

Fig. 16.7   Complexity of a system managed through configuration and definition of business rules [BNG Business Suite]

determinants of the success of implementation. The implementing team must frequently communicate project goals and statuses to the organization and system stakeholders. Attention must be paid to the training of users and system documentation. If a project is not properly managed, it may overrun its costs. As per one survey (see Exhibit 16.5), 52.7% of the projects cost 189% of their original estimates. The cost of these failures and overruns are just the tip of the proverbial iceberg.

A poorly managed information system project invariably results in the following:

Time slippage   Due to poor planning and sluggish acceptance of the systems, projects drag on beyond the stipulated time frame. Though most system implementation projects get delayed, they are still considered successful if they are able to deliver the desired results.

Cost overrun   The cost of the system implementation project is directly proportional to time and labour efforts. Thus, a delayed project costs more than a project completed on time.

Technical shortfall   Technical shortfalls also result in a performance below expectations. Surveys indicate information system implementations are short on performance and do not satisfy the key performance indicators set in the planning stage of implementation.

Thus, implementation of information systems involves meticulous planning, project management skills, and risk management. Well thought-out roll-out strategies will ensure successful implementation of new information systems in the organization.

SUMMARY

Implementation of MIS is a complex process and involves various steps. As in any project management, MIS implementation also requires meticulous planning and control measures. In the process, time and cost estimates are obtained. The task involved is to define objectives that are measurable against performance, once the system is implemented. Prior to implementing a new MIS, one has to set objectives, define key performance indicators (KPI), gather organizational support, and commit resources. KPIs are the benchmark for testing the success of an MIS, once the solution has been implemented and stabilized in the organization. On successful completion of MIS implementation, the accrued benefits and outcomes are compared with these benchmarks. The benefits in terms of quantity are easy to measure and monitor. Therefore, quantify the benefits of more efficient transaction processing and unified data model to the extent possible. It is important to create a politically conducive environment as there might be personal interests in companies that do not want a transparent system to be in place.

Implementation poses unexpected organizational challenges and changes in its structure and culture. The ERP implementation endeavour must be supported by key employees and stakeholders in the organization. Sometimes, the reason behind failure of implementation of new systems is half-hearted support in terms of mobilization of resources—time, manpower, and money.

Based on product specifications finalized during the design stage of MIS development, companies evaluate hardware and software. Benchmarking simulates the processing of a given job on several computers and evaluates their performance. The managers can develop their own evaluation factors for each category of products.

The pre-implementation steps involve system analysis, system design, and development of software. The final stage of deployment is called implementation. The implementation stage in MIS deployment performs the last few critical activities that are necessary for the system to go live. Implementation of a new MIS mainly involves installation, training, testing, data conversion, handholding support, and roll-out.

Implementation roll-out refers to the process of switchover from an old system to the new system. It is also known as conversion or changeover. There are various methodologies and approaches to system implementation in the organization. Implementation approach encompasses the sequence in which the ERP package is implemented and rolled-out to various business units. The following are the most popular choices that an organization can make—big bang, pilot, phased, and parallel.

As implementation of MIS and enterprise applications involve huge resources in terms of cost, time, and manpower, ensuring their success is of prime importance for the management. The following four factors influence the outcome of MIS implementation:

- The roles of users in the implementation process
- The degree of management support for the implementation effort
- The level of complexity and risk of the implementation project
- The quality of management of the implementation process

KEY TERMS

Big bang approach When all the modules of the system are implemented at one go across all functional departments and business units of the company.

Change management Managing the process of change in people, organization, business processes, and organizational culture during system implementation.

Data porting Importing of data from other systems (e.g., legacy software) to the new ERP.

Gap analysis Mapping of the existing business processes with the software functionality and the best practices in the industry.

Implementation roll-out The sequence and strategy in which the ERP package is implemented across the organization.

Key performance indicators (KPI) Setting benchmarks that are checked with the actual performance after a system is implemented.

Legacy software Software developed over a period of time and used in the organization.

Network diagrams Charts that can provide a clear picture of the plan and benchmark.

Parallel approach The new system is implemented and operated in parallel with the old system.

Phased approach A modular approach in which the modules of the systems to be implemented are grouped or segmented.

Pilot approach   All modules are implemented across one key department or business unit.

Query application   Applying a query for extraction of desired information from a database.

System analysis   The study, identification, and documentation of business requirements and chalking out of the project work plan.

Total cost of ownership (TCO)   The entire cost of buying and implementing a system.

CONCEPT REVIEW QUESTIONS

1. What is meant by system implementation? Discuss the various implementation strategies.
2. What do you understand by KPIs? How are they important for evaluating the information system?
3. What kind of organizational preparedness is required when implementing ERP systems?
4. What are the various implementation challenges faced by organizations? Explain any two in detail.
5. As a systems manager, how will you evaluate the hardware and software for new information systems in your organization?
6. Discuss the steps involved in implementation. Are these steps sequential in nature?
7. Discuss the various ERP implementation roll-out approaches. Which strategy do you think is best for an IS implementation?
8. What are the various factors that influence the outcome of the implementation?
9. What leads to implementation failure? List the causes you think may cause an implementation failure.
10. Write short notes on the following:
    (a) Big bang approach
    (b) Pilot approach
    (c) Key performance indicator (KPI)
    (d) Benchmarking
    (e) Handholding support
    (f) Customization

CRITICAL THINKING QUESTIONS

1. 'The best of systems may fail if they are not properly implemented.' Critically examine this statement.
2. While evaluating a software system, an organization should look at the 'best fit'. Explain this statement in detail. Do you think vice versa, that is, should an organization be the 'best fit' for a new system?
3. Search the web and other sources and find out large Indian companies where ERP implementation failed. Try to find out the causes for the same.

MIS DEVELOPMENT

Krishna N. Bhatt is the director of a multi-speciality hospital in New Delhi. The hospital was established in 1995 with a modest beginning. Today, the hospital has 450 beds, 18 specialities, 150 resident doctors, 300 visiting specialists, and around 600 paramedical staff. The hospital runs on a five-storey building and has two wings. There is a vast area marked for parking and the two basement levels are reserved parking spaces. The casualty ward runs 24 hours a day. There is an outpatient section, which is manned by around 300 doctors. There is an estimated inflow of 4500 patients who come for treatment every day. The other infrastructure in the hospital is the presence of four test laboratories, which conduct around 60 types of pathological tests. There are four pharmacies on the ground floor and two cafeterias for the visiting public. Besides this, there are four cafeterias on the fifth floor for doctors and other hospital personnel. These cafeterias serve subsidized food to the staff and also serve the dual purpose of acting as lunch rooms and tea-break rooms. The hospital has made enormous investments in state-of-the-art medical equipment and ultra-modern machines that have been imported from various countries.

Since the hospital began operating, the management had computerized departments such as outpatient department (OPD) registration, stores operations, and pharmacies. However, Bhatt was not able to get a perfect picture of the operations, including the status of beds, engagement of specialists, and operation theatres. He wanted to know about the placement of costly machinery and equipment. Even the daily receipts from OPD consultancy and inpatient billing was known only at the end of the month, when all ledgers were compiled and a statement was submitted to the chairman. The chairman decided to implement a hospital information management system that could provide summaries and detailed reports on all aspects of the operations, daily registration of patients, status of occupied and available beds, inventory of medicines and operation equipment, schedule of doctors' deployment, and availability of specialists.

Exercise

The director of the hospital approaches you to design and implement a comprehensive hospital management system that could meet all of his requirements today, and would suffice the needs of the next ten years. Plan an MIS implementation while setting clear objectives, KPIs, and choose the right roll-out strategy. List the various reports that you would like Bhatt to see every day on his table.

REFERENCES

Alter, Steven, *Information Systems—The Foundation of E-business*, Pearson Education, Singapore, 2004.

Chakraborty, Partha, 'ERP demystified', *DataQuest*, December 1998.

Davis, Gorden and Margethe Olson, *Management Information Systems*, McGraw-Hill, Singapore, 1996.

Doll, William J., 'Avenues for top management involvement in successful MIS development', *MIS Quarterly*, March 1985.

Goyal, D.P., *Management Information Systems—Managerial Perspectives*, Macmillan India Ltd, Delhi, 2006.

Jaiswal, Mahadeo and Monika Mittal, *Management Information Systems*, Oxford University Press, New Delhi, 2004.

Jawadekar, Waman S., *Management Information Systems*, Text and Cases, Tata McGraw-Hill, New Delhi, 2008.

Kalakota, Ravi and Marcia Robinson, *E-Business: Roadmap for Success*, Addison-Wesley, MA, 1999.

Laudon, Ken and Jane Laudon, *Management Information System*, Pearson Education, Singapore, 2002.

O'Brien, James, George Marakas, and Ramesh Behl, *Management Information Systems*, Tata McGraw-Hill, New Delhi, 2007.

Gartner, Inc.: Magic quadrant for midmarket and tier 2-oriented ERP for product-centric companies, www.gartner.com, last accessed on 4 June 2009.

IT project failures blog: Study: 68 per cent of IT projects fail, www.zdnet.com/blog/projectfailures, last accessed on 5 January 2012.

Krigsman, Michael, CEO, Assurenet, '5 critical points for ERP success', http://www.erp.asia/erp-failures.asp, last accessed on 23 March 2011.

http://www.focus.com/briefs/information-technology/, last accessed on 12 June 2010.

CASE STUDY 1

Romjeet Electronics: How MIS Implementation Failed

Romjee Electronics (name changed) is a Gurgaon-based company that is involved in manufacturing electronic and electrical products such as voltage stabilizers and power supplies. The company expanded its business into plastic-moulded products. With the new business in hand, the company grew remarkably and achieved a turnover of ₹980 million in the financial year ending March 2010. In the plastic moulding division, the company manufactures products only on order. For many of their customers, they are original equipment manufacturer (OEM) suppliers. The marketing and sales department of the company works overtime to get large orders from new customers. Thus, they keep adding new customers frequently. Romjee Electronics quotes the price based on product design and specifications submitted by the customer. The price is calculated taking into account the cost of the mould (which is a capital investment); the mould serves a couple of thousand impressions. Once the contract is finalized, the design and engineering department approaches the customer with the final specification of the product for approval. Then, production planning is done for the entire lot. Based on the cost of the material, the total raw material requirement is calculated and a schedule of delivery is given to the client. Out of the entire raw material, there are products that are manufactured as well as bought from the market. The complete production involved three stages—moulding, assembly, and packing. The goods are delivered in a packaged condition. To aid the production process, moulding machines, moulds, raw plastic, bought-out material, and colours are used. There are a number of orders in hand while the number of injection moulding machines and moulds are limited.

Problem

Though the company was using a software system for billing and another one for bookkeeping, there was hardly any management information system that could provide the management with daily reports on the number of jobs in hand, the number of batches, engagement of moulding machines, assembly lines, power requirement, etc. At any point of time, the management was not sure if the raw material available in the store was enough for the next batch of production. The procurement system was also manual and depended on the intuition and discretion of the purchase manager. Secondly, the designs of these products were complex and required meticulous planning for material and machines. The status of a job on the assembly line was known only to the managing director when he/she asked for a specific report. The department used to take four hours to compute the same. Any instant information was a distant dream.

Solution Area

Subsequently, the management decided to engage a software development firm to develop an MIS system that could provide the required reports and also alert messaging at the right junctures, so that the users could take appropriate remedial actions wherever required.

Solution

A software development firm was shortlisted to carry out the said job. The firm carried out a detailed system study and user requirement analysis. The software vendor firm already had an enterprise software solution that matched many of the requirements of this company. A gap analysis was done by the vendor's team. It was agreed to develop the functions for gaps. In order to quickly deploy the solution, the vendor decided to customize their product for the company.

Most of the time, the interaction of the vendor's technicians was done with the systems manager at Romjee, as there was no task force or joint implementation team constituted for the same. Based on the inputs from the systems manager, changes were made to the software. There was no proper coordination and the functional heads and users were hardly available for discussions with the technicians. The system was installed at the office of the company. The systems manager was the lone point of contact at the company. There was no team of managers overseeing the MIS implementation. The managing director of the company was the supreme authority for taking important decisions and resolving disputes. The vendor had deployed two consultants for implementation. Once the system was installed and configured, the users were given training.

Outcome

Users were instructed to create documents such as purchase order, sales confirmation, production scheduling, and material requirement note, but they found the system 'difficult' and 'incomplete'. A few others felt that the new system was 'time-consuming'. After creating one or two documents in the new system, they switched back to the manual system. The production planning department, which handled the most critical process of material planning and production scheduling, was more comfortable using a whiteboard and pen in the meeting room. They found the automated scheduling 'typewriter-like' in the newly develop MIS software. The users were then instructed to run the system in parallel and enter the data in their 'spare time', which they hardly had. The accounts manager took printouts of some statement of accounts of some suppliers; however, to his surprise, he found some entries 'missing' in the accounts ledger. On investigation, the users opined that the system had 'washed' the entries, while the consultants concluded that the users had never entered those transactions. This was a turning point for the worse. The users, backed by their department heads, presented to the managing director of the company that the new system was not workable. The software vendor firm alleged that the users and middle-level managers were hardly interested in implementing the new system. They had resisted the change.

The blame game continued for some time. Finally, the managing director decided to discontinue the project, which had formally never taken off.

Discussion Questions

1. What went wrong in the implementation of new systems at Romjee Electronics?
2. What were the factors responsible for MIS failure?
3. What do you suggest as a system consultant for revival and reimplementation of the new system?
4. Review this case and suggest how this failure could have been avoided.

(Example based on author's personal experience (name changed).)

CASE STUDY 2

Computerization in Banks in India: The Issue of Resistance to Change

Until 1983, there was no major breakthrough in mechanization and computerization in the banking industry. In September 1983, an agreement was made between the Indian Banks' Association and the All India Bank Employees' Association on the installation of electric/electronic machines (other than computers), microprocessors, and mainframe computers to support specified functional areas in branches, zonal offices, and head offices. In July 1983, the Reserve Bank of India (RBI) had appointed a committee on mechanization in the banking industry, popularly known as the Rangarajan committee. The major recommendations of the Rangarajan committee were as follows:

- The committee recommends that the process of mechanization should encompass activities at the branch, regional, and head office levels, with emphasis varying from one level to another.
- At the branch level, a system will have to be designed to ensure generation of data as a by-product of the operations at the branch level.
- Branch-level mechanization should be implemented under either model I (stand-alone electronic ledger posting machines with attached memory modules) or model II (single microprocessor-based system of large capacity) of the mechanization process.

The findings of a study of employees' resistance to automation and the outcome of discussions with trade unions stated, 'whereas the Committee focussed its attention on banking operations, that is, the task, the organizational structure of banks, and the technology, or the procedures, it failed to take into account the effects and implications of the task change on the other variable, namely, the people of the organization.'

The findings attempt to understand the emerging work organization and work behaviour of clerks who operate the machines. It uses a systems approach and is based on interviews carried out in a city's branches where electronic accounting machines (EAMs) have been installed. The implications of organizational development were drawn. The EAMs were then introduced in the cash, credit, and current accounts departments of selected branches of a nationalized bank. Although the departments that were mechanized were the same and the brand of machines installed the same, the performance of the departments differed even among branches with comparable workloads. The impact of EAMs on branch functioning varied. The only variable components among the machines were people.

EAMs and Nature of Work—Rigour in Adherence to Procedure and Instructions

With the introduction of EAMs, operators' discretion has been severely curtailed. Decision rules and procedures of the bank are now embedded in the EAM programs. Deviations are not possible without proper authorization. Even individual judgements are now governed by decision rules, that is, procedures. Deviations are separately recorded on a day-to-day basis. Prior to the introduction of EAMs, the procedures that were laid down were not followed rigorously, nor was any record maintained of deviations. At times, deviations were justified under the guise of better customer service. Machine operators used their discretion in passing the cheques, although they were not authorized to do so. 'When we knew that a customer's account operation was good, we accommodated his request, passed his cheques...', said the employees.

Standardization of Work

With the introduction of EAMs, interest application practices have been standardized. Earlier, different branches were following different practices for application of interest and issue of statements to customers. A sense of this loss is reflected in the response of one operator, 'When we were manually applying interest, we knew what we were doing; now everything happens behind the screen, the machine alone knows what is being done.'

With the introduction of EAMs, an efficient standard has been set and embedded in machine programs. Machine operators cannot leave a day's work incomplete; the next day's work cannot commence if all the activities of the previous day are not completed. Thus, emphasis is now laid on the efficient closing of the day's work.

For example, earlier, if vouchers were released late by one department, then the work of other departments was held up and was completed the next day. Such adjustments are not always possible now. The departments are more closely interconnected, and tardiness in one department affects others much more severely.

The EAMs have introduced a new, information-based technology in place of the earlier experience-based one. Information now appears on a visual display screen; it is, therefore, necessary for individuals who operate the machines to pay close attention to the screen. Responding to the information on the visual display screen requires increased mental involvement.

EAMs and Work Behaviour—Social Interaction Process

Since the EAMs need low temperature and a dust-free atmosphere, they are kept in air-conditioned rooms in most of the branches. Even in centrally air-conditioned branches, they are housed in separate enclosures with additional air-conditioners. This changed layout has affected social interaction to such an extent that one has to make an effort to reach those working on the EAMs.

Now, information is stored on floppies. Only an authorized person can operate the EAM and get the information. Thus, availability of information is restricted. Even authorized persons need either an operator or operating knowledge of the machines to read the information. Prior to the introduction of EAMs, maintenance of cordial interpersonal relations among the employees was important for task accomplishment. Employees were used to bantering while doing their work.

Employees' Response to Change

The changes themselves do not matter; what matters is the human response to these changes. To assess the response, interviews were conducted. The salient findings are listed here:

- Employees did not respond to changes as individuals; they responded as members of a group. This phenomenon is perhaps peculiar to the banking industry where most of the employees are members of one organized group or another.
- Perceptions of change, as an impediment to or a facilitator of efficient customer service, directly influenced the performance of the individual and that of the department.
- The performance, in this context, was measured in terms of speedy and accurate completion of day-to-day work.

- Performance was adversely affected in branches where employees perceived the introduction of EAMs as an impediment to efficient customer service and smooth running of the department.
- The new information-based technology has changed the meaning of work, level of satisfaction, and extent of involvement.

Computerization is being resisted by a group of employees. The interviews indicate that the apprehension is not about what computers or we can do, but what computers will do to us. Hence, the focus of attention and effort should be on employees and their responses rather than on the change. Timely management of the transitional problems, which are bound to arise when an important change is brought about, is crucial.

Discussion Questions

1. What were the major challenges in computerization of banks in India?
2. Why do you think that the IBA and Bank Employees' Association needed an agreement for automation, which was termed as 'mechanization'?
3. 'Today, any bank of repute cannot survive without an online application, let alone automation.' Do you agree with this statement? Why or why not? Support your answers with examples.
4. As a systems manager for a new bank, you have been entrusted with the responsibility of implementation of a 'customer-centric' online application. Describe the complete process of implementation that you will spearhead.

Sources:

Bhatnagar, D., 'Some organizational ramifications of computerization', *Indian Management*, 24(2), 1986, pp. 32–38.

Saha, Kakoli, 'Computerization in banks: Implications for organizational development', Vikalpa, Vol. 11, No. 3, July–September 1986, http://www.vikalpa.com/pdf/articles/1986, last accessed on 29 January 2013.

Part V

Management and Challenges of MIS

- Information Security Management

- Ethical and Societal Challenges of IT

- Information Systems Leadership

- Managing Global Systems

Information Security Management

> With Internet access proliferating rapidly, one might think that the biggest obstacle to electronic commerce would be bandwidth. But it's not; the number one problem is security. And part of the problem is that the Internet was developed for interoperability not impenetrability.
>
> —KAYTE VANSCOY

LEARNING OBJECTIVES

After studying this chapter, you will be able to

- identify information security threats
- differentiate among threats posed by hackers, malicious software, and internal sources
- understand the measures to be taken for controlling security threats and vulnerabilities
- identify the tools and technologies for securing information systems
- design an information security policy framework for an organization
- explain how to develop and use information system controls, risk assessments, security policies, disaster recovery plans, and IT security audits

EXHIBIT 17.1

Information Security: Headache for the CIO?

In the early history of America, there was a man named Willie Sutton who was an infamous bank robber. When he was asked why he robbed banks, he sarcastically replied, '... because that's where the money is'. While this answer may have been fabricated, it aptly captures the choice of target. More than 70 years later, the metaphor applies to how cybercriminals target corporate information stores—this is where the data is. The difference between a high-profile bank heist and the theft of millions of confidential records by cybercriminals is that there are many other points of entry to the information store, further complicated by remote accessibility.

Major companies including Microsoft, Wells Fargo, BJ's Wholesale Stores, and Cisco Systems, have had to deal with the growing costs of information security exposures. From intellectual property leaks to incredible cases of identity theft, the costs and risks of these crimes are growing exponentially. The US Federal Trade Commission estimates that identity thefts cost US consumers $5 billion and a whopping $48 billion to US companies. The US chamber of commerce estimated that the Fortune 1000 companies lost $49 billion in intellectual property disclosures in 2003. In order to protect themselves and survive, companies must rapidly adopt, what the security industry sees as evolving into a paradigm shift, emerging information security technologies. These technologies are information-focused rather than network-focused and can monitor for the first time, what information is leaving the company's perimeter, rather than looking for attackers coming in.

Although technologists will make critical decisions about what products hitting the market place earn the best-of-breed status, surprisingly, this adoption will not be pushed by technologists. The adoption will be pushed by the board of directors, CEOs, and CFOs of publicly-traded companies who will make information security issues an inherent component of a company's corporate governance policy.

Cyber espionage, along with privacy violations and social networking attacks facilitated by the increased use of mobile and tablet devices, will be the source of increased security threats in the coming years. This was revealed by PandaLabs, Panda Security's anti-malware laboratory in its predictions of the top security trends to watch out for in 2012.

Cyber espionage targeting companies and government agencies around the world will dominate corporate and national information security landscapes, and jeopardize the integrity of classified and other protected information. Trojans are expected to be the weapon of choice for hackers focused on these highly sensitive targets.

Sources:

Ahuja, Ratinder Paul Singh, 'Information security—An issue for the boardroom', May 2004, http://www.siliconindia.com/magazine_articles/Information_Security__An_Issue_for_the_Boardroom-CAV285981583.html, last accessed on 7 January 2012.

'Biggest security threats in 2012 are cyber espionage, privacy violations', January 2012, http://www.cxotoday.com/story/biggest-security-threats-in-2012-are-cyber-espionage-privacy-violations/, last accessed on 7 January 2012.

Bhargava, Sunil, 'Information security: Tough to protect?' http://www.siliconindia.com/magazine_articles/Information_Security_Tough_to_protect-AYVQ618825550.html, last accessed on 31 January 2013.

Exhibit 17.1 illustrates how information security threat is a multi-faceted phenomenon. The threats range from theft of confidential records, intellectual property leaks, personal identity thefts, espionage, and privacy violations. These threats have caused loss of millions of dollars to businesses. Most organizations worldwide have, at some point of time, been affected by information security threats. In this chapter, we will discuss security issues, threats, challenges and the various ways to provide security control measures.

As businesses have metamorphosed into e-enterprises with heavy use of information systems and technologies, the gains of e-enablement (e.g., faster access to information, data sharing over a large network, etc.) are accompanied by data and information security issues. In this age of the Internet and cloud-computing, businesses are prone to the risk intangible assets such as critical information and valued data, which may further pose threats to the very sustenance of the business. According to Ahuja (2004), the protection of these assets has gone unnoticed for a long time. From intellectual property, trade secrets, financial reports, and competitive pricing, to initial public offering (IPO) or mergers and acquisitions (M&A) information, these are the intangible assets, if leaked, prematurely diminish the market cap and eat away at shareholder equity.

According to Jaiswal (2004), information and communication technologies, particularly the Internet, have reduced costs and resulted in productivity gains. At the same time, business systems and information networks are exposed to a variety of serious security threats from internal corporate networks and the Internet.

INFORMATION SECURITY THREATS

E-businesses thrive on information technology (IT), which consists of hardware, software, networks, the Internet, and the web. With the emergence of the Internet and the web, information systems have assumed global dimensions. Thus, information security threats, too, have a global angle to them. We have seen that attacks on popular sites such as Yahoo!, Amazon, and e-Bay have put the focus of such businesses on security. Similarly, a few years ago, the websites of the Federal Bureau of Investigation (FBI) in the USA and Bhabha Atomic Research Centre (BARC) in India were hacked and their contents modified. Another major deterrent to e-commerce activity is the growing perception that Internet transactions are inherently insecure.

We have come across instances of hackers getting personal and credit card information and codes from a payment gateway site, resulting in the fraudulent use of credit cards. There are growing concerns about the use of credit cards in online transactions. If B2C commerce is to succeed, online payment concerns need to be addressed.

Information security concerns are not limited to the Internet; other areas such as abuse of employee access, unauthorized access by outsiders, virus attacks, theft or destruction of computer resources, and leak of proprietary information also fall under its purview. Organizations experienced breaches in information security and, as a result, there were setbacks to business operations and loss of reputation or embarrassment to the organization, as illustrated in Table 17.1.

Such complex networks with different technologies, and access to internal employees and external stakeholders (customers, vendors, etc.) make information systems more vulnerable to various threats. Systems are vulnerable to intentional or unintentional action by internal or external users. Intentional action on systems may be directed towards theft, copying, and damaging or corrupting information and systems. This may lead to serious work disruptions, unauthorized

Table 17.1 Information security lapses

Type of breach	%	Recent example
Virus attacks	78	Indian cyberspace was attached by Trojan Beebone in July 2013.
Employee access abuse	52	IBM India sacked employees for overstating revenue in July 2013.
Unauthorized access by outsider	23	Facebook exposed contact information of users because of a bug in the download function, which was detected in June 2013.
Theft/Destruction	23	Many incidences of data theft have been reported from call centres/ITES businesses.
Leak of proprietary information	18	Apple filed lawsuits for leaking pre-release version of a Mac OS X.

Sources: Infosecurity, Livemint, Firstpost, TechRepublic

EXHIBIT 17.2

Information Systems Security: Heavy Loss to Businesses

According to a survey sponsored by Symantec, attacks against endpoints are costing the average organization around $4,70,000 annually.

The costs from endpoint attacks include the following: IT labour costs to recover from the attack; loss of organizational, customer, and employee data; and damage to brand, according to a survey of 1425 organizations worldwide, conducted by Applied Research for Symantec. There is not a single solution that will prevent all attacks. However, with a multi-layered strategy, organizations can strengthen their endpoint security position. This was the view put forth by Elisha Riedlinger, principal product manager, Symantec. 'Companies that implement best practices are the companies that fare better regarding endpoint security', he added.

Critical information systems become unavailable due to various forms of attack. Ernest & Young's information security survey, 2002, reveals that around 76% of the respondents experienced unexpected unavailability.

Despite this, only 47% of the Indian companies (as compared to 53% globally) have a business continuity plan. Over half the respondents do not have agreed recovery timescales, which could mean wide expectation gaps in the event of business interruption.

The two main causes cited by Indian companies for the unavailability of systems are as follows:

- Malicious technical acts by outsiders (26%)
- Third party failure (14%)

Sources:
Periera, Brian,'Information security: A new approach', *Network Magazine*, April 2003, http://www.networkmagazineindia.com/200304/cover1.shtml, last accessed on 11 January 2012.
http://www.infosecurity-magazine.com/view/23085/endpoint-attacks-cost-firms-close-to-half-a-million-dollars-annually/, 9 January 2012, last accessed on 11 January 2012.

transfer of information to competitors, and heavy financial losses, as described in Exhibit 17.2. All these threats can be grouped under the following groups: hacking, malicious software, and internal threats.

Hacking

Hacking is an act that is carried out to gain unauthorized access to a computer system. The individual or group of individuals doing so is called a hacker. When used to explain cracking into computer systems, the term has a criminal connotation. Hackers break into computer systems by finding weaknesses in the security systems, cracking passwords, or taking advantage of the features of the Internet that make it an open system.

According to Laudon (2010), hacking activities have broadened beyond mere system intrusion to include theft of goods and information, as well as system damage, cyber-vandalism, intentional disruption, defacement, or even destruction of a website or corporate information system. Exhibit 17.2 illustrates how businesses worldwide bear the losses caused due to attacks on their information systems by hackers.

Hackers use various attacking methods such as spoofing, denial-of-service, and social engineering. Spoofing is an attack on the system in which hackers misrepresent themselves or redirect the web link to an address other than the actual one. In denial-of-service attack, hackers flood a network server with false requests or communications that causes the network to crash. As a result, the system is not able to process genuine requests for service. If a busy e-commerce site is shut down, it can cause heavy loss to the business. Attackers may flood a network with large volumes of data, deliberately consume a scarce resource, disrupt physical components of the network, or manipulate data in transit.

Table 17.2   Common hacking tactics used by attackers

Tactic	Description
Denial-of-service	An attempt to make a computer or network resource unavailable to the intended user. This can be done by flooding a website with too many requests for information, which can effectively clog the system. This can slow down the performance or even crash the site. This is the most common prank on the networks.
Scams	A deliberate attempt to lock a computer through malware to extract confidential information such as passwords, server information, personal information, or even lure users to pay money.
Spoofing	A malicious act of masquerading and falsifying, thus tricking the user to reveal critical information such as passwords or credit card numbers.
Social engineering	A tactic of manipulating people to divulge confidential information such as passwords, bank personal identification number (PIN), and other critical business information.
Sniffer	An eavesdropping program that covertly searches individual packets of data as they pass through the Internet, capturing passwords or the entire content.
Trojan horse	A malicious software that is non-self-replicating and resides in an apparently harmless program and attacks some vulnerable software or systems to steal information.
Malicious applets	Small programs that attack the local system of a web user. These software misuse a user's computer resources by launching denial-of-service attacks, invading privacy, sending fake e-mails, or stealing passwords.
War dialling	A tactic by a program that automatically sends unwanted packets of data to the network or dials thousands of telephone numbers through a modem connection.
Logic bombs	Instructions in a computer program that triggers a malicious act or stops a program on a particular date or time.
Buffer overflow	A tactic to clog the memory of the system by sending more data to the temporary storage area than it can hold.
Password crackers	Software that attempt to decipher or guess passwords

Intruders with malicious intentions trick employees into revealing their passwords or sensitive information, while pretending to be legitimate members of the same group who need the information. This practice is called social engineering. Social engineering may be practised by hackers as well as insiders. Hackers can use any of several hacking tactics illustrated in Table 17.2.

Malicious Software

Malicious software includes all types of viruses, Trojan horses, worms, and spyware. The word 'malicious software' is used to denote programs, which when executed, would cause undesired results on the system. These programs are transmitted through networks, the Internet, e-mails, and during the installation and transfer of other infected software. Users cannot detect them until they come across some damage or inefficiency in the system. Viruses and worms are self-replicating programs that hide in legitimate software and spread across the network. These malicious programs can cause data loss, system downtime, and denial-of-service. Due to virus attacks, data files might get corrupted, thus resulting in loss of data. Sometimes, the data files do not get corrupted, but the system files are infected, which results in system closures. Denial-of-service occurs if the system does not allow the performance of a particular task because of a virus infection.

The most dreaded malicious software is the worm. These are independent programs that copy themselves from one computer to another on the network. Worms and viruses also infect mobile phones. Viruses are serious threats to enterprise information systems because many wireless devices are now connected to the systems. Exhibit 17.3 illustrates how viruses not only cause financial losses to businesses, but also damage government's nuclear programmes.

A new trend in the unauthorized peeping into others' lives is supported by spyware. Spyware is a small program that installs itself on computers to monitor the user's web surfing activity and transmits the information to its source. The primary motive behind tracking users' web habits is to offer personalized goods or services through advertising. Laudon (2010) argues that Web 2.0 applications such as blogs, wikis, and social networking sites (Facebook and MySpace) have emerged as new conduits for malware or spyware. These applications allow users to post software code as part of the permissible content; such codes can be launched automatically as soon as a web page is viewed.

Internal Threats

Information security threats are not only external; there are serious internal threats as well. These threats include misuse of employees' access to information and system crashes. Unauthorized access to systems by employees is tantamount to hacking by insiders. Employees have access to privileged information, and the absence of sound security measures may lead to misuse of such information. A disgruntled employee may vandalize the system or leak critical

EXHIBIT 17.3

Viruses that are Out to Destroy Nuclear Sites

First, there was the Stuxnet computer virus that wreaked havoc on Iran's nuclear program in 2010. Now, it is the turn of 'Duqu', which, researchers said, appears to be quite similar, says a report by security firm Symantec. Iran said it had detected the Duqu computer virus that experts say is based on Stuxnet, the so-called 'cyber-weapon' discovered in 2010 and was believed to be aimed at sabotaging the country's nuclear sites. The head of Iran's civil defence organization told the official news agency, IRNA, that computers at risk at all the main sites were being checked and that Iran had developed software to combat the virus. 'We are in the initial phase of fighting the Duqu virus', Gholamreza Jalali, the head of Iran's civil defence organization, was quoted as saying. 'The final report which says which organizations the virus has spread to and what its impacts are has not been completed yet. All the organizations and centres that could be susceptible to being contaminated are being controlled', he said.

Stuxnet is a malicious software that targets widely-used industrial control systems built by Siemens. It is believed to have crippled the centrifuges that Iran uses to enrich Uranium for, what the United States and some European nations have alleged, a covert nuclear weapons program. Cyber experts say its sophistication indicates that Stuxnet was possibly produced by the United States or Israel. The new Duqu computer virus is designed to gather data from industrial control system manufacturers to make it easier to launch an attack in the future by capturing information including keystrokes. 'The attackers are looking for information such as design documents that could help them mount a future attack on an industrial control facility. Duqu does not contain any code related to industrial control systems and is primarily a remote access Trojan (RAT). The threat does not self-replicate', Symantec said.

Sources:
'First came Stuxnet; now there's Duqu', posted on 19 October 2011, http://biztech2.in.com/news/security/first-came-stuxnet59-now-theres-duqu/119382/0, last accessed on 27 August 2012.
'Iran says it has detected Duqu', http://biztech2.in.com/news/security/iran-says-it-has-detected-duqu/120832/0, posted on 14 November 2011, last accessed on 27 August 2012.

information to a rival business house. The abuse of employee access to information systems is very high. It can cause leak of key business information, revenue loss, and embarrassment to the organization. It is one problem that is difficult to resolve and is usually overlooked by the management.

For example, the case study at the end of this chapter illustrates how, in March 2002, in the US, a 'logic bomb' deleted 10 billion files in the computer systems of an international financial services company. The incident affected over 1300 of the company's servers throughout the country. The company sustained losses of approximately $3 million, the amount required to repair the damage and reconstruct the deleted files. Investigations by law enforcement professionals and computer forensic professionals revealed that the 'logic bomb' had been planted by a disgruntled employee who had recently quit the company because of a dispute over the amount of his annual bonus.

Hardware, software, and network failures are not very uncommon. The crashing of systems causes non-availability of the system, disruption of work to the users, and data loss to the organization. Hardware, software, and network failure are caused due to poor quality of equipment/tools, poor maintenance, and erroneous user action. Systems also crash because of faulty power supplies.

CONTROLLING SECURITY THREATS AND VULNERABILITIES

Due to the vulnerability of the electronic medium, information system assets need more protection and control than the other assets in an organization. An organization can take up various measures for controlling security threats and vulnerabilities. These measures can either be preventive or detective. Preventive controls inhibit unauthorized users from free access to computing resources. Detective measures are taken once the threat has penetrated the system. Scanning and disinfecting the system is essential for viruses and worms. Spyware is a detective measure. As the dependence on information systems increases, security management becomes an important task. According to O'Brien (2007), the goal of security management is accuracy, integrity, and safety of all information system processes and resources. Thus, effective security management can minimize errors, frauds, and losses in the information systems that interconnect today's companies and their customers, suppliers, and other stakeholders.

Organizations can adopt various security tools and technologies to protect their information systems. These controls include firewalls, encryption, digital signatures, physical access control, antivirus software, passwords, e-mail scanning, secure socket layers, etc.

Firewall

Firewall is an important technology to protect systems from the Internet and network-based threats. As the Internet is inherently weak in security, corporate networks become vulnerable to misuse and attack. Firewalls are placed to control access between a corporate network and an external network like the Internet. A firewall is a combination of hardware and software that is deployed to protect corporate networks from unauthorized access over the Internet.

A firewall serves as a security person that protects the organization's corporate network from unauthorized access by providing a filter, and screens all network traffic for a password and authorization code before allowing transmission in and out of the network. A firewall uses screening technologies such as packet filtering, stateful inspection, network address translation, and application proxy filtering.

Packet-filtering   This technique examines and filters Internet protocol (IP) packets, according to predefined filtering rules, based on the source/destination IP address and the port number on the packets.

Stateful inspection   This provides additional security by determining whether the packets are part of an ongoing dialogue between a sender and the receiver.

Network address translation   This provides another layer of protection over packet filtering and stateful inspection. Network address translation technology conceals the IP addresses of the organization's internal host computer to prevent sniffer programs from penetrating and misusing the network.

Proxy-server firewall   This is an intermediary for user requests, setting up a second connection to the desired resource.

Figure 17.1 illustrates an Internet/intranet firewall system for an organization.

Encryption

Encryption has become a popular way of protecting data and other communications over the Internet, intranet, and extranet. Encryption is the process of transforming plain text or data into scrambled text that cannot be deciphered by anyone other than the sender and the intended recipient. Encryption uses special mathematical algorithms, known as keys, to transform the message into a scrambled code before transmitting and then decodes it when received. According

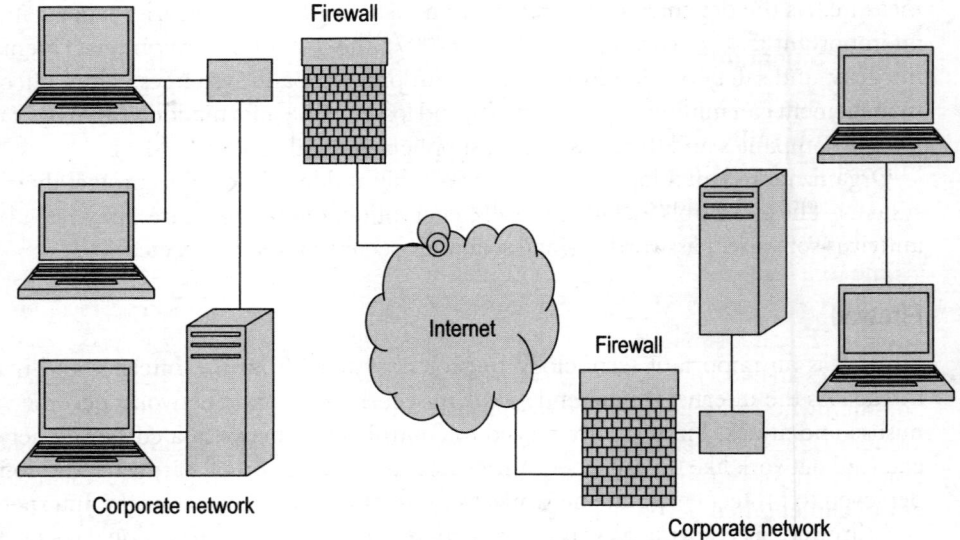

Fig. 17.1   Corporate networks protected by firewalls

Fig. 17.2   Encryption and decryption using public key infrastructure

to Rothfeder (1997), the most widely used encryption method uses a pair of public and private keys unique to each individual. For example, an e-mail can be scrambled and encoded using a unique public key for the recipient that is known to the sender. After the e-mail is transmitted, only the recipient's secret private key can unscramble the message. Figure 17.2 illustrates how encryption is used for data security.

There are several encryption software available with vendors. The main standards are RSA (from RSA data security) and pretty good privacy (PGP). Software programs and operating systems such as Microsoft Windows XP, Novell Netware, and Lotus Notes offer encryption features using RSA standards.

The two most widely used encryption methods for Internet traffic on the web are secure sockets layer (SSL) and secure hypertext transfer protocol (S-HTTP). SSL technology is used for client and server computers to manage encryption and decryption activities as they communicate during a secure web session. The SSL protocol was developed by Netscape Communication in 1994 to provide secure communication over the Internet. It is now accepted as the de facto standard for secure Internet communication.

S-HTTP is another protocol used for secured data flow over the Internet. This technology is limited to websites and it makes the site fully secure. However, SSL is applicable for secure communication between any two computers.

Digital Signatures

Digital signatures are the electronic equivalent of traditional handwritten signatures and are, thus, trustworthy. Any document, if signed in a normal way, would be easy to copy and forge. In order to avoid duplication and forgery, digital signatures are created using the public key cryptography technology. The digital certificate system uses a trusted third party, known as certification authority (CA), to validate a user's identity. VeriSign, IdenTrust, eTrust, etc., are some well-known certification authorities in the world.

The CA creates and issues digital certificates, also considered legal verifications, to each user offline. The information about the subscriber or user is fed into the server of the CA, which generates an encrypted digital certificate containing owner identification information and a copy of the owner's public key. The certificate authenticates the ownership of the public key. The sender signs the document with his/her private key, which is available to the sender only. The message thus transmitted over the Internet is in encrypted form. The recipient of the message or document then decodes the messages with the CA's public key.

For example, credit card information on the Internet used for e-commerce transactions are secured by a digital signature system. Additionally, the e-governance initiative of the government in India in the income tax and company affairs departments has resulted in the acceptance of digitally signed copies of taxation and statutory reports of companies.

Physical Access Control

Threats to information systems can be thwarted by preventing unauthorized access to systems by internal or external persons. Access control consists of policies and procedures that an organization uses for authorized and authenticated entry into their premises. Authentication is the process of establishing that the person accessing the system is genuine. Authentication is generally done by password-protected access. New generation technologies such as tokens, smart cards, and biometric identification have emerged, which are extensively being used for access control.

A smart card is a device containing a chip with an access code written on it. The reader can read the card and permit or deny access. Biometric authentication uses systems that read and interpret individual human traits, such as fingerprints, irises, and voices, in order to grant or deny access. Fingerprints and facial recognition technologies have just started and are used in security applications and access control. Laptops are also being manufactured with fingerprint identification devices.

According to Pereira (2003), there has been a paradigm shift in security measures in the wired world from 'denial-of-access' to granting access to all on a 'need to know' basis. This shift has resulted in higher importance being given to access controls and stronger means of authentication. The means of authentication currently in vogue include dual factor authentication, one-time passwords, digital signatures, etc. Organizations across the world are realizing that password-based authentication is not adequate to address the risks arising as a consequence of this paradigm shift.

Virus Defences

Information systems can be protected against virus attacks by deploying antivirus software. Antivirus software act as both defensive and detective measures against virus attacks on corporate information systems. They check the computer systems for computer viruses and remove them. Antivirus software also act as deterrents and scan files, mails, or messages before they are downloaded onto the system. However, the software detects and removes only those that are known to the scanner. Infection by a new virus will go undetected by the software. Hence, antivirus vendors promote regular updates.

According to Jayanthi (2008), there are a few trends that are driving the market towards proactive protection. The first is a gradual transition of the security systems towards products that promise intrusion prevention. Most security product vendors merely provide intrusion detection with limited ability for automatic action. Considering its limited capacity to prevent attacks proactively, intrusion detection technology would probably be history in a very short period. Enterprises are increasingly looking for reliable and comprehensive intrusion prevention packages that can be trusted to stop the viruses rather than just give alerts about intrusions in the network.

Hackers find it easy to intrude e-mails and infect the information system. Regular monitoring of e-mails by using antivirus systems and content monitoring software is necessary to protect the corporate information system.

EXHIBIT 17.4

Cyber Espionage and Privacy Violations: Biggest Security Threats in Future

McAfee and PandaLabs have unveiled their 2012 threat predictions report, outlining the top threats in information security that McAfee foresees in the coming years.McAfee Labs predicts that attacks involving political motivation or notoriety will also make headlines, including high-profile industrial attacks, cyber warfare demonstrations, and hacktivist attacks targeting public figures. 'Over the past year, the general public has become more aware of some of these risks, such as threats to critical infrastructure or the impact of hacktivism as they gain international media attention. In the meantime, we continue to see cybercriminals improving their toolkits and malware and are ready to make a significant impact in 2012', said Vincent Weafer of McAfee.

'We live in a world where all information is in digital form and is easily accessible if you know how. Today's spies no longer need to infiltrate a building to steal information. As long as they have the necessary computer skills, they can wreak havoc and access even the best-kept secrets of organizations without ever leaving their homes', said Luis Corrons, technical director, PandaLabs. The following were said to be the major trends in cyber attacks:

- Industry experts expect to see 'legal' spam and a technique known as 'snowshoe spamming' to continue growing at a rate faster than illegal phishing. Legal spam refers to sending e-mails with a sender's address, unsubscribe notification, and a disclaimer. Snowshoe spamming is a technique in which a spammer uses a wide array of IP addresses to spread out the spam load.

- As an increasing number of users handle their finances on mobile devices, attackers will bypass PCs and target mobile banking applications.
- Hackers require malware that attack the hardware layer; this will enable them to gain greater control and maintain long-term access to the system and its data. Sophisticated hackers will then have complete control over hardware.
- Virtual currency, sometimes called cyber currency, has become a popular way for people to exchange money online. These online 'wallets' are not encrypted and the transactions are public, making them an attractive target for cybercriminals.
- Organizations and individuals tend to trust digitally signed certificates; however, recent threats such as Stuxnet and Duqu used rogue certificates to evade detection. This trend will strengthen in the years to come.
- Governing bodies around the globe are taking greater interest in establishing rules for Internet traffic. McAfee Labs expects to see more instances where future solutions are hampered by legislative issues.
- Advances in operating systems moves will put hackers 'down and out.'

Sources:
http://www.cxotoday.com/story/biggest-security-threats-in-2012-are-cyber-espionage-privacy-violations/, last accessed on 1 February 2013.
http://biztech2.in.com/news/security/threat-predictions-for-2012/124212/, last accessed on 7 January 2012.

Major antivirus vaccine manufacturers and vendors include Symantec, McAfee, Trend Micro, PC-ciline, AVG, and QuickHeal (Exhibit 17.4). They also offer protection against spyware and offer integration with firewalls and web security.

Fault-tolerant Computer Systems

Organizations use fault-tolerant computer systems, which have redundant processors, peripherals, and software that provide continuous uninterrupted service in the event of system failure. According to Laudon (2010), fault-tolerant computers have special software routines or self-checking logic built into their circuitry to detect hardware failures and automatically switch to a backup device. Replacement or repair of a part when the system is working does not hamper the processing of systems. The mirroring feature of the server automatically switches the request to the backup server, if the primary server fails. For example, high-end servers offer the feature

Table 17.3 Fault tolerance in computer-based information systems

Areas	Potential threats	Fault-tolerant methods
Software—systems and applications	Shutdowns, errors, and slowdowns	Availability of application-specific redundancy, work-abound, and roll back to previous checkpoint; and system auto correction on reboot
Hardware—systems and peripherals	Shutdowns, hanging, and slowdowns	Availability of redundant systems, hard disks, and processors; auto-switchover, multiple processors-based systems, RAID-compliant and implemented systems
Databases	Data errors, data corruption, and data-wash	Database repair system, periodical automatic system-driven backup of files, safe updates, complete transactions systems, replication of critical data on different media and sites, archiving, backup, retrieval
Networks	Transmission errors, network breakdowns, and communication failures	Reliable controllers, encryption based on SSL certificates, availability of alternative routing system, automatic error-detection and error-correction systems, alternative source of Internet connectivity, multiple Internet service providers (ISPs)

of hot-swappable hard disks and fault-tolerant systems. Neumann (1995) outlined some of the fault-tolerant capabilities used in many computer systems and networks, which are illustrated in Table 17.3.

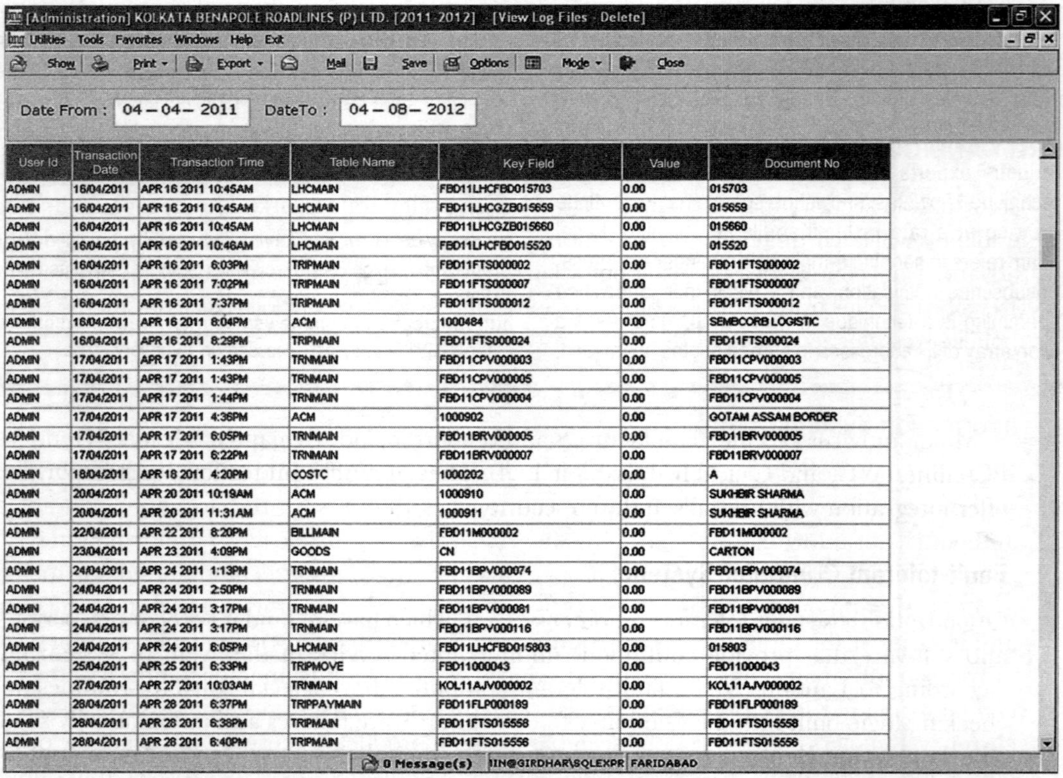

User Id	Transaction Date	Transaction Time	Table Name	Key Field	Value	Document No
ADMIN	16/04/2011	APR 16 2011 10:45AM	LHCMAIN	FBD11LHCFBD015703	0.00	015703
ADMIN	16/04/2011	APR 16 2011 10:45AM	LHCMAIN	FBD11LHCGZB015659	0.00	015659
ADMIN	16/04/2011	APR 16 2011 10:45AM	LHCMAIN	FBD11LHCGZB015660	0.00	015660
ADMIN	16/04/2011	APR 16 2011 10:46AM	LHCMAIN	FBD11LHCFBD015520	0.00	015520
ADMIN	16/04/2011	APR 16 2011 6:03PM	TRIPMAIN	FBD11FTS000002	0.00	FBD11FTS000002
ADMIN	16/04/2011	APR 16 2011 7:02PM	TRIPMAIN	FBD11FTS000007	0.00	FBD11FTS000007
ADMIN	16/04/2011	APR 16 2011 7:37PM	TRIPMAIN	FBD11FTS000012	0.00	FBD11FTS000012
ADMIN	16/04/2011	APR 16 2011 8:04PM	ACM	1000484	0.00	SEMBCORB LOGISTIC
ADMIN	16/04/2011	APR 16 2011 8:29PM	TRIPMAIN	FBD11FTS000024	0.00	FBD11FTS000024
ADMIN	17/04/2011	APR 17 2011 1:43PM	TRNMAIN	FBD11CPV000003	0.00	FBD11CPV000003
ADMIN	17/04/2011	APR 17 2011 1:43PM	TRNMAIN	FBD11CPV000005	0.00	FBD11CPV000005
ADMIN	17/04/2011	APR 17 2011 1:44PM	TRNMAIN	FBD11CPV000004	0.00	FBD11CPV000004
ADMIN	17/04/2011	APR 17 2011 4:36PM	ACM	1000902	0.00	GOTAM ASSAM BORDER
ADMIN	17/04/2011	APR 17 2011 6:05PM	TRNMAIN	FBD11BRV000005	0.00	FBD11BRV000005
ADMIN	17/04/2011	APR 17 2011 6:22PM	TRNMAIN	FBD11BRV000007	0.00	FBD11BRV000007
ADMIN	18/04/2011	APR 18 2011 4:20PM	COSTC	1000202	0.00	A
ADMIN	20/04/2011	APR 20 2011 10:19AM	ACM	1000910	0.00	SUKHBIR SHARMA
ADMIN	20/04/2011	APR 20 2011 11:31AM	ACM	1000911	0.00	SUKHBIR SHARMA
ADMIN	22/04/2011	APR 22 2011 8:20PM	BILLMAIN	FBD11M000002	0.00	FBD11M000002
ADMIN	23/04/2011	APR 23 2011 4:09PM	GOODS	CN	0.00	CARTON
ADMIN	24/04/2011	APR 24 2011 1:13PM	TRNMAIN	FBD11BPV000074	0.00	FBD11BPV000074
ADMIN	24/04/2011	APR 24 2011 2:50PM	TRNMAIN	FBD11BPV000089	0.00	FBD11BPV000089
ADMIN	24/04/2011	APR 24 2011 3:17PM	TRNMAIN	FBD11BPV000081	0.00	FBD11BPV000081
ADMIN	24/04/2011	APR 24 2011 3:17PM	TRNMAIN	FBD11BPV000116	0.00	FBD11BPV000116
ADMIN	24/04/2011	APR 24 2011 6:05PM	LHCMAIN	FBD11LHCFBD015803	0.00	015803
ADMIN	25/04/2011	APR 25 2011 6:33PM	TRIPMOVE	FBD11000043	0.00	FBD11000043
ADMIN	27/04/2011	APR 27 2011 10:03AM	TRNMAIN	KOL11AJV000002	0.00	KOL11AJV000002
ADMIN	28/04/2011	APR 28 2011 6:37PM	TRIPPAYMAIN	FBD11FLP000189	0.00	FBD11FLP000189
ADMIN	28/04/2011	APR 28 2011 6:38PM	TRIPMAIN	FBD11FTS015558	0.00	FBD11FTS015558
ADMIN	28/04/2011	APR 28 2011 6:40PM	TRIPMAIN	FBD11FTS015556	0.00	FBD11FTS015556

Fig. 17.3 System log displaying events of data entry, modification, or deletion

Other Security Measures

There are several security measures that organizations commonly use to protect business systems and networks. These include both hardware and software tools such as monitoring computer usage, keeping backup files, and e-mail monitoring. These systems offer detective and preventive measures and are handy when something goes wrong in the information systems.

Organizations must monitor the usage through specialized security monitoring software systems. These systems monitor computer systems and network, and protect them from unauthorized use, theft, and destruction. Figure 17.3 displays a log file about usage, maintained by a software in an enterprise system. According to Jawadekar (2007), monitoring keeps track of users' access and files referred, read, and changed. The tracking is called 'system log' and provides information on how the system is used by whom and when. E-mails are easy conduits for virus and hacking attacks. E-mail monitoring is done to reduce this threat. Organizations must enforce policies against illegal, damaging, and unwanted messages across the corporate network.

A backup files system is the traditional way of coping with system failures. Backup files are duplicate files of data and programs that are copied to a safe media and location; they are retrieved and restored when the original files are destroyed or corrupted. For example, ITC Wills maintains a backup of important transaction data every hour and keeps it at three different physical locations.

As we know, the greatest risk to information systems is from internal sources. Hence, the organization must conduct proper evaluation of employees at the time of selection and appointment by checking past records and references.

SECURITY AND CONTROL POLICY FRAMEWORK

Information security management calls for a firm policy framework. The best of technologies and tools will fail if there is no organization-wide security policy. The organization must define in advance what control measures to adopt when the information systems are at risk. A comprehensive IS security policy framework encompasses information system controls, risk assessments, security policies, disaster recovery plans, and security audits.

Information System Controls

Every organization, depending on their information systems, should enforce valid information system controls. These are techniques and devices that ensure the accuracy, validity, and authenticity of information system activities. According to O'Brien (2007), information systems controls must be developed to ensure proper data entry, processing techniques, storage methods, and information output. Thus, IS controls are designed to monitor and maintain the quality and security of the input, processing, output, and storage activities of any information system.

For example, many controls can be introduced while designing an information system. There can be formatted screens for input, beeps on errors, and validation on fields such as date and currency. Retailers across the globe scan barcodes on products to ensure total accuracy of input data. Optical character readers are built into the systems used by banks for accurate input of cheques.

Risk Assessment

An organization's preparedness for meeting security challenges will depend on how the risks have been analysed and assessed. The organization allocates resources for information security after assessing the vulnerable assets and risks.

Stuart (1992) defines information risks management as the process of estimating potential losses due to the use of or dependence on automated information system technologies, analysing potential threats and system vulnerabilities that contribute to loss estimates, and selecting cost-effective safeguards that reduce risk to an acceptable level.

Risk management is a process that starts with identification of risks. The risks are then analysed and prioritized so as to resolve the most critical one first. The risks are assessed to determine what will be lost if a breach in security occurs. The organization will allocate resources to buy tools and technologies to mitigate the risk accordingly. Then, the organization determines safeguards for the threat and develops tools. Table 17.4 illustrates the process of risk management.

All risks may not be anticipated and assessed. However, the risks must be assessed in quantitative terms, to the extent possible. For example, the security manager can assess loss in terms of the cost of restoration if the enterprise data is lost. Similarly, the risk involved in system downtime may be in terms of lost man-hours, which can be easily converted into cost to the organization. According to Jaiswal (2004), among the many possible quantitative methods, a defensible one is to compare the cost of preventing a loss or damage to the cost resulting from the loss. When the total probability of the loss occurring and the loss in itself exceeds the burden of avoiding it, the loss avoidance measure should be implemented.

For example, if the loss caused due to a hard disk crash is a maximum of ₹1,00,000, the company will invest in the mirroring technology, which will make last minute data available in the fault-tolerant system. This may cost the company ₹20,000. If the loss of data is just ₹10,000, the organization may decide on a daily backup of data, which may cost very little.

Security Policy

An information security policy is more involved with the awareness in the organization about handling and accessing information systems. Once the risks are identified and assessed, the organization needs to develop an information systems security policy. An effective security

Table 17.4   Risk management processes followed by an organization

Risk management process	Description
Risk identification	Study of information technology and information system infrastructure and associated threats
Risk analysis	Classification of threats and prioritization and ascertaining loss potential in the e-business
Risk assessment	Determining what will be lost if a security breach occurs, defining acceptable and non-acceptable risks
Risk resolution	Identification of safeguards, development of tools and technologies, and implementation of safeguards
Risk monitoring	Periodic reviews to identify ineffective, non-functional or redundant safeguards, update the risk analysis and reduction plan

policy combines physical security measures such as controlled access for protection of hardware and software, and security awareness throughout the organization. According to Laudon (2010), a security policy consists of statements ranking information risks, identifying acceptable security goals, and identifying the mechanisms for achieving these goals. A security policy specifies an organization's acceptable security standards and the personnel who can have access to these important information systems assets. The policy defines an acceptable use of information resources and computing equipment such as desktop, laptop, software, and the Internet.

For example, an organization should have a policy on how financial transactions be handled over the Internet. It must be part of the security policy that states which employee handles what part of the sensitive information. If employees can log into the corporate data server from their homes or while travelling, the security guidelines for accessing the same should be laid down.

The information security policy is also implemented through the authorization management of information systems. Information systems, supported by enterprise applications, come up with authorization modules that represent an organization's security policy. Authorization systems define where and when a user is permitted to access certain parts of a corporate database, a website, or an application. The users' work area is defined while assigning them the rights and privileges to work. Figure 17.4 illustrates how a security policy is implemented in e-business.

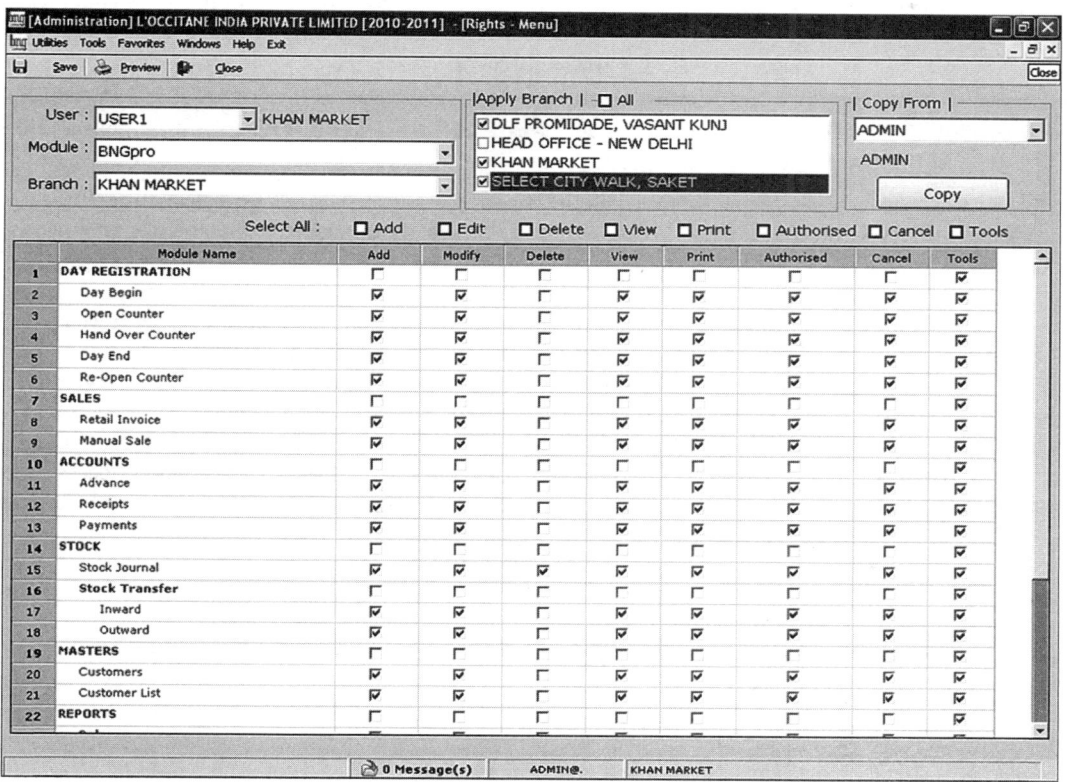

Fig. 17.4   Rights and privileges of authorization module in e-business applications

Disaster Recovery Plan

Though an organization may adopt the best of policies, tools, and techniques to secure information systems, there is an element of risk due to unforeseen circumstances, and unpredictable and uncontrollable causes damaging the information system resources in the organization. Many e-commerce retailers, airlines, and banking operations are crippled even if the systems are down for only a few hours. Therefore, organizations develop disaster recovery plans and business continuity plans to recover from such outages. A disaster recovery plan is a plan of action to recover from the impact of collapse of information systems; a business continuity plan focuses on how the organization can restore business operations after the disaster.

For example, Ramco Systems maintains a backup of their clients' data at three different locations, as a disaster recovery plan and to serve as emergency backup facilities.

According to Jawadekar (2007), a disaster recovery plan includes the following measures:

- Alternative processing arrangements
- Duplicate and offsite storage of data, hardware, and software
- Choice of systems and applications that should run

Exhibit 17.5 illustrates how Daiwa Capital Markets developed a disaster recovery plan by collaborating with IBM's work area recovery solution. In case of an emergency, the company can simply use the alternative processing arrangements with IBM without hampering any work.

EXHIBIT 17.5

Daiwa Capital Markets: Disaster Recovery Plan

Daiwa Capital Markets India Pvt. Ltd signed an agreement with IBM for a disaster recovery plan by leveraging IBM's work area recovery (WAR) solution.

As per a study from Regus, a provider of workplace solutions, while Indian businesses are galloping in the wake of economic liberalization contributing significantly to the country's growth, sadly, they fall short of planning for a disaster recovery plan (DRP). Nearly 50% of the businesses in India do not have a DRP in place for their IT infrastructure and more than 60% have no business continuity for their workplace requirements, the survey revealed. In India, 400 companies participated in the Regus survey conducted in the metro cities of Mumbai, New Delhi, Bengaluru, and Chennai.

However, Daiwa Capital Markets is a company among the remaining 50% that values a DRP. It is an investment banking company that offers integrated financial services. The new solution will help the company in the recovery of their work environment and will also offer round-the-clock technical support. The new IT set-up will act as an alternative backup site from where business operations can

resume and function even during disruptions that may arise due to unforeseen circumstances.

Daiwa was interested in an alternative workplace to mitigate the risk if its primary office became unavailable. As part of its compliance plan, the company needed an enclosure with dedicated seats, which would help maintain confidentiality and physical security of the work area. With dedicated seats, Daiwa was assured of lower turnaround time.

'In the highly competitive capital markets sector, where our business is dependent on our ability to process larger number of financial transactions continuously to meet service-level agreements as well as cater to sudden spikes in trading, any unplanned downtime can mean significant financial losses, besides important intangibles such as loss of reputation and damage to brand value. Additionally, we did not want to invest in building an alternate work area and keep it unused till disaster strikes. Choosing IBM's infrastructure recovery services not only ensures an alternative work environment to minimize loss of employee productivity and meets our implicit need for continuous

(Contd)

Exhibit 17.5 (Contd)

operations, but also helps in increasing our risk tolerance while giving us the flexibility to deal with our mission-critical operations', said Sammeer Saurabbh, executive director–IT, Daiwa Capital Markets.

This unique proposition from IBM will add value to Daiwa's overall business strategy by employing rigorous health and safety standards along with the best practices from IBM that offers IT equipment as a service. IBM will be managing Daiwa's disaster recovery project while conducting periodic disaster recovery drills with the company to ensure compliance to internal as well as regulatory norms.

'In a global economy, as the number of natural as well as manmade disruptions is on the rise, work area recovery is a key part of a business continuity plan. Today, businesses are increasingly affected by the regulatory environment and need to maintain high levels of availability and disaster preparedness. Through our infrastructure recovery services, we are

providing a comprehensive disaster recovery and business continuity solution to Daiwa to meet their continuity requirements and also enable their employees to stay productive at all times', said K.S. Raghunandan, director, integrated technology services, global technology services, IBM India.

Sources:
'Daiwa Capital Markets joins hands with IBM', 14 November 2011, http://www.cxotoday.com/story/daiwa-capital-markets-joins-hands-with-ibm/, last accessed on 13 January 2012.
'Daiwa Capital Markets leverages IBM's war for DR', 14 November 2011, http://biztech2.in.com/news/business-continuity-disaster-recovery/daiwa-capital-markets-leverages-ibms-war-for-dr/120872/0, last accessed on 13 January 2012.
'Nearly 50 percent of Indian businesses unprepared for disasters', 10 December 2011, http://www.cxotoday.com/story/nearly-50-percent-indian-businesses-unprepared-for-disasters/', last accessed on 13 January 2012.

The disaster recovery plan must specify the following:

- Which section of employees will participate in disaster recovery?
- What will be the duties of such employees participating in disaster recovery?
- What alternative hardware, software, and facilities will be used?
- Which applications will be processed on a priority basis?

Information Technology Security Audit

Information systems security is not a one-time job. As newer threats and innovative hacking techniques are invented by cybercriminals, security must be audited and upgraded to meet the new challenges. Auditing can be done by the organization's internal auditors, supported by IT specialists or by a qualified external auditing firm. The objectives of such an audit is to evaluate whether proper and adequate security measures and policies have been implemented and are working as per the desired plan. IT security auditing involves verifying the accuracy and integrity of the software, correctness of the input data, and accuracy of the output.

Another way of auditing is ascertaining the audit trail. Today, most enterprise business applications offer an audit trail functionality. Audit trail is an output provided by applications that allow a transaction to be traced through all stages of its information processing. The audit trail function traces the steps through which the transaction is processed. If the integrity of flow is tested and found correct, then the system is said to be reliable in quality assurance. Software such as security monitors, operating systems, and network control programs offer audit trail features. Such an audit trail not only helps auditors check errors and frauds, but also helps information system security experts track and evaluate the hackers' attack on corporate networks.

Table 17.5 explains some of the steps one can take to protect computers from hacking and other cybercrimes.

Thus, a comprehensive IS security policy framework calls for information system controls during data entry, processing, and output. The security policy must create awareness about

Table 17.5   Guidelines to protect computer system resources from cybercrimes

Threat areas	What to do
Computer defence	• Keep your system software updated with patches and upgrades. • Use the latest version of web browser and email software. • Use antivirus and Firewall software and update it often to keep destructive programs off your computer.
Protection of sensitive personal information	• Don't divulge sensitive information on social networking sites. • Don't write what you don't want to see on the wall/bill board. • Be selective in acceptance of friend/follower requests.
Password protection	• Protect wireless router with strong password. • Use a hard-to-guess password that contains a mix of numbers and letters, and change it frequently. • Use different passwords for different websites and applications to keep hackers guessing.
Safety during online transactions	• Keep your online net-banking password strikingly different from email passwords. • Make credit card transactions only at secured websites and send the numbers only to secured sites. • Don't allow online merchants to store your credit card information for future purchases.
Extra caution	• Use a security program that gives you control over 'cookies' that send information back to websites. • Install firewall software to screen traffic if you use DSL or a cable modem to connect to the Internet. • Don't open email attachments unless you know the source of the incoming message.

potential security issues and control mechanisms. In the event of any unforeseen security threat, there must be a disaster recovery plan in the organization. All security threats, control measures, and risks can be assessed through security audits.

SUMMARY

As e-businesses are growing with the support of technology, business systems and information networks are exposed to a variety of serious security threats from internal corporate networks and the Internet. Information security concerns are not only limited to the Internet, but also other areas such as employee access abuse, unauthorized access by outsiders, viruses attack, theft or destruction of computer resource, and leak of proprietary information. All these threats can be grouped under hacking, malicious software, and internal threats.

Hacking is carried out to gain unauthorized access to a computer system. Hackers use various attacking methods such as spoofing, denial-of-service, and social engineering, among others. Malicious software include all types of viruses, Trojan horses, worms, and spyware. Internal security threats involve misuse of employees' access to information and system crashes. Hardware, software, and network failures are not very uncommon.

Organizations can adopt various security tools and technologies to protect their information systems. These controls include firewalls, encryption, digital signatures, physical access control, antivirus software, passwords, e-mail scanning, secure socket layers, etc.

Firewall is an important technology to protect systems from the Internet and network-based threats. Encryption of data has become a popular way to protect data and other communications over the Internet, intranet, and extranet. Encryption is the process of transforming plain text or data into scrambled text that cannot be deciphered by anyone other than the sender and the intended recipient. The two most widely used encryption methods for Internet traffic on the web are SSL and S-HTTP. The digital certificate system uses a trusted third party, known as the certification authority (CA), to validate a user's identity.

Access control consists of policies and procedures that an organization uses for authorized and authenticated entry into the premises. Authentication is generally done using passwords, biometrics, smart cards, etc., for ensuring protected access. Information systems can be protected against virus attacks by deploying antivirus software. Organizations use fault-tolerant computer systems, which have redundant processors, peripherals, and software that provide continuous uninterrupted service in the event of system failure. Other measures include both hardware and software tools such as monitoring computer usage, keeping backup files, and e-mail monitoring.

Information security management calls for a firm policy framework. A comprehensive IS security policy framework encompasses information system controls, risk assessments, security policies, disaster recovery plans, and security audits. Information systems (IS) controls must be developed to ensure proper data entry, processing techniques, storage methods, and information output. Information risks management is the process of estimating potential losses due to the use of or dependence on an automated information system technology.

An information security policy has more to do with the awareness in the organization about handling and accessing information systems. An effective security policy combines

physical security measures like controlled access for protection of hardware and software, and security awareness throughout the organization.

A disaster recovery plan is a plan of action to recover from the impact of collapse of information systems while a business continuity plan focuses on how the organization can restore business operations after a disaster. IS security must be audited and upgraded to meet the new challenges. The auditing can be done by the organization's internal auditors, supported by the IT specialists or by a qualified external auditing firm.

KEY TERMS

Antivirus vaccine   Small programs used to detect, prevent, and remove viruses from a computer system.

Business continuity plan   Focuses on how the organization can restore business operations after a disaster.

Cryptography   The science of encryption of data during transmission.

Cybercriminals   Hackers, thieves, and other elements who steel information or damage a computer system.

Denial-of-service   An attack by hackers in which they flood a network server with false requests or communications that causes the network to crash.

Digital signatures   Electronic equivalent of traditional handwritten signatures using encryption technology to authenticate a document.

Disaster recovery plan   A plan of action to recover from the impact of collapse of information systems.

Fault-tolerant computer systems   Computer systems having redundant processors, peripherals, and software that provide continuous and uninterrupted service in the event of system failure.

Firewall   Combination of hardware and software that protects the corporate network from unauthorized access by providing a filter, and screens network traffic for passwords and authorization codes before allowing transmission in and out of the network.

Hacking   Breaking into computer systems by finding weaknesses in the security systems, cracking a password, or taking advantage of the various features of the Internet.

Information security policy   Awareness in the organization about handling and accessing information systems.

Intellectual property   Software and other such assets whose ownership rights are vested with the creator and protected by laws.

IS controls   Designed to monitor and maintain the quality and security of the input, processing, output, and storage activities of information systems.

IT security audit   Verifying the accuracy and integrity of the software, correctness of the input data, and accuracy of the output in an IS.

Malicious software   Programs such as viruses, which when executed, would cause undesirable results in the system.

Risk assessment   The process of estimating potential losses due to the use of or dependence upon information system technology.

Secure hypertext transfer protocol   Also called S-HTTP, used for secured data flow over the Internet.

Spoofing   An attack system in which attackers misrepresent themselves or redirect the web link to an address other than the actual one.

Social engineering   A practice by intruders with malicious intentions who befriend employees and others into revealing their passwords or sensitive information, while pretending to be legitimate members of the same group who need the information.

Spyware   A small program that installs itself on computers to monitor the user's web surfing activity and transmits the information to its source; used for advertising, also called malware.

Secure sockets layer   Also called SSL, a protocol used for client and server computers to manage encryption and decryption activities as they communicate during a secure web session.

CONCEPT REVIEW QUESTIONS

1. What is information security management? What types of security threats are faced by business

organizations?

2. How can an organization control security threats

and vulnerabilities? Outline the major tools and technologies adapted by businesses.

3. What is a firewall? Explain its functioning.

4. How do encryption and digital signature technologies work?

5. How can information systems be protected by physical access control?

6. What is a security policy? What are the various policies that an organization should develop for protection of information systems?

7. How can risk assessment be done for an organization heavily dependent on information technology?

8. What is a disaster recovery plan? What should the plan for disaster recovery be in case of an IS failure?

9. What do you understand by an IT security audit?

CRITICAL THINKING QUESTIONS

1. 'Insider security threats are more alarming and frequent than external attacks.' Do you agree with this statement? Why or why not?

2. Is there any gain in the development and proliferation of malicious software like viruses? Who benefits from the virus menace?

3. Nearly 50% of the businesses in India do not have a disaster recovery plan in place for their IT infrastructure and even more than 60% have no business continuity plan. What do you think is the reason for this approach?

4. In the name of security policy, most IS managers do nothing more than adding and deleting names from the user authorization list. A security policy signifies much more than this. Substantiate your answer with examples.

MIS DEVELOPMENT

Indian businesses are galloping in the wake of economic liberalization, contributing significantly to the country's growth. Sadly, they fall short of planning for a disaster recovery (DR), finds a study from Regus, a provider of workplace solutions. Nearly 50% of the businesses in India do not have a DR plan in place for their IT infrastructure and even more than 60% have no business continuity for their workplace requirements, the survey revealed. In India, 400 companies participated in the Regus survey, conducted in the metro cities of Mumbai, New Delhi, Bengaluru, and Chennai.

Hurricane Sandy in the US in 2012 caused an estimated damage of $62 billion; the major earthquakes in Japan, the Philippines, Italy, and Afghanistan caused loss of lives and economy. Natural disasters—floods, avalanches, lightening, flash floods, and cyclones—in India have resulted in loss of men and material. The catastrophic spate of disasters that occurred in 2011 and 2012 have driven the issue of DR to the top of boardroom agendas, highlighting the huge cost to businesses that natural disasters and their aftermath can cause. Although these are extreme examples, the consequences of common events such as fires and vandalism can also seriously damage a business. While Indian businesses have shown remarkable resilience in the wake of natural disasters such as earthquakes,

tsunamis, and terrorist attacks in the past, the Regus survey shows that Indian businesses lack a conscious DR plan. Nearly 43.5% of the companies from India believe that the cost of DR prohibits their planning. However, a significant 63.5% companies in India were ready to buy a workplace DR facility if the option is priced affordably.

In order to take the pulse of global business preparedness, the survey canvassed the opinions of over 12,000 business people in 85 countries and found that a significant proportion of firms are taking a huge risk with their shareholders' assets and failing to take proper precautions. Compared to India, nearly 45% of businesses globally do not have a DR plan in place for their IT and 55% have no business continuity plan for their workspace requirements. The research reveals that across the globe, around half the firms have no formal business continuity strategy for their IT or workforce. With reports indicating that the average incident can cost up to $5,00,000 this lack of planning could spell disaster for many firms.

Most businesses appear to run this risk due to the high perceived cost of DR but also report that they would be willing to pay a monthly fee to access a workplace DR facility in case of an emergency.

This is an important indication that although too

many businesses are taking a gamble, their mentality is changing. As affordable products and services become available around the globe, it is likely that more businesses will finally stop hoping for the best and seriously start planning to prepare for the worst.

Exercise

- What are the information security issues highlighted in the aforementioned news?
- Conduct a risk assessment for an e-commerce retailing firm like 'Ferns-n-Petals'.
- Develop a disaster recovery plan and a business continuity plan for Bombay Mercantile Cooperative Bank Ltd (www.bmcbankltd.com) having 51 branches, but no ATM, netbanking, or phone banking system.

REFERENCES

Bill, Joy, 'Report from the cyberfront', *Newsweek*, 21 February 2000.

Davis, Gorden and Margethe Olson, *Management Information Systems*, McGraw-Hill, Singapore, 1996.

Jaiswal, Mahadev and Monika Mittal, *Management Information Systems*, Oxford University Press, New Delhi, 2004.

Jawadekar, Waman, *Management Information Systems*, Tata McGraw-Hill, New Delhi, 2007.

Laudon Ken, Jane Laudon, and Rajanish Dass, *Management Information System*, Pearson Education, Singapore, 2010.

Neumann, Peter, *Computer Related Risks*, ACM Press, New York, 1995.

O'Brien, James A., George M. Marakas, and Ramesh Behl, *Management Information Systems*, Tata McGraw-Hill, New Delhi, 2007.

Rothfeder, Jeffrey, 'No privacy on the net', *PC World*, February 1997.

Stuart, Katzke, *A framework for computer security risk management*, National Institute of Standards and Technology (NIST), US Department of Commerce, Study paper on information security, October, 1992.

Turban, Efraim, Jay E. Ronson, and Ling-Peng Liang, *Decision Support Systems & Intelligent Systems*, Pearson Education, Singapore, 2005.

VanScoy, Kayte, 'What your workers are really up to', *Ziff Davis Smart Business*, September 2001.

Ahuja, R.P.S., 'Information security–An issue for the boardroom', 31 May 2004, Silicon India Magazine, http://www.siliconindia.com/magazine_articles/Information_Security__An_Issue_for_the_Boardroom-CAV285981583.html, last accessed on 7 January 2012.

Jayanthi, Sridhar, 'Day Zero: How do you stop a security attack?', Silicon India Magazine, 13 November 2008, http://www.siliconindia.com/magazine_articles/Day_Zero_How_do_you_stop_a_security_attack-BZT231104874.html, last accessed on 7 January 2012.

Periera, Brian, 'Information security: A new approach', *Network Magazine*, April 2003, http://www.networkmagazineindia.com/200304/cover1.shtml, last accessed on 15 January 2012.

www.firstpost.com, www.infosecurity-magazine.com, www.livemint.com, www.techrepublic.com, last accessed on 15 January 2012.

CASE STUDY

Banking Sector: Insider Threats Keeping Them on their Toes

From insider threats to social engineering and phishing attacks, the banking sector today has to be prepared to deal with security woes on multiple fronts. Research shows that insider threat is a major threat to information security in the banking sector.

'Insider threat study' conducted at Carnegie Mellon University, US, suggests that most of the security breach incidents examined in the banking and finance sector were not technically sophisticated or complex. Most incidents required minimal technical skill to be carried out and were perpetrated by non-technical personnel with little computer knowledge or training. This suggests that it is important for organizations to secure their networks from the full range of users, from persons responsible for data entry to management to system administrators. In other words, they typically involved exploitation of non-technical vulnerabilities such as business rules or organization policies (rather than vulnerabilities in an information system or network) and were carried out by individuals who had little or no technical expertise.

In India, Hitesh Mulani, chief information security officer, Yes Bank, apprises on the evolving threats in the banking sector and the factors determining the same.

What is the biggest new-age security threat faced by the banking industry today?

Insider threats have been and continue to be the single largest threat that all banks are faced with. While there are multiple tools to avert threats such as network and data security to a reasonable extent, insider frauds continue to evolve with various technology platforms and keep information security functions at banks on their toes at all times.

In 1996, in US, two credit union employees worked together to alter credit reports in exchange for financial payment. As part of their normal responsibilities, the employees were permitted to alter credit reports based on updated information the company received. However, the employees intentionally misused their authorized access to remove negative credit indicators and add fictitious indicators of positive credit to specific credit histories in exchange for money. The total amount of fraud loss from their activities exceeded $2,15,000. The risk exposure to the credit union was incalculable.

Broadly speaking, what are the major factors influencing governance strategies in the banking industry today?

The major factor that influences governance strategies is the constantly evolving threat landscape, which now includes a range of threat vulnerabilities on different platforms. The strategy needs to provision for this. The governance strategies are also required to incorporate steps that ensure regulatory and compliance requirements are met. We realize that there is a constant need for direct access to top management and so independent reporting structures have to be built. And, since the risk appetite of organizations is limited, especially in the banking industry, information security must be ingrained into every process/function of the banking business.

Online and mobile banking have become indispensable to banking today. What security threats do you see with the proliferation of these channels?

Security threats posed by online and mobile banking include lack of fool-proof mechanisms for non-repudiation of end-users and customers; exposure of the service to one and all—including those who do not need it, but can still 'knock at the doors' and try to penetrate. Finally, there is the perpetual threat from the flow of data through multiple third party service providers and from virus/Trojans/spyware.

Mobile application security testing forms an integral part of the strategy to secure mobile financial services. Apart from this, the application architecture and network architecture form an important part of a secure set-up of mobile financial services.

How acute is the insider threat as compared to the external one in the banking and financial industry?

Statistics vary regarding the prevalence of cases perpetrated by insiders compared to those perpetrated by individuals external to the targeted organizations. Nevertheless, insiders pose a substantial threat by virtue of their knowledge of and access to their employers' systems and/or databases, and their ability to bypass existing physical and electronic security measures through legitimate means.

In US, in March 2002, a 'logic bomb' deleted 10 billion files in the computer systems of an international financial services company. The incident affected over 1300 of the company's servers throughout the US. The company sustained losses of approximately $3 million, the amount required to repair damage and reconstruct deleted files. Investigations by law enforcement professionals and computer forensic professionals revealed the logic bomb had been planted by a disgruntled employee who had recently quit the company because of a dispute over the amount of his annual bonus.

How important is identity and access and management? Should it be the key priority on a bank's agenda?

It has to be a key factor on every bank's agenda, given that the insider threat is always looming around. Provisioning and de-provisioning, and most importantly, frequently changing profiles are a constant bone of contention that leave a few gaping loopholes in the security fabric from time-to-time.

In the US study, many incidents were committed by 'insiders'—individuals who were, or previously had been, authorized to use the information systems they eventually employed to perpetrate harm. Efforts to estimate how often companies face attacks from within are difficult to make. Many believe that insider attacks are under-reported to law enforcement agencies or prosecutors. Companies may fear the negative publicity or increased liability that may arise as a result of the incidents. Or, they may believe that the harm suffered would not be sufficient to warrant criminal charges.

Do you see social engineering as a major threat to the banking sector? What should be done to curb security threats arising from social engineering?

Social engineering is a major threat, and the only possible way to curb it seems to be via robust security awareness programs at all levels, both inside and outside the bank—for internal users, vendors, and partners as well as the customers. Besides, there are very few means of curbing the menace of new-age social engineering techniques like phishing through real-time monitoring. Hence, better end-user vigilance via greater security awareness is the most effective mechanism.

In the US study, most incidents in the banking and finance sector report required minimal technical skill to carry out and were perpetrated by non-technical personnel with little computer knowledge or training. This suggests it is important for organizations to secure their networks from the full range of users, from persons responsible for data entry to management to system administrators. In addition, many of the cases involved the exploitation of inadequate or non-existent practices, policies, and procedures, including both those addressing technical practices and non-technical ones.

What makes risk management critical for the banking sector?

With the proliferation of multiple channels and continued focus to further reach out to customers via new and innovative channels, and the increasingly competitive products being offered in the banking space, risk management has become indispensable to the banking function. It needs to be rigorously practised in true spirit in all functions of the bank.

As the US study reveals, since many of the insider attacks reviewed in this study took place at the office during normal working hours, it may help to train all staff with the goal of creating a culture of security in which suspicious or indicative behaviours are detected, monitored, reported, and investigated. Employees must know not only what to look for, but also how to report activity that raises concern. Such a culture can create self-reinforcing security in which insider activity is more likely to be detected before major damage is done, and can make employees think twice about engaging in insider activity in the first place because of increased awareness and monitoring. At the same time, it would be counter productive to create an environment of mistrust. It should be made clear that preventing or limiting the damage due to insider attacks is to the mutual benefit of the organization and its workforce.

Discussion Questions

1. Are insider security threats more alarming than hacking and virus attacks? Explain in the light of this case study.
2. What kind of disaster recovery plans must be developed by banks to meet the challenges of such breaches in information security?
3. How can banks carry out risk assessment and prepare a disaster plan?
4. Is banking and financial sector more prone to insider threats than any other sector? Substantiate your answer with real-life examples.

Sources:

'Insider threats constantly keeping banks on their toes', Interview 20 December 2011, http://biztech2.in.com/interviews/security/insider-threats-constantly-keeping-banks-on-their-toes/114962/0, last accessed on 1 February 2013.

'Illicit cyber activity in the banking sector', Study Document August 2004, Carnegie Mellon Software Engineering Institute, Pittsburg, www.cert.org/archive/pdf/bankfin040820.pdf, last accessed on 13 January 2012.

Ethical and Societal Challenges of IT

> *Privacy means different things to different people. In general privacy is the right to be left alone and the right to be free from unreasonable personal intrusions. Privacy has been a legal, ethical, and social issue in many countries ... Personal values constitute a major factor in the issue of ethical decision making. The study of ethical issues in management support systems is complex because of its multidimensionality.*
>
> —EFRAIM TURBAN

LEARNING OBJECTIVES

After studying this chapter, you will be able to

- define the ethical and social issues connected with systems
- understand the various legal, privacy, and ethical issues
- describe accountability and liability issues
- be aware of the Internet challenges to privacy
- learn about intellectual property rights, copyrights, and patent issues
- analyse the impact of information technology on the quality of life
- highlight the important provisions of the Information Technology Act 2000

EXHIBIT 18.1

Privacy: Getting Over it in the Internet Age

The public has always been fascinated by the lives of top executives—what they do, what they read, where they holiday, and how much they spend on luxuries. Does it have an end? No. The media goes into a frenzy to get a top secret about any celebrity, which can be splashed on TV and the Internet. Don't the personal lives of top executives deserve some privacy? Or does it have to be on display like a museum artefact?

The trend was triggered by the founder of a company, which has been making waves everywhere—Apple. When Steve Jobs decided to keep the details about his health to himself, it was dutifully observed by his company; the details became public only after his death. Insider information about the captains of companies has a direct binding on the price of the stocks of the companies. For example, when the Enron scandal came to light, the shareholders lost nearly $11 billion, for stocks which had hit a high of $90 per share in mid-2000, leading the shares to fall to less than $1 by the end of November 2001. The announcement of Steve Jobs' last leave led to Apple's stock plummeting by 8% in the international markets and later, by 2%.

Scott McNealy, chief executive officer, Sun Microsystems, once quoted. 'You have zero privacy anyway. Get over it.' In the Internet age, individuals have zero privacy. Their privacy is infringed on by social networking sites. Major networking sites like Facebook have started taking note of it. In August 2011, in Bengaluru, Facebook declared a major overhaul to its users' control over their privacy on the site. The changes make sure that the items posted on the site would now have their own sharing settings, determining who could access or see them.

The changes also ensure that persons tagged in a posting such as a photo or video have the option to confirm or remove their identity before it appears on their profile. This would also eliminate the ill effects of spiteful tagging used by some to add other people's name to unpleasant images.

Facebook has brought about major privacy changes for its users. Earlier, members could not tag someone who was not a Facebook friend. Facebook has abandoned this rule. It would now allow users to tag people who are non-friends by seeking their prior approval before the tags appear on their profiles.

In a blog post on the current revamp, Facebook described its previous policy as 'awkward' and 'broken'. However, the new one could bring its own headaches, from raising new privacy concerns (do people really want strangers tagging them in photos?) to offering a potential new avenue for spammers to reach out to users.

Sources:
Adapted from 'You have zero privacy anyway, get over it', SiliconIndia, posted on 3 November 2011, http://www.siliconindia.com/shownews/You_have_Zero_Privacy_Anyway_Get_Over_it-nid-96568-cid-100.html?, last accessed on 15 March 2012.
'Facebook announces a major privacy revamp', SiliconIndia, posted on 24 August 2011, http://www.siliconindia.com/shownews/Facebook_Announces_Major_Privacy_Revamp, last accessed on 15 March 2012.

Information technology (IT) has opened a Pandora's box as it has become easier to peep into the lives of people in the public domain, as illustrated in Exhibit 18.1. You can see how personal information about the health of Steve Jobs had an impact on the business of Apple Inc. We come across numerous instances of personification, replication, and sales of unauthorized personal data of individuals on social networking sites. There are many unauthorized accounts on Twitter, Facebook, etc., which impersonate well-known people in public life. For example, it is said that there are around 10–12 accounts related to the PM or PMO on Twitter. This is referred to as personification by unknown people. People can tag unknown people and non-friends and are thus aware of their activities on the Internet. Social networking sites have become a major source of personal data collection. People post their activities, status, hobbies, etc., which are tracked, collected, and distributed for business gains. These activities have raised many legal, ethical, and social issues.

In this chapter, we will discuss ethical and social issues of information systems (IS) and IT. The web has threatened individual privacy and highlighted privacy issues. Similarly, implementation of systems reduces labour costs by reducing jobs and creating strife in the society. We will try to understand how these issues should be taken care of by systems managers and tackled by laws and statutes.

ETHICAL AND SOCIAL ISSUES CONNECTED WITH SYSTEMS

Every business manager has the responsibility of promoting ethical use of IT in the workplace. As part of their ethical responsibilities, managers should efficiently perform the role of a vital human resource in the business system. Earlier we discussed that business managers take decisions supported by information systems. Thus, while taking business decisions, ethical and social dimensions must be considered for the larger good of the organization and society.

The issues of ethics in the conduct of business are taken care of in the day-to-day functioning of the organization. There are ethical principles that can serve as the basis for ethical conduct by managers, end-users, and information system professionals. Many organizations have charted out detailed policies for the ethical use of technology by their employees. Various organizations such as the Association of Information Technology Professionals (AITP), Association of Computing Manufacturers (ACM), and association of professionals in the computing field have their codes of conduct. Exhibit 18.2 displays parts of the AITP and ACM's code of conduct.

EXHIBIT 18.2
AITP and ACM Code of Ethics and Standards of Professional Conduct

AITP Standards of Professional Conduct
In recognition of my obligations to my employer, I shall

- avoid conflict of interests and ensure that my employer is aware of any potential conflicts.
- protect the privacy and confidentiality of all information entrusted to me.
- not misrepresent or withhold information that is germane to the situation.
- not attempt to use the resources of my employer for personal gain or for any purpose without proper approval.
- not exploit the weakness of a computer system for personal gain or personal satisfaction.

In recognition of my obligations to society, I shall

- use any skill and knowledge to inform the public in all areas of my expertise.
- to the best of my ability, ensure that the products of my work are used in a socially responsible way.
- support, respect, and abide by the appropriate local,

state, provincial, and federal laws.
- never misrepresent or withhold information that is germane to a problem or a situation of public concern, nor will I allow any such known information to remain unchallenged.
- not use knowledge of a confidential or personal nature in any unauthorized manner to achieve personal gain.

ACM Code of Ethics and Professional Conduct
Professional responsibilities:

- Strive to achieve highest quality effectiveness and dignity in both the process and product of professional work.
- Acquire and maintain professional competence.
- Know and respect existing laws pertaining to professional work.
- Accept and provide appropriate professional review.
- Conduct a thorough evaluation of computer systems and their impact including analysis of possible risks.
- Honour contracts, agreements, and assign responsibilities.

(Contd)

Exhibit 18.2 (Contd)

- Improve public understanding of computing and its consequences.

Organizational leadership imperatives:

- Articulate social responsibilities of members of an organizational unit and encourage full acceptance of those responsibilities.
- Articulate and support policies that protect the dignity of users and others affected by computing systems.

- Manage personnel and resources to design and build information systems that enhance the quality of working life.
- Create opportunities for members of the organization to learn the principles and limitations of computer systems.

Sources:
http://www.computing.dcu.ie/~renaat/ca613/Notes/Wk5Bowyer-Chap03.pdf, http://www.eecs.wsu.edu/~holder/courses/cse 4317/lectures/chapter_3.pdf, last accessed on 28 May 2013.

The ethical and societal challenges of IT have legal, privacy, and ethical dimensions. Exhibit 18.3 illustrates these issues with examples.

EXHIBIT 18.3

Ethical and Social Dimensions of Information Technology

Social issues connected with systems	Examples
Legal issues	• Is an electronically signed contract or an unsigned computer generated document valid in a court of law? • Are e-mail communications admissible in a court of law? • What is the value of an expert opinion in court if the expertise is encoded in a computer? • Who is liable for wrong information provided by an information system? • What happens if a manager makes a disastrous decision by relying on computer information? • Can a software or hardware vendor be held liable for damages caused due to a system crash? • Can the management force experts to contribute their expertise to build a knowledge base?
Privacy issues	• Is unsolicited information in the form of e-mail an infringement on individual privacy? • What information should a person reveal to others on the web? • What information is private if extracted from the web? • What kind of surveillance can an employer use on his/her employees? • What information about individuals should be kept in databases? • What kind of information does a person or an organization have the right to obtain, and under what conditions and safeguards?
Ethical issues	• Who owns intellectual property rights? How should one handle software piracy? • Under what circumstances can one use proprietary databases? • Who is the owner of information in an organization? • How can we compensate for reduction in jobs due to information system implementation? • How do we manage workplace safety and work stress in an IT environment? • How do we tackle non-work related use of the Internet and e-mails by employees?

Legal Issues

The introduction of IT and IS in organizations has raised many legal issues (e.g., admissibility and validity of electronic documents, correspondence, and contracts in the eyes of the law). According to Turban (2005), the questions concerning liability for the actions of intelligent machines are just beginning to be considered. In the 1990s, computers took over airline ticket reservation, which was considered an unfair step by the agents, as people had quick access to computers and the system could complete the job much faster than an agent or broker.

There are legal issues associated with computer communications, software, and use of the Internet. There are rules related to the use of computer networks, unauthorized access, data privacy, and spamming. Software licencing issues are guided by the intellectual property and copyright laws. The issues related to software licences, end-user licence agreements, free software licences, and open-source licences may involve discussion of product liability, professional liability of individual developers, warranties, contract law, trade secrets, and intellectual property.

There are laws on censorship and freedom of expression, and rules on public access to government information and individual access to information. The legal issues relate to what data must be retained for law enforcement, and what may not be gathered or retained for privacy reasons.

Other complex legal issues may crop up. For example, can a software vendor be held liable for an erroneous information based on which a wrong decision is taken by the manager, resulting in damages. Will the enterprise itself be held responsible for not testing the system adequately before entrusting it with sensitive data?

Privacy Issues

Privacy is the right of an individual to not disclose a certain amount of information about the self or allow it to be shared only with his/her consent, and with the assurance that it would be protected and treated as it were with the owner of the information.

Personal information of an individual and bank, credit, or debit card details, etc., can be easily collected during transactions; IT has made it easier for such details to be tracked and distributed. IT is capable of finding access to this data, and download and process it to create an information database about an individual without his/her knowledge. This is known as privacy violation or infringement.

While individuals are expected to take care of their personal information, the IT industry advocates certain standard ethical practices to ensure its privacy (Jawadekar 2008).

- No secret record should be maintained about individuals after use.
- No use can be made other than that of the specified original purpose.
- If another use is required, consent of the individual has to be obtained.
- Allow individuals the right of inspection and correction.
- The organization and processing system are responsible for the integrity of the secret data.

The definition of privacy violation has expanded due to the emergence of new technologies such as the Internet and mobile telephony. Privacy violation also occurs due to unsolicited e-mails, SMSes, and phone calls. This is called spamming. Spamming remains economically viable because advertisers have no operating costs beyond the management of their mailing lists, and it is difficult to hold senders accountable for their mass mailings. As the barrier to entry is very low, spammers are numerous and the volume of unsolicited mail has become very high. In 2012, the estimated figure for spam messages was around seven trillion worldwide. The costs, such as lost productivity and fraud, are borne by the public and Internet service providers, who are forced to add extra functionalities to cope with the deluge. Spamming has been the subject of legislation in many jurisdictions.

Exhibit 18.4 illustrates how an individual's privacy is in danger because of unsolicited mails, messages, and phone calls.

EXHIBIT 18.4

Spamming: How to Guard your Privacy

Unsolicited e-mails and mobile messages have become a menace for the peace-loving individual. Various governments and the telecom regulatory authority of India (TRAI) do their bit to control this menace. Regulating the SMS limit is one of the options. In September 2011, Suw Charman-Anderson wrote in *Firstpost* that TRAI's 100 SMS limit will not solve the spam problem. She said that TRAI needs to work with the mobile phone providers to tackle the problem. Perhaps, she had no clue about the Indian operators. This may be the reason why TRAI has the 100-SMS limit.

In August 2012, the government of India banned mass messaging and limited the number of messages to five. This action of the government was the result of rumours spread by mass messaging, which triggered an exodus of people belonging to the north-east from Bengaluru and Pune.

India has become the top spam-spewing nation in the world according to computer security firm Sophos' 2012 Dirty Dozen report, which lists the top 12 countries from where most spam originate.

India has leapt to the top of the spam chart in less than a year, rapidly eclipsing the US. The volume of junk mail that originated from India during the first three months of 2012 exceeded the volume coming from the US. Nearly 10% of all the junk mail sent across the web originates from or passes through computers in India, said the data protection firm.

'If you have a spam in your inbox, there is an almost one in 10 chance that it was relayed from an Indian computer', said Graham Cluley, senior technology consultant at Sophos.

Boston-headquartered Sophos said India has risen to the top of the spam chart because of the rapid growth of Internet users in the country and computers that are not properly protected.

'The latest stats show that, as more first-time Internet users get online in growing economies, they are not taking measures to block the malware infections that turn their PCs into spam-spewing zombies', said Cluley.

Facebook and Twitter Spread Junk Mail

Spammers are increasingly finding traditional e-mail spam ineffective. Hence, they are turning to social networks to spread spam campaigns. Here is the bad news—basic marketing spam has decreased, but the amount of messages that spread malware or that represent more targeted attempts to phish usernames, passwords, and personal information is increasing.

'While traditional marketing spam may appear to be no more than an annoyance, offering pills that have questionable claims or get-rich-quick schemes, they can often lead to more serious threats to your personal information', said Cluley.

Facebook, Twitter, and Pinterest were all being hit with increasing regularity by spammers, warned Sophos.

Dirty Dozen

Sophos estimates that about 9.3% of all junk mail travels through Indian computers. In second place is the US (8.3%) while South Korea (5.7%) ranks third. Indonesia tied with Russia (5.0%) at fourth place, while Italy (4.9%), Brazil (4.3%), Poland (3.9%), Pakistan (3.3%), Vietnam (3.2%), Taiwan (2.9%), Peru (2.5%), and other countries (41.7%) rounded out the rest of the Dirty Dozen.

Fighting Spam

Sophos said companies should update their corporate virus protection, and run a consolidated solution at their e-mail and web gateways to defend against spam and viruses. One should also defend home computers and laptops with licensed virus protection products, to prevent becoming part of a botnet used for the purpose of sending spam.

(Contd)

Exhibit 18.4 (Contd)

India's new position as king of spam among countries was also confirmed by spam reports from other security vendors such as Kaspersky Lab and Trend Micro.

Sources:
Choudhury, Uttara, 'India is world's top spammer; here's how

you can guard yourself', 25 April 2012, http://www.firstpost.com/tech/india-is-king-of-the-spam-world-287627.html, last accessed on 1 September 2012.
Soans, Ivor, 'Tata Indicom in bed with spammers', posted on 29 September 2011, www.firstpost.com/tech/tata-indicom-in-bed-with-spammers, last accessed on 1 September 2012.

Ethical Issues

Ethics refers to the principles that guide or define whether an action taken is morally right or wrong. Ethics is about values and human behaviour. According to Laudon (2010), information systems raise new ethical questions for both individuals and societies because they create opportunities for intense social change and, thus, threaten existing distribution of power, money, rights, and obligations. Like any other technology, IT too can be used to develop social progress, as well as commit crimes and degrade the social system.

The ethical issues in business have become a subject of discussion as new-age frauds have come into light. The Satyam fraud in 2009 shocked the entire corporate world in India. Exhibit 18.5 throws light on the issue and how such issues should be dealt with.

EXHIBIT 18.5

Satyam Computers: A Problem of Ethical Deficit in Business

Satyam was a strong brand that had been created with a name that meant truth, was respected by its customers, and was attractive to very high quality talent. The independent directors on the board were people with top credentials and the auditors were one of the top four names in the business. Yet, both the size of the deceit and the length of time it went on for were remarkable, leading to a justifiably strong and loud outcry.

Satyam faced a crisis of 'unimaginable proportions', its interim chief executive said a day after the chairman revealed that profits had been inflated for years.

In India's biggest corporate scandal in memory, chairman Ramalinga Raju resigned on 7 January 2009, after disclosing that about $1 billion, or 94% of the cash and bank balances on the company's books at the end of September did not exist. The company's shares plunged nearly 80%. The scandal, which some analysts dubbed 'India's Enron' (after the collapsed US energy firm) has cast a cloud over foreign investment in Asia's third-largest economy and over its once-booming outsourcing sector. Raju, who founded the company in 1987, said no other board member was aware of the irregularities at Satyam.

A team from the securities and exchange board of India (SEBI) arrived at the company's headquarters in Hyderabad to try and discover how the fraud could have been hidden for so long. Mumbai's benchmark stock index tumbled more than 7% and the Indian Rupee fell after the Satyam bombshell. The New York stock exchange (NYSE) halted trading in Satyam's shares (SAY) indefinitely. Some investors in Satyam's American depositary receipts have already filed class action suits against the firm in March 2009, lawyers said.

Ram Mynampati, the interim CEO of Satyam, said he was shocked by the disclosures, and added that he and other board members relied on the audited results. The company's auditing firm, PricewaterhouseCoopers said its audit had been carried out in accordance with standards and it would cooperate with regulators. Merrill Lynch, which Satyam appointed as an advisor, terminated the relationship on exposure of the fraud, adding it had found material related to accounting irregularities.

Frauds of such magnitude may also increase investors' nervousness about weak corporate governance and oversight in emerging markets, which are reeling from the

(Contd)

Exhibit 18.5 (Contd)

global financial crisis. Ram Mynampati said that Satyam had contacted its top 100 customers, who account for almost 80% of the revenue, and had received expressions of support. Satyam specializes in business software and backoffice services for clients such as General Electric and Nestlé.

Sources:
'Satyam Computers fraud brings India in to question', *USA Today*,

8 January 2009, http://www.usatoday.com/money/world/2009-01-08-satyam-computer-fraud_N.htm, last accessed on 30 January 2012.

Sinha, Janmejaya, 'A problem of ethical deficit', Boston Consulting Group India, http://www.livemint.com/2009/01/11205630/A-problem-of-ethical-deficit.html, last accessed on 30 January 2012.

http://www.karmayog.org/newspaperarticles/newspaper articles_22038.htm, last accessed on 30 January 2012.

The advent of the Internet and the web has given rise to and expanded the scope of users and business managers in carrying out unethical practices. The Internet and e-business technologies have made it easier to assemble, integrate, and distribute information, posing new concerns about appropriate use of customer information, privacy, and protection of intellectual property rights (IPR).

The lesson to be learnt is that reputation will matter more to companies. This will be true in India and abroad. A company's reputation will command a premium and can become a source of gaining a competitive advantage. Customers will be willing to pay more to deal with firms they believe will not cheat them or go bust because of skimming by owners and CEOs. For service businesses or in businesses where there are long-term contracts with dependencies over time, customers will look for trustworthiness of partners. The importance of building, nurturing, and fortifying a company's reputation will be reinforced. Building a reputation always takes time, is difficult, and does not happen on its own. Leaders need to recognize its importance and understand that if they want to create companies that last and survive, they will need to invest in the reputation of their brand. It will require companies to create a culture in which honesty is rewarded. In pursuing targets, cutting ethical corners is never tolerated and is not allowed to become an excuse for non-performance. Anecdotes and stories that form part of the firm's history need to reinforce this value.

ACCOUNTABILITY AND LIABILITY ISSUES

Who can be held accountable for a mistake committed by a computer system? Can the machine or the developer of the system be held liable for damages caused due to failure of the systems? Privacy, property ownership, and legal issues are taken care of by various laws and actions of the government and the industry; however, the issue of accountability and liability of a system user, developer, or system vendor are still not addressed. The basic question is—who will be held responsible if anything goes wrong with the system? There are a number of people involved at different stages of designing, development, implementation, and usage of a system.

For example, UK Royal Mail's computer network crashed in December 2011. As a result, customers at 12,000 branches were unable to pay bills, send presents, or access their savings accounts. According to news reports, the cause of the computer glitch was the overload of customers at the 12,000 branches making online transactions on the system. As card payments were also affected by the computer glitch, people were unable to access savings, which further infuriated hapless customers (*Gadgets Lane*, 13 December 2011).

The entire process of transaction handling is operated by users, Internet service providers, payment certification agencies, network operators, and system vendors. Can they be sued for a wrong done by a computer?

For example, the head of Mizuho Bank, the retail banking unit of Japan's second-largest lender, Mizuho Financial Group, resigned in June 2011, following a massive computer glitch. Mizuho was hit by the glitch in March 2011 after accounts were flooded with donations for a magnitude 9.0 earthquake and tsunami in north-east Japan that killed up to 28,000 people. The computer troubles forced shutdown of Mizuho's automatic teller machines (ATMs) and disrupted transactions, adding to the woes of businesses and households already badly shaken by the disasters (Reuters India edition, April 2011).

These are sundry cases of computer systems going wrong. They reveal the difficulties faced by system personnel who are responsible for the systems developed by them. The Mizuho Bank head who was, in fact, a benign user, took the responsibility upon himself and resigned. Having said this, who else would you expect to resign and pay liabilities in such cases?

Software and machines are also used as services. If an ATM fails to deliver the service it is designed for, and the customer faces inconvenience and economic problems, the manufacturer of the ATM cannot be held responsible. The laws are yet to focus on issues and challenges posed by software failures.

EXHIBIT 18.6

Indian Techies Arrested: Accountability of Software Producers?

On 13 December 2002, Arun Jain, chief executive officer, Polaris Software Labs, and Rajiv Malhotra, vice-president, of the company, heading the bankware products division, were arrested in Indonesia and charged with criminal embezzlement by Bank Artha Graha (BAG). Both of them managed their way back to India after some tough diplomatic wrangling. The Indian government's finesse in handling the issue was praised.

Polaris was awarded a contract worth about $1.3 million in 2001 to install a banking application for BAG. The bank alleges that Polaris had promised the new system could go 'live' within four months after work commenced in January. According to BAG allegations, the promised timeline of four months was never met and Polaris was unable to set the system up properly, despite extending the system integration dateline to September 2002. Subsequently, according to a BAG statement, the bank, in accordance with its rights under the agreements, issued a letter to Polaris on 27 November 2002 terminating the agreement with immediate effect. The statement says, under the terms of the contract, the bank is entitled to a refund of $6,62,000 dollars by 4 December 2002 for terminating the agreement due to default or failure of the system. The bank believes that it is also entitled to claim damages for Polaris' breach of the agreements.

Jain, on his return from Jakarta, where he was detained for a week, said the detention seemed to be 'pre-planned and premeditated', going by the swift events that immediately followed on his landing in Jakarta to solve a commercial dispute with the bank. Jain said he would have settled the case by paying money to BAG, 'which I didn't want to do. I did not want to bend backward to settle the issue'.

He said that Polaris had offered to pay $6,62,000 back to the bank by way of settlement, but they wanted $10 million as compensation. 'In future, whenever we want to do business with a developing country, we will be consulting the Indian embassy there before venturing into such a business proposition', he added. A complaint had been filed by the

(Contd)

Exhibit 18.6 (Contd)

Indonesian police against Polaris under Section 372 and 378 (dishonesty and fraud). The police were also examining whether the present case was a civil or a criminal one.

After returning to India, Jain said that he planned legal action against the Indonesian bank whose complaint had led to the arrest. 'We had gone there with the intention to resolve the commercial dispute between Polaris and the BAG. Unfortunately, the turn of events led to an unwilling detention for us. Also the bank sought compensation across the table', Jain said on 25 December 2002, in Chennai. 'The Polaris board will take into consideration all these events and take appropriate legal action including a defamation suit against the bank for our harrowing experience these last 12 days', he said.

Later, in a first of its kind, in 2003, the Malaysian police detained and allegedly roughed up nearly 200 Indian software workers on charges of violating visa rules. Most of them carried proper visas and Malaysian authorities later apologized to India for the wrongful detentions. The Indian embassy planned to lodge a formal protest note with the Malaysian government about the engineers' detention.

It was not long after that the Chennai-based Radiant Software faced legal battle from Oracle on the copyright issue. Ultimately, Radiant Software went out of business as a consequence of the problems. Similarly, the Russian software firm, Elcomsoft, is battling a case in California where a software professional, Dmitry Sklyarov, was arrested while on a tour of the US. The case is still going on.

These cases indicate the accountabilities and liabilities of software vendors towards their clients and society.

Sources:
'Arrest pre-planned and premeditated', *The Tribune*, 26 December 2002, http://www.tribuneindia.com/2002/20021226/biz.htm#1, last accessed on 11 February 2012.
'Indonesian bank, Polaris seek to settle dispute', 20 February 2003, *Economic Times*, http://articles.economictimes.indiatimes.com/2003-02-20/news/27513578_1_bank-artha-graha-rajiv-malhotra-polaris-executives, last accessed on 11 February 2012.
'Malaysia arrests techies, HCL, MEA deny', http://portal.bsnl.in/bsnl/asp/content%20mgmt/html%20content/hotnews/hotnews48831.html, last accessed 10 February 2012.
http://www.naavi.org/cl_editorial/edit_17_dec_02_01.html, 17 December 2002, last accessed on 11 February 2012.

Can responsibility, accountability, and liability be fixed on system developers? It is difficult to hold software producers directly responsible for their software products. Exhibit 18.6 illustrates how Indian software producers were arrested in foreign lands for different reasons.

INTERNET CHALLENGES TO PRIVACY

The emergence of the Internet and web technology has posed newer challenges to individual privacy. The more the world gets connected through internetworks, manifold is the increase in the individual's risk to privacy exposure. E-mail messages can be intercepted and vested interests can have access to personal data captured at retail stores, on social networking sites, and other such places. Even corporate data that is stored in the corporate server, but accessed by users globally, can be tracked. The data entered, processed, and sent across the Internet passes through different computer systems installed on the network across the globe. These systems are capable of keeping track of such communication and can also capture and store the communication reference and identities. This activity of capturing data, monitoring its use, and storing happens without the knowledge of users. The case study at the end of the chapter illustrates how personal data is collected and used by social networking sites such as Facebook, Google, and MySpace.

The online activities of an individual can be recorded. The activities include what searches are made, which websites and webpages are visited, and what has been bought over the Internet. This is done without the knowledge of netizens. There are tools available, which can monitor and track the visits of a person to webpages. The tracking data is useful for businesses to offer their products and advertisement campaigns. This is done through tracking cookies. For example, Google collects information of a surfer by planting cookies as illustrated in Exhibit 18.7.

EXHIBIT 18.7
Privacy: Do not Expect it Online

As per the new privacy policy of Google, they may collect the following types of information when the user is using the search engine:

Information you provide When a user signs up for a Google Account, they ask them for personal information. They may combine the information the user submits under his account with information from other Google services or third parties to provide better experience and improve the quality of services. For certain services, they may give the user the opportunity to opt out of combining such information. Users can use the Google Dashboard to learn more about the information associated with their account. If a person uses Google services in conjunction with his/her Google Apps Account, Google provides such services along with the user's domain administration. The administrator will have access to your account information including your e-mail.

Cookies When a surfer visits Google, he/she sends one or more cookies to his/her computer. Google claims that they use cookies to improve the quality of their service, including, for storing user preferences, improving search results and ad selection, and tracking user trends (i.e., how people search). Google also uses cookies in its advertising services to help advertisers and publishers serve and manage ads across the web and on Google services.

Log information When a surfer accesses Google services via a browser, an application or any other client, Google's servers automatically record certain information. These server logs may include information such as his/her web request, his/her interaction with a service, Internet Protocol address, browser type, browser language, the date and time of his/her request and one or more cookies that may uniquely identify his/her browser or account.

User communications When the user sends e-mail or other communications to Google, the company may retain those communications in order to process his/her enquiries and respond to his/her requests. When the user sends and receives SMS messages to or from one of Google's services that provides an SMS functionality, the latter may collect and maintain information associated with those messages, such as the phone number, the wireless carrier associated with the phone number, the content of the message, and the date and time of the transaction. Google may use people's e-mail addresses to communicate with them about its services.

Affiliated Google services on other sites Google offers some of their services on or through other websites. Personal information that you provide on those sites may be sent to Google in order to deliver the service. They process such information under the new privacy policy, which came into force in January 2012.

Third party applications Google may make available third party applications such as gadgets or extensions through its services. The information collected by Google when the user enables a third party application is processed under the new privacy policy. Information collected by the third party application provider is governed by their privacy policies.

Location data Google offers location-enabled services, such as Google Maps and Latitude. If the user utilizes those services, Google may receive information about your actual location (e.g., GPS signals sent by a mobile device) or information that can be used to approximate a location (such as a cell ID).

Sources:
http://www.google.co.in/intl/en/policies/privacy, last accessed on 30 January 2012.
http://timesofindia.indiatimes.com/tech/news/internet/Googles-privacy-policy-raises-hackles/articleshow/11639316.cms, last accessed on 30 January 2012.

Cookies are small files that are automatically stored on the computer's hard drive when a user visits a certain website. You can see these cookies in the Internet temporary folder in your computer. The cookies update information about the visitor, his/her interests, the web browser software being used, and track visits to a website. The particular website, when visited again, finds the person's activities in the past from the planted cookies. This helps the website customize its offerings and advertisements as per the interests of the visitor. For example, when you visit and buy a book on amazon.com, the next time, the website suggests a book of interest to you. Similarly, when you book an air ticket at makemytrip.com, the next time, the site, if visited from the same computer and browser, displays the same origins and destinations.

INTELLECTUAL PROPERTY RIGHTS, COPYRIGHTS, AND PATENTS

Information system products are intangible in nature, and created by individuals and organizations. These software systems, designs, layouts, etc., are termed intellectual property (IP) and are similar to works of art, literature, music, cinema, etc. Unauthorized replication, distribution, and use of these products are easy but unethical in nature. Unauthorized distribution and use can cause enormous financial loss to the organizations who have invested in research and development of such products. To safeguard the interests of genuine owners, countries have enacted various laws and statutes. Some of the intellectual property rights (IPR) are protected through the copyright act and patent laws.

Software pose challenges to intellectual property laws as this is available in the digital media and easy to replicate. Software and information products can be easily copied, altered, and reorganized in a new format, which makes it difficult to prove theft in a court of law. For example, a new web page can be designed by copying and drawing various images, styles, and designs from a variety of sources already authored by someone else.

Copyrights

Copyright laws protect IP from being copied and prevent its unauthorized use by others. The violation of copyright comes under penal laws and attracts heavy penalty under the law. Unauthorized copying of computer software is known as software piracy and is considered a theft.

The Indian Copyright Act 1957, which was extensively amended in 1994, protects computer software against piracy. Though there is no mention of computer software in the Act, it is supposed to be classified under artistic work. As per the Act, copyright is a right given by the law to the creators of literary, dramatic, musical, and artistic works, producers of cinematograph films, and sound recordings. In fact, it is a bundle of rights including, inter alia, rights of reproduction, communication to the public, adaptation, and translation of the work. There could be slight variations in the composition of the rights depending on the work.

Copyright infringement is punishable under Section 63 of the Indian Copyright Act, which states that offence of infringement of copyright or other rights conferred by this Act are punishable. Any person who knowingly infringes or abets the infringement of the copyright in a work, or any other right conferred by this Act, shall be punishable with imprisonment for a term which shall not be less than six months but which may extend to three years and with fine which shall not be less than ₹50,000 but which may extend to ₹2,00,000.

The Indian Copyright Act does not comprehensively cover IT products like software. It covers works of literature, art, and music. The intricacy of technology products needs to be considered while drafting a comprehensive copyright Act like the Computer Software Copyright Act 1980 of the United States of America. Even today, there are arguments that say that software or IT products are not 'products' but services. Can a service be copyrighted? There are many aspects of software-related intellectual property that need refinement along with the laws governing them.

Patents

Ideas can be patented but not copyrighted. A 'patent' grants the registered owner exclusive monopoly on the idea behind the product for 20 years, sufficiently protecting the interests of the owner or inventor of the product. The idea behind such laws is to reward hard work and research effort, and to make the wide commercial use of the product viable by granting licences to others who wish to produce the same.

The key drivers of patent laws are originality, novelty, and invention. Earlier, software systems were not seen as patentable processes; however now, they have gained acceptance after a US court ruling. Since software (perceived as a work of art and literature) is protected by copyrights, patenting is not in much demand in India.

IMPACT OF INFORMATION TECHNOLOGY ON QUALITY OF LIFE

On the one hand, IT has positively affected organizations in terms of profitability, sustenance, competitive advantage, and performance; on the other hand, it has had negative impacts in some areas and the quality of life of individuals. These effects are beyond cybercrimes and intellectual property-related issues. Computers and IT have changed the basic fabric of society and introduced new ways of social interaction, communication, and employment. The application of new-age technology has affected life at the workplace and beyond it, which includes personal life, employment, and health of the individual.

Workplace Interaction and Culture

IT usage at the workplace has brought down personal interaction among co-workers, as most of the processes dealing with transaction, conversation, and communication are automated using tools such as enterprise systems, artificial intelligence, and knowledge base systems. With technology taking front stage, individual creativity, and analytical and decision-making skills have been adversely affected. E-mails and messaging have reduced interpersonal interactions, as even small and unimportant issues are dealt with them. With limited interaction, individuals have become isolated, thus affecting human behaviour.

For example, the finance director of a company maintains most of the communication with the chairman through e-mails. He/She hardly has any personal interaction with the chairman and is thus devoid of the personal warmth of the relationship.

Similarly, key decision-making is vested with the information empowered central leadership in the organizational hierarchy. Even the smallest of decisions are made by the higher management as they have easy access to information facilitated by technology.

Personal Life—Family, Work, and Leisure

Though 'anywhere computing' has helped the fast-paced executive in the performance and delivery of his/her duty, ubiquitous computing has taken a toll on the family life of the individual. Computing, powered by the Internet, has blurred the line separating professional life from family life. Business applications on mobile technologies have added extra impetus to the 24 × 7 work culture.

For example, we now see people logged on to their computers or smartphones, replying to e-mails from home or while travelling, and executives authorizing transactions from their laptops while on a leisure trip with family.

Family and friends have always been a source of support to individuals. However, nowadays people tend to spend more time on computers—surfing, gathering information, or simply for entertainment—which takes people away from family and friends. Research findings suggest that too much computer indulgence by children and teenagers leads to obsession and even harmful anti-social behaviour.

Employment Loss

Computerization is widely perceived to be anti-employment, especially in the public sector. We have discussed that while implementing enterprise solutions, business process reengineering (BPR) is aimed at simplifying processes and discarding redundant and unproductive processes. It eventually leads to saving of labour cost by cutting jobs. In such situations, middle-level managers and operations-level workers lose their jobs. According to economist Jeremy Rifkin (1993), we are entering a new phase in history—one characterized by the steady and inevitable decline of jobs. Just as the steam engine replaced slave labour in the 19th century, new intelligent technologies of the IT, biotechnology, and nanotechnology revolutions are fast replacing mass wage labour in the 21st century.

The number of people underemployed or without work is rising sharply as millions of new entrants into the workforce find themselves marginalized by an extraordinary high-technology revolution. Sophisticated computers, robotics, telecommunications, and other cutting-edge technologies are fast replacing human beings in virtually every sector and industry. In the past seven years alone, 14% of all the manufacturing jobs in the world have disappeared, as more and more human labour has been replaced with intelligent, automated technology. A similar technology-related displacement is occurring in the white collar and service industries.

According to Rifkin (1993), 'Many jobs are never coming back. Blue collar workers, secretaries, receptionists, clerical workers, sales clerks, bank tellers, telephone operators, librarians, wholesalers, and middle managers are just a few of the many occupations destined for virtual extinction'.

In India, there had been stiff resistance in the 1980s and 1990s from various public sector employees against introduction of computers and automation of workflow processes. They believed that computerization would lead to job cuts and thus, widespread unemployment. It is true that automation reduces labour engagement and has an adverse effect on employment. However, proper policies and planning can help organizations redesign work to minimize job cuts and reengage manpower in fruitful employment. At the macro level, the IT and IT-enabled services (ITES) sector may generate more jobs than what would be reduced by the application of information technologies in the business and government sectors.

Health Risks

Certain groups of people are exposed to repetitive jobs while working with computers. For example, data entry operators perform the same task throughout the day. This work is repetitive and monotonous and leads to professional stress. This is known as repetitive stress injury. It results from working with a computer keyboard. Repetitive stress injury is not the only illness computers cause. Back and neck pain, leg stress, and foot pain also result from poor ergonomic designs of workstations.

A survey in southern California in September–October 1999 by Rosen and Wiel (1999) indicated a new-age illness called technostress that was related to stress induced by use of computers. The symptoms include aggressiveness, impatience, hostility towards other humans, and fatigue. According to experts, computer users tend to believe that other human beings should behave like computers in providing instant responses, and be attentive, emotionless, and obedient.

INFORMATION TECHNOLOGY ACT 2008—KEY HIGHLIGHTS

The Information Technology Amendment Act 2008, as the new version of Information Technology Act 2000 is often referred to, has provided additional focus on information security. It has added several new sections on offences, including cyber terrorism and data protection.

The IT Act 2000, which was passed by the Parliament, contains cyber laws. This Act aims to provide the legal infrastructure for e-commerce in India. Cyber laws have a major impact on e-businesses and the new information economy in India. Thus, it is important to understand the various perspectives of the IT Act and what it offers.

The IT Act 2000 also aims to provide a legal framework so that legal sanctity is accorded to all electronic records and other activities carried out by electronic means. The Act states that unless otherwise agreed, an acceptance of contract may be expressed by electronic means of communication and the same shall have legal validity and enforceability. Earlier, there were no laws to deal with cybercrimes and electronic information was not valid and enforceable in a court of law.

The IT Act 2000 addressed the following issues:

- Legal recognition of electronic documents
- Legal recognition of digital signatures
- Offences and contraventions
- Justice dispensation systems for cybercrimes

The government of India brought major amendments to IT Act 2000 in the form of the Information Technology Amendment Act 2008. As this Act addresses the issue of cyber security, this has been highly appreciated by the technology community.

Section 69 of the Act empowers the central and state governments to intercept, monitor, or decrypt any information generated, transmitted, received, or stored in any computer resource, if it is necessary to do so in the interest of the sovereignty or integrity of India. The government can also secure assistance from computer experts in decrypting and deciphering data.

In view of the growth in transactions and communications carried out through electronic records, the Act seeks to empower government departments to accept filing, creation, and retention of official documents in the digital format. The Act has also proposed a legal framework for the authentication and originality of electronic records and communications through digital signatures.

From the perspective of e-commerce in India, the IT Act 2000 and its provisions contain many positive aspects. Firstly, the implications of these provisions for the e-businesses would be that e-mail would now be a valid and legal form of communication in our country that can be duly produced and approved in a court of law. Companies shall now be able to carry out e-commerce supported by legal infrastructure provided by the Act.

Digital signatures have been given legal validity and sanction in the Act. This has created scope for the entry of companies into the business of certifying authorities and issuing digital signature certificates. The Act now allows the government to issue notification on the web, thus heralding e-governance. The Act enables companies to file any form, application, or any other document with any office, authority, body, or agency owned or controlled by the appropriate government in electronic form by means of such electronic form as may be prescribed by the appropriate government. The Act also addresses the important issues of security, which are very critical to the success of electronic transactions.

Under the Act, it will now be possible for businesses to have a statutory remedy in case anyone breaks into their computer systems or network and causes damages or carries out unauthorized copying of data.

SUMMARY

Every business manager has the responsibility of promoting the ethical use of IT at the workplace. The ethical responsibility of managers includes properly performing their role as a vital human resource in the business system. It covers legal, privacy, and ethical issues in business. Privacy is the right of an individual to not disclose a certain amount of information about the self or allow it to be shared with their consent and with the assurance that it would be protected and treated as it were with the owner of the information. Ethics refers to the principles that define whether an action taken is morally right or wrong. Ethics is about values and human behaviour.

The issue of accountability and liability of a system user, developer, or system vendor are still not addressed. The basic question is—who is held responsible if anything goes wrong with the system? The emergence of the Internet and web technology has posed newer challenges to individual privacy. Online activities of an individual can be recorded. The activities include what searches are made, which website and web page is visited, and what has been bought over the Internet.

Software poses challenges to intellectual property laws, as this is available in the digital media and easy to replicate.

Copyright laws protect intellectual property from copying and unauthorized use by others. Violation of the copyright comes under penal laws and attracts heavy penalty under the laws. The Indian Copyright Act does not comprehensively cover IT products like software. The Act covers works of literature, art, and music. The intricacy of technology products needs to be considered while drafting a comprehensive copyright Act. A 'patent' grants the registered owner exclusive monopoly on the idea behind the product for twenty years, sufficiently protecting the interests of the owner or inventor of the product.

Though IT has improved business performances, it has had negative impacts on some areas and the quality of life of individuals. The areas affected besides the workplace are personal life, employment, and health of the individual.

The Information Technology Amendment Act 2008, the new version of the Information Technology Act 2000, has provided additional focus on information security. It has added several new sections on offences including cyber terrorism and data protection. Information Technology Act 2000 addressed the following issues—legal recognition of electronic documents, legal recognition of digital signatures, offences and contraventions, and justice dispensation systems for cybercrimes.

KEY TERMS

Copyrights The legal rights of a creator or owner of intellectual property that protects them from copying and unauthorized use by others.

Cyber terrorism The use of the Internet for spreading illegal messages and rumours that cause unrest in the society.

E-governance Abbreviation for electronic governance, implies technology driven governance for delivery of government services to the citizen and businesses.

Ethical responsibility Responsibility to promote ethical use of information technology at the workplace.

Internet cookies Small files that are automatically stored on the computer's hard drive when a user visits certain websites.

Patents Registering an idea and concept behind a product and granting the registered owner exclusive monopoly on the idea behind the product for twenty years.

Privacy violation Collection of information and data about a person without his/her knowledge.

Social networking sites Websites that promote and share ideas by groups of people having common interests.

Technostress An illness or stress induced by computer usage.

CONCEPT REVIEW QUESTIONS

1. What are the various ethical and social responsibilities of businesses? Elaborate on the ethical responsibilities of systems.
2. What kind of legal, privacy, and ethical issues have cropped up because of IT?
3. What are the social responsibilities and liabilities of IT professionals?
4. Explain why it is so difficult to hold software services liable for failure in performance or harm to users.
5. What is privacy and how is it challenged by the Internet? Explain with examples.
6. What are intellectual property rights? Explain copyrights and patents.
7. How has information technology had a negative impact on life? Give suitable examples.
8. Describe the IT Act 2000. What are the key provisions of the Act?

CRITICAL THINKING QUESTIONS

1. 'Though IT has brought about efficiency in businesses, it has reduced the dignity of life.' Do you agree with this statement? Why or why not?
2. 'Privacy and Internet are opposite poles.' Critically examine this statement and suggest ways to protect privacy in the Internet age.
3. Exhibit 18.5 illustrates a real-life case where IT professionals were arrested for reasons such as non-performance of 'contractual obligation' or 'visa issues'.

Can a similar stance be taken for 'non-performance' by a software system?
4. The IT Act 2000 does not cover the burning issues of spamming, privacy protection, etc. Why doesn't India have an anti-spam law as yet?
5. The Copyright Act 1957, amended in 1994, still lacks in power to deal with software piracy issues. Suggest what action should be taken to protect software piracy in India?

MIS DEVELOPMENT

Study and analyse how IT has affected (both positively and negatively) one's

- office and work culture
- family life
- social life
- employment opportunities

Browse the Internet further for news and research in this area. Create a table comparing the good that IT has brought to mankind and the challenges we face in the aforementioned areas. What do you see? Are the benefits and positive impacts outnumbering the challenges?

REFERENCES

Jawadekar, Waman, *Management Information System*, Tata McGraw-Hill, New Delhi, 2008.

Laudon, Ken, Jane Laudon, and Rajanish Dass, *Management Information System*, Pearson Education, Singapore, 2010.

O'Brien, James A., George M. Marakas, and Ramesh Behl, *Management Information Systems*, Tata McGraw-Hill, New Delhi, 2007.

Turban, Efraim, Jay Aronson, and Ting-Peng Liang, *Decision Support Systems and Intelligent Systems*, Pearson Education, New Delhi, 2005 .

'IT Act of India 2000', http://www.cyberlawsindia.net/ Information-technology-act-of-india.html, last accessed on 5 February 2012.

'Mizuho Bank head to resign over computer glitch', http://

in.reuters.com/article/2011/04/23/idINIndia-5652 7920110423, last accessed on 10 February 2012.

Rifkin, Jeremy (1993), 'End of Work', http://www.foet. org/lectures/lecture-end-work.html, last accessed on 5 February 2012.

Rosen and Weil, 'A comparison of Y2K attitudes in USA and Slovakia', December 1999, http://www.technostress.com/ y2kusaslovakia.htm, last accessed in September 2012.

http://timesofindia.indiatimes.com/tech/news/internet/ Computer-glitch-halts-presses-in-New-Zealand/articleshow/ 9454764.cms, last accessed on 10 February 2012.

http://www.gadgetslane.com/royal-mail%E2%80%99s-computer-glitch-affects-12000-post-offices-123948.html, last accessed on 10 February 2012.

CASE STUDY

How Facebook/Google Uses your Personal Information

As of March 2012, Facebook's worth is estimated to be at least $75 billion. However, unlike other big-ticket corporations, it does not have an inventory of widgets or gadgets, cars, or phones. Facebook's inventory consists of personal data—yours and mine.

Facebook makes money by selling ad space to companies that want to reach us. Advertisers choose key words or details such as relationship status, location, activities, favourite books, and employment, and then Facebook runs the ads for the targeted subset of its 845 million users. If you indicate that you like cupcakes, live in a certain neighbourhood, and have invited friends over, expect an ad from a nearby bakery to appear on your page. The magnitude of online information that Facebook has of each of us for targeted marketing is stunning. In Europe, laws give people the right to know what data companies have about them, but that is not the case in the United States.

Facebook made $3.2 billion in advertising revenue in the year 2011, which formed 85% of its total revenue. However, Facebook's inventory of data and its revenue from advertising are small potatoes compared to some others. Google took in more than 10 times as much, with an estimated $36.5 billion in advertising revenue in 2011, by analysing what people sent over Gmail and what they searched on the web, and then using that data to sell ads. Hundreds of other companies have also staked claims on people's online data by depositing software called cookies or other tracking mechanisms on people's computers and in their browsers. If you have mentioned anxiety in an e-mail,

done a Google search for 'stress', or started using an online medical diary that lets you monitor your mood, expect ads for medications and services to treat your anxiety.

Google, the web giant, has introduced a new privacy policy that will allow it to track your move on the web. Google says that the new privacy policy will allow it to offer better services, including more relevant search results. However, web experts have raised concerns over the potential misuse of data and breach of privacy. According to Google's new privacy policy that has come into effect from 1 March 2012, the company is 'getting rid of over 60 different privacy policies across Google services and replacing them with one that's shorter, easier to read' and something that will enable it to 'create intuitive experience across Google'. Unlike in the past when Google had allowed users to choose personalized services, this time there is no option to opt out.

'Our new privacy policy makes clear that, if you are signed in, we may combine information you have provided from one service with information from other services. In short, we will treat you as a single user across all our products, which will mean a simpler, more intuitive Google experience', said Alma Whitten, Google's director of privacy, in a post on the company's official blog.

Whitten gave an example of how this information will be used. 'We can make search better—figuring out what you really mean when you type in Apple, Jaguar, or Pink. We can provide more relevant ads too', she wrote. 'We can provide reminders that you are going to be late for a meeting based on your location, your calendar, and an understanding of what the traffic is like that day. Or ensure that our spelling suggestions, even for your friends' names, are accurate because you have typed them before.'

The privacy policy from Google is at the heart of its new business strategy as it works to keep the search engine relevant and its services fresh in the face of social networking websites such as Twitter and Facebook. It is also prompted by the proliferation of devices such as smartphones and tablets. However, privacy experts are not amused. Sunil Abraham, director of centre for Internet and society, said the new changes are not good for a consumer's privacy.

'I understand that Google collects the data so that it can build a 360 degree profile of a user and based on the information serve relevant advertisements. However, there is no reason for them to store this data for long. Storing data makes it prone to misuse by authorities as well as corporations', said Abraham. Another problem, he said, is that different services are used for different purposes. 'I do not want my bakery shop owner to know what kind of medicines I buy from the nearby medical store', said Abraham.

The data collected at social sites is being used by other agencies as well. The internal revenue service in US searches Facebook and MySpace for evidence of tax evaders' income and whereabouts, and US citizenship and immigration services have been known to scrutinize photos and posts to confirm family relationships or weed out sham marriages.

Sometimes, employers decide whether to hire people based on their online profiles, with one study indicating that 70% of recruiters and human resource professionals in the United States have rejected candidates based on data found online. A company called Spokeo gathers online data for employers, the public, and anyone else who wants it. The company even posts ads urging 'HR recruiters—click here now!' and asking women to submit their boy friends' e-mail addresses for an analysis of their online photos and activities to learn, 'Is he cheating on you?'

Your application for credit could be declined not on the basis of your own finances or credit history, but on the basis of aggregate data—what other people whose likes and dislikes are similar to yours have done. If guitar players or divorcing couples are more likely to renege on their credit card bills, then the fact that you have looked at guitar ads or sent an e-mail to a divorce lawyer might cause a data aggregator to classify you as less credit-worthy. In 2007 and 2008, the online advertising company NebuAd, contracted with six Internet service providers to install hardware on their networks that monitored users' Internet activities and transmitted that data to NebuAd's servers for analysis and use in marketing.

For an average of six months, NebuAd copied every e-mail, web search, or purchase that some 4,00,000 people sent over the Internet. Other companies such as Healthline Networks Inc., have in-house limits on what private information they will collect. Data aggregators' practices conflict with what people say they want. A 2008 Consumer Reports poll of 2000 people found that 93% thought Internet companies should always ask for permission before using personal information, and 72% wanted the right to opt out of online tracking.

A study by Princeton survey research associates in 2009 using a random sample of 1000 people found that 69% thought that the United States should adopt a law giving people the right to learn everything a website knows about them. The citizens need a do-not-track law, similar to the do-not-call one.

Discussion Questions

1. What are the ethical, legal, and privacy issues highlighted by this case?
2. If you know what is being captured and tracked about you, it does not amount to privacy violation. Do you agree with this statement? Why or why not?
3. Do you agree that personal information is no more 'personal' in the era of social networking and collaborative knowledge creation? Substantiate your answers with real-life examples.
4. Social networking has given rise to a new form of advertising, that is, social marketing. Do you agree that there is no personal harm if your advertiser knows your personal tastes and preferences?

Sources:

Andrews, Lori, 'How Facebook uses your data', *New York Times*, 6 February 2012, reproduced by *The Times of India*, 6 February 2012, http://timesofindia.indiatimes.com/tech/news/internet/How-Facebook-uses-your-data/articleshow/11775188.cms, last accessed on 15 March 2012.

Anwar, Jayed, 'Google's privacy policy raises hackles', 26 January 2012, http://timesofindia.indiatimes.com/tech/news/internet/Googles-privacy-policy-raises-hackles/articleshow/11639316.cms, last accessed on 15 March 2012.

http://www.google.co.in/intl/en/policies/privacy/, last accessed on 15 March 2012.

19

Information Systems Leadership

> *Enterprises seeking ways to improve the ERP/business application support organization should look beyond strategies aimed at a tactical reduction in support costs. IT has become the single biggest source of productivity improvements in our economy, yet many business executives view the IT organization as a cost centre that should be minimized. This is not surprising since, for many enterprises, annual support costs for ERP and other large business applications can be 10% to 30% of the initial implementation budget.*
>
> —GARTNER RESEARCH REPORT

LEARNING OBJECTIVES

After studying this chapter, you will be able to

- understand the evolution of the information system (IS) function
- appreciate the management of the IS function
- be aware of the profile and role of a chief information officer (CIO)
- understand the challenges faced by a CIO

EXHIBIT 19.1

Lanco Infratech: It's all about People, Process, and Technology

Lanco Infratech, which has been successful in marching ahead of its competitors such as Tata Power, Reliance Power, and Adani Group, in becoming the biggest private sector power generator in the country, is being recognized as a force to reckon with.

Headquartered in Gurgaon, Lanco is a 25-year old group and is concentrated on engineering, procurement, and construction (EPC), power, solar and other natural resources, and infrastructure development. Post its initial public offer (IPO) in November 2006, Lanco became a listed company. The company attained a gross revenue of ₹11,265 crore in March 2011. It is fast emerging as one of the top three power developers in the private sector in India with 4410 megawatt (MW) under operation, 4968 MW under construction, and 7103 MW of projects under development.

The company's information systems department is being handled by a veteran chief information officer (CIO), Ajay Kumar Dhir, who headed the same department in OP Jindal Group, prior to his stint in Lanco. Known for his out-of-the-box thinking, Dhir is a man of vision who is spearheading the company to the next level of growth. He clearly believes in the philosophy of 'walking the talk'. Brimming with new ideas, he is perceived as someone who has evolved from being a pure technocrat to a business enabler. In an interview, Dhir talks about ICT deployments, communication strategies, CIO concerns, etc. and shares his views on the plans and vision that he has laid out for the company. He delves into his responsibilities, elucidates how he is gearing up for the challenges coming his way, and shares his priorities for the future.

What are your key responsibilities in your role as Group CIO of Lanco Infratech?

Lanco is a very large and diversified group with interests in power (thermal, hydro, and solar), mining, EPC, construction, and real estate. The company has a global footprint and is expanding very fast, with over 40 locations in India and abroad. As the group CIO, I am responsible for information technology (IT), information security, governance, risk and compliance, SAP implementation, creating a shared services organization for IT and SAP, and most importantly, ensuring that the IT strategy and initiatives are totally aligned with the organization's mission and objectives.

What challenges do you foresee in your role?

IT is all about people, processes, and technology. The biggest challenge and opportunity is to create a world class technologically leveraged organization within a fixed time frame, with the best processes and the right people skills and capabilities. Another challenge, or rather, an area of attention, is creating the right climate and framework for IT within the organization, and effective use of the investments made so far.

Tell us about your top priorities for the year at Lanco Infratech.

We wish to achieve the following—create the IT vision and roadmap for the group across all entities and business verticals; stabilize the existing SAP implementation and drive it in new businesses and regions globally; create a world-class technology infrastructure, which will help the organization become more agile; standardize processes across the group; build a robust framework of governance, risk management and compliance; create a shared services organization that caters to the group-wide requirements for IT infrastructure management and SAP; and build a corporate data centre and a world-class team.

How do you compare your role at Jindal with Lanco Infratech, considering the change in the industry vertical?

The role is quite similar to what I have been doing over the last several years, in Jindal and elsewhere. I now look to deliver exceptional value to the organization with my skills and experience of almost three decades and having worked in diverse industries and environment in India as well as abroad. My passion is to work with people, create best in class systems, and help organizations get the maximum return on investment (ROI) from their IT assets. With a large scale of operations and diverse business, it is a very interesting profile and I am very excited about the same.

What are your top concerns as a CIO of one of the major private groups?

As a CIO, it is very tough to single out one concern. There are many priorities that I have to keep in mind while discharging my duties. However, if you ask me to share some

(Contd)

Exhibit 19.1 (Contd)

of them, then they are to keep doing more with less. To innovate, I keep urging teams to think out-of-the-box like a fish out of water. Performance of the team translates into the performance of the company; therefore, I keep motivating the team to perform well and better. It is also imperative for me to connect with the business and the people, equally. In my role, I have to see that I help the organization be more agile and nimble. I keep constant check on myself to align the four main pillars—people, processes, business, and technology—to work in the best interest of the company and of course to create a risk assured framework.

What processes and innovations have you deployed in your organization to make it more effective?

Innovation is a continuous journey; one has to start somewhere and explore. We are using industry standard processes for managing our core initiatives in IT and SAP. There is a framework for fostering, recognizing, and rewarding innovation and there are many noteworthy initiatives that have been deployed across the organization.

Security is very crucial for a company. How do you manage the security and reliability concerns?

Security is very imperative for a company. So, we have a well-defined policy for information security and IT governance. This is our IT/IS blue book and is called information systems policy and procedures (ISPP). This is being implemented across the organization in a phased manner, with proper communication, and in an inclusive manner.

Sources:

Raval, Abhishek, 'IT is all about people, processes, and technology', BizTech, 10 February 2012, http://biztech2.in.com/interviews/people/it-is-all-about-people-processes-and-technology/101022/0, last accessed on 8 February 2013.

Singh, Archana, 'Interview with Ajay Dhir, Lanco Inftratech', 24 August 2011, http://voicendata.ciol.com/content/speak/111082401.asp, last accessed on 12 February 2012.

http://www.lancogroup.com/DynTestform.aspx?pageid=4, last accessed on 30 August 2012.

As seen in Exhibit 19.1, the information systems department,headed by the CIO at Lanco Infratech plays a key role in setting-up IT infrastructure, information security, governance of the IT systems, compliance and risk mitigation efforts, enterprise application implementation, and ensuring that the IT goals and objectives are aligned with the organizational missions and vision. The CIO is responsible for creating an efficient IT organization, introducing innovations in IT, motivating the team to perform, and coordinating between the business and people in the organization. The interview with the seasoned CIO highlights the roles, responsibilities, and tasks of the IT function of the modern business organization.

In this chapter, we will discuss how information systems organization evolved as a function of business management, managing various aspects of IT in the organization, and roles and responsibilities of the head of the IT department.

EVOLUTION OF INFORMATION SYSTEMS FUNCTION

Information systems functions have undergone fundamental changes over the past decade. The IS function has migrated from the back office to the executive committee, from the cost centre to the revenue driver, and from the support centre for other functions in the business to the strategic cornerstone in the e-business organization. Over a period of time, the IS function has come to be known by various names such as electronic data processing (EDP), management information system (MIS), IT, and systems—the primary function of which remains to manage computer operations.

Traditionally, system managers who oversaw IT/IS functions used to report to finance managers. Since most of the MIS was focused on finances and operations, it was treated as a sub-function of finance. As information systems grew and assumed critical importance in the organization, the systems function was headed at the director-level known as chief information officer or CIO. Figures 19.1 and 19.2 illustrate this evolution.

The Internet and enterprise solutions have changed and moved IT from a back-office personal productivity tool to a business strategy tool. The enterprise and collaboration tools have brought in new levels of automation, creating the need for IT strategic planning and control, architecture development and monitoring, and manpower management. The IT function has assumed a critical role, as information is treated at par with any other resource such as material, human resource, machine, or finance. The information resource management concept focuses on management, availability, and usage of information. Information is viewed as a key resource and investment in IT is made to gain a competitive advantage. Thus, information management is an approach to organizing and integrating the diverse elements of an IS.

IS leadership is a critical area for organizations today because of their increasing dependence on IS, both for operational stability and for enablement of process innovation and business strategy. IS leadership is distinctive from general leadership because the CIO is expected to combine IS technical skills with a deep understanding of the organization across all functions from operational to strategic.

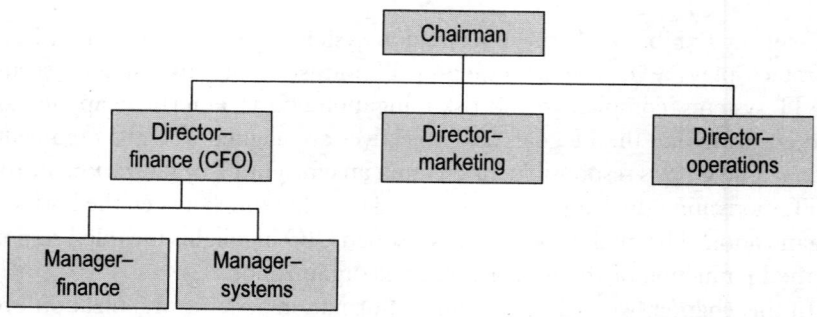

Fig.19.1   Organizational structure in the early stages of development

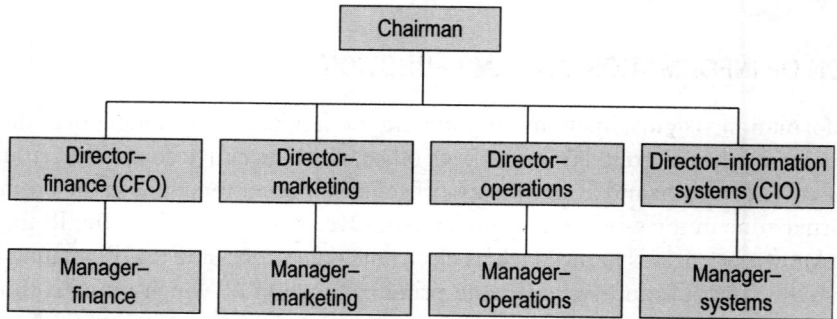

Fig.19.2   Organizational structure giving prominence to information systems

MANAGEMENT OF INFORMATION SYSTEMS FUNCTION

In the early stages of computing, the primary role of the IS function was to support the other functions in the organization. As IT became indispensable and critical, the functions became more strategic in nature and the title of the IS head graduated up from MIS executive to CIO and chief technology officer (CTO). According to a study in the US by Applegate and Elam (1992), the major activities of an IS executive were IT strategic planning and control, IT architecture management and standards development, human resource management (HRM), and IS operations. As per this study, an increasing number of IS executives reported directly to the CEO, and only a few were members of the senior management/strategic policy committee.

The IS functions, as envisioned in the modern e-business organization, are described as follows:

Managing Information Systems Operations

Information systems operation management refers to the task of purchase, maintenance, and use of hardware, software, networks, security systems, etc. System administrators perform a number of periodical tasks required for the stable and effective working of IT systems and to ensure data and information security. This includes ensuring that the hardware, software, and network infrastructure is up and running. The related activities include hardware replacements, repairs, network optimization, operating system updates, patches, and configuration changes, performing backups and restores, system monitoring, and troubleshooting, etc.

Organizations regularly upgrade their systems and the responsibility for this task lies with the IT department. It is necessary to make a comprehensive technical and financial analysis of the likely improvements before buying and installing new IT products and solutions.

For example, the IT department of the Transport Corporation of India (TCI) Ltd always strives to upgrade its systems and has been able to set new benchmarks for the logistics industry in the country.

Managing Application Development Projects

The application development function of an IT department depends on the scale and business style of the company. Smaller companies opt for ready-to-use software. Bigger and specialized businesses need more custom-built software. If the organization goes for in-house application development, the task of the IT department would involve managing a software design and development workflow that includes system study, designing, coding, modifying, debugging, testing, and documenting of the application. Managing application development requires managing and coordinating activities of teams of system analysts, developers, testing engineers, and domain experts working on a system development project. The IT department ensures timely and cost-effective completion of such projects.

The IT department takes initiatives to carry out strategically important projects to improve the company's IT infrastructure. Usually, such projects are performed by IT specialists and are monitored and controlled by the CIO and other functional heads such as the CFO or even the chief executive officer (CEO). Thus, the IT supervisors manage the technological aspect and other business supervisors control the financial, time, and strategic parts of the project. For example, the IT department of Max Healthcare Ltd managed the development and implementation of electronic health record software.

Managing User Services

Large organizations have a number of users of hardware, software, Internet, intranet, e-commerce portals, etc. These users require the support of the IT department in troubleshooting, maintenance, and training. Many companies have set up support desks as a part of the IT department, which provides help to users. These tasks are taken care of by the respective technology experts. For example, a hardware replacement or repair is looked after by the hardware engineer, while software-related support of bug fixing is taken care of by the software support engineer. These IT experts and their tasks are illustrated under the HRM function of an IT organization.

For example, Archies Limited maintains an IT organization consisting of around 10–12 system experts and technicians, who provide all kinds of user services for its 200 retail locations and nine warehouses. Similarly, TCI, the largest freight mover and logistics company in India, maintains a large IT organization consisting of around 200 personnel. The organization develops its own software and maintains the large base of hardware, huge network scattered over the country, and user base.

Human Resource Management of Information Technology

The success and failure of an IT organization depends on the quality of its people. It is always the greatest challenge for the human resource manager to recruit, train, and retain IT experts. The IT organization helps to organize, retain, and train qualified personnel in this highly technical field. The IT organization consists of various technically qualified personnel. Some of the experts and their jobs are as follows:

IT Director/CIO   Strategic planning, budgeting, department management, purchasing, interpersonal relationships, coordination with CFO/CEO, etc.

Network administrator   Managing network services and servers

Database administrator   Managing and maintaining databases

Webmaster   Coordinating content, managing web software, server, and graphics, editing, designing graphic and web communications

Hardware engineer   Setting-up, maintaining, repairing, and upgrading hardware and equipment

System analyst   Developing specifications and helping users during implementation of new software

Software support engineer   Providing troubleshooting, handholding, and first-level support to users.

PROFILE OF CHIEF INFORMATION OFFICERS

Though CIOs are responsible for the overall functioning and management of all IT functions in an organization, they are not supposed to manage day-to-day information services and support. The

EXHIBIT 19.2

State of the Indian CTO: Closer to the Top

Chief information officers (CIOs) mostly do not report to the CFO any more. Only 40% of our respondents did that, clearly reflecting their coming into their own. This depicts a more strategic role of IT in an organization, rather than being only an expense. If CIOs report to a managing committee/CEO or the COO, then their role is more towards growing the business or making a positive impact in some way. Moreover, the penetration of IT in the business has increased multifold and so has the understanding of the CIO of the business processes of the company. She/He is one of the few people in the company who touches all aspects of the business—be it the supply chain, marketing, sales, production, HR, finance, or strategic decision-making. That CIOs are increasingly sought out by their business counterparts to help make business decisions is clearly reflected in what we found—65% of our respondent CIOs say that they are on the management committees of their organizations.

On the other hand, the verdict is still out on IT being considered a cost centre in the organization. About half the CIOs say that IT is still a cost for the company, while the other half either do not consider it as a cost centre or they are undecided. In comparison with last year's survey, this is a 6% increase in companies that consider IT as a cost centre.

CIOs in India report that their IT budgets are expected to grow 12.8% in 2012, while CIOs globally expect flat growth, according to a global survey of CIOs by Gartner Inc.'s executive programmes. CIOs from India said their budgets support business strategies concentrating on growth and innovation. CIOs increasingly see technologies such as analytics/business intelligence, mobility, cloud and social networking in combination rather than isolation to address business priorities. Changing the customer experience requires changing the way the company interacts externally rather than operates internally.

Sources:

Channana, Geetaj, 'State of the Indian CTO', 11 January 2011, http://www.thectoforum.com/content/state-indian-cto, last accessed on 18 February 2012.

'Indian CIO IT budgets outshine global counterparts', 6 January 2012, http://biztech2.in.com/news/innovation-amp;-leadership/indian-cio-it-budgets-outshine-global-counterparts/126502/0, last accessed on 18 February 2012.

CIO is the top executive responsible for strategic use of IT in business. He/She concentrates on IT planning and strategy and ensures that IT helps the company meet its strategic business objectives.

Accordingly to Jaiswal (2004), the 'information' part of the CIO's job is getting increasingly important. The effective and strategic use of common enterprise-wide information requires someone with a cross-functional perspective. CIOs have taken a leadership role in reengineering their organizations' business processes and the underpinning IT infrastructures to achieve more productive, efficient, and valuable use of information with the enterprise.

The Indian corporate world appreciates the role of the CIO and hence most companies place the CIO at a senior level. For example, Star India, Reliance Capital, Raymond, Bajaj Electricals, Welspun, Thermax, Tata Chemicals, Ambuja Cement, etc., have CIOs reporting to the CEO. Exhibit 19.2 illustrates the findings of a study showing how the Indian CIO/CTO is moving towards the top management and is instrumental in strategic business planning.

ROLE OF CHIEF INFORMATION OFFICERS

The role of a CIO is rapidly evolving. From the 'MIS guy' of close to a decade ago to a business support functionary, CIOs are fast becoming important business enablers. The ones who are thinking and articulating business are finding themselves on management committees, and even the board. They are becoming instrumental in shaping the future of their organizations.

According to Desiderato (2010), when running an IT organization, CIOs and other IT leaders must focus on the broader picture. Their mission is clear—the CIO is foremost a business leader—one who relentlessly delivers IT in support of business objectives, while continually seeking to drive down overall costs.

The CIO plays many roles in the organization. These roles can be grouped under two broad categories—general leadership roles and IS leadership roles.

General Leadership Roles

A CIO belongs to the senior management group and is at the helm of the IT affairs. He/She is responsible for making information available where and when it is required, taking decisions related to IS planning and deployment, playing an interpersonal leadership role, and for hiring, training, and motivating IT personnel.

Informational Role

The CIO is the owner, custodian, initiator, and implementer of IS in the organization. He/She is responsible for dissemination of the required information to the internal and external stakeholders such as peer groups, top management, suppliers, customers, government, and the media. Every user group in need of some information looks up to the CIO and expects him/her to provide the same. The CIO is responsible for data management and information governance.

The criticality of the information role has given birth to concepts, such as master data management and enterprise information management strategy, which are the foundations of the information governance programme. Master data management is a technology-enabled business discipline in which business and IT organizations work together to ensure the uniformity, accuracy, stewardship, semantic consistency, and accountability of an organization's official and shared master data assets.

Decisional Role

The CIO takes all the decisions related to an IT organization, human resources, deployment, and acquisition. He/She influences the overall strategy and translates the organization's business strategies into information system actions. He/She is a complete entrepreneur who understands the needs of the business and develops solutions that change business situations. The CIO monitors and scans the environment and keeps himself abreast of the latest happenings in the technology space. He/She takes decisions to implement the latest technology in the organization. The responsibility of raising an IT organization lies with the CEO, who takes care of hiring, training, supervising, and motivating IT personnel. It is the CEO who takes decisions regarding allocation of human, financial, and information resources. He/She defines IT budgets and takes control measures.

Interpersonal Role

The CIO develops a working relationship between IT and other business functions in the organization. The modern CIO is expected to cross the boundaries of departments and become involved in other management functions such as marketing, production, distribution, and finance. He/She plays the role of a spokesperson not only for the IT function, but also for the organization as a whole. In large organizations, the CIO is in charge of thousands of people and is bestowed with a heavy annual budget. The position requires strong organizational leadership and financial management skills, and an ability to balance short-term realities against long-term objectives. The

CIO should be able to communicate the business case to the technical team and the technical issues to the business people.

For example, Ajay Dhir, CIO, Lanco Infratech says, 'Performance of the team translates into the performance of the company, therefore, I keep motivating the team to perform well and better. It is also imperative for me to connect with the business and the people, equally. In my role, I have to see that I help the organizations be more agile and nimble. I keep constant check on myself to align the four main pillars—people, processes, business, technology—to work in the best interest of the company.'

Information Systems Leadership Roles

Information systems leadership involves designing blueprints for the IT roadmap of the organization. On the one hand, it involves being an architect and a change agent; on the other hand, it calls for monitoring the affairs and measuring the performance of IS systems. Innovation is something that should come naturally to the CIO. The IS leadership role requires the CIO to be innovative and he/she needs to add value to the business. Every IT initiative is carefully analysed by the CIO in an inclusive manner, with total cost of ownership (TCO), RoI, and KRA being the focus areas. Strategic planning and aligning IT with organizational goals, integrating systems and processes, and implementing security and privacy measures are still the top three priorities for CIOs. Exhibit 19.3 illustrates the key roles.

EXHIBIT 19.3
CIO Strategies for Success

The economic slowdown has accelerated enterprise transformation and India is now shifting into focusing on newer strategies for management and IT. The role of a CIO is no more restricted to handling IT issues; he/she is slowly becoming the key business driver. CIOs are responsible for shaping up the future of technology through their intelligent insights and address strategic initiatives and also manage businesses successfully across industries and verticals. The role of a CIO has changed from being an information officer to being an innovative officer. In a strategy summit, CIOs highlighted the following skill sets:

- Setting clear and smart goals
- The planning and budgeting skills of CIOs and involving their teams during this process for success of any project
- Defining key result areas (KRAs) in advance, so that there is no ambiguity
- Communicating with all stakeholders and planning the strategy of communication
- Playing along with team and not as an individual
- Deploying, selecting, and training the right person for the job
- Focusing on past mistakes and managing change skills

- Leading from the front during a crisis
- Celebrating small successes with the team
- To drive the business forward, the CIO needs to see technology from the business angle and not vice versa
- Aligning his/her KRAs with the business KRAs and business achievements should drive CIO bonuses
- Change management is vital for the success of any new initiative and the CIO has to drive change management as much as the business
- At times, the CIO also has to reorient the business understanding of technology and sell the benefits of technology to the business
- Return on investments are a reality and even transformational technology has to pass the RoI test

Source:
'CIO strategies for success: Topflight CIOs explain their priorities', *Silicon India*, http://www.siliconindia.com/shownews/CIO_Strategies_for_Success_topflight_CIOs_explain_their_strategic_priorities_for_2011-nid-102531-cid-69.html/2, last accessed on 22 February 2012.

According to Desiderato (2010), 'CIOs must innovate with the business and continually demonstrate the competence, strength, and value of the IT organization. All of this is going on while budgets are being challenged, e-mails are piling up, and the leadership team is tending to the careers and morale of a complex mix of highly intelligent programmers, analysts, and IT support staff.'

Solution Architect

Information systems managers, with greater operating responsibility, act as chief architects responsible for strategic planning and aligning IT goals with the organization's goals and objectives. Many IT organizations neither have a defined architecture strategy nor a stated evolutionary plan. The long-term objective must be built with sound architectural guidelines. The CIO must have an architectural strategy as well as an infrastructure upgrade strategy, based on the mission of the business. As the business grows and the needs of the organization grow proportionately, IT cannot remain static. The CIO must have an IT strategic plan that is constructed along the business strategy plan.

For example, Meheriar Patel, CTO and head, IT, Globus, says, 'Build resilient architecture, for future ready business demands. Make information technology lead from the front and make a difference for this growth to success.'

Change Leader

CIOs must function as change agents and initiate the process of business process reengineering. According to Jaiswal (2004), CIOs must work harder to escape the organizational status quo, and venture out of their technologist comfort zone to put the plan into action. A CIO must keep enhancing this influence by making sure that they understand the strategies of the internal customers and finding people who can help them. The CIO should consider implementing a culture that values the continuous improvement of the IT organization. This is crucial in helping the CIO and the IT staff avoid complacency. IT teams are complex, and technology and good businesses are also evolving. If IT organizations do not continually raise their game, their performance will be mediocre.

A CIO's initiative to develop transformation programmes is an effective approach and should be done on a regular basis. It should not be assumed that transformational programmes are projects that may eventually come to an end. The IT organization must make clear to the organization that continuous improvement is the true goal. Like many of the other success ingredients, transformation, or continuous improvement, must be inculcated into the culture of the IT organization.

Monitoring Information Technology Operations

One of the major responsibilities of the CIO is to establish and maintain the credibility of the IT organization. According to Desiderato (2010), 'Run the shop effectively—it seems basic and unglamorous, but this is the most fundamental principle of running IT. Nothing will undermine the credibility of IT leadership more than instability and a broken platform. Without predictable, reliable, and stable systems and infrastructure, permanent progress is not possible. Transformation goals cannot be achieved, building new software (on a broken platform) becomes more difficult, and multi-sourcing grows immensely more complicated and risky'.

We have discussed in Chapter 3 as to how IT can be used for strategic advantage and bringing in efficiency and efficacy. The IT department should not only focus on providing better service to the users across the business but also help businesses operate better. Thus, the CIO should explore running their business like a service operation rather than a cost centre and develop metrics that track and evaluate the performance of the IT staff, equipment, and applications.

The major part of a CIO's role is to ensure that equipments are put on optimum utilization and the IT staff is performing efficiently. The user must be made aware of the opportunities arising

Table 19.1 Common benchmarks for IT functions against which performance can be measured

Process/Benchmark area	Example of benchmark
Technical	• Number of projects completed in a given time • Number of projects done on time and within budget • Lines of code per developer per month • Average machine capacity utilization • Occurrences of defects/errors in a period of time • Overall satisfaction in project development
Service	• Satisfaction of users with IS function • User satisfaction in response to problem-solving • Manager satisfaction with speed of system development • Percentage of problem-solving in the first instance/contact • Average time taken in problem solution • Number of problems attended to per IT person per month • Total number of problems handled • Overall satisfaction in service area
Human Resource	• Percentage of IS staff with technical degrees • Percentage of IS staff with advanced degrees • Training sessions organized for non-IS staff • Courses taken by IS employees to enhance their skill • Overall satisfaction in human resource development
Financial	• Percentage of cost for telecommunications • IT expense as percentage of revenue • IT investment as percentage of assets • IS payroll with respect to company payroll • IS payroll as a percentage of IS budget • Percentage of IS expense in R&D • Value of an in-house project compared with direct cost involved • Overall satisfaction in budgetary allocations to IS
Operations	• Average number of job handled (e.g. number of invoices + accounting vouchers entered + purchase orders created + material receipts note + salary vouchers produced, etc.) • Average machine time engaged per employee per period • Percentage of employees having a workstation • Average downtime of machines • Percentage of errors in data entry by the staff • Overall satisfaction in data-entry operations

as a result of technical innovations, and how the new systems can help them in performance of their duties.

Measuring Performance

Organizations tend to see IT departments as cost centres; and thus use cost-oriented evaluations such as decreasing costs or RoI. IT is managed on cost-driven, rather than value-driven metrics. Thus, the performance of an IT organization is measured in terms of RoI, TCO, or KRA. The CIO's role includes initiating the process of measuring performance and evaluating it against certain benchmarks. Although organizations benchmark IS/IT functions for a variety of reasons, the reasons most commonly cited include justifying the company's investment in IT, evaluating the performance of the IS group and its management, and improving the IS functions within the organization. Benchmarking may also be done as part of a more extensive cost assessment or cost reduction effort, a total quality management (TQM) programme, or a strategic planning effort. The budgeting process periodically motivates IS managers to perform some benchmarking. Most organizations subject development and acquisition of new systems to stringent RoI hurdles.

With the increasing popularity and availability of outsourcing services, many organizations require a justification for usage of the existing systems as well. CIOs can measure the performance of IT functions using the benchmarking criteria suggested in Table 19.1.

CHALLENGES FACED BY CHIEF INFORMATION OFFICERS

The CIO, on the one hand, has to establish an IT organization that helps the business achieve strategic advantage, and on the other, has to satisfy the expectations of the senior policy makers in the organization. As discussed earlier, they have to transform the general attitude towards IT from a cost-centric to a value-centric approach. There are many challenges that a CIO has to face. For example, according to the CIO of Lanco Infratech (Exhibit 19.1), the biggest challenge and opportunity that a CIO faces is to create a world class, technologically leveraged organization within a tight time frame, with best-in-class processes, and the right people skills and capabilities. Another challenge, or rather, an area of attention is to create the right climate and framework for IT within the organization, and effective use of the investments made so far.

Many leadership challenges arise due to the technology–business interface. The expectations of business may surpass the delivery by IT organizations. For example, the CIO may never want to hear that a slow-moving IT organization is preventing a new product from coming to the market or enabling competitors to gain a leg-up. This is problematic because the software development life cycle or the complexity of what is being built often takes longer than the comfort of business executives.

To combat this problem, the CIO must implement a culture of inclusion. The CIO must involve the stakeholders in the innovation process. The earlier an IT organization is involved with innovation, the faster it can figure out how to deliver business value. Bringing IT professionals to the table during the incubation stage of innovation can help them better understand requirements and give the architects a chance to figure out how best to build a design strategy that can move at the speed of business.

The biggest challenge for a CIO is the failure of IT projects. Projects may fail because of various reasons, but the responsibility lies with the information head. Exhibit 19.4 illustrates findings of research on how and why IT projects fail.

EXHIBIT 19.4

IT Failures and Causes

Research highlights that only one in eight IT projects can be considered truly successful (failure being described as those projects that do not meet the original time, cost, and quality requirements criteria). For example, the cost of project failure across the European Union was €142 billion in 2004.

The research looked at 214 IS projects at the same time, and interviews were conducted with a selective number of project managers to follow up issues or clarify points of interest. The period of analysis during 1998–2005 covered the number of IS projects examined across the European Union. Of the initial 214 projects studied, 23.8% were cancelled. What is even harder is to get all the project protagonists agree on what caused the failure and where the responsibilities lie (they can, of course, lie outside the project team). Of course, every project insider or outsider has his own version, and those versions, almost inevitably, 'cancel out'. IT project failure is not just occasional, a few impressive examples are presented hereafter. The best

documented project failures are the ones involving 'public money'.

According to a study by Tata Consultancy Services, the following were revealed:

- Some 62% of organizations experienced IT projects that failed to meet their schedules.
- Some 49% suffered from budget overruns.
- Some 47% had higher-than-expected maintenance costs.
- Some 41% failed to deliver the expected business value and RoI.

Business-critical software and services projects are clearly failing to deliver on the business objectives they set out to achieve. They take too long, cost too much, and are riddled with defects. A research by the Chartered Institute of IT, Singapore, revealed the following failed project value in millions of Euros.

Value range in millions (€)	Number of projects	Percentage (%)	Accumulative percentage (%)
0–1	51	23.831	23.831
1–2	20	9.346	33.177
2–3	11	5.140	38.317
3–5	33	15.421	53.738
5–10	4	1.869	55.607
10–20	87	40.654	96.261
20–50	6	2.804	99.065
50–80	2	0.935	100.000
Totals	214	100.00	100.000

In February 1988, hardware problems caused the Bank of America to lose control of several billion dollars of trust accounts. All the money was eventually found in the system but all 255 people—the entire trust department—were fired as all the depositors withdrew their trust money.

In 1987, the California Department of Motor Vehicles (DMV) launched a major project to revitalize their drivers'

license and registration application process. By 1993, after $45 million dollars had already been spent, the project was cancelled.

Prudential Europe terminated a $50 million contract with Unisys following the collapse of its Unite project, which aimed to deliver real-time processing of policies and pensions over the Internet.

(Contd)

Exhibit 19.4 (Contd)

In 1994, American Airlines settled their lawsuit with Budget Rent-A-Car, Marriott Corp., and Hilton Hotels after the $165 million car rental and hotel reservation system project was dumped.

Sources:

Krigsman, Michael, 'IT failures', 12 December 2007, http://www.zdnet.com/blog/projectfailures/tata-consultancy-new-it-failure-stats-and-coo-interview/531, last accessed on 20 February 2012.

http://www.tcs.com/aboutus/research_survey.html, last accessed on 20 February 2012.

http://www.it-cortex.com/Examples_f.htm, last accessed on 20 February 2012.

http://www.bcs.org/content/ConWebDoc/19584, last accessed on 20 February 2012.

SUMMARY

Information systems (IS) leadership functions have undergone fundamental changes over the past decade. The IS function has migrated from the back office to the executive committee and from being a cost centre to a revenue driver. The Internet and enterprise solutions have changed and moved IT from a back-office personal productivity tool to a business strategy tool. The enterprise and collaboration tools have brought in new levels of automation. As the IT became indispensable and critical, the functions became more strategic in nature and the title of the IS head graduated up from MIS executive to CIO and CTO.

The IS functions, as envisioned in the modern e-business organization, include managing IS operations, managing application development, managing user services, and managing the human resource of IT. The IS operation management refers to the task of purchase, maintenance, and use of hardware, software, networks, security systems, etc. The task of an IT organization involves managing software design and development workflow that includes system study, design, coding, modifying, debugging, testing, and documenting of the application. Large organizations have a number of users of hardware, software, Internet, intranet, e-commerce portals, etc. These users, every now and then, require the support of the IT organization in troubleshooting, maintenance, and training. The IT organization helps organize, retain, and train the qualified personnel in this highly technical field.

The CIO is responsible for the overall functioning and management of all IT functions in an organization. He/She is the top executive responsible for the strategic use of IT in business. He concentrates on IT planning and strategy and ensures that IT helps the company meet its strategic business objectives.

The CIO plays many roles in the organization. These roles can be grouped under two broad categories—general leadership roles and IS leadership roles. CIOs are responsible for making information available to where and when it is required, take decisions related to IS planning and deployment, and play an interpersonal leadership role. They are responsible for hiring, training, and motivating IT personnel. Information systems leadership involves designing blueprint for the IT roadmap of the organization. On the one hand, it involves being an architect and change agent, and on the other, it calls for monitoring the affairs and measuring performance of IS systems. Innovation is something that should come naturally to the CIO.

The CIO, on the one hand, has to establish an IT organization that helps the business achieve strategic advantage, and on the other, satisfy the expectations of the senior policymakers in the organization. Many leadership challenges arise due to the technology–business interface. The expectations of business may surpass the delivery by an IT organization. The biggest challenge for a CIO is the failure of IT projects.

KEY TERMS

Change leader   CIOs function as change agents to initiate the process of business process reengineering.

Chief information officer   The systems function is headed by personnel at the director-level known as the CIO.

Cost-centric approach   The approach that perceives IT as a cost centre in the organization.

Decisional role   The CIO's decision-making roles related to the IT organization.

Information governance   The CIO's role as the owner, custodian, initiator, and implementer of IS.

Information systems leadership   The role of the CIO as a leader in the organization.

Informational role The role of a CIO in dissemination of the required information to the internal and external stakeholders such as the peer groups, top management, suppliers, customers, government, and the media.

Interpersonal role The role in a working relationship between IT and other business functions in the organization.

IS operation management The task of purchase, maintenance, and use of hardware, software, networks, security systems, etc.

Key result areas Benchmarks set for measuring the performance of an IT initiative.

Return on investment The issue of value of benefits with comparisons to investments on IT is RoI.

Solution architect The responsibility to act as chief architects responsible for strategic planning and aligning IT goals with organizations goals and objectives.

System administrators The IT staff that maintains the systems and is responsible for system security.

Total cost of ownership TCO refers to assessing total costs including hidden costs.

User services Services demanded by users from the IT organization.

Value-centric approach The concept of IT seen as a value added service in the organization.

CONCEPT REVIEW QUESTIONS

1. How has IS evolved as a function of the management? Discuss.
2. What are the various functions of the IS department?
3. What are the roles and responsibilities of a head of the IS function?
4. Explain the IS leadership role of a CIO.
5. Discuss the role of a CIO in aligning the IT objectives with the business objectives.
6. Elaborate on the role of a CIO as a change agent.
7. What are the challenges faced by a CIO/CTO?

CRITICAL THINKING QUESTIONS

1. 'A CIO can help bridge the gap between the users, technologists, and the board.' Comment.
2. 'The CIO has more possibility to become a CEO.' Do you agree with this statement? Why or why not?
3. 'CIOs, do not align with the business; be in the business.' Substantiate this statement with appropriate examples.

MIS DEVELOPMENT

Visit various websites for the CIOs, of the CIOs, and by the CIOs. One of the popular Indian sites offering news, articles, blogs, interviews, debates, case studies, videos, and various technical zones is www.cio.in. There are other Indian and international sites catering to the CIOs such as www.thectoforum.com, www.cxotoday.com, www.cio.com, www.siliconindia.com, www.cioinsight.com, and www.biztech2in.com. Find out some more sites. Compare the contents of these sites as what they offer and where they differ.

Exercise

1. Explore what the CIOs have to say about the roles, responsibilities, challenges, and rewards of being a technology officer.
2. Identify the CIOs who have played the role of change agent/change leader well, and have been instrumental in bringing in business process reengineering.

REFERENCES

Applegate, Lynda M., and Elam, Joyce J., 'New information systems leaders', *MIS Quarterly*, Vol. 16, No. 4, Minneapolis, December 1992.

Gorden, Davis, and Margethe Olson, *Management Information*

Systems, McGraw-Hill, Singapore, 1996.

Jaiswal, Mahadeo and Monika Mittal, *Management Information Systems*, Oxford University Press, New Delhi, 2004.

O'Brien, James A., George M. Marakas, and Ramesh Behl,

Management Information Systems, Tata McGraw-Hill, New Delhi, 2007.

Don, Desiderato, 'A 10-step playbook for CIO success', 26 June 2010, http://www.cioinsight.com/c/a/Strategy/A-10Step-Playbook-for-CIO-Success-701122/, last accessed on 22 February 2012.

Gartner Research, http://www.gartner.com/technology/cio-priorities/erp-support.jsp, last accessed on 12 February 2012.

Gorden, Steve, Study Paper 'Benchmarking the information system function', 1994, Center for Information Management Studies (CIMS) Babson College, http://faculty.babson.edu/gordon/papers/F94BENCH.HTM, last accessed on 12 February 2012.

Logan, Debra and V.P. Gartner, *MDM critical to achieving effective information governance*, 20 January 2012, http://biztech2.in.com/news/storage/mdm-critical-to-achieving-effective-information-governance/125552/0, last accessed on 18 February 2012.

CASE STUDY

TCI: CIOs Discuss Priorities, While IT Helps Create New Benchmark

The transport and logistics industry makes up for 13% of India's GDP; yet it is among India's most immature and inefficient sectors. While the industry is plagued with poor infrastructure, differential taxes, and unregulated competition from unorganized players, it also faces unprecedented losses from operational inefficiencies. As market leaders, the ₹2250 crore TCI has taken upon itself to create more order from this chaos. The CIO strategies summit, organized by Silicon India on 23 June 2011, at the ITC Grand Central at Mumbai, focused on what the IT industry can assimilate in the coming years, driving innovation and generating business growth, CIO skill sets to meet management expectations, and many such aspects.

Can you describe some of the challenges that the Indian logistics industry faces?

A joint study by TCI and IIMC conducted to assess operational efficiencies shows that one of the biggest impediments to the industry has been delays at checkposts and in-transit. These delays relate to filling in forms required by various government departments, etc. Logistics companies and the government should work toward adopting an approach like the Transports Internationaux Routiers (TIR) Convention prevailing in the European countries. This allows seamless and borderless truck-based trade across all international road transport unions (IRUs) member-nations.

For example, it was noticed that on simulating the movement of a truck load from a factory near New Delhi to a factory near Dhaka under the TIR system, direct savings were as much as ₹15,000 per truck. The savings include the elimination of three days of waiting, a reduction in customs transaction charges, and lower man-hours. If the industry automates the processes of checking and filling government documents, it will help service providers integrate their operations with partners and customers for better visibility and control.

What challenges does TCI face? How is IT helping?

The challenges faced by us are similar to those ailing the industry. In a sector where many small-time players provide a cost advantage, we are trying to focus on a customer-centric delivery model which encourages the adoption of new services and technology to ensure customer satisfaction and loyalty. Our wide network of dealers, partners, and the vast expanse of our operations motivated us to integrate our ERP systems with that of our customers and partners to enable better service delivery and the tracking of SLAs. This process has helped us integrate several processes in the supply chain and share information including demand signals, forecasts, and inventory with all our stakeholders. Additionally, by implementing bar codes on our stock-keeping units (SKUs), we have changed the way we manage our distribution centres.

In a set-up like ours, integration, automation, and communication are key words. Our company has over 5,000 interdependent employees; hence, we have tried to ensure that all our data—including truck departures, material availability, scheduling, route planning, and clients—is available in real time on the intranet so that the flow of information between various departments is seamless and error-free.

What are the new technologies that are reshaping the industry?

The widespread adoption of warehouse management systems and GPS-enabled fleets are forcing more customers to look away from their 'store-and-transport' mindsets to real supply chain management.

The latest GPS freight tracking technology allows us to monitor freight location, condition, and security all from a central location. This radically changes the way fleets are managed. RFID is another technology that can revolutionize the industry. The RFID supply chain is an effective solution that can extensively control and track business processes, and reduce error rates and warehouse labour costs. I feel warehouse automation is one technology that will soon become a rising trend. IT is the lifeline of all our functions. It provides us with visibility and control in a highly-scattered operational environment.

How is the industry, especially logistics, benefitting from these technologies?

The use of GPS freight tracking has helped us immensely in improving on-time delivery with real-time information on estimated arrival times, load locations, and the status of a delivery. It also helps us minimize risks and losses with the help of on-board sensors that immediately notify us when assets are compromised.

We are also exploring telematics, which is a combination of an advanced vehicle tracking system through GPS, mobility, dashboards, decision support systems, etc. At TCI, we believe in developing an intelligent supply chain, which can help our customers achieve just-in-time management of supplies. A proper mix of RFI, telematics, and inventory management through warehouse automation can help us reduce miscellaneous overheads significantly.

What priorities do you see for an Indian CIO?

There are many issues that a CIO has to tackle. With the changing IT scenarios, the priorities are changing every year. The top three IT priorities remain unchanged from many years. These priorities are strategic planning and aligning IT with organizational goals, integrating systems and processes, and implementing security and privacy measures.

Aligning with the priorities, CIOs still spend most of their time dealing with business executives, which is 1.5 times more than the time spent on dealing with their teams or vendors. This represents an increased thrust in aligning IT closely with the business to ensure better returns. CIOs are no doubt growing in their role, budgets are on the rise, and so are the opportunities to shift from one company to another, in pursuit of bigger challenges. So, things are looking up. The new time will see a clear sense of the resolution of the age-old debates of business IT alignment and the need for better communication with C-level peers that still plague the community. Perhaps, one is being a tad too

optimistic, but we hope that the community will take heart from the positive sentiments in the market and methodically work through these problems in the coming year.

Do you think that the Indian CIO is ineffective?

While CIOs are moving up the ladder, there are various reasons why they are still ineffective. The one reason for ineffectiveness is the IT budget. Companies tend to keep only a small amount for IT spending. The other reason is aligning IT with business goals and disconnect with other C-level peers in the company. Research shows that CIOs still do not understand business that well and cannot communicate well with their peers. All senior CIOs stress on the importance of communication skills in the CIO. They must speak to the business in the language that they understand and not in IT jargon, which will be dismissed without much thought.

As Sandeep Phanasgaonkar, CIO, Reliance Capital says, 'CIOs have to play a dual role and speak two different languages. They must speak the language of business while speaking to business leaders and while speaking to their technology managers they must get their hands dirty and translate that business into a language of technology that the IT managers can understand.'

What are the game changers for a CIO?

New technologies such as cloud-based services, social media, and virtualization give CIOs tools to change IT's direction, strategy, and operational profile to pursue growth and continued cost reduction strategies. Adoption of these technologies has accelerated and is accelerating changes in the role, structure and purpose of IT.

Pratap Gharge, executive vice-president and CIO, Bajaj Electricals, addressed cloud-based services and social networking, and said, 'Cloud computing is becoming more and more adoptable and affordable and it can be definitely a game changed emerging technology. Social networking is growing very fast and hence corporate cannot ignore it. The platform of social networking can be used for several applications such as listening to customers and marketing.

Discussion Questions

1. What are the issues highlighted in this business case?
2. What are the priorities of a CIO, as seen by the industry leaders?
3. How does a CIO help the logistics company TCI create new industry benchmarks?
4. Do you think CIOs in India are ineffective, as small and

mid-tier organizations are still wary of spending on IT?

Sources:

Channana, Geetaj, 'State of the Indian CTO', 11 January 2011, http://www.thectoforum.com/content/state-indian-cto, last accessed on 20 February 2012.

'CIO strategies for success: Top-flight CIOs explain their strategic priorities for 2011', http://www.siliconindia.com/shownews/CIO_Strategies_for_Success_topflight_CIOs_explain_their_strategic_priorities_for_2011-nid-102531-cid-69.html/2, last accessed on 22 February 2012.

Roy, Debarati, 'Interview of Chander Agarwal, ED-TCI', http://www.cio.in/ceo-interviews/it-helps-tci-create-new-industry-benchmarks, last accessed on 20 February 2012.

http://www.tcil.com/pdfs/chander_nterview-CIO.pdf, last accessed on 20 February 2012.

20

Managing Global Systems

What makes the Internet and the world wide web so important for international business? This interconnected matrix of computers, information, and networks that reaches tens of millions of users in over one hundred countries is a business environment free of traditional boundaries and limits. Linking to an online global infrastructure offers companies unprecedented potential for expanding markets, reducing costs, and improving profit margins at a price that is typically a small percentage of the corporate communications budget. The Internet provides an interactive channel for direct communication and data exchange with customers, suppliers, distributors, manufacturers, product developers, financial backers, information providers—in fact, with all parties involved in a given business venture.

—MARY CRONIN

LEARNING OBJECTIVES

After studying this chapter, you will be able to

- identify global challenges and opportunities
- define global IT strategies to meet the challenges
- describe the global IT systems and their applications
- ponder over global technology issues

EXHIBIT 20.1

Essar Group: Implementing Large-scale Citrix VDI Solution

The Essar Group implements large-scale citirix VDI solution to provide 5000+ users with enhanced information security, faster scalability, and flexibility to work from anywhere and at anytime.

Essar Group is a multinational conglomerate and a leading player in the sectors of steel, oil and gas, power, BPO, telecom, shipping, ports, and projects. The company announced desktop virtualization implementation with Citrix in December 2011. The Mumbai-headquartered business giant, with operations in more than 25 countries across five continents, employs 75,000 people, and had revenues of USD 17 billion in 2011. The group continues to expand its global footprint, focussing on markets in Asia, Africa, Europe, the Americas, and Australia. Essar invests significantly in the latest technology to drive forward and backward integration in its businesses, and on leveraging synergies between these businesses. It also focusses on in-house research and innovation to be a low-cost manufacturer with high-quality products and innovative customer offerings.

As per Essar's multinational business approach, businesses depend heavily on their information systems to help them integrate their global business activities. Managing a business of such astronomical proportions calls for a flexible IT infrastructure that is agile enough to meet the changing global business requirements and support business growth. Trends such as IT consumerization, worker mobility, cloud computing, and work-shifting mean that more people are accessing enterprise desktops, applications, and data from numerous places across the globe, in more ways than ever before. The geo-economic, political, and cultural challenges that a global business offers induced implementation of such technologies that helped Essar to go for virtualization of the desktop applications. Additionally, virtual computing is rapidly becoming a foundational element of the security strategy for organizations of all kinds. With Citrix's Desktop Virtualization, Essar has been able to reap the benefits of application virtualization and streaming features for enabling faster responses to business requirements for applications.

Dilip Oommen, CEO, Essar Steel says, 'Essar was among the first companies to embrace SAP. The ERP has helped us greatly get an end-to-end visibility of the status of customer orders. It has also helped us control credit effectively and track every batch or unit of material. Sec-

ond, by implementing i2 solutions, we have got excellent tools to optimize capacity utilization, thus allowing us to manufacture in a more profitable manner. It also gives us complete visibility and control through the manufacturing process. Finally, our information systems are now being leveraged to crunch the cycle time from steel melting to cash realization.' Now, Essar group plans to move its 90–95% workforce to Citrix XenDesktop and Citrix NetScaler platforms and aims to complete implementation of virtual desktops for 40,000 users. Citrix XenDesktop and Citrix NetScaler with on-demand application delivery is expected to save the company more than 40% in desktop computing costs by enabling easy, centralized management of desktops and applications and reducing the need to upgrade expensive hardware.

Users will benefit from enhanced productivity as Citrix solutions transforms any Windows, web, or SaaS application into an on-demand service that can be accessed by any user on any device anywhere with unparalleled simplicity and scalability. The solution utilizes a building-block approach, which can then scale to thousands of virtual desktops delivering the application to any device in any workplace environment, supporting a rich user experience, and provides IT with additional security and control.

Jayantha Prabhu, chief technology officer, Essar Group said, 'Various issues in multinational business management prompted us to go for virtualization of our systems. Implementing a complete virtual desktop infrastructure requires expertise in desktop deployment and migrations, application virtualization, security, system management, and storage design. The great combination offered by Citrix allowed us to attain business agility, application flexibility, and infrastructure efficiency.'

Sources:
'Essar Group implements large-scale Citrix VDI solution', http://www.cio.in/news/essar-group-implements-large-scale-citrix-vdi-solution-205692011, 15 December 2011, last accessed on 17 January 2013.

'Essar Group implements Citrix VDI solution', http://www.ciol.com/Storage/Cloud-and-Virtualization/News-Reports/Essar-Group-implements-Citrix-VDI-solution/158043/0/, posted on 20 December 2011, last accessed on 11 March 2012.

Oommen, Dilip, 'The IT recipe for profits in Essar Steel', http://www.cio.in/view-top/it-recipe-profits-steel, last accessed on 11 March 2012.

(Contd)

Exhibit 20.1 (Contd)

Press note, http://www.businesswireindia.com/PressRelease. asp?b2mid=29460, 14 December 2011, last accessed on 11 March 2012.

www.varindia.com/14dec2011_16.htm, last accessed on 28 February 2012.

Essar's initiatives to upgrade their information systems (IS) by implementing Citrix virtual desktop technology brought all the users and applications online. As described in Exhibit 20.1 on Essar's multinational business approach, businesses depend heavily on their information systems to help them integrate their global business activities. Going with the global trends such as large-scale IT deployment over the enterprise, worker mobility, cloud computing, and so on, Essar Group standardized and brought the applications to one platform, instead of developing web-based applications for each business unit and business process across the globe. With this initiative, Essar Group will be able to save significant costs on desktop hardware, software, and applications. Employee productivity is bound to improve with the global deployment of IT.

In this chapter, we will discuss the international dimensions of creating and using information systems, the various challenges and issues involved, and the global strategies for IT to support organizations of a global nature.

Global information systems refer to a basic system architecture that a multinational organization uses to manage the information requirement of its international businesses. When implementing information systems globally, a multinational organization has many objectives and faces challenges in doing so. According to Gunson (2008), multinationals looked towards reengineering and cost cutting, and often combined their ERP project with the breaking down of country barriers for manufacturing sites and centres of distribution. As the 1990s progressed, other impediments became evident—the Y2K and the Euro—that brought along software application issues. Towards the end of the decade, ERP was seen to be a trampoline for Internet technology, and solutions such as supply chain management (SCM) and customer relationship management (CRM) came to the fore.

GLOBAL BUSINESS—CHALLENGES AND OPPORTUNITIES

Survival of business and the urge to expand to newer markets are some of the reasons that are inducing organizations to go global. Globalization causes many local businesses to merge with well-networked and resourceful corporations. These businesses strengthen their profitability, mitigate risks, and consolidate operations by extending their manufacturing or marketing activities in a number of countries. According to Shankar (2008), consider a multinational manufacturing company that does business in a number of countries. A substantial amount of its resources is committed to international business, it engages in international production in a number of countries, and has a worldwide perspective in its management. By branching out to multiple countries, the company can continue growing and reduce the risks it might face, even if conditions in one country change drastically.

For businesses to grow and sustain in the international market, they have to face many political, cultural, geographical, and economic challenges. Such factors can include social and cultural

Table 20.1   Common challenges to the development of global systems

Challenges	Examples
Political	Commercial regulations, data transmission and privacy laws, varying accounting, electronic data interchange (EDI) and telecommunication standards
Cultural	Nationalism, regionalism, customs, social attitudes, and linguistic differences
Geographical	Physical distances, availability of Internet, efficient bandwidth, people's acceptance of IS, shortage of skilled technicians, and language barriers
Economic	Variations in economies, cost of living, living standards, currency value, and fluctuations

values, political and legal systems, business activities and economic conditions, standard setting processes, capital markets, and forms of ownership. While designing and developing information systems strategies for a global environment, the management must consider these environmental challenges. Table 20.1 lists the most common and powerful challenges to enable the development of global systems.

The rules and regulations of governments across the globe can pose *political challenges*. These laws are meant for governing the movement of information, information privacy, origins of software and hardware, and radio and satellite telecommunications. For example, European countries have very strict laws related to data transmission across the border and privacy of citizens. Some countries prohibit the processing of financial information outside their countries and others have their own accounting standards and practices, which pose challenges in implementation of uniform information systems.

According to Biehl (2005), although there are significant benefits in implementing international accounting standards and is increasing in importance, there are still many challenges to further development and authoritative implementation. To best understand these challenges, one must look at the factors that influence the development of accounting regulations. Therefore, global companies having presence in these countries prefer to develop information systems within each country to avoid the cost and uncertainty of moving information across national boundaries.

Cultural challenges are posed by individualistic schools of thinking in the form of religious, nationalist, ethnic, and regional perspectives. According to Laudon (2010), at the cultural level, making judgments and taking action on the basis of narrow or personal characteristics rejects the very concept of shared global culture and rejects the penetration of domestic markets by foreign goods and services. People with different cultures produce different social expectations and hence, varied regulations. For example, the *swadeshi* cultural movement in India calls for self reliance in the use of goods made only in India. To safeguard this culture, the government has made regulations to protect certain goods, which cannot be produced in any other country or there cannot be any direct foreign investment in those kinds of industries.

Geographical challenges are posed by physical distances, availability of sufficient Internet bandwidth, phone network, manpower, and language barriers. Physical distances, though shortened by telecommunication and jet travel, still pose problems in flying an IT technician to fix a bug urgently. With different time zones, no communication can happen in real time. For example, when a user confronts a problem in Manhattan at 2 p.m., the IT specialist in Mumbai may be sleeping. The other issue is related to reliable telecommunication networks. Countries such as USA and Japan offer very reliable telecommunication network, while South Asia and

Eastern Europe lack such infrastructure. Language still remains a significant barrier. Countries such as China, Korea, Japan, Russia, Germany, and France still prefer their native language. Therefore, software may have to be developed with local language interfaces before a new information system is implemented and accepted by the users.

Economic challenges are presented by variation in economies of different countries. There are problems related to differences in the cost of living and labour costs in various countries. The value and fluctuations of currency can disturb planning and projections. For example, a $5 hamburger in USA by McDonalds will not sell at ₹250 in India. The company will reduce cost to make the product sell in such countries. The hamburger that could fetch profits in the US may be a loss-making proposition in India. As such, the company may not like to invest much in IT in loss-making countries. Thus, all of these economic challenges must be addressed when developing a global IT strategy.

Like challenges, international businesses offer opportunities in strategic IT deployment. A global information system strategy facilitates bringing in uniformity in business processes across the world. Implementation of such IS strategies necessitate business process reengineering to make the organization efficient and effective. No doubt, many efficient Indian businesses have acquired companies abroad and established themselves in the league of multinational companies (see Table 20.2). As illustrated in Exhibit 20.1, Essar's implementation of Citrix solutions transformed Windows, web, or SaaS applications used by the organization into an on-demand service that could be accessed by any user on any device anywhere with unparalleled simplicity and scalability. The solution scaled to thousands of virtual desktops delivering the application to any device in any workplace environment, supporting a rich user experience, and provided Essar's IT organization with additional security and control.

For example, the case study at the end of the chapter illustrates how Videocon aptly used SAP solutions to enable strategic decision-making as an agent of change for business transformation, and successfully managed global expansions, resulting in Videocon being awarded 'best consumer section implementation of SAP'.

Table 20.2   List of a few Indian multinational companies

Indian multinationals	Acquisition/Presence	Revenue (in ₹ Crore)
ONGC Videsh	16 countries	22,700
Tata Steel	Corus Steel, 26 countries	1,32,900
Reliance Industries	Flag Telecom, Bermuda Trevira, 36 countries	3,20,000
Tara Starbucks	Tetly, Good Earth, Jemca, Vitax	6600
Motherson Sumi	Visicorp, Peguform, 24 countries	14,900
HCL Technologies	31 countries	20,800
Tata Communication	DishnetDSL, Teleglobe	14,200
Hindalco Industries	Straits Ply, Novelis, 13 countries	80,800
Suzlon Energy	33 countries	21,100
Tata Motors	Daewoo, Hispano Carrocera, Jaguar-Land Rover	1,65,700
Ranbaxy	RPG (Aventis) Laboratories, Betapharm	9700
Jubilant Lifesciences	5 countries	4300
Tata Consultancy Services	44 countries	49,300
Infosys Technologies	Expert Information Services, 11 countries	33,700
Tata Chemicals	Brunner Mond, General Chemical	13,700
Wipro	NerveWire Inc, US	45,360

Global Information Technology Strategies

Global IT strategies are based on global business strategies. Organizations adopt various business strategies to operate global businesses, which are related to control, decision-making, and autonomy. According to Hill (1998), in order for companies to function effectively in different countries, strategies need to be developed to manage them effectively. According to Prof. Lynch (2012), global strategy is a shortened term that covers three areas—global, multinational, and international strategies. Essentially, these three areas refer to those strategies designed to enable an organization to achieve its objective of international expansion. Although many strategies can be used, the three major strategies that firms follow when they are involved in international business can be discussed as global strategy, multinational strategy, and international strategy.

A multinational strategy is applied when the organization is involved in a number of markets beyond its home country. However, it needs a distinctive strategy for each of these markets because of different customer demands and competition. The foreign subsidiaries of such organizations operate autonomously. Multinational strategy believes in central financial powers but decentralization of production, sales, marketing, etc., in the unit countries. The products and services in different countries are adapted to suit local market conditions. They take advantage of the availability of resources and market potential in various countries. This strategy is attractive for multinational organizations and has been put into effect at Monsanto, Hewlett-Packard, General Motors, Chrysler, Intel, Nescafé, etc.

International strategy has been primarily designed for the home market but is considered suitable for international markets to meet certain objectives. These organization's foreign subsidiaries are autonomous but are dependent on the head office for new processes, products, and ideas. International food companies such as McDonald's, Kentucky Fried Chicken (KFC), and Coca-Cola fit into this type of business strategy. These companies develop their products in the mother country and then market and even produce the goods globally through franchisees or their own production units. They adapt a decentralized approach for IS implementation. According to Olson (2005), decentralization is an attractive way to approach ERP implementation in multinational operations because it provides the flexibility to cope with local needs, while operating within an overall unified framework.

In a *global strategy*, the organization's value-added services are managed from a global perspective, without referring to national borders, and making use of local competitive advantages. In this strategy, the organization treats the world as one market and one source of supply with little variation. They are transnational in approach. According to Mische (1995), many firms are moving towards transnational strategies in which they integrate their global business or IT applications through close cooperation and interdependence between their international subsidiaries and their corporate headquarters. Laudon (2010) opines that transnational firms are stateless, truly globally managed firms that may represent a larger part of international business in the future. Transnational firms have no single national headquarters but instead have many regional headquarters and perhaps a world headquarters. Companies such as Cisco and Siemens are examples of transnational firms.

The management of global organizations supports a federal structure in which there is a strong, central core group managing decision-making, with distribution of powers and authority to all

Table 20.3   Examples of Indian multinational companies and their IT strategies

Organization	Expanse	IT strategiess	IT environment
Videocon Industries	India, China, Poland, Italy, Mexico	Multinational	Global network, ERP SAP R/3 implemented
Essar Group	More than 25 countries across the globe	Transnational	Global network, ERP SAP, i2, and Citrix solutions implemented
Bharti Airtel	19 countries across Asia and Africa	Multinational	Global network, ERP Oracle Financials, and Oracle HRMS implemented
ONGC	11 countries	Multinational	Networked projects, ERP SAP R/3, MySAP implemented
Ranbaxy	46 countries	Transnational	Global network, ERP SAP R/3, SAP ECC6 implemented
Aditya Birla Group	36 countries	Multinational	ERP SAP R/3, AFS, Oracle Fin, Mfg, indigenous ERP in group companies
Bharat Forge	Six countries	Multinational	ERP SAP, Legacy systems, indigenous ERP in group companies
Infosys	More than 20 countries	Multinational	Globally connected, ERP SAP R/3, Oracle

global divisions. Davenport (1998) argued that a federalist structure (where different elements of the organization had their own versions of an ERP system linked together at a high level) was a way to cultivate unique competitive advantages. In this approach, regional units tailor their operations to meet local requirements and regulatory authorities. However, federalism imposes customization to meet these local needs, which is usually unattractive from the perspectives of cost and schedule risk.

Table 20.3 lists Indian multinational companies and the IT strategies they have adopted.

Global Information Technology Systems

In global information systems, the core systems are globally networked and meet the requirements of the management across the organization. The compulsions of global businesses drive deployment of IT systems across the organization. According to O'Brien (2007), the applications of IT developed by global companies depend on their global business/IT strategies and their expertise and experience in IT. However, their IT applications also depend on a variety of global business drivers. This means that business requirements are dependent on the nature of the industry and its competitive or environmental forces. Business drivers such as customers, products, operations, resources, and collaborations necessitate the deployment of global IT systems. For example, in the airline and hotel industries, it is necessary to implement online reservations and transaction processing systems as they have international customers, and access to these systems is required from any place. Ives (1991) proposed some of the business drivers (summarized in Table 20.4) that make global IT a competitive necessity for global businesses.

There are standard applications in the areas of finance, accounting, and office productivity that international organizations use for their operations. At the globalization stage of growth, an organization requires changes in some of the most standard operations—financial or human resource management. This calls for development and implementation of universally accepted systems. As global competition increases, organizations opt for e-commerce and e-business

Table 20.4   Business reasons why global IT is required

Business drivers	Description	Examples
Global operations	Parts of production are done in multiple countries because of suppliers, factories, and collaboration with other companies	Woodland procures leather from Italy, manufactures in China, tests in India, and sells in the US
Global products	Similar products and services, which are manufactured or sold across the globe	Airline and hotel reservations; Coca-Cola sells to customers worldwide, 80% of revenue from outside the US.
Global resources	Raw material, equipment, and facilities available in multiple regions/countries	Samsung manufactures its products in different countries having its facilities
Global customers	Customers in many countries for the same product	Infosys has many banks as its customers who have branches in many countries

applications that include enterprise systems, supply chain management, and customer relationship management systems.

The major task ahead of a transnational organization is to encourage local users to support global systems. The organization can adapt an approach of development of global systems, giving opportunity to major system groups across the globe and then consolidate and replicate the system in the organization. This can generate a sense of ownership in a transnational effort; however, it cannot be assumed that each group is capable of developing a high-quality system. Another approach that the organization can adapt is the creation of a global centre of excellence. This centre, supported by technology groups worldwide, can identify and specify business processes, define information requirements of various user groups, and develop a global system that is acceptable to users across the organization.

GLOBAL TECHNOLOGY ISSUES

Once organizations have defined their global business models and information strategies, they work on hardware, software, and networking issues. In an international environment, these issues pose grave technical challenges. However, the following issues have been identified by Carton (2003):

- Shifting to new systems can be a painful learning process, requiring unlearning old ways of working.
- Subsidiaries of multinational firms are often faced with the changes imposed, rather than designed.
- Implementation of IS usually lead to integration of data, which has the effect of centralizing ownership, away from the multinational subsidiary.
- IT support is also often centralized (as a way to reduce IT cost), while responsibility for accurate data entry is shifted back to the point of entry, increasing the responsibility and work of the subsidiary.
- System implementation can often change the balance of power within organizations, usually favouring central administration at the expense of subsidiaries.

In multinational system implementations, each subsidiary faces unique conditions, complicating the process. According to Olson (1998), the multinational implementation of enterprise solutions in different countries complicates business process reengineering, which is an important part of system deployment as

- the need to reflect different costs of doing things may change the best practices in the country;
- there are different legacy practices across countries (because various units in different countries may have developed and implemented their own information systems over a period of time);
- additional constraints may be imposed on business process reengineering due to varying regulations;
- there may be cultural resistance to change; and
- there may be variance in users' computer experience.

All these challenges are also faced in the domestic IS strategy, but they are more intense in case of international implementation. We can summarize these issues as computing platforms, connectivity issues, software localization, database sharing, etc.

Computing Platforms

One of the major challenges is to find a standard global computing platform when there is a lot of variation from unit to unit and country to country. Computing platforms encompass the technology infrastructure of hardware, software, data resources, telecommunication networks, and computing facilities that support global business operations. For example, integrating systems that run on diverse operating systems (Linux, Windows, and Unix), and on diverse hardware (IBM, Sun, and HP) is not only a technically complex job but also involves political and cultural issues. Similarly, application software available in one country may not find support mechanisms in another country. As international brands such as SAP and Oracle have a global presence, most multinational companies opt for enterprise systems from them, as mentioned in Table 20.2.

Another issue of establishing computing facilities for a multinational organization is no less challenging. Global organizations contract systems integrators for establishing data centres. This issue is now partially taken care of by third party data management vendors and cloud computing infrastructure.

Uniform computing platforms also refer to standardization of data and technical issues. For example, in India, the financial year is usually the April–March period, that is, the financial year begins in April and ends in March the following year. However, in USA, it is from January to December, that is, it coincides with the calendar year. Multinational companies will have to standardize the financial year for making a global profit and loss statement.

Connectivity Issues

Connectivity is another challenge in international IS management. Though universal acceptance and availability of the Internet largely reduced the networking problem, it does not guarantee seamless operations as all units may not use the same application and the bandwidth availability may not be the same in all countries and units. Managing international data communications networks, including the Internet, intranet, extranet, etc., is a key global IT challenge. For example, an online application run by a transnational company may require a particular telecommunication

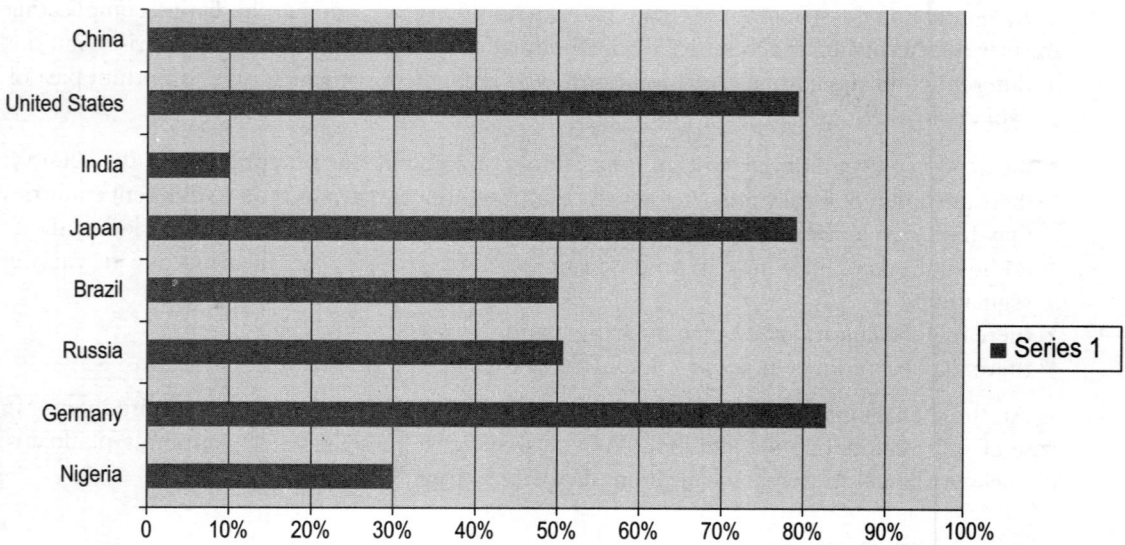

Fig. 20.1   Penetration of the Internet in the top 10 countries of the world as on December 2012.
Sources: http://www.worldometers.info/world-population/, www.internetworldstats.com/stats.htm,
http://www.populationmatters.org/, www.wikipedia.org

bandwidth. This application may run well in advanced countries offering very high bandwidth Internet, but may be pathetically slow in countries where the Internet penetration is low and not supported by good bandwidth connectivity. Figure 20.1 shows the global penetration of the Internet; it can be observed that there is low penetration of the Internet in developing countries.

The Internet and the world wide web have now become vital infrastructure in international business and e-commerce. The Internet has transcended boundaries and limits, and has paved the way for a 'global village'. The Internet provides a low-cost innovative channel for communications and data exchange within and outside the global organization. Though the Internet user population across the world is growing, much needs to be done to increase access to the Internet in developing countries, particularly India where the Internet users are just 8.4% of the population, as depicted in Table 20.5.

Multinational giants have minimum trust in the security aspects of the Internet. They generally use private networks and Internet-based virtual private networks (VPN) to communicate sensitive data. According to Laudon (2010), an increasingly attractive alternative is to create global networks based on the Internet and Internet technology. Companies can create global intranets for internal communication or extranets to exchange information more rapidly with business partners in their supply chain.

Software Localization

Regional cultural preferences, government regulations, and linguistic issues pose software localization challenges. Localization is a process of adapting computer software to different languages, regional differences, and technical requirements of a target market. It is also referred to as internationalization and is the process of designing a software application so that it can

Table 20.5   Internet usage and population statistics

S. no.	Country	Internet population (Dec 2012)	Rank (No. of users)	Total population (Jan 2013)	Internet penetration	Rank
1.	China	568,192,066	1	1,388,608,351	40.92%	102
2.	United States	254,295,536	2	320,988,006	79.22%	28
3.	India	151,598,994	3	1,257,789,012	12.05%	164
4.	Japan	100,684,474	4	127,089,884	79.22%	33
5.	Brazil	99,357,737	5	200,980,559	49.44%	86
6.	Russia	75,926,004	6	142,698,290	53.21%	81
7.	Germany	68,296,919	7	82,698,612	82.59%	22
8.	Nigeria	55,930,391	8	175,429,228	31.88%	128
9.	United Kingdom	54,861,245	9	63,136,265	86.89%	14
10.	France	54,473,474	10	64,291,280	84.73%	24
11.	Mexico	44,173,551	11	122,875,163	35.95%	114
12.	South Korea	41,091,681	12	49,262,698	83.41%	21
13.	Indonesia	38,191,873	13	250,955,828	15.22%	154
14.	Philippines	37,602,976	14	99,023,881	37.97%	118
15.	Egypt	36,881,374	15	82,548,951	44.68%	99
16.	Vietnam	36,140,967	16	92,000,723	39.28%	111
17.	Turkey	35,990,932	17	75,267,637	47.82%	97
18.	Italy	35,531,527	18	60,990,277	58.26%	68
19.	Spain	33,870,948	19	46,926,963	72.18%	45
20.	Canada	29,760,764	20	35,181,704	84.59%	16
Total top 20 countries		1,852,853,453		4,738,743,312	39.10%	
Total world		1,916,723,448		7,162,119,434	26.76%	

Sources: http://www.worldometers.info/world-population/, www.internetworldstats.com/stats.htm, http://www.populationmatters.org/, www.wikipedia.org

be adapted to various languages and regions without engineering changes. Thus, software localization refers to modifications in software to meet local language needs, government rules and regulations related to taxation, and country-specific accounting procedures and standards. The international organization may face questions such as which user interface to keep, whether the international information system has multiple language interfaces, if it can generate reports in the local language or in English, and the rate of acceptance level if a universal language like English is proposed for all input and output forms.

Much of the user resistance to change comes if the user interface is not liked by them or they have been more comfortable with the old interface. User productivity and efficiency is increased when interfaces are in the users' native language. Users in countries such as China, Germany, and France are not comfortable with the universal language as English. How user support by the international vendor of a system and language can become issues is illustrated in Exhibit 20.2, which highlights these issues in case of implementations at salesforce.com.

According to Collins (2001), software localization is based on market research in each country as well as inputs from usability testing in the target country. Knowledge about many aspects of a country are obvious and immutable characteristics (e.g., language); other aspects are subtler and subject to cultural shifts (e.g., the meaning of colours). Besides language change, software localization has to take into account contents, currency, time and date formatting, measurements,

EXHIBIT 20.2

Salesforce.com: The Global Issues with Global CRM

As of March 2009, Salesforce.com, the global CRM giant, had more than 55,000 enterprise customers, 1.5 million individual subscribers, 30 million lines of third-party code, and hundreds of terabytes of data all running on 1,000 machines. Salesforce relied on data stored in only 10 databases that run on about 50 servers. It held several patents on the ways to index the tens of millions of rows of raw data. However, its secret weapon was the 'optimizer', which queried the databases and made sense of all the data.

Managing the operations of a global organization of that magnitude is not an easy task. Supporting that number of customers globally poses challenges of a very high degree. Salesforce had to work relentlessly to improve services and retain customers in the highly competitive Cloud CRM space.

Salesforce.com has made a series of changes to its support services that include the removal of certain features from the standard tier, but the company says that overall it will provide a better experience for customers.

The company offers two kinds of services to their customers—standard support and premier support. Standard support is included at no charge with all Salesforce.com editions. Premier support costs 15% of the licence list price for professional and enterprise edition users, while a Premier + tier costs 25% of the licence list for professional and enterprise users and is included with the unlimited edition (Salesforce.com).

First, phone support for standard support customers would now be focussed on 'severity one' issues. A severity one issue is where no user is able to access the system. Dean Robison, senior vice-president for global services, said, 'We want to change the service experience. We want to make sure that when you log a case, you get an expert.'

'What we saw was the opposite issue', said George Hu, COO of Salesforce. 'People were taking critical issues and logging them through the portal. If it is a real critical issue, we want you to pick up the phone and call us. Still, I think you could talk to us for any issue', he said.

Salesforce.com is also 'scaling back, or better refining its developer support capabilities, Robison said in the video interview. Standard support customers will be able to log development bugs and issues with Salesforce.com, he said. 'We will capture that and get the information back to you when and if we are able to solve and remove that bug.'

Meanwhile, premier support customers still get a higher level of support, including code troubleshooting. 'This is the differentiation between standard and premier', said Robison.

Thirdly, Salesforce.com is taking the resources it had devoted to its standard support chat channel and diverting them to the premier channel, he said. Chat will no longer be an option for standard support customers.

Premier plan users get around-the-clock phone access with a two-hour response time, as well as expanded training resources (Salesforce.com). They may also get an assigned support representative if they have enough CRM licences or subscription fees. Premier+ adds in a series of administrative services.

Sources:
Kanaracus, Chris, 'Salesforce.com shakes up standard support plan features', 9 February 2012, http://www.cio.in/news/salesforcecom-shakes-standard-support-plan-features-223932012, last accessed on 21 January 2013.
Schonfeld, Erick, 'The efficient cloud: All of salesforce runs on only 1,000 servers', 23 March 2009, http://techcrunch.com/2009/03/23/the-efficient-cloud-all-of-salesforce-runs-on-only-1000-servers/, last accessed on 21 January 2013.
http://www.salesforce.com/in/, last accessed on 22 April 2012.

address layouts, numeric formats, colour schemes, images and sounds, navigation systems, and telecommunication compatibility issues.

For example, an English phrase translated into Hindi may require up to 80% more space. English has 26 letters in the alphabet while Asian languages like Chinese have more than 50,000 characters. In addition, the question mark (?) in English is translated as a semicolon (;) in Greek. The contents may also require change. For example, comparing two brands during advertising is legal in USA, but is not permitted in countries like China. Time and data formats vary from one country to another. The unit of measurement followed the world over is the metric form, that is, centimetre and metre; however in USA, measurements are in inches and feet. Similarly, in India, temperature is measured in degree Celsius, while in USA, it is Fahrenheit. The address styles in India and USA also differ in the sequence of name, surname, house number, street number, state, and country. Countries such as China and Bulgaria use the reverse style of addresses on the envelope. They first write the state, followed by city, street number, and house number. The numerical formatting in USA involves a comma being used after every 1000th place (for e.g., 1 million is written as 1,000,000); in India, the comma is placed after every 100th place (for e.g., 1 million is written as 10,00,000 or 10 lakh). Similarly, colours have different meanings and connotations in different countries. The uses of images and sounds also differ among cultures; for example, the use of the flag symbol, thumbs up, etc., are not allowed in middle-east countries.

Database Sharing

Whose data is it, anyway? Global data access and sharing has always been an issue in global business operations. Many countries view trans-border data transfer as violation of national sovereignty and business loss as data transfer may avoid custom duties and regulations. The data transfer may also be seen as privacy violation. Data access on the world wide web has been an issue of regulation and also a battleground for governments across the globe. Restrictive policies by various governments severely inhibit growth of e-commerce in those countries.

Therefore, global information systems cater to the requirement of multinational corporations, meeting the global challenges related to politics, economics, culture, and geography. Global information systems align with global business strategies adopted for control, decision-making, and business autonomy in international, multinational, and global business environments.

We have thus completed the study of information systems and have understood how they help manage a business successfully by making the right decisions and gaining a competitive advantage in the modern business environment. We touched upon various components of IT and the latest trends in hardware, software, database, and telecommunications. Students have gained insight into various decision support systems and knowledge management initiatives. The role of people and IT leadership was discussed. We learnt how IT has affected our lives and has had an impact on society.

SUMMARY

Global information systems refer to a basic system architecture that a multinational organization uses to manage the information requirement of its international businesses. Multinationals looked towards reengineering and cost cutting, and often combined their ERP project with the breaking down of country barriers for manufacturing sites and centres of distribution. The needs of business survival and the urge to expand to newer markets are some of the reasons that are inducing organizations into going global. Globalization causes many local businesses to merge with well-networked and resourceful corporations.

For businesses to grow and sustain in the international market, they have to face many political, cultural, geographical, and economic challenges.

The rules and regulations of governments across the globe can pose political challenges. Cultural challenges, on the other hand, are posed by individualistic schools of thinking in the form of religious, nationalist, ethnic, and regional perspectives. Economic challenges are because of problems related to differences in the cost of living and labour costs in various countries.

Global IT strategies are based on global business strategies. Organizations adopt various business strategies to operate global businesses, which are related to control, decision-making, and autonomy. The three major strategies that firms follow when they are involved in international business are multinational strategy, international strategy, and global strategy.

In global information systems, the core systems are globally networked and meet the requirements of the management across the organization. The compulsions of global businesses drive deployment of IT systems across the organization.

In an international environment, hardware, software, and networking issues pose grave technical challenges. These issues are discussed under computing platforms, connectivity issues, software localization, and database sharing issues. Computing platforms encompass the technology infrastructure of hardware, software, data resources, telecommunication networks, and computing facilities that support global business operations. Managing international data communications networks, including the Internet, intranet, extranet, etc., is a key global IT challenge. Software localization is the process of adapting computer software to different languages, regional differences, and technical requirements of the target market. Global data access and sharing has always been an issue in global business operations.

KEY TERMS

Computing platform   Refers to the technology infrastructure of hardware, software, data resources, telecommunication networks, and computing facilities that support global business operations.

Global information systems   The core systems are globally networked and meet the requirements of management across the organization.

International strategy   Foreign subsidiaries are autonomous but are dependent on the head office for new processes, products, and ideas.

IT consumerization   When employees bring their own devices (BYOD) to work and use them to share files and data inside and outside the office, it is called the consumerization of IT, which includes the use of third-party cloud services and applications such as cloud storage and social media.

Legacy practices   The use of various software solutions developed over a period of time.

Multinational strategy   Strategy where foreign subsidiaries operate autonomously; they believe in central financial powers but decentralization of production, sales, marketing, etc., in the unit countries.

Software localization   Process of adapting computer software to different languages, regional differences, and technical requirements of a target market.

Transnational strategy   Strategy in which the organization's value-added services are managed from a global perspective, without referring to national borders, and taking the benefit of local competitive advantages.

Virtual computing   The concept of sharing physical and logical resources of a computer system such as hard disk, memory, software as done in cloud computing.

Work-shifting   The 'anywhere office', where work is no longer tied to an office. Sharing business resources via telecommunication, online tools, and technology, to shift work to any place one likes.

CONCEPT REVIEW QUESTIONS

1. Explain why companies expand beyond a country's border.
2. What types of challenges are faced when designing a strategy for an international business?
3. What types of global IT strategies can be adopted by a multinational organization?
4. What information systems/applications are relevant to a transnational corporation?
5. What are the global technology issues? Explain in detail the issue of software localization.

CRITICAL THINKING QUESTIONS

1. 'Globalization has posed new opportunities as well as challenges.' Explain this statement with respect to the information systems strategy.
2. 'There is no concrete demarcation and differentiation among multinational, international, and transnational strategies.' Critically examine this statement.
3. If you were the CIO of a company operating in many countries, what criteria would you use to determine whether an application should be developed as a global application or a local application?
4. How would cultural, political, and geo-economic challenges affect a multinational company's use of the Internet?

MIS DEVELOPMENT

As referred to in this chapter and previous chapters, there are a number of enterprise software packages—SAP, Baan, MfgPro, Oracle Manufacturing, Oracle Financial, Microsoft Dynamic NAV, Microsoft Dynamic AX, Microsoft Dynamic GP, mySAP, SAP By Design, Ramco Marshal, Ramco On Demand, Infosys Finacle, TCS Bancs. Visit the websites of all these manufacturers and EPP providers. Make a list of the products with

their features and compatibility of their applications in global organizations.

Create a chart if their implementation poses any challenge on the political, cultural, geographical, and economic fronts. Figure out if they pose any global technology issue and satisfy the localization needs of a global organization. Do all of them offer user interfaces in English, Mandarin, Arabic, Spanish, and French?

REFERENCES

Carton, F. and Adam, F., 'Analysing the impact of enterprise resource planning systems roll-outs in multi-national companies', *Electronic Journal of Information Systems Evaluation*, Vol. 6, No. 2, IBIMA Publishing, 2003.

Cronin, Mary, *Global Advantage on the Internet*, Van Nostrand Reinhold, New York, 1996.

Davenport, T. 'Putting the enterprise into the enterprise system', *Harvard Business Review*, July–August, 1998.

Gunson, John and Jean-Paul de Blasis, 'Implementing ERP in multinational companies: Their effect on the organization and individuals at work', Study Paper, University of Geneva, 2005.

Hill, C.W.L., *International Business: Competing in the global marketplace*, Irwin McGraw-Hill, New York, 1998.

Ives, Blake and Sirkka Jarvenpaa, 'Application for global information technology: Key issues for management', *MIS Quarterly*, March 1991.

Laudon, Ken, Jane Laudon, and Rajanish Dass, *Management Information System*, Pearson Education, Singapore, 2010.

Mische, Michael, 'Transnational architecture: A reengineering approach', *Information Systems Management*, Winter, 1995.

Olson, Davil L., B. Chae, and C. Sheu, 'Issues in multinational ERP implementation', *International Journal of Services and Operations Management*, Vol. 1, No. 1, Buckinghamshire, 2005.

O'Brien, James A, George M Marakas, and Ramesh Behl, *Management Information Systems*, Tata McGraw-Hill, New

Delhi, 2007.

Sankar, Chetan S. and Karl-Heinz Rau, *Implementation strategies for SAP R/3 in a multinational organization*, Cyber Tech Publishing, Hershey, PA, 2006.

Umle E. J., R. R. Haft, and M. M. Umle, 'Enterprise resource planning: Implementation procedures and critical success factors', *European Journal of Operation Research*, Amsterdam, May 2003.

Biehl, Markus, 'Implementing global information systems', *Case Paper, Schulich School of Business*, Toronto, http://www.yorku.ca/mbiehl/files/Global_IS_Implement_CACM.pdf, last accessed on 2 April 2012.

Collins, Rosann Webb, 'Software Localization: Issues and methods', The 9th European Conference on Information Systems, Slovenia, June 2001, http://is2.lse.ac.uk/asp/aspecis/20010021.pdf, last accessed on 25 March 2012.

Lynch, Prof. Richard (2012), http://www.global-strategy.net/categories/Whatisglobalstrategy, last accessed on 2 September 2012.

Wall Street Journal, IBEF Research, http://www.ibef.org/artdispview.aspx?in, last accessed on 10 March 2012.

www.internetworldstats.com/stats.htm, www.population matters.org, www.worldometers.info/world-population, last accessed on 5 March 2012.

www.wikipedia.org, last accessed on 9 February 2013.

CASE STUDY

Videocon: Indian Multinational Giant Awarded for ERP Implementation

In 2007, Videocon, one of the best customers of SAP, was given the SAP ACE 2006 award in recognition of implementing a templated SAP best practices-based solution across five countries using global ASAP methodology within a short period of five months. Videocon has won such a coveted award from SAP AG for the second consecutive year. Earlier,

the company won the award in the category 'best consumer sector implementation (consumer products)' in 2006.

Organization

Videocon is an Indian multinational industrial conglomerate with interests all over the world. The group has 17 manufacturing sites in India and plants in China, Poland, Italy, and Mexico. It is also the third largest picture tube manufacturer in the world. The group is a $4 billion global conglomerate. Today, the group operates through six key sectors—consumer electronics, mobile phone, colour picture tube, oil and gas, direct-to-home (DTH) TV, and telecommunication. The brand trust report, 2011, ranked Videocon as the 42nd most trusted brand in India among the top 300 brands.

'The company is weighing the option of floating subsidiaries for the international operations and creating a new global brand', K. R. Kim, vice-chairman and chief executive of Videocon (global operations),told Business Standard. 'Videocon earns about $300 million through international operations with some presence in Europe. In contrast, LG earns about 70% of its revenues from international markets. Keeping this in mind, we will add capacity through organic and inorganic expansion', said Kim.

Videocon has already acquired Nordmende in the European markets. It is likely to introduce the international brand as a premium label in India. The company also contract-manufactures for multiple brands such as Electrolux, Kelvinator, Sansui, Akai, and Hyundai, apart from owning the flagship brand, Videocon. Videocon also aims to make one million mobile devices by 2013. 'Initially, we will outsource handset production and then explore manufacturing possibilities in India. The handsets will be retailed in the overseas markets as well', Kim said.

Global IS

Videocon has emerged as the first company in India to have successfully implemented mySAP (ERP version 2004) across the organization. This installation combines all the futuristic modules—enterprise portal (EP), business warehousing (BW), customer relationship management (CRM), and human capital management (HCM)—amongst others. Thus, it is one of its kind in India. Videocon has spent close to ₹25 crore to upgrade IT systems at workplaces and install mySAP. mySAP Germany has also categorized Videocon as the ramp-up partners (upgraded customers) for this state-of-the-art execution. Videocon Group has also provided its 1500+ sales staff with laptops to enable them to always carry office work and respond effectively to business requirements.

Pradeep Dhoot, President, Videocon, said, 'Videocon has aptly used SAP solutions to enable strategic decision-making, as a change agent for business transformation and to manage success growth and global expansions.

In the dynamic world, keeping abreast with the market forces is of paramount importance. The mySAP project at Videocon was initiated and driven by the vision of a work environment where every employee will be empowered with knowledge, information, statistics and data that would facilitate in taking faster decisions.'

Award

Videocon won the SAP ACE award in 2007 for 'implementing a templated SAP best practices-based solution' and the 'best consumer sector implementation (consumer products)'. Instituted on the occasion of SAP completing a decade of operations in India, SAP ACE 2006 received 156 nominations from 85 organizations from India and Sri Lanka for awards in 16 categories. The SAP ACE 2006 award was held to recognize the maturing IT usage by Indian enterprises. The award is a reaffirmation of the growing maturity of IT adoption in Videocon group of companies. It underlines how IT is being leveraged at Videocon for effective business transformation and for consolidation of its global spread. It bears testimony to the fundamental practice at Videocon to achieve excellence in its operational efficiencies while delivering strong return on investment to its stakeholders.

The award ceremony was attended by senior management from SAP, partners, and a good representation of customers. Henning Kagermann, CEO, SAP AG and Leo Apotheker, deputy CEO, SAP AG, presented the awards. The top management, including board members and senior IT personnel from across SAP's customer base, participated enthusiastically and was in attendance to receive the awards.

This was the first edition of SAP's annual awards in recognition of customer excellence. An expert panel adjudged Videocon as the winner in the said category after a detailed panel discussion.

Reward

Pawan Kalra, joint president, Videocon Industries Ltd, who had spearheaded this project in Videocon received the award. On the occasion, he said, 'The SAP system implementation has increased proficiency, better service deliveries to customers, and expedited response to the market dynamics. Relentless efforts, undivided attention, and the spirit of core team members resulted in the successful completion of the mySAP project in a record time.'

Kalra added, 'In today's dynamic world, keeping abreast with the market forces is of paramount importance. The mySAP project at Videocon was initiated and driven by the vision of a work environment where every employee will be empowered with knowledge, information, statistics and data that would facilitate in taking faster decisions, increased proficiency, better service deliveries to customers and expedited response to the market dynamics. Videocon has aptly used SAP solutions to enable strategic decision-making, as a change agent for business transformation and to manage our multinational growth.'

Discussion Questions

1. Describe the multinational strategy Videocon used for IS implementation.
2. Explore what type of organizational structure is being used by Videocon.
3. What could be the reasons that Videocon upgraded to mySAP ERP?
4. How have information systems helped Videocon's transition into a global business model?

Sources:

Deshpande, Tejal A. and Nevin John, 'Videocon plans major global retail foray under VC brand', http://www.business-standard. com/india/news/videocon-plans-major-global-retail-foray-under-%60vc%60-brand/323865/, Mumbai, 23 May 2008, last accessed on 5 March 2012.

SAP ACE 2007—Award, http://www.infodartindia.com/news.html, last accessed on 22 January 2013.

'Videocon honoured with SAP Special Recognition', http://news. oneindia.in/2007/09/11/videocon-honoured-sap-special-recognition.html, September 11, 2007. last accessed on 5 March 2012.

http://www.videocon.com, last accessed on 25 February 2011.

Index

Related Titles

Strategic Management
9780198070795

N. Chandrasekaran, Director, Centre for Logistics and Supply Chain Management, LIBA, Chennai and **P.S. Ananthanarayanan**, visiting faculty, BIM, Trichy, and LIBA, Chennai

Strategic Management is a comprehensive textbook that has been written in a student-friendly style, includes discussions on concepts and research in the field, and provides a balanced approach to the subject.

Key Features
- Provides a brief to readers on how to overcome risk-based challenges when applying new strategies
- Includes 40 case studies on major Indian and global companies including Indian Oil Corporation Ltd, Reliance Industries Ltd, and Oracle Corporation.

Operations Research
9780198075479

Pradeep Prabhakar Pai, Associate Professor, Chetana's Institute of Management and Research, Mumbai

Operations Research: Principles and Practice is a comprehensive textbook that explains the concepts and managerial applications of OR lucidly, with the help of graphs, tables, and numerous solved examples.

Key Features
- Discusses topics such as sensitivity analysis for a minimization problem, activity-on-node (AON) method of network analysis for a deterministic project, theory and method of oddments to solve game theory problems, trans-shipment problems, and an introduction to non-linear programming problems
- Equips students with the skills required for making rational business decisions using operations research techniques/models

E-business
9780198069843

Parag Kulkarni, CEO and Chief Scientist at EKLaT Research, Pune, **Sunita Jahirabadkar**, Assistant Professor, Department of Computer Engineering, Cummins College of Engineering, Pune, and **Pradip Chande**, Group Director, TRUBA Group of Institutes, Indore

E-Business is a comprehensive textbook that integrates e-commerce with the strategic aspects of e-business, using numerous examples, exhibits, figures, and case studies.

Key Features
- Includes chapters on knowledge management and business intelligence in e-business, Internet security, Internet payment, and website development
- Discusses contemporary issues and current trends such as mobile computing, m-commerce, Internet banking, and the IT Act, 2000

Title by the Same Author

Other Related Titles